INDEPENDENT TRAVELLERS

NEW ZEALAND

THE BUDGET TRAVEL GUIDE

Other titles in this series include:

Independent Travellers Australia
The Budget Travel Guide

Independent Travellers Britain and Ireland
The Budget Travel Guide

Independent Travellers Europe by Rail
The Inter-Railer's and Eurailer's Guide

Independent Travellers Thailand, Malaysia and Singapore
The Budget Travel Guide

Independent Travellers USA
The Budget Travel Guide

INDEPENDENT TRAVELLERS

NEW ZEALAND

THE BUDGET TRAVEL GUIDE

Christopher and Melanie Rice

Thomas Cook
Publishing

Published by Thomas Cook Publishing,
a division of thomascook.com Limited
PO Box 227
Unit 15/16
Coningsby Road
Peterborough
PE3 8SB
United Kingdom

Telephone: 01733 416477
E-mail: books@thomascook.com

ISBN 1 841573 68 X

Head of Publishing: Donald Greig
Series Editor: Edith Summerhayes
Text design: Tina West
Layout and copy-editing: Wendy Wood
Cover design: Liz Lyons Design, Oxford
Cover layout: Studio 183, Thorney, Peterborough
Proofreader: Susi Bailey
Maps supplied by: Polly Senior Cartography
New maps prepared by Lovell Johns Ltd, Witney, Oxfordshire

Text typeset in Book Antiqua and Gill Sans using QuarkXPress
Colour repro: Z2 Reprographics, Thetford
Text revisions: Cooling Brown
Printed and bound in Italy by Legoprint S.P.A.

Mini CD design: Laburnum Technologies Pvt Ltd, New Delhi, India
CD manufacturing services: business interactive ltd, Rutland

First edition (2000) written and researched by:
Christopher and Melanie Rice

First edition edited by:
Wendy Wood

Update research for 2004 edition:
Grant Bourne
Sara Mason-Parker

Mini CD written and researched by:
Grant Bourne

Transport information:
Peter Bass, Editor, and **Reuben Turner**
Thomas Cook Overseas Timetable

The Authors

Christopher and Melanie Rice have travelled widely. They have written numerous travel guides and articles, featuring destinations such as Russia, the Czech Republic, Eastern Europe, Turkey, Berlin, the Algarve and islands in the Dodecanese. They have contributed to several Thomas Cook publications, including *Signpost Brittany and Normandy*. Chris and Melanie are also well-known children's authors with more than 30 titles to their credit.

Grant Bourne is a New Zealander whose passion for travel has taken him through much of Europe, Africa, Asia and the Near East. He has written and illustrated travel guides and articles in both German and English. Now living in the Rhine Valley, Germany, he frequently returns home for extended visits.

The authors and Thomas Cook Publishing would like to thank the following for their help during the production of this book:

Larry Dunmire, Dave Allen, Ethel Davies, Caroline Jones and Spectrum Colour Library for the photographs used in this book, to whom the copyright belongs.

The Thomas Cook Archives for supplying the historical illustrations.

Stephen Griffith, New Zealand Tourist Board, Wellington; Gareth Powell; Fran Robinson; Grant Bourne and Michael Albert.

AUTHORS – ACKNOWLEDGEMENTS

Thomas Cook's *How to See New Zealand* brochure of 1936–37

All photographs supplied by Larry Dunmire, except for those credited below (to whom copyright belongs).

Colour section pp. 64–65 (i) harbour bridge, Ethel Davies; yachts, Spectrum Colour Library.
pp. 352–353 (ii) Lake Manapouri, Dave Allen; walker in rainforest, Caroline Jones.

Cover photograph:
Jon Arnold Images/Alamy

HELP IMPROVE THIS GUIDE

This guide will be updated each year. The information given in it may change during the lifetime of this edition and we would welcome reports and comments from our readers. Similarly we want to make this guide as practical and useful as possible and are grateful for any comments, criticisms and suggestions for improving future editions.

A free copy of this guide will be sent to all readers whose information or ideas are incorporated in the next edition. Please send all contributions to the Series Editor, *Independent Travellers New Zealand*, Thomas Cook Publishing, at: PO Box 227, Unit 15/16, Coningsby Road, Peterborough, PE3 8SB, United Kingdom, or e-mail: books@thomascook.com.

Legend for Town Maps

Motorway & slip road
Main road & mall — VULCAN LANE
Other road
Footpath
Railway
Tram route
One-way street
Bus station
Parking area
Ferry route
Place of interest — Art Gallery
Information centre
Hospital
Police station
Post office
Hotel — CARLTON (H)
Park
Library
Golf course
Built-up area
Place of worship

Legend for National Park Maps

Major route — 4
Minor road & track
Footpath
National park
Place of interest
Peak — 466 m

CONTENTS

GENERAL INFORMATION

ROUTES & CITIES

NORTH ISLAND

p. 58

Routes are shown in one direction only but can, of course, be travelled in the opposite direction. See pp.16–17 for a diagrammatical presentation of the routes.

SOUTH ISLAND
p. 261

REFERENCE SECTION

SPECIAL FEATURES

INTRODUCTION

Though only a little larger than Britain and about the same size as the US State of Colorado, New Zealand offers as great a variety of scenery as you'll find anywhere. It's also relatively empty – the population is a mere 4 million, less than half that of London. Bearing in mind that 50 per cent of New Zealand's inhabitants live in the three cities of Auckland, Christchurch and the capital, Wellington, it's clear that there's still plenty of room for visitors.

Most tourists associate New Zealand with Australia, yet it's important to remember that the two countries are as far apart as, say, London and Moscow or New York and Denver; the people are different too. New Zealand comprises two main islands, helpfully named North and South. Apart from Stewart Island, just off the southern coast, there's a scattering of dependencies across the Pacific, including the Chatham Islands, Campbell Island, Tokelau and Raoul Island in the Kermadecs, not forgetting a 414,000 square kilometre chunk of Antarctica, administered as the Ross Dependency.

Being an island country, New Zealand has a great deal of coastline, in fact more than 15,000 kilometres. It's also extremely mountainous. What many people don't realise is that on the North Island, Ruapehu, Ngauruhoe and Tongariro are active volcanoes, while Taranaki and Rangitoto are considered dormant. The South Island too has some spectacular snow-covered peaks, more than 30 of which rise to over 3000 metres. The highest is Mount Cook (3754 metres), known to the Maoris as Aoraki, the 'Cloud Piercer'. Apart from coastline and mountain scenery, New Zealand boasts miles of pristine beaches, glacial lakes and fiords, majestic rivers and vast tracts of primeval forest and native bush. Amazingly, even today there are some isolated spots that may never have seen a human being.

New Zealand Quick Facts

Official Name

New Zealand (English); Aotearoa (Maori)

Capital

Wellington

The Flag

The New Zealand flag was introduced in 1869 and officially adopted in 1901. The British blue ensign reflects the country's colonial heritage, while the emblem of the constellation of the Southern Cross reflects its geographic location.

Anthems

God Defend New Zealand

God Save the Queen

New Zealand Geography

Area

270,534 sq km

Highest Point

Mount Cook (Aoraki)

3754 m (12,316 ft)

above sea level

Lowest Point

Sea level along the coast

Population

4 million

Blessed with this superabundance of natural riches, New Zealanders are understandably keen to preserve them. 'Greenies' to a man and woman, they cherish their unique environment – a larger percentage of the country is designated National Park than anywhere else in the world. If you have the energy, it will soon be possible to walk from one end of each island to the other and you can bet your bottom dollar that the country's more fanatical trampers (the local term for hikers) will be doing just that.

New Zealand's colonial history is relatively short. Captain Cook didn't plant the British flag here until 1769, just seven years before the American Declaration of Independence, and it was another 30 years before the first settlers began to put down roots. The Maoris, on the other hand, had already been living in Aotearoa, the 'Land of the Long White Cloud', for more than 700 years when Cook arrived. The colonials soon became adept at exploiting the Maoris' tribal divisions and their lack of familiarity with western technology. Within a century of Cook's arrival, the indigenous population was in danger of losing its traditional way of life altogether as the colonial farmers prospered after buying up huge tracts of Maori land and resources. In the last 20 years or so, the Maoris have made a comeback and most fair-minded New Zealanders support the new policy of biculturalism. You'll now find greater use of Maori place names for example – there's even some support for rechristening the country Aotearoa.

One of the great formative influences on New Zealand was the relationship with Britain. Until the early 1970s, 'The Trip', the rite-of-passage, for almost every New Zealander was to England. New Zealand may well have been 'God's own Country', but Britain was, to some degree, still the motherland. Since then, Britain has tried to forge a new identity within the European Union and so has forced New Zealand to redefine its own role in the world. Like its neighbour Australia, it is now happy to see itself as a Pacific power with a modern go-getting economy, born of a newly discovered self-confidence. Soon you will be arriving in this exciting and vibrant country.

INTRODUCTION

HOW TO USE THIS BOOK

Independent Travellers New Zealand combines expert advice with details of 33 different routes, cities and areas, each in its own self-contained chapter. The book reflects the astonishing variety of scenery to be encountered in New Zealand and the range of activities available. The chapters vary in approach, each bringing out the best ways to see and enjoy that part of the country. Of the route chapters, some recommend particularly scenic rail journeys, flights, four-wheel-drive tracks and boat trips around the coastal areas. Most of the roads selected are covered by New Zealand's excellent bus networks.

As well as giving clear driving instructions and public transport details, each route chapter suggests touring bases and describes the most important attractions in detail. The remaining chapters feature cities or attractions considered worthy of a longer stay. Each has detailed information on how to get there, getting around by local transport and how to make best use of your time. All chapters offer suggestions for budget-friendly accommodation and places to eat as well as how to find local entertainment highlights.

ROUTE MAPS

A clear route map shows the layout of possible journeys in each chapter.

ROUTE DETAIL

From Auckland take State Highway 1 through the suburbs of Albany, Silverdale, Orewa and Waiwera to **Warkworth**. 66 km

ROUTE DETAIL

Route details and approximate cumulative mileages are given.

PRICES (IN NZ$)

Food (average for a main course, not including drinks or dessert)

$	$10–$15
$$	$15–$25
$$$	$25 and above

Accommodation (double room/ two persons)

$	up to $60
$$	$60–$130
$$$	over $130

HOW TO USE THIS BOOK

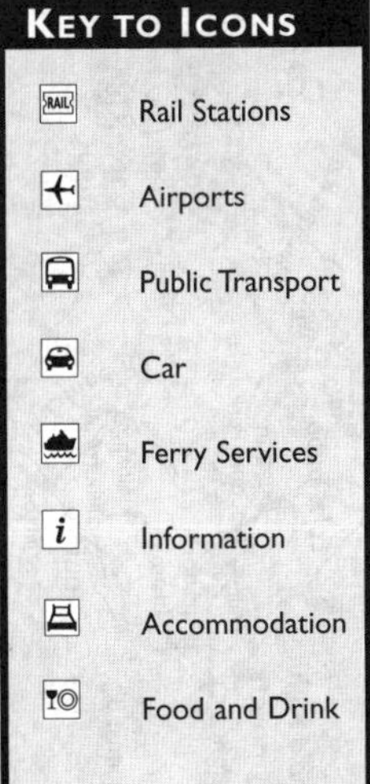

The order of these routes and cities moves from Auckland and the north, southwards through the North Island to Wellington. From here the routes cross to the South Island and continue southwards, ending with Stewart Island.

Most chapters are accompanied by a map, showing the route or city or area, and the stops en route are described in the text. Each also has a route description and a summary of ways to get there in the form of a table showing bus and train schedules and a list of driving and public transport approaches. The public transport details are given with the appropriate *OTT* table number – the relevant table in the *Thomas Cook Overseas Timetable* (see p. 51), which lists bus, rail and ferry schedules.

Throughout the book you will see notes and tips in the margins. These provide added information and suggest places to stop en route. There are also day-trips from the main destination and details of boat trips, walking tours and other activities. Finally, there's the suggestion of an onward route connecting this with other chapters.

PUBLIC TRANSPORT DETAILS

Mode of travel, journey time, frequency of service and *Thomas Cook Overseas Timetable* (*OTT*) table numbers are given.

BALCLUTHA – INVERCARGILL
OTT TABLE 9819

TRANSPORT	FREQUENCY	JOURNEY TIME
Bus	3 daily	2hrs

BALCLUTHA – GORE
OTT TABLE 9819

TRANSPORT	FREQUENCY	JOURNEY TIME
Bus	3 daily	1hr 5mins

GORE – INVERCARGILL
OTT TABLE 9819

TRANSPORT	FREQUENCY	JOURNEY TIME
Bus	5 daily	55mins

Note: There is an extra bus on Fridays

PACIFIC OCEAN
Tasman Sea
North Island
Cape Maria van Diemen
North Cape
Parengarenga Harbour
Te Kao
Rangaunu Bay
Awanui
Kaitaia
Cape Brett
Russell
Kawakawa
Whangarei
Dargaville
Waiotira
Needles Point
Hauraki Gulf
Paparoa
Kaipara Harbour
Colville Channel
East Coast Bays
Mount Roskill
Takapuna
Waitemata
Auckland
Manukau
Thames
Bay of Plenty
Paeroa
Cape Runaway
Tauranga
Te Araroa
Hamilton
Matata
Whakatane
East Cape
Te Awamutu
Putaruru
Te Puia
Albatross Point
Tokoroa
Kawerau
Opotiki
Rotorua
Waikato
Awakino
Lake Taupo
Taupo
Huiarau Range
North Taranaki Bight
Gisborne
New Plymouth
Tongariro National Park
Waitara
Wairoa
Cape Egmont
Mahia Peninsula
Stratford
Hawke Bay
Napier
Eltham
Ruahine Range
Hawera
South Taranaki Bight
Taihape
Cape Kidnappers
Hunterville
Hastings
Wanganui
Marton
Cape Farewell
Palmerston North
Dannevirke
Collingwood
Tasman
Levin

NEW ZEALAND
South Island
SOUTH PACIFIC
OCEAN
Karamea Bight
Richmond
Lower Hutt
WELLINGTON
Cape Palliser
Blenheim
Seddon
Cape Campbell
Ward
Westport
Buller
Reefton
Spenser Mts
Wairau
Greymouth
Hokitika
Puketeraki Range
Waiau
Kaikoura
Cheviot
Harihari
Southern Alps
Rakaia
Waipara
Pegasus Bay
Christchurch
Mount Cook
Canterbury
Banks Peninsula
Akaroa
Haast
Jackson Head
Ashburton
Canterbury
Bight
Mount Aspiring
Omarama
Timaru
Milford Sound
Lake
Wanaka
Waitaki
Waimate
Wanaka
Lake Te
Anau
Queenstown
Oamaru
Doubtful Sound
Alexandra
Hampden
Fiordland
National Park
Lake
Wakatipu
Roxburgh
Palmerston
Waikouaiti
Manapouri
Clutha
Lumsden
Port Chalmers
Dunedin
Otautau
Winton
Gore
Balclutha
Cape
Providence
Riverton
Invercargill
Foveaux Strait
Bluff
Oban
Stewart Island
Port Pegasus
Southwest Cape

ROUTE MAP

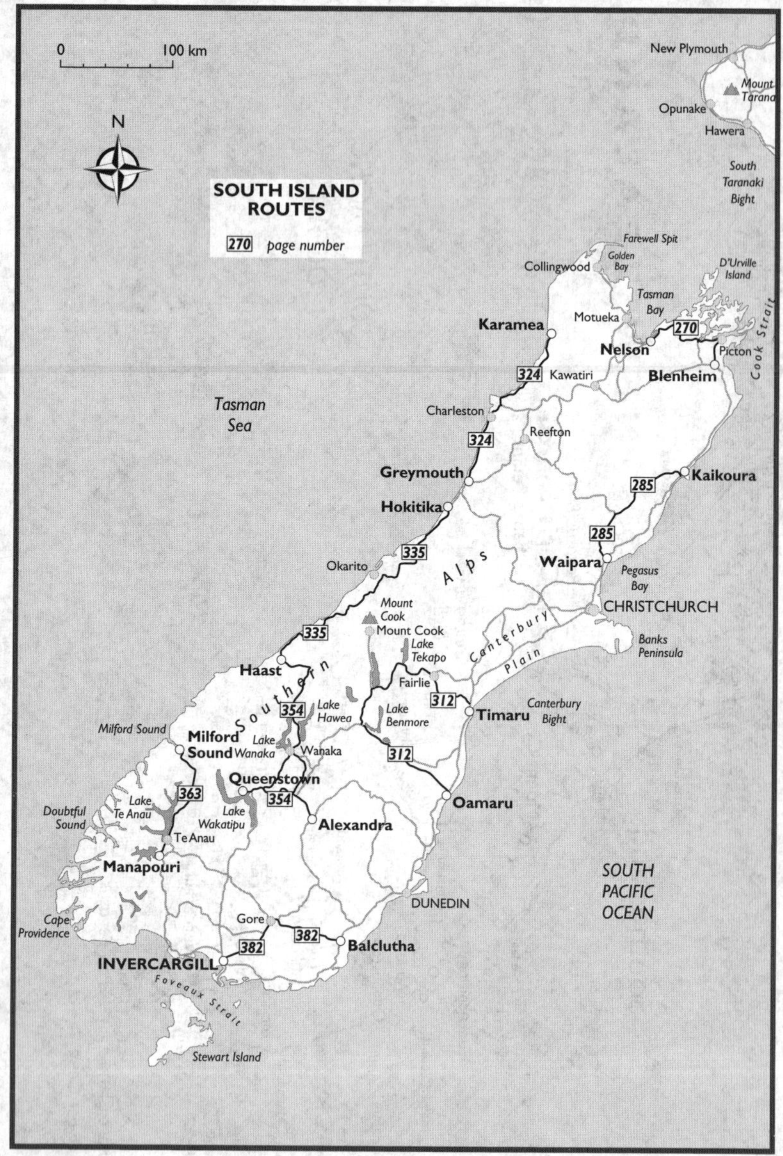

0
100 km
N
SOUTH ISLAND ROUTES
270 page number
New Plymouth
Mount Taranaki
Opunake
Hawera
South Taranaki Bight
Farewell Spit
Golden Bay
Collingwood
D'Urville Island
Tasman Bay
Motueka
Karamea
270
Nelson
Picton
Cook Strait
324
Kawatiri
Blenheim
Tasman Sea
Charleston
324
Reefton
Greymouth
Kaikoura
285
Hokitika
285
335
Okarito
Alps
Waipara
Pegasus Bay
Mount Cook
Mount Cook
CHRISTCHURCH
335
Canterbury
Lake Tekapo
Banks Peninsula
Plain
Haast
Southern
Fairlie
354
Lake Hawea
312
Timaru
Canterbury Bight
Lake Benmore
Milford Sound
Milford Sound
Lake Wanaka
Wanaka
312
Queenstown
363
354
Oamaru
Lake Te Anau
Lake Wakatipu
Alexandra
Doubtful Sound
Te Anau
Manapouri
SOUTH PACIFIC OCEAN
DUNEDIN
Cape Providence
Gore
382
382
Balclutha
INVERCARGILL
Foveaux Strait
Stewart Island

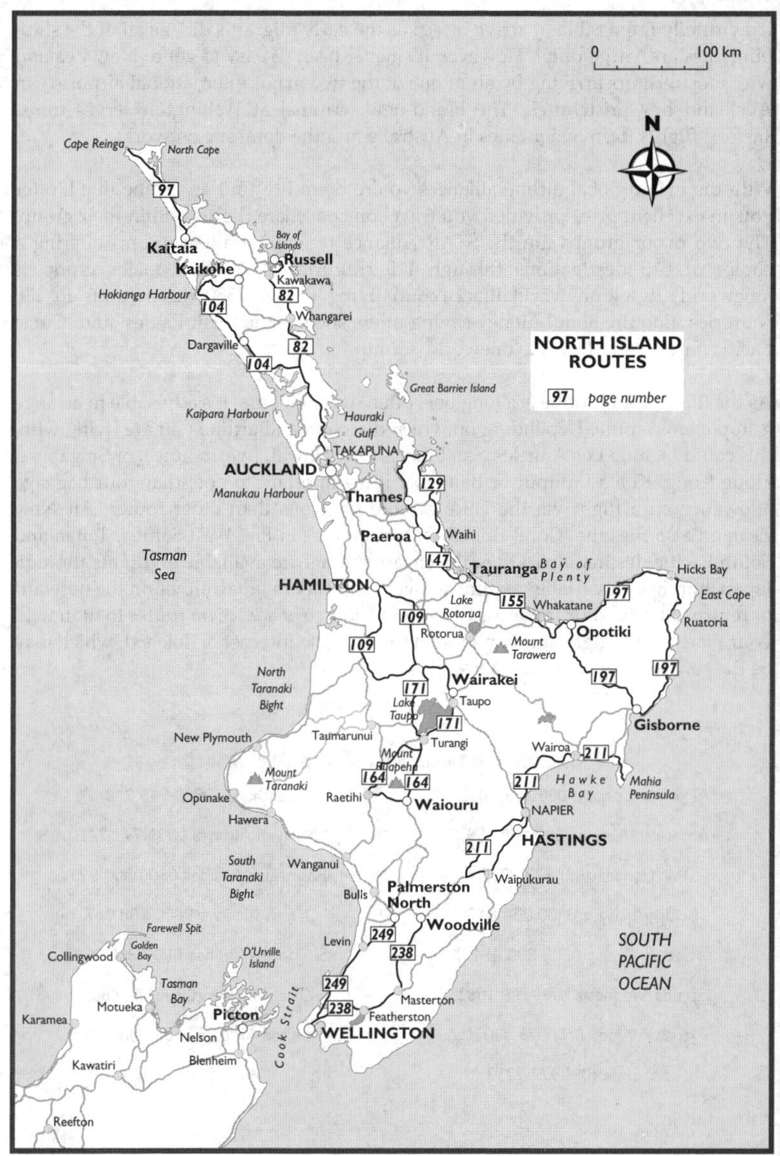

NORTH ISLAND ROUTES
97 page number
0 100 km
N
Cape Reinga
North Cape
97
Kaitaia
Bay of Islands
Russell
Kaikohe
Kawakawa
Hokianga Harbour
82
104
Whangarei
Dargaville
82
104
Great Barrier Island
Kaipara Harbour
Hauraki Gulf
TAKAPUNA
AUCKLAND
129
Manukau Harbour
Thames
Paeroa
Waihi
Tasman Sea
147
Tauranga
Bay of Plenty
HAMILTON
Hicks Bay
197
East Cape
155
Whakatane
Lake Rotorua
109
Rotorua
Ruatoria
Opotiki
109
Mount Tarawera
North Taranaki Bight
171
Wairakei
197
197
Lake Taupo
Taupo
171
Gisborne
New Plymouth
Taumarunui
Turangi
Wairoa
211
Mount Ruapehu
Mount Taranaki
164
164
211
Hawke Bay
Mahia Peninsula
Opunake
Raetihi
Waiouru
NAPIER
Hawera
HASTINGS
211
South Taranaki Bight
Wanganui
Waipukurau
Palmerston North
Bulls
Woodville
Farewell Spit
249
Golden Bay
Levin
D'Urville Island
238
SOUTH PACIFIC OCEAN
Collingwood
Tasman Bay
249
Motueka
238
Masterton
Picton
Featherston
Karamea
Nelson
WELLINGTON
Cook Strait
Blenheim
Kawatiri
Reefton

REACHING NEW ZEALAND

It's virtually impossible to arrive by sea as the early migrants did, as all of the shipping lines are 'cargo only'. However, it's never been so easy to get to New Zealand with most visitors arriving by air at one of the two major international airports – in Auckland or Christchurch. The brand-new terminal at Wellington serves trans-Tasman flights from major cities in Australia and the domestic network.

With the major global airline alliances you're bound to find an airline that'll offer you an excellent price provided you travel on codeshare flights within their group. The two major groups are the STAR Alliance (www.star-alliance.com) offering a choice of 815 destinations through 115 countries. The other major group is 'oneworld' (www.oneworldalliance.com) flying to over 550 destinations in 130 countries. Enquire about money-saving offers such as the 'Visit Passes' and 'Circle Pacific' fares offered by the 'oneworld' Group.

As the flight from Europe is a long one, often over 26 hours, it's advisable to arrange a stopover en route. Depending on which direction and airline you are flying with, this could include Los Angeles, San Francisco or Hawaii (westbound), or Singapore, Hong Kong, Kuala Lumpur or Bangkok. It is important to note that your baggage allowance on a flight via the USA is more generous than other routes. Air New Zealand also flies the 'Coral Route' with stopovers in Fiji, West Samoa, Tonga and South Pacific destinations. Often the cheapest seats are available on flights through Japan, but these invariably require an overnight stay in Japan either on the outward or return journey. Your travel agent is a good source of advice on routes to fit in with your plans and budget, but don't forget to check the Internet or Teletext, which may be the best sources of bargain fares.

CONTACT TELEPHONE NUMBERS IN AUCKLAND

Air New Zealand 0800 737 000

American Airlines 0800 887 997

Air Canada (09) 977 2210

British Airways 0800 274 847

Cathay Pacific 0508 800 454

Garuda Indonesia (09) 366 1862

Japan Airlines (09) 379 3202

Lan Chile (09) 977 2233

Lufthansa 0800 945 220

Malaysia Airlines 0800 777 747

Polynesian Airlines 0800 800 993

Qantas Airways 0800 808 767

Singapore Airlines 0800 808 909

Thai Airways (09) 377 3886

United Airlines 0800 508 648

REACHING NEW ZEALAND

Auckland airport, with both domestic and international terminals, is located 23 kilometres south of the city and you should allow around 40 minutes' travel time to the city centre. Christchurch and Wellington airports are both around 20 minutes from their respective city centres. Public transport from airports is well provided for at all locations and includes taxis (usually surcharged after 2200) and Super Shuttle coach services - these can be pre-booked and make drops en route to the city centre.

Once in New Zealand you may need to contact your carrier to change your flight arrangements. Air New Zealand has Travelcentres in all major towns; alternatively contact any TAANZ travel agent and they will be able to help. Note that there may be a charge levied for alterations to your plans. There is a NZ $25 tax levied at the airport on departures.

TRAVELLING BY AIR

Unless you book air travel within New Zealand as part of your ticket package you will find that, despite promotional fares, domestic air travel purchased locally is relatively expensive on the two major carriers, Qantas Airways (formerly Ansett) and Air New Zealand. However both airlines offer Air Passes for non-residents with an international air ticket to and from New Zealand.

More Tips on CD

Check the CD for lots of extra links and tips on travel to and around New Zealand, and much more besides.

How to Contact Qantas Airways

On the Internet: www.qantas.co.nz

Within NZ:

Qantas Airways Travel shops in major centres or toll-free 0800 808 767

Abroad:

Australia – toll-free: 13 13 13

UK – 0845 7 747 767

USA/Canada – toll-free: 1800/227-4500

South Africa (Johannesburg): 011 441 8550

All other countries: contact your local Qantas agent.

For example, Air New Zealand offers the South Pacific Airpass, which is also a good way to add an extra destination or two to your New Zealand trip. It allows flights within New Zealand, between New Zealand and Australia, between New Zealand and the Pacific Islands and within the Pacific Islands on Air New Zealand operated flights. The Airpass is divided into four domestic and three international zones. The minimum number of flight coupons is two, the maximum number ten. Additional coupons can be purchased in New Zealand. For details consult your local travel agent.

Qantas Airways offers the Boomerang Pass. This is great not only for flights within New Zealand (single-zone pass), but also for flights throughout Australia and the Pacific Islands (multi-zone pass). Contact a Qantas or British Airways agent for details.

There are a number of smaller carriers that operate domestically, such as Origin Pacific Airways, tel: 0800 302 302, also on the web at www.originpacific.co.nz, offering competitive fares to destinations including Christchurch, Nelson, Wellington, Palmerston North, Napier, New Plymouth, Hamilton and Auckland. Great Barrier Airlines, tel: 0800 900 600 (www.gbair.co.nz) has flights from Auckland and North Shore to Great Barrier Island, other islands in the Hauraki Gulf and the Coromandel Peninsula. A relative newcomer is the budget airline Freedom Air, tel: 0800 600 500 (www.freedomair.co.nz), with cheap flights between the main centres and also trans-Tasman flights.

HOW TO CONTACT AIR NEW ZEALAND

On the Internet: www.airnz.co.nz

Within NZ:

Air New Zealand Travel Centres in major shopping centres, or call toll-free: 0800 737 000

Abroad:

Australia toll-free: 13 24 76

UK: 0800 028 4149

USA toll-free: 800/262-1234
Los Angeles only: 310/615-1111

Canada toll-free (English): 800/663-5494 or (French) 800/799-5494
Vancouver only: 604/606-0150

TRAVELLING BY TRAIN

DETAILS ON TRANZ SCENIC TRAIN SERVICES WITHIN NZ:

www.tranzrail.co.nz or www.tranzscenic.co.nz

Freephone: 0800 872 467 daily 0700–2100

Fax: 04 472 8903

Outside NZ, tel: 64 4 495 0775 or fax: 64 4 472 8903.

OTT – see page 51

A train journey through New Zealand simply can't be bettered as you encounter dramatic country that's inaccessible by road. Tranz Scenic's modern and powerful trains provide comfort and relaxation with service staff on hand to help. So sit back on your sheepskin lined seat for a memorable journey!

You can book your tickets in advance through any travel agent, Visitor Information Centres and selected railway stations, or freephone 0800 872 467. Off-peak discount fares are available on most services, but are limited in number and must be purchased within New Zealand - take note of varying refund conditions, important if your plans are fluid.

There are day return excursions and concession fares available for children, Senior Citizens, Students, and Backpacker or HI/YHA members upon presentation of proof of age or membership cards.

Tranz Scenic sells the 'Best of New Zealand' Pass for independent travellers. This gives access to all train services, cross straits services on the Interislander and the Lynx, InterCity Coachlines and steam train journeys on the Kingston Flyer and the Taieri Gorge/Newton track to and from Dunedin and Queenstown. Each route has been costed in Best Points and you pre-purchase sufficient points to meet your needs. Current prices are $499 for 600 points (worth $630 of travel), $646 for 800 points and $783 for 1000 points. Passes can be purchased outside New Zealand at your local travel agent, or within New Zealand, tel: 0800 NZ BEST (0800 692 378), e-mail: bestpass@tranzscenic.co.nz, visit a Tranz Scenic Centre or see a travel agent. If you are coming from the UK, you can buy them before you leave from Austravel on 020 7287 0212. They are valid for six months starting from the date of your first journey. An unused pass is valid for four months from date of purchase. The pass also gives you discounts on a range of sightseeing experiences.

There are five stages to travelling around New Zealand with your 'Best of New Zealand' Pass. Firstly, you can actually book each journey by phone. Call free on 0800 692 378, at least 24 hours before departure. At peak times of the year it is a good idea to book sooner as seats are not guaranteed. You then tell the staff your pass number and the journey you would like to book, and they will confirm the reservation and also let you know how many Best Points you are using. Then, when the time comes to travel, there is actually no need for a ticket as your pass itself is enough, and should be shown to staff at check-in. If you run short of points on your holiday, you can

North Island

• *The Overlander* – Auckland to Wellington & vice versa daily. Major stop at Hamilton. 11-hr trip.

• *The Northerner* – Auckland to Wellington & vice versa overnight with accommodation on reclining seats. 11-hr trip.

South Island

• *The TranzCoastal* – return journey from Christchurch to Picton each day. Connecting with the 1330 Interislander departure to Wellington, and meeting the 0930 Interislander departure from Wellington. Major stop at Kaikoura. 4½-hr trip.

The TranzAlpine – acknowledged as one of six Great Train Journeys in the world. Return journey from Christchurch to Greymouth each day. Major stop at Arthur's Pass. 4½-hr trip.

purchase a top up of either 20, 100 or 200 Best Points to keep you going. Families or groups should note that you can put everyone's points on a single Family or Group Pass, which means that booking is greatly simplified as you only need to quote one number.

The pass also gives you access to coach travel with Great Sights New Zealand and InterCity Coachlines. The Interislander ferry provides a year-round link between the North and South Islands. It is a relaxing and pleasant cruise across Cook Strait and through the beautiful Marlborough Sounds. Those in a hurry can also make use of the fast ferry, the Lynx.

The actual train journeys can be pretty impressive too. Travelling in either direction between Dunedin and Queenstown couldn't be more exciting with the combination of the Taieri Gorge and the Newton Track and Trail. This train, *The Taieri Gorge Limited* (www.taieri.co.nz), goes over giant viaducts of iron and stone. Then a Newton Coach driver will take you through Central Otago to or from Queenstown.

Perhaps one of the most famous is the *TranzAlpine Express*, which travels daily from Christchurch to Greymouth. The journey takes around 4 hours and leaves Christchurch at 0900 daily. It has an observation car, and serves snacks and morning tea. The train starts off crossing the agricultural wealth of the Canterbury Plains and starts its climb at Springfield. On the 231-kilometre journey the train goes through 19 tunnels. At the Arthur's Pass station there is normally a change of engines and then you go through the 8.5 kilometre-long Otira tunnel. The train then descends down past Lake Brunner to Greymouth - a magical journey.

You can only purchase a ticket at a Tranz Scenic ticketing outlet, and you should be at the station at least 20 minutes before the advertised departure time. (Trains will depart early if all booked passengers have been checked in by the train crew!) Not all stations sell tickets, so check when booking. Refreshments - light meals, snacks, confectionery and hot and cold drinks are available on all services, and all trains except the *Northerner* are fully licensed. Smoking is not permitted on any service. Bicycles are charged at $10 per journey and places must be booked in advance as space is limited.

TRAVELLING BY FERRY

CRUISES

It's possible to cruise around New Zealand. Most cruises start in Auckland and take in the sights of the Bay of Islands, Rotorua (a day trip from Tauranga) Napier/Hawkes Bay, Wellington, Marlborough Sounds, Fiordland, Dunedin and Christchurch. Contact your travel agent for details when planning your trip.

Competition across Cook Strait (which divides the North and South Islands) is sadly lacking, with only the Interisland Line's ferries competing with the airlines and some smaller operators. Don't forget to ask when booking for the best deal available.

Part of Tranz Rail Holdings, the Interisland Line (tel: 0800 802 802; www.interislandline.co.nz) operates the Interislander Ferry and Lynx catamaran services, both connecting with the Tranz Scenic trains. A free courtesy bus is available from the station to the ferry terminal in Wellington and Picton.

The Lynx fast ferry operates throughout the year, departing from the Waterloo Quay terminal in downtown Wellington. The drop-off point for car rentals is, however, the Interislander terminal, so allow at least 15 minutes extra for a free transfer from here to the Lynx terminal. The advantage of the slower Interislander ferries is that they allow you the opportunity for a 3-hour cruise up the beautiful Queen Charlotte Sound admiring the scenery. Sailing times for the Interislander and Lynx ferries are as follows.

ARATERE AND *ARAHURA* FERRY SAILINGS

From Wellington: 0130 (except Sun and Mon), 0600, 0930*, 1400 and 1730 (all daily).

Returning from Picton: 0530 (except Mon), 1000 (except Mon), 1330**, 1800 and 2130 (all daily).

Always check timetables prior to departure.

* this service connects the 0735 arrival in Wellington of the Northerner from Auckland, and the 1340 TranzCoastal to Christchurch.

** the 0730 train service from Christchurch connects with this ferry to Wellington, and the Northerner overnight service to Auckland.

LYNX FAST FERRY SAILINGS

From Wellington: 0800, 1530 daily.

From Picton: 1130, 1900 daily.

Ferry services to the Islands in the Hauraki Gulf – Waiheke, Rangitoto and Kawau etc. are run by Fullers from Auckland Ferry Building. Subritzky Lines takes cars from Half Moon Bay, Auckland to Waiheke. Information at the Auckland Visitor Information Centre.

Stewart Island (see the final chapter of this book) can be reached on the Foveaux Express ferry service, a 60-minute trip from Bluff. Tel: 03 212 7660, fax: 03 212 8377; www.foveauxexpress.co.nz; e-mail: foveauxexpress@southnet.co.nz.

TRAVELLING BY COACH

New Zealand's national passenger network is run by InterCity Coachlines. NZ owned and operated, it offers services to almost anywhere on a frequent timetable with daily departures. For independent travellers there are various travel passes allowing you to cross NZ taking in specified destinations at your leisure. Local travel agents or Visitor Information Centres will have details on the four nationwide coach passes, as well as on the 'Travel Pass', which allows you to combine rail, ferry, coach and air over 5, 8, 15 or 22 days. Bookings toll-free on 0800 33 99 66, online at www.travelpass.co.nz or e-mail: res@travelpass.co.nz.

Newmans Coach Services is a privately owned company that has been in operation for over 120 years, linking major centres. Their coaches are a bit more luxurious than InterCity's, and come equipped with a restroom, air conditioning and video entertainment. Apart from their own sightseeing day trips to attractions like Waitomo Caves and Milford Sound, they also participate in the 'Travel Pass' scheme with InterCity (see above). Bookings on Auckland, tel: 09 913 6200, Wellington, tel: 04 499 3261, Christchurch, tel: 03 374 6149, Rotorua, 07 348 0999. Information on www.newmanscoach.co.nz.

You can e-mail InterCity Coachlines or have a look at their website:

e-mail:
info@intercitygroup.co.nz
website:
www.intercitycoach.co.nz

For the more adventurous independent traveller, try the Magic Travellers Network. Their coaches, which use knowlegeable, friendly drivers travel on a variety of fixed routes taking in major attractions including many of the National Parks and their walks. You decide the pace you travel, getting off where and when you want for as long as you want. Passengers tend to be a mixture of nationalities with an average age in the mid-20s, and share a love of active outdoor pursuits.

Magic Bus can also book accommodation and activities. Prices start from $99 for a minimum two-day trip to the Bay of Islands. There are a few points to remember if you are travelling with Magic:

If you get off the coach, then book the next sector with your driver. If you change your mind, then just ring Magic direct and inform them of your change.

Magic provides you with a selection of hostels around New Zealand that have been recommended by past travellers. Your driver will make every effort to book that accommodation for you and can drop you off and pick you up from that hostel. If you need special requirements for your room though, you are advised to ring them personally as well.

More Magic services are put into use in the summer so you are advised to keep a close eye on the timetables so that you are aware of all the opportunities available. For more details contact Magic Bus, tel: 64 9 358 5600, fax: 64 9 358 3471; www.magicbus.co.nz; e-mail: info@magicbus.co.nz.

Kiwi Experience is an alternative coach transport network designed especially for backpackers and like-minded travellers to get you off the beaten track. Similar to Magic Bus, they can be likened to a tour that allows you the flexibility to jump on and off the coach at any point along the route. They claim to attract lots of passengers that like to party non-stop! They guarantee cheaper prices in the UK than in New Zealand and offer a 5 per cent discount with the VIP, YHA, Nomads or ISIC card. You can book through travel agents, or contact Kiwi Experience, tel: 64 9 366 9830, fax: 64 9 366 1374; www.kiwiexperience.com; e-mail: enquiries@kiwiex.co.nz.

Connections for 18 to 35s also operate activity orientated tours in New Zealand for 18–35-year-olds. The various tours range from 6 to 15 days and are fully inclusive of hotel/lodge accommodation, as well as many activities and most meals. Check their website at www.connections1835.com.au; e-mail: mail@connections1835.com.au.

On South Island, Atomic Shuttles operate competitively priced daily coach services for independent travellers. Bookings can be made through most hostels, travel agents and information centres, or contact the main office in Christchurch, tel: 03 322 8883 (24 hours), fax: 03 349 3868; www.atomictravel.co.nz; e-mail: atomic@caverock.co.nz.

There are numerous shuttle buses running across both main islands; for further listings check www.newzealandsites.com/travel/transportation/bus-services.

For all coach bookings and enquiries in the UK, contact the Travellers Contact Point: 2–6 Inverness Terrace, Bayswater, London W2 3HX; tel: 0207 243 7887; www.travellers.com.au; e-mail: info@travellersuk.com.

DRIVING

CAR AND CAMPERVAN HIRE The minimum age for car hire is 21 and there is likely to be an excess on the insurance if you are under 25. Avis, Hertz and Budget are all represented in New Zealand as well as many smaller companies which, while cheaper, may not offer the flexibility of the big players. Budget travellers might consider hiring second-hand cars - a cheaper, if less reliable option. Most cars are modern automatic saloons, though it is also possible to rent four-wheel-drive vehicles.

Widely used, campervans are compact and appeal to the independent-minded traveller. Booking through a tour operator can produce the best deals. There are sites for campervans all over the country, typically charging a small fee per night. If you hire one, insist on a thorough briefing before you depart. Nationwide operators include Maui Rentals (tel: 0800 651 080; www.maui-rentals.com), Kea Campers (tel: 0800 520 052; www.keacampers.com) and Britz NZ (tel: 0800 831 900; www.britz.co.nz). Prices range from NZ$70 to $300 per day, depending on length of hire, comfort and season. Prices often include insurance, breakdown services, unlimited kms and GST.

DOCUMENTS New Zealand is one of only a few countries where collision damage waiver (CDW) is compulsory and it will be automatically included in the motor insurance policy. Note that you may not be insured for travel on unsealed roads, certainly not for the Ninety Mile Beach or Skippers Canyon. If you're planning to travel in Coromandel check your insurance carefully before you set out.

New Zealand happily accepts most driving licences but it is never a bad thing to get an international licence from your motoring organisation. It does not cost much, it looks impressive, and you can never have too much documentation. Whichever form you use, drivers must be in possession of a current approved overseas or international licence at all times - even tourists will be subject to on the spot fines for not having their licence.

OFF-ROAD DRIVING Some of the roads in New Zealand are graded tracks. This is especially true in the north of the North Island. Although these roads are very safe and driveable, some hire cars do not insure their cars for off-road driving. In other words, you cease to be insured the moment you go onto an unmetalled road. It is therefore important that you discover what the insurance on your car hire covers. If necessary you should take out extra insurance (some rural roads are unmetalled, so this is advisable).

BRIDGES Many bridges in New Zealand are only one lane wide. A sign with a large white arrow in a blue square indicates priority. A round red-edged sign indicates you must give way to oncoming traffic. In truth, you will find that the roads carry such a small amount of traffic that this is never a problem.

TERMINOLOGY Some road terms may not be familiar. Speed humps or traffic calmers are called judder bars in New Zealand. Signs painted on the surface of the road to warn you of coming hazards are painted in reverse order, presumably on the basis that you will read them one at a time as you come to them. In fact, you tend to take them in at a single glance and find yourself puzzling over 'ahead road major'.

ACCIDENTS The rules regarding accidents are pretty much the same as in other countries. Never admit liability. Get the full details from the other driver, including insurance policy number and issuer, driving licence and address. Report accidents immediately (but certainly within 24 hours) to your hire company. If anyone is hurt, inform the police immediately.

BREAKDOWNS Most hire companies will let you have anything fixed on a car up to a limit of about $100. After that you need to contact them for authority. If you do break down your best bet is to contact your car hire company, which will typically have a freephone number to call. If you are out of calling range and broken down a long way from anywhere, the next vehicle along will almost certainly try to help you. In this regard New Zealanders are quite remarkable.

DRIVING CONDITIONS New Zealand roads are generally easy to drive, though extra care should be taken on gravel roads – rural roads that are not tar-sealed. Also bear in mind that multi-lane highways are the exception, so be careful when overtaking, especially on the country's many hilly roads. All in all, by simply exercising the care you would at home, you will be able to enjoy an accident-free holiday.

DRINKING AND DRIVING LAWS Do not even think about drinking and driving in New Zealand. There is a theoretical limit of 80 mg of alcohol to 100 ml of blood but there is a very active campaign to lower that limit and the police are absolute tigers. New Zealand simply does not tolerate drunk drivers.

FUEL This is readily available but it is a good practice to fill up as soon as the needle gets to the halfway mark. There is nothing worse than driving along what appears to be an endless highway with the needle hovering around empty. All hire cars take unleaded petrol. Few garages are self-service. Someone will come out, fill the car for you, clean the windscreen and offer to check your oil. You may have forgotten that such courtesies existed. They do in New Zealand.

PARKING In keeping with the rest of the world, New Zealand suffers from parking problems in the larger towns and cities. In some places, like Hamilton and Auckland, the only way to deal with it is to leave your car in a long-stay car park and walk everywhere. Other places are somewhat easier. In many places parking at a 45-degree angle to the kerb is standard. As almost anyone parks 'nose in', they reverse out, so driving past such parked cars requires extra care and attention.

In some towns there are parking meters and if you overstay your payment you will get a ticket. Do not think that having a hire car will save you – you will get a supplementary charge on your credit card account at a later stage as a nasty reminder.

POLICE The recently introduced Highway Patrol enforce local speed limits with the aid of speed cameras. What you need to do is to change mental gear and realise that you are driving in a country where the roads can be narrow and frequently very winding and that the speed limits suggested are pretty sensible.

ROAD SIGNS All road signs follow standard international practice. The only one that you might not be familiar with is the LSZ sign – for Low Speed Zone – which means that you must drive at 50 kph (30 mph) in adverse conditions. Otherwise the 100 kph (60 mph) limit applies.

LIGHTS New Zealand drivers seem to switch to dipped lights as soon as there is any loss of visibility. This sensible idea means that dipped lights are used during heavy rain and in the late afternoon, just as the light is fading. Motor cycles drive permanently on dipped beams.

AUTOMOBILE CLUBS Many automobile clubs have reciprocal agreements with the automobile Association in New Zealand. In Britain the AA, in Australia the NRMA, RVAC and others all have such arrangements, so check with your organisation before you go. Where reciprocal arrangements exist, you can visit any New Zealand office and come away with a bundle of free maps and guides.

SEATBELTS Everyone has to wear seatbelts, front and back, with only the very pregnant excused. There is a heavy fine for infringement.

SECURITY Car theft does happen, of course, but don't be over concerned. Take the usual precautions: lock up when you leave your vehicle, and don't leave valuables visible.

MOTOR MUSEUM You will see more elegant old vehicles on the road than anywhere else in the world. It is like a moving motor museum. The cars are not, however, kept as museum specimens. They are used every day. In one day near Hamilton it is possible to see a Riley 1.5 c. 1951, an MG TF, a Morris Cowley, a Jaguar XK120, a Railton and a Swallow Doretti. If you are a car lover, it is really an unexpected bonus.

A FINAL HINT If you are driving on both islands leave one vehicle at the point of departure and pick up a replacement at the point of entry on the next island. Don't bother taking your car over on the ferry – it's not worth the hassle.

RULES OF THE ROAD

Driving in New Zealand is really quite hassle-free, provided you observe a few sensible precautions. Read all the documentation supplied by the rental company; drive on the left; wear your seat belt at all times; don't drink and drive.

The left-hand rule

It's vital to remember when driving in New Zealand that the rule at intersections is different to anywhere else. On approaching an intersection where you intend to turn left, you must give way to traffic coming from the right and all traffic opposite you at an intersection or traffic lights. The only exception is when a green arrow allows you to proceed. Most hire companies supply diagrams to demonstrate this quaint eccentricity.

Considering the narrowness of many roads the accident rate is commendably low. On many narrow roads there are passing bays where slow traffic can pull over to permit safe overtaking. The speed limit on open roads is 100 kph, in built-up areas and low speed zones (LSZs), 50 kph. The fine for speeding varies depending on the degree by which the limit was exceeded. The maximum fine is $630 and the police are especially eagle-eyed on the approaches to towns.

Many bridges in New Zealand are single track. They are indicated by a circular 'Please Give Way' sign, a large arrow indicating which direction has priority and a smaller one showing which should give way. These signs are positioned some distance from the bridge and you should start braking as soon as you see one.

TAXIS

Taxis are metered. They operate from ranks or, for an extra charge, can be ordered by phone. Hailing them in the street is not usual. Two or three people sharing an airport taxi may work out cheaper than taking the shuttle bus.

CYCLE TOURING

This is an excellent way to see the country with its many quiet roads and varied scenery. While the South Island is more mountainous than the North, paradoxically you'll find that, overall, gradients are easier on the South Island. Unfortunately, New Zealand road builders tended to build 'up and over' so expect some strenuous bicycling!

It's so easy and economical to rent bikes in New Zealand that it's hardly worth all the trouble of bringing your own. If you're planning on touring for more than two months, there's a buy back scheme whereby 50 per cent of the price is refunded if the bike is returned in reasonable condition – for details see Natural High at www.cyclenewzealand.com. All major towns and tourist resorts have cycle rental companies.

THE CYCLING RULES OF THE ROAD

Give way to traffic turning from the right.

Always wear a helmet (compulsory).

Give way to cars and trucks.

Note also that cycling is illegal on all National Park tracks and on motorways.

RECOMMENDED

Northland circuit – a 12-day tour taking in all the sights north from Auckland to Cape Reinga along the east coast returning along the west.

Coromandel circuit – 7–9 days from Auckland around the Peninsula, either returning to Auckland or continuing to Rotorua or Whakatane in the east Bay of Plenty.

Rotorua to Wanganui via Lake Taupo, National Park and then down the 'River road' alongside the magnificent Whanganui River and National Park to Wanganui.

The West Coast to Nelson – 10–12 days from Wanaka across the Haast Pass and up the West coast of the South Island ending in Nelson.

Christchurch to Mt Cook and Queenstown – 6–9 days Lakes and Mountains tour.

More information from **Pedallers' Paradise NZ Cycle Touring Guide Books**. These books by Nigel Rushton retail at $12 in NZ, and cover highway profiles, gradient descriptions, distances, services, local attractions and alternative routes. Other useful guides published in New Zealand include **New Zealand by Bike** Bruce Ringer, Reed Books ISBN 0 7900 0367 8 (also available in the USA, Canada and the UK) and **Classic New Zealand Mountain Bike Rides** Paul, Simon and Jonathan Kennett ISBN 0 9583490 10. For information on South Island cycle touring holidays and bike hire see www.cyclenewzealand.com, and for mountain biking in general visit www.mountainbike.co.nz.

ROUTE PLANNING

The quickest way to cross between the two islands is to fly but a cheaper, and more scenic, option is to take the ferry across Cook Strait.

The mountainous terrain of both Islands means that travellers hoping to see all of New Zealand in one trip find themselves winding round in circular loops. Most international flights arrive in Auckland. From here it is possible to explore the Northland by driving or taking a bus. Northliner and InterCity Coachlines head through Warkworth, Whangarei, Paihia, Kerikeri and Mangonui to Kaitaia. From here the only way to reach the northern tip, Cape Reinga is by four-wheel drive excursion - assuming you want to drive along Ninety Mile Beach. Otherwise you can follow State Highway 1F all the way to the top in an ordinary car, though note that the last section is unsealed. Return via Paihia, then Kaikohe, Opononi, Dargaville and Brynderwyn to Auckland.

To see the rest of the North Island head south from Auckland. The train goes through Hamilton to Taumarunui, then via the Raurimu Spiral to Palmerston North and from there along the Kapiti Coast via Levin to Wellington.

For a more comprehensive coverage, make use of the road network. Buses from Hamilton call at New Plymouth on the west coast before going on to Wanganui. From here State Highway 4 heads back northwards via the Mangawhero Valley to National Park. At this point State Highway 47 crosses to Taurangi and Lake Taupo. Skirt the lake to the volcanic region of Rotorua before returning to Hamilton.

To see the eastern side of the island, take State Highway 26 to Thames on the Coromandel. This area is not well served by public transport, but buses follow State Highway 25 which loops round the peninsula via Coromandel town and Whitianga to Waihi. From here State Highway 2, known as the Pacific Coast

INFORMATION

One of the great things about travelling in New Zealand is the amount of detailed information which is available to guide and reassure you on your trip. There are over 90 information centres coordinated by the NZ Tourist board, forming the Visitor Information network. Each of the visitor centres, listed in this guide under the respective towns, can provide you with local safety advice as well as recommending insurance services if you decide to take part in an activity like bungy jumping.

Highway follows the Bay of Plenty through Tauranga and Whakatane, then crosses Eastland to Gisborne and Hawkes Bay. From here you can continue south on State Highway 2. InterCity and Newmans buses cover most of the region and Tranzit buses connect the towns near Wellington.

Routes round the South Island are dictated by the topography – there are only a few crossings of the central divide. From Blenheim both the railway line and State Highway 1 follow the east coast through Kaikoura, Christchurch (where the passenger train ends), Timaru, Oamaru and Dunedin to Invercargill.

From Invercargill State Highway 6 is the main road to Queenstown. West Coast InterCity and Mount Cook Landline buses operate along this route. State Highway 94, the only road to Fiordland National Park and Milford Sound turns off outside Lumsden. From Queenstown State Highway 6 crosses the Haast Pass and descends to the shoreline, passing Mount Cook and the Fox and Franz Josef Glaciers en route to Greymouth.

One way to appreciate the magnificent mountain crossings is to take the TranzAlpine Express from Greymouth through Arthurs Pass to Christchurch. Fifty kilometres further north at Waipara, take State Highway 7 past Hanmer Springs, so as to cross the Lewis Pass on your way back to the west coast. To complete the circuit of the island, take State Highway 6 from Westport to Tasman Bay, then Blenheim.

ACCOMMODATION

Advance bookings are recommended during the peak holiday season (from Christmas to the end of January, and during school holidays). Otherwise it's pretty much go as you please. Hotels within a group (see p. 406) will offer a free onward reservation prior to your departure. Many hotels offer special reduced rates at weekends (Fri–Sun) depending on the location and season – always ask.

Hotels All hotels should provide a fully licensed bar and restaurant. All rooms have en suite bathrooms. While they do not generally have cooking facilities, there are tea and coffee making machines.

Motels A motel will consist of self-contained units, usually with full cooking facilities enabling guests to prepare their own meals. Most units have en suite bathrooms and many properties have laundry facilities and spa or swimming pools.

Guest Houses A guest house or small hotel is often a converted older building with a certain charm. What it lacks in facilities, it usually makes up for in the warmth of the welcome.

Holiday Homes Imagine a fully equipped house with a private garden and a beach-front view! Such a home can be booked either in NZ or online and is not too expensive, especially for a group. A good alternative for families, or those who want to spend more time in one place. The book *Baches and Holiday Homes to Rent*, by Mark and Elizabeth Greening can be bought in NZ, or ordered from their website at www.holidayhomes.co.nz. For more online listings throughout New Zealand contact www.holidayhouses.co.nz.

Holiday Parks A holiday park has communal kitchens, toilets, showers and laundries. A wide variety of accommodation is available, such as camping sites, cabins, tourist flats and backpacker style lodges.

Farm Stays A farm or homestay offers an opportunity to experience a slice of New Zealand life. On a farm you can join in the activities: milking, kiwi fruit harvesting etc. Tariffs usually include breakfast.

Backpackers Backpackers accommodation takes the form of small, simply furnished rooms or dormitories, with shared kitchen facilities and a lounge, either in purpose-built hostels or as part of a larger complex. The two big networks are Budget Backpackers Hostels (BBH) and VIP Backpackers Resorts. Instead of a membership card, like the YHA, they offer (for a fee) special discount cards. In the case of BBH, it is the BBH Club Card (which also doubles as a phone card), whereas VIP Backpackers Resorts offer the VIP Backpacker Discount Card. These cards enable discounts with the major NZ transport companies and at various attractions. Free accommodation booklets from both organisations can be obtained in NZ.

YHA is the oldest and largest international network of hostels, with 64 hostels in New Zealand. There are many discounts available to YHA members in New Zealand, plus many offers that you can take advantage of before you go. Non residents can buy a membership in New Zealand for $30. Note that in most New Zealand YHAs, sleeping bags are not permitted, although blankets and duvets are provided. More details at www.yha.org.nz. In 2001, Hostelling International introduced a free online booking service which allows travellers to check out hostel facilities and make bookings up to six months in advance: www.hostelbooking.com.

YMCA/YWCA hostels are found mainly on the North Island in the main centres. On the South Island there are hostels in Christchurch, Invercargill, Dunedin and Timaru. The YMCA is open to individuals and families and some YWCA hostels will also accommodate men. For more details visit the YMCA website at www.ymca.org.nz. Information on the YWCA is available at www.ywca.org.nz.

Qualmark, 'the independent sign of quality', is the official independent quality classification system for New Zealand tourist accommodation and shopping. It's a joint venture between the New Zealand Tourist Board (NZTB) and the Automobile Association of New Zealand (NZAA). The accommodation ratings are based on facilities, rather than price and are colour-coded as follows: black (hotels), red (motels and self-catering), blue (bed and breakfast and homestays), green (camping sites, holiday parks, backpacker lodges).

There are two rival guides available in New Zealand: *AA New Zealand Accommodation Guide*, and *Jasons Motels and Motor Lodges New Zealand*. The AA guide lists hotels, motels, resorts, B & Bs, guest houses, home and farm stays, holiday parks, camping grounds, hostels and backpacker lodges. It features Qualmark ratings (see earlier). Complimentary copies are available to AA members, and can usually be picked up at an establishment featured in the guide. Alternatively, they may be purchased from Visitor Information Centres at $13.90 or from the following websites: www.aaguides.co.nz or www.nz-accommodation.co.nz. *Jasons Motels and Motor Lodges* guide is free and can be obtained from Visitor Information Centres and the motels or motor lodges mentioned. It can also be ordered direct from the publisher (postal fees payable for those living outside New Zealand or Australia): Jason Publishing, PO Box 9390, Newmarket, Auckland 1031; tel: 64 9 912 8400, fax: 64 9 912 8401; www.jasons.co.nz; e-mail: admin@jasons.co.nz.

CHILDREN

Children are welcome in New Zealand and well catered for. Supplies of baby foods, nappies and other essentials are widely available, and the water is clean and safe to drink everywhere. Adequate protection from the sun is absolutely essential as New Zealand has high levels of damaging ultraviolet rays.

All the major skiing resorts have a children's programme, with special clubs, trainers, childminders, etc. Hotels and motels provide cots for youngsters on request, while most restaurants will be happy to serve children's portions.There are plenty of parks and playgrounds where children can run wild, and there are several purpose-built attractions, like Splash Planet in Hastings and Rainbow's End, in Auckland. In a country that's noted for its adventure activities and outdoor sports, children will never be lost for something to do. Overall, New Zealand has a great and wonderful tradition of childcare, born of the sense that children represent the country's future.

CLIMATE

In New Zealand the warmest months are January and February and the coldest, June and July. The long summer holidays for school children extend over Christmas through January and demand for all services is high throughout that period.

Surrounded by sea, New Zealand enjoys a temperate climate, the North Island being marginally warmer than the South. Summer temperatures average 17°C but can soar to over 30°C. There are heat-waves but they're not a regular feature of New Zealand weather. Winter temperatures average 8°C and rarely fall below zero, except in the Southern Alps of the South Island.

CLIMATE QUICK FACTS

Temperate climate

Summer average 17°C

Summer high 30°C

Winter average 8°C

Winter low 0°C

North Island is marginally warmer than the South.

Rainfall varies according to the geography, with the West Coast and the Southern Alps receiving the most, often in spectacular deluges that can bump annual rainfall averages in a single day. Summer tends to be the drier season in the north, winter in the far south.

DISABLED TRAVELLERS

All new public buildings (including hotels etc.) are required by law to provide adequate access for the disabled. When travelling around the country, disabled persons will find that many transport operators will cater for their needs, or even offer them special discounts. However, note that urban buses are rarely equipped with wheelchair facilities.

GUIDE DOGS

A six-month quarantine period applies to guide dogs.

Disability Resource Centres will provide information on facilities at regional attractions. Contact the Disability Resource Centre, PO Box 24-042, Royal Oak, Auckland; tel: 09 625 8069, fax: 09 624 1633; e-mail: drc@disabilityresource.org.nz.

If you have documentation confirming disability you may be entitled to a New Zealand Mobility card – for which a charge is made. This will permit parking in specially designated areas. You will need to bring a medical certificate with you as official confirmation of your disability. For further details tel: 0800 227 2255, fax: 07 853 9765; www.ccs.nzl.org; e-mail: admin@waikato.ccs.org.nz.

FOOD AND DRINK

One of the advantages of eating out in New Zealand is that you always know you will be eating the freshest and finest ingredients. There's a wonderful choice of vegetables, the fish on your plate will often have been caught only hours earlier and New Zealand lamb is renowned throughout the world for its superb quality. Kiwi fruit, with its distinctive hairy skin and succulent green flesh, is now widely exported, but it's still worth sampling the real thing. If you're driving around the country and are looking for something to quench your thirst, load up with fruit from one of the roadside stalls. It's cheap and healthy and you can pat yourself on the back for helping the local economy.

It is a sadness that you will probably never taste one of the great delicacies of New Zealand – *toheroa soup*. This is made from a succulent shellfish once abundant on the beaches of North Island – Ninety Mile Beach was a favourite spot hunting ground. The dish became so popular that the shellfish, in danger of extinction, have been declared a protected species.

SOME NATIONAL SPECIALITIES

During your visit you should look out for some of the national specialities – venison (cervena) is a lot more palatable than the fatty muttonbird, a Maori delicacy still available on Stewart Island. Of the fresh fish, the locals' favourite is snapper, but blue cod, grouper, John Dory and tuna can also be recommended. Shellfish enthusiasts should try paua (abalone), tuatua (clams), Bluff oysters, green-lipped mussels and crayfish.

While New Zealand was never exactly renowned for the subtlety and sophistication of its cuisine, more imaginative minds are now at work introducing new, more adventurous, culinary trends. The mainstays – steaks, roast lamb and salmon – become more flavoursome when cooked in sesame oil with coriander and lemon grass. These Pacific Rim influences are in a nutshell what give New Zealand cooking its originality.

Coffee is the most popular non-alcoholic drink and café latte is well on the way to becoming a national beverage. It's often served in a huge bowl with an accompanying Anzac biscuit, made from golden syrup and oatmeal. Cappuccinos, usually served with sprinkled chocolate, and mochaccino, are other favourites.

New Zealand also has its own soft drink called L&P (Lemon and Paeroa), a refreshing, if sweet, mixture of lemon and mineral water.

Beer is a standard New Zealand drink. The Lion Nathan brewery produces Steinlager, one of the world's most garlanded beers. Look out for the more interesting and esoteric brews now being introduced under the influence of the growing micro-brewery movement.

In recent years New Zealand has made great strides as a wine-producing country. If you're interested in tastings and exploring wine cellars, the main vineyards are concentrated west of Auckland and in Gisborne, Hawke's Bay, Martinborough, Marlborough, Canterbury and Central Otago. Generally speaking, the whites such as Sauvignon Blanc are superior to the reds, although the producers are starting to do great things with the Pinot Noir grape.

MICRO-BREWERIES

For many years the Kiwi beer drinker's world was a very small one indeed. Compared with Europe, the choice of local beers was limited. Most brands sold were produced by one of the big nationwide breweries; that usually meant either Dominion or Lion Breweries. However, in recent years the situation has taken a turn for the better. Throughout the country dozens of small breweries have emerged, some of them producing brews refreshingly different from the mainstream brands.

A feature of many of these new, handcrafted beers is the emphasis placed on natural, non-pasteurised ingredients. They are often brewed without the addition of any sugars, chemicals or preservatives. The brewers also show an enthusiasm for European- or British-style beers and are producing a few very credible ales and wheat beers.

You are bound to come across a few interesting brews on supermarket shelves, but for some others you will have to go to the source. Good choices in Auckland are the Loaded Hog (p. 67) and Shakespeare Tavern, 61 Albert St. In the Taranaki region drop in at White Cliffs Breweries (4.5 kilometres north of Urenui, on Highway 3) and sample Mike's Mild Ale. Worth a mention in the South Island are the Dux de Lux bar, Christchurch (p. 297), and the Pink Elephant Brewery, Rapaura Rd, Renwick, Marlborough. For more tips chat to the patrons at the local pub.

HIKING

THE WHANGANUI RIVER JOURNEY

Although not a classic tramp, the canoe trip down the Whanganui river between October and April is classified as a Great Walk, with River Journey passes covering the use of all facilities on the river.

Hiking, or 'tramping' as it is known in New Zealand, gives you the opportunity to enjoy some of the world's last unspoilt places. There are thousands of kilometres of marked track, including the 'Great Walks' (see p. 40) and if these are crowded during the summer, there's a choice of lesser known, but equally scenic, routes to fall back on.

A network of back country huts has been established to provide overnight accommodation, ranging from category 1 with stoves, mattressed bunks, toilet and washing facilities to category 4 - usually simple shelters for getting out of the rain. Availability is on a first come-first served basis, so it's best to take a tent, just in case! Fees are paid by pre-purchased tickets from any Department of Conservation (DOC) office or Visitor Centre. Currently costing $5 each, you'll need one or two per night depending on the hut classification. Put the stub in the box on arrival and show the other part on your pack. An annual pass for just $65 saves money and hassle if you're doing a lot of tramping! Note that the pass is not valid for the 'Great Walks'.

The DOC also maintains over 120 campsites. Serviced sites are provided with flush toilets, hot showers, tap water, kitchen and laundry facilities, while standard sites have cold running water, toilets and fireplaces. Basic sites are places to pitch a tent with cold water on tap. Camping is permitted on all tracks, except the Milford Route. On the 'Great Walks' stay within designated areas - this is important to protect the native forests and purity of the streams and lakes.

Leaflets and park guides available at National Park Visitor Centres or local DOC offices will help you plan your tramp. Full details of DOC campsites and the hut system can be obtained from any DOC office or the Head Office at PO Box 10 420, Wellington; tel: 04 471 0726, fax: 04 471 1082; website: www.doc.govt.nz.

THE LANDSCAPE

The landscapes of New Zealand are dominated by the ranges of mountains and hills that run through both islands. There are 223 named peaks of more than 2300 metres, the highest being Mt Cook in the South Island, and over 75 per cent of the country lies more than 200 metres above sea level. This rugged topography has given rise to a huge variety of landforms and ecological zones; the only temperate-zone habitat not found here is true desert. Additionally, no inland location lies more than 110 kilometres from the sea.

THE TRAMPING EXPERIENCE

It's been a hot day, that climb over the last ridge has left the knees a bit wobbly, but now a cool breeze brushes your cheeks and you pause for a quick gulp from your water bottle. Another 10 minutes through a damp gully flanked by tree ferns and then, over a rise, you spot it – sunlight reflecting off a corrugated-iron roof reveals the goal of the day, a park hut scarcely visible amidst a sea of green.

The last short stretch to the hut is sometimes the hardest. Again you lose sight of it as the track descends, only to climb again almost immediately. Some 4 hours have passed since you started and it would be great to down your load finally and remove those sweaty boots. Around a bend and it's suddenly in front of you: brown-painted weatherboards, a generous veranda and, above all, the promise of a well-earned rest.

Sitting back with a freshly brewed cup of tea, the back of your T-shirt still damp from the backpack, you might ask yourself was all the effort worth it? Most would reply in the affirmative. For one thing the food always tastes great after a long day's tramping. Even the simplest meal of crackers and cheese will taste wonderful to a ravenous tramper. But joys of the tummy aside, there is really no better way to come into contact with the country's magnificent natural scenery or to meet its people. Any Kiwi trampers you meet are usually only too willing to share their knowledge with you. Over a hot cuppa they might not only give you some good tips for other tramps, but they might even invite you to their home.

After the evening meal some might play a round of cards by candlelight, others might just sit outside and yarn. Such evenings in the bush can be magical. Often you can stare up at a clear star-studded sky that seems so near you can almost touch it. Only the sound of insects, or perhaps a morepork (native owl), disturbs the tranquillity.

Tomorrow is your last day on the track and then it's back to civilisation. After just a few days in the bush, you are surprised at how quickly you were able to forget the hassles of daily life. More relaxed than you've ever been in a long time, you fall asleep as soon as you hit the pillow. The next day's tramp requires an early start and, as much as you've enjoyed it, you're yearning for a sip of cold beer in town.

TOPOMAPS

Remember to carry the appropriate 'Topomaps' for the track you are walking. The best for detail, they are available from the Department of Survey & Lands Information shops in key centres. Other useful maps are 'Parkmaps' and 'Trackmaps'.

THE GREAT WALKS The following are designated by the Department of Conservation as New Zealand's most famous tramping tracks. Most tracks take two to four days to complete and are well signed so getting lost is not a problem! Great Walks hut passes from the DOC are required for stays in huts and campsites. There is no camping on Milford Track.

Lake Waikaremoana Track, Te Urewera National Park – a 46-kilometre easy–medium walk in either direction over four to five days. An area of remote forested wilderness around the crystal-clear waters of the lake, with an abundance of native birdlife, fine beaches and good trout fishing. You must have a booking prior to starting this walk – DOC Aniwaniwa Visitor Centre, Te Urewera NP, Private Bag 2213, WAIROA. Booking desk, tel: 06 837 3900; e-mail: ureweraInfo@doc.govt.nz. Track transport: Big Bush Holiday Park (tel/fax: 06 837 3777) provides an 'on demand' shuttle service from Wairoa to the lake. Waikaremoana Guided Tours (tel: 06 837 3729, fax: 06 837 3845) offers a water taxi service from Waikaremoana Motorcamp.

Tongariro Northern Circuit, Tongariro National Park – circling the perfect cone-shaped Mt Ngauruhoe in the Tongariro Heritage Park, this four-day walk takes in active volcanic areas and hot springs. Do not attempt in winter. Track transport: One of the various options is Alpine Scenic Tours. They depart from Turangi to the track entry points, tel: 07 386 8918, fax: 07 386 8397; www.alpinescenictours.co.nz.

Abel Tasman Coast Track, Abel Tasman National Park – an easy-grade three- to five-day tramp, popular in summer, with wonderful coastal scenery, golden sandy bays and safe swimming. Track transport: one of the various options is Abel Tasman Coachlines, tel: 03 548 0285 or 03 528 8850; www.nelsoncoaches.co.nz/abeltasman.

Heaphy Track, Kahurangi National Park – an easy to medium 76-kilometre tramp in the north-west Nelson area, through mountain beech forest and ending on a nikau palm-fringed beach. Track transport: Kahurangi Bus Services, tel: 03 525 9434; fax: 03 525 9430; www.kahurangi.co.nz; e-mail: inquiries@kahurangi.co.nz.

RECOMMENDED BOOKS

New Zealand's Top Tracks, Mark Pickering, 1997, Reed Books, ISBN 0 7900 0589 1. A guide to DOC's Great Walks.

101 Great Tramps in New Zealand, Mark Pickering and Rodney Smith, revised 1998, ISBN 0 7900 0637 5.

A Tramper's Guide to New Zealand's National Parks, R Burton and M Atkinson, 1998, Reed Books, ISBN 0 7900 0622 7.

Look After the Land

• Protect plants and animals – treat the forests and birds with care, they are unique and often rare.

• Remove rubbish – take it in and take it out!

• Bury toilet waste – where there are no facilities, bury toilet waste in a shallow hole well away from waterways, tracks, campsites and huts.

• Keep streams and lakes clean – when washing, take the water and wash well away from water sources. Allow the water to drain into the soil. Do not return polluted waste water to a stream or lake.

• Take care with fires – portable fuel stoves are preferable to lighting a fire. Be aware of any fire bans that may be in place, especially in the summer months – and if you need to light a fire keep it small, and make sure it is out by dousing well and checking the ashes are out before leaving.

• Keep to the track – it helps protect fragile and often rare plants – and you won't get lost in the bush either!

• Consider others – all trampers have the right to enjoy the environment in peace.

• Respect our cultural heritage – many parks contain *taonga* (treasures), features of great significance and cultural importance to the Maori peple who have lived here for over 1000 years. Five of our national parks have been designated World Heritage Sites.

• Enjoy your visit – but as you leave check whether the next visitor to the area will know that you've been there. *Toitu te whenua* – leave the land undisturbed.

Look After Yourself

• Remember that walking in New Zealand's back country could be different from what you've experienced before. Choose a tramp that matches your level of fitness and experience, remember to carry the right gear and follow basic safety rules. DOC staff will be able to advise you on suitable routes based on your fitness, the weather and the time of the year.

• Beware – giardia is found in most lakes and streams. Before drinking always boil for a minimum of 3 minutes, chemically treat or use a giardia-rated filter.

• Always make sure you have good-quality walking boots, a comfortable backpack, wet-weather gear and warm clothing (even in summer), high-energy food with extra rations, and a first-aid kit. A portable stove, candles, torch and eating utensils are also important.

• Tramp with at least one other person – more if possible – and always leave a note of your plans at the Visitor Centre before starting. Use the visitor hut book to record your intentions along the way and the names of fellow trampers – this could be invaluable if help is needed.

• Despite a mild climate remember that the weather is notorious for changing extremely quickly, and heavy rain, snow and high winds can hit mountains even in summer (Nov – March). Do not be afraid to turn back if you are inadequately prepared. If disaster strikes and you need assistance in a remote area, send two people for help to the police or DOC, and stay alert to attract searchers' attention.

Routeburn Track, Mt Aspiring and Fiordland National Park - a medium-grade three-day walk. New Zealand's renowned alpine traverse with magnificent views, rainforest and subalpine scrub. Must be prebooked through Fiordland NP office in Te Anau (see Milford Track, below). More information from Kiwi Discovery, Camp St, Queenstown, tel: 03 442 7340, fax: 03 442 7349; www. kiwidiscovery.com/tracks; e-mail: info@kiwidiscovery.com. Track transport: from Queenstown with The Backpacker Express, tel: 03 442 9939; fax: 03 442 9940, and also Kiwi Discovery.

Milford Track, Fiordland National Park - 'The finest walk in the world', this award-winning route is a four-day 'one way only' easy walk from Te Anau to Milford.Very popular and must be prebooked. Bookings for Milford and Routeburn through Fiordland NP Centre, PO Box 29, Te Anau; bookings tel: 03 249 8514, fax: 03 249 8515; e -mail: greatwalksbooking@doc.govt.nz. Track transport: Can be arranged by Kiwi Discovery, Camp St, Queenstown; tel: 03 442 7340, fax: 03 442 7349.

Kepler Track, Fiordland National Park - the newest 'big track' finished in 1988 to a very high standard and offering a four-day medium loop with longer alpine sections between Lakes Te Anau and Manapouri. Track transport: either walk to the start (about 45 minutes) from Te Anau, use one of the boat services to Brod Bay, or catch the Kepler Track Shuttle Bus, tel: 03 249 7777.

Rakiura Track, Rakiura National Park - a three-day medium-grade 36-kilometre track on Stewart Island where there is almost no dry season - be warned! But certainly an excellent place for viewing native birdlife. Track transport: from Invercargill fly to Stewart Island, once there it's easy to walk to the start of the track. Contact Stewart Island Flights, tel: 03 218 9129, fax: 03 214 4681; e-mail: info@ stewartislandflights.com.

MAORI CULTURE

Maori culture is a real highlight for the visitor to New Zealand. The Maoris have been involved in the tourism industry since 1870 and 1880 when the Tuhourangi people - a sub-tribe of the Te Arawa confederation of tribes - south of Rotorua owned the Pink and White Terraces, which were impressive and beautiful layers of thermal pools. Visits to these pools were operated on a commercial basis. Even when these pools were destroyed by the eruption of Mt Tarawera in 1886, Rotorua is still a centre for Maori tourism. High-class entertainment here can be seen at numerous venues, often accompanied by a 'hangi' (a typical Maori feast).

A guided tour of any part of New Zealand by a Maori will provide the guest with an interpretation of the country's geographical features and history that is unique and interesting. The tourism industry recognises that the Maoris are a very important part of the attraction of New Zealand as a destination, and Maori faces and aspects of the culture can be seen in most promotions.

Maori people see the world not simply in terms of the physical, but also the spiritual realms. These are concepts difficult to explain in English – but the basic premise is that the Maoris believe everything in nature has a certain spiritual essence.

MAORI PEOPLE

Maoris are a tribal-based people. Oral history indicates that they first established themselves in Aotearoa New Zealand between 25 and 30 generations ago.

Knowledge of ancestry and the ability to name each generation is a key to identity of the Maori culture.

There are between seven and nine large tribal regions – although tribal boundaries are a matter for discussion between different tribes and different versions of history!

There are about 160 tribal and sub-tribal groups.

Each has a distinctive genealogy and a definite attachment to a specific piece of land.

Traditional crafts include carving and weaving, but today's artists also make use of contemporary art forms.

Maoris place particular emphasis on hospitality. Perhaps from a proverb: 'What is the most important thing in the world? It is people, people, people'. This is a value that holds the Maoris well within the tourism industry.

The Maoris acknowledge the permanence of land and the need to care for the land in a way that will ensure sustainability of life in the long term. Tribal boundaries are explained in terms of geographical features. Their genealogical connection to the land is important to all Maoris.

MONEY

The New Zealand dollar is divided into units of 5, 10, 20 and 50 cent coins. There are also $1 and $2 coins and notes in denominations of $5, $10, $20, $50 and $100.

Thomas Cook Traveller's Cheques free you from the hazards of carrying large amounts of cash. Foreign exchange desks are found in many Thomas Cook travel shops, which provide foreign exchange facilities and will change currency and traveller's cheques (free of commission in the case of Thomas Cook Traveller's Cheques). They can also provide emergency assistance in the event of the loss or theft of Thomas Cook Traveller's Cheques.

Major credit cards are accepted by most businesses in New Zealand, although as in most countries, cash is appreciated in smaller establishments. ATMs (automatic teller machines) are widespread, and can be used to withdraw cash if you have a PIN number with your credit card.

OPENING HOURS

Banks are open Mon–Fri 0930–1630, except public holidays.

Bureaux de Change, found in most major resorts, are open long hours and often at weekends.

Most shops open Mon–Fri 0900–1730, and Sat 0900–1230 (or until 1630 in the larger centres). Late-night shopping is until 2030 or 2100 on one night of the week (usually Thursday or Friday). In larger towns many supermarkets and some retail stores keep longer hours and are open seven days. This also applies to petrol stations throughout the country, some of which are open 24 hours. Convenience stores (dairies) usually open daily 0700–2200.

MUSEUMS

Throughout New Zealand there are two kinds of museums. First there are those in the cities which are of a very high standard and which, typically, are open Mon–Sat 0900–1700. Some of them are also open on Sundays. This especially applies to the glorious new Te Papa in Wellington, the finest museum in New Zealand.

Then there are the small museums run by the historical societies of the smaller towns. Often you will find that they are open only on one Sunday in a month from 1000 until 1100. As they are run by volunteers you can hardly complain. Many of them are interesting but you will find that quite a few consist of little but displays of early agricultural equipment. On the other hand there are some small museums that are fascinating, intelligent, amusing and well run.

NATIONAL PARKS

Entrance to every national park is free, and they are open right through the year. Every national park has an office - sometimes several - staffed by rangers who are enthusiastic, concerned and helpful. Where camping is allowed in national parks - it is not always the case - it is normally in designated areas. National parks are the responsibility of the Department of Conservation (DOC). They publish some splendid small guides on specific features, which are available at all good information offices at low prices.

FLORA

Centuries of exploitation at first by the Maoris and then, more devastatingly, by European settlers have transformed a land that was once almost entirely covered by forest. Prior to logging in the 19th century, great kauri forests dominated the north of the North Island. Other parts of the island were blanketed by equally impressive podocarp forests. Comprised of native conifers such as totara, rimu and kahikatea, this type of forest has remained virtually unchanged for over 190 million years. In the cooler South Island it was the native beech forest that reigned supreme, except for the west coast, where again podocarp species dominated.

Fortunately, the logger's axe is no longer encroaching on New Zealand's unique forests. Recognising that its trees and wildlife are a finite and valuable resource, the country now preserves a third of its total land area in the form of parks and other protected areas. In this respect New Zealand is a leader when it comes to environmental protection.

A characteristic feature of the native forest is the abundance of ferns. There are some 180 species of fern, though the ones that capture most interest are the lovely tree ferns. Two species found throughout the country are the ponga, or silver fern, and the mamaku. The former is easily recognised by the silver-coloured underside of its fronds and grows up to 10 feet high. The mamaku has a black trunk and is the tallest of the tree ferns, reaching a height of 20 metres.

Other notable trees include the beautiful pohutukawa, which is found in coastal areas and flowers bright red around Christmas time; the yellow-flowering kowhai, a favourite of nectar-eating birds such as the tui; and the nikau palm, New Zealand's only native palm tree. Nikaus are found on both main islands, but they prefer the warmer regions of the North Island.

The country's alpine regions are home to over 600 species of plant. A curiosity is the strange-looking vegetable sheep (it looks like a sheep from a distance), a member of the daisy family unique to New Zealand. Down on the coast native flax is common, and on some dunes you might see the grass-like pingao, which is unrelated to any other plant in the world.

FAUNA

New Zealand's untouched forests were once without land mammals. Only a few species of bat flitted through the trees, otherwise the forest was the realm of birds. In the absence of ground-dwelling predators some lost the ability to fly, filling ecological niches that elsewhere were occupied by mammals. Now-extinct moa browsed bushes like giraffes, and tiny, flightless wrens once scuttled about in place of mice.

But the arrival of man, and the animals he brought with him, proved to be a disaster for many native birds. Especially hard hit were the flightless species, which stood little chance against the rampages of rats, cats and weasels. Of the few that have so far survived, the majority are counted among the country's most endangered animals. Even kiwis, a national symbol, are endangered in many parts of their habitat. Extremely rare is the kakapo, the world's heaviest and only flightless parrot. Also very rare is the takahe, which was re-discovered a little over 50 years ago. Only the flightless weka has managed to retain a fairly healthy population. Around forest huts in the South Island they are still a common sight, often coming quite close to investigate (and possibly steal) any shiny objects.

If the above sounds somewhat depressing, it is perhaps pertinent to add that the nation's forests are by no means empty of birdsong. Conservation programmes in recent decades have enabled some declining bird populations to increase and a few birds have done quite well, despite competition on the part of introduced animals. Relatively common birds you are likely to spot on a walk along one of New Zealand's bush tracks include fantails, tui, native pigeons and bellbirds. The kaka parrot is on the increase in some areas and the world's only mountain parrot, the kea, may often be seen in alpine regions.

Away from the forest, on the coast, visitors will also find an interesting array of wildlife. Apart from several species of penguin, you are likely to glimpse fur seals and even huge elephant seals on shore. In the coastal waters dolphins are quite common and around Kaikoura mighty sperm whales are a major attraction.

As far as reptiles are concerned, there are roughly 30 species of lizard in New Zealand, as well as the unique tuatara. Many visitors will be relieved to know that there are no poisonous snakes, though there is a poisonous spider known as the katipo. Fortunately it is rarely encountered and the bite is seldom fatal.

The only wild mammals of any size are all introduced. They include a few species of deer, wild pigs, possums and chamois in the alpine regions. All may be hunted for sport and they are all considered pests in the national parks.

Dogs are not allowed into any national park. Some of these parks are serious wilderness areas and you would be well advised to take advice from the rangers on the prevailing conditions and take any necessary precautions before embarking on an ambitious expedition.

OUTDOOR ADVENTURE

The selection of outdoor activities in New Zealand is pretty much unbeatable, and not all of them are expensive. Cycling, surfing and tramping are practically free if you have your own gear; and the price of a trip to the ski slopes or the golf course will certainly be a pleasant surprise to those used to European rates. Major attractions, like bungy jumping, white-water rafting and jetboating, will cost a fair amount, as you would expect.

Most sporting activities can be booked through tourist information offices, at your hostel in New Zealand, or directly through commercial operators. Some backpacker hostels offer discount rates for guests. If you want to check out prices in advance, speak to a specialist travel agent or contact the New Zealand Tourism Board at New Zealand House, Haymarket, London SW1Y 4TQ; tel: 020 7930 1662 or 0906 910 1010 (£1 per minute).

BLACK-WATER RAFTING Glide underground through worm-lit caves in Waitomo. Cost is around $70. Website: www.black-water-rafting.co.nz.

BUNGY JUMPING The one everyone wants to know about! Queenstown, Taupo, Mangaweka, Hanmer Springs and Auckland. Costs from $80.

CANOEING AND KAYAKING Both very popular in New Zealand. Canoeing is done in open, two-person canoes, and kayaking in narrow, one-person craft. This is possible at all levels according to the river – tranquil cruises or heaving rapids – whichever you prefer. Queenstown, Wanaka, Whanganui River. Cost is from $30.

CAVING Can either be done through a commercial operator or through a caving club. Waitomo, Westport, Nelson are just a few of the locations.

FISHING From big game to trout, fishing is popular and available in many places in New Zealand. The best months are January to May (boat fishing is March to November). For game fishing, you will need to charter a skippered game boat, which provides everything from bait to refreshments. Otherwise you will need to purchase a fishing licence.

ADRENALIN JUNKIES

The adrenalin is surging through your body as the last few steps to the platform are taken. 'Why the heck am I doing this?' is a question that flies through most heads before the plunge. Your palms are sweaty, your lips dry and it feels as though a great swarm of butterflies has taken possession of your stomach.

'Okay mate, smile for the camera,' grins one of the bungy crew. At that moment you're not sure whether it's going to be a smile or a grimace that's snapped for posterity. 'Are you ready?' Daft question, you think, but you nod your head anyway and move closer to the edge. Over 100 metres below, the abyss is awaiting you. The countdown begins and, pushed by a final rush of adrenalin, you dive.

Some let out a scream when they make the plunge. Others remain silent, as nothing but air embraces them and they hurtle downwards at over 100 kph to the river below. Then, just when impact seems imminent, the rubber cords attached to your ankles pull you back and you bounce like a helpless doll in the hands of a demented puppeteer. The whole thrill has lasted little more than 7 seconds.

But these 7 seconds had it in them! Everybody who has jumped seems to be overwhelmed by a feeling of intense well-being. It's a high that can last for days and is produced by hormone-like substances known as endorphins that the body releases at the instant you overcome your fear.

Not everybody manages the bungy jump. Some turn back at the last moment, not yet ready to face the abyss. But that also takes courage; recognising your limits. Those who do spring are a varied bunch. From bronzed outdoor types, to petite Japanese women and obvious indoor types with nascent pot bellies. What they all share is a lust for the immediate thrill, along with the desire to know if they can take themselves to the limit.

It's a calculated risk, this mini-adventure. The knowledge that thousands before you have done it, and survived, reassures and motivates. Those who've experienced such a thrill are often hungry for more. For these adrenalin junkies New Zealand is an eldorado of possibilities. Tandem skydiving, white-water rafting or jetboating all are just a ticket away.

The New Zealand Professional Fishing Guides Association is pleased to give advice and quotes to anglers. Fishing is mainly concentrated on the east coast of the North Island, including Bay of Islands, Tutukaka, Whangaroa, Whitianga, Major Island, Whakatane, Lake Rotorua, Lake Taupo and Southern Lakes (trout). Websites: www.fishnz.co.nz; www.fishing.net.nz; www.nzpfga.com.

Golf New Zealand has more than 400 golf courses, many of them not too expensive. There are many near Taupo and Waitangi, in the Bay of Islands. Green fees range from $5 in some country areas to $100 at more exclusive city courses.

Horse Riding Horse riding is a great opportunity to get right out into the wilderness. Kaikoura, Westland, Wanaka, Taupo, Taranaki. Prices range from $25 an hour to $360 for a two-day trek. Websites: www.ridenz.com; www.truenz.co.nz/horsetrekking.

Jetboating Ride the incredible Hamilton jetboats, invented in New Zealand, for a huge thrill that luckily requires no skill! From Queenstown, jetboating can be combined with helicopter and raft trips. Other locations include Taupo, Whanganui river, Waimakariri, Rangitaiki River and Waikato River below the Huka Falls. Costs from $50.

Mountain Biking A great way to see the country: you can stick to the roads or head off into some forest parks and designated off-road tracks. Cycling is not permitted in national parks. Expect to pay about $20 a day or $90 a week.

River Sledging The latest craze. Sledgers ride polystyrene sleds with just a wetsuit and a helmet for company. Kawarau River, near Queenstown. Costs from $90 a ride.

Rock Climbing Rock climbing is a popular sport, pursued in quarries and up artificial walls, as well as mountains. Auckland, Te Awamatu, Southern Alps.

Sailing Kiwis love the water (if you need proof take a look at Auckland's double harbour any time over the weekend). The Bay of Islands is a popular sailing spot, but almost every coastal town will have an active yacht club and charter operator. You can hitch up with a local club for free, or charter from about $80 per day. Auckland, Northland, Hauraki Gulf, Lake Taupo, Marlborough Sounds. For charters also check out the following website: www.charterguide.co.nz.

Scuba Diving There is some fascinating sea life to be seen. Wreck diving is available and Fiordland offers relatively easy access to rare black coral. Poor Knights Islands Marine Reserve (Whangarei), Sugar Loaf Island Marine Park (New Plymouth), the Bay of Islands, Hauraki Gulf, Marlborough Sounds.

SEA KAYAKING This is increasingly popular and a good alternative to coastal tramping in sheltered areas. Bay of Islands, Coromandel, Abel Tasman National Park, Fiordland. From $40 a day.

SKIING A major winter sport, with fields open in the North and South Islands from June to October. There are many small cheap club fields operating in South Island. Larger operators include Whakapapa and Turoa in Tongariro National Park, Mt Hutt, Coronet Peak and the Remarkables in the South Island. In general, they are smaller than the European fields, but they are still of a high standard. Lift passes are around $70 a day at major fields (they'll be much less at the clubs).

SKYDIVING This is a popular activity in New Zealand. Paihia and Queenstown are the best spots.

SURFING New Zealand surfers are a hardy bunch and can be found riding the waves all year round, even in the icy waters off Dunedin. Auckland (east and west coasts), Gisborne, Taranaki, Dunedin, Kaikoura and the west coast all have good breaks.

TEAM SPORTS Every weekend and at the end of most working days, Kiwis head for the sports fields to indulge in everything from rugby and soccer to touch rugby, beach volleyball and netball. Settle anywhere for more than a week or two and you'll be able to hook into a team of one kind or another - see local newspapers or tourist offices for contacts. Costs no more than a few dollars per game.

WHALE WATCHING This allows you to get close to a killer whale, a sperm whale or dolphins off the coast of Kaikoura. Weather is an important factor, so it is best to allow a few days to be sure that you spot one of these superb animals.

WHITE-WATER RAFTING This is very popular and lots of fun. You can usually choose between either a half-day trip or a three- to four-day adventure. Rivers are graded from 1 to 6 (not raftable) according to difficulty. No experience is required (just a shot of bravery!). There are opportunities in Queenstown, the Whanganui River, the Rangitikei and many places in the North Island. Cost is from $80 a day.

WINDSURFING Like sailing, windsurfing is tremendously popular in New Zealand, and people surf on all lakes and around the coast, sheltered or not. Lessons are readily available at Lake Taupo, Auckland, southern lakes and Bay of Islands to name just a few.

PACKING

When packing for a trip to New Zealand, it is more a question of what to leave out rather than what to take. New Zealand is a very informal country. Men are never really likely to need a tie, unless you are going to one of those restaurants where style is more important than the food. A suit isn't needed either: a blazer and slacks for the men is the equivalent of formal dressing. Ladies also dress informally and quite casually. You will, however, need a truly waterproof - and not just shower-proof - coat of some kind, preferably with a hood.

READING

Referred to throughout this guide as the **OTT**, the *Thomas Cook Overseas Timetable* is published every two months, price £10.50 per issue. Indispensable for independent travellers using public transport in the New Zealand, it contains timetables for all the main rail, bus and ferry services, plus details of local and suburban services. It is available from UK branches of Thomas Cook, by mail order, phoning (01733) 416477 in the UK, or on the website www.thomascookpublishing.com. In North America, contact ST Travel Publications, 3959 Electric Rd, Suite 155, Roanoke, VA 24018; tel: 1 (800) 322-3834; www.travelknowledge.com; e-mail: sales@travelknowledge.com. A special edition of the *Overseas Timetable* is available from bookshops and from the outlets given above - the *Thomas Cook Overseas Timetable Independent Traveller's Edition* includes bus, rail and ferry timetables, plus additional information useful for travellers. Please note that the OTT table numbers very occasionally change - but services may easily be located by checking the index at the front of the *Overseas Timetable.*

FICTION The best known New Zealand author is Katherine Mansfield, which was the pen name of Katherine Middleton Murry. She was born in Wellington and raised in New Zealand. In her short life - she lived only 35 years - she wrote a series of works that are reminiscent of Chekhov.

In most bookshops you can also see a display of the works of the late Barry Crump. The best of these is *A Good Keen Man*. Barry Crump's memory is revered in New Zealand, and his books give a very accurate flavour of the country.

Finally, Ngaio Marsh, the detective writer and the distinguished theatre director, was also a Kiwi.

FAY WELDON

It is not generally known that the novelist Fay Weldon is also a New Zealander, having been born and raised on the Coromandel Peninsula.

SAFETY

New Zealand is not a crime-free zone but provided you apply common-sense rules, you should not experience any problems during your stay. It is supposed to be one of the safest countries in the world for travellers. However, just to be cautious, travel with as few valuables as possible; don't leave items such as cameras visible on car seats or unattended on the beach while you swim and remain reasonably vigilant. Hotels and motels normally provide facilities for storing items best not left in rooms.

No particular vaccinations are required for travel in New Zealand. Take out medical insurance before you travel: it's relatively cheap and saves a lot of hassle. Accidental injury may be covered by New Zealand's government-run Accident Compensation and Rehabilitation scheme and this may help with some medical expenses but it is not comprehensive.

Normal holiday insurance will not extend to bungy jumping, white-water rafting, skiing, snowboarding and other activities that can result in broken bones. Make sure you take out extra cover – especially if you are skiing as the costs of recovering accident victims from the slopes can be horrendous.

SHOPPING

New Zealand may not be a shopper's paradise, but there are some interesting products available. Worthwhile souvenirs include hand-knitted sweaters, garments made from possum fur, sheepskin products, original pottery, jade work and other jewellery. However, on the whole you come to New Zealand for scenery, sport and food.

Many coffee shops appear to have been designed with a 1960s look. You might think that this is the result of clever new-wave retro designing. You would be wrong. New Zealanders, when it comes to coffee shop design, stay with what they find comfortable.

SMOKING

Smoke-free environments, regulated by law, are relatively common in New Zealand as a result of the high percentage of deaths due to cancer. (One in four New Zealanders die of the disease, and 87 per cent of lung cancer deaths are due to smoking.) Tobacco advertising is banned, and sponsorship is only allowed providing a tobacco related sponsorship is not acknowledged. Travellers should note that smoking is forbidden on domestic internal flights (non-smoking rules may also apply to international flights both inbound and out of New Zealand depending on the airline). Smoking is also forbidden on buses – local or national, in passenger booking offices and waiting lounges except where a smoking area has been designated and clearly marked. When eating out in licensed restaurants, a hotel or bar you will find designated non-smoking areas. At least half of the available seating (sometimes more) is specifically allocated to non-smokers and clearly signed as such. The fine for smoking in an undesignated area is $400 per person.

Duty-free allowance is 200 cigarettes or 50 cigars, or 250 grams tobacco, or a mixture up to 250 grams, and you must be over 17 years of age to purchase. Other non-tobacco smoking products are illegal/not permitted and under no circumstances should you attempt to import these.

SPEAKING NEW ZEALAND STYLE

If you are planning on starting your tour of New Zealand on a good footing, then it is probably a good idea to brush up on some of the lingo.

Like most places in the world where English is spoken, it is not quite in its original format. There is an old 'fish and chips' joke – where Australians tease New Zealanders that they pronounce it 'foosh and choops'. That does provide quite a useful guideline! In general, New Zealanders are very laid back and this is reflected in their language.

Some Kiwi vocabulary:

Bach: a country or seaside retreat, which can range from a shack to a large and palatial mansion.
Chilly bin: an essential part of New Zealand life, being an insulated case for carrying picnic supplies (and, more importantly beer) to the beach and sporting events.
Chunder: the result of an excessive intake of beer (vomiting is also referred to by several other terms, for instance technicolour yawn).
Greasies: splendidly descriptive New Zealand word for fish 'n' chips.
Kiwi: colloquial term for all New Zealanders.
Marae: a Maori word generally referring to the open space in front of a meeting house, though it is also loosely used to include the surrounding buildings as well.
Pakeha: a Maori word now referring to non-Maori New Zealanders.
Scull: to knock back your drink very quickly – probably derived from the Scandinavian *skol*.
Shout: to offer to pay something for somebody, often a drink at the pub; e.g. 'It's my shout' (It's my turn to pay for the drinks).
Ute: a car-sized pick-up truck (contraction of utility van).

PRONOUNCING MAORI PLACE NAMES

Many New Zealand place names are Maori and it is very helpful when asking for directions to be able to pronounce them correctly. Each Maori syllable ends with a vowel. There are five vowels – a, e, i, o, u – which can be short or long:

a – as in father

e – as in when

i – as in ee in meet

o – as in fort

u – as in oo in boot

If there are two vowels together then they are each given their own sound but run together slightly.

For example, ai is ah-ee but will sound like the i in high.

There are 11 consonants: m, h, k, m, n, p, r, t and w, which are pronounced as in English, ng as in singer, and wh, pronounced either as wh or a very soft f.

Luckily, most Maori place names have been assimilated to English pronounciation anyway, following your instincts on vowel length.

SPECIAL DAYS

New Zealand doesn't have any big ethnic festivals. Waitangi Day, commemorating the peace treaty signed between the Maori and the Europeans in 1840, is commemorated on 6 February but even in Waitangi itself the celebrations can be muted, or even non-existent, following a series of serious demonstrations by Maori activists.

25 April is Anzac Day, a very important date, as New Zealand sent, as a percentage of its population, more troops to both World War I and II than any other Allied country. On Anzac Day, if you have served in the forces, you pin your medals to your chest and you march to the memorial service. You can then go and sink a few ales and renew old friendships and frolic in the streets without fear of interference by the police.

For a complete listing of the National Holidays, see the Directory section in the back of this book. A detailed events calendar is provided on the CD.

SPORT

New Zealand is sports mad. Every sport that you can think of is played here, and played at a very high level. In rugby union, the country moves from interest to total obsession. The All Blacks, the New Zealand Rugby Union side, are revered as gods as long as they keep winning. Sometimes, very rarely, they have a losing streak and the country goes into deep mourning. At some time during your visit you will be asked your opinion of the All Blacks side. No matter what you actually think, it would be a very generous diplomatic gesture to say that this is the greatest rugby team that the world has ever seen. Such consideration will make your visit much more enjoyable.

TIPPING

Tipping is not customary in New Zealand. Service charges are not included in restaurants and hotel bills as a matter of policy and in some cases a tip can seriously offend. The best advice is to use your own discretion, but to see tipping as the exception rather than the rule.

EXCEPTIONS

The top restaurants and international hotels might expect tipping. In those cases, a good guideline is 10 per cent.

WATER

Nowhere in the world, it is claimed, can you drink purer water than in New Zealand. In Christchurch the water is often nominated as the purest city water in the world. That people still buy bottled water merely shows the power of advertising. However, some rivers and streams have been contaminated by giardia parasites. During a hike always boil or treat the water beforehand.

WINE

Bringing wine into New Zealand is not worthwhile. It is cheaper and better to buy it locally. Auckland, Wellington and Christchurch airports have duty-free shops in their arrivals areas, so you do not have to carry the goods with you from the airport you departed from.

TIMELINE OF NEW ZEALAND HISTORY

Around AD 1000	Arrival of the Polynesian people later known as Maoris, via double-hulled canoes, on the shores of New Zealand. They live off the land, fishing and hunting flightless birds such as the moa.
c.1300–1400	The Maoris establish settlements mainly around the coast of the North Island and visit Stewart Island and the southern coast. They develop into a tribal society, one tribe defending itself from another by building forts (*pa*) on hill-tops. They live in villages and grow crops such as the *kumara* (sweet potato).
1642	The Dutch East India Company sends Abel Tasman to explore the region. His first sight of New Zealand is Golden Bay, South Island. After an altercation with local Maoris he sails up the coast before returning home. The Dutch call the territory Staten Landt, then Nieuw Zeeland.
1769–70	Captain James Cook explores New Zealand on board the *Endeavour* and plants the British flag. After initially meeting hostility, he establishes friendly relations with the Maoris. Only from this time on do they actually refer to themselves collectively as Maori, meaning 'normal'. They call the foreigners *pakeha*.
1772–78	Cook returns to New Zealand several times and writes a report encouraging other European visitors. Meanwhile, French explorers also make expeditions to the territory.
1790–1820	First phase of European settlement. First sealers, then whalers set up coastal stations and encampments. They're joined by a motley population of adventurers and escaped convicts from Australia.
1814	Arrival of the first Christian missionaries from New South Wales.
1820	Founding of Russell (Kororareka).
1820–35	'Musket Wars'. Maori tribes get hold of European guns and use them to settle their own territorial disputes. Meanwhile, law and order threatens to break down completely in both communities. Jurisdiction of New South Wales courts extended to the British in New Zealand.
1833	James Busby is appointed British Resident after several North Island tribes appeal directly to King William IV to protect their lands. Busby receives no armed support from the Governor of New South Wales and is powerless to act.
1835	Charles Darwin describes the population of Russell as 'the very refuse of society'.
1839–43	William Hobson is instructed to establish British rule in NZ as a dependency of New South Wales. Edward Gibbon Wakefield's New Zealand Company plans to colonise the country with 'planned settlements' at Wellington, Nelson and New Plymouth. Some 19,000 settlers arrive under the scheme.
1840	Governor Hobson persuades North Island Maori chiefs to sign the Treaty of Waitangi, transferring sovereignty to the British in return for guaranteeing Maori land rights. Differences between the English and Maori versions of the document lead to friction, which continues to this day.

TIMELINE OF NEW ZEALAND HISTORY

1841	New Zealand is declared a separate colony from New South Wales. Auckland becomes the capital.
1844	Hone Heke, one of the first chiefs to sign the Waitangi Treaty, cuts down the British flagpole at Kororareka (Russell), beginning the 'war in the North'.
1852	The Constitution Act establishes colonial government with six provincial councils and a national parliament. Effectively, the Maoris are excluded from the decision-making process.
1858	Increasingly frustrated by colonial rule, the chief of the Waikato Maoris, Te Wherowhero, is declared king in an effort to prevent more land sales. The protest leads to violence and the outbreak of war.
1860–70	New Zealand Wars between British and Maoris coincide with gold fever on the west coast of the South Island.
1893	As the settler communities prosper, New Zealand is the first country in the world to give women the vote after a campaign led by Kate Sheppard.
1907	New Zealand is declared a Dominion of the British Empire.
1914–18	World War I. ANZAC troops from New Zealand and Australia are deployed by the British against the Ottoman army in the Dardanelles and suffer huge losses at Gallipoli in April 1915.
1939–45	New Zealand fights on the Allied side in World War II.
1947	In appreciation of the role played by New Zealand forces during the war, the country is granted full independence.
1973	Waitangi Day becomes an official public holiday. New Zealanders are divided whether to mark it with celebrations or protests.
1975	The Treaty of Waitangi Act sets up tribunals to hear Maori land claims against the Crown. Land March from Te Hapua (Northland) to the Parliament Building in Wellington.
1985	Sabotage by French Secret Service of Greenpeace vessel *Rainbow Warrior* in New Zealand waters.
1987	NZ Prime Minister David Lange bars ships carrying nuclear warheads from New Zealand harbours as part of his campaign against French nuclear testing on the Moruroa Atoll.
1996	Introduction of Mixed Member Proportional Representation. The balance of power in the resulting coalition is held by the New Zealand First party and its part-Maori leader, Winston Peters.
1998	Financial and economic disaster hits Auckland's business community following a 9½-week power failure. Thousands of businesses are affected.
2000	NZ is one of the first countries in the world to report the non-event of the Y2K computer bug. Team NZ wins the America's Cup for the second time running.
2002	Helen Clark's Labour party wins the election for the second time running.
2003	NZ hosts the America's Cup and is defeated by Swiss challenger *Alinghi*, a yacht captained by a New Zealander!

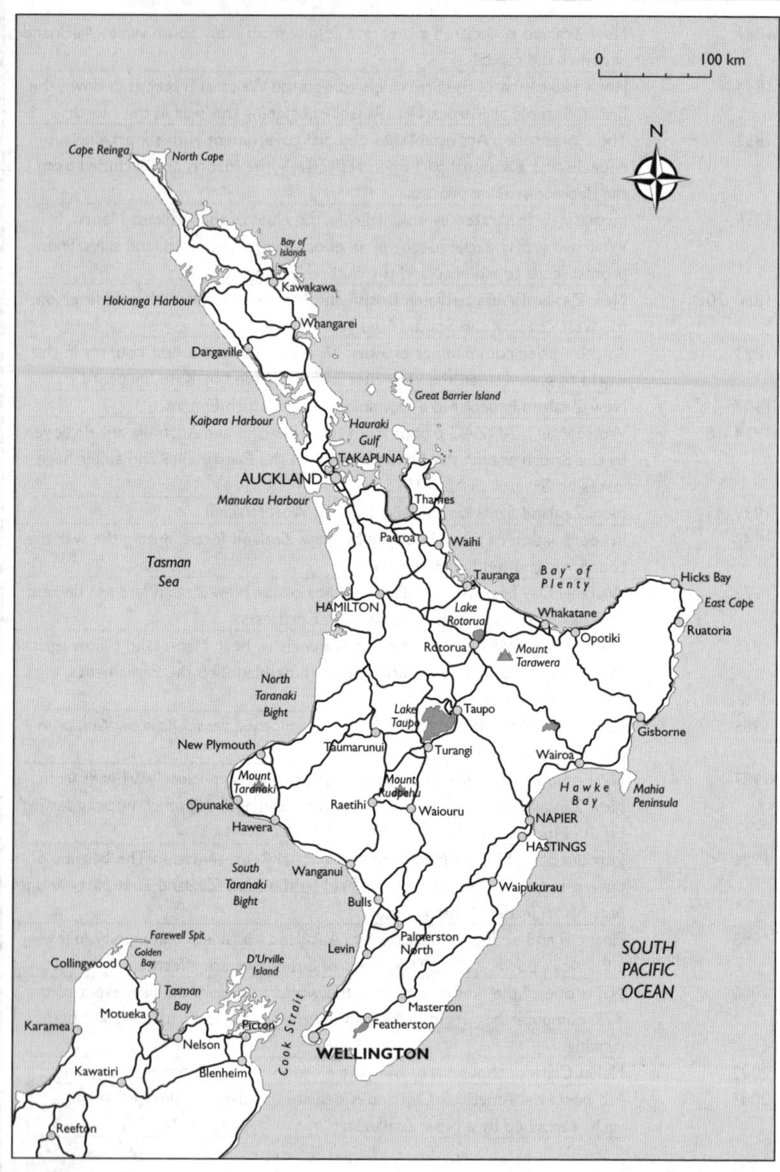

0
100 km
N
Cape Reinga
North Cape
Bay of Islands
Kawakawa
Hokianga Harbour
Whangarei
Dargaville
Great Barrier Island
Kaipara Harbour
Hauraki Gulf
TAKAPUNA
AUCKLAND
Manukau Harbour
Thames
Paeroa
Waihi
Tasman Sea
Tauranga
Bay of Plenty
Hicks Bay
East Cape
HAMILTON
Lake Rotorua
Whakatane
Opotiki
Ruatoria
Rotorua
Mount Tarawera
North Taranaki Bight
Lake Taupo
Taupo
Gisborne
New Plymouth
Taumarunui
Turangi
Wairoa
Mount Taranaki
Mount Ruapehu
Hawke Bay
Mahia Peninsula
Opunake
Raetihi
Waiouru
NAPIER
Hawera
HASTINGS
South Taranaki Bight
Wanganui
Waipukurau
Bulls
Farewell Spit
Golden Bay
Palmerston North
Collingwood
D'Urville Island
Levin
SOUTH PACIFIC OCEAN
Tasman Bay
Motueka
Masterton
Karamea
Picton
Featherston
Nelson
Cook Strait
WELLINGTON
Kawatiri
Blenheim
Reefton

North Island

North Island is packed with features worth visiting, and in particular Northland, forming the irregularly shaped, 240 kilometre-long peninsula that juts out at an odd angle from the North Island's top corner. Stretching out towards the equator and bisecting the 35th parallel – hence putting it on the same latitude as Sydney – Northland revels in a mild climate that has earned it the nickname of the 'winterless north'.

Northland has a rich historical legacy that reflects its position as the birthplace of New Zealand. It was here that the first Polynesian explorers settled, later to be followed by the Europeans on their whaling ships. Ancient legends, tribal battles and European colonists are all woven in the fabric of Northland. The main resort area in Northland is the scenic Bay of Islands, where 800 kilometres of coastline shelter the 150 or so offshore islands that give the area its name.

There are no resorts on the islands themselves; most accommodation surrounds the bustling town of Paihia, a pleasant town that is efficiently geared up to cope with its annual summer influx of 70,000 visitors. Alongside Paihia is Waitangi, the site of the 1840 treaty signing that formed such a pivotal role in the country's history. Just to the north of the Bay of Islands are the orchards of citrus and kiwi fruit that surround the township of Kerikeri, which boasts two of the country's oldest buildings, one in stone and the other wooden. Their age, however, pales into insignificance when compared with nature's own work in the form of the magnificent kauri trees in forests on the west side of the peninsula at Waipoua.

From Paihia it is a long journey up to one of the most isolated spots in New Zealand, Cape Reinga. In Maori legend, this was just the starting point for an even longer journey, as it was from here that the spirits of the dead set out across the oceans to Hawaiki, the ancestral homeland.

North Island: Our Choice

Parnell, Auckland
Browse through the shops, people-watch in the cafés

Waipoua Forest Sanctuary, Northland
Unique kauri forest

Russell, the Bay of Islands
An ideal base for the Cream Trip

Hahei, Coromandel
Fantastic beaches and picturesque Cathedral Cove

Tiritiri Matangi Island, Hauraki Gulf
Some of the world's rarest birds in their natural habitat

Rotorua and lakes
Maori culture, beautiful lakes, thermal activity

Tongariro National Park
Volcanoes and great walking

Whanganui River
Travel the river on a restored riverboat or by canoe

Napier
Stroll around the art deco city, visit the nearby gannet colony

East Cape road
Beautiful coastal scenery, dozens of lovely bays to visit

Mount Bruce National Reserve
Takahe and other rare birds

Museum of New Zealand, Wellington
Entertaining presentation of the country's history and people

How Much You Can See in a ...

Week (7 days)

Day 1. Auckland Day 2. Coastal drive to Coromandel township, then Hwy 25 to Whitianga Day 3. From Whitianga detour to Hahei or Hot Water Beach, then via Tauranga to Rotorua Day 4. Rotorua Day 5. Hwy 5 to Taupo (en route Waiotapu Thermal Wonderland and Wairakei), then around Tongariro National Park on Desert Road (Hwy1) via Waiouru, Ohakune and Raetihi to Wanganui Day 6. To Wellington along Hwy 1 Day 7. Wellington

Fortnight (14 days)

Day 1. Auckland Day 2. To Paihia Days 3–4. Paihia, Bay of Islands Day 5. To Kauri Coast via Kaikohe, then further south to Warkworth Day 6. To Otorohanga and Waitomo Caves via Hamilton Day 7. To Rotorua via Mangakino (en route Pureora Forest Park) and Tokoroa Day 8. Rotorua Day 9. To Taupo Day 10. To Wanganui Day 11. To New Plymouth, then return to Wanganui following road around other side of Mount Egmont Day 12. To Palmerston North, then via Woodville to Mount Bruce and Masterton Day 13. To Wellington Day 14. Wellington

Month (28 days)

Days 1–2. Auckland Day 3. To Paihia Days 4–5. Paihia (bus trip to Ninety Mile Beach) Day 6. To Mangonui, Doubtless Bay Day 7. To Kaitaia, then south along Kauri Coast to Dargaville, and then on to Warkworth Day 8. To Coromandel township Days 9–10. Coromandel Day 11. To Whitianga, then down to Tauranga and Rotorua Days 12–13. Rotorua Day 14. To Waihau Bay (East Cape) Day 15. To Gisborne Day 16. Gisborne (day trip to Lake Waikaremoana in Urewera National Park) Day 17. To Napier Day 18. To Taupo on SH5 Day 19. To Whakapapa Village in Tongariro National Park Day 20. Whakapapa Village Day 21. To Otorohanga and Waitomo Caves Day 22. South to New Plymouth on SH3 Day 23. New Plymouth Day 24. To Wanganui Day 25. Wanganui Day 26. To Wellington on SH1 Days 27–28. Wellington

For most visitors, Auckland is the entry point to New Zealand. The only true city in the international sense, Auckland is quite unlike the rest of the country. Although chock-full of tourist attractions, it's not a tourist city *per se* but a thriving cosmopolitan metropolis that accepts visitors with warmth and friendliness, albeit in a matter-of-fact, offhand manner.

Built on a series of hills that turn out to be extinct volcanoes and overlooking twin harbours, Auckland is undeniably beautiful. As always, in this part of the world, the scenery transcends the architecture.

The harbour (Auckland is almost completely surrounded by water) is a real gem. To the north Waitemata extends into the Hauraki Gulf and the Pacific, while to the south Manukau reaches out to the Tasman Sea. Sailing is the leading past-time for locals and on a sunny weekend you can barely make out the water for the forest of spinnakers and genoas. Not for nothing is Auckland known as the 'City of Sails'.

The isthmus on which Auckland stands was a much fought-over place in Maori times. The traditional name, Tamaki-makau-rau, means 'Tamaki of a hundred lovers' (or 'Tamaki of the many rivers', depending on who you are talking to) and has now been incorporated into the welcome signs at Auckland's Mangere airport.

An Urban Sprawl

The population of Auckland currently stands at around 1 million – pretty puny by world standards. In terms of area, however, it ranks as one of the largest cities on earth – a low-rise urban sprawl, straddled by the harbours of Waitemata to the east and Manukau to the west.

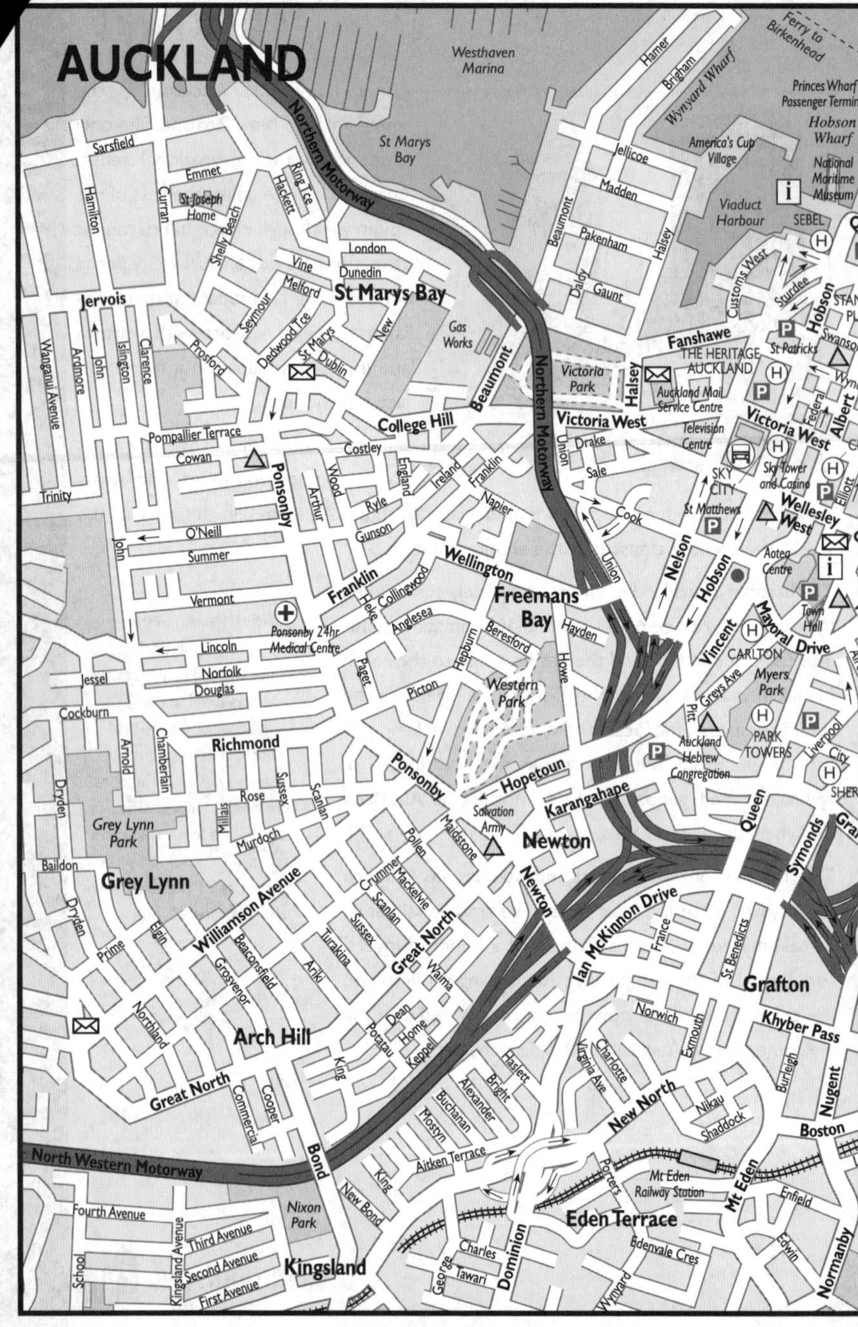

AUCKLAND
Westhaven Marina
Ferry to Birkenhead
Hamer
Brigham
Wynyard Wharf
Princes Wharf Passenger Terminal
Hobson Wharf
St Marys Bay
Northern Motorway
America's Cup Village
National Maritime Museum
Sarsfield
Emmet
Ring Tce
Hackett
St Joseph Home
Jellicoe
Madden
Viaduct Harbour
SEBEL
Hamilton
Curran
Shelly Beach
Beaumont
Pakenham
Halsey
London
Vine
Dunedin
Melford
St Marys Bay
Daldy
Gaunt
Customs West
Sturdee
Hobson
Jervois
Seymour
Dedwood Tce
St Marys
New
Gas Works
Fanshawe
THE HERITAGE AUCKLAND
St Patricks
Swanson
Wanganui Avenue
Ardmore
John
Islington
Clarence
Prosford
Dublin
Beaumont
Victoria Park
Halsey
Auckland Mail Service Centre
Wyndham
Albert
Federal
College Hill
Victoria West
Television Centre
Victoria West
Pompallier Terrace
Costley
Union
Drake
Cowan
Ponsonby
Wood
England
Ireland
Franklin
Sale
Sky Tower and Casino
SKY CITY
Elliott
Trinity
Arthur
Ryle
Napier
Cook
St Matthews
Wellesley West
O'Neill
Gunson
John
Summer
Wellington
Union
Nelson
Hobson
Aotea Centre
Franklin
Collingwood
Vermont
Heke
Freemans Bay
Town Hall
Anglesea
Mayoral Drive
Ponsonby 24hr Medical Centre
Hepburn
Beresford
Hayden
Vincent
Lincoln
Norfolk
Paget
Howe
CARLTON
Jessel
Douglas
Picton
Western Park
Greys Ave
Myers Park
Cockburn
Pitt
PARK TOWERS
Liverpool
City
Richmond
Arnold
Chamberlain
Ponsonby
Hopetoun
Auckland Hebrew Congregation
Dryden
Rose
Sussex
Scanlan
Karangahape
Queen
Millais
Salvation Army
Maidstone
Symonds
Grey Lynn Park
Murdoch
Pollen
Newton
Baildon
Crummer
Mackelvie
Grey Lynn
Williamson Avenue
Scanlan
Newton
Dryden
Sussex
Ian McKinnon Drive
Elgin
Beaconsfield
Turakina
Great North
France
St Benedicts
Prime
Grosvenor
Ariki
Waima
Grafton
Northland
Norwich
Exmouth
Khyber Pass
Arch Hill
Potatau
Dean
Home
Keppell
Charlotte
Virginia Ave
Haslett
King
Bright
Alexander
Great North
Commercial
Cooper
Buchanan
Mostyn
New North
Nikau
Shaddock
Burleigh
Nugent
Boston
North Western Motorway
Bond
Aitken Terrace
Porters
Mt Eden Railway Station
Mt Eden
King
Enfield
Fourth Avenue
Nixon Park
New Bond
Third Avenue
Kingsland Avenue
Eden Terrace
Second Avenue
Kingsland
Charles
Edenvale Cres
Edwin
School
First Avenue
George
Tawari
Dominion
Wynyard
Normanby

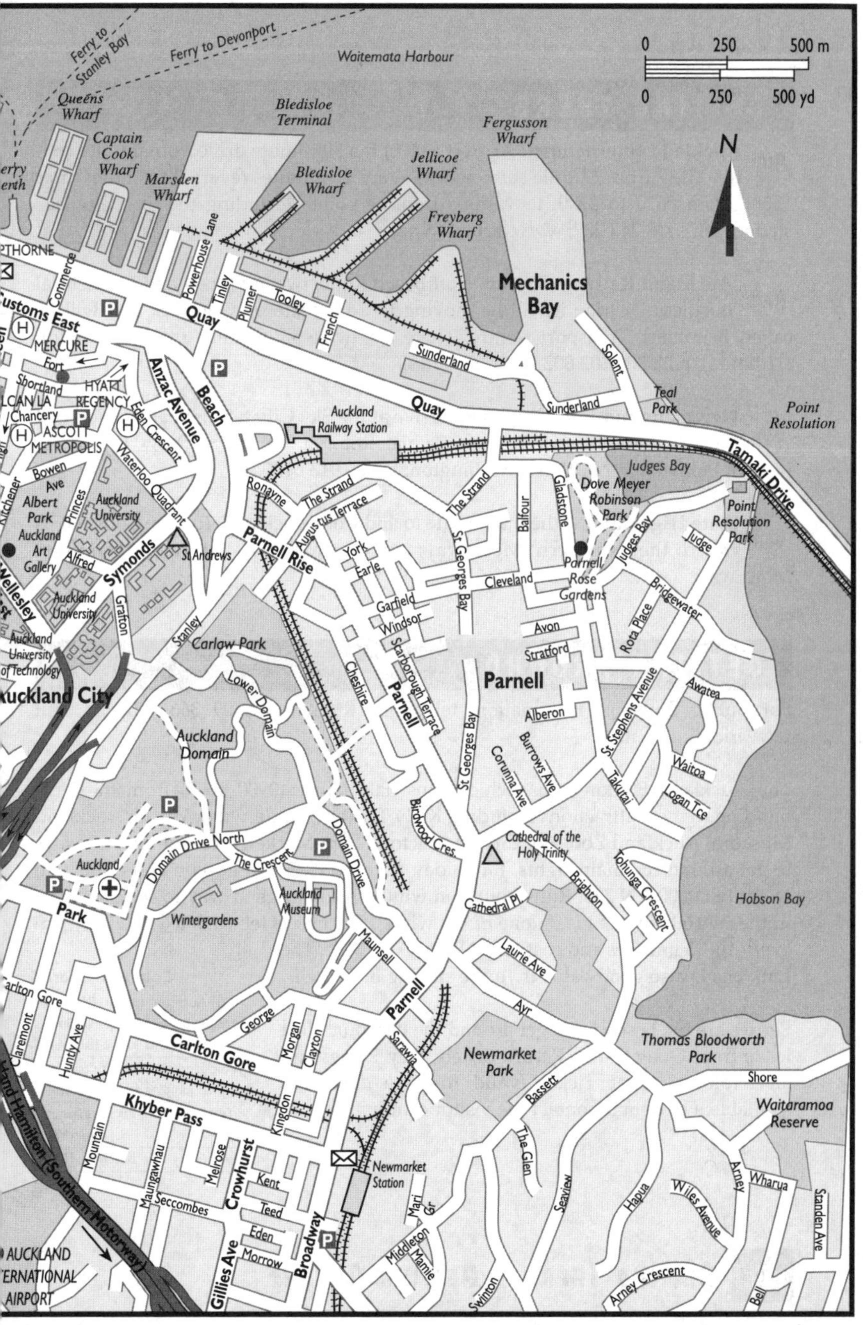

GETTING THERE

AIR **Auckland International Airport (AKL)** is a 50-minute drive from the city centre. The Airbus Shuttle service runs every 20 minutes (every 30 minutes after 1800), from 0620 to 2200, to various transfer points including the Sky City bus station, tel: 0508 247 287; www.airbus.co.nz.

RAIL **Auckland Railway Station** is off Beach Rd, between Parnell and the Central Business District; it will be moving to a new site on Queen St and will be called Britomark Transport Centre. There are twice-daily trains from Wellington (11 hours); tel: 0800 802 802 for train times.

BUS **Newmans and InterCity buses** arrive at the Sky City terminal at Hobson and Victoria Street. Services from Paihia, Rotorua, Tauranga, New Plymouth, Napier, Palmerston North and Wellington; tel: 09 913 6100.

CAR **State Highway 1** is the main route to and from Auckland. Running north it is called the Northern Motorway; southwards, the Auckland Hamilton Motorway.

GETTING AROUND

For public transport information, telephone Rideline on 09 366 6400 or visit www.rideline.co.nz.

The Auckland Explorer bus, which runs half-hourly (0900–1600) from the ferry building to most attractions including Kelly Tarlton's Underwater World, Auckland Museum, Auckland Zoo, Sky City and Victoria Park Market, is one of the best ways to get around the main sights. Buy a day ticket for $25 and hop on and off as you wish. Tel: 0800 439 756. Runs hourly in winter. Another good way to see the sights in the central city area is on one of the white Link buses; tel: 09 366 6400. They run every 10–15 minutes and cost only NZ$1.20 per ride. The Link bus is also good value if you're staying in Parnell.

Ferries are the best way to get around the harbour. Most leave from Quay Street. Return tickets, Day Passes and an Explorer Super Ticket (valid for five days) are available. For details contact the visitor centre.

Colour Section

(i) Auckland (pp. 61–81): the harbour bridge and city skyline; yachts in the harbour

(ii) Auckland: the Sky City tower; inset: rap jumping at the Novotel

(iii) View from Mt Maunganui (p. 157)

(iv) Ninety Mile Beach (p. 101)

& BAR

NIK

Fullers

INFORMATION

Auckland Visitor Centre (AVC) 287 Queen St; tel: 09 979 2333, fax: 09 979 2334, e-mail: reservations@aucklandnz.com. Open Mon–Sun 0900–1700.

New Zealand Visitor Centre Viaduct Basin, cnr Quay and Hobson Sts. Open daily 0930–1730.

Airport AVC International Airport Terminal open daily 0500 until the last flight; tel: 09 275 6467. Accommodation arrangements and friendly and informed advice.

POST AND PHONES There are numerous post offices in the city, but *Poste Restante* mail can be collected from the Wellesley Street Post Shop (CPO), 24 Wellesley Street (tel: 09 379 6714; open Mon–Fri 0830–1700).

ACCOMMODATION

Albert Park Backpackers $ 27–31 Victoria St East; tel: 09 309 0336. Located in the centre but away from the noise.

Alan's International Backpackers $ 2 Churton St, Parnell; tel: 09 358 4584; e-mail: international.bp@xtra.co.nz. Female dorms and internet/e-mail service.

Auckland Central Backpackers $ 9 Fort St Downtown; tel: 09 358 4877, fax: 09 358 4872. Very busy, 24-hr reception.

Auckland International YHA $ 5 Turner St; tel: 09 302 8200, fax: 09 302 8205. A new hostel with good, clean facilities, by Queen St.

Central City Backpackers $ 26 Lorne St; tel: 09 358 5685, fax: 09 358 4716; e-mail: ccbnz@xtra.co.nz. Central but quiet location.

City Central Hotel $$ cnr Wellesley and Albert Sts; tel: 09 307 3388, fax: 09 307 0685. Excellent hotel located in the heart of the city with budget-priced rooms. Those at the back are spacious and less noisy.

City Garden Lodge $ 25 St Georges Bay Rd, Parnell; tel: 09 302 0880, fax: 09 309 8998; e-mail: city.garden@compuweb.co.nz. A lovely hostel originally built for the Queen of Tonga. Set in attractive gardens with good kitchen facilities and cheap internet.

Grafton Oaks Hotel $$ 121 Grafton Rd; tel: 09 309 0167, fax: 09 377 5962. Next to the Domain and within easy walking reach of the city. Sky TV in cocktail bar, motorway access and tennis and golfing facilities nearby.

Kiwi International Hotel $$ 411 Queen St; tel: 0800 100 411, fax: 09 379 6496; www.kiwihotel.co.nz. Unremarkable but central hotel, overlooking Myers Park and with off-street parking.

Lantana Lodge $ 60 St Georges Bay Rd, Parnell; tel: 09 373 4546. A lovely small, quiet and friendly hostel with good facilities including internet.

Park Towers Hotel $$ 3 Scotia Pl; tel: 09 309 2800, fax: 09 302 1964; www.parktowers-hotel.co.nz. Excellent value hotel with light-filled airy rooms, some with views over the city. (Within walking distance of Queen St.)

Parnell Inn $$ 320 Parnell Rd, Parnell; tel: 09 358 0642. Pleasant accommodation located among restaurants.

FOOD AND DRINK

There is no shortage of restaurants in Auckland. **Devonport, Ponsonby** and around the **Quay** are all good areas, but if you want to concentrate on one area, make it **Parnell**.

Alligator Pear Restaurant $ 211 Parnell Rd; tel: 09 307 2223. Open 1730–late daily except Mon. Advertised as New Zealand cuisine with a Mediterranean flavour, the menu is eclectic to say the least. BYOW and licensed.

Antoine's $$$ 333 Parnell Rd; tel: 09 379 8756. Formal, *à la carte* dining, featuring French cuisine. Licensed. Closed Sunday.

Dragon Boat Restaurant $$ Atrium-On-Elliot, Elliot St; tel: 09 379 6996. Dim sum and tasty Cantonese and Szechuan dishes.

Food for Life $ 423 Queen St; tel: 09 300 7585. Extremely inexpensive, pure vegetarian food – including all-you-can-eat option. Lunch only, closed weekends.

Iguaçu Restaurant and Bar $$$ 269 Parnell Rd, Parnell; tel: 09 358 4804. Smart brasserie, regarded by many to be the best restaurant in Auckland for the price. Licensed.

Katsura Restaurant $$ Carlton Hotel, cnr Mayoral Drive and Vincent St; tel: 09 366 5628. Quality Japanese cooking.

Kermadec Ocean Fresh Restaurant $$$ 1st Floor, Viaduct Quay, Viaduct Basin; tel: 09 309 0412. One of the best seafood restaurants in Auckland.

La Bocca Di Mare $$ 251 Parnell Rd; tel: 09 300 3260. Open for brunch at weekends, lunch and dinner seven nights a week. Italian cuisine, strong on seafood. Licensed and BYOW.

The Loaded Hog $ 204 Quay St, Viaduct Basin; tel: 09 366 6491. Part of a New Zealand chain offering snacks and light meals. Brews its own beer.

Maruhachu Restaurant $$ 123 Parnell Rd; tel: 09 357 3535/6. Japanese restaurant serving excellent sushi and other traditional dishes with a bias towards seafood dishes. Sake, but also a wide range of New Zealand wines. Closed Sunday.

Oh Calcutta $$ 151 Parnell Rd; tel: 09 377 9090. Open for lunch Wed–Sun, daily for dinner. Licensed and BYOW. Authentic Indian food from a tandoori oven.

Sawadee $$ 42A Ponsonby Rd, Ponsonby; tel: 09 376 0320. Possibly the best Thai restaurant in New Zealand. Great atmosphere.

Tuatara Bar & Grill $$ 198 Ponsonby Rd, Ponsonby, tel: 09 360 0098. Trendy, if noisy, café serving good food. Licensed.

HIGHLIGHTS

The city's main thoroughfare, running north and south from the waterfront to the suburb of Newtown, was built along the floor of a valley which is why the side streets climb steeply away from the main road. **Queen Street** has many of the best shops and restaurants, as well as two tourist information offices, offering free maps and brochures.

About halfway up Queen St you'll find Aotea Square, where the Council Buildings, the Old Town Hall, and the Aotea Centre Cultural Complex are all located.

The square is very close to the **Auckland Art Gallery**, a beautiful old building dating from 1888 that houses the largest collection of New Zealand paintings in the world. Some of them date back to the time of Captain Cook, including a canvas by William Hodges who travelled with the explorer on his voyages. Also featured are paintings by New Zealand's best-known artist, Frances Hodgkins. Main gallery is free, for the New Gallery there is an entrance fee; open daily 1000–1700.

Two suburbs especially attractive to visitors are the meticulously restored Victorian glories of Parnell and Ponsonby. Ponsonby offers splendid views and both are full of excellent restaurants. In Parnell, look out for the wooden **Gothic Revival Cathedral of St Mary** (open Mon–Fri 1000–1600), considered by many to be the finest of its kind, and the **Kinder House** (2 Ayr St; tel: 09 379 4008; open Mon–Sat 1100–1500), said to be haunted by the original owner's brother, who was murdered by his wife's lover in Sydney.

AUCKLAND AMBASSADORS

Dressed in blue vests, white shirts and white hats, the Auckland City Ambassadors roam the Central City area with the aim of helping and informing tourists. Don't hesitate to ask an Ambassador if you are lost, or are looking for a bus, shop, etc.

COAST TO COAST WALKWAY

The signposted walk between Waitemata and Manukau harbours crosses the Auckland isthmus. It takes about 4 hours to complete, but you can always cheat and hop on a bus if you get tired. Albert Park, Auckland University, Auckland Domain, Mount Eden and One Tree Hill are among the sights you'll pass on the route. A free brochure is available from the AVC.

In the same street is **Ewelme Cottage** (14, Ayr St; tel: 09 379 0202; open Fri–Sun 1030–1200, 1300–1630), built in 1863–64 by the vicar of Howick, the improbably named Reverend Vicesimus Lush. Much of the original furniture and fittings have been preserved and the house is surrounded by a delightful rambling garden.

The **Auckland Domain**, to the west of Parnell, is a large park near the city centre. It contains the Winter Garden, with glasshouses full of tropical plants. Located on a hill in the south-east part of the Domain is **Auckland Museum**, which boasts the world's largest collection of Polynesian artefacts, as well as fascinating displays on New Zealand's natural history. Among the star exhibits is a 30 metre-long Maori war canoe, carved from a single totara tree some 150 years ago.

The exhibition of Maori art is considered to be one of the most significant in the world. It includes Hotunui, a meeting house with fine carvings depicting the Ngati Maru tribe. Even more splendid are the spectacular storehouse carvings discovered in a cave at Te Kaha and now decorating the front wall of museum's central gallery. The collection also includes artistic treasures from Polynesia, Melanesia and Micronesia. Open daily 1000–1700. Free, but donations welcome.

The two best views of the city can be had from **Mount Eden**, a 200 metre-high volcanic structure and the highest point in Auckland, and **One Tree Hill**, which takes its name from the lonely pine tree that grows on the summit. Beside the tree you'll see a 21-metre obelisk erected by Sir John Logan Campbell, known as the Father of Auckland because of his important role in the city's early development. The pine replaced a totara tree, held sacred by the Maoris since around 1600. In recent years there has been at least one attempt by Maori activists to cut down the pine tree and replant a totara – it is said that only when the pakeha succeeds in growing a totara on the site, they will be truly *tangata whenua*, people of the land. One Tree Hill was immortalised in a hit song by the Irish band, U2.

PARKS AND GARDENS Auckland has at least a dozen parks within easy driving distance of the city centre, including from the 64-hectare

Regional Botanical Gardens (near the southern motorway) and the 110-hectare Long Bay – a busy seaside park with a kilometre-long beach, cliff-top walk, café and children's adventure playground (Gladstone and Judges Bay Rds; tel: 09 303 1530; open daily 0800–dusk). **Eden Garden** is only five minutes from the centre of town by car with a magnificent showing of rhododendrons in October (24 Omana Ave, Epsom; tel: 09 638 8395; open daily 0900–1630).

BEACHES Auckland is blessed with beaches lying within the city limits and within easy reach. They are handily designated by geographical area – East, West and North. Closest to hand are the east coast beaches along Tamaki Drive on the south side of the harbour. They are safe for children but tend to become crowded on sunny days (two beaches highly spoken of are **Takapuna** and **Mission Bay**). The black-sand beaches on the west coast are also popular, but as the sea can get rough here they are not suitable for children. **Piha** lies some 40 kilometres from Auckland and offers an ideal combination of powerful surf and a sheltered lagoon. South of Piha is **Whatipu**, which is sheltered by the sand bar that protects Manukau Harbour. **Bethells** is the pick of the northern beaches with good surfing, while nearby **Karekare** was used as a location for the opening sequences of the film *The Piano*.

TAKE CARE

Remember that on Auckland's west coast the surf is fun but tremendously powerful.

THE PIANO BEACH

Made famous by the opening sequences of Jane Campion's award-winning film *The Piano*, Karekare Beach lies roughly 36 kilometres west of Auckland. The easiest way to get there is with a rental car, or join a tour from Auckland. Scenic Pacific Tours, tel: 09 634 2266 or 0800 698 687, fax: 09 634 0222; www.scenictours.co.nz; e-mail: info@scenictours.co.nz; they offer a full-day tour that includes Karekare Beach.

DAY TRIPS

DEVONPORT One of the most charming and relaxed of Auckland's suburbs is **Devonport**. Perfect for an evening stroll, you can enjoy the views by following the 'Old Devonport Walk' (pick up a brochure from Tourist Information); alternatively you can while away the time considering which of the dozens of restaurants deserves closer scrutiny. If you're looking for something to do, there's a **Naval Museum** on Spring St which recounts the history of the local base, or you can inspect the twin volcanic peaks in North Head and Mount Victoria. The latter was once a Maori fort while North Head was heavily fortified in the 19th century to protect Auckland from a Russian invasion which never materialised. Open daily 1000–1630. Ferries to Devonport depart from Quay St about every 30 minutes from 0615–1945 (journey time 15 minutes), then hourly Mon–Fri until 2330.

Howick Historical Village This living history museum has, deservedly, won several tourist awards. It is a restored fencible (a soldier liable only for service at home) compound dating from the middle of the 19th century. There are over 30 authentic buildings including a thatched sod cottage, a village store, forge, church and school. The guides are dressed in period costume although you may find the Swatch watches slightly anachronistic! Lloyd Elsmore Park, Bells Rd, Pakuranga; tel: 09 576 9506; open daily 1000–1600.

Glenbrook Vintage Railway Take the expressway south from Auckland, then turn right onto route 22. The railway is part of the **Glenbrook Farm Park**, some 50 minutes drive from the city in an area with other attractions including the vintage sailing scow Jane Gifford. The classic steam train runs most Sundays and public holidays and you can luxuriate in the splendid wood-panelled carriages. Check the schedules at the Waiuku Information Centre; tel: 09 636 9361 or 09 236 3546.

Wine Trail A number of tour companies offer escorted visits to local vineyards, but following a tried and tested route. If you want to avoid the tour groups, a better idea might be to work out your own itinerary – the Visitors Centre has a helpful brochure.

Auckland's vineyards are centred around two attractive towns – **Henderson** and **Kumeu**, both only 20 kilometres or so from the city centre and easily accessed. The Henderson wineries were initiated by immigrants from the Dalmatian Coast who originally came to collect kauri gum. Many of their descendants are still running the

The Fathers of Auckland

Auckland was founded by two pioneer-adventurers, Bill Webster and John Logan Campbell. Webster was an American whaler who very probably jumped ship before setting up a trading station at the entrance to the Waiau River. Campbell was a local doctor who was persuaded by Webster in 1840 to purchase land on the site of present-day Auckland with a view to transferring the capital there from Coromandel. The venture required considerable vision, as there were no more than 150 Europeans resident in New Zealand at the time. Campbell, now known as the father of Auckland, went on to found the Auckland Savings Bank and, in due course, became Superintendent of the Auckland Province. Billy Webster was eventually forced to leave New Zealand, penniless, landless and indebted to Sydney merchants. A newspaper of the time pronounced that he had 'overstepped the bounds of prudence in playing out his commercial transactions.' Perhaps; but he had also helped in the birth of one of the southern hemisphere's great cities.

vineyards. However, the largest winery in Henderson, **Corbans**, was founded by a Lebanese family at the turn of the last century. Most enterprises welcome visitors and offer samplings as a way of promoting sales. Pleasant Valley Wines (322 Henderson Valley Rd and Babich's (Babich Rd, Henderson) are recommended. In Kumeu try **Matua Valley Wines** (Waikoukou Valley Rd, Waimauku) where there's a good restaurant; also Nobilos (Station Rd, Haupai), Kumeu River (Highway 16, Kumeu) and the Selak Winery (Old North Rd, Kumeu) all with reputations in the making.

VILLAGES IN THE WAITAKERE RANGES

The extinct volcanic cones (there were once 36 of them) were ideal for the building of pas, fortified Maori villages. Maori tradition attributes the volcanic activity to a war between fairy peoples of Hunua and Waitakere. The Waitakere tohunga, or witch doctor, caused the isthmus to erupt as a Hunua war party crossed the intervening plain.

Directions: Take the north-western motorway, route 16, from central Auckland, leaving at the Waterview exit. Continue to head west until you arrive at the small village of Titirangi, gateway to the Waitakere.

WAITAKERE RANGES Right on Auckland's door step, the **Waitakere Ranges Regional Parkland** covers an area of more than 16,000 hectares of native forest and coastline – the city's lung in fact. One side of the park faces onto **Manukau Harbour** the other faces out towards the **Tasman Sea**. You can access the park from about 80 points around the perimeter, but the most convenient is via the town of **Titirangi**. The Visitors Centre (open 0900–1700; tel: 09 817 7134) is located about 5 kilometres away on **Scenic Drive** some 5 kilometres beyond that. Here you will find all the information you need about the park, the nature trails etc. and the rangers are also on hand to help.This scenic mountain range west of Auckland is a favourite walking and picnic spot for locals. The 20-minute **Arataki Nature Trail** is a great introduction to kauri (a species of pine) and other native trees. If you have more time, take the **Auckland City Walk**, the highlight of which is **Cascade Falls**.

Despite being so close to the city the terrain is very rugged and some of the tracks would tax an experienced walker, known locally as a tramper. Don't be put off if you don't feel you qualify as there are plenty of easy, all-weather walks especially in the north of the park and on the shores of Manukau Harbour itself. On the way you can enjoy the forest, waterfalls and spectacular harbour and ocean views.

OTHER THINGS TO SEE AND DO

AUCKLAND ZOO The animals can be seen in their appropriate natural habitat from savannah to rainforest. Other highlights include an aviary of indigenous birds, a nocturnal kiwi house and a children's farm. For those wanting to make a day of it, there are cafés and picnic areas as well as a tramway link to the Museum of Transport and Technology. Great North Road; tel: 09 846 7020. Open daily 1000–1700, last admissions at 1630.

AUCKLAND ZOO KIWIS
You may not be able to see the kiwi birds in the nocturnal house at Auckland Zoo as they are very shy. You are more likely to see the local birdlife in the walkthrough Qantas New Zealand Aviary. The park has over 900 animals kept in enclosures as like as possible to their natural habitats.

KELLY TARLTON'S UNDERWATER WORLD AND ANTARCTIC ENCOUNTER Visitors are led along a submerged transparent tunnel to meet the fish face to face in a variety of habitats. The aquarium is one of the world's largest and borrows one of Auckland's storm water holding tanks beneath Tamaki Drive. The Antarctic Encounter re-creates Scott's expedition of 1911–12 and features the hut at McMurdo Sound as well as a ride on a snow cat through a deep-freeze environment. Look out for the penguin colony and other marine life sea. 23 Tamaki Drive, Orakei; tel: 09 528 0603 or 0800 805 050; open daily in summer 0900–2200, last entry at 2100; in winter 0900–1800, last entry 1700.

MOTAT (MUSEUM OF TRANSPORT & TECHNOLOGY) A 10-minute drive from downtown Auckland, the MOTAT is located along Great North Rd at Western Springs. A must for technology fans, the museum houses vintage cars, trams and an exhibit on Richard Pearse, who Kiwis claim learned to fly before the Wright brothers! At a separate site (both sites are connected by a working tramline) you can view vintage aircraft and trains. The tramline also provides a connection to Auckland Zoo. Open daily except Christmas 1000–1630 (last admission); tel: 09 846 0199 or 09 846 7020 (24-hour infoline).

NATIONAL MARITIME MUSEUM Have you ever wondered what it was like to travel steerage class in the 1800s? You'll find the answer here, along with a fascinating collection of historic boats from New Zealand and Polynesia. The boat building workshops – not forgetting New Zealand's 1988 America's Cup challenger – are a reminder of Auckland's continuing obsession with the sea. Open daily, winter 0900–1700, summer 0900–1800; tel: 09 373 0800 or 0800 725 897.

RAINBOW'S END **Rainbow's End** is a noisy fairground that will keep the children happy for hours. The roller coaster isn't the world's highest but the corkscrews, dips and dives are more than enough to set the passengers screaming. Corner Great South and Wiri Station Rds, Manukau City; tel: 0800 438 672, open daily from 1000.

RANGITOTO ISLAND If Rome was built on seven hills, Auckland stands on seven extinct volcanoes. The last eruption occurred about 800 years ago on Rangitoto island. You can get there by ferry and, providing you are relatively fit, clamber to the top from where you will be able to enjoy spectacular views of the city. Boats leave from Pier 3. The trip takes 45 minutes – allow 2 hours for the climb to the summit. (See p. 80.)

A CLOSER LOOK

For a close-up look at the harbour you might consider a kayaking tour. Fergs Kayaks (12 Tamaki Dr., Okahu Bay; tel/fax: 09 529 2230; www.fergskayaks.co.nz) hires out kayaks for half-day tours, or you can opt for a full-day guided tour to Rangitoto Island.

SKY TOWER Part of the Sky City complex, this tower in downtown Auckland is hard to miss as it rises to a height of 328 metres, thus making it the tallest building in the southern hemisphere. At the top is a revolving restaurant, along with an outdoor observation level that offers fantastic views over the city and harbour. The brave can stand on glass floors and admire the city directly beneath their feet. The even braver can actually jump off the tower (tel: 0800 759 586; www.skyjump.co.nz). In Sky City there is also a casino, a state-of-the-art theatre for performing arts and a variety of restaurants and bars. Open 0830–late (casino 24 hours); tel: 0800 759 2489.

STARDOME OBSERVATORY View the skies of the southern hemisphere through a 500-millimetre Zeiss telescope (Wed, Thur, Sat). The Stardome Planetarium, within the same complex, is also worth a visit. Situated on the lower slopes of One Tree Hill. Open for planetarium shows in the evenings Wed–Sat; tel: 09 624 1246; www.stardome.org.nz.

AUCKLAND HARBOUR BY BOAT The city sprawls along the shores of Waitemata and Manukau harbours and the Hauraki Gulf. Waitemata Harbour is spanned, to the east, by the Auckland Harbour Bridge, which links Freeman's Bay, on the southern side, and Northcote, on the northern.

AUCKLAND BRIDGE CLIMB

A 2½-hour climb along walkways and curving arches takes you 65 metres above the harbour. At the top you are rewarded with great views of the Gulf islands and the city skyline. The bridge climb has been personally tested by the NZ prime minister, Helen Clark! For ages ten and over; tel: 0800 000 808 or 09 377 6543; www.aucklandbridgeclimb.co.nz.

The easiest way to experience the harbour atmosphere is to take a 15-minute **ferry** ride to Devonport, where there's a splendid beach as well as Auckland's race course. There are stunning views of the city both ways. If you become hooked, there are numerous services exploring almost every conceivable part of the harbour at low cost.

Timetables and destinations are available at Fullers Cruise Centre on Quay St; tel: 09 367 9111; e-mail: enquiries@fullersakl.co.nz. Harbour cruises (2 hours) leave from Pier 3 at 0930 1145 and 1400.

Skipper & Charter Boat Owners Hire Services charter out bare boats – that is,you go sailing by yourself – and also offer skippered cruises (tel: 09 442 2004, fax: 09 442 2055).

The Great Outdoors

Auckland Adventures offer a variety of outdoor experiences around the city. They include half-day outings with wine tastings, day trips to see the gannets at Muriwai beach and a full-day mountain bike adventure. Tel: 09 379 4545, fax: 09 379 4543; www.aucklandadventures.com.

The ***Søren Larsen*** is a rigged 19th-century brigantine with 12 sails. It leaves from the docks near the National Maritime Museum and during the cruises you will have the opportunity to set the sails and take a turn at the wheel (tel: 09 411 8755 for more details). Alternatively, if you're looking for something a bit more thrilling, the ***NZL 40*** was built for the America's Cup in 1995 (although was not finished in time to race). This is the Ferrari of yachts, and whether you're an expert sailor or a first timer you'll gasp in awe when the crew explain the statistics of the yacht's design – it's one giant stressball. The two-hour sailing experience leaves from the Viaduct Basin most days; tel: 0800 724 569.

A place where you can learn to sail is at the Rangitoto sailing centre (Royal Akarna Yacht Club, Okahu Bay; tel: 09 479 1846). The boats for hire are small day sailers, ideal for exploring the relatively safe area around the harbour. They do complete sailing introduction courses lasting two or three days. For more information check their website at www.sailingnz.co.nz.

Viaduct Harbour and Cup Village

This was where all the super yachts were moored during the America's Cup 2003. It's still worth a look, even when there's no big regatta, as the chances are you'll be able to spot a boat that's worth more than your house and car together. The village is right next to the Maritime Museum, on Viaduct Harbour.

SHOPPING

Often referred to by its initials as VPM, **Victoria Park Market** (Victoria St West; open daily) has a mixture of stalls and upmarket shops. Many of the stalls have an alternative air about them, offering such items as home made wax candles, crystals and aromatherapy scents. The big plus however is the delightful garden area with umbrella-shaded seating. A range of interesting shops and arcades can be found along and around **Queen St** while more specialised shopping centres and markets are situated all over Auckland. The AVC has some useful brochures.

NIGHTLIFE

Auckland has a vibrant music scene with at least 40 major gigs on the go each weekend, more if you count all the pubs and taverns. A major clubbing area downtown is around **Vulcan Lane** and **High Street**. Few clubs charge admission.

Alhambra Restaurant & Bar Three Lamps Arcade, 283 Ponsonby Rd, Ponsonby; tel: 09 376 2430; live jazz and blues Thur–Sun nights. Restored cinema with stunning views of Auckland city and harbour.

Cause Célèbre & The Box 33–35 High St; tel: 09 373 4321. Typical night club featuring jazz bands.

The Power Station 33 Mt Eden Rd, Mt Eden; tel: 09 377 7666. The place to go to for alternative rock concerts.

The Temple 486 Queen St; tel: 09 377 4866. Regular pop/rock sessions normally starting around 2100. Happy hours are the main attraction before then. Good, original Kiwi music.

There are several open-air venues where you can hear music with no charge. Tel: 09 379 2020 for details. The venues include:

Molly Green Reserve on Mount Roskill

Myers Park

Tahaki Reserve on Mount Eden

THEATRE

The Edge is Auckland's main centre for arts and entertainment and encompasses the Aotea Centre, The Civic, Auckland Town Hall and Aotea Square – all within seconds of each other. A range of programmes operate including comedy festivals, shows and opera; tel: 09 307 5033.

CINEMAS

The main cinema area is around the junction of Queen and Wellesley Streets. During the International Film Festival in July, arthouse and foreign films are screened in a variety of cinemas throughout the city. A new giant-screen Imax cinema is located in the Force Entertainment Centre, near Aotea Square, Queen St.

EVENTS

Auckland hosts a range of events throughout the year. The AVC's '**Auckland – Alive & Happening**' lists most of these.

AUCKLAND REGATTA Auckland is the yachting centre of New Zealand, with more than 80 per cent of the country's registered boats. The regatta takes place on the Monday closest to 29 January in a tradition that extends back more than 150 years. More than a thousand boats take part in the races, from dinghies to cruisers.

BMW AUCKLAND MARATHON More than 50,000 runners take part in the annual run around Auckland's waterfront on the third Sunday in October. There's also a half marathon and wheelchair event. Tel: 09 575 1616.

ELLERSLIE FLOWER SHOW The largest flower show in the southern hemisphere takes place at the end of November in the Auckland Regional Botanic Gardens in Manukau City. Tel: 09 309 7875. Throughout the year, flower-lovers can also visit the Auckland Domain, to the east of Parnell, a large park near the centre of the city, that houses the Winter Garden, which has several glasshouses crammed full of tropical plants.

A CITY TO INSPIRE ART AND LITERATURE

The oldest art galleries and museums in the country are found in Auckland. The Auckland City Art Gallery was founded in 1888, and the Auckland Institute and Museum opened in 1852. Both contain notable collections.

New Zealand has more than 1000 libraries, and the Auckland Public Library is one of the jewels in New Zealand's crown, containing about 1.2 million volumes, including Maori works.

At some point during your visit you will conclude that Auckland is one of the most attractive cities in the world. You will not be the first traveller to think that. Rudyard Kipling, in his *Song of the Cities*, wrote a final stanza, headed 'Auckland', which reads, in part:

Last, loneliest, loveliest, exquisite apart –
On us, on us, the unswerving season smiles
Who wonder 'mid our fern why men depart
To seek the Happy Isles.

This is actually a very poor example of Kipling's work, but the thought is there. Auckland is lovely, exquisite and apart.

THE ISLANDS OF THE HAURAKI GULF

Hauraki means 'wind from the north', but in reality the waters of this vast bay on the eastern edge of Auckland are sheltered on three sides, making it popular with yachtsmen. During the summer months locals and visitors flock to the beaches and forests of the **Hauraki Gulf Maritime Park**, which embraces 47 islands, some fully developed commuter territory, others the protected refuges of plants and wildlife. Most islands are open to visitors and each has something distinctive to offer.

Kawau Island and Waiheke Island are favoured by sun-seekers while islands like Rangitoto and Great Barrier are a popular haunt of trampers. The **Department of Conservation in Auckland** administers the islands and provides information at the Visitors Centre Ferry Buildings, Quay St; tel: 09 379 6476. For details of ferry services, contact Fullers Cruise Centre (next door); tel: 09 367 9111.

FERRY TO GREAT BARRIER ISLAND

The ferry trip from Auckland to the island takes about two hours and sails twice weekly with extra sailings in summer (tel: 09 367 911 for details; www.fullers.co.nz; e-mail: enquiries@fullers.co.nz). It's quicker to get there by air – **Great Barrier Airlines** is a scheduled airline with regular departures from Auckland. The flight is itself a great sightseeing experience.

Great Barrier Island is the furthest from Auckland. Half the area is administered by the Department of Conservation and at Port Fitzroy, the DOC maintains an office with information and maps; tel: 09 429 0044. Besides surf beaches and hot springs, the island boasts more than 8000 hectares of regenerating kauri forest growing on the rugged mountain slopes and there are walking tracks criss-crossing the area. Some walks are pretty taxing and can take anything up to six hours to complete, but if time is short there are plenty of less strenuous alternatives.

The cormorants that give **Kawau Island** its name can stlll be seen sunning themselves on the rocks off shore. Kawau was purchased by Sir George Grey, a Governor and later Premier of New Zealand, in 1863 for the princely sum of £3700. Grey was an avid collector of trees, plants and animals from around the globe and a few of his more unusual imports have survived including Chilean palms, coral trees and wallabies – you might even hear the odd kookaburra. The Governor's residence, Mansion House, became a hotel after his death but has recently been restored in period style and is open to the public. Opening hours vary.

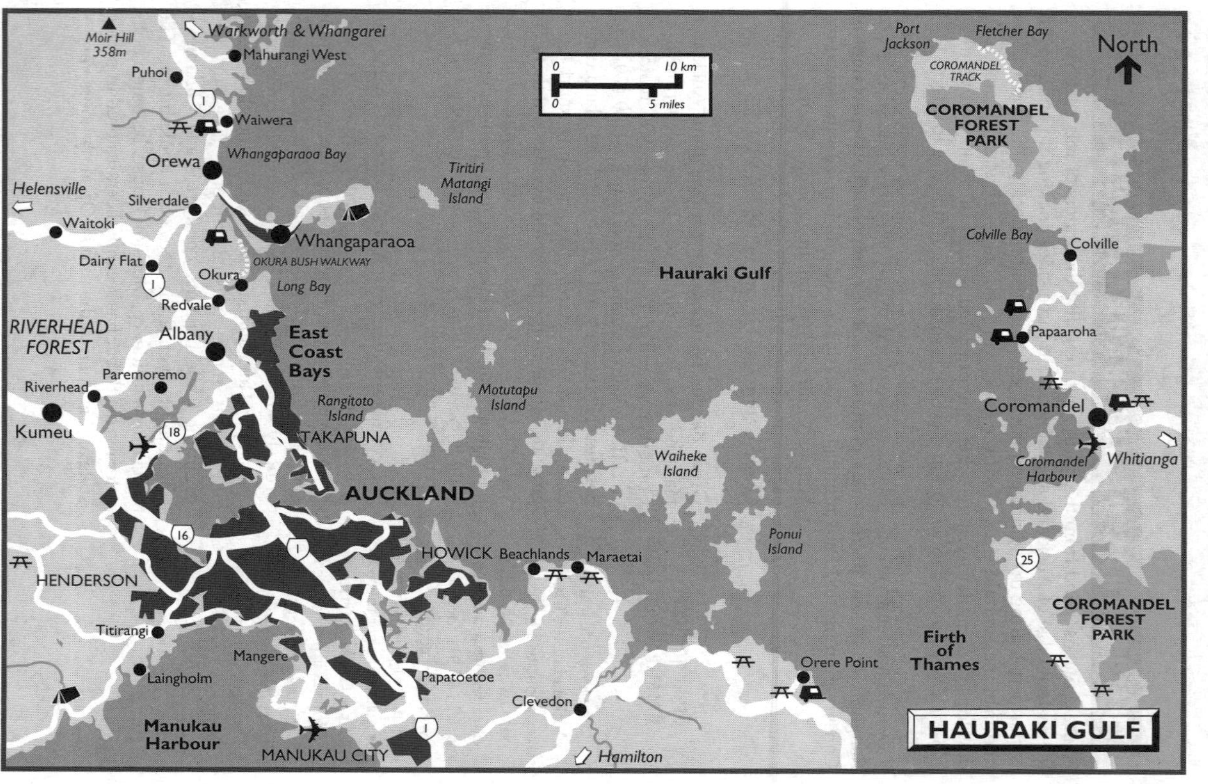
HAURAKI GULF
North
0
10 km
0
5 miles
Moir Hill 358m
Warkworth & Whangarei
Mahurangi West
Puhoi
1
Waiwera
Orewa
Whangaparaoa Bay
Helensville
Silverdale
Waitoki
Whangaparaoa
OKURA BUSH WALKWAY
Dairy Flat
Okura
Long Bay
Redvale
RIVERHEAD FOREST
Albany
East Coast Bays
Paremoremo
Riverhead
Kumeu
18
Rangitoto Island
TAKAPUNA
AUCKLAND
16
HOWICK
HENDERSON
Titirangi
Laingholm
Mangere
Papatoetoe
Manukau Harbour
MANUKAU CITY
Tiritiri Matangi Island
Motutapu Island
Hauraki Gulf
Waiheke Island
Ponui Island
Beachlands
Maraetai
Clevedon
Hamilton
Orere Point
Firth of Thames
Port Jackson
Fletcher Bay
COROMANDEL TRACK
COROMANDEL FOREST PARK
Colville Bay
Colville
Papaaroha
Coromandel
Coromandel Harbour
Whitianga
25
COROMANDEL FOREST PARK

AN EXCURSION TO TIRITIRI MATANGI

Only a short cruise from downtown Auckland is the tiny island wildlife sanctuary of Tiritiri Matangi. Here bird watchers have the unique opportunity of seeing a few of the world's rarest birds. But even if your interest in avifauna is limited to stuffed turkey, it is still a great way to escape the noise of the city for a day. There are shady bush walks and even a pretty beach of glistening white sand. Best of all, it is guaranteed to be free of holiday crowds.

Travelling to the island involves an early morning start. Equipped with a picnic lunch (there is no food available on the island), togs, repellent, good walking shoes and plenty of sunscreen, you board a comfortable launch, which then whisks you over the clear blue waters of the Gulf to the island. En route there is a good chance of spotting a variety of marine life; penguins and dolphins are commonly seen.

At the jetty passengers are greeted by conservation officers, who give a brief introduction to Tiritiri Matangi. Those who have booked the 1-hour guided walk (optional) are then led off for an instructive tour of the island. At almost every step the guide is able to draw your attention to the local residents (which you might otherwise miss) – a tui perched nearby, or perhaps a tiny North Island robin, barely visible in a dark thicket.

However, for many years what was left of the island's native forest hardly resounded with birdsong. From the 1850s onwards, European farmers cleared much of the bush and converted it to pasture. Deprived of their natural habitat many native birds disappeared. This situation continued until the 1970s, when the last stock was removed, and the island became a scientific reserve.

After a massive replanting project, the island is once again cloaked in regenerating native forest. Unwanted predators were removed and conservationists were able to reintroduce the native birds successfully. Visitors are now almost certain to see such rarities as the red crowned parakeet, the saddleback and the kokako. In many cases it is possible to get amazingly close to the birds, as in the absence of danger they are much less shy than on the mainland.

The guided walk invariably ends at the historic lighthouse. Here visitors can buy souvenirs and drinks. This is also a good place to observe flightless takahe, as they are always to be seen nibbling grass near the shop. On the way back to the wharf, a good tip is to follow the Wattle Track. Drinking troughs along the way will allow more close-up views of the birds.

Information: Fullers Cruise Centre, Ferry Building, Quay Street, Auckland; tel: 09 367 9111; www.fullers.co.nz; e-mail: enquiries@fullers.co.nz. Book at least two days ahead.

To get a flavour of what the island was like before Grey's time visit **Bon Accord harbour** with its miners' cottages, smelting house, mine shafts, and other remnants of the copper industry which flourished during the 1840s and 1850s. Ferries to Kawau leave from Quay Street in Auckland, but the shortest crossing is from Sandspit, east of Warkworth. Try Matata Cruises; tel: 0800 225 292 or Kawau Kat Cruises; tel: 0800 888 006 within Auckland, otherwise dial 09 425 8006.

FOOTPRINTS IN THE LAVA

Rangitoto was created by volcanic activity, probably starting around AD 1100 and continuing uninterrupted for more than 700 years. These last eruptions were low on the Richter scale and you can still see footprints in the hardened lava where the local Maoris stood around watching the fireworks!

Rangitoto Island is now a nature reserve with an amazing pohutukawa forest. There are more than 200 species of native plant here, including 40 varieties of fern. A narrow causeway links Rangitoto to Motutapu – 'sacred island' to the Maoris – where the DOC is currently running a programme of reforestation. The ferry from Auckland leaves Fullers Cruise Centre on Quay St at 0930 and 1145, returning at 1230 and 1500 with additional services during the holiday season. (Journey time 45 minutes). Guided tours of the island are available.

Rangitoto has numerous accessible paths for walkers, the most important of which is the Rangitoto Summit Track, a 900-metre boardwalk at the top of the mountain from where there are wonderful views of the Hauraki Gulf.

Other popular tracks on Rangitoto include the Kidney Fern Walk, a verdant wonderland of ferns of all shapes and sizes, and Kowhai Grove, best in the spring when the Kowhai flowers.

The second-largest island in the Gulf, **Waiheke**, is also one of the country's smallest winemaking districts. Some of the best Cabernets in New Zealand are produced here and most wineries are open to visitors for tastings. If you don't mind splashing out, stop for a meal at the Mudbrick Vineyard and Restaurant, Croll Vineyard, Church Bay Rd (2 kilometres west of Oneroa); tel: 09 372 9050, which serves excellent Mediterranean cuisine, washed down with a selection of local wines.

There are some superb white-sand beaches on the northern coast of Waiheke including Oneroa, Palm Beach and Onetangi – all safe for swimming. Alternatively, if you're looking for something more adventurous snorkelling, surfing, wave skiing and boogie boarding are all available, with mountain biking for land lubbers.

The island's Information Centre is at Oneroa, 10 minutes' walk from the ferry. Here you will also find the **Whittakers Musical Museum**, a collection of antique organs, pianolas, accordians, mouth organs and the like. Each day at 1300 the Whittakers give a concert-demonstration of the instruments (about 1½ hours). A little further along the road at Ostend there's an excellent crafts and produce market on Saturday mornings.

Waiheke is the most accessible of all the islands. Fullers operate frequent 30-minute ferry services to Matiata Wharf at the western end. If you're planning to stay on the island for a few days, the Subritzky Shipping Line runs a car ferry from Auckland (Half Moon Bay). Tel: 09 534 5663.

i **Waiheke Visitor Information Centre**, 2 Korora Rd, Oneroa; tel: 09 372 9999, fax: 09 372 9919; e-mail: waiheke@iconz.co.nz.
Waiheke Booking Centre, Oneroa; tel: 09 372 3377, fax: 09 372 7229; can organise accommodation on the islands along with your transport there.

Hekerua Lodge Backpackers $ 11 Hekerua Rd, Little Oneroa, Waiheke; tel/fax: 09 372 8990; e-mail: hekerua@ihug.co.nz. In a lush setting, close to beach, shops and restaurants. This hotel has basic rooms, some shared, but facilities include swimming pool, barbecue, games room and cyber café.
Midway Motel $$ Ostend, Waiheke Island; tel: 09 372 8023 or 0800 372 8023, fax: 09 372 9669. Facilities include spa, gym and indoor heated swimming pool. All rooms have TV.
Omaru Bay Lodge $$$ Orapiu Rd, Waiheke Island; tel: 09 372 8291; fax: 09 372 2673; e-mail: omarubay@xtra.co.nz. All rooms have en suite facilities and verandas with views of the bay. Breakfast, lunch and dinner included in price.
Onetangi Beach Front Apartments $$–$$$ 27 The Strand, Onetangi, Waiheke; tel: 09 372 7051, fax: 09 372 5056; e-mail: info@onetangi.co.nz. Situated right next to beautiful Onetangi beach, these self-contained units have all the comforts. Kayaks can be hired.
Pohutukawa Lodge $$ Pa Beach, Tryphena Great Barrier Island; tel: 09 429 0211, fax: 09 429 0117. This large wooden homestead by the beach offers bed and breakfast accommodation and a backpackers' lodge.
Waiheke YHA $ Seaview Rd, Onetangi, Waiheke; tel/fax: 09 372 0971; e-mail: robb.meg@bigfoot.com. Warm and friendly. Great views, mountain bikes available and all bedding is free.

Stony Batter Walk

One of many great walks on Waiheke, this one is located at the eastern tip of the island. Stony Batter is the site of World War II gun emplacements. There are fantastic views, an interesting little museum and lengths of stairs and tunnels to explore. Bring a torch!

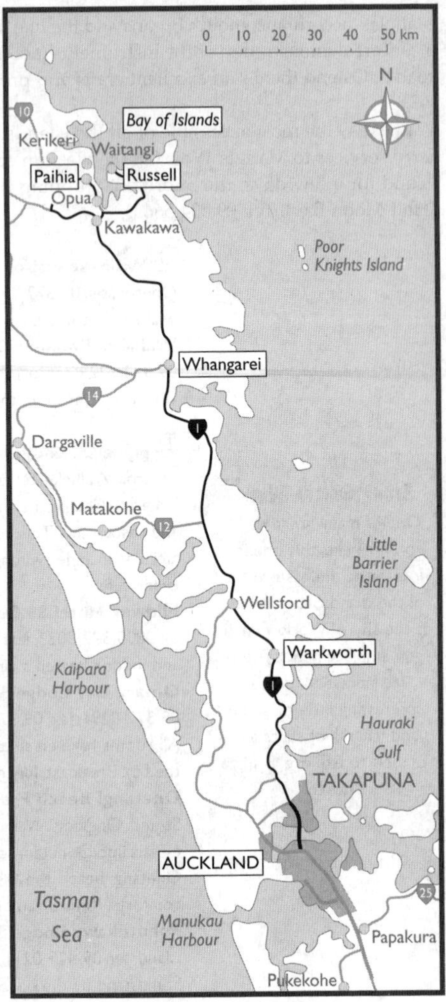

Route Detail

From Auckland take State Highway 1 through the suburbs of Albany, Silverdale, Orewa and Waiwera to **Warkworth**. 66 km

Continue north through Wellsford, Kaiwaka, Brynderwyn, Braigh and Ruakaka to **Whangarei**. 170 km

Continue through Hikurangi, Whakapara and Kawakawa. (Here there are turnings to the right to the seaside resorts of Ngunguru Bay, Sandy Bay and Whangaruru Harbour.) At Kawakawa, follow State Highway 11 via Opua to **Paihia**. 237 km

Alternatively, you can take a car ferry direct to **Russell** from Opua. It leaves every 10 minutes from 0650.

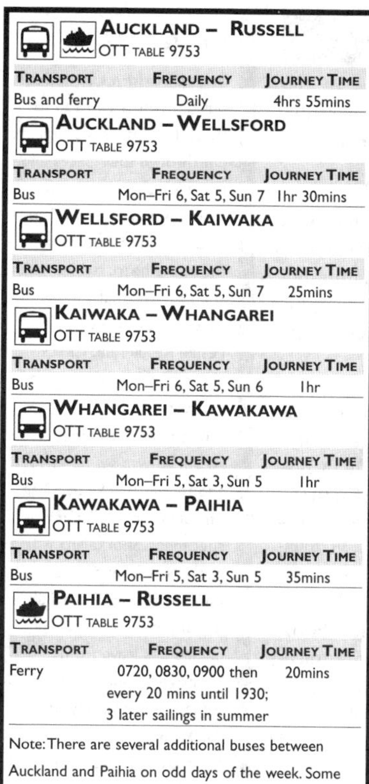

Auckland – Russell
OTT table 9753

Transport	Frequency	Journey Time
Bus and ferry	Daily	4hrs 55mins

Auckland – Wellsford
OTT table 9753

Transport	Frequency	Journey Time
Bus	Mon–Fri 6, Sat 5, Sun 7	1hr 30mins

Wellsford – Kaiwaka
OTT table 9753

Transport	Frequency	Journey Time
Bus	Mon–Fri 6, Sat 5, Sun 7	25mins

Kaiwaka – Whangarei
OTT table 9753

Transport	Frequency	Journey Time
Bus	Mon–Fri 6, Sat 5, Sun 6	1hr

Whangarei – Kawakawa
OTT table 9753

Transport	Frequency	Journey Time
Bus	Mon–Fri 5, Sat 3, Sun 5	1hr

Kawakawa – Paihia
OTT table 9753

Transport	Frequency	Journey Time
Bus	Mon–Fri 5, Sat 3, Sun 5	35mins

Paihia – Russell
OTT table 9753

Transport	Frequency	Journey Time
Ferry	0720, 0830, 0900 then every 20 mins until 1930; 3 later sailings in summer	20mins

Note: There are several additional buses between Auckland and Paihia on odd days of the week. Some buses only stop at Kawakawa on request.

The northernmost peninsula of New Zealand, Northland, is packed with things to see and do. It's a pleasant hour's drive from Auckland, although you'll no longer see any hibiscus along the coast of that name.

Russell, one of the most attractive towns in the country, was also the first capital. It seems to have undergone the most amazing of transformations. Once known as the 'Hell Hole of the Pacific', it's now advertised as the perfect destination for romantic weekends. Russell makes an ideal touring base for exploring Ninety Mile Beach and the Far North region.

The historic Treaty of Waitangi, which transferred sovereignty to Britain while maintaining the pretence of Maori land ownership, was signed near Paihia. Learn all about this seminal event in New Zealand's development by visiting the superb Waitangi Treaty House.

New Zealand is equally mindful of its maritime heritage. The Bay of Islands is an outstanding example of the country's 'Marine Parks' strategy, where fishing as well as commercial and other invasive developments are prohibited to encourage wildlife.

The Treaty of Waitangi

In January 1840 Captain William Hobson arrived in New Zealand, charged with the task of putting an end to the land wars between the Maoris and the settlers. On 5 February he presented a draft treaty to a gathering of Maori chiefs assembled near the home of the British Resident James Busby at Waitangi. After debating the issue for 24 hours they agreed to sign the following day, so accepting the governorship of Queen Victoria. The Treaty was eventually signed by 500 Maori leaders.

WARKWORTH

Warkworth is a small town on the banks of the Mahurangi River. The focal point is the harbour, where the wharves are cluttered with yachts during the summer season.

Its founder, John Anderson Brown, was born in a town of the same name in Northumberland, UK. When he arrived in 1843, he said the sweep of the Mahurangi River reminded him of the River Coquet near his birthplace. Many of the streets are named after prominent Northumberland families and villages.

In front of **Warkworth Museum** on Tudor Collins Drive are two kauri trees, one of them 800 years old and 12 metres tall. The Parry Kauri Park was bought by residents because someone was, of course, going to cut the trees down. The museum itself has an impressive display of kauri gum and local timbers. Tel: 09 425 7093; open daily 0900–1600 in summer, to 1530 in winter.

Some 3 kilometres out of town is the **Satellite Earth Station**, the hub of New Zealand's telecommunications network. There's an audiovisual display in the Visitors' Centre explaining the technology behind the three enormous satellite dishes. Tel: 09 425 8059; open daily, 0900–1500.

WARKWORTH–AUCKLAND RIVALRY

For a long time the only communication between Warkworth and Auckland was by ship, creating a deadly rivalry between two local shipping companies. On two occasions at least the fierceness of the competition led to major collisions between the ships. On the second occasion, in 1905, the *Claymore*, a vessel belonging to the MacGregor Steamship Company, ran into, and sank, the *Kapanui* (owned by the Settlers) in Waitemata Harbour.

EN ROUTE

Sheepworld, 4 kilometres out of town, is devoted to sheep farming. Sheepdogs are put through their paces and there are shearing demonstrations. You're allowed to feed the lambs, but it may tug at the heart strings when you discover that lamb is the speciality of the nearby Leslee Restaurant. Check Sheepworld's craft shop for souvenirs.

Goat Island Marine Reserve was set up in 1978 and thrives thanks to a ban on fishing and collecting specimens. Snorkelling is possible here and scuba diving is also available. Full-day and half-day boat excursions leave from Warkworth and are good value. The University of Auckland's Marine Laboratory is based on Goat Island.

A 40-minute detour from State Highway 1 (turn off just north of Wellsford) will bring you to Mangawhai Heads. Follow the coast road from here to Langs Beach and Waipu Cove for bracing views of Bream Bay and the Hen and Chicken Islands, habitat of rare birds like the wattled saddleback. The road rejoins the Highway at Waipu.

Royal Mail Run

This 1½-hour cruise departs Sandspit, near Warkworth, at 1030 daily. Apart from enjoying the beautiful coastal scenery, you also get to visit Kawau Island and historic Mansion House. Kawau Kat Cruises, tel: 09 425 8006 or 0800 888 006.

Horse Riding

Pakiri Beach Horse Riding, 35 minutes north-east of Warkworth (tel: 09 422 6275), offers routes along deserted beaches and coastal hills. Rides last from 1 hour to a full day and you will be provided with a horse suited to your expertise. All you need is sturdy footwear and long trousers.

i **Warkworth Visitor Information Centre** 1 Baxter St; tel: 09 425 9081, fax: 09 425 7584; e-mail: service@warkworth-information.co.nz.

Warkworth Inn $ Queen St; tel: 09 425 8569, fax: 09 425 9696; e-mail: wwinn@maxnet.co.nz. Established in 1862, this traditional bed and breakfast hotel is good value.

Walton Park Motor Lodge $$ 2 Walton Ave; tel: 09 425 8149, fax: 09 425 8564; www.waltonpark.co.nz; e-mail: enquiries@waltonpark.co.nz. Friendly motel with swimming pool and licensed restaurant.

Bridge House Lodge $$ 16 Elizabeth St; tel: 09 425 8351. Historic building, candlelit dining.

Cruise in Café $$ Sandspit Wharf; tel: 09 425 9475. Fresh fish specialities. Breakfast, lunch and dinner daily, except Tues. BYO and licensed.

Puhoi Village

About 55 kilometres north of Auckland, and only a short detour off State Highway 1, is the historic settlement of Puhoi Village. The area was first settled by German-speaking Bohemian immigrants in 1863 and many of their descendants still live in Puhoi to this day. The village is actually quite unique in that it is one of the few localities that has preserved something of its national origins.

The biggest attraction here is the Puhoi Pub, a fine two-storey colonial building on a hill above the Puhoi river. Apart from being a great place for a cold beer, it is also filled with relics from the old pioneering days. Particularly interesting is a collection of historical photos and documents, including the district's first liquor licence issued in 1879. Other reminders of the colonial past can be seen in the Church of St Peter and Paul and in a small museum close by.

A canoe trip along the meandering Puhoi river is great fun. In the old days before proper roads, the river was the easiest way to reach the isolated settlement. This leisurely paddle will take you through farmland, mangrove swamp and native forest. Contact **Puhoi River Canoe Hire**, tel: 09 422 0891.

Whangarei

The main city of Northland, Whangarei (population 44,000) is a commercial centre and port rather than a major tourist destination, though it does contain some of the finest beaches in New Zealand. Founded in 1842, most of the population moved to Auckland for protection during the Maori wars which began soon afterwards. Whangerei remained a sleepy backwater until the 1960s since when it has grown by leaps and bounds.

The climate around Whangarei is sub-tropical with 2000 hours of sunshine a year and an average rainfall of 1555 millimetres. The volcanic soil has given birth to an abundance of plants and vegetation, best appreciated in the beautiful parks and gardens. Particularly noteworthy are **Cafler Park** and **Rose Gardens**, in the town centre and the popular picnic spot, **Mair Park** (Rurumoki St). From here there are well-marked trails to Parahaki, once a Maori fort. The views from here are spectacular and well worth the hour's climb.

Side Trip

Beyond the suburb of Tikipunga, the road passes the impressive Whangarei Falls before reaching the coast at Ngunguru Village, a small resort at the head of Whangarei's beautiful sandy beaches. Over the hill is the harbour and marina of Tutukaka, the gateway to Poor Knights Islands. The road then follows the coast past the popular surfing beaches of Matapouri and Woolleys Bay, while tracks lead down to Whales Bay and other secluded coves among the pohutukawa trees. At Sandy Bay the road turns inland to meet State Highway 1 to Whangarei.

In the centre of town is an attractive waterfront development called Town Basin. Here you'll find the **Clapham's Clocks Collection**, the largest of its kind in the southern hemisphere (open daily 0900–1700). Like most harbour developments around the world the main interest lies in the yachts moored along the promenade, although you'll also find the predictable range of specialty shops and restaurants.

Organised Excursions

The Visitors Centre organises excursions to Abbey Caves to see glow-worms (2 hours) in the limestone caves, and fishing trips in Whangarei Harbour.

Sticking with the clock theme, try the **Kauri Clock Factory**, Nell Place (off Dyer St), Otaika, Whangerei; tel: 09 438 8884. Preserved kauri wood, some 50,000 years old, is made into clocks at this factory. Guided tours are available, and there is also a showroom and a shop. Open Mon–Fri 0800–1700, Sat–Sun 0900–1600.

Whangarei Falls

The Whangarei Falls lie 5 kilometres northeast of the town, at Tikipunga. The 25-metre falls are created by an old basalt lava flow and you can observe them from two viewing platforms.

Northland Breweries, 104 Lower Dent St; tel: 09 438 4664; open Mon–Sat 0900–1400, offers tours and free tasting. It is a microbrewery producing three traditional

EN ROUTE

To Whangaruru Harbour leave State Highway 1 at Whakapara and follow the signs to Oakura Bay – a delightful spot for dolphin watching, swimming, boating, fishing and diving.

Whananaki Trail Rides, Hailes Rd (off Highway 1); tel: 09 433 8299. Organised horse treks on the east coast. Everything from 1 hour to two to five days.

beer varieties, without the use of chemicals. The Northland draught is particularly well spoken of.

The highlight of **Whangarei Museum** (Clarke Homestead & Kiwi House, Maunu, 6 kilometres out of town, tel: 09 438 9630) is the nocturnal kiwi house – the perfect opportunity to take a closer look at New Zealand's national emblem. The surrounding 25 hectares of farmland and bushwalks are also worth exploring. Another worthwhile excursion is to the **Mangrove Boardwalk**, starting at Ewing Rd, just off the Ted Elliot Memorial Pool car park. Caution: when exploring mangroves insect repellent is a must.

Just 6 kilometres out of town, the **Moirs Hill Walkway** tracks through native bush and plantation (allow 3 hours). The views of the Hauraki Gulf are well worth the effort. For a change of scenery, take the route running through the Pohuehue Scenic Reserve.

i **Visitor Information Centre** 92 Otaika Rd, Tarewa Park (2 km out of town); tel: 09 438 1079, fax: 09 483 2943; e-mail: whangarei@clear.net.nz.

Central Court Motel $ 54 Otaika Rd; tel/fax: 09 438 4574. Central location next to a licensed restaurant.
Cherry Court $$ 35 Otaika Rd; tel: 438 3128, fax: 09 438 7972. Comfortable motor lodge with swimming pool, indoor private spa and barbecues.
Cheviot Park $$ cnr of Western Hills Drive and Cheviot St; tel: 09 438 2341, fax: 09 438 0442. Motor Lodge with outdoor pool, private spa and barbecue facilities. Welcomes disabled.
Flames International Hotel $$ Waverley St; tel: 09 436 2107, fax: 09 436 2107. Quiet accommodation with sea views and access to beautiful beaches. Facilities include bar and licensed restaurant.
Whangarei YHA Manaki Tanga $ 52 Punga Grove Ave; tel: 09 438 8954, fax: 09 438 9525; e-mail: yhawhang@yha.org.nz. A small hostel set in spacious grounds overlooking the harbour. Internet facilities.

Bogart's Restaurant $ cnr Cameron and Walton St; tel: 09 438 3088. Coffee shop and restaurant in laid-back New Zealand style. BYO and licensed.
Killer Prawn $$ Bank St, next to the Strand; tel: 09 430 333. Open daily for lunch and dinner. The ultimate in specialist restaurants and the winner of several awards. Licensed.
Reva's $$ Town Basin; tel: 09 438 8969. Open daily for brunch, lunch and dinner. Also a bar.
Serenity Café $ 45 Quay St. Offers an all-day breakfast, 20 flavours of ice-cream, waffles and great espresso. Open from 0700.

PAIHIA AND WAITANGI

Paihia, just across the water from Russell, is often considered to be its poor relation – but just try telling the locals that. In truth, there's not much to the place itself apart from a long string of motels, but Paihia is next door to the Waitangi National Reserve, a beautiful park with buildings and exhibitions relating to the Treaty of Waitangi (see pp. 83 and 96). Paihia is a good jumping-off point for exploring the delights of the **Bay of Islands**.

The centrepiece of the Waitangi National Reserve, just north of Paihia, is the **Treaty House** where the Treaty of Waitangi was signed in 1840. The historical importance of the treaty lies in the way it defined the attitudes of New Zealanders of European descent – the pakeha – towards the Maoris. Presented to the world at large as a model of equitable treatment, its flaws appear obvious only in retrospect.

The house, together with 400 hectares of gardens, was purchased by the Governor General, Lord Bledisloe, in 1932, who then gifted it to the nation as a national historic site.

BAY OF ISLANDS VINTAGE RAILWAY

A vintage steam train, pulled by a J-Class locomotive, runs between Opua and Kawakawa through beautiful scenery. The pick-up point is on the main street of Kawakawa. The journey takes about 45 minutes and there are two or three trains daily. Tel: 0800 802 805. At the time of writing the train was non-operational, but it is hoped it will return to the tracks in the near future. The Kawakawa station is now a museum.

POOR KNIGHTS ISLANDS

The waters around the islands of Tawiti-Rahi and Aorangi were rated one of the best diving spots in the world by no less an authority than Jacques Cousteau. The fish are not the only attractions: you'll also come across schools of dolphins, blue penguins and various species of whale on their annual migrations. Local seabirds include gannets and shearwaters.

Several companies offer excursions to the Poor Knights Islands and diving is possible all year round, although November to late April is probably the best time. Snorkelling is equally rewarding if you don't fancy scuba diving.

Knight Diver Tours operates trips to the Poor Knights daily throughout the year (www.poorknights.co.nz). Knight Line (Whangarei; tel: 0800 288 882) offers day trips for scuba diving and wetsuit snorkelling plus sea kayaking.

HUNDERTWASSER'S LOO

Seldom has the sound of flushing chains flushed so many faces with pride as in the small town of Kawakawa. Located inland on State Highway 1, the town was usually bypassed by tourists on their way to Paihia and the sea, sun and fun of the Bay of Islands. The only attraction was the vintage steam train, puffing its way up the town's main street from the coastal resort of Opua. But that has changed; Paris has its Louvre but Kawakawa now has its new public loo – the most original in the entire land.

Designed by Austrian-born artist Frederick Hundertwasser, it features coloured tiles, coloured windows made from wine bottles, bulbous pillars and a grassy roof – and there is not a straight line in sight. In fact many of the tourists who now queue up in front of it are more interested in clicking a photo of the facilities than in using them. Most are amazed to find a public privy that doubles as an objet d'art. Even more wonder how it ended up in an obscure place like Kawakawa.

Hundertwasser first arrived in New Zealand way back in 1973. He liked what he saw of the country, decided to stay, and eventually bought himself a 450-hectare farm, just a few kilometres outside of Kawakawa. A 'greenie' long before the term became popular, he followed his ecological bent by, among other things, planting his land with native trees and equipping his home (a converted cowshed) with an organic toilet and a grass roof. Though he frequently returned to Austria, he would spend at least several months of the year in New Zealand, relishing the relative anonymity of his rural hideaway.

Prior to the loo, Hundertwasser was best known for his 'koru flag', an alternative flag for New Zealand. Designed in 1983, and based on a Maori spiral motif (*koru*), it was never officially accepted. Other architectural projects he had planned, including a design for the new Te Papa museum in Wellington, never came to fruition. The loo is, therefore, his first public building in the Southern Hemisphere.

The artist died in February 2000 of a heart attack, and has been buried on his beloved Kawakawa property. However, the flag and the lavatory may not be the last mementoes of Hundertwasser in New Zealand. Before his death he completed designs for various business premises in Kawakawa. If local business people can raise the cash, a number of shop fronts will be refurbished in Hundertwasser style, and some of the pressure might finally go off the loo – to the relief of those who really need to use it!

EVENTS

In August more than 50 jazz bands come to town for one of the country's liveliest festivals. In September there is an opportunity to sample local food and wines when over 40 producers display their wares at the festival on the shores of the Bay of Islands.

Beautifully preserved, it's a must-see for anyone visiting New Zealand. The highlight of the exhibition is the magnificent **Ngatokimatawhaorua**, a 35 metre-long Maori war canoe. One of the largest of its kind in the world and capable of carrying up to 80 warriors, it was carved from three massive kauri trees in the Puketi forest. An excellent audio-visual presentation outlines the events surrounding the signing of the Treaty, though arguably from the pakeha point of view. The reserve (also beautifully preserved) is well worth exploring. Allow yourself time to take the boardwalk through the mangrove forest to the Haruru Falls. (Don't forget the insect repellent.)

Another place worth a look is **Kelly Tarlton's Museum of Shipwrecks**. New Zealand's pioneering wreck diver has given his name to this museum on the *Tui*, a three-masted barque moored at the Waitangi Bridge. An exhibition of booty from salvage operations off the Northland coast includes some jewellery lost by the Rothschild family. Open daily.

Bay Adventurer Backpackers $ 28 Kings Rd; tel: 09 402 5162, fax: 09 402 2163, www.bayadventurer.co.nz, e-mail: bayadventurer@xtra.co.nz. An excellent new hostel in a beautifully landscaped setting. Facilities include a large pool, spa and Internet. For a bit more luxury there are also self-contained apartments. Recent winner of the BBH National Quality Award and hard to beat for the price.

Casa Bella $$ MacMurray Rd; tel: 09 402 7387, fax: 09 402 7166. Comfortable motel, pleasantly arranged round a Spanish-style courtyard. Heated swimming pool and spa.

Paihia Holiday Motor Inn $$ Joyces Rd; tel: 09 402 7911, fax: 09 402 7729. Hotel in a peaceful bush setting, 300 m from the centre. Licensed restaurant and bar, swimming pool, spa pool and barbecue.

Pipi Patch Backpackers Lodge $ 18 Kings Rd; tel: 09 402 7111. Close to beach and shops. Winner of a tourist award.

The area is a bit thin on eateries although you will find fresh fish on the menu in most cafés. Service though is variable.

Bistro 40 $$ 40 Marsden Rd, Paihia; tel: 09 402 7444. Waterfront restaurant, next to the old Stone Church. Excellent seafood and the wine list includes some first rate New Zealand whites.

The Boat Restaurant & Bar $$ Waitangi; tel: 09 402 7018. Brash restaurant in a landlocked ship on the way to the Treaty House. Part of the Museum of Shipwrecks.

Twin Pines Restaurant and Bar $$ Puketona Rd, Haruru Falls, Paihia; tel: 09 402 7195. Open daily for lunch and dinner. The setting is a beautifully restored mansion built from kauri wood. The home-brewed beer is a plus.

SHOPPING

Cabbage Tree, Williams Rd, Paihia; tel: 09 402 7318; open daily. Voted one of the best shops in New Zealand, Cabbage Tree specialises in New Zealand-made products, including the famous Swandri 'swannies', and will ship worldwide to avoid problems with excess baggage.

Waikokopu Café $$ Treaty Grounds, Waitangi; tel: 09 402 6275. Restaurant overlooking the beach in the grounds of the Treaty House. Vegetarian and children's menu. Serves excellent coffee. Open daily 0900–1700, longer in summer.

BAY OF ISLANDS

The maritime park comprising more than 150 islands and sheltered bays boasts a cornucopia of marine life, enriched by the warm waters of the tropical South Pacific. Consequently the Bay is one of New Zealand's most popular big-game fishing grounds, with catches including blue and black marlin, broadbill, tuna, kingfish and sharks.

GAME FISHING

Zane Grey (1872–1939) did more than anyone to popularise big-game fishing in the Bay of Islands. Born in Zanesville, Ohio, Grey abandoned a career as a dentist to pioneer the Western as a literary genre and his novels eventually became best sellers.

Another major attraction in the Bay of Islands is dolphin and (sometimes) whale watching. Those in the know will recognise common and bottlenose dolphins as well as minke, brydes and killer whales. Remember that if you want to ensure success with whale-spotting, it is a good idea to set aside at least a couple of days as sightings are heavily dependent on the weather.

TRIPS AROUND THE BAY All the boat operators take conservation seriously and go to great pains not to intrude on the marine environment. Most of the commercial vessels in the bay are licensed by the DOC and part of the hiring fee goes to dolphin research. The two main booking operators for cruises, swims with dolphins and trips to Ninety Mile Beach are:

Fullers, Paihia; tel: 09 402 7421 or 09 403 7866 (Russell), fax: 09 402 7831; www.fullers-bay-of-islands.co.nz.

Kings Dolphins Cruises and Tours, Paihia; tel: 0800 222 979 (reservations) or 09 402 8288, fax: 09 402 7915; www.dolphincruises.co.nz; e-mail: info@dolphincruises.co.nz.

The award-winning **Dolphin Discoveries** (NZ Post Building, Paihia; tel: 09 402 8234, fax: 09 402 6058; www.dolphinz.co.nz; e-mail: dolphin@igrin.co.nz) offers four-hour trips twice daily at 0800 and 1230.

The Cream Trip

The Cream Trip is one of the last Royal Mail boat runs left in New Zealand. From September to May departures are from Paihia daily at 1000 and Russell 10 minutes later (June and September: Mon, Wed, Thur and Sat.) The boat meanders in and out of numerous small bays and inlets delivering and collecting the mail and dropping off stores where required. As a concession to visitors there's a detour to Black Rocks, unusual volcanic formations jutting out into the sea, and to Urupukapuka Island, where snacks and meals are available at the Zane Grey café. You can book the Cream Trip with Fullers in Paihia, tel: 09 402 7421. (You won't need seasickness tablets for this trip as the waters en route are mostly sheltered.)

Awesome Adventures (Maritime Building, Paihia; tel: 09 402 6985, fax: 09 402 7832; www.awesomeadventures.co.nz) offers an extra trip free if you're unlucky enough not to see a dolphin or whale. Typically you sail in a purpose-built catamaran and there are even opportunities to go swimming with the dolphins (an unforgettable experience). The trip includes a visit to Urupukapuka Island, where you can either stop over for a few hours, or take a further ride in an underwater viewing vessel to observe the seabed.

Coastal Kayakers, Paihia; tel: 09 402 8105 operates guided tours exploring the mangrove forest and the Haruru Falls (4 hours), Motumaire Island and the Waitangi coast (one day) or Urupukapuka Island (two days with an overnight camp).

Great Escape, Opua; tel: 09 402 7143. For the independent-minded who would rather explore the Bay of Islands under their own steam, Great Escape in Opua hires out small sailing boats. (If you are not completely confident you can join a flotilla.) Opua is just a short drive from Paihia and the hiring costs are very reasonable.

The ***R Tucker Thompson*** is a tall ship replica of an old schooner. All members of the crew are expected to assist in the sailing and rigging of the vessel. Fullers; tel: 09 402 7421.

If you want to sail but would prefer someone else to do the serious work for you, Vanessa McKay has over 50,000 ocean kilometres under her belt. Her boat leaves Paihia at 1000 and Russell at 1020. Carino Day Sailing, tel: 09 402 8040.

Alternatively, you can try your hand at big game fishing. There's a large number of charter vessels to choose from, for instance the Bay of Islands Swordfish Club, tel: 09 403 7857.

Paihia Dive Williams Rd, Paihia; tel: 09 402 7551. Scuba diving in the Bay of Islands, including a trip to the wreck of Greenpeace's boat, the *Rainbow Warrior*.

Ski-Hi Tandem Skydive, Watea Airfield, Haruru Falls; tel: 09 402 6744. Drop from between 3000 and 4000 metres over the Bay of Islands. Free pick-up available.

i **Bay of Islands Information Bureau**, Entrance to wharf, Marsden Rd, Paihia; tel: 09 402 7345, fax: 09 402 7314; e-mail: visitorinfo@fndc.govt.nz. They'll also have info on all the local events: e.g. 2nd weekend of August – the Bay of Islands rocks to the sounds of the Jazz and Blues Festival.

RUSSELL

THE FLOGGING PARSON

In February 1830 two Maori ladies fell out over the favours of a whaling captain. The fight gradually escalated into a full-scale war between two tribes. More than 100 warriors were killed on the beach in the first day alone. Eventually the situation was brought under control thanks to the intervention of missionaries, led by Samuel 'The Flogging Parson' Marsden.

Edward Markham, artist and writer, conveys something of the atmosphere of the time in New Zealand, in *Recollections of It*. He wrote:

'Thirty to five-and-thirty sail of whalers come in for three weeks to the Bay, and 400 to 500 sailors require as many women, as they have been out one year ... And even the relations of those who are living as servants with the missionaries go to Pihere and bring them away, in spite of all their prayer lessons. These young ladies go off to the ships and three weeks on board are spent much to their satisfaction, as they get from the sailors a fowling piece for the father or brother, blankets, gowns and as much as they would from the missionary in a year.'

There are a number of ways to get to the lovely town of Russell, which lies just across the water from Paihia. Those with cars will find the most direct route from Auckland will be to turn off State Highway (SH) 1 at Kawakawa and then continue on SH 11 to Opua. Here a car ferry crosses roughly every 10–15 minutes to Okiato, just 12 kilometres south of Russell. Otherwise, if you have more time, there is a scenic coastal route that follows the Old Russell Road – leave SH 1 at Whakapara (north of Whangarei) and continue via Oakura and Rawhiti to Russell. The unsealed Waikare Road that leaves SH 11 at Taumarere, a few kilometres north of

STRANGE BUT TRUE?

Russell was originally known as Kororareka, which according to legend means 'sweet penguin'. The story goes that a Maori chief was wounded in battle and asked for some penguin soup. As he sipped the broth he is said to have murmured, '*Ka reka te korora*', which translated means 'How sweet is the penguin'. Strange but true?

FERRIES TO RUSSELL

Passenger Ferry from Paihia

Departs Paihia Wharf 0720, 0830, 0900 then every 20 minutes until 1730, 1830 and 1930. Runs until 2230 in summer.

Car Ferry from Opua (just south of Paihia) 0650–2200 every 10 to 15 minutes.

Kawakawa, is a long, bumpy alternative. For those staying in Paihia there are regular passenger ferries to Russell. They leave from Paihia Wharf in town every 20 minutes.

Nowadays Russell has almost an excess of charm. This was not always so. In the 1820s whalers, sealers and traders made full use of the sheltered anchorage where they encountered a motley population of escaped convicts, deserters and sailors who had jumped ship. The mayhem which ensued is revived every New Year's Eve when Aucklanders traditionally come here to celebrate!

In a sense, Russell is a living museum. Its most impressive monument is the splendid weatherboard Christ Church, built in 1836 and probably the oldest-surviving church in New Zealand. (Charles Darwin donated money to the building fund when he visited the Bay of Islands around this time.) Inside the church you can still see bullet holes made by Hone Heke and his warriors when they ransacked Russell in 1844. Note the beautifully embroidered kneelers and the Maori and Settler graves in the church grounds.

The **Pompalier House** on the waterfront was built from rammed earth in 1839–41. It was first used as a Roman Catholic mission, and later as a printing press. (The name derives from J B F Pompalier, a French bishop who printed the first Catholic religious text in Maori.)

The house is now an award-winning museum in an historic garden setting, operated by the New Zealand Historic Places Trust. The Strand, tel: 09 403 9015. It is open open most days 1000–1700, but confirm the opening times near your visit by phone, as they are liable to change.

The **Duke of Marlborough Hotel** on the waterfront is in proud possession of the oldest liquor licence in the country, dating from 1840 – for more than 13 years before that date the pub had been operating without a licence!

Another place of interest to look out for on the Strand is the prestigious Bay of Islands Game Fishing Club, founded in 1924.

Russell Museum itself is independent and self-funding. The exhibits include a magnificent 1:5 scale model of Captain Cook's ship *Endeavour*, some of Zane Grey's fishing tackle and a handful of Maori artefacts. 2 York St, tel: 09 403 7701; open every day 1000–1600.

Flagstaff Hill is where Hone Heke and his warriors battled with the settlers in the 1840s (see p. 96). The current flagpole was erected in 1857 by the Maoris as an act of reconciliation. On 12 days of the year the flag of the Confederation of Tribes flies proudly to remind residents of Russell's turbulent history.

CAPE BRETT TRIP

Half-day cruises leave for Piercy Island at the entrance to the Bay of Islands, passing through the hole in the rock at Cape Brett. For more information, contact Fullers; tel: 09 402 7421.

About 1 kilometre beyond Flagstaff Hill at the end of the peninsula is **Tapeka Point Historic Reserve**, the site of a Maori *pa* (fortress) offering great views of the Bay. If you walk on for one more kilometre, you'll come to Oneroa Bay where the sheltered beach area is safe for swimming.

i **The Visitors Centre** on the waterfront is run by the Department of Conservation. It is well stocked with information not only about Russell, but the whole of the Northland region. Bay of Islands Maritime and Historic Park Visitor Centre, The Strand; tel: 09 403 9003.

Arcadia Lodge **$–$$** Florance Ave; tel/fax: 09 403 7657. This hotel in a historic wooden house with beautiful gardens has been receiving visitors for more than 100 years. Dormitories as well as bed and breakfast accommodation. No children, but free kayaks!
Hananui Lodge Motel **$$** The Waterfront; tel: 09 403 7875, fax: 09 403 8003. Beautifully located motel, overlooking the beach.
Motel Russell **$** 16 Matauwhai Bay Rd; tel: 09 403 7854, fax: 09 403 8001. Close to the beach and in a quiet garden setting, the motel has its own pool and spa. Scooters for hire.
Russell Top Ten Holiday Park **$** Longbeach Rd; tel: 09 403 7826 or 0800 148 671, fax: 09 403 7221; www.russelltop10.co.nz; e-mail: russelltop10@xtra.co.nz. An excellent holiday park with attractive gardens and very good facilities.

GOOD PUBLICITY

'The inhabitants in this Bay are far more numerous than in any other part of the country that we had before visited ... they seemed to live together in perfect amity ... The Bay affords us good anchorage, and refreshment of every kind.'

Captain James Cook with the first positive tourist report on Russell, 1769

Duke of Marlborough Hotel **$$$** Waterfront, Russell, tel: 09 403 7829, fax: 09 403 7828; open daily for lunch and dinner. Dine out in grand style in one of the oldest pubs in New Zealand (Somerset Restaurant). In the summer there are tables on the open veranda overlooking the water, while in the winter customers move indoors to warm themselves by the log fire.

The Gables $$$ The Strand; tel: 09 403 7618. Top-of-the-range diner with romantic candlelit rooms.

Gannets $$ York St; tel: 09 403 7990. Poor lighting, amateurish, if enthusiastic, service, but fish to dream about.

Sally's Restaurant $ 25 The Strand, Russell; tel: 09 403 7652. Waterfront dining.

MAORI GRIEVANCES CONCERNING THE TREATY OF WAITANGI

The Maoris had numerous grievances concerning the Treaty of Waitangi which they had signed in 1840 (see p. 83). Not only were the terms inaccurately translated, but even the concept of land ownership was understood differently by the Maoris.

When they began to understand the implications of the treaty, the Maoris started to protest. In July 1844 Hone Heke Pokai led a band of warriors to Russell where they destroyed a flagpole as the most obvious symbol of British rule. It was immediately re-erected but torn down repeatedly until, in March 1845, the town was abandoned by the residents and laid waste by the Maoris.

Although more than 150 years have passed since the treaty was signed, it is still a bone of contention and protests against commemorating Waitangi Day (a national holiday in New Zealand) continue to break out sporadically.

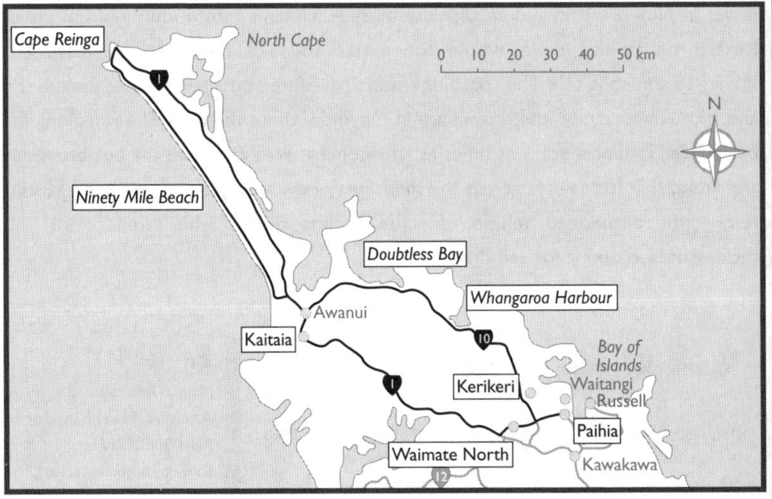

Paihia – Kaitaia
OTT table 9753

Transport	Frequency	Journey Time
Bus	2 daily	2hrs

Paihia – Mangonui
OTT table 9753

Transport	Frequency	Journey Time
Bus	2 daily	1hr 30mins

Mangonui – Kaitaia
OTT table 9753

Transport	Frequency	Journey Time
Bus	2 daily	40mins

Cape Reinga

Cape Reinga, at the tip of North Island, is sacred to the Maoris as the stepping off point to the hereafter. To the south lies Ninety Mile Beach, one of the most exhilarating drives in New Zealand and an absolute must. A full day's return journey from either Russell or Paihia, it's a whole lot easier to take the bus and leave the driving to someone else. The coach operators have fitted out special buses for the trip and, more importantly, the drivers are in the know about the tides. The run along the beach itself is almost scary at times as an incoming wave can catch the bus broadside and literally lift it sideways across the sand. Every now and again you will see a rusting ruin – the abandoned vehicle of some hapless tourist who came to rue his recklessness in opting for self-drive.

Cape Reinga by Bus

Although it is possible to explore the Aupouri Peninsula by car, the bus tour is far the better option and the easiest way to enjoy the drive along Ninety Mile Beach, a must on any itinerary but totally unsuited to private cars, even four-wheel drives. You can pick up a bus virtually anywhere in Northland but the most convenient spot is Paihia, where two major lines operate from the centre of town. Bus routes vary according to the tides, but you should get to see at least some of the major sights. The following is a fairly typical itinerary.

Depart about 0730 for Waimate North (sometimes there's a detour to Kerikeri). From here the bus makes its way through the Puketi Kauri Forest to Kaitaia, before turning onto Ninety Mile Beach. This stretch of road is little more than a track. At the northern end the bus crosses the Te Paki Quicksand Stream, the only point of access to the tip of the island and Cape Reinga.

The return route follows the main peninsula road with possible detours to Doubtless Bay and Mangonui Harbour. Towards the end of the trip you'll notice the deep and near-landlocked Whangaroa Harbour before returning to Paihia. Operators from Paihia include **Fullers** (tel: 09 402 7421, fax: 09 402 7831; www.fullers-bay-of-islands.co.nz; e-mail: reservations@fullers-bay-of-islands.co.nz) and **Dune Rider** (tel/fax: 09 402 8681; www.dunerider.co.nz; e-mail: dunerider@xtra.co.nz).

En Route

Many buses call at the **Ancient Kauri Kingdom** (tel: 09 406 7172; www.ancientkauri.co.nz), a commercial enterprise that recovers enormous kauri logs from the swamps before making them into furniture. Some of these logs have lain underground for up to 30,000 years.

Cape Reinga by Car

If you leave out Ninety Mile Beach, it is possible to drive to the lighthouse at Cape Reinga along State Highway 1F from Kaitaia. Bus tours along the beach also start from Kaitaia, and make for a less tiring day than those starting in Paihia – see accommodation listings under Kaitaia for operators.

WAIMATE NORTH AND AROUND

The site of the first inland mission station in New Zealand (established by Samuel Marsden in 1830), this once volcanically active area is now some of the most fertile farmland in the Northland. Paths lead through the **Puketi Kauri Forest**, parts of which are more than 1000 years old.

Only a few years younger than the Mission House at Kerikeri, the Waimate North Mission House is New Zealand's second-oldest surviving building. Though the site for the mission was chosen in 1830, it was not until 1831 that the house itself was built with the help of local Maoris. One of the aims of the resident missionaries was to teach the Maoris English agricultural methods. Already by 1834 the country's first flour mill was operating and wheat was being supplied to other mission stations. When Charles Darwin visited in 1835, he was much impressed with what was New Zealand's first European-style farm.

Even though it is possible to look around the historic house at your leisure, it is nevertheless worthwhile first to take advantage of a guided tour. It costs nothing extra and the guide is invariably a mine of information, revealing many fascinating details that would otherwise be missed. At the end of this brief tour you will have a much better appreciation of what it was like to live, in an isolated mission station, during the early days of settlement.

KAITAIA

The main town of the far north of Northland was founded by Croatian settlers who came there in search of kauri gum. With a good selection of shops and restaurants, it is a useful stopping point before venturing into the wilds of Cape Reinga.

i **Far North**, Jaycee Park South Rd, Kaitaia; tel: 09 408 0879, fax: 09 408 2546; e-mail: fndckta@xtra.co.nz.

Capri Motel $$ 5 North Road; tel: 09 408 0224 or 0800 422 774, fax: 09 408 0086; e-mail: caprimotel@xtra.co.nz. Comfortable self-contained units with Sky TV. Can organise tours to Cape Reinga.

Main Street Backpackers $ 235 Commerce St; tel: 09 408 1275 or 0508 624 678; e-mail: mainstreet@xtra.co.nz. Maori-run backpackers, where you can learn lots about Maori culture. Can organise tours to Cape Reinga.

Sierra Court Motor Lodge $$ 65 North Rd; tel: 09 408 1461 or 0800 666 022, fax: 09 408 1436. Motel in extensive and pleasant grounds with swimming pool, spa, laundry, games room and children's playground.

KERIKERI

Kerikeri lies 22 kilometres to the north-west of Paihia and was the site of a Maori *pa* (fort) ruled over by Hongi Hika, a fearsome chief who nevertheless welcomed early proselytisers from the English Church Missionary Society in 1823. Nowadays, it's a small, rather sleepy town of fewer than 3000 people. Kerikeri's importance lies not in the town itself but in the basin of the same name, (just down the hill from the shopping centre). It was here that the first translation of the New Testament into Maori was made and a Maori dictionary was compiled, effecting the introduction of Christianity to New Zealand.

THE ARAROA WALKWAY

The first stage of a continuous long-distance walk, from one end of New Zealand to the other was opened in February 1995. It stretches between Kerikeri and Waitangi. The walk conceived by the Te Araroa (meaning the 'long pathway') Trust, and will eventually extend all the way from North Cape to the Bluff (to be completed by December 2005).

The **Stone Store** was built by missionaries in 1832–35 and replaces an older wooden structure that had probably been here since 1819. For a time Bishop Selwyn used the top floor as a library. On display in the store is the first plough in New Zealand, which was pulled by a team of six oxen back in 1820. Open daily during the summer 1000–1700; closed Thur–Fri in winter; tel: 09 407 9236.

A ROUND OF GOLF?

Then visit the attractive 18-hole Kerikeri Golf Club on GolfView Rd; tel: 09 407 8837, fax: 09 407 8875.

Next door is the **Kerikeri Mission House**. Dating from 1822, it's the oldest building in the country. For the first ten years of its life it was used by the staff of the Church Missionary Society; it is now known as Kemp House after the family that lived here from 1832 until 1974, when it was handed over to the Historic Places Trust. Even in the 20th century, one member of the family, Miss Gertrude Kemp, kept a light in her window to guide boats up the river basin. This tradition probably dated from the time when the house was built.

At 1 Landing Road there is an authentic replica of a **Maori fishing village**, reputed to have been the home of Rewa, the great Maori chief. The reconstruction was built in 1969 (access by way of the Visitor Centre; open daily 1000–1600). Just across the inlet is the fortified

SHOPPING

Baa-Baa Enterprises, Inlet Rd, Kerikeri; tel: 09 407 9597. Handmade sheepskin slippers with individual painted designs.

Origin Art & Craft Co-op, State Highway 10 (turn left off Kerikeri Rd, direction airport); tel: 09 407 1133. Shop for pottery, handcrafted shoes, woodcraft and much else besides. Open daily 1000–1700.

The Chocolate Factory Kerikeri Rd; tel: 09 407 6800. Free viewing and tasting before you shop. Mailing service too.

Maori *pa* (fort) belonging to Hongi Hika, who once ruled over most of the North Island. Finally, the **Kerikeri Rainbow Falls** are 4 kilometres out of town, off the Waipapa Rd on Rainbow Falls Rd – a 10-minute stroll from the car park.

Department of Conservation, 34 Landing Rd; tel: 09 407 8474.

Abilene Motel $$ 136 Kerikeri Rd; tel: 09 407 9203, fax: 09 407 8608; e-mail: abilene@kerikeri-nz.co.nz. Set in beautiful grounds with a children's play area and swimming pool. Close to shops and restaurants

Central Motel $$ 58 Kerikeri Rd; tel: 09 407 8921 or 0800 867 667, fax: 09 407 8005; e-mail: ewrigley@voyager.co.nz. Close to town centre. Studio and family units, games room, swimming pool and spa.

Colonial House Lodge $$ 178 Kerikeri Rd; tel: 09 407 9106, fax: 09 407 9038; e-mail: colonial.lodge@xtra.co.nz. 1–2-bedroom cottages in a garden setting, 1500 m from town.

Hone Heke Lodge $ 65 Hone Heke Rd; tel/fax: 09 407 8170; e-mail: honeheke@xtra.co.nz. Close to shops. Free pickup from bus.

Kerigold $$–$$$ Kerikeri Rd; tel: 09 407 3200, fax: 09 407 3201; e-mail: kerigoldchalets@xtra.co.nz. Deluxe chalets set in an avocado and citrus orchard, not far from the town centre.

Kerikeri Farm Hostel $ On SH 10; tel: 09 407 6989; e-mail: kkfarmhostel@xtra.co.nz. Located on a citrus orchard.

Butler's Restaurant and Bar $–$$ Stone Store Basin; tel: 09 407 8479. Beautifully situated opposite the Stone Store, with a reasonably priced café lunch menu and more expensive à la carte dining in the evenings.

Marx Garden Restaurant $$$ Kerikeri Rd; tel: 09 407 6606. Open for lunch Fri, Sat, Sun from 1200–1400. Dinners are served Tues–Sun from 1730.

Rocket Café $ Kerikeri Rd; tel: 09 407 3100. Voted one of Northland's best cafés and also a delicatessen.

NINETY MILE BEACH

In fact, only 60 miles (90 kilometres long), Ninety Mile Beach is one of the greatest and most unusual bus drives in the world! The Te Paki Quicksand Stream, a small river which runs between sand dunes, is the only access point. Usually the bus will stop near a sand dune to allow the passengers to go surfing down the face of the dune. There's no ecological damage as the dunes are continuously being replaced by sand blowing across the peninsula.

QUAD YOUR WAY DOWN...

The only safe way of seeing Ninety Mile Beach without going on a bus tour is to 'quad' your way down. Drive to Ahipara – roughly the start of the beach – where you can then hire a quad (a four-wheel motorbike) and, after directions, explore the beach at your leisure. Contact Ahipara Adventures Centre at Pine Tree Lodge Motor Camp, Takahe St, Ahipara; tel: 09 409 2005. A word of warning: these bikes do not have power steering and it requires considerable exertion to swing the bar over so that they go exactly where you intend.

CAPE REINGA

The Cape is marked by a lonely white lighthouse that has been in use since 1941. Its warning beacon is now solar powered; it flashes every 12 seconds and can be seen some 35 kilometres away. This is just as well, as about ½ kilometre offshore the Tasman Sea meets the South Pacific Ocean in a stormy turmoil that, even on a calm day, is dangerous to shipping.

In clear weather, the views extend over a seemingly endless expanse of ocean to the **Three Kings Islands**. The first European to sight this isolated group was the explorer Abel Tasman in 1643. Much closer at hand, just below the lighthouse on a wind- and wave-battered promontory of rock, is a venerable 800-year-old pohutukawa tree. According to Maori tradition, the spirits of the dead depart through its roots into the ocean, on a final journey to the spiritual homeland of Hawaiki. For this reason, the Cape is of great spiritual significance to the Maori people.

NO ORDINARY BUS

The buses that follow the route along Ninety Mile Beach are specially constructed for the job. The engine is moved inside the body of the bus and the chassis is tipped up at the tail to give extra clearance. The whole chassis is then galvanised. At the end of every trip, while the passengers are enjoying a cup of coffee, the bus is carefully hosed down to remove all salt water. Each night it is returned to the depot to be given another hosing down – every week it has a thorough greasing.

With these precautions the devastating effects of driving on the beach are kept at bay and the buses enjoy a long and useful life. No car would be able to stand up to this treatment.

DOUBTLESS BAY

According to the brochures this is 'The ultimate Northland Destination' – and it's undeniably popular. Swimming, surfing, diving, kayaking, sailing and water skiing are all possible on the numerous safe beaches, which range from sheltered coves to sand and surf. At the centre of the bay, the picturesque fishing village of Mangonui has not yet been overwhelmed by commercial development and it's claimed that this is where you can get the best fish and chips in New Zealand.

'Here the clocks seem to tick slower, the calendar turns more slowly. In the Northland the pace of life is slower than in the rest of New Zealand. And no one in the whole country is in a desperate hurry. In the Northland we do not have stress. Nor do the visitors after a week up here.'

Jonathan Gage, interview in the *Sydney Morning Herald*, April 1968

WHANGAROA HARBOUR

Created by volcanic activity, the harbour is backed by towering cliffs, broken by cascading waterfalls and rocky coves. Known as the 'Marlin Capital', Whangaroa has a **Big Gamefish Club** (American angler and author Zane Grey was a founder member); but the waters around the harbour are also a breeding ground for scallops and oysters. The historic pub, Marlin Hotel (tel: 09 405 0347) is just one place where you can sample the local fishy delights.

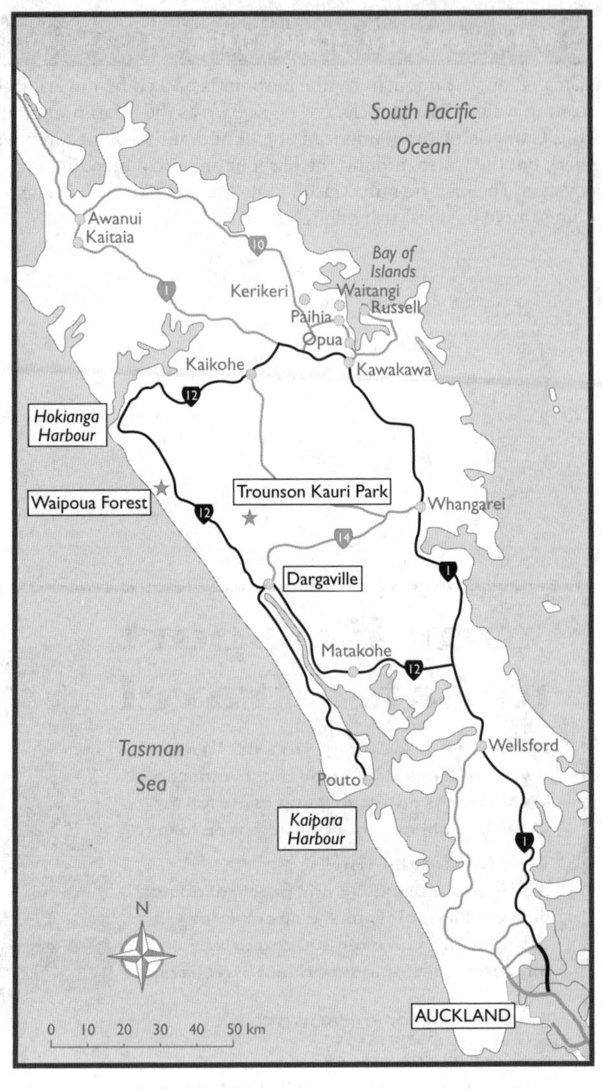
South Pacific
Ocean
Awanui
Kaitaia
10
Bay of
Islands
1
Kerikeri
Waitangi
Russell
Paihia
Opua
Kaikohe
Kawakawa
12
Hokianga
Harbour
Waipoua Forest
Trounson Kauri Park
Whangarei
12
14
Dargaville
1
Matakohe
12
Wellsford
Tasman
Sea
Pouto
Kaipara
Harbour
1
N
0 10 20 30 40 50 km
AUCKLAND

From Hokianga Harbour to Kaipoura Harbour, the west coast of Northland has everything: from wildlife reserves and watersports opportunities to picturesque inlets, peaceful rural settlements, undeveloped parkland and empty beaches.

This region of great natural beauty also contains the last remaining tracts of the ancient kauri forest, which once covered large areas of the northern North Island – the Trounson Kauri Park, and the Waipoua Forest Sanctuary. If you want to find out more about the kauri, the museum at Matakohe is a must-see. In the 19th century this noble tree became the focus of unwanted attention when shipbuilders from all over the world recognised its suitability for making the spars and masts of sailing ships. In time, the demand led to the serious depletion of the region's forests. Nevertheless visitors can still hike through kauri trails as well as farmland, unspoilt coastland and hill country. For further details contact the Visitor Information Centre in Dargaville, capital of the kumara-growing region.

ROUTE DETAIL

Begin by taking State Highway 1 from Auckland to Ohaeawai, then turn south on State Highway 12 to Kaikohe.

From Kaikohe follow State Highway 12 to Opononi and Omapere at the mouth of **Hokianga Harbour**. The road now swings inland through **Waipoua Forest Park**. Shortly after Katui it is possible to make a detour to **Trounson Kauri Park**. Otherwise the highway continues parallel to the coast to **Dargaville**.

From Kaikohe – Dargaville 141 km

South from Dargaville, State Highway 12 follows the Wairoa River to Kaipara Harbour, then continues through the villages of Matakohe and Paparoa to join State Highway 1. From here you can return to Auckland. You could detour from Dargaville by taking the road along the west side of **Kaipara Harbour**, and the narrow peninsula separating it from the Tasman Sea. Just before Rototuna, 30 kilometres on, the tarmac ends but the unsealed road is drivable as far as Pouto on the edge of the harbour.

Return Journey 100 km

HOKIANGA

This historic harbour was also known as Te Kohanga o Te Tai Tokerau ('the nest of the northern tribes') and most Maori people trace their ancestry to this settlement. The rolling hills around the harbour are dotted with small villages, including the shipbuilding centre, Horeke, and historic Rawene, which are among New Zealand's oldest European settlements. Nearby are the beaches of Opononi and Omapere.

A car ferry, known as **Kohu Ra Tuarua**, now crosses Hokianga harbour. It leaves Rawene on the half-hour from 0730 and returns from the Narrows near Kohukohu on the hour (last sailing 2000). For more information or bookings contact the **Hokianga Information Centre** at Omapere (tel: 09 405 8869, fax: 09 405 8317; e-mail: fndchka@xtra.co.nz).

WAIPOUA FOREST SANCTUARY

A protected forest covering an area of 15,000 hectares, Waipoua contains 75 per cent of New Zealand's remaining kauri trees, some of them up to 2000 years old. The largest, and most famous, **Tane Mahuta** ('Lord of the Forest'), estimated at between 1200 and 1400 years old, is only a short walk from the road and is accessible by wheelchair. The forest only survived because of public protest. When the last of the kauri was being harvested in 1952, a petition signed by more than 70,000 people convinced parliament to set aside a large area of the forest as a sanctuary. The caretaker's cottage, built at the beginning of the 20th century, has been preserved as a museum. Tracks, such as the **Yakas, Lookout** and **Waiotemarama Kauri and Waterfall Walks**, criss-cross the forest. There are also some superb coastal routes offering views across the sand dunes.

TROUNSON PARK

This 573-hectare park lies 32 kilometres north of Dargaville. The 40-minute loop walk takes visitors from the parking and picnic area through the forest by way of a number of picturesque streams and kauri stands to the **Four Sisters** – two trees each with two trunks. Guided night walks are a special attraction here, allowing visitors the opportunity to encounter glow-worms, possums and, of course, kiwis in their native habitat. (Trounson is now one of the best kiwi breeding sites in New Zealand, with about 200 birds all told.)

CLENDON HOUSE

Built in the 1860s for James Reddy Clendon, witness to the Treaty of Waitangi, ship owner, magistrate and member of the first Legislative Council. The house (in Rawene) became a museum in 1972. Clendon Esplanade, tel: 09 405 7874. Open 1000–1600.

DARGAVILLE

Dargaville was founded in 1872 and became a borough in 1908. The town takes its name from Joseph McMullen Dargaville, an emigrant from Ireland who worked as a bank clerk in Australia before moving to New Zealand, where he eventually rose to the elevated rank of bank inspector. After resigning he got involved in the kauri timber business and bought the land where the town now stands.

Because of its location near the forest and the Northern Wairoa River (once navigable to the sea), Dargaville's economy centred around kauri logging, gumdigging, shipbuilding and shipwreck-salvage.

The **Maritime Museum**, in Harding Park is mainly devoted to shipwrecks (common along this part of the coast). The most intriguing relic is a couple of masts from *Rainbow Warrior*, the Greenpeace ship sunk by the French Secret Service for taking too close an interest in their nuclear tests. (Open daily 0900–1600; tel: 09 439 7555.)

EN ROUTE

To walk the entire Hokianga–Waipoua Coastal Track will take three days, but it is possible to 'do' shorter stretches: for example from Hokianga Harbour to Waimamaku Beach (approximately 4 hours) or to the Kawerua exit (6 hours).

For the adventurous, just south of Dargaville the Tokatoka Peak, the core of a 180 metre-high volcano, is a 20-minute climb.

i **Kauri Coast Information Centre** Normanby St; tel: 09 439 8360, fax: 09 439 8365; e-mail: info@kauricoast.co.nz.

Awakino Point Lodge $$ State Highway 14; tel/fax: 09 439 7870. Located among orchards and gardens, this motel, only 2 minutes from town, also provides breakfasts.
Dargaville Motel $$ 217 Victoria St; tel/fax: 09 439 7734 or phone 0800 466 835. Ideally situated for exploring the area. Some units have good river views. Disabled visitors welcomed.
Dargaville VIP Holiday Park $ 10 Onslow St; tel/fax: 09 439 8296; e-mail: dargavilleholidaypark@xtra.co.nz. Facilities include kitchen complex, outdoor BBQ and TV lounge. Internet/e-mail is available. Free pickup from town and bus depot.
The Greenhouse Hostel $ 13 Portland St; tel: 09 439 6342, fax: 09 439 6327; e-mail: m.stevens@clear.net.nz. Close to shops and in a garden setting.

KUMARA

Dargaville is the centre of a major kumara-growing region. *Kumara* is the Maori name for the sweet potato, which forms an important part of the traditional Maori diet.

Hobsons' Choice Motel $$ 212 Victoria St; tel: 09 439 8551, fax: 09 439 8553. New motel with swimming pool and spa baths. Breakfasts available.

Kauri House Lodge $$$ Bowen St; tel/fax: 09 439 8082. Large wooden hotel with en suite rooms, billiard room, library and swimmimg pool.

Sample local delicacies such as *tuatua* (clams), *kumara* (sweet potato) and fresh fish.

Blah, Blah, Blah Café $ 101 Victoria St; tel: 09 439 6300. Varied menu featuring gourmet pizzas. Open 0900–late, Sun from 1600.

Seaview Café $ 13 Baylys Coast Rd; tel: 09 439 4549. Enjoy your meal while gazing out over the sea.

The Steak House $ 138 Victoria St; tel: 09 439 8460. Juicy NZ steaks.

BAYLYS BEACH (RIPIRO BEACH)

For a different experience try Baylys Beach Horse Treks, tel: 09 439 4531.

New Zealand's longest driveable beach (by four-wheel drive) extends 100 kilometres south of Dargaville from Maunganui Bluff to Pouto Point at the entrance to Kaipara Harbour. The shoreline is perfect for surfing and sand tobogganing as well as digging for tuatua.

Beachcombers may want to scour the sand near the 100-year-old wooden lighthouse for relics from the estimated 153 wreck sites.

KAIPARA HARBOUR

Once a shipbuilding area, the harbour is now a quiet, rural sort of place. Many of the local settlements have attractive spots for lunch; for example in **Paparoa**, try the dairy by the village green, the Old Bank Building or the Old Post Office Guest House. **Matakohe** has an old church (1867) now used as the church hall, but also a fascinating Kauri and Pioneer Museum, which traces the history of the Kauri coast and the local trade in timber and gum. There's also a shop selling kauri souvenirs and, opposite, the Gumdiggers Tea Rooms. Open daily 0900–1700.

Kauri Country Safaris run 3-hour excursions into the forest where you can try your hand at bushworking, using original antique tools, and taste 'black billy tea' and scones. Tel: 0800 246 528.

Route Detail

Hamilton lies at the junction of State Highway 1, from Auckland to Taupo, and State Highway 3 to New Plymouth. Travel south on State Highway 3, through Ohaupo, Te Awamutu and Tokanui, where the road crosses the river Puniu and the township of Kiokio en route to the sheep and cattle rearing area known as King Country. About 8 kilometres south of Otorohanga, a small turning to the right leads to Waitomo and the caves (see p. 113).

Return to State Highway 3 and continue south through Te Kuiti before turning left on to State Highway 30 to cross the Pureora Forest Park. Continue driving through Kopaki, Mangapehi and Pureora as far as Maraetai (just off the main route).

From here a partly unsealed road heads northwards to State Highway 1. Turn left when you reach the Highway to return to Hamilton via Cambridge.

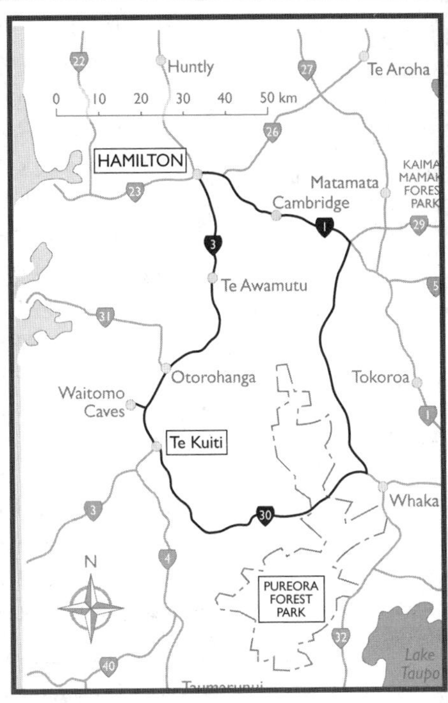

Hamilton – Te Kuiti

OTT tables 9750/9758

Transport	Frequency	Journey Time
Train	2 daily	54mins
Bus	2 daily	1hr 15mins

Hamilton – Otorohanga

OTT tables 9750/9758

Transport	Frequency	Journey Time
Train	2 daily	40mins
Bus	2 daily	55mins

Otorohanga – Te Kuiti

OTT tables 9750/9758

Transport	Frequency	Journey Time
Train	2 daily	16mins
Bus	2 daily	20mins

Note: There is a daily bus between Waitomo Caves and Auckland. Another bus connects at Otorohanga with the 0830 train from Auckland (1043 at Hamilton) that goes to the caves; see OTT 9767.

EN ROUTE

From Ngaruawahia, take a short detour west and after 23 kilometres you'll discover Waikato's 'hot spot', the **Waingaro Hot Springs**. Here you can zoom down the Big Splash waterslides or laze in the thermal pools and spas. You could even spend the night in a caravan or motel unit. Open daily from 0900–2200; tel/fax: 07 825 4761; e-mail: waingaro.hot.springs@clear.net.nz.

Hamilton lies at the edge of the Waikato region, 129 kilometres south of Auckland in the heart of the North Island. Known for its lush vegetation and rolling countryside, the Waikato is one of the world's richest dairying and agricultural regions, fed by the river of the same name as it flows from Lake Taupo to the sea at Port Waikato. The area, particularly Hamilton, was originally inhabited by the Tainui tribe, who abandoned their settlements when the first Europeans arrived (the 4th regiment of the Waikato Militia was attracted by the promise of land). Throughout Waikato's history the river was the primary means of communication – until 1878 that is, with the arrival of the railway. Roads followed later. The Tainui's influence is still very much in evidence – at Ngaruawahia, just beyond Hamilton, for example, you'll find the home of the Maori queen and the impressive Tarangawaewae Marae on River Road.

Aside from its river (the longest in New Zealand) and dairy farming, the Waikato province is also famous for racehorse breeding and for Neil Finn, of Split Enz and Crowded House fame, who was born in the town of Te Awamutu.

HAMILTON

The growth of modern Hamilton has been spectacular and it's now New Zealand's fifth largest city and a major commercial and industrial centre. It's also home to Waikato University and Polytechnic, as well as the Agricultural Research Institute. It is pretty much the hub of the Waikato, and provides a good base for exploring the province's forest reserves and beaches to the west, and its leisure lakes and farm stays in the east. Nothing in the Waikato region is more than an hour's drive from the city.

The mighty Waikato River, which bisects the city, is used by water-skiers and rowers and is flanked by some nice parks.

An ideal place to start your visit is the **Waikato Museum of Art and History** on the corner of Grantham and Victoria Streets, one of New Zealand's most dynamic and innovative museums. Here you can immerse yourself in the region's Tainui Maori culture and discover the history of the Waikato. There are also temporary exhibitions of modern New Zealand and Australian art, and the 140-year-old war canoe, Te Winika, is on show. Tel: 07 838 6533; open daily, 1000–1630, closed Christmas. On the same site is '**EXSCITE**' a new 'hands-on' interactive Science and Technology centre providing hours of absorbing entertainment for all ages. Information, tel: 07 838 3470 , fax: 07 838 3497; www.exscite.org.nz.

Inevitably in a city overlooking New Zealand's longest river, there's no shortage of activities involving the Waikato River. The historic paddleboat, **MV *Waipa Delta***, made her maiden voyage on the river in 1877. Nowadays she departs from the Memorial Park Jetty and there's a choice of cruises. The leisurely 2-hour cruise with buffet lunch departs at 1230, or, if time is pressing, you could opt for the 1-hour afternoon tea cruise (departs 1500). In the evenings you can enjoy dinner on board with live entertainment – the 3-hour cruise departs at 1900; tel: 07 854 7813 or 0800 472 3353, fax: 07 854 9419; www.waipadelta.co.nz.

Alternatively, a more exciting way to see the river is by jet boat tour with **Camjet Jet Boat Tours**, tel: 07 843 6114 or 0800 226 538; www.camjet.co.nz.

Set on a scenic stretch of riverbank, off Cobham Drive, you'll find **Hamilton Gardens**, a major green space with around 100 different themed gardens and numerous seasonal attractions and exhibitions. (There's always something new to see here.) Tel: 07 838 6782, fax: 07 856 2132; www.hamiltongardens.co.nz.

EN ROUTE

Travel south on State Highway 3 and you'll pass through Otorohanga. Stop here for a guided tour of the **Kiwi House and Native Bird Park**, where every visitor is assured of seeing active birds in their natural environment. Set in 2.5 hectares of bush, the house is also home to numerous other rare and unusual bird species. Tel: 07 873 7391, fax: 07 873 7356; www.kiwihouse.org.nz. Open daily 1000–1700.

THE FORGOTTEN FOREST

One interesting feature in the zoo is the Forgotten Forest, a fascinating attempt to simulate New Zealand's natural environment, as it was before the arrival of humans.

Hamilton Zoo (8 kilometres from the city, take State Highway 53 towards Raglan) is a new-style zoo, renowned for its generous habitats and enlightened approach to conservation. You can see a host of endangered and exotic species and there's also a chance to explore the largest free-flight conservation aviary in Australasia as well as New Zealand's forgotten forest. Here in 'The Forgotten Forest' more than ten endangered native bird species inhabit a fern valley. Tel: 07 838 6720; open seven days a week 0900–1700.

Hamilton has a burgeoning nightlife, which belies its reputation as an overgrown farming town. Most of the pubs and clubs are on or around Victoria St.

Not forgetting the shops: catering for the wallets of wealthy farmers, Hamilton has also become something of a shopping oasis.

EN ROUTE

Surfers should keep an eye out for Raglan, New Zealand's most renowned surfing spot. West of the harbour town are the surf beaches of Whale Bay and Manu Bay. The Indicators, at the northern end of Manu Bay, is rated as the best left hand break in the world.

i **Hamilton Visitor Information Centre** cnr Bryce and Anglesea Sts; tel: 07 839 3580, fax: 07 839 3127; e-mail: hamiltoninfo@wave.co.nz.

Department Of Conservation (Waikato Conservancy Office) 18 London St; tel: 07 838 3363, fax: 07 838 1004.

Otorohanga Visitor Information Centre 87 Maniapoto St; tel: 07873 8951, fax: 07 873 8398; e-mail: otovin@xtra.co.nz.

Commercial Hotel $, 287 Victoria St; tel: 07 839 4993 or 0508 266 468, fax: 07 834 2389.

Hamilton YHA $ 1190 Victoria St; tel: 07 838 0009, fax: 07 838 0837. Central location, overlooking Waikato River.

J's Backpackers $ 8 Grey St; tel: 07 856 8934; www.jsbackpackers.co.nz; e-mail: biddlem@xtra.co.nz. Close to Hamilton Gardens, internet access.

Le Grand Hotel $$$ 237 Victoria St; tel: 07 839 1994 or 0800 534 726, fax: 07 839 7994. Central grand-style hotel in a historic building.

Mill Lodge Motor Inn $$ 135 Ulster St; tel: 07 839 3143 or 0800 803 135, fax: 07 839 4361. Quiet modern motel, close to restaurants in the centre.

Cazbar & Caffe $$ The Marketplace (off Hood St); tel: 07 838 0998. Snacks and main meals. Live music Tuesdays, Thursdays and Saturdays. Licensed.

Sahara Tent Café & Bar $–$$ 254 Victoria St; tel: 07 834 0409. A taste of the Middle East in Hamilton. Good takeaway menu.

WAITOMO

CAVE TOOBING

Tumu Tumu Toobing is a cave rafting experience billed as suitable for ages ten and upwards. For details, tel: 0800 924 866 or 07 878 7788.

Further south, just off State Highway 3, you'll discover Waitomo Caves, one of New Zealand's premier attractions. The Waitomo Shuttle bus (tel: 0800 808 279) connects with coaches and trains at Otorohanga, or if you're coming from Taupo and Rotorua, take the Waitomo Wanderer, tel: 07 873 7559.

Before exploring the caves themselves, visit the **Museum of Caves**; open daily; tel: 07 878 7640.

In the course of a century the **Glow-Worm Caves** have played host to more than 1 million visitors from all over the world. Take a magical boat ride through Glow-Worm Grotto where the light from a myriad of these tiny insects is reflected in the water deep underground. Aranui Cave, 3 kilometres away, is a bonus. Here you can admire the beautifully delicate limestone features – a natural marvel. Both caves are well lit with good paths, handrails and informative local guides. Tours for the Glow-Worm Cave leave every half-hour from 0900–1700 and for Arunui Cave at 1000, 1100, 1200 and 1500; tel: 07 878 8227, fax: 07 878 8858; www.waitomocaves.co.nz.

For those seeking thrills and spills there are a number of options:

Waitomo Adventures Ltd, tel: 07 878 7788 or 0800 924 866, fax: 07 878 6266; www.waitomo.co.nz. This is the only company that offers '**The Lost World**', a spectacular, award-winning trip involving a 100-metre abseil down through the Lost World Cave. For the inexperienced there's a 4-hour trip where you're harnessed to a professional. The 1½-day trip includes instruction on the first day followed by a physically and emotionally challenging 7-hour adventure on the second.

Also offered by Waitomo Adventures is **Haggas Honking Holes** – where you abseil down a waterfall, climb over fantastic rock formations, view glow-worms and much more.

Black Water Rafting offers a professionally guided underground cave tubing experience. For the Rafting I trip, the original exhilarating 'glow-worm glide', allow 3 hours. Or, for the Rafting II adventure, a combination of abseiling, glow worm floating, caving and climbing, allow 5 hours. Afterwards you can take a hot shower, and then relax over soup and a round of toast at the Black Water Café. Tel: 07 878 6219 or 0800 228 464, fax: 07 878 5190; www.black-water-rafting.co.nz.

Waitomo Down Under promises 'serious fun' with a choice of three different adventures. You can combine the caves and glow worms experience with a spot of local Maori culture at the Tokikapu Marae. The company is operated by the descendants of the native chief who introduced the caves to the Europeans more than 100 years ago. Wetsuit, gloves, helmet and sarcastic guide are all supplied. Tel: 07 878 7788 or 0800 102 605, fax: 07 878 6565.

Around Waitomo there are a number of easy bush walks. Contact the Visitor Centre for details. There's also horse trekking (tel: 07 878 7649) and a visit to **The Shearing Shed**, tel/fax: 07 878 8371, where you can pet a fluffy Angora rabbit or see a variation on sheep shearing – rabbit shearing! To see the real thing, pop up the road to **Woodlyn Park**, tel: 07 878 5255, where you can also help train a farm dog and watch demonstrations.

i **Visitors Information Centre,** Waitomo Caves; tel: 07 878 7640, fax: 07 878 6184; e-mail: waitomomuseum@xtra.co.nz.

There's a wide range available, from the elegant Waitomo Caves Hotel to the usual choice of motels and backpackers' hostels. You could even stay in a restored 1950s railcar!

Juno Hall $ Waitomo Caves Rd (1 km from Waitomo); tel: 07 878 7649. Courtesy van to Museum of Caves and camping allowed in grounds. Horse trekking available.

Waitomo Caves Hotel $$$ by the Museum of Caves; tel: 07 878 8204, fax: 07 878 8205. Grand hotel with fully refurbished rooms, restaurant and bar. Backpacker dormitories ($) in YHA annex.

PUREORA FOREST PARK

About 55 minutes from Waitomo on State Highway 30 (in the direction of Rotorua) is the **Pureora Forest Park**, little known but accessible from State Highways 30, 4 and 32. This hidden wonderland of magnificent native forest is home to the endangered kokako – a forest bird with a distinctive early morning song. Tiny Hochstetter's frogs dwell on the forest floor, though they are so well camouflaged you would be lucky to glimpse one. You will see stunning scenery, a variety of native fauna and flora, and very few humans - a refreshing feature after the major tourist attractions.

The area was devastated by the Taupo eruption of AD 186 and native forests subsequently flourished on the ash-enriched soils.

Pureora is a rare survivor of the kind of forest that once covered vast tracts of the North Island. Today it's surrounded by acres of farmed exotic woodland. One of New Zealand's most significant conservation battles took place here in 1978 when protesters 'took to the trees' to prevent mass-scale destruction of the Pureora. This radical action led to a government-imposed moratorium and eventually to the end of native forest logging in the park.

Today you can visit the Tree Top Protest site and climb the 12-metre Forest Tower nearby for a better perspective of the tree canopy. This is also a perfect spot for observing native birds, especially in the early morning. The site is a 10-minute drive from the Pureora Field Centre with detailed information on the area. One feature is the Buried Forest which, after disappearing in a volcanic eruption 1800 years ago, was accidentally rediscovered by a bulldozer in 1983.

There are three easy walks (30 minutes) in the Pureora, suitable for all ages and with good opportunities to view the magnificent native trees for which it is renowned. Details of Totara, Rimu and Waihora Lagoon walks can be found in the Forest Park brochure along with other more demanding tracks. Finally, as a memento of your trip to the North Island, leave the car in the Link Road car park, cross the road and follow the short flat track to a cairn marking the 'Centre of the North Island'– a photo for your album!

i **Te Kuiti Visitor Information Centre** Rora St; tel: 07 878 8077, fax: 07 878 5280; e-mail: tkinfo@voyager.co.nz. **Pureora Field Centre** (DOC) tel: 07 878 4773.

WHERE NEXT?

From Hamilton or Te Kuiti, take Hwy 3 south-west to New Plymouth (see p. 116). OTT table 9758 details coach services between the towns.
State Highways 1 and 5 take you south-east from Hamilton; it is about 100 km to Rotorua (see p. 180); the journey can also be made by coach – OTT table 9756 gives timings.

NEW PLYMOUTH

The Taranaki region is just about the most deserted corner of the North Island. New Plymouth is a small but elegant coastal town with a population of around 50,000. It lies at the junction of State Highway 3 and, despite its isolation, has a prosperous and contented feel. Rising above the town are the northern slopes of the most beautiful mountain in New Zealand, Mount Taranaki. This is the centre of one of the most important dairy regions in the country, but there's also a small petrochemical industry, founded on the offshore oil and gas fields.

This area was much favoured by the Maoris in pre-European times and well settled, but raids and local wars drove out many of the tribes, leaving it sparsely populated. The first European settler, Dickie Barrett, arrived in 1828 and married a Maori woman, Rawinia Waikaiua. Despite this intermarriage, the relationship between the Maoris and the pakeha in the area was always a troubled one and the colonists felt the need to form a militia in 1855. Misunderstandings led to war five years later and a conflict that spluttered on for more than 20 years.

GETTING THERE AND GETTING AROUND

AIR **New Plymouth Airport** lies north-east of the city. Withatruck buses run a 10-minute shuttle service into the centre.

CAR **State Highway 3** passes through New Plymouth from Wanganui in the south and Te Kuiti in the north.

BUS **Okato Bus Lines** operate a comprehensive local service. Their depot and information office is at 32 Queen St. InterCity coaches leave from the travel centre at the corner of King and Queen Sts. Local buses are also operated by **New Plymouth City Services**, tel: 06 758 2799.

INFORMATION

New Plymouth Visitor Information Centre cnr of Liardet and Leach St; tel: 06 759 6080, fax: 06 759 6073; e-mail: info@newplymouth.govt.nz. Also information is available from the **Department of Conservation** 220 Devon St West; tel: 06 758 0433.

POST AND PHONES The main post office is at 21 Currie St. Open Mon–Fri 0900–1700.

ACCOMMODATION

Devon Hotel $$ 390 Devon St East; tel: 06 759 9099, fax: 06 758 2229. Smart hotel with heated swimming pool, spa and bar. Restaurant serves buffet-style evening meal. Off-road parking.

Egmont Lodge YHA $ 12 Clawton St; tel: 06 753 5720, fax: 06 753 5782; www.taranaki-bakpak.co.nz; e-mail: egmontlodge@taranaki-bakpak.co.nz. A short walk from town. Full kitchen facilities. Check the website for two other excellent backpackers in the vicinity.

Flamingo Motel $$ 355 Devon St West; tel/fax: 06 758 8149. Friendly central motel with indoor and outdoor pools. Disabled visitors welcomed.

Henwood House $$ 122 Henwood Rd, (5 km east on State Highway 3); tel/fax: 06 755 1212. Comfortable bed and breakfast hotel in a Victorian homestead with extensive gardens and lounge with veranda.

Sunflower Lodge $ 25 Ariki St; tel: 06 759 0050, fax: 06 759 0051; e-mail: jrsanders@xtra.co.nz. Central location, private bathrooms and free tea and coffee.

Wave Haven $ 1518 Main Rd Oakura, Taranaki; tel/fax: 06 752 7800. A good backpackers, ideal for surfers.

FOOD AND DRINK

Andre L'Escargot $$$ 37–43 Brougham St; tel: 06 758 4812. Upmarket restaurant serving classic French food. Licensed.

The Carriage $ Oakura, State Highway 45; tel: 06 752 7277. Café in a converted railway carriage serving a good range of snacks and sandwiches.

Portofino $$ 14 Gill St; tel: 06 757 8686. Good Italian fare – book well in advance. BYO and licensed.

Steps $$ 37 Gover St; tel: 06 758 3393. Mediterranean specialities – main meals as well as a good variety of snacks. Open Tues–Fri for lunch and dinner. BYO and licensed.

HIGHLIGHTS

The history of New Plymouth can be read in some of the buildings. The oldest is the **Wesleyan Mission Girls School** at Moturoa. No one is quite sure when it was constructed, but it was very likely built in 1869.

NEW PLYMOUTH

Pukekura Park (on Liardet St) is definitely a contender for the best park in New Zealand. It was transformed from the wilderness by volunteer labour, a process that began in 1876, two years before the dam was built to form the main lake. The park's attractions include Poet's Bridge, the bandstand, the Queen Victoria Diamond Jubilee Fountain, the fernery and the tea kiosk, from where there are splendid views of Taranaki in clear weather.

Brooklands Park lies next to Pukekura and boasts a natural amphitheatre seating more than 16,000 people (the lake in front of the stage reflects sounds and images). It was here, in the very centre of the park, that the first resident magistrate, Captain Henry King, lived in the 1840s. You can still see what is left of the house – little more than the fireplace and chimney (the remainder was burned down during the Maori wars). Also within the park is a massive puriri tree, said to be over 2000 years old.

The Gables is the last survivor of four colonial hospitals built by Governor George Grey between 1846 and 1848 with the benign aim of encouraging the Maoris to take advantage of the Western medical facilities. This didn't work out because in 1854 a local chief died in the hospital from stab wounds and the institution was declared tapu (taboo). This may not have been altogether a bad thing as the resident surgeon is on record as describing the hospital as 'cold, draughty and inadequate'. It served better as a military command post during the Maori wars, and later became an old peoples' home. Early in the 20th century, it was bought by a local businessman who eventually donated it (along with the adjoining Brooklands Park) to New Plymouth. It is now used as a workshop and display premises by the Taranaki Society of Arts.

JACK OF ALL TRADES

At one time many buildings in New Plymouth boasted weatherboard cladding. This is now rare. One of the best remaining examples is the Flight Family House which is now used by New Plymouth Girls' High School grounds as part of the school's art department. (Until 1984 the building stood on Eliot Street.) The house was built in 1868 by Josiah Flight, who was at various times resident magistrate, provincial sub-treasurer, coroner, collector of customs, bank director and militia officer!

The construction of **St Mary's Church** began in 1842 and was completed in September 1846, using rocks brought up from the beach. It is probably the oldest stone church in the country. Originally a small building measuring 15 metres by 10 metres, it was later enlarged and strengthened. During the Maori Land Wars in the 1860s the church also served as a magazine. The original bell is still in use and hangs outside the church. Both the exterior and the interior are beautifully designed and inside you can see the regimental colours of many of the European forces as well as some of the Maori battalions.

If you follow the Heritage Trail (a free Heritage Walkway brochure is available at the Information Centre, but you'll also need to get hold of a proper map of the town) you'll come to the **Alpha Flour Mill** in Baines Terrace. This was the city's first mill, and opened in February 1843 with millstones made from rocks taken from the beach. The Heritage Trail is a circular walk beginning at Pukeariki Landing, next to the Centre City Shopping Complex in Gill St, and takes a leisurely 2 hours.

HEN AND CHICKENS

The Hen and Chickens is a row of private houses not open to the public, built to accommodate the various branches of the Hirst family. They are built to a basic plan but with individual variations. Hirst named the row York Terrace, but the Hen and Chickens soubriquet has stuck!

The excellent **Taranaki Museum** on Ariki St contains some splendid Maori wood carvings and relics of the Polynesian migration. These include an anchor and an adze, both said to have come up from the original Tokomaru canoe, dating from the time of the first Polynesian migration six centuries ago. Open Mon–Fri 0900–1630, weekends 1300–1700. Free admission.

New Plymouth

Oil was first discovered at Moturoa in 1866. The original oil field continued to yield for more than a century and only closed in 1972. The **Alpha well** in New Plymouth - one of the earliest in the world - opened in 1865, primarily to produce gas. You can see a beam pump at the end of Bayly Rd, a relic of the Egmont Oil Well.

West Country Settlers

In 1841 the town was surveyed and settled by the Plymouth Company, an appropriate name as many of the new arrivals came from villages in Devon and Cornwall in the west of England. An obelisk in Pioneer Rd overlooks the spot where, on 31 March 1841, the first Plymouth Company arrivals came ashore at Ngamotu beach from the ship, *William Bryan*. When the monument was unveiled in 1911 no fewer than 43 of the original Plymouth Company immigrants were still alive to attend the ceremony.

The **Sugarloaf Islands Marine Park** is a protected area of some 8 square kilometres, where you can see seals, dolphins and even humpback whales on their way to their breeding grounds. There are numerous bird species and over 70 different species of fish. The islands are the remnants of an ancient volcano and were used in pre-European times as fortifications by and against marauding Maori tribes. Several of the islands, including Paritutu, Mikotahi, Mataora, Motu-o-Tamatea and Pararaki, were reinforced with palisades, huts and water catchments. The best way to see the Islands - most are closed to the public - is to take a cruise with Chaddies Charters, which uses an old English lifeboat, tel: 06 758 9133.

A little way out of town, Te Henui is a gentle signposted walk of about 3 kilometres that starts at the Waiwaka Reserve. The route follows the Te Henui stream through some beautiful scenery and past the Pukewarangi *pa* (fort) site.

Events

Feb/March – Taranaki Festival of the Arts. Classical and jazz concerts, ballet, theatre, cabaret and much else besides. Takes place in alternate years; the next festival is in 2005. Great fun for all ages and not to be missed.

Nightlife

The club scene centres on **'Devon Mile'** (the stretch of Devon St between Dawson and Eliot Sts).

The Grapevine cnr Currie and Devon St; tel: 06 757 9355. A wine bar and café. Serves Kiwi and Malaysian cuisine. Open Tues–Sun 1700 until late.

The Mill 2 Courtenay St; tel: 06 758 1935. Four large bars in a converted flour mill with discos and live bands at weekends.

EGMONT NATIONAL PARK

The Egmont National Park, the second oldest in New Zealand, was created in 1900. It covers 33,000 hectares of parkland and the North Egmont Visitors Centre, within the park, lies roughly 27 kilometres south of New Plymouth. There is a remarkable 140 kilometres of pathway in total. Get hold of the **Department of Conservation booklet: Walks in the Egmont National Park** and the **Egmont National Park Map** (Infomap 273–09).

MOUNT EGMONT OR TARANAKI?

In 1986 the government ruled that both names were equally valid. However, as is common in New Zealand nowadays, the Maori form, Taranaki, is moving into favour as the name of choice.

MOUNT TARANAKI

Taranaki is one of the most perfectly formed mountains in New Zealand. Unfortunately it's often shrouded by cloud and mist and only rarely reveals its beauty.

Taranaki is imbued with Maori legends. One of these relates the story of the creation of the mountain. All the mountains of the North Island were originally gathered together in one place; all were male except for pretty Pihanga. Male mountains were in constant competition for Pihanga's attentions. Eventually, two of them, Taranaki and Tongariro, came to blows and Taranaki was driven away towards the west coast - which is where it has remained to this day. A more prosaic, but geologically credible explanation is that Mt Taranaki is the youngest of three large volcanoes lying on one fault line. It rises to 2518 metres and, despite the fact that it has not erupted for some 350 years, is still reckoned to be dormant rather than extinct.

If you are fit and relatively experienced it is possible to climb to the summit and get back in one day. However, the weather can be very changeable; check with the park rangers before setting off. In winter you will need ice axes, crampons and ice climbing experience.

EN ROUTE

Some 29 kilometres from New Plymouth, on the Upper Carrington Rd, is the world-famous Pukeiti Rhododendron Trust consisting of 360 hectares of colourful blooms. Apart from rhododendrons – at their best between September and November – you can see giant rata, magnolias, camelias, viburnums, acers and many more species. Tel: 06 752 4141. Open April–Sept 1000–1500, Oct–March 0900–1700.

THE TARANAKI HERITAGE TRAIL

One way of exploring the foothills of Mount Taranaki is to follow the Taranaki Heritage Trail by car. It's well signposted and more than half of the 238-kilometre route around the mountain is coastal. Stop at each of the sites along the way and you have a full day's trip. The route can be taken in either direction and goes from New Plymouth to Waitara, Urenui, Stratford, Oakura, Okato, Opunake, Manaia, Patea and then back to New Plymouth.

WANGANUI AND THE WHANGANUI RIVER

Wanganui lies on the river of the same name – well, not quite. An important colonial settlement, Wanganui lies at the centre of a rich farming area, served by the small port of Castlecliff at the mouth of the river.

The best way to get an overview of the area is to take the Durie Hill elevator by the side of the City Bridge. An elaborately carved Maori gateway marks the entrance to the 200-metre tunnel, blasted into the hillside in 1919. From here the elevator climbs 66 metres to the summit. (Alternatively, if you're feeling energetic, you can run up the 176 steps to the top!) Open weekdays 0730–1900 and Sunday 1300–1800. The view from the Memorial Tower (open daily 0800–1800) takes in much of the coast of the South Island, as well as Mounts Taranaki and Ruapehu.

A Little History: Wanganui Vs Whanganui

It's not a spelling mistake – strangely enough, the river is spelt differently to the town. Wanganui was in fact one of the most important early European settlements in New Zealand. Indeed, it was one of the most prosperous. You can get a feel for this prosperity by viewing some of the mellow and elegant gardens in the town.

The peak year in Wanganui's history was probably 1926. After that it declined in population and did not stop to pick up steam again until after World War II.

Originally the town was called Petre after Lord Petre, one of the directors of the New Zealand Company. But difficulties between the Maoris and the Company meant that this name was in dispute for quite some time. When these arguments were settled, the name Wanganui was officially adopted for the town.

Colonel William Wakefield of the New Zealand Company took charge of the land purchase negotiations at Wanganui. The 'naked savages' were presented with a ragtag of items, including looking-glasses, pipes, blankets and jew's harps in return for the sale of 16,000 hectares. The Maoris, regarding this as an act of generosity on Wakefield's part, rather than payment for the land, made him an equivalent gift of 30 pigs and 10 tonnes of potatoes. Wakefield later insisted that these offerings had been paid for separately and were unconnected with the land 'purchase'.

Behind Queen's Park and the **Sarjeant Gallery**, which has a representative selection of New Zealand paintings (open 1030–1630 during the week and 1300–1630 at weekends), are the **Moutoa (Pakaitore) Gardens**. This is where the local land agreements were signed, although the Maoris have never accepted that the square was included in the deal. The park was deliberately chosen as the scene of a peaceful protest in 1995 in the belief that the police had no power of arrest on the site. After a four-month occupation the matter was settled in the High Court, but the Gardens have been a focus of renewed protest as recently as April 1999.

St Paul's Memorial Church in Anaua St (also known as Putiki Church) is one of the finest Maori churches in New Zealand. Built in 1937, the interior has some magnificent wood carving.

The **Whanganui Regional Museum** opened in 1895 and was at one time the largest museum of its kind, reflecting the importance of the town. The collection of Maori artefacts here is remarkable and includes a 23-metre war canoe, Te Mata-o-Hoturoa, dating from 1810, with bullets embedded in the hull. There are also ten articulated moa skeletons. Open Mon–Sat 1000–1630 and Sun 1300–1630.

It was in Cox Gardens in 1962 that Peter Snell set the world record for running a mile in 3 minutes 54.4 seconds. Above the gardens is a watch tower used by the Fire Brigade from 1800 onwards to keep an eye on the city. It now houses the town clock.

Another of the town's finest gardens is Virginia Lake, on St John Hill, 1.5 kilometres north of town. It is named after Virginia Water in Surrey, England, and is open all day during the week, including Saturday morning and Sunday afternoon.

INFORMATION

Wanganui Information Centre 101 Guyton St; tel: 06 349 0508, fax: 06 349 0509; e-mail:info@wanganui.govt.nz.

Department of Conservation Office cnr Ingestre and Hill St; tel: 06 345 2402, fax: 06 345 8712.

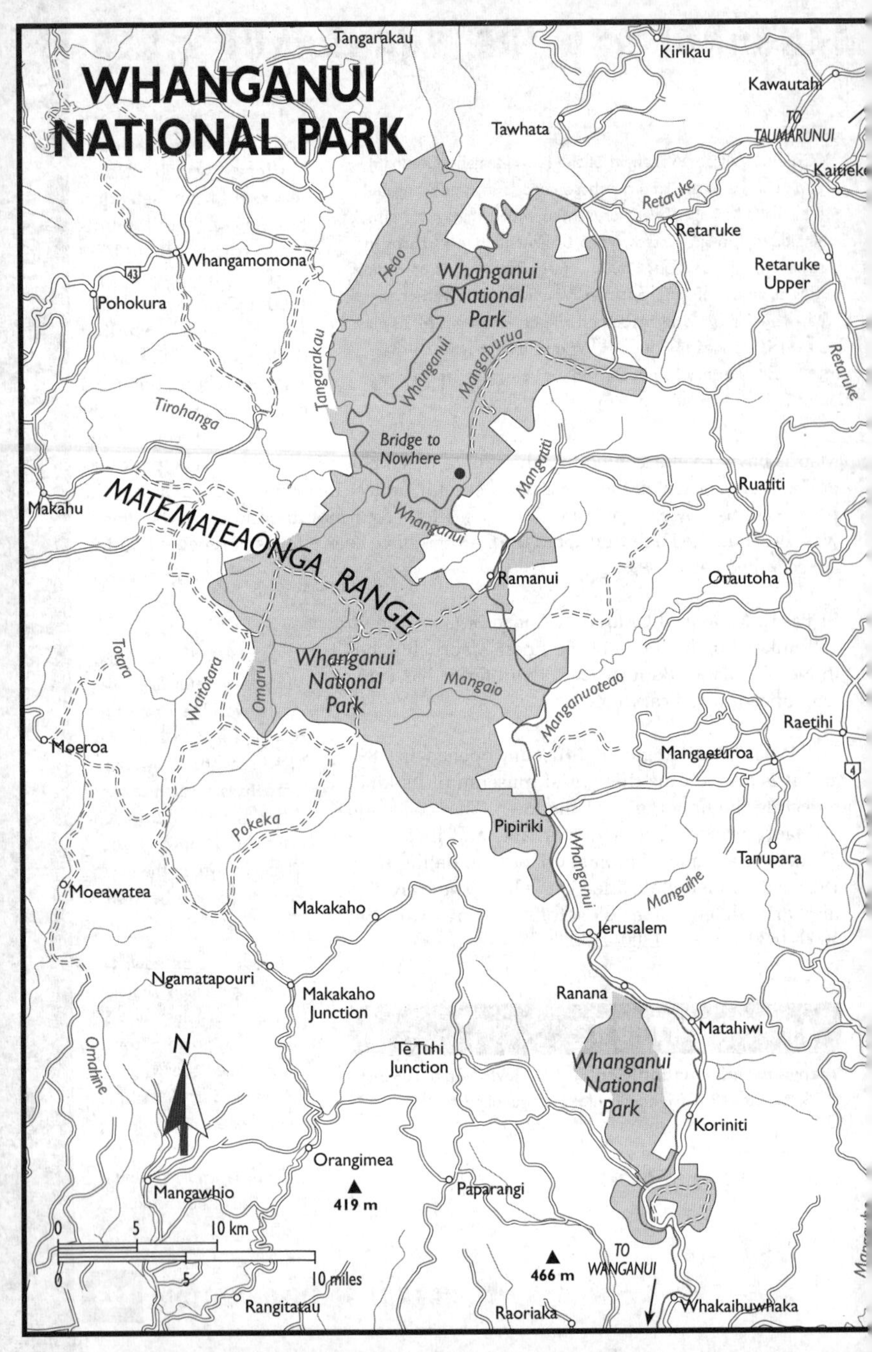
WHANGANUI NATIONAL PARK
Tangarakau
Kirikau
Kawautahi
TO TAUMARUNUI
Kaitieke
Tawhata
Retaruke
Retaruke
Retaruke Upper
Retaruke
Whangamomona
43
Pohokura
Heao
Whanganui National Park
Tangarakau
Whanganui
Mangapurua
Tirohanga
Bridge to Nowhere
Mangatiti
Ruatiti
Makahu
MATEMATEAONGA RANGE
Whanganui
Ramanui
Orautoha
Totara
Waitotara
Omaru
Whanganui National Park
Mangaio
Manganuoteao
Raetihi
Moeroa
Mangaeturoa
4
Pokeka
Pipiriki
Whanganui
Tanupara
Moeawatea
Mangaihe
Makakaho
Jerusalem
Ngamatapouri
Makakaho Junction
Ranana
Matahiwi
Omahine
N
Te Tuhi Junction
Whanganui National Park
Koriniti
Orangimea
419 m
Mangawhio
Paparangi
0
5
10 km
0
5
10 miles
466 m
TO WANGANUI
Rangitatau
Raoriaka
Whakaihuwhaka

ACCOMMODATION

Avenue Motor Inn $$ 379 Victoria Ave: tel: 06 345 0907, fax: 06 345 3250; www.theavenuewanganui.com; e-mail: theavenue@xtra.co.nz. Spacious airy rooms, Facilities include swimming pool, bar, café and restaurant.

Bushy Park Homestead $–$$ 796 Rangitautau East Rd, Kai Iwi, RD8; tel/fax: 06 342 9879; www.bushypark-homestead.co.nz; e-mail: bushypark.homestead@xtra.co.nz. Pleasant 1906 house with a mere 95 hectares of land.

Grand Hotel $$ 99 Guyton St; tel: 06 345 0955, fax: 06 345 0953; www.thegrandhotel.co.nz; e-mail: the-grand-hotel@xtra.co.nz. Good-value old-style hotel with bars and restaurant.

Riverside Inn $–$$ 2 Plymouth St; tel/fax: 06 347 2529. Large bed and breakfast hotel with backpackers dormitories. Good location by the river.

Tamara Backpackers $ 24 Somme Pde; tel: 06 347 6300, fax: 06 345 8488; www.tamaralodge.com; e-mail: tamaralodge@paradise.net.nz. Lodge overlooks Whanganui River. Facilities include internet access and free bikes. Close to town.

Wanganui Motor Lodge $$ 14 Alma Rd; tel: 06 345 4742 or 0800 800 544, fax: 06 345 0235. Good-sized units, spa and swimming pool, restaurant and bar.

FOOD AND DRINK

A New Name For Tutaenui

Thirty-eight kilometres to the south-east of Wanganui is the town of Marton. The original Maori name for this area was Tutaenui, meaning dung heap. In 1869 the settler townfolk resolved to change the name to Marton, after the birthplace of Captain Cook.

Riviera $$ Upokongaro, 11 km outside of town on State Highway 4; tel: 06 345 6459. Superb Italian food with fresh pasta and ice cream. Licensed. Dinner Wed–Sun. Lunch Thur–Sun.

Rutland Arms $ 48–52 Ridgeway St (on the corner of Victoria St); tel: 06 347 7677. Pub-style restaurant with large courtyard.

Zanzibar's $$ Victoria Court, 92 Victoria Ave; tel: 06 345 5900. Modern New Zealand cuisine. Licensed and BYO. Open Mon–Fri 0900–late, Sat 1000–late.

WHANGANUI NATIONAL PARK AND RIVER

The main attraction of Whanganui National Park is, of course, the river that gave it its name. Within the park's boundaries, the country's longest navigable river flows through one of the most remote areas of wilderness on the North Island. This wild region is best experienced on a canoe journey between Taumarunui and Pipiriki, or by shouldering your backpack and hiking for several days along one of the main tracks. If time is short, then the trip along the River Road is also rewarding.

THE RIVER'S HISTORY The Whanganui River flows for 290 kilometres from Mount Ngauruhoe to the Tasman Sea. Fed by the Ongarue, Tangarakau, and Ohura, it negotiates its way around 239 rapids, passing through some of the most picturesque scenery in New Zealand as it does so. The Whanganui is impassible to large ships because of a sand bar near the town, but small boats are able to navigate almost the entire length of the river and it is a near-perfect stretch of water for canoeing. The Whanganui was vital for Maori communications and defences and forts were built along the entire length of the river bank. Europeans began arriving in the area in 1831, among them one Jim Rowe, who is said to have traded in preserved Maori heads. It seems only natural justice that he should end up beheaded by the Maoris themselves.

Prior to the opening of the Main Line Trunk Railway in 1908, the 'river route' was an important tourist attraction on the route between Auckland and Wellington. When Thomas Cook and Son opened an office in Auckland in 1899, their representatives signed a contract with Hatrick's paddle-steamer company for carrying passengers on the Whanganui (including overnight accommodation at the Pipiriki hotel, also owned by Hatrick's at the time). In 1904 the 'New Tourist Route' was advertised worldwide as follows: 'This voyage through the magnificent canyon of the Whanganui River, takes one into the very heart of Maoriland, past scenes of exquisite beauty which linger in the mind forever. Every tourist should visit the Whanganui - its loveliness is beyond compare.' The River was also advertised in the brochures, rather improbably as the 'Rhineland of Maoriland.'

FOLLOWING THE RIVER...

For an interesting drive from Wanganui follow the River Road along the banks of the River as far as Pipiriki, a journey of 80 kilometres. Leave Wanganui via State Highway 4, which climbs over Aramoana, with some amazing views of the river, before dropping to Oyster Shell Bluffs. The River Road branches off to the left passing through Atene, Koriniti, Ranana and Jerusalem. After 72 kilometres you'll see the Omorehu Waterfall Lookout, a delightful spot for a picnic with views over the gorge. The road peters out at the tiny settlement of Pipiriki. To return to Wanganui take the small but drivable road to Raetihi, where you can pick up State Highway 4.

NB. There are no petrol stations on the River Road. Stock up before leaving Wanganui.

There was a slump in the tourist trade in the 1920s as visitors were enticed away to the Chateau Hotel at Tongariro. In 1934 Hatrick's business received a further blow as the mail contract was transferred from the steamer to the new River Road.

The riverside **Hipongo Park** was presented to the citizens of Wanganui by a local Maori chief, Walter Hipongo. It's a place of great natural beauty with towering, fern-clad cliffs, eroded by streams tumbling into the river. There are plenty of places to picnic among the natural bush. The park was once the site of Putakataka Pa, a Maori fort, renowned for never having been captured.

On the way to Hipongo, boats from Wanganui pass '**Kemps Pole**' (on the left bank as you go upstream), erected in November 1880 by Major Kemp, a Wanganui chief. Kemp claimed ancestral rights to lands along the Whanganui and the pole

THE *WAIMARIE* RIVERBOAT

The name *Waimarie* means 'Good Fortune', which is certainly something this grand old lady, the last working paddle steamer on the Whanganui river, has experienced. The restoration and recommissioning of this elegant riverboat – a millennium project for the Riverboat Centre in Wanganui – has been the highlight of an already illustrious career. Visitors can take a trip upriver on the restored PS *Waimarie* and learn a little more of its fascinating history.

The *Waimarie* was originally named the *Aotea*, and was registered as No. 1 in the Ships Register of 1900 in Wellington. She arrived as '60 packages plus a steamer's boiler' from London and was assembled in Wanganui, making her maiden voyage on 29 June 1900. Two years later the *Aotea* was sold to A Hatrick & Co. for the sum of £2000 (a bargain – shortly afterwards she was valued at £4000 without repairs!) and renamed the *Waimarie*. Thirty-four metres long with room for 260 passengers, she worked the busy water highway for nearly 50 years, operating a ferry service, conveying goods and livestock, and collecting and delivering the post to river settlements. At the height of Hatrick's business empire, the *Waimarie* was one of 12 company riverboats plying the waters of the Whanganui.

Eventually the *Waimarie* was laid up, and in 1952 sank at her berth on Settlers Wharf in Wanganui. The superstructure was removed, but the hull remained firmly embedded in the mud for more than 40 years. Then in January 1993 her hull was salvaged by a team of energetic volunteers and members of the Whanganui Riverboat Restoration and Navigation Trust Inc. The ship was reassembled in the Riverboat Centre, following the original design and manufacturing methods as closely as possible. Here you can see a fascinating photographic and video exhibition of the salvage, and displays on the riverboat era. Open Mon–Sat 0900–1600, Sun and public holidays 1300–1600.

(Toko-maru) indicated that the river route was closed to Europeans unless they held a signed pass. This requirement was set aside in 1883 when the surveyors for the railway started work, but Kemps Pole still stands.

RIVER TRIPS The *Waimarie* (see p. 127) is now in service again as a cruise boat. Excursions leave from the Hatrick wharf in the heart of Wanganui, for cruises lasting 2 hours. Full details can be obtained from the Visitors Information Centre in Wanganui or direct from the **Riverboat Centre** at 1A Taupo Quay opposite Moutoa (Pakaitore) Gardens; tel/fax: 06 347 1863; www.riverboat.co.nz.

TRAMPS IN THE PARK The trek along the **Matemateaonga Walkway** is definitely worth considering, though it takes four days to complete. The **Mangapurua Track** is equally impressive, runs for 40 kilometres, and can be covered in 3½ days. A shorter walk is the 45-minute jaunt from the Mangapurua Landing in Wanganui to the Bridge to Nowhere. Contact the Visitors Information Centre for details.

JERUSALEM In 1885 Mother Mary Joseph Aubert founded the community of the Daughters of our Lady of Compassion in this appropriately-named village. The sisters took care of local orphans and farmed and made medicines from ancient Maori herbal recipes, which they sold in Wanganui. More recently, in the 1960s, James K Baxter, poet and reformed alcoholic, established a mission for dipsomaniacs and drug addicts. He insisted on calling it a community, not a commune, because, as he wrote in his Jerusalem Day Book: 'Communes are the work of Mao Tse Tung.' It was here that James Baxter composed his *Jerusalem Sonnets,* which are still in print.

EN ROUTE

Numerous firms operate jet boat and canoeing trips on the river between Pipiriki and Taumarunui; the following is a selection: Bridge to Nowhere Jetboat Tours; tel/fax: 06 385 4128; Wades Landing Outdoors, tel: 07 895 5995 or 0800 226 631, fax: 07 895 7995; www.whanganui.co.nz, offer jet boating and canoeing trips from Whakahoro to Pipiriki. Wairua Hikoi Tours; tel: 06 345 3485 runs one- to two-day guided canoe tours from Pipiriki; with a Maori guide and marae visits. Blazing Paddles Tours, tel: 07 895 5261 or 0800 252 946, fax: 07 895 5263; www.blazingpaddles.co.nz offer one- to five-day trips in Canadian kayaks.

WHANGANUI RIVER TRIP

Classified as a 'Great Walk', the 145-kilometre river trip from Taumarunui to Pipiriki takes an average of five days to complete by canoe. For more information contact: DOC, 74 Ingestre St, Wanganui; tel: 06 345 2402, fax: 06 345 8712.

THAMES – WHITIANGA
OTT TABLE 9757

TRANSPORT	FREQUENCY	JOURNEY TIME
Bus	2 daily (not Sat, Nov–Mar)	2hrs 30mins

THAMES – COROMANDEL
OTT TABLE 9757

TRANSPORT	FREQUENCY	JOURNEY TIME
Bus	2 daily Mon–Fri, 1 Oct–Apr	1hr 10mins

COROMANDEL – WHITIANGA
OTT TABLE 9757

TRANSPORT	FREQUENCY	JOURNEY TIME
Bus	Daily (not Sat, Nov–Mar)	1hr 5mins

Note: There is no direct service from Whitianga to Coromandel. Connecting services operate from Whitianga to Hahei.

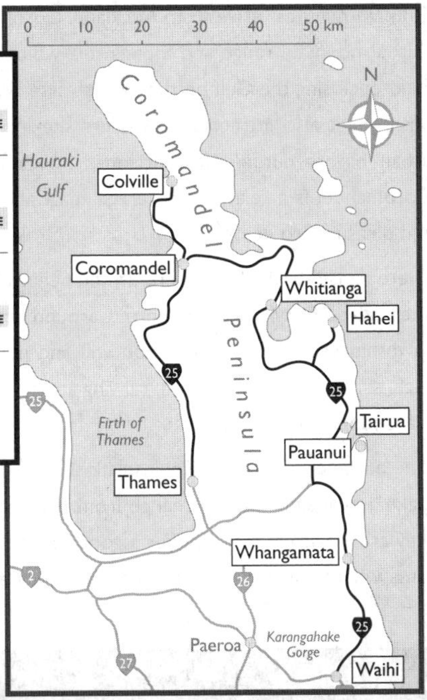

Notes

There are two buses daily from Waihi to Paeroa. Two buses run daily between Paeroa and Thames, both directions, with an additional evening bus on Fridays and Sundays; OTT table 9757.

ROUTE DETAIL

Thames is 115 km east of Auckland: take Highway 2 towards Mangatarata, then Hwy 25 to Thames. Coming out of Thames head north on State Highway 25, which hugs the mountains on one side and the sea on the other. It passes through a series of small settlements – Whakatete Bay, Ngarimu Bay, Thornton Bay, Te Puru, Waiomu, Ruamahanga and Tapu.

At Tapu you can detour onto the Tapu–Coroglen road, which crosses the peninsula from east to west. Part of it is unsealed road and in places it is very steep. However, it is well maintained and driving is not a problem, although you may, on occasion, meet large timber trucks.

From Tapu the State Highway 25 follows the coastline through Waikawau and Kereta to Coromandel. 57 km

If you want to continue up the peninsula from here, take the small road west at the far end of town to Colville, returning to Coromandel via Waikawau and Kennedy Bay – a round trip. Just before Coromandel, State Highway 25 turns and crosses the peninsula to Matarangi Beach and then to the seaside resort of Whitianga; next it curves inland around the harbour to Coroglen and Whenuakite. Here you can take a short detour to the seaside town of Hahei. The main road heads down the east coast to Tairua, then through the Tairua Forest until Whangamata, before continuing inland to Waihi.

The Coromandel

Only 90 minutes' drive from Auckland, Coromandel is named for a harbour, a township, a mountain range and a peninsula which extends northwards from the Hauraki Plain, enclosing the Gulf on the eastern side. The terrain is mainly rugged, undeveloped bush, yet it also attracts Aucklanders seeking to escape the traffic fumes and other urban blights during the Christmas holidays. For the rest of the year, however, Coromandel is a relatively deserted, magical area, full of history, of places to explore and pleasures to enjoy.

There's a laid-back atmosphere on the peninsula, which over time has created its own alternative lifestyle, mainly centred around art and craft. At places like Coromandel township, Waihi and Thames, you will find numerous craft workshops specialising in such things as wood and bone carving and pottery – in some cases you can watch the craftspeople at work.

One of the charms of the Peninsula is that all the towns are of a very modest size, and make a peaceful, relaxing change from the hectic scene of nearby Auckland. Small as they are, however, they all offer a good range of accommodation and plenty of restaurants where you can enjoy a balmy summer's evening after a day on the beach.

Thames

Thames is a town of something less than 7000 inhabitants – in the glory days of the gold rush in the 19th century, the population was almost three times that many. You can still get a feel of its past from the old wooden buildings on the main street. The town lies on the Firth of Thames and the site was originally spotted by Captain Cook, who sailed to the mouth of the Waihou River before exploring by long boat. It was Cook who rechristened the Waihou the Thames, noting a resemblance between the two rivers that has eluded later travellers. The Maori name for the river has prevailed.

Like so many other towns in Australia and New Zealand, Thames grew to prominence because of its gold and timber. The local timber was the kauri; it still exists, though in much-diminished quantities. Gold was discovered early in the 1850s, but an arrangement had to be reached with the local Maoris before serious prospecting could start. An agreement was not reached for another decade – the first major strike occurred on 10 August 1867. There followed a gold stampede, with the town quadrupling in size almost overnight to around 20,000 – half as much again as the population of Auckland. Now there are only four pubs in Thames; at the height of the gold rush there were nearly 100.

BY BOAT AND PLANE

A weekly ferry runs between Auckland and the Coromandel Peninsula from March to November. Gulf Ferries Ltd; tel: 09 379 0092 or 0800 888 006. For those in a hurry, Air Coromandel fly to several destinations on the Peninsula, tel: 09 256 6500.

EN ROUTE

The Coromandel Peninsula is known for its gemstones. In Wilderness Gems, 13 River Rd, Ngatea; tel: 07 867 7417, you'll find a warehouse full of rock crystals from around the world. As well as a viewing window that allows you to peep into the carving and grinding workshop, there's a shop selling items made from marble and polished stones. Open 0900–1700. Free admission.

The early settlements of Thames and Grahamstown were originally connected by a railway line. This has now been re-opened by the **Thames Small Gauge Railway Society** and trains operate every Sunday pretty much throughout the year (tel: 07 868 6678).

Most of the other attractions in this pleasant town are connected in some way or other with the gold rush. Definitely worth seeing is the **Thames Mineralogical Museum and School of Mines** on the corner of Cochrane and Brown Streets. Mine managers were trained here until 1954 and in the course of the exhibition of historical photographs and mineralogical samples you will learn all about the business. Open daily 1100–1600. You could follow this up with a visit to the **Thames Historical Museum** on Pollen Street, which offers a fascinating glimpse into the life of the town. Open daily 1300–1600; closes at 1500 in winter.

You'll see numerous reminders of the gold rush as you wander around the streets of Thames. Just behind the Power House, on the corner of Bell and Campbell Streets, is the **Queen of Beauty Pump**, which used to drain the mines in the old days. Prepare to be deafened when you visit the Thames Gold Mine and Stamper Battery (tel: 07 868 8514) to the north of the town, on the main road. Apart from the demonstration (mercifully lasting only a few minutes at a time), there is a mineshaft, with model figures, in a tableau. Visitors are invited to enter the shaft - but it is not for anyone suffering from claustrophobia. Open daily throughout the year 1000–1600.

POETIC NAME

The name Coromandel comes, not from the Coromandel Coast of India as many people think, but from HMS *Coromandel*, the vessel that sailed into the harbour in 1820 to collect kauri wood spars for the Royal Navy. As it happens, the ship was also carrying Samuel Marsden ('The Flogging Parson'), who richly deserved a reputation as a magistrate on par with the English Judge Jeffries. Marsden was heading for Thames, the start of his overland trip to Tauranga to establish the first Christian mission in New Zealand.

Thames Information Centre 206 Pollen St; tel: 07 868 7284, fax: 07 868 7584; e-mail: thames@ihug.co.nz.

Coastal Motor Lodge $$ 608 Tarura Rd; tel: 07 868 6843, fax: 07 868 6520. This was one of the first motels in New Zealand, and has been superbly updated. Enormous rooms with fully equipped kitchens. Opposite the yacht club.
Rolleston Motel $$ 105 Rolleston St; tel: 07 868 8091, fax: 07 868 8783. A moderately priced motel with studio and family units.
Sunkist Lodge Backpackers Hostel $, 506 Brown St; tel: 07 868 8808.
Valley View Homestay $ Kauaeranga Valley Rd; tel/fax: 07 868 7213. The meals here are made using organically grown food. River swimming and hiking close by.

As Coromandel is the centre of the alternative lifestyle in New Zealand, almost all the restaurants use organic foods and for once vegetarians can enjoy the luxury of choosing from the mainstream menu. The cafés in Coromandel town also make the best café latte on the planet.
Food For Thought $$ Pollen St; tel: 07 868 6065. This café-delicatessen offers good food, coffee and a wide variety of teas. Open Mon–Fri 0730–1600; Sat mornings only.
The Gold Bar & Restaurant $$ 404 Pollen St; tel: 07 868 5548. Sells salads, pastas, snacks and main meals. Licensed. Good service. Open Tues–Fri at 1130, Sat–Sun at 1700 till late.

TWITCHERS AND THE COROMANDEL

The protected wetlands such as the Kopuatai Peat Dome attracts flocks of migratory birds which, in turn, attract squadrons of ornithologists. There is a bird hide off Brown Street, near the town centre, which overlooks the mangrove swamps.

THE COROMANDEL FOREST PARK

Established in 1971, the forest covers an area of 73,000 hectares, stretching 100 kilometres along the Coromandel Peninsula. The mountain range of the same name, which forms the backbone of the peninsula, runs northwards to the highest peak, Mount Moehau (892 metres). The most popular part of the park is Kauaeranga Valley, which has picnic spots, camp sites, swimming holes and some 50 kilometres of walking track. It's an easy 30-minute stroll to the attractive Hoffman's Pool. Orokawa Bay is spectacular and contains the Orokawa Scenic Reserve – 145 hectares of native bush. At the far end of the bay a bush track heads inland to the William Wright Falls.

GUIDED WALKS

One of the best known of the companies offering guided walks is Kiwi Dundee Adventures, PO Box 198 Whangamata; tel: 07 865 8809; e-mail: kiwi.dundee@xtra.co.nz. The two- to five-day tours enable you to experience the full beauty of the Coromandel countryside.

EN ROUTE

An unsealed, scenic road crosses the peninsula from Tapu. After about 6.5 kilometres you'll come to the Rapaura Watergardens (tel: 07 868 4821), set in a secluded valley surrounded by native forest. There are 14 ponds covered in water lilies and surrounded by landscaped gardens with waterfalls within easy walking distance. Monet would have loved them. Open daily 1000–1700. Another 3 kilometres down the road a sign before a small bridge points to the 'square kauri'. Climb the steps for a close up view of this giant 1200-year-old tree.

The Old Thames $$ 705 Pollen St; tel: 07 868 7207. Traditional family-style restaurant with a broad range of dishes. Try pavlova, a local dessert of meringue topped with fruit and cream. Licensed. Open 1700 daily until late.

Sealey Café $ 109 Sealey St; tel: 07 868 8641. Snacks and main meals are served in a relaxed atmosphere. Open early until late. BYO.

WALKS IN THE COROMANDEL FOREST PARK

From Thames, a road (unpaved for part of the way) runs inland through the rugged Kauaeranga Valley. The name means 'No crossing here'. After about 13 kilometres, you'll come to an information office run by the Department of Conservation (tel: 07 867 9080). There are displays on kauri logging and you can also pick up printed guides outlining walks in the area. At the end of the fairly tough Kauaeranga Kauri Trail is the Pinnacles Hut, where you can stay overnight. The very fit could manage the walk in a day. There are several shorter walks, including Billygoat Landing, a 20-minute stroll of 1.5 kilometres with fine views of the 180-metre Billygoat Falls.

COROMANDEL

Coromandel itself is a lovely little town with a single main street and an atmosphere so laid-back it is almost somnolent. Though by no means a big town, indeed scarcely a town at all (the population is under 1000), it's an arty place with well over 100 studios and ateliers displaying their wares. As you might expect, Coromandel is geared less to sightseeing than to idle strolling and leisurely lunches in any one of the excellent sidewalk cafés. There's a great choice for vegetarians and the prices are very reasonable.

To imagine what Coromandel was like in its glory days you have to remember that it was once a string of tiny settlements. Visitors would disembark at high tide at Fureys Creek stone jetty, then known as the 'Lower

THE GROWTH OF COROMANDEL

Timber trading started here as early as 1794 when the first sawmillers arrived on *The Fancy* and set up shop. Three years later the Dunlop family moved in and founded Dunlop's Harbour, one of the first European settlements in New Zealand. Then came the gold prospectors. There was also a thriving trade in seafood: by the turn of the century, 24 tonnes of mussels were being shipped to Auckland every week.

Town'. What is now Moehau Takeaways and Tearooms was originally the ground floor of the Moehau Hotel, an impressive two-storied building. The Golconda Hotel still looks much as it did originally. The local night spot was the Star and Garter (since demolished), where the entertainment included floor shows and dancing girls.

Away from that Lower Town, on the road to Long Bay, was a 'tent city' known as Belleview. The main settlement of Coromandel was in the area of the Coromandel Hotel, originally a two-storey building. The old hospital is at the junction of Main Street and Kapanga Road. Opposite lived Dr Berkinshaw, the local surgeon, whose daughter, Fay Weldon, is one of New Zealand's better known novelists. The family home, a colonial mansion, still stands.

Coromandel still exudes prosperity, maybe because it lies on the only fertile plain this side of the peninsula. Presumably some of the wealth accumulated in the gold-rush era and from kauri logging is still in circulation. A reminder of Coromandel's past is the **School of Mines Museum** (tel: 07 866 7251; open daily 1100–1600 (summer), 1100–1500 (winter).

GOLD FEVER

Gold prospecting in New Zealand did not follow the pattern of the Californian gold rush of 1848 or that of New South Wales in 1851. Although the existence of gold was already known in the 1850s, the Maoris were firmly opposed to the mining of the land. Also, when prospecting began, it was necessary to extract the gold from quartz using a chemical process – nuggets and gold reefs were very rare in New Zealand. The largest piece of gold, discovered in the Rocky River, weighed slightly less than 10 ounces, so few miners made money by panning. Mining involved the use of stampers to grind down the rock – a serious financial investment. Individual prospectors, looking for alluvial finds, soon exhausted the meagre supplies to be found in the rivers, and generally took jobs with local companies. In New Zealand then, miners collected pay packets and there were no fortunes to be made.

EN ROUTE

Some 3 kilometres out of Coromandel is Long Bay Reserve, a beach with a camping and picnic site. Signposted tracks allow you to explore the area more easily.

'An area of totally unspoiled beauty with scenery so spectacular it takes your breath away.'

Farley Maxwell, *On Travelling South*, 1957

GARDENS OF COROMANDEL

The peninsula is one of great natural beauty. The **Driving Creek Gardens** were created over 70 years ago and consequently many of the native and exotic trees originally planted are now fully matured. The trees are under-planted with bromeliads, orchids and many varieties of lily. The commonest shrubs include camellias, rhododendrons and magnolias. Open Oct–May 0900–dusk; tel: 07 866 8704 in advance rest of year.

This is one of five gardens within easy reach of Coromandel town and the Visitor's Centre has a brochure detailing them all.

The others are: **Taraire Grove Gardens**, only 1.5 kilometres north of the town; **Harmony Gardens**, about 5 minutes south of the town on the coast road to Thames (309 Road) – a private garden running along the bank on the Waiau River with an amazing collection of rhododendrons and azaleas (tel: 07 866 8835; open daily in summer; rest of year by appointment); **Waiau Waterworks**, a whimsical garden, further along the 309 Road, full of Heath Robinson-style eccentric gadgets, worked by waterpower (tel: 07 866 7191; open daily mid-Sept to June 0900–1700). The latest addition is **Waitati Gardens**, along Buffalo Road and opposite the Stamper Battery. Created by a local florist, it includes a range of native plants. Another plus is the stunning view of Coromandel Harbour. Tel: 07 866 8659 for opening times.

i **Coromandel Information Centre,** Council Building, 355 Kapanga Rd; tel: 07 866 8598, fax: 07 866 7285; e-mail: coroinfo@ihug.co.nz.

The Central Motel $$ 50 Wharf Rd; tel/fax: 07 866 8709. Central location on the site of the Star and Garter, a rip-roaring pub in the old days.

Coromandel Court Motel $$ 365 Kapanga Rd; tel: 07 866 8402 or 0800 267 626, fax: 07 866 8403. Right in the centre of town just behind the Coromandel Information Centre.

Coromandel Hotel $ 611 Kapanga Rd; tel: 07 866 8760, fax: 07 866 8241. A lively pub with rooms to let, also a bistro (open Mon–Sat and Sun during the summer).

Tui Lodge Backpackers $ 60 Whangapoua Rd (SH 25); tel: 07 866 8237. Around 800 m from town in a tranquil setting. Free tea, coffee and bikes.

Wyuna Bay Motel $$ 2640 Wyuna Bay Rd; tel/fax: 07 866 8507. A small quiet motel on the beach. Safe swimming and boat ramp.

Admirals Arms $$ 146 Wharf Rd; tel: 07 866 8272. Serves an excellent meal.

Buffalo Lodge $$$ 860 Buffalo Rd; tel: 07 866 8960. Up-market, prize-winning place with excellent vegetarian specialities. Open for dinner Thur–Sun from 1800. Closed May–Sept. Bookings essential. BYO.

Coromandel Café $ Kapanga Rd; tel: 07 866 8495. Serves light meals and, arguably, the best café latte in New Zealand, presented in bowls you could swim across. Just one of these will set you up for the day. Open in summer 0700 until late, in winter reduced opening hours.

Pepper Tree Restaurant and Bar $$ 31 Kapanga St; tel: 07 866 8211. The name is apposite as the restaurant is shaded by a large old pepper tree. Serves great local seafood and alternative organic dishes. Veranda tables and live bands on summer weekends.

SHOPPING

Everything in Coromandel township is arts and crafts, and in particular, pottery. The wares are on sale in over 100 studios and ateliers. This is not bad going when you consider that the population of the entire town is not much over 1000!

If you're not keen on studio-shopping, call in at the Weta Design Store (46 Kapanga Rd; tel: 07 866 8823) which has a wide range of work by contemporary New Zealand artists.

In general, Coromandel does have its attractions, but the best way to spend time here is to stroll idly around the town, taking a long lunch in one of the excellent sidewalk cafés, which offer great food – much of it vegetarian – at very reasonable prices.

DRIVING CREEK RAILWAY

It all began in the early 1970s. Barry Brickell – artist, conservationist, developer and engineer – had a dream and set out to realise it on a tract of land 3 kilometres north of Coromandel Township at 140 Driving Creek Road. Taking advantage of the readily available supplies of yellow plastic clay (created by the weathering of old volcanic rock), Brickell set about building a pottery workshop, which was soon turning out terracotta pots, tiles and sculptures. Fuel to fire the kilns wasn't a problem either as the migrants who had arrived here from the Californian goldfields back in the 1850s had planted non-native pine trees. As the fast-growing pines were felled and transported to the kilns, 'BB' was able to restore the land to its original state, replanting the slopes with kauri and other indigenous species.

To access the clay and wood and to transport the young trees up the hill, BB built a narrow-gauge mountain railway. To accomplish this minor feat of engineering he first had to overcome a series of seemingly insuperable obstacles. First of all the tortuous route had to be surveyed and tracks cut through the scrub. Next, the construction of the earthworks involved not only the use of a bulldozer, but much back-breaking labour with a pick and shovel. Finally, two tunnels had to be cut through the hillside, then landscaped by hand and replanted.

Before the passenger service became operational in 1990, BB had to confront one more problem. To negotiate the steeper curves of the climb, an unusually narrow gauge (just 381 millimetres) had been used in constructing the track. Now this required the building of specially designed trains in the railway's own workshops. The most ambitious of these, a double articulated three-unit job, manages the twists and turns of the line so well that it fully lives up to its name of the Snake.

The final section of the line was completed in June 1995 after 20 years of hard slog and considerable expense. BB's gamble had paid off, but not quite in the way he intended. For while the returns from the pottery have been steadily diminishing, the Driving Creek Railway has become a major tourist attraction, carrying 30,000 passengers in 1998. There are plans to extend the line further through a third tunnel and two more reverses to get the train up to the high plateau. A visitor facility with refreshments is also in the pipeline.

FACTS AND FIGURES

The main line to the summit features four large viaducts, three reversing points and two horseshoe spirals. The average gradient is about 1 in 26. One of the unique features of the railway is the double-deck viaduct, the two levels being connected by a spiral. The main span is 14 metres and the total length of track, 46 metres. The construction of this section alone took two years. On a return trip the train passes over the viaduct four times in different directions on both levels!

It's a 1-hour trip along the track to the ridge-top terminus from where there are panoramic views of the Hauraki Gulf, Coromandel township and the hills to the east. Apart from the fabulous forest scenery and fascinating railway there's a working pottery, a tile and brick-making workshop and a craft shop. Open daily with train departures at 1000 and 1400 (with 1200 and 1600 services during the peak summer months). Tel/fax: 07 866 8703; www.drivingcreekrailway.co.nz.

All proceeds from the railway go towards the restoration of the kauri forest.

COLVILLE AND BEYOND

The drive to Colville is one of the best in New Zealand and reason enough for a visit to the Coromandel Peninsula. Colville itself lies 28 kilometres from Coromandel. Before moving on from here, call at the Colville General Store and Café to top up with petrol refreshment and supplies (it's the last stop on the peninsula). The store is eccentrically eclectic, stocking, among other things, homoeopathic remedies and health foods.

From Colville the road is unsealed, but well maintained. It is 29 kilometres to Port Jackson following a coast that faces the Hauraki Gulf and is close to paradise. There are gates along the way, which should be carefully closed after the car has passed through. After Port Jackson, a blip rather than a village, the road continues along the coast of the Colville Channel with a stunning backdrop of lupins. It ends at Fletchers Bay, a beautiful pohutukawa-shaded cove. From here you could leave the car and trek across the corner of the Coromandel Forest Park, or climb to the 150-metre high Needles for spectacular views. To return to Colville, you must retrace your route through Port Jackson.

Alternative Healing

The Coromandel Peninsula is a centre of alternative healing.

At Manaia, south of Coromandel township on State Highway 25, is Mana Retreat Centre; tel: 07 866 8972. Courses offered here include yoga, meditation and the Hakomi method of psychotherapy. The Plains Healing Centre runs courses on everything from aromatherapy to holistic pulsing and medical dowsing. It's located at 463 Hauraki Rd, Turua, 13 kilometres from Thames on the Hauraki Plains; tel: 07 867 5315).

EN ROUTE

Whitianga is home to the Mercury Bay Boating Club, one of the contenders in the 1988 America's Cup. The race is commemorated in a small museum run by the local historic society. (Open in summer 1000–1500, in winter to 1400.)

WHITIANGA

Whitianga faces Mercury Bay, so called because it was from here that Cook observed the transit of the planet Mercury, one of the many reasons for his expedition. It was also at Whitianga that, following orders, Captain Cook took possession of New Zealand 'in the Name of the King of Great Britain'. The Union Jack was hoisted on 15 November 1769. By coincidence, it was also here that Kupe, the leader of the first Polynesian expedition, came ashore in about AD 950.

A SPECIAL NOTE ABOUT DRIVING

The roads are scenic, winding and panoramic, but the grandeur of the scenery can sometimes be so distracting as to be hazardous. Most of the roads crossing the spine of the peninsula are ungraded and steep, but not difficult to traverse. Make sure you have proper insurance before leaving.

Today Whitianga is a pretty seaside town, small and easy to explore on foot and overlooking an estuary that makes a safe anchorage. In the height of the summer season Whitianga is jam-packed with holidaymakers heading for the six local beaches, all within walking distance of the town. One of the most attractive is **Buffalo Beach**, which extends for 4 kilometres and is safe for children (though it can get rough in winter). The beach takes its name from HMS *Buffalo*, which was wrecked here in a gale in 1840.

Opposite lies **Ferry Landing**, site of the original town. The passenger-only ferry (daily from 0730–1830, 1930 and 2130 with extra crossings at the height of the season) saves a road trip of over 30 kilometres. The wharf at Ferry Landing is thought to be one of the oldest in the country, although the original stone blocks have long been concreted over. It is worth taking the trip just to climb to Shakespeare's Lookout, from where you can enjoy amazing views over the whole of Mercury Bay. (There is is also a memorial to Captain Cook.)

SPORT

Fishing – Whitianga's fishing fleet specialises in crayfish, but big game fishing is also available through charter hire.

Scuba diving – a specialist is Cathedral Cove Dive, 3 Margaret Place, Hahei, Whitianga; tel: 07 866 3955. Trips to the Marine Reserve in Mercury Bay as well as to outlying areas.

Whitianga Tourist Information 66 Albert St, Whitianga; tel 07 866 5555, fax: 07 866 2205; e-mail: whitvin@ihug.co.nz. Open Mon to Fri from 0900–1700 and Sat from 0900–1300. Open seven days a week in the summer holidays.

Buffalo Peaks Backpackers Lodge $ 12 Albert St; tel: 07 866 2933; fax: 07 866 2944.

Mercury Bay Beachfront Resort $$ 111 Buffalo Beach Rd; tel: 07 866 5637 or 0800 225 022, fax: 07 866 4524; website: www.beachfrontresort.co.nz. The only motel directly on the beach.

The Waterfront $$ 2 Buffalo Beach Rd; tel: 07 866 4498, fax: 07 866 4494. Newest beachfront accommodation.

Café Nina $$ 20 Victoria St, Whitianga; tel: 07 866 5440. Open daily for breakfast and dinner. Reputedly the best coffee in Whitianga. This trendy café is in a 100-year-old miner's cottage and serves breakfast and brunch at weekends. You can eat outdoors in the summer and indoors by the fireside in the winter. Curry night is on the last Friday of the month.

Doyles $$$ 21 The Esplanade; tel: 07 866 5209. Expensive restaurant overlooking the beach. Dinner only in winter, breakfast, lunch and dinner Oct–Apr.

The Esplanade $$ 10 The Esplanade, Whitianga; tel: 07 866 4263. Open daily 0900–2300, from 0830 until late on weekends. Indoor and outdoor dining with splendid harbour views. Varied international menu.

On the Rocks $$ 20 The Esplanade, Whitianga; tel: 07 866 4833. Open daily lunch and dinner. Literally on the waterfront with views across Mercury Bay. Fish dishes with vegetarian meals also available. Where possible, eat outside. Licensed with a good selection of New Zealand wines.

Shopping: If you can't find anything that takes your fancy in the souvenir shops, you can learn to carve your own work of art at Bay Carving, The Esplanade, Whitianga; tel: 07 866 4021 or 0800 158 864.

Side Trip to Mercury Bay

Mercury Bay offers some of the finest fishing as well as the most spectacular sights to be found anywhere in the world. The waters around Tuhua Island (Mayor Island) off the Coromandel Peninsula contain whopping snapper, kingfish and gamefish. Captain Cook spotted the island on London's Lord Mayor's Day, hence the name. Tuhua is the Maori word for obsidian, a dark glasslike volcanic rock prevalent on the island once widely used for making axes and arrowheads.

Cathedral Cove Kayaks (tel: 07 866 0500) offers full- and half-day trips to the Marine Reserve. Sea kayaks are safe, non-intrusive and unthreatening to local wildlife. You could even sail out at sunset and continue paddling under the stars.

The Mercury Bay Museum explains why the transit of the planet Mercury was so important to Captain Cook's expedition. Open daily summer 1000–1600; Sun, Tues, Thur in winter.

HORSEBACK EXPLORATION INTO THE COROMANDEL

Just outside Coroglen, on the Rangihau Road, halfway between Whitianga and Tairua, is the Rangihau Ranch (tel: 07 866 3875), which specialises in guided horse treks into the Coromandel Ranges following the original packhorse trails of the 1800s. The treks last from one to several hours and you don't need to be an experienced rider. You'll save yourself a lot of discomfort by wearing tights under your jeans!

The outback sheep station, Twin Oaks Riding Ranch (Kuaotunu Rd, Whitianga; tel: 07 866 5388) also offers rides through the native bush and farmland with panoramic views of Mercury Bay and the Pacific Ocean. Again, no previous riding experience is necessary.

More unusually, the Ace Hi Horse Treks (on the State Highway at Whitianga; tel: 07 866 4897; e-mail: acehitreks@xtra.co.nz) offers not only one- or two-hour guided treks but also a pub-crawl on horseback – you stay the night at the pub, which is probably just as well.

Further up the peninsula at Coromandel (on the main road to Colville) is White Star Horseback Riding (tel: 07 866 6820). The rides to the ridge allow views of the Pacific Ocean and the Hauraki Gulf – and on a clear day, even the centre of Auckland.

CATHEDRAL COVE

The Cathedral Cove Recreational Reserve was presented to the nation in 1971 by Vaughan Harsant. It covers some 34 hectares and can be reached either on foot or by boat. Except at high tide, the cove is accessible only through the cathedral, a gigantic arched cavern that penetrates the headland between the two coves. The cathedral is about 20 metres wide and 10 metres high and was formed by sea action. To get to Cathedral Cove follow State Highway 25 to Whenuakite, turn off in the direction of Hahei, and then follow the signs to the car park. From here it is a 35-minute walk. The walk from Hahei beach takes around an hour.

HAHEI

Hahei has perhaps the best beach on the Coromandel Peninsula, protected by a series of offshore islands, with sand tinged pink by shells. It's part of a marine reserve and perfect for scuba-diving. You can also visit the vast **Cathedral Cave** at low tide. A little way to the south is **Hot Water Beach**, well known for its surfing as well as for its thermal spring. Steam can be seen rising from the open sea at high tide. For two hours either side of low tide you can dig your own bath and sink into the hot mineral water – wonderfully relaxing for mind and body. Hot Water Beach is one of the few places on the Peninsula with any serious thermal activity.

PANNING FOR GOLD

David Philips in Coromandel (tel: 07 866 8987) is one of many firms offering explorations into the bush to visit historic gold diggings. You also learn how to pan at the site of New Zealand's first gold discovery. Sharon Johansen's Guiding Adventures (PO Box 76, Pauanui Beach; tel: 07 864 8731) also has a good reputation.

PAUANUI AND TAIRUA

These two popular resorts face each other across the Tairua estuary (linked by a ferry) and are considered by some to be a little too developed. The setting though is spectacular, with Mt Pauanui offering splendid views from its 387-metre summit. Canoe safaris are available on the Tairua River.

i **Pauanui Information Centre** tel: 07 864 7101.
Tairua Information Centre tel: 07 864 7575.

The Purangi Winery $$ on the road to Cooks Beach; tel: 07 866 3724. Open Oct–Apr, lunch and dinner, May–Sept Mon–Fri lunch only, Sat–Sun lunch and dinner. Wine bar selling fruit and normal wines and liqueurs made from kiwi fruit and other fruits; also snacks and main meals.

WHANGAMATA

Whangamata means Obsidian Harbour, and is so called because pieces of this glass-like mineral, used for making axes and arrows, were frequently washed here from Mayor Island. The harbour now offers chartered boats for game fishing off the

EN ROUTE

Take State Highway 25 south until you see the signposted turn-off to the Wentworth Valley Road. Follow the road 4 kilometres to the car park/campsite that marks the start of the track to Wentworth Falls (5 kilometres, an easy hour's walk).

nearby islands. It is also an ideal place for canoeing: canoes can be hired from the **Estuary Mini Market**, Marie Crescent; tel: 07 865 8788.

The surfing in New Zealand is generally a well-kept secret, but Whangamata with its magnificent 4-kilometre beach is an undiscovered surfers' paradise. There's any variety of breaks and rides, often in excess of 300 metres. (The bar at the harbour end of the beach is the best place for breaks, but you could also try out the waves nearer the surf club.) The beach is patrolled during the holiday season. The surfing attracts thousands during the summer holidays when the population increases tenfold. The rest of the year it is very quiet.

Local shops provide equipment as well as advice on surfing and you can get more information from the **Whangamata Information Centre** (616 Port Rd; tel: 07 865 8340).

'On Coromandel some of New Zealand's loveliest beaches rest in uncrowded comfort under a benign sky. A few people might be fishing from the shore, others might be walking in the distance. But mainly, it is quiet, serene. A place for wandering up and down slopes, over paths, through the trees, along the shore.'

Jean de Lille, *Discovery*, 1963

Whangamata is the base for one of New Zealand's best-known tourist ventures: **Kiwi Dundee Adventures** (PO Box 198, Whangamata; tel: 07 865 8809; www.kiwidundee.co.nz) is run by Doug Johansen and his partner, Jan Poole, and they provide most of the serious eco-tours on offer in the area.

Ocean Beach extends 3.8 kilometres from the harbour entrance to the mouth of the Otahu River and, again, is patrolled during the holiday season. The shore is protected by offshore islands: at low tide you can walk to the largest of these, **Hauturu**.

Just to the north of Whangamata is **Opoutere Beach** with 5 kilometres of white-sand dunes and not a single house or sign of civilisation in sight. To get there, park at the beginning of Ohui Road and walk through the forest – a ten-minute stroll – crossing a wooden footbridge to the beach. Inshore lies Wharekawa Harbour, an area of estuarine mudflats and mangroves and home of the Wharekawa wildlife refuge, where there is excellent bird-watching.

Whangamata Information Centre 616 Port Rd; tel/fax: 07 865 8340; e-mail: info-whangamata@xtra.co.nz.

Cedarwood Motel & Motor Lodge $$ 413 Port Street; tel: 07 865 9211, fax: 07 865 9237. Spacious units and a bistro.
Whangamata Motel $$ 106 Barbara Ave; tel/fax: 07 865 8250. Three minutes from the beach and 100m from the main shopping area. Inexpensive.

Nickel Strausse $$$ Wentworth Valley Rd; tel: 07 865 7468. A winery restaurant serving food with a Bavarian emphasis. Closed Mon.
Pinky's $ 703 Port Road; tel: 07 865 9961. Bar and restaurant.
Puka Park Resort $$$ Mount Ave, Pauanui (north of Whangamata); tel: 07 864 8088 or 0800 785 272. Open daily breakfast, lunch and dinner. The cooking is New Zealand Pacific with Asian influences and has won several awards. The seafood is uniformly excellent. Licensed.

SCUBA DIVING ON THE PENINSULA

There are lots of scuba-diving opportunities within easy reach of Whangamata, including the Alderman Islands (40 minutes in a fast boat), coastal sites from Cape Colville to Whitianga and Tairua, Slipper Island, Dogger Bank and the Mercury Islands. The Alderman Islands are rich in fish life and offer several wall dives. Dogger Bank is a 5 kilometre-long reef with deep crevasses. Fishing is also possible in most of these places (within the legal limits) but nowhere in the Te Whanganui A Hei (Cathedral Cove) reserve.

Jim Hope (17 Pacific Dr., Tairua; tel: 07 864 8511) offers diving courses and diving cruises on the MV *Taranui*, which will take 19 passengers on a day trip.

THE HAURAKI PLAINS

The Plains are directly south-east of Auckland and encompass the towns of Miranda, Waihi and Ngatea. At Miranda there are hot springs.

The **Sea Bird Coast**, as it's called, extends as far as the Coromandel Peninsula. In the early 1900s the Hauraki Plains were still a large swamp between the Waihou and Piako Rivers. In 1908 an Act of Parliament provided for the draining of much of the swamp and the reclaimed land was allocated to soldier-settlers. Today there are more than 64,000 hectares of highly productive dairy land, protected by stop banks and floodgates.

You will also find, however, extensive wilderness wetlands such as the Koputai Peat Dome, which attract flocks of wading birds in the autumn and winter (and in turn, squadrons of bird watchers).

EN ROUTE

Miranda Hot Springs, west of Thames, between Miranda and Waitakaruru. Thermal pools, sauna and picnic area open daily 0900–2100; tel: 07 867 3055.

The Firth of Thames, especially around Miranda, is one of New Zealand's most important coastal habitats for shore birds, with shallow estuarine waters, shellbanks, grass flats, mangrove forest and saltmarsh. The average bird population is around 25,000, but when the migratory species arrive in the summer (mid-Oct to mid-Mar) numbers may increase to over 40,000. One of the most common visitors is the protected bar-tailed godwit, from Siberia and north-west America. About 10 per cent of the 100,000 godwits descending on New Zealand stay in the Firth, some remaining over the winter.

Living alongside the godwits are the lesser knots, Arctic waders favouring the sandy flats – numbers vary from 2000 to 11,000. Other regulars include the Pacific golden plover and ruddy turnstone. A number of endangered New Zealand species are also known to visit the Firth from the south: the New Zealand dotterel and black stilt, the South Island pied oystercatcher and the pied stilt. The wrybill (on the protected list since 1940) arrives from the river beds of

VISITING A FISHERY

Kaiaua Restaurant $$ East Coast Rd, Kaiaua; tel: 09 232 2776. Open daily.

On the route from Auckland to Coromandel, this café has twice been awarded the title 'New Zealand's Best Fish and Chip Shop'. Kaiaua catches its own fish and you have the option of a take-away or eating out on the veranda. Bliss!

Canterbury at the end of December. The numbers build until August, when 90 per cent of the population heads southwards again.

The best place to see the birds is the **Miranda Shorebird Centre** (East Coast Rd, just north of Miranda; tel: 09 232 2781), one of the world's great migratory bird habitats. The walking trails and bird hides offer superb views of the Firth of Thames and the avian life, and there's a very helpful information centre here too.

Another place of interest on the Hauraki Plains are the **Ngatea Water Gardens**. Here you will not only get to see more birds, but also fountains and waterfalls set in a beautiful garden landscape. The gardens are situated south of Thames at Bratlie Place, Ngatea; tel: 07 867 7275. Open daily 1000–1700; closed July and Christmas.

Route Detail

From Paeroa there are two possible routes to Tauranga.

Paeroa – Auckland via State Highway 2 122 km

Or, a longer route travels inland: leave Paeroa on State Highway 26, passing through Tirohia and Mangaiti before reaching Te Aroha. There the road heads west through Waitoa and on to Tatuanui. At the junction with State Highway 27 turn left and follow the road south through Waharoa and Matamata to Hinuera. Just beyond the village, take another left onto State Highway 29, which crosses the Kaimai Range.

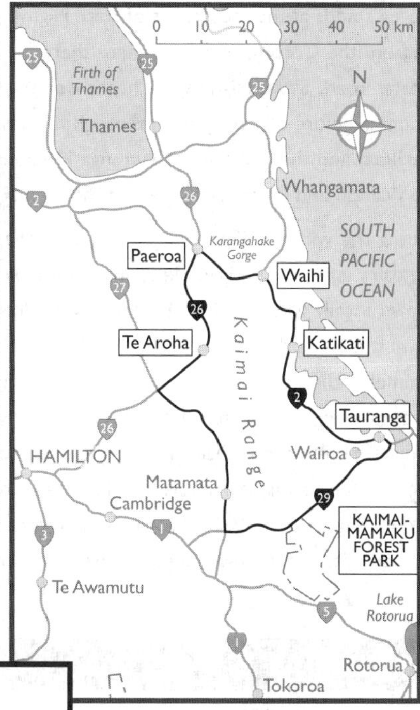

Paeroa – Tauranga
OTT TABLE 9757

Transport	Frequency	Journey Time
Bus	3 daily	1hr 30mins

Paeroa – Waihi
OTT TABLE 9757

Transport	Frequency	Journey Time
Bus	3 daily	20mins

Waihi – Katikati
OTT TABLE 9757

Transport	Frequency	Journey Time
Bus	2 daily	20mins

Katikati – Tauranga
OTT TABLE 9757

Transport	Frequency	Journey Time
Bus	2 daily	50mins

Note: There are extra services on Fridays and Sundays.

PAEROA – TAURANGA

Paeroa stands at the crossroads of State Highway 2, from Auckland, and State Highway 26, from the Coromandel. From here there are two possible routes to Tauranga. The coastal road, State Highway 2, heads south, passing through Waikino, **Waihi** and Waimata before dropping down through the attractive Athenree Gorge on the way to **Katikati** and the coastline of Tauranga Harbour. The alternative inland route follows the Waihou and Paiko rivers west of the Kaimai Range.

During the winter, a fierce wind roars over the Kaimai Range, between Tauranga and the dairy lands of the Hauraki Plains. With typical New Zealand understatement, it is known locally as the Kaimai Breeze – some 'breeze', for it has been known to bring down the odd airliner! Fortunately, the Kaimai presents a gentler face to visitors in the summer – the best time to explore the beautiful Karangahake Gorge (by steam train if you prefer), the forested hills of Kaimai Mamaku Park (an excellent drive) and the birdlife of the Hauraki Plains (especially on the coastal region near Miranda or Waihi). Some of the towns have interesting histories, like the genteel spa of **Te Aroha** or the gold-mining town of Waihi. If you're looking for something a bit more exciting, head for the port city of Tauranga – a good base if you intend spending some time in the area.

PAEROA

This little town on the banks of the Ohinemuri River, has a population of around 4000. The name can be translated as 'Long Mountain Range', a reference to the Coromandel Mountains just to the north. In New Zealand Paeroa is famous for the fizzy drink known as L&P (Lemon and Paeroa) – the mineral springs add zest to the flavour. As you drive into town, you can't help but notice the grotesque oversized bottle in the main street, at the junction of State Highways 2 and 26.

Paeroa is a country town servicing an agricultural area that specialises in dairy farming. It started out as a river port - steamships used to come up the Waihou River bringing goods to and from Auckland. Paeroa prospered following the discovery of gold just a few kilometres from the town, on the Komata Reef where there was a highly productive, if short-lived, mine.

Tarariki Pottery makes an interesting visit. Reservoir Rd; tel: 07 862 7380 (in the bush near the Tarariki River). There are demonstrations for visitors and a gallery of stoneware and terracotta.

Paeroa Information Centre 1 Belmont Rd; tel/fax: 07 862 8636.

Paeroa Casa Mexicana $$ 71 Puke Rd; tel/fax: 07 862 8216. Motel in attractive garden setting. Breakfasts and evening meals available.
Paeroa Hotel $ Belmont road; tel: 07 862 7099. Large wooden building with comfortable, if basic, rooms, café-restaurant (Delanies) and bar.

The Lazy Fish $ 56 Belmont Rd; tel: 07 862 8822. Lunch Wed–Sat, dinner daily except Tues. Large helpings. BYO.
Tui Coffee Lounge $ 18 Belmont Rd; tel: 07 862 8379. Open for lunch Mon–Sat and dinner (Fridays only). Licensed.

KAIMAI RANGE

The country inland from Tauranga is dominated by the Kaimai Range, which extends south-eastwards from the Coromandel Mountains as far as the Mamakus in the south. The longest railway tunnel in New Zealand runs through the Kaimai, for 9 kilometres. It was begun in 1969 and was in operation within seven years.

THE KAIMAI BREEZE

A terrible understatement, this refers to the frighteningly strong wind that blows over the Kaimai Range, between Hauranga and the Hauraki Plains. It was credited with bringing down an aeroplane in 1963.

KAIMAI–MAMAKU FOREST PARK

Stretching from the Karangahake Gorge (State Highway 2) south to State Highway 5 near Rotorua, the Kaimai–Mamaku Forest Park invites exploration with an extensive network of over 300 kilometres of track; varied plant and animal life, and abundant evidence of a fascinating past.

Gold was first discovered in the north Kaimai in 1869, leading to over 50 years of intensive mining. Kauri logging began at the same time, continuing into the 1940s. The Kauri Loop Track takes you up an old tramline to the two largest remaining kauri trees in the park, while mining evidence is clear on the easy Karangahake walkway off SH2.

The Karangahake Gorge is a pleasingly verdant valley carved out by the Ohinemuri River. A walkway through the gorge follows part of a disused railway line, including a 1-kilometre brick-lined tunnel. Buses are on hand to pick up and put down hikers at either end of the route. Tracks also lead up to Mt Karangahake from here (4-hour return trip).

Gold Mining in the Gorge

From 1875 to 1918 the Karangahake Gorge was a major gold mining area and is still littered with abandoned machinery and equipment. Recent technological improvements have made it possible to reopen some of the old mining areas – in 1992 an American company went into production at Waitekauri, and is currently mining around 100,000 ounces of gold and 37,000 ounces of silver annually.

Te Aroha on SH26 at the base of Mt Te Aroha (952 metres) is the main access point for numerous forest and bush tramps, where visitors are likely to see or hear many forest birds. These include the kokako (rare but here), whio (blue duck), bush robins, bellbirds, tui, kereru (wood pigeons) and fantails. North Island kaka are occasionally heard. The park is also home to small populations of Hochstetter's frog, the long-tailed bat and the rare Coromandel stag beetle.

It is also the starting point for exploring the Waiorongomai Valley, an extensively developed gold-field with mines, tramlines, inclines and tunnels – beware of dangerous mine tunnels and shafts. Lower valley walking is comparatively easy, while the upper valley is steeper.

After a walk in the bush enjoy a soak at the Hot Soda Water Baths in Te Aroha and watch the Mokena geyser as it erupts roughly every full hour (details under Te Aroha in the next section).

The south of the Park is less developed and the natural beauty of the area is evident at the towering Wairere Falls, where the Wairere stream falls 153 metres off the plateau – a 1½-hour return walk, starting just off Goodwin Rd, 6 kilometres south of Gordon on the Gordon–Okauia road. This track was important to the Maoris as it allowed access to Tauranga harbour and the sea.

Signposted off State Highway 29 is a track to the Rapurapu kauri trees. This is one of the most southern stands of the ancient trees, reached through attractive bush country.

TE AROHA

This quiet dairy-farming town was once a fashionable Victorian spa. The buildings in the Domain have been refurbished and it is possible to capture some of the period atmosphere as you stroll round the bathhouses, drinking fountains and well-kept grounds.

Te Aroha Soda Spa Baths: Individuals or couples can soothe tired limbs in one of the five private spa pools, whereas larger groups prefer the traditional bathhouse. There is also an outdoor soda spa and a freshwater swimming pool within the complex. Open daily 1000–2200; tel: 07 884 8717; www.tearohapools.co.nz.

BENEATH THE SPA

Te Aroha Museum in an old sanitorium below the spa baths (tel: 07 884 8052) takes up the Victorian theme, with exhibits that include two early lavatories, several wind-up gramophones, photographs of the town in its heyday and an early spa poster. Open 1100–1600 on weekends and public holidays. Tour parties any day on request.

Just beyond the baths is the **Mokena Soda Geyser**, the only hot soda-water geyser in the world. From the geyser tracks lead to **Mt Te Aroha**, a three- to four-hour walk through bush to the viewing platform at Bald spur, followed by a steeper climb to the summit. From here there's a superb vista across the Bay of Plenty and on a clear day it is even possible to see Mt Taranaki 245 kilometres to the west. (The road to the summit is private, but a small bus transports visitors in the summer.)

i **Te Aroha Information Centre** 102 Whitaker St; tel: 07 884 8052, fax: 07 884 8259; e-mail: infotearoha@xtra.co.nz. They also have useful information on the Kaimai-Mamaku Forest Park.

Te Aroha Holiday Park $ 217 Stanley Rd (off State Highway 26); tel/fax: 07 884 9567. Beautiful site with swimming pool, cabins and tourist flats.

Te Aroha Motel $$ 108 Whitaker St; tel/fax: 07 884 9417; e-mail: davliz_aarcady@xtra.co.nz. A comfortable motel close to the Domain and the town's facilities. Breakfasts available on request.

Café Banco $$ 174 Whitaker St; tel: 07 884 7574. As the name suggests, the café occupies the premises of a former bank. Open Wed–Sun.

Domain House Restaurant $$ 1 Wilson St; tel: 07 884 9675. Dating from 1906, the verandaed house serves à la carte specialities.

Mokena Restaurant $$$ 6 Church St; tel: 07 884 8038. Popular licensed restaurant, serving a smorgasbord from 1800. Booking advised. Open Thur–Sun.

GOLDFIELDS STEAM TRAIN

Between Waihi and Waikina you can ride a 7-kilometre stretch of track on the Goldfields Steam Train, a narrow-gauge mine railway run by the Victoria Battery Tramway Society (tel: 07 883 8251). Departures daily at 1100, 1230 and 1400 (journey time 20 minutes each way).

The station is located at the Victoria Battery site alongside the Karangahake Walkway. The trains were built to serve the largest quartz-crushing plant in the southern hemisphere (used in gold extraction). The locomotive in the transformer room is a converted Model T Ford. Souvenirs and refreshments available.

WAIHI

Waihi, 'The Town with a Heart of Gold', was originally a mining community. For years the Martha Mine (in the centre of town) was one of the richest producers in the world – total output exceeded 8 million ounces of gold. The mine closed in 1952 but reopened in 1988. It still manages to produce 75,000 ounces a year of gold as well as 650,000 ounces of silver. Open for tours during the week (tel: 07 863 8192 to check times and make a booking).

Waihi also has a museum in Kenny Street (open 1000–1600 weekdays and 1330–1600 at weekends, closed Sat in winter) with plenty of background about gold mining, using models and displays. There's a special section on the famous Waihi strike, which brought the whole operation to a standstill in 1911.

Waihi Information Centre Seddon St, Waihi; tel: 07 863 6715. Open daily 0900–1700.

Chez Nous $ 41 Seddon Ave; tel: 07 863 7538. Friendly bed and breakfast establishment with clean, comfortable rooms.

Golden Cross Hotel $ cnr Rosemont and Kenny St; tel: 07 863 6306. Provides backpacker accommodation. Also a live music venue.

Shalmar Motel $$ 40 Seaforth Rd, Waihi Beach; tel/fax: 07 863 5439. Spacious motel, handy for the surfing beach, shops and restaurants.

Waihi Motel $$ Tauranga Rd; tel: 07 863 8095, fax: 07 863 8094. Central motel with fair-sized units.

Grandpa Thorn's $$ 4 Waitete Rd; tel: 07 863 8708. Genuine New Zealand cooking with lamb specialities. Booking essential as tables are at a premium. Closed Sun evening and Mon, otherwise open 1800 until late.

Waitete Orchard Winery and Café $ Waitete Rd; tel: 07 863 8980. Open from 0830 to 1730 or later depending on business. Knockout organic food and fruit juice as well as naturally brewed beer. BYO. Organic fruit and veg on sale.

WAIHI BEACH

This tiny hamlet was planned as a retirement settlement for miners. Every summer visitors descend on the place to enjoy the 10 kilometre-long beach (it's pretty empty for the rest of the year). At the north end is a bird sanctuary, Pohutukawa Park. From here a track leads over the headland and down a steep path to Orokawa Bay (not suitable for swimming) – a 2-hour return walk.

KATIKATI

This otherwise unexceptional town has an amazing collection of murals running right along the main street, turning the place into a kind of open-air art gallery. The idea originated in 1990 when plans to divert State Highway 2 away from the town threatened the little community with commercial death. To avoid this fate, the decision was taken to brighten the place up with murals. There are currently 30 of them. You can buy a brochure explaining each mural at the information centre.

EN ROUTE

The Morton Estate on State Highway 2, 5 kilometres from Katikati, is a colonial-style house and winery. Vineyards stretch up the mountain slopes behind the restaurant (tel: 07 552 0620) and the ends of the rows are planted with roses in the French manner. The Chardonnay and sparkling wines are recommended. Open daily 1000–1700.

i **Katikati Information Centre** 36 Main Rd; tel: 07 549 1658, fax: 07 549 1798; e-mail: enquires@katikati-info.co.nz.

Katikati Naturist Park $ 149 Wharawhara Rd; tel: 07 549 2158 or 0800 4567 567; www.katikati-naturist-park.co.nz; e-mail: sampsons@ihug.co.nz. A nudist resort 3 km from Katikati. Provides a range of accommodation from tent sites to comfortable cabins.

WHERE NEXT?

From Tauranga you could head south-east on State Highway 2, and then take the signed right turn to Rotorua (see p. 180) and Lake Rotorua. This area has the main attraction that it is set on a volcanic plateau, right in the heart of the North Island's thermal belt. The result is an extraordinary range of hot springs, geysers and boiling pools.

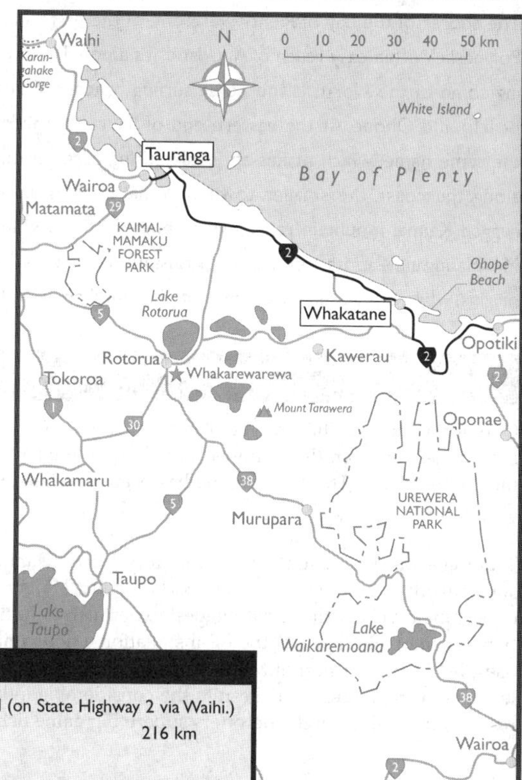

ROUTE DETAIL

Tauranga – Auckland (on State Highway 2 via Waihi.) 216 km

From Tauranga, State Highway 2 (also known as the Pacific Coast Highway) continues to follow the shoreline of the Bay of Plenty, passing the surfing beaches of Omanu and Papamoa along the way. It then turns inland towards Te Puke, the self-styled 'kiwifruit capital of the world', before continuing to Otamarakau where it rejoins the coast. At Matata, take the small coast road through Thornton, passing the airport on the way, to the resort of Whakatane.

To join up with the East Cape Route, p. 197, leave by the south-east route and return to State Highway 2 which now winds around the edge of Ohiwa Harbour. Continue through Kutarene and Waiotahi to Opotiki, the easternmost town of the Bay of Plenty.

Note

There is one bus daily from Whakatane to Opotiki, to link to the East Cape Route, p. 197.

Tauranga – Whakatane

The shores of the Bay of Plenty were one of the first landing sites of the Maoris from Polynesia. Within easy reach of Auckland, it's a popular spot with holidaymakers, boasting some of the North Island's best surfing beaches, including Mt Maunganui (Ocean Beach) and Ohope. At the eastern end of Tauranga harbour is the lively port city of the same name, which makes an ideal touring base for exploring the region. Further along the coast, the smaller town of Whakatane is an equally popular resort. The rugged Kaimai mountain range, which borders the bay, and the steep-sided dome of Mt Maunganui at its centre, are constant reminders of the landscape's volcanic origins, while out at sea lurks the mist-shrouded active volcano, White Island.

TAURANGA

One of the busiest cities in New Zealand, Tauranga occupies a 3-kilometre neck of land projecting from the south-eastern shore of the harbour, which opens out onto the Bay of Plenty. The Maori name has been translated variously as 'resting place' and 'safe anchorage'.

Tauranga was designated a city in the early 1960s. Its mild climate and rich volcanic soils have transformed it into a major agricultural district and citrus fruit centre – especially kiwifruit, the fourth biggest export earner in the country. Less decorative parts of the landscape are the oil installations, flour mills and factories. Tauranga uses the deepwater port of Maunganui, 8 kilometres to the north-east, now more or less a suburb of Tauranga. Despite the considerable industrial activity, the seaside resort is tranquil enough and offers superb big game fishing.

Beaches...

Tauranga's beaches are uniformly superb and those on the inland side are protected. The Mount has two major beaches almost abutting one another: Ocean Beach is 15 kilometres long and one of the finest surfing beaches in the country. Mount Maunganui Beach, on the other side of the peninsula, boasts several kilometres of golden sand ideal for sunbathing.

Within the almost land-locked Tauranga Harbour you will also find numerous sheltered bays, safe for swimming. Two of the best are Omokoroa (21 kilometres to the west of Tauranga) and Pahioa (22 kilometres).

Elms Mission

Tauranga was first settled by European missionaries in 1834. Two years later, the Church of England established **Elms Mission Station House** in Mission Street (the first house in the area). The gardens and grounds are open to the public daily; the house is open Sunday 1100–1400.

Early settlers in Tauranga saw the potential of the fertile land and soon found themselves in bitter conflict with the local Maori tribes, who had previously been fighting with one another. **Tauranga Community Historic Village** on Seventeenth Avenue re-creates Victorian colonial life with its own steam train, blacksmiths shop and other working displays. There's also a large collection of Maori relics as well as a range of old farming equipment. Open 0900–1700 weekdays.

Otemataha Pa is the burial place of victims of the Land Wars of 1864–65. Another relic from that era is the once-fortified site of **Monmouth Redoubt**, dating from 1864. It was from here that the troops set out for the Battle of **Gate Pa** (see box on p. 158), about 5 kilometres from the city, on the road to Greerton. At the corner of Dive Crescent and McLean Street is the **Te Awanui** war canoe, carved from kauri wood in 1973, and brought down to the harbour for cermonial occasions.

Mt Maunganui – known locally as 'The Mount' – has given its name to Tauranga's lively resort, situated at the end of a peninsula on the far side of the harbour. You can climb Maunganui (232 metres) in about an hour – it's pretty exhausting on a hot day, but the view from the top makes the effort well worthwhile.

Tauranga is an excellent resort for hiking. There are over 20 waymarked walks in the area, all described in a pamphlet available from the Information Centre. One of the most enjoyable follows the shoreline of the **Waikareao Estuary** from the end of Maxwells Road and takes around 2 hours. This track connects with **McCardles Bush Boardwalk** – there are mangroves en route, so don't forget the insect repellent.

The **McLaren Falls Park** (11 kilometres from Tauranga on State Highway 29) has well-signed walks through native bush, with natural pools for swimming and canoeing.

The **Puketoki Scenic Reserve**, Whakamarama is a 32-hectare reserve with tracks through the bush. (Turn off the main road 14.5 kilometres west of Tauranga at the Te Puna Stream.)

With its 24-kilometre beach, excellent surfing, shop, pub (but little else) **Matakana Island** makes a good day trip from Tauranga, but you'll have to be prepared to get up early. The 'Forest Lady' leaves from The Strand, Mon–Fri at 0645, returning at 1545 (a 15-minute journey). The Matakana ferry leaves from Omokoroa, just to the west of town daily at 0745, returning at 1600.

THE HEROINE OF GATE PA

Tauranga has a bloody history. On 29 April 1864, a combined force of 1650 soldiers and sailors of the British Navy, supported by artillery, stormed Pukehinahina Pa above Tauranga. The fort was defended by just 250 Maoris; even so they inflicted considerable losses on the British in fierce hand-to-hand fighting. The encounter later became known as the Battle of Gate Pa.

Amongst the defenders of the *pa* was the female warrior, Heni-te Keri-Karamu. A veteran of earlier conflicts, she fought on this occasion while carrying her baby on her back. During a lull in the fighting Heni heard the cries of the British wounded outside her trench and responded by taking them water. The settlers claimed that far from being an act of charity, this was a curse, following the biblical injunction contained in Romans 12:20: 'Therefore, if thine enemy hunger, feed him. If he thirst, give him drink: for in doing so thou shalt heap coals of fire on his head.'

For the very active, white-water rafting on the raging Wairoa river is considered some of the best available in the country. One operator is **Wet 'n' Wild Rafting;** tel: 07 348 3191 or 0800 462 7238, fax: 07 349 6567; www.wetnwildrafting.co.nz.

The other major attraction of Tauranga is the beach life. The beaches here are constantly superb and on the inland side are totally protected. The Mount (Mt Maunganui) has two major beaches almost abutting each other: Ocean Beach and Mount Maunganui Beach. Within Tauranga Harbour itself (using the name for a geographical feature rather than a port) there are also numerous sheltered beaches, for the harbour is almost landlocked. Two of the best are Omokoroa (21 kilometres to the west of the town) and Pahioa (22 kilometres in the same direction).

Tauranga does not forget one type of sustenance either: **Mills Reef Winery** (on Moffat Rd, Bethlehem, 6 kilometres from Tauranga city centre on State Highway 2) produces some good Chardonnays, but also Rieslings, Sauvignons and sparkling wines. There are tasting rooms (open 1000–1700 daily) and a 45-minute tour. The restaurant (open 1100–1500,

EN ROUTE

Kiwifruit Country (6 kilometres from Te Puke on State Highway 2) offers a 30-minute tour of the orchards and processing plant, followed by a visit the souvenir shop, café etc. Open daily 0900–1700; tel: 07 573 6340, fax: 07 573 6345; www.kiwifruitcountry.co.nz.

1800–late) overlooks the vineyards. Tel: 07 576 8800 or 0800 645 577, fax: 07 576 8824; www.millsreef.co.nz.

Tauranga Information and Visitors Centre 95 Willow St; tel: 07 578 8103, fax: 07 578 7020; e-mail: trgvin@tauranga.govt.nz.
Mt Maunganui Visitor Information Centre Salisbury Avenue; tel: 07 575 5099. Or contact Tauranga Visitor Centre.
Department of Conservation 253 Chadwick Rd; tel: 07 578 7677, fax: 07 578 1634.

Academy Motor Inn $$ 734 Cameron Rd; tel: 07 578 9103 or 0800 782 922, fax: 07 578 9133; www.academymotorinn.co.nz; e-mail: enquiry@academymotorinn.co.nz. Well-equipped rooms with spa baths and Sky TV. Heated swimmimg pool and secure parking – good value.
Avenue Eleven $$ 26 Eleventh Ave; tel/fax: 07 577 1881, www.avenue11.co.nz; e-mail: avenue11tauranga@yahoo.co.nz. Small family-run motel, centrally located, with good views and stylish rooms.
Cobblestone Court $$ 86 Chapel St; tel: 07 576 9028 or 0800 506 306, fax: 07 576 1397; e-mail: glenmur@xtra.co.nz. Located just 100 m from the harbour and walkway. Small swimming pool.
Fitzgerald's Irish Inn $$ 463 Maunganui Rd, Mt Maunganui; tel/fax: 07 575 4013. Friendly, comfortable B&B hotel.
Harbour View Motel $$ 7 Fifth Ave E; tel: 07 578 8621, fax: 07 578 7123. Quiet location close to the beach.
Pacific Coast Backpackers $ 432 Maunganui Rd, Mt Maunganui; tel/fax: 07 574 9601 or 0800 666 622; www.pacificcoastlodge.co.nz; e-mail: pacificcoastbackpackers@xtra.co.nz. Free bikes and pickup. Also organises and books local activities. Close to beach.
Tauranga Central Backpackers $ 62–66 Willow St; tel/fax: 07 571 6222 or 0800 116 126; e-mail: centralbackpack@xtra.co.nz. Central location close to bus depot. Internet access.
Tauranga YHA $ 171 Elizabeth St; tel: 07 578 5064, fax: 07 578 5040; e-mail: yhataur@yha.org.nz. Cosy hostel in a garden setting in the centre of the city. Internet access.

Astrolabe $$ 82 Maunganui Rd, Mt Maunganui; tel: 07 574 8155. Nightclub with bar and restaurant serving a range of dishes, including steak, fish and pasta.

BARRY CRUMP

Journalist, deer culler and pig hunter Barry Crump's first book, *A Good Keen Man,* was published in 1960. It succeeded like no other in conveying a sense of what it means to be a New Zealander. Other titles followed, including *Hang on a Minute Mate* and *One of Us*. Crump returned from the South Island to settle in the Bay of Plenty in 1996 and died of a heart attack a few months later.

Since then Crump has become a national icon, despite the fact that literary critics write disparagingly of his work. One guide recently referred to him as 'New Zealand's John Wayne.'

Deano's Bar & Grill $$ 305 Maunganui Rd; tel: 07 575 6675. Claims to have biggest steaks in the region. Open daily lunch 1200–1400, dinner 1800–2200.
Grumpy Mole Saloon $$ 41 The Strand; tel: 07 571 1222. Cowboy western bar that also serves food.
Harbourside Brasserie and Bar $$ The Strand; tel: 07 571 0520 or 0800 721 714. Imaginatively presented seafood. Good local wines.
Hot on the Rocks $ 61 The Strand; tel: 07 577 6518. Eat all you can for one price.
Shiraz $ Corner of Wharf St and Strand; tel: 07 577 0059. Small, popular café serving Middle Eastern and Mediterranean specialities. Booking essential.

Sport

Big game fishing is a major attraction and you can charter fishing trips throughout the year. Enquire at Tauranga Big Game Fishing Club, Sulphur Point; tel: 07 578 6203.

Tauranga Dolphin Company (tel: 07 578 3197; www.swimwithdolphins.co.nz) operates a day cruise that facilitates, but doesn't guarantee, swimming among the dolphins.

White-water rafting on the raging Wairoa River is only for the experienced. Contact **Wet 'N' Wild Rafting**, tel: 07 348 3191.

Bungee Rocket (tel: 07 578 3057; www.bungeerocket.com), in Tauranga, will catapult you to a height of 50 metres in 1 second, after which you can enjoy the drop.

Horse rides are available from Papamoa Adventure Park, Papamoa Beach (tel: 07 542 0972; e-mail: papamoa.adventure.park@xtra.co.nz). Climb to an ancient Maori *pa* site that offers superb views over the Bay of Plenty.

Mayor Island

This cone-shaped dormant volcano, with a marine reserve on its north coast, offers visitors some pleasant walks through the forest. Boats leave from Tauranga, Mt Maunganui and Whakatane and land in Opo Bay on the south coast. There are regular services throughout the summer. The trip takes 2 hours.

Colour Section

(i) Trout fishing on Lake Taupo (p. 177); a pier on the Coromandel Peninsula (pp. 129–146)

(ii) Bungy jumping on the Waikato River

(iii) Rotorua (pp. 180–195): Lake Rotorua; a Polynesian spa

(iv) Wellington (pp. 224–237): Old Government Building

TAUPO
BUNGY N.Z.

WHAKATANE

The town at the mouth of the Whakatane river serves as the commercial centre for the eastern end of the Bay of Plenty. In the hinterland are the forests that supply the town's paper mills and timber processing plants. Whakatane is Maori for 'to play the part of a man'. The story goes that when the lead canoe of the Mataatua Maori was approaching land back in the 14th century the daughter of the Chief Toroa, **Wairaka**, grabbed a paddle and helped guide the canoe ashore. Although this was forbidden by Maori custom, Wairaka was defiant, saying, '*Me whakatane au i au*', meaning, 'I will act as a man.' A statue of Wairaka now stands at the Whakatane Heads at the mouth of the river. In fact, the Mataatua were probably not the first Maori explorers to arrive here. It's believed that the famous adventurer and navigator, **Toi te Huatahi**, landed at Whakatane during his visit to New Zealand in the 12th century. It has even been suggested that Toi built a fort on the Heads and there are the remains of two *pa* on this site. However, no conclusive date has yet been determined for their construction. A splendid circular footpath, called **Nga Tapuwae O Toi**, leads to the original earthworks, then around Kohi Point to Ohope Beach – a comfortable walk of 7 hours but you can join or leave at any point along the route. Maps are available from the Visitor Centre.

The first European resident was Philip Tapsell, who established a store here in 1830. In 1865 the Hau Hau rebellion led the government to declare martial law throughout the area and four years later, Te Kooti, a Maori insurgent, launched an attack on the town from the impregnable Urewera Country. He was held up by a small redoubt manned by a French flour miller, Jean Guerren, and six men, but after two days and nights, the settlers were finally overrun. Te Kooti and his men then sacked Whakatane and set fire to the town. There is a memorial to Guerren 5 kilometres south on the main road to Opotiki, appropriately incorporating a stone from his mill.

... AND MORE BEACHES

The Whakatane area boasts some superb beaches. To the west of the town is the 18 kilometre-long Ohope beach, a great favourite with surfers. It's backed by the beautiful pohutukawa – sometimes known as the New Zealand Christmas Tree because it blooms during the festive season. At the end of the beach is Ohiwa Harbour, famous for its shellfish, including oysters.

Running through the centre of Whakatane is the main drag, The Strand, while at the Boon Street crossing you will find the small **Whakatane Museum and Gallery** (open

Tue to Fri 1000–1630). Also in the centre of the town is a small park that contains a memorial to the dead of World War I and the Potaturoa rock, a Maori sacred place. Here you'll also find a model of the canoe, Mataatua, in which Wairaka and her fellow explorers arrived, and karaka trees, said to have grown from seeds that arrived with the expedition.

DOLPHIN-SWIMMING One popular attraction in Whakatane is dolphin-swimming. Dolphins Down Under (92 The Strand; tel: 07 308 4636) provides all the necessaries, including hot showers after the trip. Check their website at www.dolphinswim.co.nz.

WHITE-WATER RAFTING White-water rafting is especially exhilarating on the Motu River, which rushes in a foaming white ribbon down to the Bay of Plenty from the Raukumara Ranges. Whakatane Raft Tours, tel: 07 308 7760 organises helicopter rides (or four-wheel drive) to the Motu and other rivers in the area.

JETBOATING Jetboating is an alternative way to enjoy the white water experience. Kiwi Jet Boat Tours (tel: 07 307 0663) is run by an ex-world champion who takes you on the Rangitaiki.

i **Whakatane Information Centre** Boon St; tel: 07 308 6058, fax: 07 308 6020; e-mail: whakataneinfo@xtra.co.nz.

Alton Lodge $$ 76 Domain Road; tel: 07 307 1003 or 0800 500 468, fax: 07 308 5438; e-mail: altonlodge@wave.co.nz. Pleasant, well-serviced motel with heated indoor swimming pool.

Karibu Backpackers $ 13 Landing Rd; tel/fax: 07 307 8276. Excellent backpackers close to shops. Free pickup.

Pacific Coast Motor Lodge $$ 41 Landing Rd; tel: 07 308 0100 or 0800 224 430, fax: 07 308 4100; e-mail: pacific.coast.lodge@xtra.co.nz. New motel, some units with own spa baths.

WHITE ISLAND

The offshore volcano was named White Island by Cook because it rarely emerges from a covering of mist – the crater lake is 60 metres below sea level and gas, ash and steam spew continuously from beneath the surface. Whakaari is still active and erupts regularly, most recently in 1992.

You can visit the island by boat with Pee Jay Charters (a 5-hour trip including lunch, leaves daily at 0830), tel: 07 308 9588 or 0800 733 529, fax: 07 308 0303; www.whiteisland.co.nz. Or, if money is no object, Vulcan Helicopters organises a walking tour, tel: 07 308 4188 or 0800 804 354; www.vulcanheli.co.nz.

Also offshore from Whakatane is Whale Island, a wildlife reserve run by the Department of Conservation.

Whakatane Hotel $ 79 The Strand; tel: 07 307 1670, fax: 07 307 1679; www.thewhaka.com; e-mail: whakatanehotel@xtra.co.nz. Colonial-style central hotel with dormitories as well as rooms. Clean, comfortable and good value.

Go Global Bar & Brasserie $$ Commerce St; tel: 07 308 9000. Brasserie-style restaurant overlooking the sacred Pohaturoa Rock. Wed–Fri lunch, Mon–Sat dinner. Licensed and BYO.

Strand Café Restaurant $$ 208 The Strand; tel: 07 307 0728. Specialises in hearty breakfasts and lunches. Open from 0600 weekdays and 0700 weekends. Licensed.

WALKING ON WATER

In 1906, a certain Rua Kenana declared himself to be the younger brother of Jesus Christ. In addition to eternal life, he offered seven wives to prospective disciples. As a practical demonstration of his divine powers he mustered his followers at Whakatane Heads so they could watch him walk on water. Just before embarking on his watery journey, he asked the gathering whether they truly believed that he was Christ's brother. There was resolute agreement. 'In which case,' he said, 'no proof is necessary and you can all go home!'

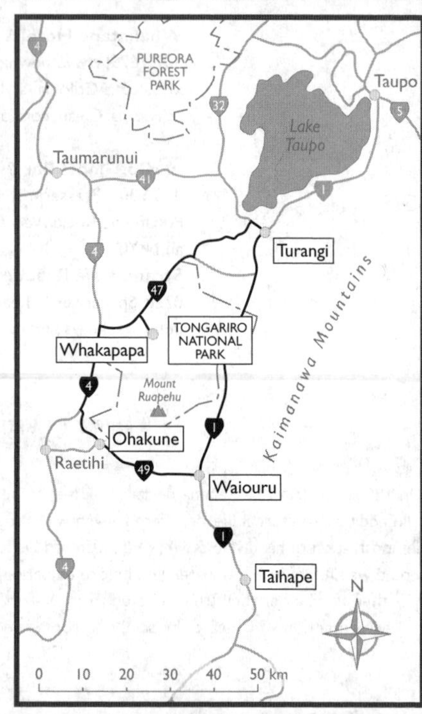

Route Detail

Waiouru is situated at the junction of State Highway 1 (the Wellington to Auckland road) and State Highway 49. From Waiouru it's possible to make a circuit of the Tongariro National Park, as well as a number of excursions into the park itself.

Leave Waiouru on State Highway 1, then head north along the eastern edge of the park to Rangipo. From here turn left onto State Highway 46, which runs between Lake Rotoaira and the Park. If you decide to take this short cut, just beyond Papakai turn left onto State Highway 47.

Alternatively, continue on State Highway 1 to Turangi (from where you could continue along the Lake Taupo circuit, see p. 171). From Turangi take State Highway 47 past Tongariro, following the western side of the park with Mt Tongariro and Mt Ngauruhoe on your left. Of several tracks into the mountains along this stretch of road, the side turning 12 kilometres beyond Taurewa (usually used by skiers) leads to Whakapapa, the only village in the park, on the lower slopes of Mt Ruapehu. Return to State Highway 47 which joins State Highway 4. Turn left onto State Highway 4 and follow the road to Tohunga Junction, where State Highway 49 leads to Waiouru via Ohakune. If you take State Highway 1 south from Waiouru, the mountainous stretch to Taihape and Mangaweka is particularly scenic.

TONGARIRO NATIONAL PARK CIRCUIT

The majestic Tongariro National Park was presented to the nation by the Maori chief Te Heu Heu Tukino IV in 1887. The first of the 14 national parks of New Zealand, it is widely regarded as the finest. There's an amazing variety of landscapes, from the luxuriant rain forest and volcanic lakes of the northern and central regions to the gentle farmland of the south.

The barren volcanic plateau south of Turangi is the reason why this stretch of State Highway 1 is known as 'The Desert Road'. A wilderness it may be, but there are fabulous views from here across the Rangipo plains. The dominant feature of the park, however, is the trio of snow-covered peaks: Mounts Tongariro, Ngauruhoe and Ruapehu, the 'three sisters' of Maori mythology.

En Route

The Tongariro National Trout Centre (3.5 kilometres south on State Highway 1; tel: 07 386 8607) is run by the Department of Conservation as a farm for rainbow trout. Eggs are stripped from the female trout and fertilised. When they hatch about a month later, they are sent on to other departmental stations before being released at one year into streams throughout the country. Open daily 1000–1500. Free of charge.

TURANGI

Turangi, originally a small fishing village to the south of Lake Taupo, has grown in line with the demands of the Tongariro Hydro Electric Power Scheme. The first station was completed in 1973 and a second has since been constructed underground. More information is available from the Turangi Visitors Centre. The new town on the foothills of Pihanga, rising to more than 1325 metres, is also a centre for the forestry industry. Nearby is the Tongariro, one of the most famous trout fishing rivers in the world.

There is a spectacular view of Lake Taupo from Highway 47 (Pihanga Saddle Rd observation point). As you approach the saddle, look out for the track signed to Lake Rotopounamu, a virgin lake with sandy beaches safe for swimming (a 20-minute walk). This is also a good spot for trout fishing and birdwatching.

Turangi Visitor Centre Ngawaka Place; tel: 07 386 8999, fax: 07 386 0074; e-mail: turangi@laketauponz.com.

Creel Lodge $$ 183 Taupahi Rd; tel/fax: 07 386 8081. Swimming pool, games room and a fish smoker on which to cook your catch.

Ika Lodge $$ 155 Taupahi Rd; tel/fax: 07 386 5538; e-mail: ikalodge@xtra.co.nz. Motel on the banks of the Tongariro with restaurant serving fish specialities.

Anglers Café $$ Anglers Paradise Resort, State Highway 41; tel: 07 386 8980. Licensed restaurant with log fire in the winter. Also rooms and a heated swimming pool.

Brew Haus Bar & Restaurant $$ Club Habitat, 25 Ohuanga Rd; tel: 07 386 7492. Bar serves beer made on the premises. Happy hour 1700–1900. Offers an *à la carte* menu and also accommodation.

Rod and Gun Restaurant $$ Bridge Tongariro Fishing Lodge, State Highway 1; tel: 07 386 8804 or 0800 887 688. One of the many restaurants and hotels catering for anglers.

TONGARIRO NATIONAL PARK

The land originally donated by Chief Te Heu Heu Tukino IV to form the National Park was a mere 2600 hectares, a fraction of its current dimensions (78,651 hectares). It was declared a World Heritage Site by UNESCO in 1991. In summer the numerous tracks and trails are utilised by casual visitors and serious hikers alike, while in winter attention is switched to the Mount Ruapehu ski fields.

The walking trails range from 10-minute saunters to full-day tramps. Most start near **Whakapapa Village**. For those fit enough to rise to the challenge, the main one-day walks are the Tongariro Crossing, Ngauruhoe Summit and Ruapehu Crater. These are not to be attempted in winter, except by experienced, properly equipped mountaineers, preferably led by a guide. The lowest of the three peaks (1967 metres) is **Mount Tongariro**. There are still numerous craters, fumaroles, mud pools and hot springs on the northern slopes,

Lord of the Rings

In his filming of the *Lord of the Rings* trilogy, New Zealand director Peter Jackson chose the volcanic landscape of Tongariro National Park for scenes involving Sauron's domain of Mordor. In order to protect the sensitive flora during the shooting of battle scenes, around 5 tonnes of carpet were laid around the slopes of Mt Ruapehu. Some of the battling orcs were played by NZ soldiers, who also lent a hand with the construction of a number of sets.

BY MOUNTAIN BIKE

The Tongariro Forest Crossing (42 Traverse), in Tongariro Forest Conservation Area, is one of the best mountain bike rides in the North Island. Contact Tongariro Hike 'n' Bike, tel: 07 386 7588.

indications that at some point in the future, a fresh eruption could occur. **Mount Ruapehu** has a lake-filled crater, warmed by the volcano. It's strongly acidic with temperatures of between 20°C and 40°C, although the summit of 2797 metres is snow-covered all year round. **Mount Ngauruhoe** (2291 metres) occasionally emits a stream of steam and gas into the atmosphere, but fortunately nothing more threatening in recent years.

A word of warning: the weather in the park is extremely changeable and this applies all year round, Anyone going walking or camping should get the latest weather and track information before leaving and should, where appropriate, register at the information centre.

MOUNTAIN TRAMPING

The most famous walk in the park is the **Tongariro Crossing**, a 17-kilometre tramp past lava flows, an active crater and the beautiful Emerald Lakes. The walk can be completed in something under 8 hours and transport is available at the start and finish. The climb to the summit of Ngauruhoe is a 16-kilometre return trip. The route is the same as the Tongariro Crossing as far as the saddle at the base of Ngauruhoe, where the climb begins. From here the mountain somewhat resembles Mount Fuji in Japan. When you reach the summit, you'll enjoy a magnificent view of the still-active crater, which last erupted in 1975. (Don't set off without a full set of maps and the advice of the park rangers.) The 6-hour track to the Tama Lakes (on the saddle between Mts Ruapehu and Ngauruhoe) allows for a refreshing swim en route. There are guided walks to the crater of Mount Ruapehu. Ruapehu Alpine Lifts takes some of the strain from the early part of the walk; during the summer, departures are from the base of the Whakapapa Ski Field at around 0930 (tel: 07 892 3738).

If time is pressing, there are several shorter tracks (of anything from 10 minutes to 2 hours) leaving from nearby the Visitors Centre.

WHAKAPAPA

The only village in the park, with a handful of cafés and hotels, Whakapapa, on the north-western slopes of Mt Ruapehu, really comes alive with the arrival of the winter snows and the skiiers. There are more than 30 runs, suited to all levels. Turoa, on the south side of the mountain, is just as extensive and boasts the country's largest vertical drop (720 metres). There's also plenty of fun for snowboarders. When there's no snow (Dec–Apr), you can still take the chairlift to have lunch at New Zealand's highest café!

Tongariro National Park Circuit

i Visitors Centre Whakapapa Village, tel: 07 892 3729, fax: 07 892 3814; e-mail: whakapapavc@doc.govt.nz. Open daily.

Walkers should seek out the **Tongariro River Walkway** (5.5 kilometres south of the town on State Highway 1). This follows a terrace above the river and was originally designed to give access to anglers. Duration: 90 minutes each way.

Tongariro River Delta Wetland Tour is an eco-tour in a flat-bottomed boat, led by experienced guides who explain the ecosystem of the delta. (Depart around dawn and dusk; tel: 07 386 6409.)

Several firms offer raft and kayak excursions on the river: **Tongariro River Rafting**, tel: 07 386 6409 and Rapid Sensations, tel: 07 378 7902 among them.

Note that Mt Ruapehu last erupted in 1996, sending a cloud of ash and dust 12 kilometres into the atmosphere – a salutary reminder that New Zealand is part of the Pacific Ring of Fire, a girdle of active volcanoes set around the Pacific Plate.

Waiouru

New Zealand's main army training base and the home of the Queen Elizabeth II Army Memorial Museum (see below), Waiouru has always had the reputation of being cold, bleak and barren – the ideal site, perhaps, for a military training camp. The chill comes with the town's altitude at 813 metres above sea level (the train station is the highest in the country). Summers on the other hand tend to be dry, dusty and hot – a rare combination in New Zealand.

Queen Elizabeth II Army Memorial Museum provides a flavour of army life past and present through a series of informative displays. There's also enough military hardware on display to satisfy the keenest enthusiast. (Open daily 0900–1630, when you can get a cup of tea and a snack on the premises.)

Fly over the Mountain

You can fly over Mt Ruapehu, observing the volcanic activity and the Waimangu Thermal Valley en route. You'll also see the Wakapapa ski fields and White Island. The return is by way of the crater known as Frying Pan Lake. Volcanic Wunderflites (tel: 07 345 6077; e-mail: wunderflites @xtra.co.nz.) is one of a number of companies offering this trip.

OHAKUNE

Inundated with skiers in season, but deathly quiet in the summer when many of the bars, clubs and restaurants close, Ohakune is the centre of a farming area (note the giant, painted carrot at the entrance to the town!).

Ohakune Mountain Road is a splendid 17-kilometre drive, climbing from Ohakune Junction to the 23-metre Mangawhero Falls.

WHAT SUITS YOU?

Ohakune has the best selection of motels, restaurants and shops, whereas Taihape is more central, but still handy for the walking tracks in the northern section of the park.

TAIHAPE

Taihape is a small rural town, serving a large farming area. The country setting, however, is stunningly beautiful and has always been a magnet for landscape artists. The town lies 33 kilometres south-east of Waiouru on the Hautapu River. Founded in 1894 as a coaching station on the track leading east to Hastings, Taihape was originally known as Otaihape, a Maori word meaning 'abode of Tai the hunchback.'

TITOKI POINT GARDEN

This is one of the most admired gardens in New Zealand. If you have a campervan you will find facilities here and farm activities are also offered. Located to the north-west of Taihape at Bells Junction. Tel: 06 388 0085. Open Wed–Sun 1000–1600 (Oct–May).

Following the end of the Land Wars in 1881, it became possible for the first time to build a railway through the heart of North Island without encountering armed opposition. There is not much to see in a town which advertises itself as the 'Gumboot Capital of New Zealand' – head straight for the rural hinterland.

From Taihape, the inland Patea Road is a tough and demanding drive to Napier. Before the arrival of the railway, this was the region's only link with the outside world. The route encounters some of the harshest terrain anywhere in the North Island and the only outposts of civilisation you're likely to come across are the sheep stations, one of which, Ngamatea, is the largest on North Island (48,000 hectares). The road covers a distance of 169 kilometres from Taihape to the hamlet of Pukeokahu, before crossing open riverine countryside to Kuripapango in the Kaweka Forest Park. From here it's downhill all the way to Napier. (Incidentally, Patea is named after a Maori who fled inland to escape the wrath of his wife's relatives after her murder.)

Rangitikei Information Centre 90 Hautapu St, Taihape; tel: 06 388 0350, fax: 06 388 1090; e-mail: rangitikei.tourism@xtra.co.nz.
The Department of Conservation Field Centre cnr Bank St and Main Rd, Mangaweka; tel: 06 388 2031.

Abba Motor Camp $–$$ Old Abattoir Rd; tel: 06 388 0718. Camping facilities and cabins in an attractive, peaceful setting on the banks of Hautapu River.
River Valley Lodge $$ tel: 06 388 1444, fax: 06 388 1859; www.rivervalley.co.nz. Beside the Rangitikei River. Also offers rafting and horse trekking.
Taihape Motels $$ cnr Kuku & Robin Sts; tel/fax: 06 388 0456. Centrally located units.

Brown Sugar Café $ Huia St; tel: 06 388 1880. Cakes and snacks. Closed Tues. Open for dinner Fri and Sat (booking advised).
DC3 Café $ State Highway 1, near Mangaweka. These tea rooms, 24 km south of Taihape, are in the fuselage of an old DC3 aircraft.
The Venison Kitchen $$ 65B Hautapu St; tel: 06 388 1011. Specialises in dishes made with local venison.

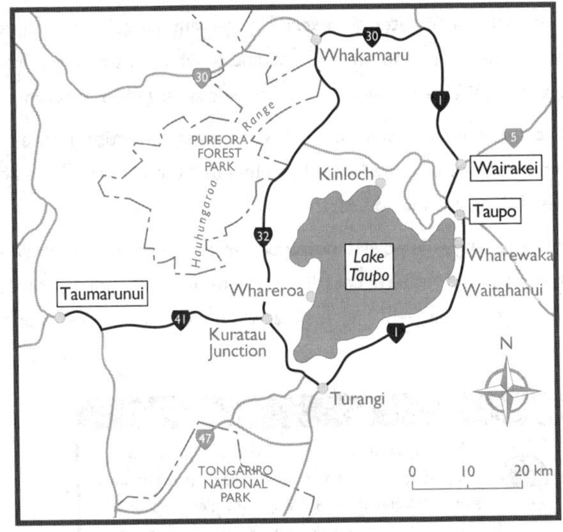

WAIRAKEI – TURANGI
OTT TABLE 9756

TRANSPORT	FREQUENCY	JOURNEY TIME
Bus	3 daily	1hr 15mins

WAIRAKEI – TAUPO
OTT TABLE 9756

TRANSPORT	FREQUENCY	JOURNEY TIME
Bus	3 daily	5mins

TAUPO – TURANGI
OTT TABLE 9756

TRANSPORT	FREQUENCY	JOURNEY TIME
Bus	3 daily	45mins

Note: This is part of the service from Auckland to Palmerston North/Wellington. Some coaches make a 25-minute rest stop in Taupo.

Lake Taupo Circuit

Taupo is the largest lake in New Zealand, covering an area of some 619 square kilometres. It was created by a series of gargantuan volcanic eruptions and is now fed by numerous rivers, the most important of which is the Tongariro. Taupo's outlet to the sea is the Waikato River, the country's longest inland waterway.

The thermal springs were already a tourist attraction in the 1880s, long before the American writer Zane Grey recommended the Taupo region as containing some of the best fishing grounds on earth.

More recently Taupo has developed into an important centre for water sports. The eastern and southern coastlines are pitted with holiday settlements, but the west coast, being relatively inaccessible, is the favourite retreat of anglers.

Route Detail

Wairakei lies at the northern end of Lake Taupo at the junction between State Highway 1 (Wellington – Auckland) and State Highway 5 (Napier – Rotorua). Leave Wairakei and head south along the Waikato Valley to the lakeside town of Taupo. 10 km

From here continue on State Highway 1 following the shoreline through Wharewaka, past the airport, and on to Te Rangiita. The road crosses a number of rivers feeding into the lake before reaching the town of Turangi at the southern tip. 50 km

From Turangi take State Highway 41 through Tokaanu to Kuratau Junction. (You can make a detour from here by continuing on SH41 to the upper reaches of the Whanganui River and the little town of Taumarunui, before returning to Kuratau Junction.)

Take State Highway 32 along the western side of Lake Taupo, east of the Hauhungaroa Range and the Pureora Forest Park. The road then continues to Whakamaru. Turn right here and briefly follow State Highway 30 across the Waikato River at Whakamaru. Turn right again onto State Highway 30, then continue to Atiamuri. Return to Wairakei on State Highway 1. 134 km

WAIRAKEI

A Local Geyser

The Geyser Valley of Wairakei Park has been a tourist attraction since the first holiday boarding house was established by Robert Graham (a former superintendent of Auckland Province) more than a century ago.

Wairakei is both a town (more properly, a suburb of Taupo) and a park, set on the west bank of the Waikato River. The town lies in the Waiora Valley, and boasts the second-largest geothermal power station in the world. Driven by heat energy from a volcanic fault running from Mt Ruapehu through Taupo, it taps into a vast underground hot-water system. The returns are fast diminishing, however, an indication that this is a finite resource.

The best way to see the local sights is via the **Huka Falls** Tourist Loop. First stop on the itinerary is the Huka Falls, 2.5 kilometres south of the town on State Highway 1. Here the Waikato River squeezes into a chasm only 15 metres across. The torrent thunders over a ledge at a rate of 22,000 litres a second, foaming over 10 metres of rock into the basin below (*huka* is the Maori word for foam).

The Taupo Observatory

The Institute of Geological and Nuclear Sciences runs the Taupo Observatory Visitors Centre (Huka Falls Loop Rd; tel: 07 374 8375), where you can find out how geothermal forces are harnessed. The centre includes an earthquake simulator and a seismograph recording activity on Mt Ruapehu. There's also an excellent account of vulcanology. Open Mon–Fri 0900–1700, Sat–Sun 1000–1600.

The effect of the torrent is particularly spectacular if you watch from the bridge crossing the falls or from one of the other vantage points either side of the river. (A 7-kilometre walk follows the river bank, ending at the Aritiatia Rapids, see p. 174.)

Practically next door, on the Huka Falls Loop Rd, is the **Wairakei Prawn Park**, where you can find out more in 20 minutes about this particular crustacean than you'd think possible. The farm breeds giant freshwater prawns in a large pond fed by warm water from the Waikato River. At the end of the tour there's a barbecue to look forward to. The 30-minute guided tours take place on the hour between 1100–1600. Booking is advisable as it is very popular; tel: 07 374 8474.

Some 4 kilometres along the Karapiti Rd is a wide valley pitted with steaming craters and pools, aptly named **Craters of the Moon**. This geological phenomenon was only revealed in the 1950s when the activity of the power station led to a massive reduction in the water level. Entry is free.

The **Aratiatia Rapids** are situated 5 kilometres from town, just off State Highway 5, and are well signposted. Once described as 'the most beautiful location on the river', the rapids are another example of the ecological impact of the geothermal plant and its unquenchable thirst for water. They no longer flow as nature intended, but are 'turned on' at certain hours for the enjoyment of visitors. (1000, 1200, 1400 and, sometimes in the summer, at 1600.) You'll hear a warning siren before the river bursts over the rapids. The show lasts for about half an hour and there are lookout points along the bank.

Taupo Bungy (tel: 07 377 1135 or 0800 888 408, fax: 07 377 1136; www.taupobungy.co.nz) drops its customers from Hell's Gate, a 50 metre-high platform above a bend on the Waikato River. (Over 65s jump free.) There is a variation called Baptism, involving a plunge into the river itself.

If you want to see how bees make honey, the **Honey Hive** (tel: 07 374 8553; www.honey.co.nz) has glass-sided hives so you can spy on the bees as they work to keep the queen happy. Open 0900–1700.

Ben Lomond Homestay $$ 1434 Pohipi Rd; tel/fax: 07 377 6033; e-mail: benlomond@xtra.co.nz. Set on 500 hectares of working farmland around 15 km from Taupo.

Wairakei Resort $$ State Highway 1; tel: 07 374 8021 or 0800 737 678, fax: 07 374 8485; www.wairakeiresort.co.nz. Motel with spa pools and heated swimming pool.

The Barn – Hot Rock Café $$ Wairakei Thermal Valley, State Highway 1; tel: 07 374 8004. Hot snacks!

The Prawn Works Bar & Grill $$ Huka Falls Rd; tel: 07 374 8474. Only open until 1700 for most of the year. Booking advisable.

An Open-air Pool

The former Maori settlement of Tokaanu is 5 kilometres to the west of Turangi at the geothermal pools. Entry to the Thermal Park is free, while the Pools (tel: 07 386 8575) on Mangaroa Rd are open daily 1000–2100. There's an open-air public pool and partly enclosed private pools.

The Hidden Valley

Just 25 minutes north of Taupo, a side road leads off State Highway 1 to the 'Hidden Valley' of Orakei Korako (tel: 07 378 3131, fax: 07 378 0371; www.orakeikorako.co.nz). Access to this thermal world of geysers and bubbling hot springs is by boat. At the bottom of Ruatapu, or Aladdin's Cave, is the Pool of Mirrors where, if you put your left hand in the water, any wish you make is bound to come true. Those with a less romantic nature might just like to dip their jewellery in the water. It seems that the pool's unique chemical composition gives it the ability to clean jewellery if it's left in the water for about 5 minutes.

TAUPO

The town enjoys a spectacular setting at the edge of the lake with views across to the snow-capped mountains of Tongariro National Park. The magical scenery is entirely the result of volcanic activity. There have been a number of violent eruptions around Taupo – those in AD 130 and AD 186 were reported in contemporary Chinese and Roman records. The eruption in AD 186 is thought to have reached a height of 50 kilometres, with volcanic rock blasted over an area of 7000 square kilometres. The explosion left a crater with a radius of 15 kilometres (now Lake Taupo).

One by-product of the volcanic activity is a proliferation of thermal springs. Taupo became a fashionable spa in the 19th century and is still going strong. The most famous baths are the **AC Baths** on Spa Rd (open Sun–Thur 0800–1700, Fri–Sat 0800–2000). AC stands for Armed Constabulary – it was here that soldiers stationed in Taupo, during the campaign against Te Kooti in 1869, came to relax. The main pool is kept at a steady 37°C but there are private pools up to 3°C warmer.

CRUISES ON THE LAKE

Most of the cruises that companies offer last at least 2 or 3 hours. But if time is short, *Ernest Kemp* (tel: 07 378 3444) is a replica steam boat offering 1-hour trips. One of the highlights is an impressive Maori rock carving, which is only accessible by boat.

For more on the town's history, visit the small but interesting **Taupo Regional Museum and Art Gallery** in Story Place near the Visitor Information Centre (open daily 1030–1630). Nearby is the old Court House, built in 1881 as a military barracks for the AC, and the **Taupo Rose Gardens**, where more than 500 bushes bloom in the summer.

Several operators offer scheduled **cruises** on the lake. The vintage yacht *The Barbary* (tel: 07 378 3444) was once owned by the hell-raising film actor, Errol Flynn. Cruise Cat Scenic Cruises (tel: 07 378 0623 or 0800 825 825) offer trips to the Maori rock carvings, as does the *Ernest Kemp* (see box above). All boats depart from the wharves at the Taupo Boat Harbour.

i **Taupo Visitor Information Centre** 30 Tongariro St; tel: 07 376 0027, fax: 07 378 9003; e-mail: taupovc@laketauponz.com.

Department of Conservation Field Centre Centennial Dr; tel: 07 378 3885.

Lake Taupo Circuit

There is a large choice of accommodation on the shores of the lake.

Action Down Under YHA Hostel $ 56 Kaimanawa St; tel: 07 378 3311, fax: 07 378 9612; e-mail: yhataupo@xtra.co.nz. Central location close to the lake. Facilities include bike hire, table tennis, video library, internet access and a spa pool.

Rainbow Lodge $ 99 Titiraupenga St; tel: 07 378 5754, fax: 07 377 1548; www.rainbowlodge.co.nz; e-mail: rainbowlodge@clear.net.nz. Only a short walk to town. Facilities include a sauna, pool table, laundry and bike hire. Good value.

Gillies Lodge $$ 77 Gillies Ave; tel/fax: 07 377 2377. Smart motel. Lake activities organised.

The Bach $$ 2 Pataka Rd; tel: 07 378 7856. 'The Holiday Home' to New Zealanders serves Italian pizzas as well as specialities such as salmon lasagne, all washed down by local wines. Dinner daily from 1800, lunch at weekends 1200–1500.

Holy Cow $ 11 Tongariro St; tel: 07 378 0040. Burgers, curries, potato wedges etc. served in a lively bar.

Misha's Italian Café $$ 28 Tuwharetoa St; tel: 07 377 6293. Traditional Italian food. Licensed and BYO.

The Thai Restaurant $$ 2 Roberts St; tel: 07 378 1139. The owner/chef, Nong, moderates the heat of the dishes for western palates, but if you are used to Thai food you can have it served the traditional way. Licensed and BYO.

Tales from a Fisherman's Log

Taupo's first western publicist, the American writer Zane Grey, fished for giant trout in Lake Taupo, later recounting his experiences in a book called *Tales from a Fisherman's Log*, which is frequently reissued. Grey recalls one occasion when his son landed 135 trout in 42 days, his brother 140 and Zane himself 87. The largest of them weighed in at more than 7 kilograms. Needless to say, the publicity generated by the book brought anglers from all over the world to Taupo.

Trout hatcheries are found throughout New Zealand because, while many of the lakes and rivers have plenty of food, they lack adequate spawning grounds. The rainbow trout of New Zealand are all descended from a single shipment of eggs from California and are considered to be the only pure strain of the species left in the world.

The best months for trying fishing yourself (no rainbow trout guaranteed!) are January to May (boat fishing March to November). For game fishing, you will need to charter a skippered game boat, which provides everything from bait to refreshments. Otherwise, make sure you purchase a fishing licence.

By Paddlewheeler and Jet Boat

You can take trips down the Waikato River by jet boat or vintage riverboat. The paddlewheeler *Otunui*, built in 1907, does daily cruises to the foot of the Huka Falls. Departure point is the Aratiatia Dam on Aratiatia Rd, just off State Highway 5, some ten minutes from Taupo. Contact 'African Queen', tel: 0800 278 336; www.paddlewheelers.net.
If you like it a bit faster, your best bet is Rapids Jet. Their visitor facilities are directly below the Aratiatia Dam on Rapids Rd, not far from the African Queen departure point. Tel: 07 378 5828 or 0800 727 437; www.rapidsjet.com.
Can't make up your mind? Then combine both with the 'Paddlewheeler & Jet Boat' package. Further information at the above addresses.

Fishing in Lake Taupo Anglers will need a Taupo trout-fishing licence, valid for a day, a week, a month or a season. Permits are available from sports stores, dairies, service stations, motels, hotels, as well as tourist information centres.

The minimum legal size for any species taken from Lake Taupo and its tributary streams and rivers is 45 centimetres. The average trout is about 1.5 kilograms. The bag limit is three trout, irrespective of species, which may only be caught during the legal fishing hours of 0500 to midnight. Nearly all rivers and streams in the district are restricted to fly fishing only. Trout are available year round and you can fish either from a boat or by casting from the shore.

The local fishing guides will be delighted to show you how and where to catch the best fish. Members of the **Taupo Launchmen's Association** (tel: 07 378 3444), located at the Boat Harbour, have more than 20 boats at their disposal and claim an 80 per cent success rate.

TAUMARUNUI

This small town sits astride State Highway 4 at the junction of the Ongarue and Whanganui Rivers. Located in the heart of 'King Country', it's almost surrounded by national parks. To the north-east lies the Hauhungaroa Range (between Taumarunui and Lake Taupo). To the south-east is Tongariro National Park, to the west, Whanganui National Park. Taumarunui was one of the last places in the region to be settled by Europeans.

Nowadays the town is very quiet, with a population of around 6500 – its sole claim to fame is that it marks the entrance to Whanganui National Park.

i **Taumarunui Visitor Centre** Railway Station, Hakiaha St, tel: 07 895 7494, fax: 07 895 6117; e-mail: info@ruapehudc.govt.nz.

Central Park Motor Inn $$ Maata St; tel: 07 895 7132 or 0800 283 030, fax: 07 895 7133. Set in spacious grounds, the facilities at this motel include spa pools, barbecue area and swimming pool.

Mahoe Motel $ State Highway 4; tel: 07 895 8988, fax: 07 895 8990; e-mail: mahoe.motel@xtra.co.nz. Licensed restaurant, 7 km south of Taumarunui.

The Food Bay $ 4 Hakiaha St; tel: 07 896 6411. Meals and takeaways. Open daily 0800–2200.

Rivers II Café $ 43 Hakiaha St; tel: 07 895 5822. Good coffee and deli-style food. Open Mon–Sat 0700–1600.

RAURIMU SPIRAL

After reaching the junction of State Highway 41 and State Highway 4, take the short detour to Taumarunui to view the working model of the Main Trunk Railway Line and the spectacular feat of modern engineering known as the 'Raurimu Spiral'. You'll find the model at the Visitor Information Centre on Hakiaha St in the Railway Station, (tel: 07 895 7494; open Mon–Fri 0900–1630 and weekends/public holidays 1000–1600).

Once you have come to terms with the concept, drive south on State Highway 4 until you see the signs to the Raurimu Spiral Look Out (on your left). To appreciate the sheer complexity of the task the early railway surveyors and engineers were confronted with, try to time your visit to coincide with a passing train (see opposite).

A Main Trunk Line, linking Wellington in the south with Auckland in the north, was the cherished dream of the 19th-century colonial treasurer, Julius Vogel. The Spiral was one of the last sections of the line to be completed and solved the problem of how to get a train down from the volcanic Waimarino plateau to the sheltered Whanganui River valley – a drop of 220 metres in under 6 kilometres of track and with a maximum gradient of 1 in 50.

The key to the riddle was provided by a senior engineer in the Public Works Office, Robert West Holmes. His solution was to build a complete circle of track, three massive horseshoe curves and two tunnels. This effectively doubled the line of sight from Raurimu to National Park from 5.6 kilometres to 11 kilometres. Work began in 1905 and the Spiral was completed two years later. The Main Line Trunk route opened for business in the autumn of 1908.

THE TUNNEL LENGTHS

The two tunnels are 384 metres and 96 metres long respectively.

The best time to view the Spiral 'in action' is when the Tranz Scenic Overlander service is on the line. The southbound train leaves Taumarunui at 1301 daily, arriving in the National Park at 1353. The northbound Overlander leaves National Park at 1418 and arriving at Taumarunui at 1511. (The Spiral is closest to National Park.) Remember that the timetable is subject to change.

WHAT DO YOU ACTUALLY SEE?

What you actually see is the train appearing from one direction, only to disappear from view and re-emerge some minutes later travelling the opposite way! It then disappears again before speeding off in the original direction (but at a height either higher or lower than its starting level): an ingenious solution to a major problem.

You can 'travel the Spiral' yourself (providing the service is on time) by catching the southbound train to National Park, then the northbound service back to Taumarunui. Full details and tickets are available at the **Visitor Information Centre** in Taumarunui. Phone the VC at around 1230 to check that the trains are running according to the schedule.

For train buffs there's a special festival in January centred in Taumarunui. The rest of the year, contact **Mainline Steam**, a company specialising in steam train trips throughout New Zealand. Occasionally they operate weekend breaks to Ohakune via the Spiral. You get to see much of the scenic heartland of New Zealand with the Army Museum at Waioru and dinner at Chateau Tongariro thrown in. In fact, the Army Museum (full name is The Queen Elizabeth II Army Memorial Museum) is certainly worth a visit: through a series of fine displays it gives a very real idea of army life through the years. There is also an extensive range of military machinery exhibited, with enough to satisfy the keenest enthusiast, including uniforms and dioramas of famous battlefields. Waioru itself is somewhat bleak and barren (some say that was why it was first chosen as an army training camp). **Mainline Steam**, Takapuna, Auckland, tel: 09 489 8360 or 0800 462 978; e-mail: j.godfrey@clear.net.nz.

ROTORUA

Rotorua is the main focus for tourism on the North Island – one of its streets, Fenton, boasts the longest stretch of motels in the whole of New Zealand. Though locals are in the habit of calling it a city, Rotorua is actually nothing more than a town and a small one at that. However, within that relatively compact area you'll find everything you need, from a wide range of accommodation to excellent restaurants, shops and – the main attraction – the Polynesian Spa.

Rotorua lies at the south-western end of Lake Rotorua and was founded in the early 1870s. The most visible industry, after tourism, is timber – the extensive tree plantations, dating from the 1920s, continue to supply large sawmills and pulp and paper plants. The Forest Research Institute was founded at Rotorua in 1947.

Rotorua's location, on a volcanic plateau at the heart of the North Island's thermal belt, is its main source of appeal. All around the town you'll find geysers and hot springs of every description. In some parts housebuilding is risky because digging the foundations leads to the release of unwanted thermal activity – some residents have woken in the night to find their front garden transformed into a hot bath. The advantage of living here is that no one has to pay central heating bills; the disadvantage is the pervasive odour of sulphur!

> 'Over all Rotoroa there is a faint aroma, not at all disagreeable, from the geysers, steam holes and other rather alarming manifestations of the nearness of Hell. The most astounding hole on this course is the short Sodom and Gomorrah hole. Here you play over a hundred yards of fissures out of which comes reeking sulphurous steam. I looked down one tiny volcano top, and it was filled with seething, boiling, gurgling, and bubbling mud.'
>
> **Alfred Viscount Northcliffe, *My Journey Round the World* (August 1921)**

GETTING THERE AND GETTING AROUND

AIR Rotorua airport, 8 kilometres north-east of town, is serviced by Air New Zealand and Mount Cook Airlines. There's a regular bus service to the centre.

BUS InterCity and Newmans Buses depart from Auckland, Wellington, Tauranga and Napier for Rotorua.

CAR By car, State Highway 1 from Auckland (through Hamilton) is the fast route. More picturesque is State Highway 2, then State Highway 33 from Tauranga, on the coast of the Bay of Plenty.

INFORMATION

Tourism Rotorua 1167 Fenton St; tel: 07 348 5179, fax: 07 348 6044; e-mail: info@tourism.rdc.govt.nz. Open daily 0800–1730. The mock-Tudor clock tower is a local landmark.

Best of Maori Tourism 1189 Fenton St; tel: 07 347 4226. Promotes Maori businesses and sightseeing trips in its souvenir and craft shop.

POST AND PHONES The main Post Office, at 81 Hinemoa St, is open Mon–Fri 0730–1730, Sat 0830–1600, Sun 1000–1500.

A TUDOR TOURIST OFFICE

The Tourist Office, located in the centre of Rotorua, looks a bit like a cross between an Austrian ski lodge and a Tudor building. It was built just after the turn of the 20th century as the Rotorua Post Office, and it holds a memorial town clock, in remembrance of Premier Richard Seddon, who died in 1906.

ACCOMMODATION

Cactus Jack BBH $ 54 Hauapa St; tel/fax: 07 348 3121.

Cosy Cottage International Holiday Park $
67 Whittaker Rd; tel: 07 348 3793. Off Lake Rd, with its own mud hole, thermal mineral pool and natural steam cooker.

Havanna Motor Lodge $$ 12 Whakaue St; tel: 07 348 8134 or 0800 333 799, fax: 07 348 8132. Good-value lakefront motel with spas and swimming pool. Disabled people welcome.

Hot Rock Backpackers $ 1286 Arawa St; tel: 07 347 8636, fax: 07 348 8616.

KiwiPaka YHA $ 60 Tarawera Rd; tel: 07 347 0931, fax: 07 347 3167. Hot thermal pool, café, travel centre; non-members are welcome.

Motel Monterey $$ 1204 Whakaue St; tel: 07 348 1044, fax: 07 346 2264. Pleasant motel in attractive grounds, with light, airy rooms. Heated swimming pool.

Ngongotaha Lakeside Lodge $$–$$$ 41 Operiana St, Ngongotaha; tel/fax: 07 357 4020; www.homestays.net.nz/ngongotaha.htm; e-mail: lake.edge@xtra.co.nz. A comfortable B&B located 10 km north of Rotorua. Situated directly on the lake, great for anglers.

Princes Gate Hotel $$ 1057 Arawa St; tel: 07 348 1179, fax: 07 348 6215; www.princesgate.co.nz. Large timber hotel. All rooms have modernised en suite facilities, some with verandas.

Royal Lakeside Novotel $$$ Lake End Tutanekai St; tel: 07 346 3888, fax: 07 347 1888. New hotel on the shores of the lake. Spa and fitness centre. Every evening Maori concert and hangi.

Spa Lodge $ 1221 Amohau St; tel: 07 348 3486, fax: 07 346 0485.

TAKE A HIKE DOWN FENTON STREET

If you are short of a hotel, take a walk down Fenton St ... it claims to be the longest street in New Zealand and it certainly could be a contender for the longest string of hotels and motels!

But if, on the other hand, you get confused by the huge choice of places in Rotorua (only a selection have been listed here) then a good bet is to head back to the tourist office, tell them your budget and it will be arranged for you.

SPAS AND HOT BATHS

Almost every hotel and motel in Rotorua has its own thermal bathing facility. Spas were all the rage in the 19th century, when the therapeutic properties of the springs were thought to be beneficial in the treatment of almost every ailment. In those days visitors would drink the waters as well as soak in them on the assumption that bad-tasting medicine does you more good. The oldest bath-house in Rotorua, in the Government Gardens, once boasted 84 baths supplied by the Rachel and Priest springs.

When faith in the benefits of spa water began to wane around the middle of the 20th century, this august establishment fell into decline and eventually closed in 1963. (The corrosive impact of hydrogen sulphide on the piping did not help matters.) Latterly there has been a revival in the tradition of hot-water bathing, and the Polynesian Spa complex on Hinemoa St, tel: 07 348 1328, still draws water from the original springs. The spa is not expensive and offers a choice of 30 hot pools, graded in temperature from 33°C to 43°C. Connoisseurs opt for the Lake Spa – five outdoor pools, overlooking Lake Rotorua. However, the temperatures in the hottest of these is such that few visitors can withstand the heat for long. After bathing there's the possibility of a water-jet massage. The Hot Springs Café offers both refreshments and full à la carte dining. Open 0600–2300. Licensed.

FOOD AND DRINK

Rotorua's excellent cafés rustle up superb coffee and snacks (vegetarians are well catered for). There's a good choice of restaurants, too, mainly clustered around the lake end of Tutanekai St.

Aorangi Peak $$ Mountain Rd; tel: 07 347 0046. Perched high above sea level, this restaurant serves New Zealand and international cuisine with local wines.

Fishspot Café $$ Eruera St; tel: 07 349 3494. Open daily 1130–1400, 1630–2100. Reputed to be the only licensed seafood restaurant in Rotorua – first class.

Kebab Café $$ 67 Arawa St; tel: 07 348 8411. Open daily 1100 until late. Middle Eastern cuisine modified for pakeha taste buds, serving the usual range of kebabs, felafel etc. Licensed and BYO.

Rendezvous Restaurant $$ 1282 Hinemoa St; tel: 07 348 9273. Award-winning BYO and licensed restaurant. The Maori chef cooks fresh food to order.

The Pig and Whistle used to be the old town police station!

Pig and Whistle $$ cnr Haupapa and Tutanekai St; tel: 07 347 3025. Open daily 1130–2130, later on Fri and Sat. This restaurant gets noisy on Fri and Sat nights, when local bands perform. Local brew on tap.

Poppy's Villa $$$ 4 Marguerita St; tel: 07 347 1700. Open seven nights. Classy restaurant in an air-conditioned Edwardian villa on the southern outskirts of the city. Winner of the Lamb Cuisine Award. Fully licensed and BYO.

Zanellis $$ 1234 Amohia St; tel: 07 348 4908. Open Tues–Sun 1800 until late. Serves a range of traditional Italian dishes – the seared scallops are memorable. Licensed and BYO.

What is a Hangi Feast?

A hangi is a Maori earth oven in which food is cooked by steam. Traditionally it's a feature of important Maori gatherings such as weddings or funerals. However, it is now often prepared for tourists at places such as Rotorua and is usually accompanied by traditional Maori songs and dances.

HIGHLIGHTS

Government Gardens is built on a small peninsula extending into the lake. The old bath-house (1908) is now the excellent **Rotorua Museum of Art and History**. Some of the original piping as well as the green and white tiles have been preserved and you can compare what you see with photographs of the building in its heyday when visitors from all over the world came to 'take the waters'. The **Te Arawa** craft exhibition includes exquisitely carved weapons and figurines made by the Arawa who were famed for their skills and artistry long before the arrival of the first Europeans. The museum also relates the cataclysmic events of the Tarawera eruption of 1886 through eyewitness accounts and photographs. (Open daily 0930–1800, in winter until 1700.) The formal gardens surrounding the gallery are partly obscured by clouds of water vapour.

The jetty next to Government Gardens is the embarkation point for trips across the lake and to Mokoia Island, one of New Zealand's inland bird sanctuaries (details on p. 186).

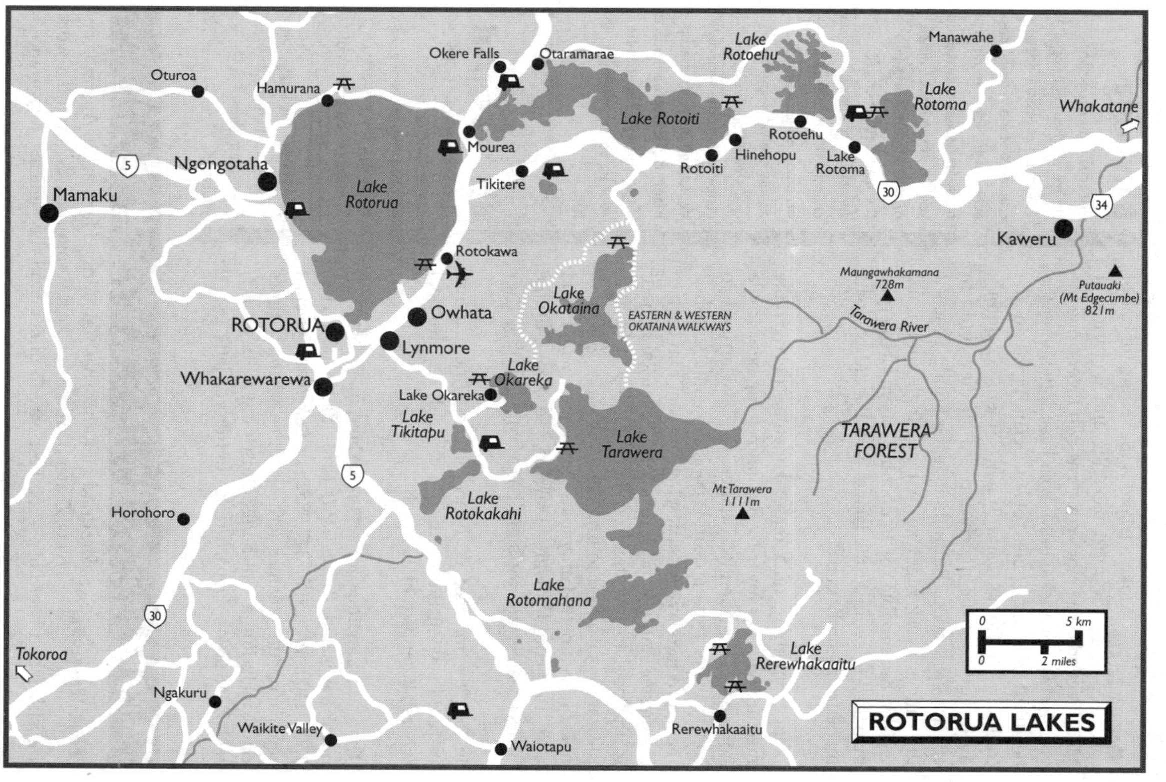

ROTORUA LAKES
0 5 km
0 2 miles
Oturoa
Hamurana
Okere Falls
Otaramarae
Lake Rotoehu
Manawahe
Lake Rotoma
Lake Rotoiti
Whakatane
Mourea
Rotoehu
Hinehopu
Rotoiti
Lake Rotoma
Tikitere
Ngongotaha
Mamaku
Lake Rotorua
Kaweru
Rotokawa
Maungawhakamana 728m
Putauaki (Mt Edgecumbe) 821m
Lake Okataina
EASTERN & WESTERN OKATAINA WALKWAYS
Tarawera River
Owhata
ROTORUA
Lynmore
Lake Okareka
Whakarewarewa
Lake Okareka
Lake Tikitapu
Lake Tarawera
TARAWERA FOREST
Lake Rotokakahi
Mt Tarawera 1111m
Horohoro
Lake Rotomahana
Tokoroa
Lake Rerewhakaaitu
Ngakuru
Waikite Valley
Waiotapu
Rerewhakaaitu

Rotorua

Mokoia Island Mokoia Island is the setting for one of the most romantic and enduring of Maori legends. The story concerns two lovers, one the young chief Tutanekai of Mokoia Island, the other the beautiful Hinemoa, also of patrician birth. In the tradition of Romeo and Juliet, Hinemoa's family disapproved of the match and did all they could to effect a separation. But although the family beached the canoes every night so that no single individual would be capable of launching them, Hinemoa managed to swim to the island with the aid of floats made from empty gourds.

Being something of a tease, Hinemoa delayed the meeting with her lover by first immersing herself in a hot pool. Coincidently, Tutanekai's slave arrived to collect water from a nearby pool. Hinemoa smashed the gourd the slave was carrying and sent him back to his master empty-handed, bringing Tutanekai himself to the pool to investigate. When he arrived he was pleasantly surprised to find his lover waiting for him naked! Eventually Hinemoa's family were won round and the couple were married, so that, unlike Shakespeare's tale, the story has a happy ending.

In fact, the romance of Tutanekai and Hinemoa has inspired several films and you can still see the pool where Hinemoa took her bath.

There are numerous cruises on the lake, many of which circle the island. Try ***Scatcat*** (trips daily 1000, 1100, 1300, 1400; tel/fax: 07 347 9852); or ***Lakeland Queen***, a replica paddle steamer (cruises three to four times daily, including a 'full-buffet cruise' and a 'tea cruise'; tel: 07 348 6634). Departures from Rotorua jetty.

Ohinemutu

Rotorua is an important centre of Maori culture. There are at least a dozen concerts of indigenous music every night, some traditional hangi feasts. On the lakeside you'll find the Maori village of Ohinemutu – originally the main settlement. A surprise is the small Anglican church with its beautifully ornamented latticework panels, the work of Maori craftsmen. Equally remarkable is the window depicting Christ, dressed in a Maori cloak and feathers. (Seen through the glass he appears to be walking on the lake.)

Get it on tape!

Don't forget your video camera and/or tape recorder when visiting Rotorua's thermal areas. The sights and sounds of bubbling mud pools, or geysers gushing huge plumes of steam, will make a great memento of your trip.

Sport

Four-Wheel Drives The quad motorbike has transformed farming in Australia and New Zealand. You can take a 90-minute ride around a working sheep and beef farm – the best way to understand the vehicles' importance in agricultural life. (You can also enjoy stunning views of Rotorua and the Bay of Islands.) This experience is offered by **Mountain Action**, 525 Ngongotaha Rd; tel: 07 348 8400. Amazingly, animals find quad-biking more acceptable than the traditional two-wheeled motorbike and dogs are more than willing to ride on the back!

EXPLORE ON HORSEBACK One of the best ways to explore the countryside – the horse watches the track, so you get to enjoy the views. There are at least three horse riding centres in or near Rotorua.

Foxwood Park on Fairbank Rd; tel: 07 345 7003 organises fully guided treks to last anything from an hour to a full day, depending on your level of experience. The horses are also matched to your abilities.

Paradise Valley Horse Riding, 643 Paradise Valley Rd; tel: 07 348 8195, offers rides over farmland with views of Lake Rotorua.

The Farmhouse, Sunnex Rd, Ngongotaha; tel: 07 332 3771, has over 100 horses to choose from and again, rides are across farmland and bush.

TROUT FISHING There are 11 lakes and several streams in the area where you can fish for trout. The best known are Rotorua, Tarawera, Rotoiti and Oikaitana. (The streams are reserved for fly-fishing only.) Lake Rotorua is open for fishing year round, the others are open from 1 October to 30 June. The streams don't open until 1 December. The Rotorua Anglers' Association has published an excellent fishing guide – *Trout Fishing Maps and Information* – available from most tackle shops and at the Tourism Rotorua Centre, which will also arrange the necessary licences. As always you'll catch more trout if you have a guide to give you a helping hand. Gordon Randle, 11 Te Ana Place; tel: 07 349 2555 guarantees results.

JET BOATING (Take State Highway 30 East to Te Ngae junction, then turn down State Highway 33.) Jet boating on the Kaituna River is a very New Zealand experience, both scenic and exciting. The boats are designed to travel at speed through shallows and rapids where feebler craft dare not venture. **Longridge Jet,** tel: 07 533 1515.

A RAINBOW TROUT FARM

If you'd rather look at trout than catch them, Rainbow Springs (State Highway 5, North) is a wildlife park with the world's finest display of rainbow and brown trout, seen through a glass-sided underwater viewer. The park has also won awards for its Nocturnal Aviary. Open daily 0800–1700.

Across the road in Rainbow Farm there are sheep dog exhibitions and sheep shearing shows (1030, 1145, 1300, 1430, 1600); tel: 07 347 9301.

MAORI ART

The traditional arts and crafts of the Maoris developed over the centuries in isolation from other Polynesian peoples. In many ways unique, the various art forms they practised achieved a level of sophistication virtually unparalleled in the South Pacific. Visitors to New Zealand will encounter Maori art in museums, on visits to meeting houses and in numerous souvenir and craft shops. The artistic traditions of the Maoris are, in fact, still very much alive, and often you'll come across fascinating modern interpretations of the age-old motifs and themes.

Some of the earliest examples of Maori art to be found in the country are the rock drawings that adorn some shallow caves and natural rock surfaces in both the North and South Islands. Most frequently found in the South Island, the oldest examples are tentatively dated as early as the 15th century. Later drawings depicting sailing ships and horses show that rock drawing was practised into the 19th century. A modern example of a rock drawing can be seen on a rock face on the shores of Lake Taupo.

As Maori culture developed over the centuries its art forms became more complex and varied. Weaving and carving flourished because of practical requirements, and the availability of suitable raw materials such as flax and wood. From flax fibres the Maoris were able to make clothing and baskets, whereas symbolic wood carvings satisfied the spiritual needs of a society whose religious values were an integral part of daily life.

One of the most distinctive features of traditional Maori art is the use of the spiral to form intricate curvilinear patterns. It was only in weaving, where geometric patterns were used, that the spiral did not occur. Another characteristic is the stylised human form. Found in many carvings it is also featured in one of the best-known Maori ornaments, a neck pendant known as the *hei-tiki*.

The highest flowering of classic, pre-European Maori art came in the late 18th century. Of the various crafts they practised it is generally acknowledged that they showed the greatest skill at wood carving. In fact, many experts assert that Maori carvers attained a beauty and perfection in their art unrivalled anywhere else in Polynesia. Reasons for this include the existence of soft, easily carved woods such as that provided by the totara tree, and the presence of jade (pounamu or greenstone) in the South Island. This hard stone enabled thin-bladed adzes and chisels to be used for much of the delicate detail work.

Probably the most remarkable showcase of Maori artistic achievement is the *whare whakairo,* or carved meeting house. This was the largest and most magnificent traditional building the Maoris ever produced. It was, and still is, a focal point of the tribe and incorporates all the most important art forms. Decorated both inside and out with intricate carvings, the interior also features painted designs on the rafters known as *kowhaiwhai* and woven reed wall panels known as *kotukutuku*.

Such a concentration of artistic endeavour was not, however, motivated by purely decorative purposes. Carvings, in particular, were a means of preserving tribal history in an oral society. These carved figures not only represented dead persons, they were actually seen as manifestations of an ancestor. Making them visible as a carving brought them into the presence of the living, thus allowing a chief to invoke their protection for the tribe. The images of ancestors on the posts lining the walls of a meeting house supported the building not just structurally, but symbolically as well.

Another art at which the Maoris excelled was *moko,* or tattooing. In contrast to other Polynesian cultures, the pattern was cut into the flesh using a bone chisel and not merely pricked in. The men were often heavily tattooed on the face, buttocks and thighs. In the case of the women, the tattoos were usually restricted to the chin and lips. In recent years the art of *moko* has enjoyed a comeback and occasionally you can see Maoris sporting traditional facial tattoos.

Apart from carving and weaving, the Maoris are also known for their songs and dances. Famous examples of dances are the aggressive-looking *haka,* as performed by the All Blacks before a rugby match, and the graceful *poi* dance. During the latter a ball made of flax (*poi*) is swung to a rhythmic chant or tune. It is often performed at Maori cultural shows in places such as Rotorua. Indeed, with a school of carving and a number of finely carved and easily accessible meeting houses, Rotorua is a great place to go for an introduction to Maori art and culture.

Rotorua

Water Sports

Rafting, kayaking, water-skiing, windsurfing and jet boating are all available on the lakes and rivers around Rotorua.

Adventure Kayaking (tel: 07 348 9451) also offer a two-day trip with an overnight camp by Lake Tarawera.

White-water Rafting The white-water ride down the upper Kaituna – about a quarter of an hour's drive from Rotorua – is reputed to be the highest commercially rafted waterfall in the world. The ride (graded 5+, where 6 is widely accepted as impossible) includes a drop of 7 metres – definitely not for the faint-hearted. One of a number of companies offering this ride is **River Rats Rafting Adventures** (tel: 07 347 6543; website www.riverratsrafting.co.nz). **Raftabout** (tel: 07 345 4652 or 0800 723 822; www.raftabout.co.nz) will pick you up in Rotorua and take you to Wairoa for a 90-minute hammering down the McLaren Falls, through Mother's Nightmare, Devil's Hole, Roller Coaster and other features. Lunch, for obvious reasons, is served after the ride. This experience is rated grade 5. The river is open for riding only 26 days of the year so you need to check ahead.

Kayaking Rotorua's lakes are best enjoyed from the quiet of a kayak. For a day on the enchanting, fern-lined Lake Okataina or an evening observing glow-worms on the banks of Lake Rotoiti, contact **Adventure Kayaking**, tel/fax: 07 348 9451.

NIGHTLIFE

The best nightlife in Rotorua is in the bars and restaurants. But the big attraction for tourists to the area are the **Hangi and Maori Concerts**. The major hotels hold stage-managed extravaganzas on Maori themes, but for the real thing join a group to an out-of-town site. Several Maori companies organise evening trips to a Maori village, usually leaving around 1800–1900. You'll be served food steamed in the hangi (earth oven), during which you'll become acquainted with traditional Maori greetings, songs, chants and dances.

Mai Ora tel: 07 348 9047, is based in a village overlooking the Whakarewa Thermal Reserve. They use natural hot water to steam the hangi.

Monkey Jo's 1263 Amohia St; tel: 07 346 1313. A bar and night club. Live music Thursdays from 2200.

Rotoiti Tours tel: 07 348 8969, visits a meeting house on the Rakeias Marae at Tapuaekura Bay on the shores of Lake Rotoiti.

Tamaki Maori Village tel: 07 346 2823, offers a hangi and concert with the possibility of an overnight stay on the marae.

LEARN HOW TO SHEAR A SHEEP

For years the New Zealand economy was dependent on the wool clip. At the Agrodome (10 kilometres out of Rotorua on State Highway 5 North) there's an hour-long stage show that includes a parade of the 19 different breeds of sheep raised in New Zealand as well as a sheep-dog demonstration and a gun shearer showing off his skills. (Note that 'gun' in the sheep-shearing context means one of the very best.) The speed and skill with which an expert shearer can strip a sheep without doing it an injury is quite remarkable. Shows are at 0930, 1100 and 1430. There are also tours of the farm. Tel: 0800 339 400; www.agrodome.co.nz.

SKYLINE GONDOLA

For panoramic views of the area, take the Skyline Gondola 900 metres up Mount Ngongotaha. Each car carries four people and the trip takes 5 minutes. At the top the adventure activities include 'zorbing' (rolling downhill in a giant inflatable ball) and a 'luge' (actually hurtling on a tea tray on wheels). Open daily 0900 until after sunset; Fairy Springs Rd; tel: 07 347 0027.

ROTORUA BUNGY

Jump from a 43-metre tower or try the Agrobungy. The latter involves being hoisted to 40 metres in a hang-gliding harness, then off you fly! At the Agrodome, tel: 07 357 4747.

ROTORUA THERMAL REGION

The Taupo Volcanic Zone includes Rotorua's thermal region, and extends from the volcanoes of Tongariro National Park to White Island in the Bay of Plenty. However, around Rotorua visitors need not fear any erupting volcanoes, as thermal activity is limited to spectacular geysers, bubbling mud pools and steaming hot springs.

WHAKAREWAREWA Whakarewarewa's full name is Te Whakarewarewatanga-o-te-ope-a-Wahiao, meaning 'the uprising of the war party at Wahiao'. (To locals it's known simply as Whaka.)

Whakarewarewa is an extensive nature park with silica terraces, geysers, bubbling mud pools and boiling springs on the banks of the Puarenga River – about 2 kilometres from Rotorua. Take one of the signposted trails to see spectacular features including the 10-metre geyser known as the **Prince of Wales' Feathers** and the 30-metre Pohutu (meaning big splash) – 'performances' take place several times a day. The entrance to the thermal area is by way of the **New Zealand Maori Arts & Craft Institute** (tel: 07 348 9047 or 0800 494 252).

As well as free lunchtime concerts at 1215 daily and the 'Maori Experience' at 1815 (including a Maori welcome, concert and barbecue), the Institute organises continuous demonstrations of traditional carving and weaving. If you like what you see, there's a shop here too.

Nearby is the **Whakarewarewa Forest**, covering an area of 4052 hectares. There's an amazing variety of tree species, including a grove of giant redwoods. **Forest Visitor Centre**, Long Mile Rd; tel: 07 346 2082. The forest is lush and wonderful mountain bike territory – contact Planet Bike Ltd; tel: 07 348 9971.

WAIOTAPU The main feature of the Waiotapu thermal reserve, 30 kilometres from Rotorua, is the multicoloured springs and terraces, accessed by walkways and informative signposting. An hour-long loop track leads past the bubbling mud basins known as the **Devil's Ink Pots,** small volcanic lakes aptly named **Artist's Palette**, and **Champagne Pool**, which flow over lime green silicate terraces. Also look out for the **Lady Knox Geyser**, activated by a ranger every day at 1015 by dropping soap into a cairn. (It's said that the geyser first erupted after prisoners, taken here to wash, accidentally activated it with soap.) Whether or not this is true, it is a scientific fact that the soap releases pressure on the geyser by breaking down the surface tension of the water. Lady Knox, incidentally, was the daughter of Governor-General Lord Ranfurly.

WAIMANGU VOLCANIC VALLEY Blown open by the Taiwera eruption of 1886, the Waimangu Valley is still highly active. Surrounded by lush vegetation, is **Frying Pan Lake**, the world's largest boiling lake, 100 metres in diameter and **Inferno Crater** (usually immersed in steam) which overflows for 2 days in every 38-day cycle. Another must see is the giant red, steaming face of **Cathedral Rocks**, although the terraces are not quite as impressive as the once famous Pink and White Terraces of Te Wairoa. There's a Visitors Centre near the entrance, open daily 0830–1700. For the price of admission, you can take a 50-minute cruise on **Lake Rotomohana** and ride on the shuttle buses that run through the valley.

A 3-D MAZE

Leave Rotorua on State Highway 30. Opposite the airport, on Te Ngae Rd, you'll find the Fairbank Maze, a traditional hedge maze which will take you about 20 minutes to negotiate. (Open daily, donation box.) For a greater challenge, try the unusual 3-D Maze, made from wooden fencing, 3 kilometres down the road. (Tel: 07 345 5275. Open daily 0900–1700.)

ROTORUA SHUTTLE SERVICES

Various companies run daily shuttle services to a number of Rotorua's main attractions, including Waimangu, Waiotapu and Whakarewarewa. The following depart from Tourism Rotorua:
Magic of the Maori Shuttle, tel: 07 349 3949;
Thermal & Cultural Shuttle, tel: 0800 287 2968.

HELLS' GATE Fifteen kilometres out of Rotorua on State Highway 30 is Hell's Gate, also known as Tikitere. This seething mass of boiling springs, mud holes and eerie sulphur vents is a guaranteed tourist draw. Also here is the **Kakahi Falls** a unique waterfall flowing at a steaming 38°C. (Open daily 0900 to 1700.) When the playwright George Bernard Shaw visited Hell's Gate he commented, 'It reminds me too vividly of the fate theologians have promised me.'

WHY IS THERE SO MUCH VOLCANIC ACTIVITY?

The simplest explanation for the concentration of volcanic activity in the Taupo region is that the earth's crust is particularly thin here, allowing rain water to permeate as far as the molten lava. The heat turns the water to steam and pressure drives it back to the surface.

Another explanation is that molten rock traps the steam and other gases to create huge expanding bubbles. These rise slowly to the surface until they burst through an escape hole. It's the gases, mainly sulphuretted hydrogen, give Rotorua its malodourous reputation.

MOUNT TARAWERA On the south-eastern shore of Lake Tarawera you'll see a line of peaks and craters left by Mt Tarawera when it last erupted in 1886. You can climb into the centre of the crater, but as the mountain is Maori Reserve, not a public park, you have no automatic right of access. The Visitors Centre will be happy to book a tour for you. The ascending road is very rough and requires a sturdy four-wheel drive vehicle and an experienced driver. The crater is knee-deep in volcanic ash but you can get to the bottom if you don't mind ruining your shoes. One company that caters for this trip is Mount Tarawera 4WD Tours (tel: 07 348 9929). If you do take a guided walk of Mount Tarawera's crater, be prepared for the fact that most visitors find it quite hard-going. Traditionally, guides have encouraged visitors to glissade down to the bottom of the crater and then climb back up to the top. If you do take this option, don't be disheartened by comparing yourself against your guide – who will doubtless race effortlessly back to the top: after all, the local air is reputed to have excellent energy-giving properties!

Today, the Te Wairoa museum brings the history of Mount Tarawera's eruption alive. It is 15 minutes by car from the town centre on Tarawera Road.

You can take a cruise on Lake Tarawera in the restored **MV *Reremoana*** (tel: 07 362 8595). The cruise lasts 45 minutes, or there's a 2½-hour trip which includes a walk through the bush to the shores of Lake Rotomahana.

TE WAIROA The Tuhourangi people, a sub-tribe of the Te Arawa confederation, had within its territory the village of Te Wairoa and the **Pink and White Terraces**, where mineral-rich water flowed down the hillside, leaving chalky deposits. When the settlers discovered them, they called them the eighth wonder of the world. This attracted the attention of Thomas Cook when he was arranging tours of New Zealand in 1870 – the Terraces were listed as a major sight that the Maoris operated on a commercial basis. Then catastrophe struck. On 10 June 1886 Mount Tarawera erupted, destroying the Terraces and burying Te Wairoa and two smaller villages under a thick sediment of hot ash and mud. More than 150 lives were lost. Today the excavated dwellings of the Buried Village are connected by a meandering pathway, set among trees and meadows beside the Te Wairoa Stream. Open daily from 0900.

OTHER LAKES IN THE AREA

There are three other lakes within easy reach of Rotorua. At the western end of Lake Rotoiti, meaning Little Lake, is the settlement of Okere. (Reached via the Tauranga Rd.) Here the Kaituna River is forced through a narrow fissure in the cliff to form a dramatic waterfall, popular with rafters. From the car park, steps lead through caves in the rocks to the side of the falls.

The more distant Rotoehu is linked to Rotoiti by Hongi's Track (1½ kilometres through bush). It's named after chief Hongi Hika, who arrived in 1823 with a band of over 1000 warriors to make war on the Arawas of Mokoia Island. As part of the trek, they had to carry their canoes over this stretch of land.

Lake Okataina is quieter, surrounded by thick bush and totally unspoilt. There's no road along the shore, just tracks and sandy beaches, best accessed by boat. Information and boat charter from Okataina Tourist Lodge, tel: 07 362 8230.

LAKE HOUSE HOTEL,

ROTORUA,

AND THE

PALACE,

Both Houses under the management of

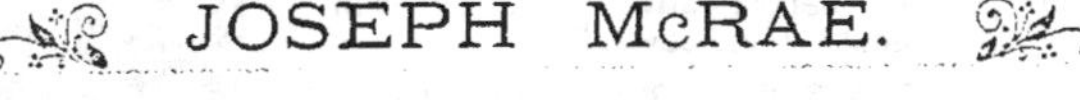

Both Hotels are most pleasantly situated, and contain every convenience for the comfort of Visitors.

——:o:——

HOT, MINERAL, & SULPHUR BATHS

in the grounds attached to both Hotels.

——:o:——

Terms Moderate.

——:o:——

Arrangements can be made for a lengthened stay.

——:o:——

Horses and Buggies for the convenience of Travellers.

——:o:——

TELEGRAMS OR LETTERS RECEIVE PROMPT ATTENTION.

——:o:——

Invalids

should not fail to pay a visit to see the Natural Wonders of this District, and to use the Baths, for the wonderful cures derived therefrom are well-known all the World over.

The altitude of the District is 1500 feet above the level of the sea.

Bona fide non-residential Tourists Granted Special

A page from Thomas Cook's *New Zealand Pocket Pamphlet,* dating from1890/91

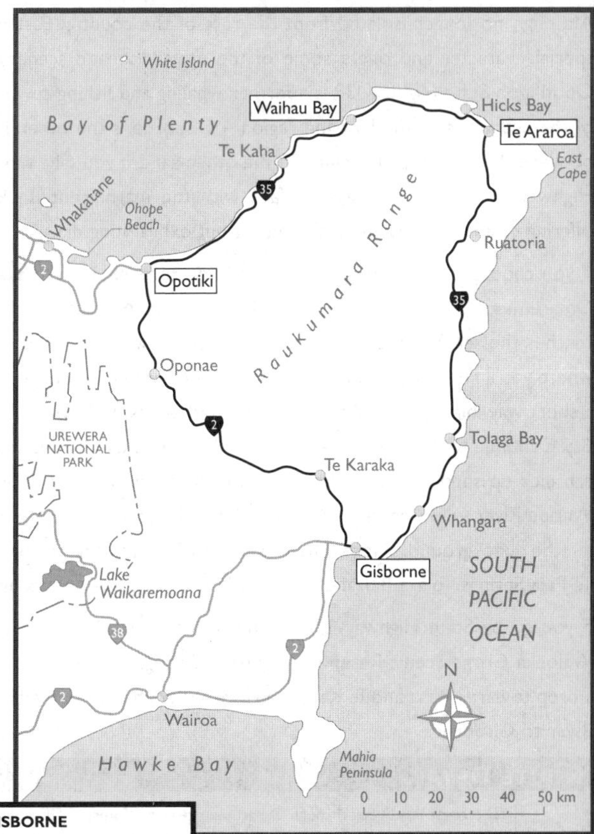

OPOTIKI – GISBORNE
OTT TABLE 9754

TRANSPORT	FREQUENCY	JOURNEY TIME
Bus	1 daily	2hrs 5mins

OPOTIKI – TE KARAKA
OTT TABLE 9754

TRANSPORT	FREQUENCY	JOURNEY TIME
Bus	1 daily	1hr 35mins

TE KARAKA – GISBORNE
OTT TABLE 9754

TRANSPORT	FREQUENCY	JOURNEY TIME
Bus	1 daily	30mins

Note: This service runs mid-afternoon.

The East Cape Route

Although no longer isolated from the rest of the country, Eastland retains its own special character and offers some of the most dramatic scenery in New Zealand. Opotiki on State Highway 35 is a former whaling and fishing town and is seen as one of the entrances to the Eastland region – Gisborne is the other. The coastal scenery between the two is spellbinding. On the other hand, if you take the inland route (State Highway 2), you'll come face to face with the magnificent Raukumara Mountains, offering dramatic vistas and a challenging but exhilarating drive.

If you choose the coast road, it will lead you through a succession of tiny villages – Omarumutu, Opape, Torere, Hawai, Houpoto and Whitianga, where the Motu River reaches the sea. The route continues through Omaio, Whanarua Bay and Raukokore, where you'll find a tourist information centre. After Waihau Bay and Whangaparaoa, it's a short way inland to Potaka, before the road bends back towards the coast at Hicks Bay. Continue to the town of Te Araroa, which has its own tourist office and where you can pick up supplies. The Highway then cuts across the East Cape to Tikitiki on the Waiapu River, following the north bank to the Ruatoria crossing, with Mount Hikurangi in the background. Here the road returns to the coast, passing through Te Puia Springs, Tolaga Bay and a string of minute seaside communities to Gisborne.

If you go by State Highway 2, then this inland road climbs through the magnificent Waioeka Gorge Scenic Reserve and passes through Wairata to Matawai. Then there's a drop towards Puha and Te Karaka, before the road follows the banks of the Waipaoa River to Gisborne.

Route Detail

The coast road goes through Omarumutu, Opape, Torere, Hawai, Houpoto and Whitianga. The route continues through Omaio, Whanarua Bay and Raukokore, and Waihau Bay; then you will reach Whangaparaoa. 113 km

From here it is a short way inland to Potaka, before the road bends back towards the coast at Hicks Bay. Continue to the town of Te Araroa. The Highway then cuts across the East Cape to Tikitiki on the Waiapu River, following the north bank to the Ruatoria crossing with Mount Hikurangi in the background. Here the road returns to the coast, passing through Te Puia Springs, and Tolaga Bay to Gisborne. 334 km

Alternatively, the State Highway 2 inland road climbs through the magnificent Waioeka Gorge Scenic Reserve and passes through Wairata to Matawai. Then there's a drop towards Puha and Te Karaka, before the road follows the banks of the Waipaoa River to Gisborne. 147 km

OHIWA HARBOUR

Some 16 kilometres from Opotiki is Ohiwa Harbour, a beautiful spot with a magnificent backdrop of pohutukawa, New Zealand Christmas trees. Unusually you'll find native black beech trees growing side by side with mangroves – they normally flourish in very different climatic conditions.

OPOTIKI

The name Opotiki derives from O-Potiki-Mai-Tawhit, a spring on the eastern bluff above Waiotahi Beach. The literal meaning is 'place of the children from Tawhiti'.

Your first stop should be the Information Centre, where you'll find all the information you need on four-wheel drives to the Motu River,with its jet-boating and white-water rafting possibilities.

At the northern end of Church Street in the town is a small and rather eccentric **Heritage and Agricultural Society Museum**. Open Mon–Sat 1000–1530, Sun 1330–1600.

In the town itself, **St Stephen's Anglican Church**, on Church St, is worth a visit. It was built by the Reverend Carl Sylvus Volkner in 1864, who later died a violent death at the hands of the Hau Hau. The pakeha version states that he was murdered, while the Maoris argue that Volkner was executed for actively supporting the settlers during the Land Wars.

A good place to stretch the legs is the **Waioeka Gorge Scenic Reserve**, some 20 kilometres south of town on State Highway 2 to Gisborne. A nice short walk here is the **Waioeka Nature Trail**. This loop track takes only 15 minutes but it goes through magnificent native bush. A great help for the uninitiated is the fact that many of the trees and plants are identified with signs. For something more strenuous, just continue down the road another 8 kilometres to the signposted parking area that marks the start of the **Tauranga Track**. The walk takes two to three hours and you have to cross a stream twice – don't attempt this when it is in flood!

An ancient tree in the Hukutaia Domain, within the town, is a puriri tree, thought to be well over 1000 years old.

Opotiki Information Centre cnr St John and Elliot St; tel/fax: 07 315 8484; e-mail: InfoCentre@odc.govt.nz.

Capeview Cottage $$$ Tablelands Rd; tel: 07 315 7877 or 0800 227 384, fax: 07 315 8055; e-mail: brianj.young@xtra.co.nz. This luxurious cottage comes with fully equipped kitchen, luxury bathroom and laundry facilities. Spectacular views of coastal scenery from the private gardens.
Central Oasis Backpackers $ 30 King St; tel: 07 315 5165; e-mail: centraloasis@hotmail.com. A kauri villa in peaceful surroundings. Close to beach, free pickup from bus, free bikes.
Magnolia Court Motel $$ cnr Bridge and Nelson St; tel: 07 315 8490 or 0800 556 246, fax: 07 315 5444; e-mail: magnolia.crt.motel@xtra.co.nz. Spacious, well-equipped units.
Opotiki Backpackers Beach House $ Appleton Rd, Waiotahi Beach; tel: 07 315 5117; e-mail: alowry@paradise.net.nz. This hostel is located 5 km west of Opotiki on SH 2. Free pickup from town. Great location directly on the beach.

Masonic Hotel $$ Church St; tel: 07 315 6115. Open for lunch and dinner.
Seymours Restaurant $$ Church St; 07 315 6173. Good-value dinner menu. Open Mon–Sat.

WATER SPORTS

Two rivers run into the harbour – the Otara and Waioeka – and both offer excellent boating and yachting: true New Zealand past times. There are numerous safe swimming beaches and bays in the area, including the popular Waiotahi, which is only 6 kilometres out of town and is patrolled by the surf club during the season.

Jet boat rides are offered along the spectacular and turbulent lengths of the Motu River, to the east of the town. These trips are not inexpensive but are certainly thrilling: powering through narrow, spectacular gorges or planing in just centimetres of water in specially designed jets makes an unforgettable experience. They also require no skill on your part.

Try Motu River Jet Boat Tours (tel/fax: 07 315 8107; e-mail: Kel.McKirdy@xtra.co.nz); you need to book at least a day ahead.

WAIHAU BAY

An idyllic setting of deserted sandy beaches and rocky headlands, Waihau Bay is safe for swimming, surfing and kayaking. If you want to stay here, **Waihau Bay Homestays**, opposite the beach, offers bed and breakfast, with a fish supper if booked in advance (tel/fax: 07 325 3674). The owners will also arrange diving, fishing and horse-trekking expeditions, and there are facilities for the disabled.

TE ARAROA

Located in an expansive bay with good surfing conditions, most of Te Araroa's facilities can be found in the holiday park (tel: 06 864 4873, fax: 06 864 4473) at the end of the beach. Twenty kilometres along the coast, an unsealed road leads to the East Cape Lighthouse, the most easterly point in New Zealand. From the promontory there are fabulous views of the ocean and the Raukumara mountain range. Beyond the Cape are a number of secluded bays (Waiapu, Tokomaru, Anaura and Tolaga), hot springs (at Te Puia) and Maori treasures (the church at Tikitiki). Swimming, surfing, walking and horseriding opportunities abound.

Te Araroa might once have been an isolated Maori settlement but nowadays it has plenty to offer the tourist other than good views. You'll find it is one of the larger towns on this piece of coastline and has a tourist information centre.

TRANSPORT ALONG COAST ROAD

Kiwi Experience (tel: 09 366 9830) offers the 'East Cape Escape' package, which allows you to get on and off as you wish. It starts in Rotorua and the minimum trip is four days. There are also shuttle services, for instance the one offered by Hicks Bay Backpacker Lodge (tel/fax: 06 864 4731; e-mail: hicksbaybackpackers@xtra.co.nz). For details of other services contact the tourist offices in Opotiki, Gisborne or Wairoa.

HAU HAU AND THE POVERTY BAY MASSACRE

The Maori Hau Hau tribe believed themselves invincible to bullets. When confronted by firearms they would hold one hand above their head, palm outward, while making a barking sound (hence 'Hau Hau'). More gruesome was their habit of carrying the heads of victims before them on long stakes as totems.

While the unique method of bullet-proofing turned out to have fatal conceptual flaws, the Hau Hau did inspire genuine fear among the pakeha, for example when they murdered the missionary, the Reverend Carl Volkner, in March 1865 at Opotiki. The propaganda of the time alleged that the Hau Hau, led by the prophet, Kereopa Te Rau, drank the reverend's blood.

Elements of the Hau Hau religion were incorporated into Rangatu beliefs – the teachings of Te Kooti Rikiraugi. Te Kooti was arrested in 1865 during the battle of Waerenga-a-hika, tried as a Hau Hau spy and deported to Chatham. Three years later, he and 200 of his followers escaped and were responsible for the Poverty Bay Massacre in which around 60 Maoris and Europeans were murdered and their houses and farm buildings burned to the ground. The tiny church at Matawhero, at the crossroads on State Highway 2, was the only building in the immediate vicinity to survive the massacre.

GISBORNE

Gisborne is the closest town in the world to the International Date Line and predictably markets itself as being the 'First To See The Light'.

Its location is Poverty Bay, the name given to the area by Captain Cook after he failed to find provisions here – no one has had any problems since!

Gisborne also lies at the confluence of the Waimata and Taruheru rivers, which join here to form the Turanganui – reputedly the shortest river in New Zealand at just 1390 metres. There are footpaths along all three waterways, which make exploring this compact yet charming town very enjoyable. The harbour was built in the 1920s by constructing a diversion wall across the Turanganui. This created a ready-made marina, now well provided with restaurants and cafés.

GETTING THERE AND AROUND

AIR **Gisborne Airport** (domestic flights only) lies on the western edge of town, 2 kilometres from the centre.

BUS **Buses** leave and arrive outside the Visitors Centre. A daily InterCity bus goes to Auckland via Rotorua. There is also a daily service to Wellington via Napier.

INFORMATION

Eastland Visitor Information Centre 209 Grey St; tel: 06 868 6139, fax: 06 868 6138; e-mail: info@gisbornenz.com.

POST AND PHONES **Books & More NZ Post** Gladstone Rd; tel: 06 867 8220 – also facilities for sending faxes and telegrams. Open Mon–Fri 0830–1700 (Wed open at 0900).

DON YOUR WETTIE

Gisborne is an excellent surfing area and you can hear surfing reports following the daily 0700 news on Radio 89FM.

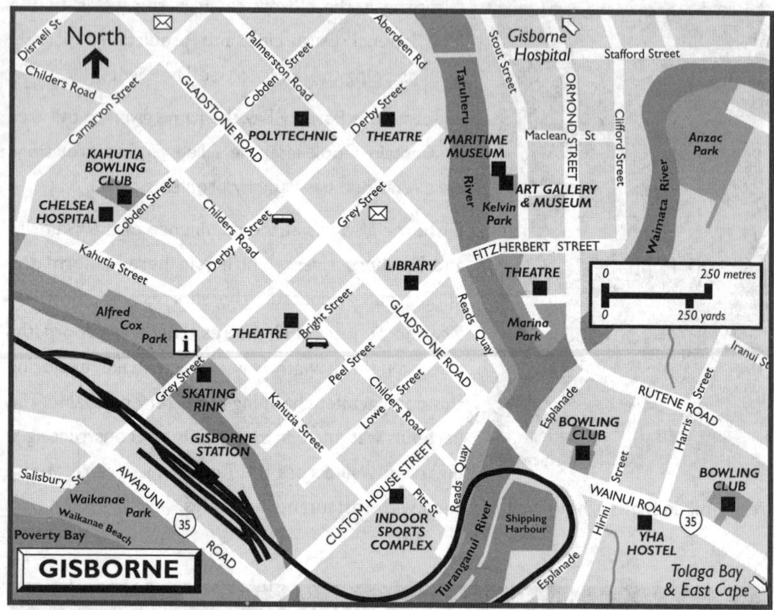

ACCOMMODATION

Blue Pacific Beachfront Motel $$ 90 Salisbury Rd; tel: 06 868 6099, fax: 06 867 0481. Motel overlooking the sea with sauna and spa pool.

Eastland Motor Lodge $$ 798 Gladstone Rd; tel: 06 868 4115, fax: 06 867 3604. Just minutes from the beach, this motel has its own saltwater pool.

Gisborne Backpackers $ 690 Gladstone Rd; tel: 06 868 1000.

Gisborne Park Hotel $$ cnr Huxley and Tyndall Rds; tel: 06 868 4109, fax: 06 867 8344. Comfortable hotel with spacious rooms and good restaurant.

Gisborne YHA Hostel $ cnr Wainui Rd & Harris St; tel: 06 867 3269.

Glen Innis Farm Stay $$ 3558 Tiniroto Rd, Hangaroa; tel: 06 863 7127. This bed and breakfast also caters for backpackers and has camping facilities. Located on a hill-country farm above the scenic Hangaroa River.

FOOD AND DRINK

Café Villaggio $$ 57 Ballance St; tel: 06 868 1611. Award-winning restaurant with cool courtyard – excellent for lunches. Licensed & BYO. Open daily.

Fettuccine Bros $ 12 Peel St; tel: 06 868 5700. Authentic Italian dishes with large helpings and vegetarian, as well as meat, sauces. Licensed and BYO. Open daily from 1800.

Landfall $$ On the wharf; tel: 06 867 2039. Local produce and wines. À la carte dining, daily from 1800 until late.

The Marina Restaurant $$$ Marina Park, Vogel St; tel: 06 868 5919. Dine on superb New Zealand cuisine while looking out over the Taruheru and Waimata rivers. Licensed. Closed Sun.

Young Nick's $$$ Centennial Marine Drive, Midway Beach; tel: 06 867 5861. Seriously good seafood and wonderful views – well worth paying extra for.

HIGHLIGHTS

Gisborne claims to be the world's most easterly city, lying less than 900 kilometres (less than 560 miles) from the International Date Line.

The first European visitor, Captain James Cook, arrived here on 7 October 1769 and a reconnoitring party was sent ashore two days later. Ominously this first contact between pakeha and native ended in bloodshed after members of the crew suspected a Maori of trying to steal a sword.

As you would expect, there are a number of monuments commemorating Cook and the crew of the *Endeavour* in the area. The **obelisk** on **Kaiti Beach** was raised by national subscription with each schoolchild contributing a penny towards its construction. It marks the spot where Captain Cook landed in 1769, but gives the wrong day. The **totem pole**, situated near the Information Centre, was donated by the Canadian government to mark the bicentenary of the landings. The **Cook Observatory**, on Kaiti Hill, is open to the public on Tuesdays (at 1930 in the winter and 2030 in the summer).

GISBORNE

One of the best views of Gisborne is from the **Titirangi Scenic Reserve,** which incorporates Kaiti Hill. This was originally a Maori *pa* and on a clear day you can see right across Poverty Bay to Young Nick's Head at the southern end. From here there are pathways leading down to the Captain Cook landing site.

Te Poho-o-Rawiri, one of the largest meeting houses in New Zealand, stands at the bottom of the hill beyond the Titirangi Reserve. The House opened in 1930 and is beautifully carved. You need permission from the Information Centre to enter the site and a donation is appreciated.

The history and culture of the area is the subject of the **Gisborne Museum and Arts Centre**. Within the grounds is Wyllie Cottage, the oldest building in Gisborne (1872). The six rooms are furnished in 19th-century colonial style. Open Mon–Fri 1000–1600, Sat–Sun 1330–1600.

Gisborne is bounded by river flats – the alluvial soil makes for wonderfully fertile agricultural land, ideal for market gardens and vineyards. The town has an excellent **Botanical Garden** in Aberdeen Rd, on the banks of the Taruheru river. A better way to appreciate the scenery is to follow the **Te Kuri** footpath (3 hours) which starts at the end of Shelley Rd and wends its way through farmland and forest.

CAPTAIN COOK

Cook, popularly called Captain Cook, was born in Marton, England, the son of a farm labourer. After spending his early years as an apprentice with a firm of shipowners, he enlisted in the British navy in 1755. Within four years he had become a master, and he spent the years 1756 to 1767 charting the North Atlantic coastal waters off Newfoundland and Nova Scotia and the Saint Lawrence River below Québec. It was two years later, in 1769, that he discovered 'Poverty Bay' and (now named) Gisborne.

WHAT'S IN A NAME?

Gisborne was named after the then colonial secretary, Sir William Gisborne, because the original Maori name – Turanganui-a-Kiwa – was often confused with Tauranga in the Bay of Plenty.

WAIKANAE BEACH

There's a statue of Nicholas Young, the first seaman on board the *Endeavour* to sight land, at Waikanae Beach, the point where the Turanganui River flows into the sea. Young, the surgeon's boy on the ship, was only 12 years of age at the time – his reward was a gallon of rum.

The beach becomes crowded during the holidays and at weekends in the summer – otherwise you can enjoy splendid isolation here.

Near the Gisborne museum is a small but interesting Maritime museum containing part of the superstructure of the *Star of Canada*, which foundered on Kaiti Beach in 1912, and was once used as a house. Open 1000–1630 weekdays, 1400–1630 weekends and public holidays.

MURRAY BALL

Gisborne is the home of well-known New Zealand cartoonist, Murray Ball. Murray's most entertaining creation, *Footrot Flats*, is set locally and was inspired by Te Kuri, Maori for 'dog'. (The cartoon's central character is the archetypal New Zealander, Farmer Wal, but it's 'Dog' who is the true hero.) The Te Kuri path passes Murray Ball's farm, where Wal lives his imaginary bachelor life.

GISBORNE WINERIES

SOLD OUT

Because Gisborne sees the light first, New Years Eve in Gisborne is a popular event each year – often hotels will be sold out well in advance. Gisborne hosts a wealth of celebrations as well, so get your tickets – and your bottles of bubbly – in early!

For an interesting side trip from Gisborne, take the Tiniroto Rd towards Wairoa in Hawkes Bay. After 53 kilometres you will arrive at Doneraille Park, a native bush reserve on the Hangaroa River with safe swimming and picnic sites. Continue to Tiniroto itself to visit Hackfalls Arboretum (tel: 06 863 7091) with its important tree collection planted round the lakes on a sheep and cattle station. The Tiniroto Lakes nearby offer first-rate trout fishing while just beyond are the Te Reinga Falls where the Hangaroa and Raikituri rivers drop into a deep ravine.

At Eastwoodhill is another Arboretum, just beyond Ngatapa, 35 kilometres west of Gisborne it is well worth a visit. Established in 1918, it's planted with an enormous collection of trees and shrubs representing both hot and cold climates. A gentle 45-minute stroll along marked paths takes in the whole of the garden (open daily 0900–1600). It's possible to tour some of the wineries in the Gisborne area - many have their own restaurants and commercial wine cellars. However, bear in mind that these are small, private vineyards so you'll need to book beforehand.

A selection of the best vineyards near to Gisborne is given below. Wine enthusiasts can get even more detailed information by enquiring at the tourist office in Gisborne and asking for a 'Wine Trail' brochure. This lists the locations and opening hours of all of the vineyards in the area, and when you can visit to try and buy wines.

Matawhero Wines Riverpoint Rd; 8 km west of Gisborne, tel: 06 868 8366; open Mon–Sat 1100–1600. Owner Denis Irwin began making wine in the mid-1970s and achieved almost instant success. Ring ahead if you want to taste wines at the vineyard, or visit the **Colosseum Wine Bar** at 4 Riverpoint Rd, tel: 06 867 4733.

Millton Vineyard 119 Papatu Rd; 15 km west of Gisborne, tel: 06 862 8680 or 0800 464 558 for appointments. New Zealand's first organic vineyard uses no insecticide or soluble fertiliser. Millton's 1992 Chardonnay was recently selected as the best organic wine in the world by an international jury.

Parker MC Smash Palace, Banks St, Gisborne; tel: 06 867 6967; open daily 1000–1800. Vineyard with its own wine bar, instantly recognisable for the full-sized DC-3 aircraft perched on the roof and the fibreglass dinosaur at the door. Parker MC produces a sparkling wine, using the Methode Champenoise, in such small quantities that customers can specify what they want in the final bottling. They also produce the elegant and drinkable First Light Red, a Beaujolais hardly known outside Gisborne.

Pouparae Park Wines 385 Bushmere Rd; tel: 06 867 7931; open daily 1000–1800. Although no grapes are actually grown on this elegant property, it's surrounded by vineyards and produces a good Chardonnay (sold at the cellar door).

Shalimar Estate Ngatapa Rd, 15 km west of Gisborne; tel: 06 862 7776; open 1300–1700, Oct–Apr. After growing contract grapes for 25 years, the estate started its own label in 1994. Cellar sales.

The Works Café (Longbush Wines) Kaiti Beach Rd, Gisborne; tel: 06 863 1285; open daily 1000–1800. This harbour-side winery and café offers cellar door tastings and you can also sample their tasty Waimata cheeses. Wines offered here originate from the Longbush vineyards.

The Hawke's Bay Wine Industry

Gisborne is known as the Chardonnay capital of New Zealand and lies at the centre of one of the country's most important wine-growing regions. About 35 per cent of the national crop of the Chardonnay grape is grown locally. The first grapes were planted in the 1850s by Marist missionaries who went on to establish the Hawke's Bay wine industry.

Friedrich Wohnsiedler, a German sausage-maker who emigrated to Gisborne at the turn of the century, switched to wine producing during World War I. By the time of his death, in the mid-1950s, the Waihirere vineyard was a major property. (It was later acquired by the giant Montana company.)

Chardonnay has to be made from at least 75 per cent chardonnay grapes. Natural factors make New Zealand Chardonnay unique. The relatively cool climate is well adapted to vine-growing, and the long autumn gives the grapes a chance to ripen slowly, concentrating the flavour to the full. The resulting Chardonnay is a subtle and full-bodied wine. Local wine-growers have done very well here and have many medals to their credit.

The First Vines

The first vines were planted by the British Resident, James Busby, in his back garden at Waitangi in the 1840s, but it has only been during the last decade that the New Zealand wine industry has come of age.

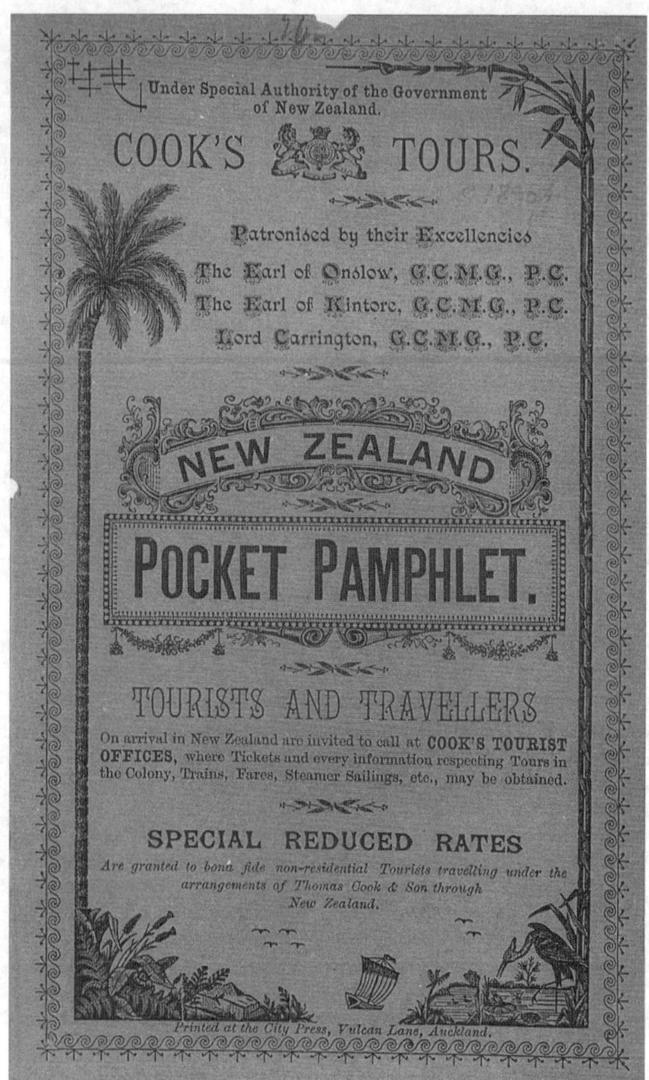

The *New Zealand Pocket Pamphlet* of 1890/91

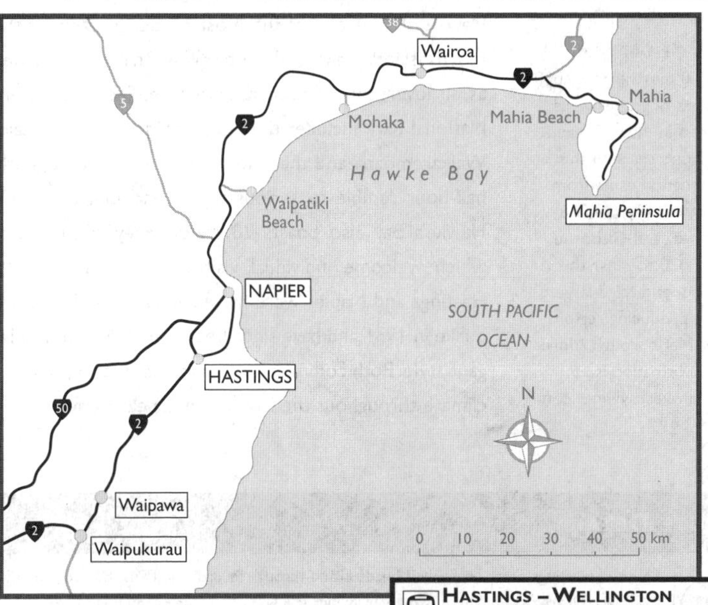

Hastings – Gisborne
OTT tables 9763/9764

Transport	Frequency	Journey Time
Bus	2 daily	4hrs 20mins

Hastings – Napier
OTT table 9764

Transport	Frequency	Journey Time
Bus	2 daily	25mins

Napier – Wairoa
OTT table 9763

Transport	Frequency	Journey Time
Bus	2 daily	2hrs 15mins

Wairoa – Gisborne
OTT table 9763

Transport	Frequency	Journey Time
Bus	2 daily	1hr 35mins

Hastings – Wellington
OTT table 9764

Transport	Frequency	Journey Time
Bus	2 daily	5hrs 25mins

Hastings – Waipukurau
OTT table 9764

Transport	Frequency	Journey Time
Bus	2 daily	40mins

Waipukurau – Woodville
OTT table 9764

Transport	Frequency	Journey Time
Bus	2 daily	1hr 15mins

Woodville – Wellington
OTT table 9764

Transport	Frequency	Journey Time
Bus	2 daily	3hrs 15mins

Hastings – Mahia Peninsula

Wine Country
In 2000 more than 80,000 tonnes of grapes were crushed in New Zealand. A lion's share of this production came from Hawke's Bay (23,886 tonnes) and Gisborne (21,820 tonnes), the second- and third-largest wine-producing regions after Marlborough. More information is at www.hawkesbaywines.com.

Hawke's Bay is one of the most attractive parts of the North Island, greatly valued by New Zealanders as well as all lovers of art deco architecture. The Te Urewera National Park includes the breathtakingly beautiful Lake Waikaremoana and the walks here range from a gentle half-hour ramble to serious three- and four-day hikes. Hawke's Bay also boasts 28 major vineyards, most of which welcome individual visitors. The twin cities of Hastings and Napier were flattened by a massive earthquake in 1931 and have since been rebuilt in a more elegant style. Both communities are tourist-friendly and the climate throughout the bay region is near perfect.

Route Detail

South of Hastings, State Highway 2 heads inland through Pakipaki and Pukehou to Waipawa. Nearby Waipukurau is marginally bigger if you count the sheep pens. Follow the Highway until the right turning onto State Highway 50 just beyond Takapau. This highway follows the edge of the Ruahine Forest Park through Ongaonga and Tikokino before returning to Hastings. Leave Hastings on the Coast Road heading northwards, passing through Clive to Awatoto on Hawke's Bay, then continue to neighbouring Napier. 25 km

From here the road follows the line of the bay to Tangoio. Just beyond Bay View is the junction with State Highway 5, which crosses the Ahimanawa Range to Taupo. Continue on State Highway 2, which winds inland to Tutira, Putorino, Kotemaori and Raupunga, then returns to the coast at Waihua. Pass through Ohinepaka to Wairoa at the river estuary of the same name. 115 km

Beyond is the inland route to Gisborne and Urewera National Park. State Highway 2 then follows the north coast of Hawke's Bay through Tuhara and Whakaki to Nuhaka where a small road turns off right through the pine trees to Opoutama on the Mahia peninsula. 155 km

HASTINGS

Along with Napier, Hastings has the fifth-largest urban population in New Zealand. It lies on the Heretaunga Plains in an area of rich farmland and the town itself is full of beautiful parks and gardens. The main street was totally destroyed in the 1931 earthquake and 93 people were killed. Thanks to the subsequent rebuilding, Hastings boasts a fine collection of art deco and Spanish-American Mission buildings. The Visitors Centre has full details of architectural trails.

The city is named after Warren Hastings, the first Governor General of the East India Company, who was later tried for corruption in one of the major scandals of the late-18th century.

SPLASH PLANET

Fantasyland is now part of the new amusement park, Splash Planet. This fully themed waterpark includes old Fantasyland favourites such as the pirate ship and space rocket, along with many new water-based activities. Highlights include thrilling waterslides, a paddle steamer, relaxing hot pools and a boating lake. Splash Planet is located on Grove Road, tel: 06 876 9856; www.splashplanet.co.nz.

i **Hastings Visitor Information** Russell St North; tel: 06 873 5526, fax: 06 873 5529; e-mail: vic@hastingstourism.co.nz.

AJ's Backpackers Lodge $ 405 Southland Rd; tel: 06 878 2302; e-mail: ajslodge@xtra.co.nz. Colonial villa with cosy BBQ area. Free pickup in Hastings area.
Elmore Lodge Motel $$ 301 Omahu Rd; tel: 06 876 8051 or 0800 356 673, fax: 06 876 8051; e-mail: j.b.nicol@xtra.co.nz. Close to ten-pin bowling, shops and restaurants.
Fairmont Motor Lodge $$ 1120 Karamu Rd North; tel: 06 878 3850 or 0800 244 144, fax: 06 878 3851; e-mail: fairmontreservations@xtra.co.nz. New motel, close to the centre, with swimming pool and double-sized spa baths.
Hastings Backpacker Hostel $ 505 Lyndon Rd East; tel: 06 876 5888; www.homepages.paradise.net.nz/medcasa; e-mail: medcasa@paradise.net.nz.
Providencia $$$ 225 Middle Rd, Havelock North; tel: 06 877 2300, fax: 06 877 3250; e-mail: nfdr.baker@xtra.co.nz. 1903 homestead in attractive orchard setting. Excellent breakfasts.
Travellers Lodge $ 606 St Aubyn St West; tel: 06 878 7108, fax: 06 878 7228; e-mail: travellerslodge@clear.net.nz.

PETANQUE POPULARITY

One of the most popular sports in the area is petanque, possibly because this is the only sport you can play while still holding a full wine glass.

Clearview Estate Winery $$ Clifton Rd; tel: 06 875 0150. Lunches only. Classic cooking with great wines from this small, coastal winery, which opened in 1989.
The Corn Exchange $$$ 118 Maraekakaho Rd; tel: 06 870 8333. Trendy, popular restaurant with a regularly changing menu, which includes a range of meat dishes (bison and venison occasionally appear); also large pizzas. Bars stay open until 0100 at weekends.
McGinty's $$ 3764 Karamu Rd North; tel: 06 876 1410. Open seven days for dinner.
Te Awa Farm Restaurant $$ State Highway 50; tel: 06 879 7602. Sample award-winning cuisine in this winery restaurant.
Thai Silk Restaurant $$ 601 Karamu Rd North; tel: 06 878 3718.
Vidal Estate Restaurant $$ 913 St Aubyn St East; tel: 06 876 8105. Café and licensed restaurant with great wines and delicious 'fish of the day'.

WAIPAWA

Located 50 kilometres south-west of Hastings on the northern bank of the river of the same name, Waipawa became the county town in 1884. It was originally called Abbotsford after F S Abbott, who took out a grazing lease on the area in the 1850s. Within ten years the farming community he founded had its own churches, hotels and local stores, and can fairly claim to be the oldest established town in Hawke's Bay. Sadly for its founder, 'Abbotsford' did not catch on and the residents changed the name in favour of the Maori Waipawa.

THE BROTHERS OF THE SOCIETY OF MARY

The first wine producers in the area, the Brothers of the Society of Mary, were a French religious order who began by producing altar wines. Recalling those early days is The Mission Vineyard and Winery at Greenmeadows, 198 Church Rd; tel: 06 844 2259. This is the oldest winery in the country, although the building was moved to its present location at the end of the 19th century. Tours (Mon–Sat 1030 and 1400) include tastings and cellar-door sales. Also try the superb food at the attached restaurant; tel: 06 844 6048.

WAIPUKURAU

Waipukurau lies 8 kilometres southwest of its smaller sister town, Waipawa. Like Waipawa it was founded as a farming community and the two have been rivals ever since. Waipukurau can either mean 'stream where the mushrooms grow' or 'many floods' – the locals shorten the name to Waipuk anyway.

You can see the town clearly from Reservoir Hill (reached from Nelson Street off Reservoir Road), once the site of a Maori *pa*. Much of the life here revolves around livestock – the sheep pens alone have a capacity of 50,000.

i **Central Hawke's Bay Visitor Information Centre**
Railway Esplanade; tel: 06 858 6488, fax: 06 858 6489; e-mail: chbinfo@xtra.co.nz.

Airlie Mount Homestay $ South Service Lane; tel: 06 858 7601, fax: 06 858 7609. A comfortable, attractively situated bed and breakfast for non-smokers.

Lochlea Farmstay $ 344 Lake Rd, Wanstead; tel/fax: 06 855 4816 or 0800 186 506; e-mail: lochlea.farm@xtra.co.nz. Stay on a working sheep and cattle farm. Free pickup from Waipukurau.

Tavistock Hotel $$ Ruataniwha St and Racecourse Rd; tel: 858 8070.

Iramatu Café 11 km south of Waipukurau on SH2; tel: 855 8364. This is a large nursery garden that also sells snacks, wine and coffee. Open daily 0600–1600.

WINE TOUR TRAILS

There are dozens of vineyards within easy reach of Hastings and Napier, mainly dotted around the southern end of the Ngaruroro River valley. For an organised tour, contact Hawkes Bay in a Glass (tel: 06 843 2478, fax: 06 843 2474; www.qualityhb.co.nz). If you prefer to work out your own itinerary, there are free maps available from the Napier and Hastings Visitor Information Centres. Every February the Harvest Hawke's Bay festival celebrates the latest wine crop.

THE WORLD'S LONGEST PLACE NAME

Near Waipukurau is the mountain range with the world's longest place name: Taumatawhakatangihangakoauauotamateaturipukakapimaungahoronukupokaiwhenuaki-tanatahu.

A translation might be: 'The place where Tamatea, the man with the big knees, who sailed all around the land, played his nose flute to his loved one.' (The loved one was his twin brother, who had died in battle.)

NAPIER

Napier, especially the area around the Marine Parade – the seafront boulevard that defines the town – has all the appearance of a British seaside resort; the major difference, of course, is that Napier is almost invariably sunny! With more than 2350 hours of sunshine annually, this tourist magnet also has ideal climatic conditions for fruit growing and viticulture.

Little remains of the 19th-century town, which was destroyed by an earthquake in 1931. The art deco buildings that rose almost literally from the ashes, have made Napier unique among New Zealand's cities. If you're interested in architecture, your first port of call should be the **Art Deco Shop,** headquarters of the Art Deco Trust, 163 Tennyson St; tel: 06 835 0022; open daily 0900–1700.

An Art Deco Walk leaves from here every day in summer at 1400 and Wed, Sat and Sun in the winter (details at the Visitor Centre and the Shop). There's also an inexpensive walk map if you prefer to explore the town at your own pace.

EN ROUTE

Ten kilometres from the centre of town on the Springfield Rd is the 33-hectare Otatara Pa Historic Reserve. Much of the original earthworks are still visible, thanks to conservation measures that have included rebuilding the palisades and the ancestral figures surrounding the *pa*. The overall impression is of a fortified Maori village exactly as it was 100 years ago – presenting formidable challenges to any would-be attacker.

At the heart of Napier, is **Marine Parade**, 2 kilometres long and bordered with Norfolk pines. Near the small local Museum is a statue of Pania of the Reef, a legendary Maori siren. There are several other attractions to be found on the Parade. The **Aquarium** is a major oceanarium with seals, penguins, sea lions and dolphins. You can even see divers hand-feeding the fish. Open 0900–1700.

THE NAPIER EARTHQUAKE

The earthquake of 3 February 1931 brought total devastation to Napier and changed the town for ever. For more information visit the Hawke's Bay Museum, Marine Parade; tel: 06 835 7781, where you can see two 20-minute videos on the terrible event and its consequences. The museum also has an excellent gallery of Maori art. Open daily 0900–1800 (summer).

EN ROUTE

Just 40 kilometres to the north of Napier is the Lake Tutira bird refuge, founded by W H Guthrie-Smith, naturalist and author. The steep Tutira walkway follows the contours of the lake to Table Mountain and offers fine views of Hawke's Bay. (9 kilometres return.)

SHELL SEEKING

The walk to Cape Kidnappers from Clifton reveals the age-old strata in the cliff face – beds of sandstone, gravel, pumice and silt representing an evolutionary history of the area. One of these layers, near Black Reef, known as Maraetotara Sand, contains more than 100 different species of fossilised shells, including many extinct types.

For more underwater entertainment, you could visit the dolphinarium, **Marineland**. Open daily 1000–1630, with dolphin shows at 1030 and 1400; tel: 06 834 4027. **Kiwi House Marine Parade** is the only place in New Zealand where you are guaranteed to see one of these shy, nocturnal creatures (the national emblem) for real. The star performer is Jeremy, who regularly struts his stuff in public. Open daily 1100–1700 with an informative talk at 1300 and feeding at 1400; tel: 06 835 7553.

If you stray 32 kilometres south-east of Napier, you will find the world-famous gannet colony at **Cape Kidnappers**. The large white Australian gannet (*Sula bassna serrator*), also known as the booby, nests here between November and February. The easiest way to get to the colony is to travel by tractor-drawn trailer along the beach from Te Awanga. A short climb and walk to the birds' nests follows. (Ask for details from **Gannet Beach Adventures**; tel: 06 875 0898 or 0800 426 638; www.gannets.com or **Gannet Safaris**; tel: 06 875 0888 or 0800 427 232; e-mail: gannetsafaris@xtra.co.nz). The season for gannet-spotting is October to late April - check at the Visitor Centre before you go.

There's also plenty of sporting opportunities in the area. Try **Riverlands Outback Adventures**, Napier; tel: 06 834 9756; e-mail: riverlnds@xtra.co.nz, who offer rafting expeditions on the Mohaka River. Or for an uplifting experience, **Early Morning Balloons Ltd**, Waipukurau; tel/fax: 06 858 8480; www.early-am-balloons.co.nz - which as the name suggests, takes you airborne over Hawke's Bay (includes a picnic lunch).

i **Napier Visitor Information Centre** 100 Marine Parade; tel: 06 834 1911, fax: 06 835 7219; e-mail: info@napiervic.co.nz.

Department of Conservation Office Marine Parade; tel: 06 835 0415.

Criterion Art Deco Backpackers $ 48 Emerson St; tel: 06 835 2059, fax: 06 835 2370; e-mail: cribacpac@yahoo.com. Centrally located in a historic art deco building. Facilities include female-only dorm, bike hire, TV room and kitchen.

Edgewater Motor Lodge $$ 359 Marine Parade; tel: 06 835 1148, fax: 06 835 6600; e-mail: edgewater-holdings@xtra.co.nz. Beachfront motel within walking distance of the centre.
Fountain Court Motor Inn $$ 411 Hastings St; tel: 06 835 7387 or 0508 411 000, fax: 06 835 0323; www.fountaincourt.co.nz; e-mail: accommodation@fountaincourt.co.nz. Nice motel in centre of town. Off-street parking, swimming pool and restaurant.
Glen-View Farm Hostel $ Aropaoanui Rd; tel: 06 836 6232, fax: 06 836 6067. Located 32 km north of Napier, off SH 2 to Gisborne. There's great horse trekking on this sheep and cattle farm. Facilities include a BBQ, swimming pool and a small shop.
Masonic Hotel $$$ cnr Marine Parade and Tennyson St; tel: 06 835 8689, fax: 06 835 2297; www.masonic.co.nz; e-mail: stay@masonic.co.nz. Classic art deco hotel, now thoroughly modernised. Restaurant and Irish pub.
Mon Logis Guesthouse $$$ 415 Marine Parade; tel/fax: 06 835 2125; e-mail: monlogis@xtra.co.nz. Smart hotel in lovely old colonial building, overlooking the sea. Restaurant and good breakfasts.
Napier YHA $ 277 Marine Parade; tel: 06 835 7039, fax: 06 835 4641; e-mail: yhanapr@yha.org.net. Good hostel next to beach.

EN ROUTE

Overlooking Napier is Bluff Hill, a 3 kilometre-long natural feature. The lookout at the end offers views right along the coast, in one direction as far as the Mahia Peninsula, in the other towards Cape Kidnappers. Captain Cook came up with the name as he sailed by in 1769.

Pierre sur le Quai $$$ 62 West Quay; tel: 06 834 0189. Open Tues–Sat. Classy French restaurant with superb seafood dishes. Licensed.
Sri Thai $$ 60 Bridge St; tel: 06 835 2299. From 1730 daily. Not authentic Thai, but a good range of spicy Asian dishes. Licensed.
Stunned Mullet $$ 209 Marine Parade; tel: 06 835 9188. Great vegetarian food as well as excellent fish, served with local wines. Try for the back courtyard if the weather is fine. Dinner every night and lunch at weekends.

LAKE WAIKAREMOANA

Dazzling Lake Waikaremoana (the name means 'sea of rippling waters') is one of the jewels of the area. To get there take State Highway 2 to Wairoa, then head north-west on the Rangiahua road to Kaitawa and the lake itself. It's possible to drive right around the northern end of the lake, but much of the road here is dirt track, so check your insurance before you set out. Buses travel from Rotorua, but not from Wairoa.

WAIROA

Lying on the banks of the river of the same name, the sleepy town of Wairoa was once a port for local sheep and dairy farmers. The kauri lighthouse on Marine Parade was moved here in 1958 from Portland Island on the Mahia Peninsula. It was built in 1877 and was originally lit by a kerosene burner. For those interested in Maori art, there's also a meeting house at Takitimu marae, decorated with carvings typical of the Gisborne area. Viewing can be arranged from the Visitors Centre.

i **Wairoa Visitors Centre**, cnr State Highway 2 and Queen St; tel/fax: 06 838 7440; e-mail:weavic@xtra.co.nz.

MAHIA PENINSULA

This barren promontory separating Hawke Bay from Poverty Bay is popular with surfers, who head for the windy east coast (fishermen and scuba divers prefer the more sheltered west side). Linked to the mainland by a narrow isthmus, the small settlement of Mahia Beach has a few campsite shops, but nothing in the way of pubs, restaurants and the like.

MORERE HOT SPRINGS

Both public and private thermal pools in an attractive bush setting. There are some easy walks in the vicinity. The springs are situated on State Highway 2, not far from the beaches of the Mahia Peninsula; tel: 06 837 8856.

THE HAWKE'S BAY EARTHQUAKE

The earthquake that devastated the Hawke's Bay area on 3 February 1931 measured 7.9 on the Richter scale. More than 600 aftershocks occurred in the following fortnight and rescue work was hampered by the continuing tremors. While the destruction spread as far as Hastings and Gisborne, Napier, at the epicentre, bore the brunt. The total death toll was 256.

After the tragedy it was discovered that the land level had risen more than 2 metres, while the sea had drained from the Aruhiri lagoon. One positive outcome was the 300 square kilometres of new land on which the airport now stands.

TE UREWERA NATIONAL PARK

Welcome to the largest, untamed stretch of native forest in the North Island. Te Urewera, New Zealand's fourth-largest National Park, is within easy reach of Rotorua, 120 kilometres along State Highway 38. The last 75 kilometres of road are unsealed, making the journey dusty and time-consuming; however, the remoteness and scenic beauty more than make up for it – watch out for roaming horses! The inaccessibility of Te Urewera has for centuries protected the local Maori tribe, known as the Tuhoe or 'children of the mist', and the park has a rich heritage of Maori legend and history. (The area was one of the last rebel strongholds in the Land Wars of the 1860s and 1870s.)

The focal point of the Park is Lake Waikaremoana, with its crystal-clear water. Here you'll find excellent swimming, canoeing, boating and trout fishing. The lake features one of the 'Great Walks', a 46-kilometre, three- to four-day tramp, mostly along the shore edge, but with one climb up the Panekiri Range, which offers panoramic views across this rugged and mysterious land.

You'll find countless native plants here, some of them rare, while the forest type varies from montane beech to mixed broadleaf woodland (along the lake) and dense rainforest. A short 2-hour return walk from the Visitor Centre in Aniwaniwa takes you up to nearby Lake Waikareita at an altitude of 800 metres. The walk from Lake Waikaremoana (580 metres) leads through a range of forest types from podocarp broadleaf to red and silver beech in the higher altitudes.

A LITTLE PARK HISTORY

Urewera was the ancestral home of a Maori people known as the Tuhoe ('children of the mist'). The first European to visit the area was British explorer William Colenso, who arrived in 1841.

At the centre of the park is Lake Waikaremoana, almost completely surrounded by bush, except on the south side, which is dominated by the dramatic Panekiri Bluff. The name is Maori and means 'Sea of the Shining Water'.

You'll notice that the forest is alive with the sound of native birds – a highlight of the Park. They include kaka, kakariki, kereru, New Zealand robins, New Zealand falcons, riflemen, tuis and bellbirds, and at night moreporks and North Island brown kiwis. Te Urewera is also home to the endangered blue wattled kokato – a large population of around 300 birds was discovered in 1991, giving hope that the Urewera is a rare bastion for this native species on the brink of extinction. Grey, mallard and paradise ducks are common along the lake and you'll come across New

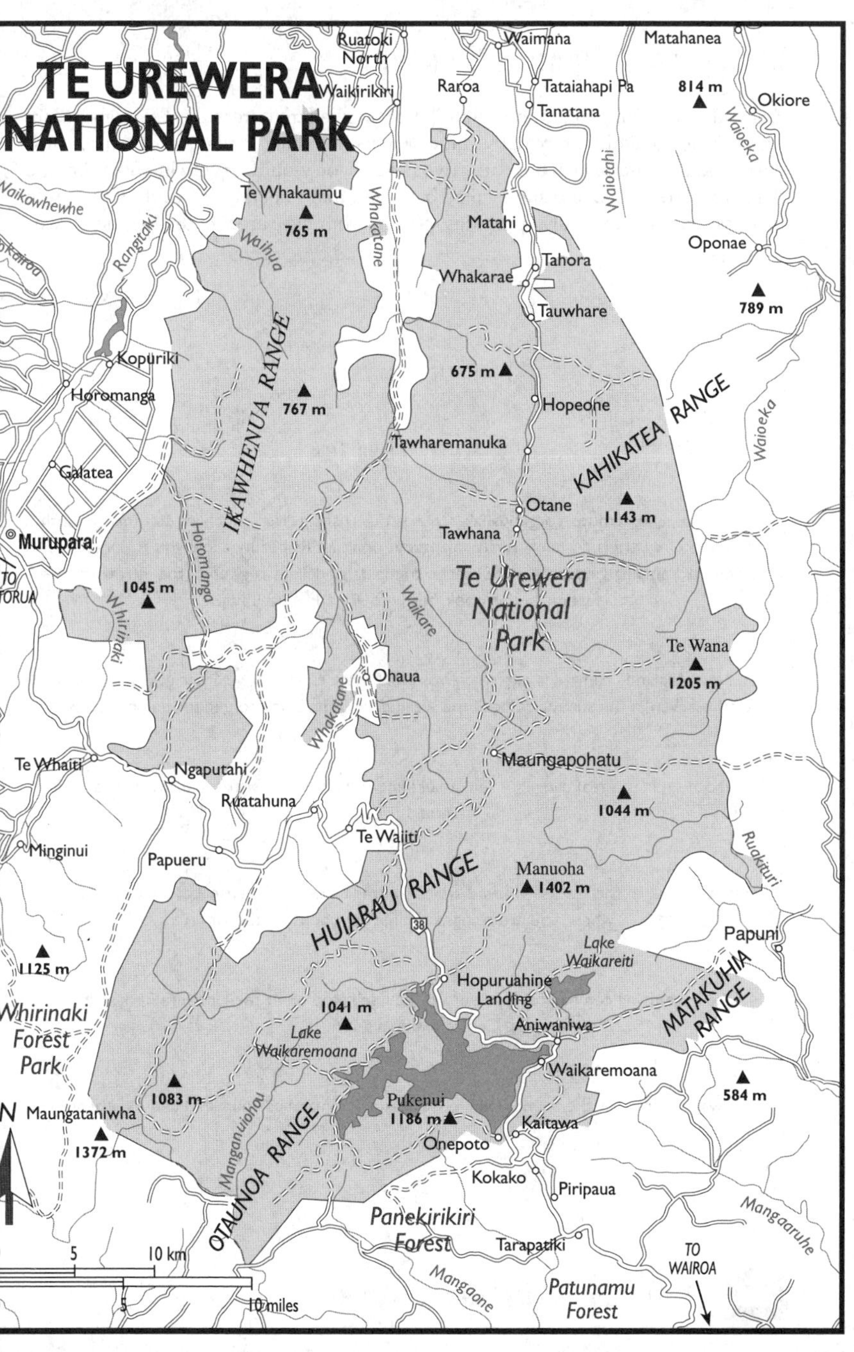
TE UREWERA NATIONAL PARK
Ruatoki North
Waimana
Matahanea
Waikirikiri
Raroa
Tataiahapi Pa
Tanatana
814 m
Okiore
Waioeka
Waiotahi
Te Whakaumu
765 m
Whakatane
Waikowhewhe
Rangitaiki
Waihua
Matahi
Tahora
Whakarae
Oponae
Tauwhare
789 m
IKAWHENUA RANGE
Kopuriki
Horomanga
767 m
675 m
Hopeone
KAHIKATEA RANGE
Tawharemanuka
Galatea
Otane
1143 m
Tawhana
Murupara
TO ROTORUA
Horomanga
1045 m
Whirinaki
Te Urewera National Park
Waikare
Te Wana
1205 m
Ohaua
Whakatane
Te Whaiti
Ngaputahi
Maungapohatu
Ruatahuna
1044 m
Te Waiiti
Minginui
Papueru
Ruakituri
HUIARAU RANGE
Manuoha
1402 m
38
Papuni
1125 m
Lake Waikareiti
Hopuruahine Landing
MATAKUHIA RANGE
Whirinaki Forest Park
1041 m
Lake Waikaremoana
Aniwaniwa
Waikaremoana
1083 m
584 m
Manganuiohou
Pukenui
1186 m
N
Maungataniwha
1372 m
OTAUNOA RANGE
Kaitawa
Onepoto
Kokako
Piripaua
Panekirikiri Forest
Mangaaruhe
Tarapatiki
0
5
10 km
10 miles
TO WAIROA
Mangaone
Patunamu Forest

Zealand scaup, kingfisher and white heron in sheltered areas. Fast-flowing rivers are home to the whio, a rare native blue or whistling duck. Birds aside, there are also deer, possums and pigs in the park. Two rarities you would be very lucky to spot are the native long-tailed and short-tailed bats. And that's not all – in addition to its role in conservation, the park provides power from its three hydroelectric power stations.

A Few Tramping Tips

Very few people, remote, gorgeous lakes, numerous rushing rivers, bubbling streams and lush bush – Te Urewera is certainly breathtaking; but don't let its beauty allow you to forget the standard tramping guidelines. A full set of tramping guidelines is given in the introductory section of this book, but here are a few useful tips.

1. New Zealand's climate is extremely volatile. Always carry wet-weather gear and warm clothes, even in the summer. Check the weather and the track conditions before you go.

2. Hypothermia is a real danger – you should know the warning signals and what to do if it should occur.

3. Always stick to the tracks – New Zealand's bush is extremely dense. Let someone know where you are going, and fill in log books on the way.

4. Take a tramping companion. If you are by yourself stop off at the Urewera Park Visitor's Centre and join a group.

5. Always check that the tramp you are embarking on matches your level and experience.

CRITERION HOTEL

HASTINGS ST., NAPIER.

THIS large and well known Hotel is acknowledged to be one of the best in the North Island, and is patronised by all the principal Tourists and travelling public.

Every attention is paid to Letters and Telegrams engaging Apartments, and the wants of the travelling public are studied down to the most minute detail.

Cook's Hotel Coupons Accepted.

P. GORMAN, Proprietor.

From Thomas Cook's *New Zealand Pocket Pamphlet*, 1890/91

WELLINGTON

The cultural, commercial and political capital of New Zealand, Wellington's reputation as the windy city is well earned. It derives from Wellington's proximity to the Cook Strait, which acts as a wind funnel for the constant westerly breezes. One way to enjoy the phenomenon is from inside a restaurant – you can watch the rain being driven up past the window. Wellington (regional population 429,000) prides itself on being a sophisticated and cosmopolitan city with the best theatre and nightlife around. The modern commercial heart is quite compact, making it easy to get about. But it's the seaward and mountain views that really impress – the drive in from the airport along Oriental Bay is one of the best there is.

Maori legend tells the story that the explorer Kupe first came across Wellington's harbour. When the first Europeans arrived in 1840 the Maoris welcomed them, hoping that they would provide protection against hostile neighbouring tribes.

The city's name commemorates Arthur Wellesley, first Duke of Wellington, the hero of Waterloo and a great supporter of the New Zealand Company scheme.

WELLINGTON TODAY

Wellington is well positioned in an agricultural region, and it is a major seaport, a rail centre, and a commercial and manufacturing hub. The main products of the area, which includes the industrial city of Lower Hutt, are transportation equipment, processed food, clothing, textiles, machinery and printed materials. In addition, tourism and government operations are of prime importance to Wellington's economic base.

Wellington contains a number of New Zealand's finest cultural and educational facilities. Among these are the National Archives, New Zealand's National Library, the Royal Society of New Zealand and the excellent Te Papa Tongarewa, the National Museum of Art, History and Maori Culture.

GETTING THERE

A Wellington Duel

Dr I E Featherston, editor of the *Wellington Independent*, fought a pistol duel with a Colonel Wakefield in Wellington in 1847. The esteemed journalist fired first and missed. Colonel Wakefield then fired into the air – the technical word for this being to delope – avowing that he could not shoot a man with seven daughters.

Air The **Airport** is 5 kilometres or a 15-minute drive from the centre of town. All services use the one terminal. Buses leave approximately every 30 minutes.

Rail The **Railway Station** is on Bunny Street by Waterloo Quay. There are mainline trains to Auckland twice daily. From the station Tranz Metro (www.tranzmetro.co.nz) runs suburban trains to Paraparaumu and also to Masterton via Upper Hutt. Half-hourly shuttle buses leave from platform 9 to the city centre.

Road Wellington lies at the junction of **State Highways 1 & 2**.

Bus **Newmans and InterCity Buses** depart from the station to Tauranga, Napier and Auckland (via New Plymouth or Rotorua).

Ferry Interislander ferries depart from the **Interislander Ferry Terminal** on Aotea Quay, whereas the Lynx fast ferry departs from **The Lynx Terminal** at Waterloo Quay. A free courtesy bus takes visitors to and from town, departing from Platform 9 at the railway station. The Super Shuttle (tel: 0800 748 885) and Co-operative Shuttles (tel: 04 387 8787) also operate a connecting service to both the ferries and airport.

GETTING AROUND

The bus service in Wellington is fast and efficient. The main pick-up point is Courtney Place. Tickets for buses and trolley buses can be purchased from the driver as you board. For serious exploring get a Daytripper Pass from the Visitor Centre.

The quickest way to get oriented is by conducted bus tour. **Wally Hammond** tours leave daily from the Information Centre in Wakefield St at 1000 and 1400, or you can be picked up at your hotel by arrangement; tel: 04 472 0869.

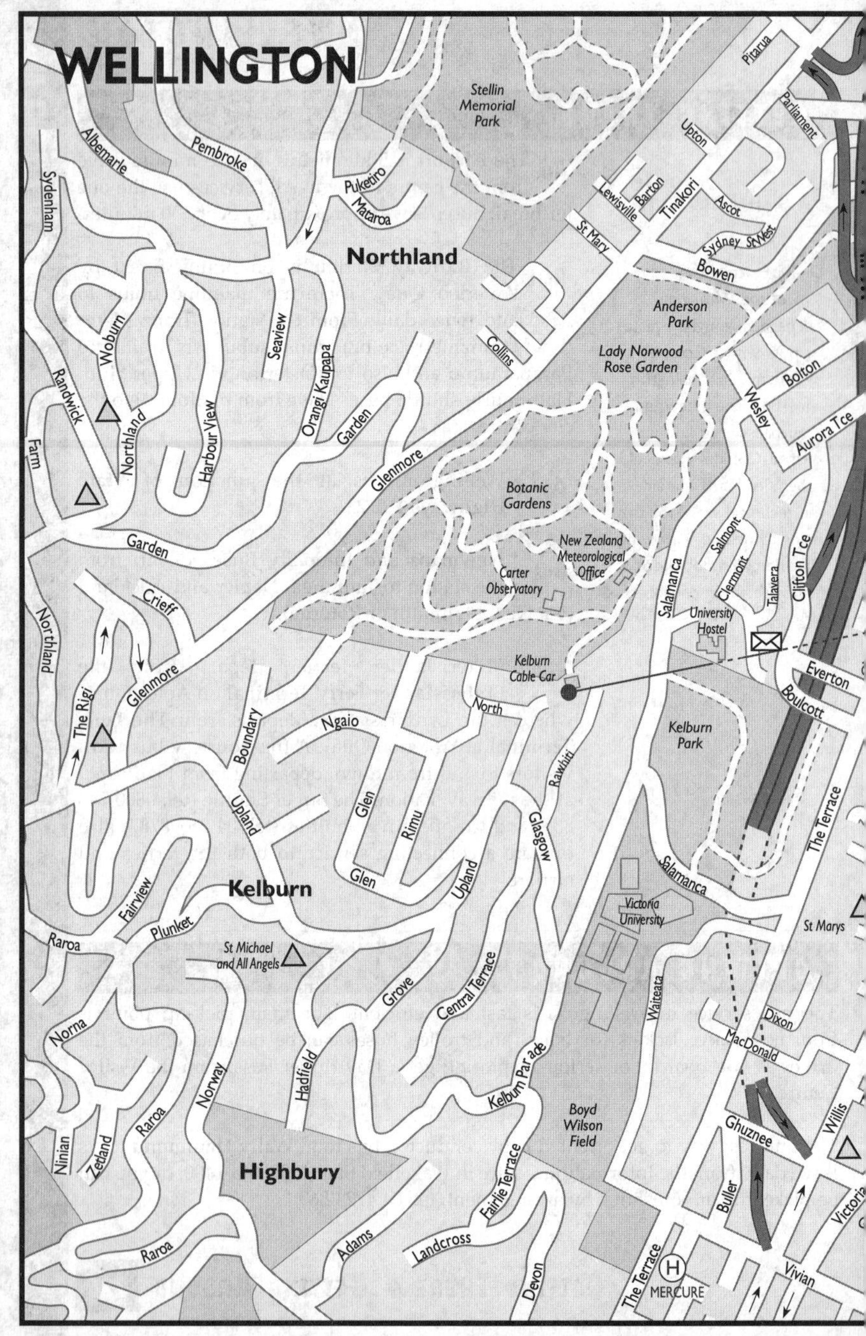
WELLINGTON
Stellin Memorial Park
Northland
Kelburn
Highbury
Anderson Park
Lady Norwood Rose Garden
Botanic Gardens
New Zealand Meteorological Office
Carter Observatory
University Hostel
Kelburn Cable Car
Kelburn Park
Victoria University
St Michael and All Angels
Boyd Wilson Field
MERCURE
St Marys
Albemarle
Pembroke
Sydenham
Puketiro
Mataroa
Pitarua
Parliament
Upton
Lewisville
Barton
Tinakori
Ascot
St Mary
Sydney St West
Bowen
Woburn
Seaview
Orangi Kaupapa
Collins
Randwick
Northland
Harbour View
Garden
Farm
Glenmore
Wesley
Bolton
Aurora Tce
Crieff
Salmont
Clermont
Talavera
Clifton Tce
Salamanca
Everton
Boulcott
The Rigi
Boundary
Ngaio
North
Rawhiti
Upland
Glen
Rimu
Glasgow
The Terrace
Fairview
Raroa
Plunket
Grove
Central Terrace
Waiteata
Dixon
MacDonald
Norna
Hadfield
Norway
Kelburn Parade
Willis
Ghuznee
Ninian
Zetland
Fairlie Terrace
Buller
Victoria
Adams
Landcross
Devon
Vivian

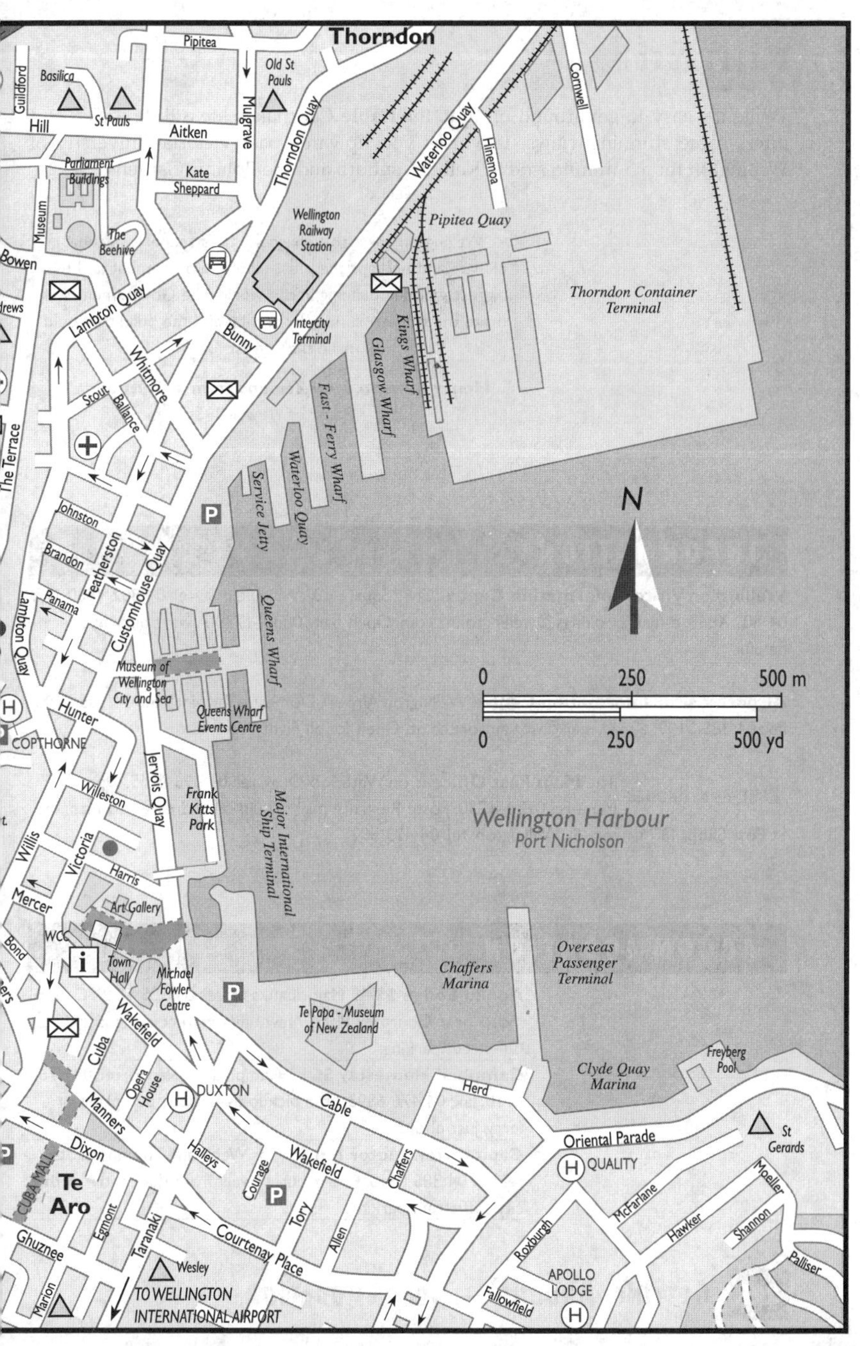
Thorndon
Pipitea
Old St Pauls
Guildford
Basilica
St Pauls
Hill
Aitken
Mulgrave
Thorndon Quay
Waterloo Quay
Cornwell
Hinemoa
Parliament Buildings
Kate Sheppard
Museum
The Beehive
Wellington Railway Station
Pipitea Quay
Bowen
Lambton Quay
Bunny
Intercity Terminal
Thorndon Container Terminal
Whitmore
Kings Wharf
Glasgow Wharf
Fast - Ferry Wharf
Stout
Ballance
Waterloo Quay
Service Jetty
The Terrace
Johnston
Brandon
Featherston
Customhouse Quay
Panama
Lambton Quay
N
Queens Wharf
Museum of Wellington City and Sea
Queens Wharf Events Centre
0
250
500 m
0
250
500 yd
Hunter
COPTHORNE
Willeston
Jervois Quay
Frank Kitts Park
Major International Ship Terminal
Wellington Harbour
Port Nicholson
Willis
Victoria
Harris
Mercer
Art Gallery
Bond
WCC
Town Hall
Michael Fowler Centre
Chaffers Marina
Overseas Passenger Terminal
Te Papa - Museum of New Zealand
Wakefield
Cuba
Opera House
Freyberg Pool
Clyde Quay Marina
Herd
DUXTON
Manners
Cable
Dixon
Oriental Parade
St Gerards
Halleys
Wakefield
Chaffers
QUALITY
CUBA MALL
Te Aro
Courage
Moeller
McFarlane
Egmont
Taranaki
Tory
Courtenay Place
Allen
Roxburgh
Hawker
Shannon
Ghuznee
Wesley
Palliser
APOLLO LODGE
Marion
TO WELLINGTON INTERNATIONAL AIRPORT
Fallowfield

Wellington

While it's easy to get around on foot, the **Cable Car** makes life a little easier, and offers some stunning views. It whisks you upwards past Victoria University of Wellington for a 5-minute ride to Kelburn suburb and the Botanic Gardens.

> 'Wellington has a good harbour, bold scenery, splendid climate and perhaps the most Liberal Government and the biggest wooden building in the world. The Government will make the biggest blunder by-and-by, and the building would make the biggest fire.'
>
> **Henry Lawson, *New Zealand from an Australian's Point of View*, 1893**

INFORMATION

Wellington Visitor Information Centre Civic Square 101 Wakefield St; tel: 04 802 4860, fax: 04 802 4863; e-mail: bookings@wellingtonnz.com. Open daily 0830–1730. Always busy but very helpful.

Airport Visitor Information Centre Wellington Airport Domestic Terminal; tel: 04 385 5100, fax: 04 385 5139; e-mail: mail@wtg-airport.co.nz. Open for all flight information.

Post and Phones The **Main Post Office** is on Waterloo Quay, tel: 04 496 4065. Open Mon–Fri 0730–1730. Poste Restante mail should be addressed to Manners St Post Shop, 43 Manners St, Wellington; tel: 04 473 5922.

ACCOMMODATION

Apollo Lodge $$ 49 Majoribanks St; tel: 04 385 1849. Central motel near Courtney Place. New units with cooking facilities. Off-street parking.

Campbell Homestay $$ 83 Campbell St, Karori; tel: 04 476 6110, fax: 04 476 6593. Free pickup from train, bus, plane or ferry. Just phone.

Capital View Motor Inn $$ Cnr Webb and Thompson Sts; tel/fax: 04 385 0515. Five minutes' walk from the centre of the city. Off-street parking.

Downtown Backpackers $ 1 Bunny St; tel: 04 473 8482, fax: 04 473 5363.

Halswell Lodge $$ 21 Kent Terrace; tel: 04 385 0196, fax: 04 385 0503. Central hotel with fully equipped rooms and motel units.

Harbour City Motor Inn $$ Cnr Victoria and Webb St; tel: 04 384 9809, fax: 04 384 9806. Easy access to ferry, airport and motorway. Well-equipped units with spa and undercover parking.

Harbour View Homestay $$ 125 Te Anau Rd, Roseneath; tel: 04 386 1043 or 0800 080 078. On the bus no. 14 route. Free pickup. Expansive views of harbour.

Hotel Ibis $$$ 153 Featherston St; tel: 04 496 1880 or 0800 700 0700, fax: 04 496 1881; e-mail: reservation@ibiswlg.co.nz. New hotel in the heart of Wellington.

Lodge in the City $ 152 Taranaki St; tel: 04 385 8560.

Rowenas City Lodge $ 115 Brougham St, Mt Victoria; tel: 04 385 7872.

Settlers Motor Lodge $$ 83–85 Hutt Rd, Petone; tel: 04 939 4088 or 0800 838 583, fax: 04 939 3168. New motel, close to the Interislander ferry terminal. Restaurant and bar.

Shepherd's Arms $$–$$$ 285 Tinakori Rd, Thordon; tel: 04 472 1320 or 0800 393 782, fax: 04 472 0523. A good-value 1870s hotel in the historic district, which has been tastefully renovated. Restaurant and bar.

Trekkers Hotel/Motel $ 213 Cuba St; tel: 04 385 2153, fax: 04 382 8873. Situated very near the centre of the city, with car parking, a café, travel service and clean if shabby rooms – all at a very low price. Excellent value.

Tinakori Lodge $$ 182 Tinakori Rd; tel: 04 939 3478, fax: 04 939 3475. A Victorian villa with large rooms and a solarium. Serves delicious breakfasts.

Wellington City YHA $ 292 Wakefield St; tel: 04 801 7280, fax: 04 801 7278.

FOOD AND DRINK

It's said that Wellington has more eateries per head of population than New York City. Naturally, New Zealand cuisine is well provided for, but ethnic and vegetarian restaurants also flourish and there's a growing brunch culture at weekends. Head for Queens Wharf and Courtney Place in the evenings.

Angkor Cambodian Restaurant $$ 43 Dixon St; tel: 04 384 9423. Open for lunch Mon–Fri 1200–1430; dinner Mon–Sat 1800 onwards. One of the few Cambodian restaurants in the southern hemisphere; the cuisine is a cross between Thai and Korean. Licensed.

Caffe L'Affare $ 27 College St; tel: 04 385 9748. Great for coffee, great for brunch. All-day breakfast menu. Licensed.

Dockside $$ Shed 3, Queen's Wharf; tel: 04 499 9900. A converted warehouse with big glass windows overlooking the harbour. The seafood dishes are especially recommended. Licensed.

The Garden Lunch Bar $ 1F Cable Car Shopping Centre; tel: 04 473 4334. Café-style cuisine, salads and sushi. Open Mon–Fri 0730–1530.

Hummingbird $$ 22 Courtenay Place; tel: 04 801 6336. Popular restaurant (bookings essential in the evening). Brunch Sat and Sun.

Imbibe Antipasto $$ 3 Swan Lane; tel: 04 385 7060. Great range of antipasto and a good selection of wines. Brunch served on Sun. Open Mon–Sat 1630 until late.

Midnight Expresso $ 178 Cuba St. More varieties of coffee than you can imagine, also cheap snacks. Mon–Sun 0800–1500.

Net Arena, Cyber Café $ 175 Cuba St; tel: 04 384 1185. One of the many Internet cafés in Wellington where you can check your e-mail while drinking a fair café latte. Open daily 1000–2000.

One Red Dog $$ 9–11 Blair St; tel: 04 384 9777. This restaurant and bar serves gourmet pizza and award-winning beers. Open daily.

Satay Malaysia $ 18–24 Allen St; tel: 04 385 7709. Staggering portions at a very reasonable price and the cuisine is genuinely Malaysian. BYO. Open daily 1730–late; lunch Wed–Fri 1200–1430.

Shed 5 $$$ 5 Queens Wharf; tel: 04 499 9069. Massive woolshed converted into a quality restaurant, café and bar. Seafood is a speciality. Licensed.

The Skyline $$$ 1 Upland Rd, Kelburn; tel: 04 475 8727. Designed by Ian Athfield, the New Zealand architect de jour whose work always arouses strong feelings, this glass-fronted restaurant with amazing views is near the Botanic Gardens. Imaginative menu with excellent seafood and vegetarian selection. There is also a café for less formal eating.

HIGHLIGHTS

Enjoying a superb waterfront site is **Te Papa Tongarewa**, opened in 1998 as the National Museum of Art, History and Maori Culture. It was designed by a team of Auckland architects. Te Papa – 'our place' in Maori – is a state-of-the-art museum, making full use of multimedia displays. The top floor is devoted to the Maori people and the exhibits include a meeting house, a war canoe and a marae where traditional tribal ceremonies are performed. The museum also includes sections on New Zealand's abundant natural resources and wildlife, including models of the huge moa bird (now extinct) and a blue whale.

There are interactive features too: there is an earthquake simulator and you can also enjoy virtual-reality bungy jumping and whale diving. The art collection includes works from New Zealand, Australia and Europe, with Rembrandt engravings and British watercolours from the 18th–19th centuries. Guided tours are available and there's fine dining at the Icon Restaurant. Tel: 04 381 7000; www.tepapa.govt.nz. Open daily 1000–1800 (late night Thursday).

The **Museum of Wellington City and Sea** on Queen's Wharf, Jervois Quay, occupies two storeys of the beautifully restored old Harbour Board building, dating from 1891. New Zealand's maritime history is traced through ship models, paintings, photographs, videos, figureheads and other artefacts. There's an intriguing section on disasters, featuring the *Titanic*, as well as the sinking of the inter-island ferry TS *Wahine*, which foundered in Wellington harbour in April 1968 with the loss of 51 lives. (In both cases, a shortage of lifeboats was a factor in the death toll.) Open daily 0930–1730 (longer in summer); tel: 04 472 8904.

A **cable car** runs from Cable Car Lane just off Lambton Quay (tel: 04 472 2199) approximately every 10 minutes Mon–Fri 0700–2200, Sat, Sun 0900–2200. The climb is 120 metres, covering a distance of 610 metres

THE COLONIAL COTTAGE MUSEUM

The Colonial Cottage Museum at 68 Nairn St, is one of the oldest buildings in New Zealand, dating back to 1858. The furnishings are in the style of the period and evoke the life for the early settlers who tried to recreate Victorian Britain in their adopted country. Tel: 04 384 9122; open daily 1200–1600; May–Dec only Wed–Sun.

WELLINGTON ARTS FESTIVAL

The most successful cultural event in the country. Features top local and international acts. Takes place biennially, next in March 2004. www.nzfestival.telecom.co.nz.

with an average gradient of 1:5. The service has been in operation for nearly 100 years and was originally steam-driven. At the summit you'll find a café and the small **Cable Car Museum**; tel: 04 471 0919; open Mon–Fri 0930–1730, Sat, Sun 1000–1630.

The **Botanic Gardens** are quickly reached from the upper terminus of the cable car. Don't miss the Lady Norwood Rose Gardens at the city end with more than 300 varieties arranged in formal beds or the nearby Begonia House. You can enjoy a coffee here as well as a wide selection of natural and organic food.

The **Cricket Museum**, Sussex St, is in Wellington's main cricket ground, Basin Reserve on Kent Terrace. If New Zealanders are not sailing or worshipping at the altar of the great god rugby, they are following the other national sport. Cricket has been played here since the first settlers arrived and the museum is replete with international cricketing memorabilia. The prize exhibit is a bat dating from 1743 – one of the oldest in existence. Open Nov–Mar 1030–1530; the rest of the year Sat–Sun only. On match days the museum is open while the game is in progress.

The **Carter Observatory**, at 40 Salamanca Rd, is a short stroll from the upper cable car terminus. New Zealand is said to be the best place on earth to view the heavens because of the clear visibility and lack of air pollution. (Tel: 04 472 8167; open daily 1000–1700.) Nearby is the **Thomas King Observatory**, which dates back from the beginning of the century and has recently been restored to its former glory with the original polished brass fixtures and fittings. There are continuous shows in the planetarium from 1015 to 1615, with night-sky viewing on Tuesday and Saturday (tel: 04 472 8167).

Old **St Paul's Cathedral**, on the corner of Mulgrave and Pipitea Streets, is a fine example of a 19th-century Gothic-style church adapted from traditional stone to timber. Since 1964, when St Paul's was saved from demolition thanks to government intervention, the former cathedral has been used for music recitals and

THE SWISS CABLE CAR

The Kelburn cable car was originally built in 1902 but nowadays it operates with modern, Swiss-built cars so is very safe. It provides fabulous views of Wellington.

BACK TO NATURE

Apart from old favourites such as lions, giraffes and chimps, the **Wellington Zoo** (tel: 04 381 6750) also offers a few home-grown oddities, including the kiwi, tuatara and giant weta. The zoo is near Newtown Park; catch the number 10 or 23 bus from downtown.

At the **Karori Wildlife Centre** you will be able to get a closer look at the native birdlife. Only a 10-minute drive from the city, it's situated in a lovely 250-hectare bush-clad valley. The exact location is 31 Waiapu Road, Karori; tel: 04 920 9200.

WATCH THE SKY

Steps lead from the downtown area to high-level terraces on the slopes of Mount Victoria (196 metres). The Maoris call this local lookout Matairangi or 'watch the sky'.

concerts as well as for weddings and funerals. Tel: 04 473 6722; open daily 1000–1700 (Oct–Mar); closed Sun (Mar–Oct).

The new St Paul's Cathedral is opposite the National Library.

The parliament buildings are an eclectic mix of architectural styles. **The General Assembly Library** (1897) is considered a Gothic masterpiece, while the Legislative Chambers (1922) are Renaissance revival. The modern Beehive, designed by Sir Basil Spence, architect of Coventry Cathedral in England, houses ministerial offices. It was completed in 1982 and is already showing serious signs of wear and tear. The Old Government Building, on the corner of Lambton Quay and Whitmore St, looks at first glance as if it was built of fine cream stone; in fact, it is the second-largest wooden building in the world. Designed by William Clayton in 1876 and framed in native rimu and Tasmanian blackwood, it is now part of the Law School of the Victoria University of Wellington.

Katherine Mansfield's birthplace at 25 Tinakori Rd, in Wellington's oldest suburb, Thorndon, is open to the public. The house was built by the famous author's father in the year of her birth, 1888. Mansfield left New Zealand for Europe at the age of 19, but many of her best-known short stories were written with this house as a backdrop – *A Birthday* or *The Aloe*, for example. Both the house and the Victorian garden have been beautifully restored and the exhibition includes numerous mementoes of the author as well as displays relating incidents from her life that she incorporated in her writing. Open daily 1000–1600.

Opposite the parliament buildings is the Backbencher Pub, where MPs gather between (or during) sittings. The building dates from 1893 and there's a lively interior with satirical cartoons and puppets of well-known MPs.

EARTHQUAKE STATISTICS

Eight years after the first European settlement was established, the town was seriously damaged by earth tremors. Following the major earthquake of 1855, which claimed 12 lives, there were further shocks in 1868, 1890, 1897, 1904, 1913, 1914 and 1942.

Like many towns in New Zealand, Wellington is built on a geological fault line. In 1855 an earthquake measuring 7.9 on the Richter Scale not only caused wholesale destruction in the city but also raised the shoreline over 60 centimetres.

Since then many of Wellington's buildings have been earthquake-proofed with 'seismic gaps' in the foundations to allow movement of 30 centimetres. In 1997 a wave of small tremors shook the city. Hopefully these subterranean rumblings were not a sign of worse things to come.

Wellington

Wellington Harbour Wellington has a superb harbour with ideal sailing conditions. Of the literally dozens of sailing tours on offer, the best, and consequently the most heavily booked, is the ***Phantom of the Straits*** – former winner of the Whitbread Round the World cup, (tel: 04 477 3503).

Some of the cruises allow you to picnic on Somes Island, a former quarantine station which is now managed by the Department of Conservation as a breeding ground for lizards, black-backed gulls and blue penguins. Another popular spot for a day trip is the beach at Days Bay. The **Evening Post Ferry** (tel: 04 499 1272) is a catamaran which leaves from Shed 5 on Queens Wharf to Days Bay, stopping at Somes Island. Departures Mon–Fri 0630–1830, Sat–Sun 1015–1700 (25-minute journey). **Dolphin Sailing Academy** (tel: 04 586 0699; www.dolphinsailing.co.nz) offers lunch and dinner cruises, as well as 3-hour harbour cruises. If you have any special wishes, they're usually quite accommodating.

The Discovery of the Harbour

Wellington's fine deep-water harbour was discovered by a Captain Herd in 1826. However, it wasn't until 1839 that Colonel William Wakefield's advance party arrived on the *Tory*, landing on the beach at Petone. The first New Zealand Company immigrants arrived four months later in January 1840.

Sport With the harbour on the doorstep, windsurfing and sea kayaking can be enjoyed right in the heart of the city. **Fergs Rock 'n' Kayaks** (tel: 04 499 8898) offers freedom or guided paddles or even a night time trip. Find them in Shed 6 on Queens Wharf, where you'll also discover a rock climbing wall; or hire inline skates for a brisk whizz along the harbour front. Windsurfers can hire gear from **Boardriders** at 53 Willis St; tel: 04 499 3655.

Red Rocks Coastal Walk

The walk starts 7 kilometres south of the city in a car park at the western end of **Ohiro Bay Parade** and follows the the coastline from Ohiro Bay to **Sinclair Head** – it's 4 kilometres there and back, so it can easily be managed in a couple of hours. The Red Rocks are made from solidified volcanic lava stained by iron oxide and are about 200 million years old. In the distance, is the snow-capped **Kaikoura Mountain Range** – simply stunning. If you're here between May and October you'll also see a colony of fur seals, the occasional dolphin and, during migration periods, possibly even a whale. Don't go too close to the seals and never get between them and the sea.

SOUTHERN WALKWAY This 11-kilometre trail around the southern reaches of the harbour takes four to five hours, but can be broken into shorter stretches. Leave from the side of Hotel Raffaele in Oriental Bay, then follow the orange arrows to Shortland Park in Island Bay. The walk offers views of the harbour and the city centre from Mounts Victoria (196 metres) and Albert (178 metres). Much of the route is shaded by the pine trees of the Town Belt Forest.

NORTHERN WALKWAY There's a similar 16-kilometre trail along the northern shore of the harbour. Again orange arrows point the way from the Botanic Garden by the cable car terminus to Johnsonville Park. The route passes through the shady Trelissick and Khandalla Parks, while from Mount Kaukau (430 metres) there are superb views over the harbour towards the Tararua Range.

THE COAST ROAD

The coast road out of Wellington continues past marinas and waterfront properties to a more exposed area of volcanic rock, with the warning that penguins may be crossing. Many local residents have penguin nests under their houses – the penguins then cease to be cute birds to be admired and become smelly pests with disgusting habits.

NIGHTLIFE

Wellington's nightlife is first rate. The bars, cafés, restaurants and clubs of Courtenay Place are as good a starting point as any.

Bar Bodega Ghuznee St. Wellington's most famous night spot has, in its time, featured most of the great New Zealand bands.

Chicago Queens Wharf; tel: 04 473 4900. Huge bar and live bands Fri and Sat nights. Giant screen to view sports events.

Hole in the Wall 154 Vivian St. Bar and nightclub where you can hear all types of music from jazz to techno. Also pool and pinball tables. Open until 0300.

Tatou Ground Floor 22, Cambridge Terrace. Two bars and popular nightspot with techno music. Open until 0600.

MUSIC

The New Zealand Symphony Orchestra, the Wellington Sinfonia, the Wellington Opera Company and the Royal Ballet Company all perform in the city, so there is usually something happening every night of the week. Check with the Visitor Centre for details.

Michael Fowler Centre, Town Hall 111 Wakefield St; tel: 04 384 3840 (ticket reservations). Orchestral and other performances.

State Opera House 111–113 Manners St; tel: 04 801 8209. Opera, ballet and musicals.

Westpac Trust St James Theatre 77–87 Courtenay Place; tel: 04 802 4060; www.stjames.co.nz. Stages opera, ballet and major musicals. Also houses the main Ticketek box office.

Some major concerts are held in the **Queens Wharf Events Centre** (tel: 04 470 0190).

LISTINGS

The free newspapers *City Voice* and *Capital Times* are available throughout the city. The daily newspapers *The Dominion* and the *Evening Post* carry listings. You can get hold of the free magazine *Wellington – What's On* from the Visitors Centre, hotels and motels.

The main events are:

Late February – Dragon Boat festival in the inner harbour

March – Biennially (on even numbered years) International Festival of the Arts; Annual Fringe Festival

July – Film Festival

'I would not, for a great deal, say anything that could even seem derogatory of Wellington. It is a place worthy of the utmost love and admiration of its citizens. In its surroundings it is peculiarly happy. They are romantic, picturesque in the extreme, which qualities, in days not so far distant, constituted a serious drawback to the city's expansion.'

F T Bullen, *Advance Australasia*, 1907

THEATRE

Wellington has an active live theatre scene, with a number of excellent professional and amateur companies - consult *What's On* for listings information.

Bats 1 Kent Terrace; tel: 04 802 4175, stages modern works and alternative theatre.

Circa cnr Taranki and Cable Sts; tel: 04 801 7992, is an excellent repertory theatre with a national reputation.

The Downstage cnr Courtenay Pl and Cambridge Terr; tel: 04 801 6946. Touring shows and in-house productions.

> While it is quite true that occasionally the city experiences three days' steady rain without a break, it is false to say that dirty or windy weather is anything like normal – in fact it would be truer to say that such climatic conditions are abnormal... Indeed, taken altogether, Wellington, apart from the delightful character of its citizens, is one of the most desirable places to live in the whole world, in my opinion.
>
> **F T Bullen, *Advance Australasia*, 1907**

CINEMAS

Embassy 10 Kent Terrace; tel: 04 384 7657. Newly restored art deco cinema screening general releases.

Hoyts Manners Mall; tel: 04 472 5182. Five-screen cinema showing mainstream movies.

Paramount 25 Courtenay Pl; tel: 04 384 4080.

Rialto cnr Cable St and Jervois Quay; tel: 04 385 1864. Art and avant-garde films as well as New Zealand archive film.

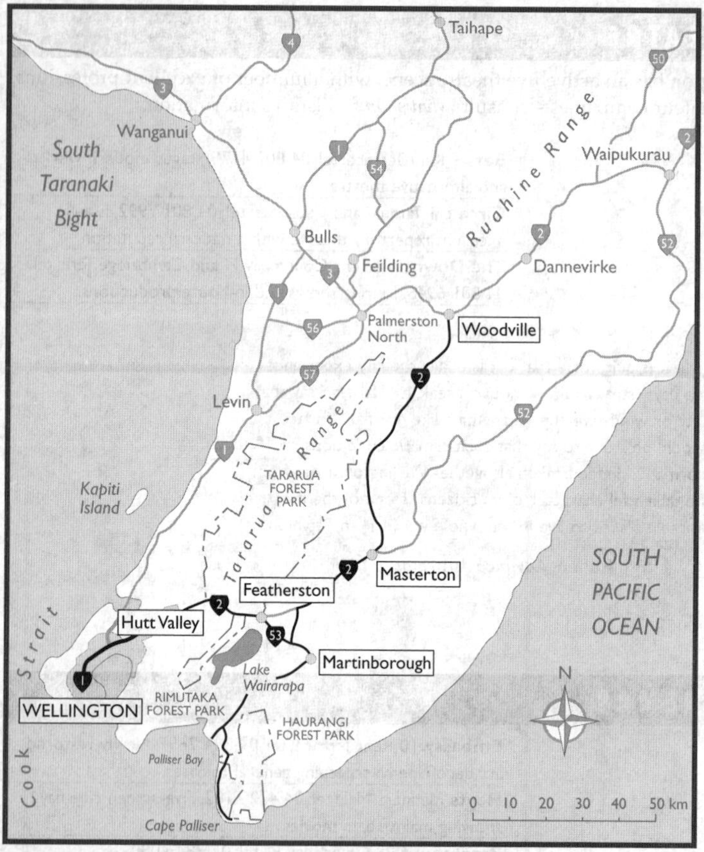

WELLINGTON – FEATHERSTON
OTT TABLE 9751

TRANSPORT	FREQUENCY	JOURNEY TIME
Train	4 daily Mon–Fri, 2 Sat–Sun	54mins

FEATHERSTON – WOODVILLE
OTT TABLE 9766

TRANSPORT	FREQUENCY	JOURNEY TIME
Bus	1 daily Mon–Fri	2hrs 50mins

WELLINGTON – MASTERTON
OTT TABLE 9751

TRANSPORT	FREQUENCY	JOURNEY TIME
Train	4 daily Mon–Fri, 2 Sat–Sun	1hr 28mins

FEATHERSTON – MASTERTON
OTT TABLES 9766/9751

TRANSPORT	FREQUENCY	JOURNEY TIME
Bus	1 daily, Mon–Fri	50mins
Train	4 daily Mon–Fri, 2 Sat–Sun	34mins

MASTERTON – WOODVILLE
OTT TABLE 9766

TRANSPORT	FREQUENCY	JOURNEY TIME
Bus	Daily	1hr 20mins

Note: Bus services from Wellington to Woodville go via Palmerston North.

Given its proximity to Wellington, the Wairarapa is surprisingly unfamiliar to tourists. Even for the locals until recent times, it only really came alive once a year, in March, when the Golden Shears Competition – the Olympics of sheep shearing – was held in Masterton. All that has now changed with the emergence of the Martinborough vineyards and the explosion in the popularity of its wines. Today the Wairarapa markets itself as a year-round visitor destination, reaching out not only to wine buffs but to tramping enthusiasts, sun worshippers and watersports fanatics with facilities that are improving almost by the month.

By Train to Masterton

Tranz Metro (www.tranzmetro.co.nz) runs suburban trains from Wellington Railway Station to Masterton via Upper Hutt.

Route Detail

From Wellington, take State Highway 2 along the Lower and Upper Hutt Valley, crossing the tail end of the Tararua Range to Mount Bruce and Featherston. From here take State Highway 53 to Martinborough. 70 km

From Martinborough one of the most popular excursions is to Palliser Bay. Follow the signs from Martinborough Square. The road runs along Lake Wairarapa to Lake Ferry before turning towards the coast and Cape Palliser.
Excursion (round trip) 70 km

An alternative route to the coast is via Haunui Wind Farm. Turn left at Tuturumuri to reach the coast at Tora.

To explore the area north of Martinborough, take State Highway 53, then the turn-off to Greytown. Here rejoin State Highway 2, continuing eastwards through Carterton, then crossing the Waingawa River into Masterton. Leaving Masterton, State Highway 2 crosses the railway at Opaki before running parallel to the Tararua Range through Mount Bruce, Eketahuna and Pahiatua to Woodville.
Wellington – Woodville 175 km

THE HUTT VALLEY

The Hutt valley runs north-west from Wellington as far as the Tararua and Rimutaka Ranges and is vital to the economic wellbeing of the city. At its heart is the Hutt River. A market gardening and farming area, Hutt also has a little industry mixed in. The total population (including the three towns of Lower and Upper Hutt and Petone) is around 150,000. To the Maoris, Hutt was a corruption of a phrase meaning 'breath of the south wind'. Sir William Hutt was a British Member of Parliament and chairman of the New Zealand Company who ironically (but all too typically) never set foot in the country.

THE MAORI NAME

Hutt is expressed much more poetically by the Maoris with its full name: Heretaunga.

THE LORD OF THE RINGS

'New Zealand, Home of Middle Earth', states the official website (www.purenz.com) of the NZ Tourist Board in a matter-of-fact manner. Before the screening of the first part of *The Lord of the Rings* trilogy in December 2001, many would have thought 'Home of Sheep' or 'Home of Businessmen Who Dress in Shorts' much more appropriate. And considering that J R R Tolkien never visited New Zealand, not a few might have found the claim presumptuous. But that was before Kiwi director Peter Jackson brought *The Fellowship of the Ring* to the cinemas, where it promptly broke-box office records both at home and overseas.

Now, it is quite obvious that New Zealand *is* Middle Earth. If Tolkien never went to New Zealand, he certainly imagined landscapes that look like New Zealand. Even Frodo (actor Elijah Wood) agrees: 'It has every geological formation and geographical landscape you can imagine . . . and some you can't'. All three films of the trilogy were shot in just 274 days at over 150 locations throughout the country. The rolling hill country near Matamata, south-east of Tauranga, became the setting for Hobbiton; the volcanic landscape of Tongariro National Park was an ideal backdrop for Mordor; and Queenstown's Lake Wakatipu was used as a location for Lothlorien. Many of these scenes were then digitally manipulated by the special-effects company Weta, based in Wellington. Scenes shot close to the capital include Helms Deep, which was filmed in a quarry near Lower Hutt.

The last film in the trilogy is due out towards the end of 2003. In view of the first two films' enormous success, the NZ government is hoping for a tourist boom. Around NZ$4.5 million has been tagged for promotions linking the film with the country. The NZ Energy Minister, Pete Hodgson, a man with a suspiciously Gandalf-like beard, has been designated to coordinate these efforts, thus earning himself the nickname 'Minister of the Lord of the Rings'.

For more information on the films, visit the following websites: www.lordoftherings.net or www.jasons.co.nz/destinationlordoftherings.

MARTINBOROUGH

The layout of Martinborough is unique. It dates from the 1870s when the founder of the town, Sir John Martin, conceived a grid pattern with a difference. Its streets radiate from a central point to represent the bars on the Union Jack! Sir John then went on to name the streets after places he had visited on his world tour. The result is curiously exotic: where else in a community of less than 2000 will you find the great cities of the world, including Venice, Dublin or New York, commemorated in this way?

To find out more about Sir John's quirks, visit the **Colonial Museum** on The Square. Open weekends and during the school holidays 1400–1600; to arrange a visit at another time, call 06 306 9796.

Martinborough is best known for its excellent wines - Sauvignon Blanc, Pinot Noir and Cabernet Sauvignon varieties are all grown locally.

i **Martinborough Information Centre** 18 Kitchener St; tel: 06 306 9043.

Claremont Motels $$ 36 Regent St; tel/fax: 06 306 9162 or 0800 809 162; www.claremont-motels.co.nz; e-mail: claremont@wise.net.nz. Massive garden with views across the countryside. Fifteen minutes from the centre of town.
Martinborough Motel $$ 43 Strasbourg St; tel: 06 306 9408, fax: 06 306 8408. Close to the centre and minutes from the vineyards and an 18-hole golf course.

Martinborough Bistro $$$ The Square; tel: 06 306 9350. Popular restaurant in the Martinborough Hotel, serving beautifully presented Pacific Rim Cuisine. Booking advised.
The Old Winery Café $$ Margrain Vineyard, Huangarua Rd; tel: 06 306 8333. Set in the heart of a vineyard, the restaurant provides modern New Zealand cuisine, accompanied by the vineyard's own award-winning wines.
The Post & Vine $$ Puruatanga Rd; tel: 06 306 8552. Open during summer 1100–1700 at weekends. Home cooking and, of course, home-grown wine.
Pukemanu Tavern and Steak House $ The Square; tel: 06 306 9606. Open Mon–Sat 1000 till late, Sun 1100.

NEW ZEALAND'S FIRST COMMERCIAL WIND FARM

The seven turbine engines of New Zealand's first commercial wind farm are clearly visible ranged along a 540-metre ridge on the road to White Rock, 21 kilometres south-east of Martinborough (follow the signs from the Lake Ferry Road). The Haunui Wind Farm is closed to the public but there is a viewing area 400 metres before you reach the site. Drive on for 11 kilometres to Tuturumuri, turning left to Tora, where the rugged, windswept coastal scenery makes this a lovely place for walking and picnicking.

MASTERTON

The first European explorers arrived here around 1841, establishing smallholdings along the coastline. They made a living from sheep farming and were left alone until the New Zealand Company became interested in selling the land the settlers had occupied illegally. The farmers offered to buy the land from the Company but its executives were not interested in small-scale transactions.

At this point the farmers' spokesman, Joseph Masters, formed the Small Farms Association to pressurise the Company into making land available at a price affordable to the poorer migrants. The association went on to petition the Governor, who was sympathetic to their plight and who helped carry the day. Two sites were chosen for settlement; one was called Masterton to commemorate Joseph Masters, the other, Greytown, in honour of the Governor.

The two communities vied for pre-eminence until the arrival of the railway decided the issue by bypassing Greytown. Masterton currently has a population of around 20,000. At one time the Canterbury Christian Society expressed an interest in establishing a church settlement in the Wairapapa Valley, but eventually chose a site on the South Island instead – today's city of Christchurch.

EN ROUTE TO PALLISER BAY

This attractive stretch of coast is a 72-kilometre drive from Martinborough by way of the stunning rock formations known as the Putangirua Pinnacles. In the bay itself you may be lucky enough to see New Zealand fur seals at close range and you can also climb the steps of the Cape Palliser Lighthouse.

The international **Golden Shears** competition, for which Masterton is best known, is the most important event of its kind. It's a good opportunity to appreciate the skills and physical strength of the 'gun shearers', who are able to strip a sheep without a cut or a ridge in under a minute.

In the town itself, **No. 30 Victoria St** is a splendid example of wooden domestic architecture in the colonial style of the late 1870s.

Hood Aerodrome, just to the south of Masterton, has a vintage aviation museum usually open on Sundays (call to check, tel: 06 377 3466).

Children will love the **Queen Elizabeth Park** on Dixon St, with its shady gardens, small deer farm and boats to rent. There's also a miniature railway with both steam and diesel engines. (Operational only during the summer, at weekends and during school holidays; 1300–1600.)

Also in the park is the **Wairarapa Arts Centre**, and within that is the tiny Stidolph Museum of Early Childhood (Bruce St; tel: 06 377 1210). It makes an interesting and curious visit.

SPORT There is some excellent diving from Riversdale Beach near Masterton. Divers Supplies (391 Queen St; tel: 06 378 6492) has local knowledge and can arrange training and tours.

Masterton is also a good centre for trout fishing: McGills Safaris (Opaki; tel: 06 378 6327), run by Linton McGill, teaches the intricacies of fly fishing. The same expertise is available at Wairarapa Hunting and Fishing (101 Queen St; tel: 06 378 8723).

Parachuting with experts is available from Skydive Wairarapa at Hood Aerodrome; tel: 0800 867 593 483; www.goleap.co.nz, with tandem sky-dives on offer for absolute beginners. This is also a major gliding area and many New Zealand records have been set from Masterton airfield.

For raft, kayak and riverbugging contact the Adventurer Centre, 76 Main Rd, Greytown; tel: 06 304 8565.

Finally, as a slight detour, try **Cavelands Farm** (Caveland Rd, off Gladstone Rd, about 11 kilometres from town), with some unusual inhabitants – glow-worms that live in the 150 metre-long farm caves. Tel: 06 372 7733 for permission to visit.

TOP SHEARERS

It used to be said that Masterton was dormant for 11 months of the year, only waking up in March for the sheep-shearing festival. It is the most important event of its kind in the world, and anyone who is asked to compete in this event is already considered to be one of the best shearers in the business.

Watching the gun shearers strip sheep perfectly in less than a minute makes it all look deceptively easy.

A WINE WARNING!

The inhabitants of Wellington know their wines and come to Masterton and Martinborough on shopping expeditions – so be prepared for lots of the vineyard stocks to sell out quickly.

i **Wairarapa Visitor Information** Centre 5 Dixon St, Masterton; tel: 06 378 7373, fax: 06 378 7042; e-mail: tourwai@xtra.co.nz.

Chanel Court Motel $ 14–16 Herbert St; tel/fax: 06 378 2877; e-mail: chanelcourtmotel@xtra.co.nz. Family-orientated motel with children's playground and licensed restaurant. Also backpackers accommodation.

Discovery Motor Lodge $$ 210 Chapel St; tel: 06 378 7745 or 0800 188 515, fax: 06 378 9467; www.discovery.co.nz;

COBBLESTONE EARLY SETTLERS MUSEUM

Just over an hour's drive out of Wellington travelling north over the Rimutaka Mountain Pass, this outdoor museum has a collection of historic Wairarapa buildings, farm machinery and horse-drawn vehicles. It was originally the Cobb & Co coach stable, founded in 1866 as a staging post on the Wellington to Wairarapa mail and passenger coach service. 169 Main Rd South, Greytown; tel: 06 304 9687; open daily from 0830.

e-mail: info@discovery.co.nz. Well-equipped studio suites with considerable style. Swimming pool and spa baths.
Masterton Motor Lodge $$ 250 High St; tel: 06 378 2585 or 0508 644 644, fax: 06 378 2587; www.masterton-motorlodge.co.nz; e-mail: info@masterton-motorlodge.co.nz. Swimming pool and tennis courts in 4 hectares of garden.

Alcatraz Bar and Grill $$ Chapel St; tel: 06 378 6993. Open Tue–Sun from 1100 until late. Café during the day, restaurant and nightspot in the evening. Licensed.
Bloomfields $$$ Lincoln Rd; tel: 06 377 4305. Lunches Wed–Fri from 1200. Dinner Tue–Sat from 1800. Imaginative restaurant, with good vegetarian choices. Licensed and BYO.
Fusions Restaurant & Bar $$ 126 Chapel St; tel: 06 370 2310.
Opal Restaurant $$ 439 Queen St; tel: 06 370 2900.
O'Tooles Slug and Lettuce Pub $ 94 Queen St; tel: 06 377 3087. Generous helpings of pub food.

WAIRARAPA WINE AND FOOD FESTIVAL

The Wairarapa wine and food festival is held annually on the third weekend in February in Solway Park Showgrounds. It's a day of top-class entertainment, with fine local wines and Mediterranean-style cuisine.

Solway Park is an appropriate location to hold the festival too – the park itself was originally the district's first vineyard, planted in 1878.

MOUNT BRUCE

The **National Wildlife Centre** at Mt Bruce (north of Masterton) offers protection to two almost extinct native birds, the takahe and the kokako. Other New Zealand bird species include the saddleback, blue duck, Auckland Island teal and stitchbird. There's also a nocturnal house with kiwi and New Zealand's 'living fossil', the tuatara, a lizard-like reptile and the last surviving member of the genus Ryncocephalia, which has remained essentially unchanged for 150 million years. Don't miss the kaka being fed daily at 1500 – they're the clowns of the forest! Open daily 0930–1600; tel: 06 375 8004.

VINEYARDS IN THE MARTINBOROUGH REGION

With few exceptions the vineyards offer cellar sales 'while stocks last' – the inhabitants of Wellington know their wines and visit Martinborough on regular shopping expeditions.

There is an excellent guide to New Zealand wines on the Internet at www.nzwine.com.

Ata Rangi, Puruatanga Rd; tel: 06 306 9570; www.atarangi.co.nz. Award-winning Pinot Noir. Open Sat, Sun 1200–1600 (Sept); Mon–Fri 1300–1500, Sat, Sun, holidays 1200–1600 (Oct–Easter).

The Claddagh Vineyard, Puruatanga Rd; tel: 06 306 9264. Tastings by prior arrangement. Open Mon–Fri 1300–1500, while stocks last.

Gladstone Vineyard, about halfway between Martinborough and Masterton; tel: 06 379 8563; www.gladstone.co.nz. Award-winning Sauvignon Blanc (vintage 1999). Visitors are welcome between Tues–Sun 1100–1700 (Sept–June). Vineyard lunches Fri–Sun from Labour Weekend (Oct) to end Mar.

Hau Ariki Wines; tel: 06 306 9360. The first Maori marae in New Zealand to make wines commercially. Visits by appointment.

Margrain Vineyard; tel: 06 306 9292; www.margrainvineyard.co.nz. With café (tel: 06 306 8333) and excellent accommodation.

Martinborough Vineyard, Princess St; tel: 06 306 9955; www.martinborough-vineyard.co.nz. Open 1100–1700 throughout the year. Known for its Pinot Noir and Chardonnay.

Martinborough Wine Centre, Kitchener St; tel: 06 306 9955. Here you can sample a wide range of wines and local produce, and on Saturdays shop at the local market.

Muirlea Rise, 50 Princess St; tel: 06 306 9332. Cellar door sales of Pinot Noir, Fri–Mon all year.

Palliser Estate; tel: 06 306 9019; www.palliser.co.nz. Open daily 1030–1600.

Te Kairanga Wines, Martins Rd (5 kilometres south-east); tel: 06 306 9122; www.tkwine.co.nz. Award-winning wines. Open for tastings daily 1100–1800. Guided tours at weekends at 1400.

Walnut Ridge, 159 Regent St; tel: 06 306 9323; www.walnutridge.co.nz. Wine shop is open for sales and tastings on weekends and public holidays in summer only, 1100–1700.

Winslow Wines, Princess St and Huangarua Rd; tel: 06 306 9648. Cellar door sales. Open daily 1000–1800.

EN ROUTE

HENLEY LAKE

To the east of Masterton is the artificial Henley Lake, a pleasant spot with walking tracks along the adjacent river.

WOODVILLE PICNIC AREAS

The town park, in Ormond St, has picnic tables, a playground and plenty of shade. Or, for a more rural spot, head out of Woodville towards Parmerston North. Just before the Manawatu Gorge, cross the bridge and drive a short distance along Ballance Rd to find another quiet picnic area.

WOODVILLE

Originally and perhaps more appropriately known as The Junction, Woodville lies 28 kilometres east of Palmerston North on the road and railway routes to Wellington. The Seventy Mile Bush from which the name Woodville derives has all but disappeared. Now the town serves the surrounding farming area.

Gottfried Lindauer, renowned for his portraits of 19th-century Maoris, spent his later years in Woodville. His headstone can be seen in the cemetery. The town park, in Ormond St, has picnic tables, a playground, toilets and plenty of shade.

i **Tararua Visitors Information Centre** 42 Vogel St; tel: 06 376 1023 or 0800 827 278, fax: 06 376 1025; e-mail: info@tararua.com.

New Central Motor Inn and Hotel $ 63 Vogel St; tel/fax: 06 376 5282. Small motel with bar-restaurant.
Ormond Street Motel $ 45 Ormond St; tel/fax: 06 376 5638. Very quiet garden setting close to the park.
Woodville Country Motel $ Vogel St; tel/fax: 06 376 5557. Recently renovated units. Breakfasts available.

Lindauer Restaurant $$ 50–52 Vogel St; tel: 06 376 4543. Large, family-style restaurant. Licensed and BYO. Open seven days from 1100 till late.

QUICK FACTS ABOUT NEW ZEALAND WILDLIFE

With the exception of two species of bat, no indigenous mammals are native to New Zealand. As far as we know, the first white settlers, who arrived early in the 19th century, found a type of dog and a black rat, both of which had been brought by the Maoris about 500 years earlier. Today, the only wild mammals are descended from deer, rabbits, goats, pigs, weasels, ferrets and opossums – all imported.

New Zealand is free from snakes, and has surprisingly few insects. There are some pretty strange creatures though – like the tuatara. This is a lizard-like reptile with a vestigial third eye, and is believed to be a survivor from prehistoric times.

EN ROUTE

Masterton is the nearest town to the Tararua Forest Park, which has a wide range of walks suited to all levels. Most of them start at Holdsworth. Note that weather conditions can change rapidly so you will need to be properly equipped. Take the advice of the ranger at the Field Centre (tel: 06 377 0700) in Masterton, or consult with the Visitor Information Centre.

WHERE NEXT?

From Woodville, you can continue through fertile country on State Highway 2, to Hastings (see p. 213), a town of beautiful parks and gardens. Further on this route is Napier, Hastings' twin city, detailed on p. 216.

MANAWATU GORGE

The Manawatu river rises in the Ruahine Range, and flows 160 kilometres through the Manawatu Gorge and across the plain into the Tasman Sea at Foxton Beach.

The Manawatu Gorge road bridge, built in 1871, is one of the great engineering feats of the age. To see it, head out of Woodville towards Palmerston North, crossing the bridge just before the gorge as far as Ballance Rd, where you'll find a quiet picnic area. At times, workmen hung from ropes from the cliff top in order to cut a way through.

You don't have to be a fresh-air freak to appreciate New Zealand, but it does help. The country is certainly a strong contender for the outdoor sports capital of the southern hemisphere, and Manawatu Gorge is no exception. To add some variety to your visit, one of the best ways of exploring the Manawatu Gorge is on horseback. Beginners are welcome, and if you have not ridden before, try wearing pantihose under your jeans to protect your legs from chafing. Timeless Horse Treks in Woodville (tel: 06 376 6157) operates through bush and river scenery near the gorge.

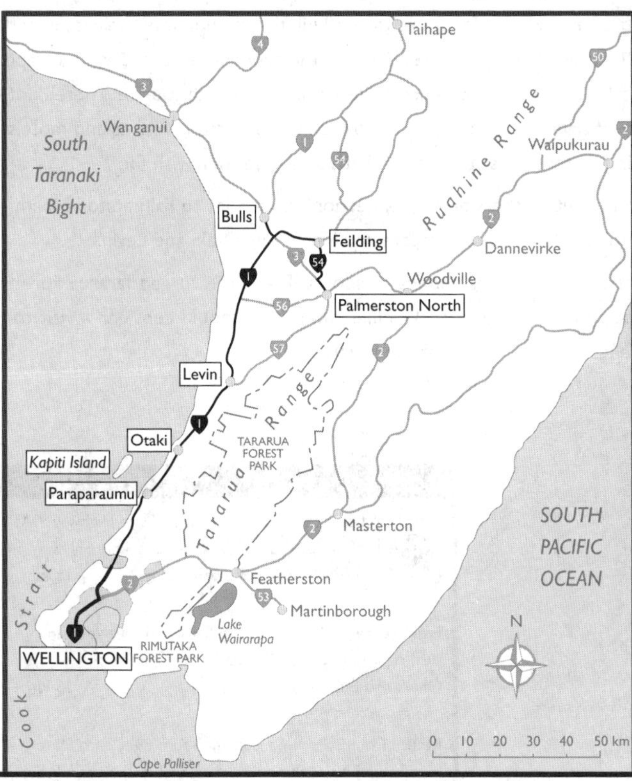

PALMERSTON NORTH – WELLINGTON

OTT TABLES 9750/9756/9758

TRANSPORT	FREQUENCY	JOURNEY TIME
Train	2 daily	2hrs 15mins
Bus	5 daily	2hrs 5mins

PALMERSTON NORTH – LEVIN

OTT TABLES 9750/9756/9758

TRANSPORT	FREQUENCY	JOURNEY TIME
Train	2 daily	35mins
Bus	5 daily	50mins

LEVIN – OTAKI

OTT TABLES 9750/9756/9758

TRANSPORT	FREQUENCY	JOURNEY TIME
Train	1 daily	20mins
Bus	7 daily	15mins

OTAKI – PARAPARAUMU

OTT TABLES 9750/9756/9758

TRANSPORT	FREQUENCY	JOURNEY TIME
Train	1 daily	23mins
Bus	8 daily	20mins

PARAPARAUMU – WELLINGTON

OTT TABLES 9750/9756/9758

TRANSPORT	FREQUENCY	JOURNEY TIME
Train	2 daily	51mins
Bus	8 daily	45mins

Note: There is 1 extra train and 3 extra buses that run on this route on Monday to Fridays only.

Palmerston North – Wellington

The Kapiti Coast extends for more than 30 kilometres north of Wellington and has a charm of its own. Popular with residents of the capital, who use it as an escape valve from the stresses and strains of urban life, it's also a hit with tourists. There's not much in the way of sights – it's mainly small townships, retirement villages and motels – but you will find all the sun, sea and sand that you would ever wish for.

You can get about via the 'Capital Connection' rail service to Palmerston North, which connects the settlements of Paraparaumu, Waikanae, Otaki and Levin.

If you're not into swimming and water sports there's the rugged Tararua Forest Park, which is popular with trampers. Wildlife enthusiasts should consider a visit to Kapiti Island, a sanctuary for native birds and lizards.

Route Detail

Leave Palmerston North on State Highway 3. At Newberry turn right, then take State Highway 54 through Te Arakura to Feilding. 15 km

From Feilding take the road to Sanson, where you can turn right onto State Highway 3, passing through Ohakea to Bulls. 35 km

Return from Bulls to Sanson, then turn right onto State Highway 1. This road now runs parallel to the coast in the direction of Cook Strait. You'll pass numerous side turnings along the way leading to beaches at Tangimoana, Himatangi Beach, Foxton Beach and Waitarere. Beyond Levin, State Highway 1 connects with more beaches at Waikara and Otaki on the way to Waikanae and the sizeable resort of Paraparaumu with Kapiti Island offshore. The final stretch takes in Plimmerton and Porirua before continuing to Wellington. 170 km

PALMERSTON NORTH

Palmerston North is named after the British statesman and prime minister, Lord Palmerston, whose administration bought the land from its Maori owners in 1864. (The suffix 'North' was added in 1871 to avoid confusion with the Palmerston in North Otago.)

Originally Palmerston North was just a rural community, but nowadays it is enlivened, particularly during term time, by the presence of the large student population who study at Massey, the second-largest university in New Zealand.

Palmerston North services a large, fairly prosperous rural community and it's also home to New Zealand's second-largest university, Massey, as well as a number of other educational and research establishments, earning it the title 'Knowledge City.' A quarter of the town's residents are consequently in the student age group, between 15 and 24. During the summer vacation (December to March) Palmerston North can be a very dull place.

When the bush was first cleared, a 6.8-hectare square was set aside to form the commercial heart of the city and it was here that the railway station was first located. Now the square is a pleasant green space, though it's also home to the **Civic Centre**, from where you can get a bird's-eye view of the town. Also in the square is a fountain installed to mark the coronation of King Edward VII and a statue of the local chief, Te Awe Awe, who fought on the government side in the Land Wars.

There's a good view of the university campus from the **Munro lookout**, a memorial to C S Munro who founded New Zealand's first rugby football club.

There's a **Rugby Museum** (tel: 06 358 6947) on 87 Cuba St with a range of memorabilia as well as videos of famous internationals, which the All Blacks invariably win, needless to say. Open Mon–Sat 1000–1200 and 1330–1600, Sun afternoon only.

The **Science Centre and Manawatu Museum** (tel: 06 355 5000) at 396 Main St was opened in 1994. One of its best features is the Maori galleries, but there's also a European settler house, an early 20th-century school room and a reconstruction of the city's first store. (Open daily 1000–1700.)

AN EARTHQUAKE SIMULATOR

In the science centre at the Manawatu museum are interactive exhibits including an earthquake simulator – enough to keep children, and parents amused all day.

The **Manawatu Art Gallery** on Main St (in the same complex as the Science Centre) was created like so many of New Zealand's public galleries, through the efforts of amateur enthusiasts. In this case the now-defunct Manawatu Society of Arts. Most of the

THE TOKOMARU STEAM ENGINE MUSEUM

Some 20 kilometres south of Palmerston North on Highway 57 is the Tokomaru Steam Engine Museum, with its collection of working steam engines, some over a century old. Tel: 06 329 8867.

THE AIRFORCE EXPERIENCE

Visit the Ohakea Wing Museum, home of the Royal New Zealand Airforce. Just 10 minutes from Palmerston North on State Highway 1; tel: 06 351 5020; www.afw.co.nz/ohakea.htm.

THE CAPITAL CONNECTION

This Tranz Scenic rail service runs between Palmerston North and Wellington Mon–Fri. Trains depart Palmerston North at 0821 and return from Wellington at 1717. The trip takes just under 2½ hours. The daily *Overlander* and *Northerner* trains also stop in Palmerston North. Tranz Metro's suburban trains stop at smaller stations between Wellington and Paraparaumu.

work is by New Zealand artists, including a representative selection of contemporary paintings and drawings by Colin McCahon, Toss Woollaston, Pat Hanly, Michael Smither and others. Open daily 1000–1700.

Palmerston North is made for strolling. **The Esplanade**, near the road to Shannon, forms a park along the shoreline of the Manawatu River, and has everything from a rose garden to a miniature railway. The Riverside Walkway runs through the park and then for 10 kilometres upriver. On the opposite bank is the spacious and leafy Massey University campus.

i **Manawatu Visitor Centre** 52 The Square; tel: 06 354 6593, fax: 06 356 9841; e-mail: manawatu.visitor-info@xtra.co.nz.

Department of Conservation 717 Tremaine Ave; tel: 06 350 9700, fax: 06 350 9701.

Alpha Motor Inn $$ cnr Broadway and Victoria Ave; tel: 06 357 1129, fax: 06 359 0188. Central and quiet with a reasonable licensed restaurant.

Ann Keith Budget Hotel & Hostel $ 146 Grey St; tel: 06 358 6928, fax: 06 355 0291; www.bacpackersnbnb.co.nz; e-mail: beds@backpackersnbnb.co.nz. Located in an old villa. Close to shops.

Aubyn Court Motorlodge $$ 360 Ferguson St; tel: 06 354 5757, fax: 06 354 5758; e-mail: aubyn.court@clear.net.nz. Smart new motel, near the university.

Grey's Inn $$ 123 Grey St; tel: 06 358 6928, fax: 06 355 0291; e-mail: ak1@clear.net.nz. Comfortable bed and breakfast hotel.

Pepper Tree YHA $ 121 Grey St; tel: 06 355 4054, fax: 06 355 4063; e-mail: peppertreehostel@clear.net.nz. Kitchen facilities, BBQ and tent sites. Close to town.

Pioneer Motel $$ 632 Pioneer Highway; tel: 06 357 7165 or 0800 274 663, fax: 06 357 7164; e-mail: jillin@clear.net.nz. Comfortable motel in nice setting. Swimming and spa pools.

Supreme Motor Lodge $$ 665 Pioneer Highway; tel: 06 356 5265 or 0800 112 211, fax: 06 356 5267; www.suprememl.co.nz; e-mail: sml@suprememl.co.nz. Heated indoor swimming pool and gym.

Aqaba $$ 186 Broadway Ave; tel: 06 357 8922. Flaming gas braziers outside. This lively pub-restaurant has an eclectic menu. Order your food at the bar.
Costa's $ 282 Cuba St; tel: 06 952 5577. Odd mixture of food, including Mexican and Thai. Licensed.
Dejeuner $$ 159 Broadway Ave; tel: 06 952 5581. Upmarket French restaurant but with New Zealand wines.
George Street Delicatessen $ cnr George and Main St; tel: 06 357 6663. Marvellous food at low prices. Mon–Wed 0730–1800, Thur–Sat 1930–2400, Sun 0830–2300.

FEILDING

Feilding was founded by the Emigrants and Colonists Aid Corporation, headed by the Duke of Manchester, and the layout of two central squares was inspired by the famous English industrial city (Feilding was one of the Corporation's directors). The Corporation bought 43,000 hectares of uncleared land, known as the Manchester Block, for £75,000 and agreed to send 2000 immigrants to the area over a five-year period. In return, the government provided free passages and guaranteed employment close to the town.

The first settlers arrived in 1874 and lived in conditions of great hardship until the bush was cleared. The project was billed as a work of charity, but the Corporation ensured a substantial profit on the investment to its shareholders.

Today Feilding is famous for its livestock sales, which take place on Fridays in the yards off Warwick St. The cartoonist Murray Ball was born in Feilding. His father played for the All Blacks, and Murray himself came close to selection at one time.

EN ROUTE

There are two splendid gardens out of town: Mount Lees Reserve, 11 kilometres down the Ngaio Rd, off Mount Stewart Rd (open Wed–Sun), and Cross Hills Gardens, 6 kilometres from Feilding on State Highway 45 (open daily from Sept–Apr 1030–1700).

Feilding Holiday Park 'Greenmeadows' $ 5 Arnott St; tel/fax: 06 323 5623. Cabins and tent sites available. Peaceful surroundings.
Feilding Motel $$ 7 Kimbolton Rd; tel: 06 323 6837 or 0800 500 474, fax: 06 323 5892; e-mail: feildingmotel@actrix.co.nz. Large motel offering breakfasts and evening meals on request.
Raceway Court Motel $$ Awahuri Rd; tel/fax: 06 323 7891. Off-street parking, restaurant and bar.

Mirrors Restaurant $$ 25 Manchester Square; tel: 06 323 4147.

BULLS

Bulls, 31 kilometres north-west of Palmerston North, is the oldest settlement in this part of Manawatu and was originally known as Rangitikei. The town was founded by James Bull, a distinguished English wood craftsman (you can see examples of his carving in the House of Commons). Bull ran the local inn and shop and the name of the township was officially changed to Bulls in 1872. Ever since, the local people have been punning on the name with gusto. Some examples: the cash machine outside the bank – 'Cash-a-Bull'; the fire station – 'Extinguish-a-Bull'; the police station – 'Const-a-Bull'; the Visitor Centre – 'Inform-a-Bull' and so on. It's said that this is the only place in the world where you can get milk from Bulls. Apart from the signs, there's little to see in the town itself. Two of the oldest buildings are **Raumai Grange Lavender Farm** (tel: 06 322 0953) on Parewanui Rd (open all year), an 1860s homestead, now a nursery and gift shop (the lavender blooms from November until April) and **Connelly Cottage**, built by Bull himself and now a restaurant and teashop.

EN ROUTE

For amazing views of Palmerston North and the Manawatu Plains, take the Pahiatua Track, a 39-kilometre road which crosses the Tararua Range en route from Pahiatua to Aokautere (the turn is clearly marked).

i **Rangitikei Information Centre** 113 Bridge St; tel: 06 322 0055, fax: 06 322 0033; rangitikei.information.centres@xtra.co.nz.

Bridge Motor Lodge $–$$ 2 Bridge St; tel: 06 322 0894, fax: 06 322 1957. Riverside hotel, ideal for walks and swimming. Also cabins and tent sites.

Flock House Hotel $$ Parewanui Rd; tel: 06 322 1045 or 0800 656 545, fax: 06 322 1991; e-mail: flockhouse@xtra.co.nz. Facilities include heated indoor pool, gymnasium, squash and tennis courts and a barbecue area.

LEVIN

Ninety-five kilometres north of Wellington, at the junction of State Highway 1 and State Highway 57, is Levin. Founded in 1889, it owes its origins to the construction of the Wellington to Palmerston North Railway. The fertile plain on which it stands was a major north–south highway for the Maoris in pre-European times, and many major battles were fought for control of the area. The name honours William Hort Levin, one of the founder-directors of the Wellington-Manawatu Railway Company.

The town (population 16,000) is a horticultural centre, at the heart of market gardens and dairy farms. The garment industry is the other main employer and you'll come across numerous factory shops selling discount clothing. **Lake Horowhenua**, on the edge of town, is a pleasant boating and picnic spot. There are two artificial islands in the lake that once supported Maori *pa* (fortified settlements).

The most popular beach is **Waitarere**, ideal for bathing with dunes and gently sloping sand. Nearby is the wreck of the sailing ship *Hydrabad*, blown ashore in 1878. It's possible to drive (four-wheel drive) from here to **Hokio Beach**, a former coaching stop on the Wellington Rd.

i **Horowhenua Visitor Centre** 93 Oxford St; tel: 06 367 8440, fax: 06 367 0558; e-mail: horowhenua.visitor@clear.net.nz.

Levin Motor Camp (Playford Tourist Park) $ 38 Parker Ave; tel: 06 368 3549, fax: 06 368 3159; e-mail: levin.motor.camp@xtra.co.nz. Tent sites and cabins. Close to the shops.

Mountain View Motel $$ The Avenue; tel: 06 368 5214 or 0800 686 683, fax: 06 368 4091; e-mail: mvmotel@nzol.net.nz. Family motel with cooking facilities, children's play area, swimming pool and licensed restaurant.

Panorama Motel $$ Main Rd North; tel: 06 368 5401 or 0800 660 220, fax: 06 368 8691. Large motel with swimming pool, spa, putting green and licensed restaurant.

Café Nua $ 7 Bath St; tel: 06 368 0777. Superb value, especially the salads. Open 1000–2200.

Raewyn's Restaurant $$ 262a Oxford St; tel: 06 368 5184. Buffet lunches and dinners – a hearty eater's delight. Licensed and BYO.

OTAKI

Otaki lies in a fruit-growing area beside the side of the Otaki River. It's the home of the first Maori University (Te Wananga o Raukawa) and was the site of an early Maori church, unfortunately destroyed by fire in 1995. Otaki is a popular vacation resort - its population almost doubles from December to March when the holiday homes fill up. The grey sand beach is safe for swimming and the waves are suitable for gentle surfing.

EN ROUTE

Himatangi Beach lies 38 kilometres south-west of Palmerston North on the State Highway 56 and extends for 10 kilometres. In the summer it's patronised by the locals, but for the rest of the year it's deserted.

EN ROUTE

Some 8 kilometres from Levin is the Papaitonga Scenic Reserve, on the lake of the same name. It's a refuge for swamp birds including Australian bitterns, black swans, spotless crakes and New Zealand dabchicks.

PARAPARAUMU

Paraparaumu, about 45 kilometres from Wellington, is the largest resort on the Kapiti Coast, although even here the population is under 2000. The town lies on the main highway, where you'll also find the **Southward Car Museum**, said to contain the largest and most varied collection of veteran and vintage cars in the southern hemisphere. (Open daily 0900–1630.)

Three kilometres from the town is Paraparaumu Beach, safe for swimming and with views out to the densely forested **Kapiti Island** (see p. 260).

Barnacles Seaside Inn $ 3 Marine Parade, Paraparaumu Beach; tel: 04 902 5856; e-mail: lin&lois@xtra.co.nz. Great views over the sea to the South and Kapiti Islands.

Le Beauchamp Homestay and Gardens $$$ 239 State Highway 1; tel/fax: 04 297 1430; www.lebeauchamp.co.nz; e-mail: lebeauchamp@xtra.co.nz. 'The Beautiful Fields' has a superb garden and its own lake and waterfall. The price includes an excellent breakfast.

Ocean Motel $$ 42 Ocean Rd; tel: 04 902 6424, fax: 04 902 6426; e-mail: oceanmotel@ihug.co.nz. Spacious hotel in beautiful grounds. Close to the beach, shops and golf course.

Paraparaumu Motel $ 65 Amohia St; tel/fax: 04 298 4476 or 0800 746 000. Handy for the car museum and the Picton ferry.

Brier Patch $$ 9 Maclean St; tel: 04 902 5586. Popular restaurant serving Creole and Cajun specialities. Open for dinner daily, lunch Wed–Fri, brunch Sat–Sun. Booking essential at weekends. Licensed and BYO.

Copperfield Seaside Motel $$ 7–13 Seaview Rd; tel: 04 902 6414. Excellent restaurant for breakfasts, offering a good range of savoury pancakes. Two minutes from the beach. BYO.

TARARUA FOREST PARK

Established in 1954, the Tararua Forest Park encompasses the Tararua Mountain Range, which divides the lower North Island. A natural playground for Wellingtonians, the park has a rugged native forest interior and offers a diverse range of activities, from overnight tramping, canoeing and river tubing adventures to shorter day walks, picnics and camping.

Colour Section

(i) The Picton Ferry (p. 264); punting in Christchurch (p. 302)
(ii) Christchurch Cathedral (p. 298)
(iii) The Kingston Flyer (p. 353)
(iv) Maori wood carving

778

TE RAUPARAHA – A MAORI NAPOLEON

Born around 1768, Te Rauparaha is considered to be one of the greatest Maori warrior chiefs of his time. A member of the Ngati Toa tribe, he migrated with his people from the ancestral homelands at Kawhia to Kapiti Island in the early 1820s. Powerful enemies he and his people had made among neighbouring tribes were a principal reason behind the move. With its good view over this part of the North Island's west coast, and separated from the mainland by a 6-kilometre 'moat', the island made an excellent stronghold.

Recognising the advantages of European weapons, Te Rauparaha quickly built up an arsenal of guns and ammunition. Thus equipped, and utilising his considerable military skills, he was soon able to dominate much of the southern part of the North Island and the northern part of the South Island. This state of affairs persisted until the early 1840s, when Europeans started to settle the region.

Because he had a reputation for savagery and treachery, Te Rauparaha was once detested and feared by many of the European settlers who had dealings with him. Above all, it was the infamous massacre near Wairau, in the South Island, that led to assertions of his brutality. In a dispute over land ownership, Colonel Wakefield of the New Zealand Company (the company that organised early settlement of the country), and 20 of his men, were killed by followers of Te Rauparaha. After speaking to the chief, and other Maori leaders who were involved, Governor Fitzroy decided that they had been unduly provoked by the Europeans. No punitive action was taken, but most colonists were incensed by the governor's decision.

Te Rauparaha's many military victories, often against numerically superior forces, have inspired some authorities to refer to him as a 'Maori Napoleon'. However, on a number of occasions he avoided direct armed confrontation by using his political skills to play off one enemy tribe against the other. No warmonger, he resorted to violence only when he deemed it necessary in the interests of his tribe.

A signatory of the Treaty of Waitangi, Te Rauparaha spent his final days peacefully at Otaki, on the west coast of the North Island. Never baptised, he remained faithful to the old pre-European Maori traditions until his death in 1849.

The terrain can be rough, providing challenges for the hardiest of trampers. Another word of warning: the weather is changeable, especially on the peaks, and can become severe at any time of the year - be prepared with warm clothing and supplies even on the shortest of walks. Overnight parties should include an experienced tramper.

There are two main access points - in the west through Otaki Forks, in the east through Holdsworth. Otaki Forks lies midway between Wellington and Palmerston North. Take the Otaki Gorge Rd, signposted off State Highway 1 south of Otaki, for 19 kilometres. (Take care on the last 5 kilometres as the road is unsealed.) Otaki can also be reached by daily bus and train services. NB *The Overlander* (Wellington-Auckland train service) no longer stops at Otaki.

TARARUA FOREST PARK INFORMATION

DEPARTMENT OF CONSERVATION:

Otaki Forks; tel: 06 364 3111

Waikanae Field Centre; tel: 04 296 1112

Masterton Field Centre; tel: 06 377 0700

There's ample evidence of the pioneering era in the Forks, with the remains of stone walls, sawmills and traces of farming activity on the river terraces. Today, this is the access point for the Southern Crossing of the Tararuas, a classic two- to three-day tramp above the bushline, suitable for intermediate/experienced hikers. There are a number of shorter walks up the river valleys ranging from 30 minutes to 3½ hours return. The Otaki is also well suited to canoeing and rafting, especially for beginners (the river is graded '2'). Further upstream, the Upper Otaki offers an excellent two- to three-day 'tubing' adventure (paddling in overinflated truck tyre inner tubes). The **River Rock** in Gorge Road (tel: 06 354 3110) runs guided trips, hires out equipment and operates a pick-up/drop-off service.

Holdsworth, the main eastern access point, lies 15 kilometres from State Highway 2. Turn onto Norfolk Rd by the Juken Nissho timber plant, 2 kilometres south of Masterton. (This becomes Mount Holdsworth Rd.) With a backdrop of some of the highest mountains in the range, Holdsworth offers forest tramps ranging from the easy to the extremely difficult. There is a series of short bush walks through native towering forest, with picnic sites along the Atiwhakatu Stream. This is the starting point for the Mt Holdsworth Circuit, a three-day alpine trek.

CAMPING IN NEW ZEALAND

The law states that camping is actually permitted on any suitable open space, other than those marked 'No Camping', or on private property subject to the owner's permission.

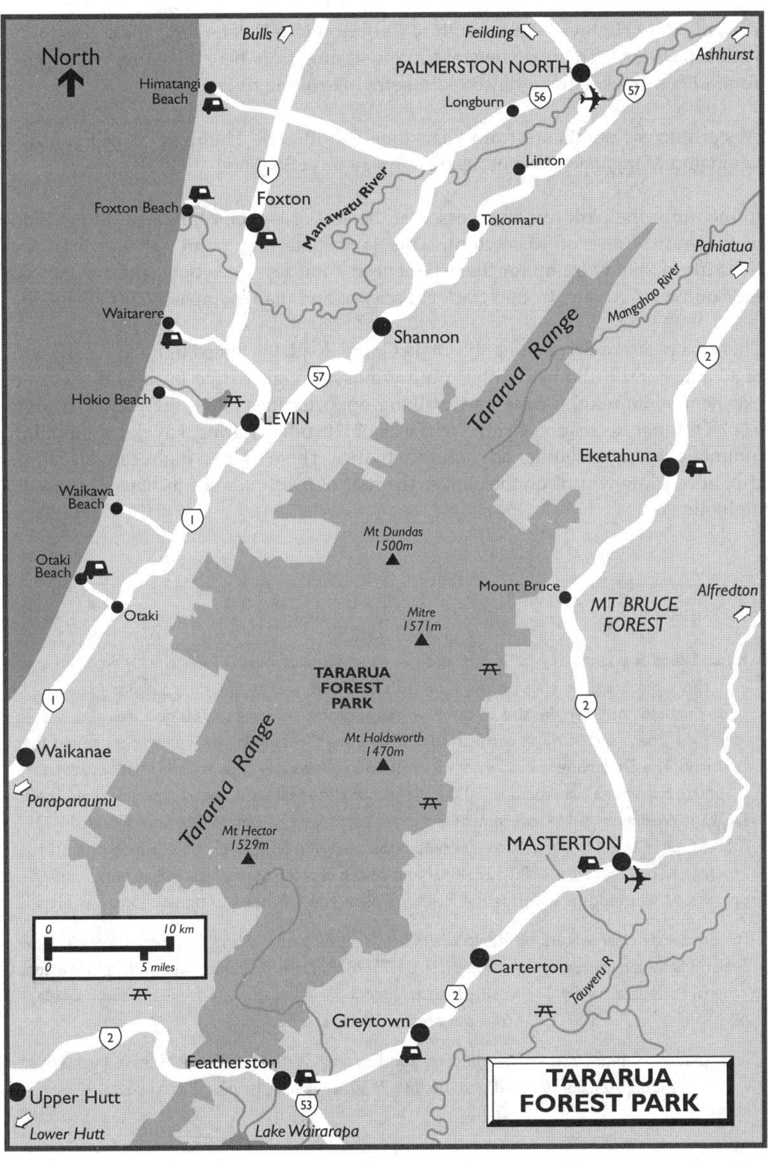
North
Bulls
Feilding
Ashhurst
PALMERSTON NORTH
Himatangi Beach
Longburn
56
57
Linton
1
Manawatu River
Foxton
Foxton Beach
Tokomaru
Pahiatua
Mangahao River
Waitarere
Shannon
Tararua Range
2
57
Hokio Beach
LEVIN
Eketahuna
Waikawa Beach
1
Mt Dundas 1500m
Otaki Beach
Mount Bruce
Alfredton
MT BRUCE FOREST
Otaki
Mitre 1571m
TARARUA FOREST PARK
1
2
Mt Holdsworth 1470m
Waikanae
Paraparaumu
Tararua Range
Mt Hector 1529m
MASTERTON
0 10 km
0 5 miles
Carterton
Tauweru R
2
Greytown
2
Featherston
Upper Hutt
53
Lower Hutt
Lake Wairarapa
TARARUA FOREST PARK

Turn off State Highway 2 just south of Carterton into Dalefield Rd for access to the **Waiohine Gorge**. There are several tramps starting from here including the popular Totara Flats Track, a three-day 38-kilometre hike along river valleys.

Western access points are from Gladstone Rd off State Highway 57 just south of Levin and Mangahao Road of State Highway 57 at Shannon.

In the north the park can be accessed at the end of Upper Waingawa Rd (14 kilometres north-west of Masterton). This is the starting point for the Northern Crossing, a 2½-day tramp for the experienced – it is less developed and wilder than the Southern Crossing (rough track experience and map/compass skills essential).

There's a pleasant drive along the Otaki Gorge Road, via State Highway 1 just south of Otaki. For 19 kilometres the route winds through native bush and there are excellent swimming, fishing and walking opportunities along the way. The River Rock Outdoor Recreation Centre, tel: 06 354 3110, offers rafting, kayaking, abseiling, mountain biking and other adventure activities. There's also a night canyon-rafting trip, lit by glow-worms on the banks. The roar of the rapids seems fiercer in the still night air.

KAPITI ISLAND

Kapiti Island is a sanctuary for endangered birds and lizards. Most of it is thickly wooded and there are dramatic cliffs on the seaward side. Kapiti was at one time a major Maori stronghold and later the site of seven whaling stations. It covers 1760 hectares and was declared a nature reserve as early as 1897. There are three major walking tracks around the island. The Department of Conservation (DOC) allows day trips to land Wednesday to Sunday, but with a maximum of 50 people per day. You will either need a permit from the DOC in Wellington, Old Government Buildings, Lambton Quay and Whitmore St; tel: 04 472 7356 (Kapiti Island bookings), or you could book a trip through one of the launch operators, such as Kapiti Tours, tel: 0800 527 484. Most of the charter companies will arrange landing permits. At weekends and during the holiday season you will need to book a long way ahead.

The amazingly clear waters off Kapiti Island are ideal for scuba diving. Operators include New Zealand Sea Adventures, Paraparaumu (tel: 04 236 8787) and The Dive Spot (7 The Esplanade, Mana, Paremata; tel: 04 233 8238). Both arrange a permit, hire out equipment and provide transport to the island and back.

Information: Kapiti Coast Visitors Information Centre, Centennial Park, 239 State Highway 1, Otaki; tel: 06 364 7620, fax: 06 364 7630; e-mail: kapiti.info@levin.pl.net.

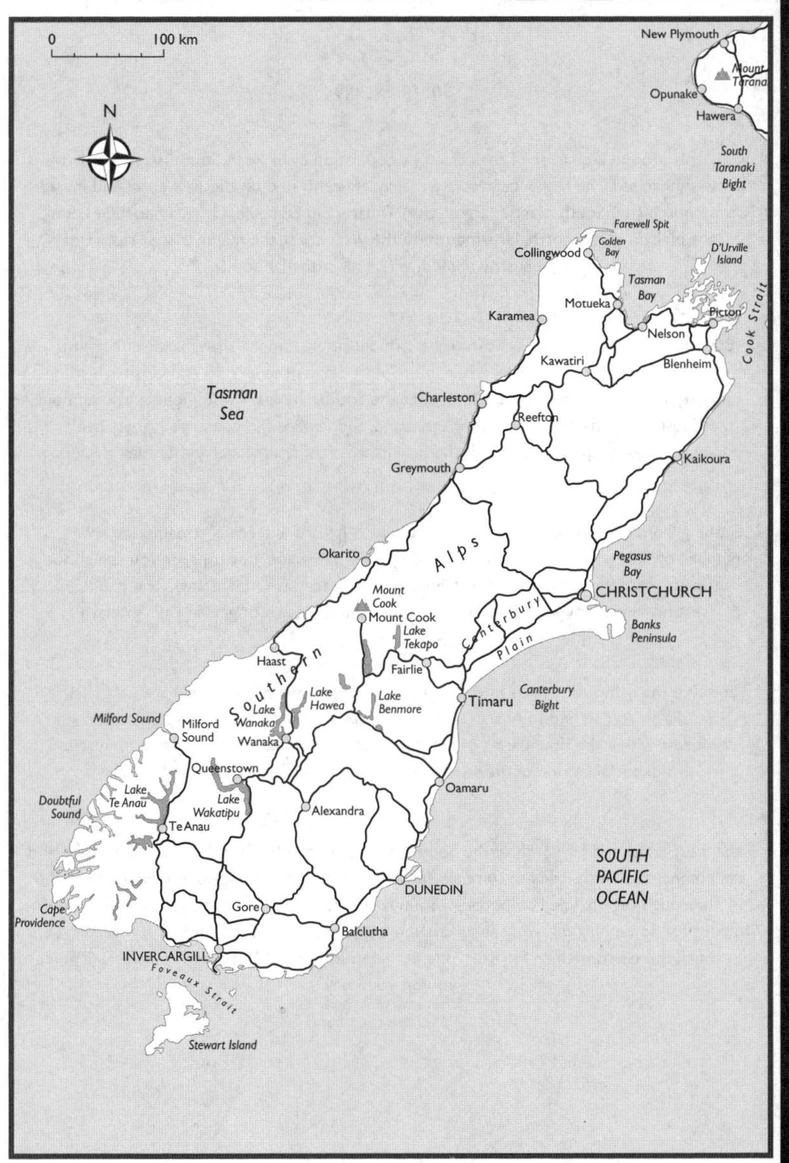
0
100 km
N
New Plymouth
Mount Taranaki
Opunake
Hawera
South Taranaki Bight
Farewell Spit
Golden Bay
Collingwood
D'Urville Island
Tasman Bay
Motueka
Karamea
Picton
Nelson
Cook Strait
Kawatiri
Blenheim
Tasman Sea
Charleston
Reefton
Kaikoura
Greymouth
Southern Alps
Okarito
Pegasus Bay
Mount Cook
CHRISTCHURCH
Mount Cook
Canterbury Plain
Lake Tekapo
Banks Peninsula
Haast
Fairlie
Lake Hawea
Lake Benmore
Canterbury Bight
Timaru
Milford Sound
Lake Wanaka
Milford Sound
Wanaka
Queenstown
Oamaru
Doubtful Sound
Lake Te Anau
Lake Wakatipu
Alexandra
Te Anau
SOUTH PACIFIC OCEAN
DUNEDIN
Gore
Cape Providence
Balclutha
INVERCARGILL
Foveaux Strait
Stewart Island

SOUTH ISLAND

With only around a quarter of the country's population living here, South Island is relatively sparsely inhabited. The larger centres are mainly concentrated on the east coast and include Christchurch (the South Island's largest city), Timaru and Dunedin. Other important centres are Nelson in the north, Greymouth on the west coast, the major tourist resort of Queenstown and Invercargill in the far south.

But what the South Island lacks in terms of population, it more than makes up for in the grandeur of its scenery. And what makes the South Island's scenery so grandiose is a stunning range of snow-capped mountains known as the Southern Alps. These mountains reach out almost along the entire length of the island, and feature the country's highest peak (Aoraki/Mount Cook), along with the magnificent Fox, Franz Josef and Tasman glaciers.

Gushing from the rugged slopes of the Southern Alps are numerous streams and rivers. A number of the rivers can be enjoyed on thrilling white water raft trips, or you can shoot through narrow river gorges in a jetboat in such places as Queenstown. The country's second-longest river (338 kilometres), the Clutha, has its origins in Lake Wanaka.

There are many beautiful lakes in the South Island, but especially beautiful are Lakes Tekapo, Wanaka, Wakatipu and Te Anau. The latter fringes a magnificent expanse of untouched rainforest within the boundaries of Fiordland National Park. It is here that trampers can experience one of the world's most famous walks, the Milford Track.

If the west coast and far south of the South Island can get a bit damp, the north of the island can compensate, with loads of summer sunshine, great beaches and superb wines from the Marlborough region. The Marlborough Sounds are a paradise for sea-kayaking and if you're looking for something big, you can always journey to Kaikoura for a look at a whale or two. In short, there's something for everyone in the South Island. The following pages will guide you on your way.

SOUTH ISLAND: OUR CHOICE

Golden Bay
Get away from it all on uncrowded beaches and in sleepy townships

Whale watching at Kaikoura
You'll never have a better opportunity to see these giants of the deep

Nelson Lakes National Park
Two lovely lakes set in alpine scenery

TranzAlpine Express
A spectacular train journey over the Southern Alps

Akaroa
A bit of French charm, away from the bustle of Christchurch city

West Coast Drive
Glaciers, pancake rocks and down-to-earth West Coast pubs. The loveliest coastal drive in the South Island

Otago Peninsula
Albatross colony, yellow-eyed penguins, great scenery and the country's only castle

Queenstown
Jump off a bridge, shoot the rapids or just sit on the lakeshore

Scenic flight over the Southern Alps
Fantastic views of glaciers, peaks and rainforest

Fiordland boat trip
Dramatic scenery

Alexandra
Off the beaten track, interesting local gold-mining towns

Catlins
Wild coastal scenery, a petrified forest, away from it all

HOW MUCH YOU CAN SEE IN A ...

WEEK (7 DAYS)

Option 1

Day 1. Picton Day 2. To Nelson Day 3. Nelson (excursion to Motueka and Abel Tasman National Park) Day 4. To Greymouth Day 5. To Arthur's Pass Days 6–7. To Christchurch (excursions to Akaroa or Hanmer Springs)

Option 2

Day 1. Fly to Queenstown from Wellington Days 2–3. Queenstown Day 4. To Mount Cook Day 5. Mount Cook Day 6. To Christchurch Day 7. Christchurch

FORTNIGHT (14 DAYS)

Day 1. Picton to Nelson Day 2. Nelson Day 3. To Greymouth via Westport and Punakaiki Day 4. Greymouth to Fox Glacier Day 5. To Queenstown Days 6–7. Queenstown Days 8–9. Te Anau (day trip to Milford Sound) Day 10. To Dunedin via Gore and Balclutha Day 11. Dunedin Day 12. To Christchurch Days 13–14. Christchurch

MONTH (28 DAYS)

Days 1–2. Picton Day 3. To Motueka (Abel Tasman National Park) Day 4. Motueka Day 5. To Blenheim via Nelson Lakes National Park Day 6. To Kaikoura Day 7. Kaikoura Day 8. To Hanmer Springs Day 9. To Greymouth Day 10. Greymouth Day 11. To Fox Glacier Day 12. Fox Glacier Day 13. To Queenstown Days 14–16. Queenstown Day 17. To Te Anau Days 18–19. Te Anau (day trip to Milford Sound) Day 20. To Invercargill Days 21–22. Trip to Stewart Island from Invercargill Day 23. To Dunedin via Catlins Day 24. Dunedin Day 25. To Mount Cook Day 26. Mount Cook (alternative: stay at Twizel) Day 27. To Christchurch Day 28. Christchurch

COOK STRAIT AND THE MARLBOROUGH SOUNDS

New Zealand's North and South Islands are divided by Cook Strait, which also connects the Tasman Sea to the Pacific Ocean and is 20 kilometres wide at its narrowest point, between Perano Head and Cape Terawhiti. Maori history recounts how many swimmers made the crossing long before the first European achieved the feat in 1962. This was Barrie Devenport, who took just over 11 hours to swim the Strait.

The first European to encounter Cook Strait was the Dutch explorer, Abel Tasman, in December 1642. Unsure whether there was a passage (although the current suggested the possiblity to him), he marked it on his chart as a bight – Zeehaens Bocht – named after one of his ships. Captain Cook was the first to chart the Strait accurately, earning him the right to name it. The Maoris call it Raukawa, which means 'leaves of the kawakawa', a decoration worn by a chief in mourning.

Cook Strait is in the Roaring Forties (see box on p. 265), but thankfully most of the time the weather is kind and the crossing is uneventful. The cost is the same as flying but you get the exhilarating sea trip thrown in. Plus, as the ferry comes into Picton you get a marvellous preview of what awaits you on the South Island of New Zealand. For Picton is a beautiful town in itself, with the added bonus that it is surrounded by the Marlborough Sounds, a series of stunning fiord-like drowned river valleys.

The only way to appreciate the Marlborough Sounds fully is to go out by boat. You can either self-drive from sites on the waterfront at Havelock or Picton, or use one of the many water taxis. Either way, it makes a very memorable experience.

THE PICTON FERRY

The magical journey between the North and the South Islands via Cook Strait takes 3 hours by ferry and should not be missed. Booking is essential. Contact Picton Tourist Information Office or **Interislander Ferry**, Wellington; tel: 0800 802 802 or 04 498 3302; www.interislandline.co.nz. The schedule is given in the *Thomas Cook Overseas Timetable*, table nos 9780/1.

Picton Harbour is 400 metres outside the town. In Wellington the Interislander ferry terminal is on Aotea Quay, 2 kilometres north, while the Lynx ferry terminal is in the centre of town.

If you're not a romantic and/or in a hurry, you could fly between the two islands for a similar price.

MARLBOROUGH SOUNDS MARITIME PARK

The unusual stretch of coastline at the north-eastern tip of the South Island - a disparate collection of tiny islands and peninsulas indented with even more miniscule bays and coves - has been designated the **Marlborough Sounds Maritime Park**. It was formed when movements of the earth's crust caused the land level to fall, allowing the sea to inundate the web of branching river valleys. Many of the islands are protected wildlife reserves, but a network of roads and tracks has been created through the peninsulas for residents of the small settlements and isolated homesteads.

To get an overview by land, take the road from Havelock to Titirangi, from where there are amazing ocean views. Allow a day to explore the 69-kilometre road fully - you can stay at the **Te Mahia Bay Resort,** tel/fax: 03 573 4089. The road is only sealed for the first 29 kilometres, but your efforts will be rewarded. Out of holiday season, the road is often deserted and the entire area is quiet and uncommercialised. There can be no better introduction to the South Island. If you're tempted to return, you will be in good company - Captain Cook stayed here five times.

It would be a mistake to miss the opportunity to view the Sounds by boat. Self-drive hire boats are available all along the waterfronts of Havelock and Picton, but it's also possible to join an excursion. Kayaking is also popular in the sheltered waters of the sound. **Marlborough Sounds Adventure Company**, Picton tel: 03 573 6078 or 0800 283 283, fax: 03 573 8827; www.marlboroughsounds.co.nz) offers guided tours that include an evening trip with barbecue; other firms include **Havelock Sea Kayaking Co**, Havelock (tel: 03 574 2114) and **Sea Kayaking Adventure Tours** (tel: 03 574 2765), based at Anikawa, Queen Charlotte Sound. For a more relaxing tour of the area, **Boat Dolphin Watch Marlborough** (tel: 03 573 8040, fax: 03 573 8040; www.dolphinwatchmarlborough.co.nz) offers twice-daily guided eco-tours of the Motuara Island bird sanctuary.

THE ROARING FORTIES

Cook Strait lies within the Roaring Forties and is subject to unpredictable weather conditions and powerful currents, which makes it one of the most dangerous stretches of water in the world. The sinking of the inter-island ferry *Wahine*, which foundered in Wellington Harbour during a storm on 10 April 1968, occurred when the vessel was blown off course by freak gale-force winds before striking Barretts Reef. Not to worry – most of the time the weather is kind and the crossing uneventful.

COOK STRAIT AND THE MARLBOROUGH SOUNDS

Queen Charlotte Sound

An important Maori trade route, now plied by Interislander Ferries, Queen Charlotte Sound was named after the niece of the Duke of Mecklenburg who married King George III of England and bore him 15 children. The 67 kilometre-long **Queen Charlotte Track** is an opportunity to get acquainted with the natural charms of the area. The path runs from Ship Cove to Anakiwa through coastal forest, coves and inlets, including a beautiful waterfall. To walk the entire track takes about four days, but if you're on a tight schedule, the boat will drop you off at one point and pick you up again at another. Everywhere there are staggering views of the Queen Charlotte and Kenepuru Sounds. Contact the Picton Department of Conservation office for further details (see p. 267).

The MV *Mavis*

The MV *Mavis* takes visitors on trips round the Sounds. Built from kauri wood in 1919, she originally worked as a mail-boat and mussel carrier. The route varies, but usually involves a spot of sightseeing, fishing, visits to mussel farms and opportunities for picnics and swimming. For more information, contact Classic Cruises, tel: 03 574 2114.

Water taxis run to various points in the Sounds from Picton and the **Cougar Line** (tel: 03 573 7925 or 0800 504 090, fax: 03 573 7926; www.cougarlinecruises.co.nz, will arrange drop-off and pick-up points for trampers. **Beachcomber Cruises** (tel: 03 573 6175, fax: 03 573 6176; e-mail: beachcomber@xtra.co.nz) offers tours of the bays, plus various other options including the mailboat trip (see below) and luncheon cruises. Also try **Tramp the Track Boat Ltd**, tel: 0800 287 267; www.charterguide.co.nz/hts/1097.htm.

Pelorus Sound

Named after HMS *Pelorus,* which explored the Sound in 1838, this is another stunningly beautiful area, with walking tracks along the banks particularly popular with anglers. The mailboat travels the length of Pelorus Sound every Tuesday, Thursday and Friday, leaving from the Havelock Marina at 0930 or from Picton at 1015. You can book it through **Beachcomber Cruises** (tel: 03 573 6175 or 0800 624 526). The boat calls at isolated homesteads and the occasional mussel farm en route, taking about 7 hours all told, so it's not ideal if you're in a hurry.

PICTON

The small port of Picton lies in the beautiful surroundings of the Marlborough Sounds, 29 kilometres north of Blenheim and 146 kilometres east of Nelson. Originally known as Newton, the town changed its name in 1859 to honour one of the generals at the Battle of Waterloo – Sir Thomas Picton.

A whaling station for a time, Picton is now a ferry terminal, providing moorings for the yachts of wealthy wine-estate owners. An old sailing vessel, ***Edwin Fox***, is currently being restored in a dry dock on Picton Foreshore. Built in 1853 from Burma teak, the clipper carried convicts to Australia and migrants to New Zealand. She was later converted into a coal hulk before suffering the ultimate indignity of serving as a breakwater. The remains were acquired by the Picton Restoration Society for 10 cents. The Visitor Centre by the mooring (tel: 03 573 6868) has displays on the history of the ship.

The new **Aquarium of the Marlborough Sounds** (open daily 0900–1700; tel: 03 573 6030), next door, pumps sea water directly into its 16 tanks, including a shark tank and touch pool.

Picton Community Museum is on London Quay (tel: 03 573 8283), and is far better than most small community museums in New Zealand. It has a collection focused on the whaling trade, which was carried on locally for over a century.

'The South Island is the stricken canoe of Aoraki, with its crew on one side forming the mountains, and its shattered, sunken prow in the north forming the sounds: Te Hoiere (Pelorus Sound) and Totaranui (Queen Charlotte Sound).'

Official explanation in the Department of Conservation publication *The Marlborough Sounds*

i **Picton Visitor Information Centre** Picton Foreshore; tel: 03 573 7477, fax: 03 573 5021; e-mail: pictonvin@xtra.co.nz.
Department of Conservation Office Picton Foreshore; tel: 03 520 3007, fax: 03 573 5021.

Aldan Lodge Motel **$$** 86 Wellington St; tel: 03 573 6833 or 0800 277 278, fax: 03 573 6091; e-mail: aldanlodge@xtra.co.nz. Clean, comfortable units close to the harbour. Children's playground.
Bell Bird Motel **$** 96 Waikawa Rd; tel/fax: 03 573 6912. Good-value accommodation in attractive setting. Breakfasts available.
Harbour View Motel **$$** 30 Waikawa Rd; tel: 03 573 6259 or 0800 101 133, fax: 03 573 6982. Watch the ferries come in from the balcony of this welcoming modern motel.
Wedgwood House **$** 10 Dublin St; tel: 03 573 7797, fax: 03 573 6426; e-mail: wedgwoodhouse@xtra.co.nz. Centrally sited youth hostel.

Whatamonga Homestay $$ 425 Port Underwood Rd (9 km north-east of Picton); tel/fax: 03 573 7192, fax: 04 472 4085; www.whsl.co.nz; e-mail: info@whsl.co.nz. Fabulous setting, overlooking Whatamonga Bay. Large rooms with en suite bathrooms. Dinner by arrangement.

The Barn Café $ High St; tel: 03 573 7440. Dine in historic surroundings to the sound of 1960s music.

Le Café $ London Quay; tel: 03 573 5588. Asian and European food served by friendly staff. Open daily 0800–2200. Closed Mon–Tues, June–Aug.

Marlborough Terranean $$ 31 High St; tel: 03 573 7122. A popular candlelit restaurant with terrace, serving quality international dishes. Licensed and BYO.

PELORUS JACK

The name Pelorus also recalls Pelorus Jack, a dolphin that used to meet and greet the ships plying between Nelson and Wellington. The government passed an Order in Council protecting the creature in 1904 and it continued to welcome sailors for another eight years.

HAVELOCK

At the head of the beautiful Pelorus Sound is Havelock, the self-styled Greenshell Mussel Capital of the World. There are 200 mussel farms in the area and Havelock is the processing centre. Havelock was founded on gold mining and timber felling. It's best known nowadays for its restaurants, which specialise in the tasty *Perna canaliculus*. Probably the best of the eateries is **Mussel Boys**, where they're served either as 'steamers' (mussels in the whole shell) or 'flats' (grilled mussels on the half shell). They are delivered to your table in a handleless saucepan and you use the shells as a pair of tweezers to drag out the flesh. The licensed café is unpretentious with wooden tables and stools – knives and forks available only on request.

BOATS FROM HAVELOCK Havelock is an ideal touring base for exploring the Marlborough Sounds (see also p. 265). For example, you can ride on one of the launches that makes the day-long trip delivering mail and provisions to farmers and campers. Alternatively, there are excursions to Tennyson Inlet, and to other places around the Sounds. Check this out with the **Havelock Outdoors Centre**, tel/fax: 03 574 2114; www.marlboroughadventures.co.nz.

'If greenlip mussels such as these were served in such quantity in a London restaurant I would have to mortgage my house to afford them.'

Clement Freud (British Liberal politician, broadcaster, journalist, author) BBC radio, 1978

Fishing The sheltered inlets of the Marlborough Sounds are ideal fishing territory. Chris Hobbs of **Marlborough Snapper Adventures,** Havelock (tel: 03 574 2911, fax: 03 574 2914; e-mail: hobzee@ihug.co.nz), takes visitors out on his boat, the 6-metre *Tamure*. Under his expert guidance it's possible to catch snapper weighing 2–9.5 kilograms on light tackle, as well as yellowtail kingfish and kahawai in season. Fishing is mainly in the Kenepuru and Pelorus Sounds. There are no guarantees you'll catch anything, but if you come back empty-handed your name will be entered into the history of Havelock.

i **Tourist Information Centre and Outdoors Centre**
Main Rd; tel: 03 574 2114; www.marlboroughadventures.co.nz. Also acts as booking agent for fishing trips and boat charters, and for the Department of Conservation.

Havelock Garden Motel $ 71 Main Rd; tel: 03 574 2387, fax: 03 574 2376; e-mail: havelockhideaway@xtra.co.nz.
Havelock YHA $ 46 Main Rd; tel: 03 574 2104, fax: 03 574 2109; e-mail: yhahave@yha.org.nz.
Havelock Motels $$ 52 Main Rd; tel: 03 574 2961, fax: 03 574 2412. New complex in town centre, with restaurant and hotel next door.

Mussel Boys Restaurant $ 73 Main Rd; tel: 03 574 2824. Open 1100–2100 in the summer, 1100–1900 in the winter.

Boat Hire

Pelorus Charters & Shipbrokers, Havelock Marina; tel: 03 574 2537. Bareboat charters. Havelock Water Taxis; tel: 03 572 9108. Boat charters for fishing, diving and scenic trips, as well as water-taxi work. Havelock Sea Charters; tel: 0800 727 007. Pelorus Sound Water Taxi; tel: 03 574 2151. *Miss Te Rawa*; tel: 03 572 9410. Marlborough Snapper Adventures; tel: 03 574 2911.

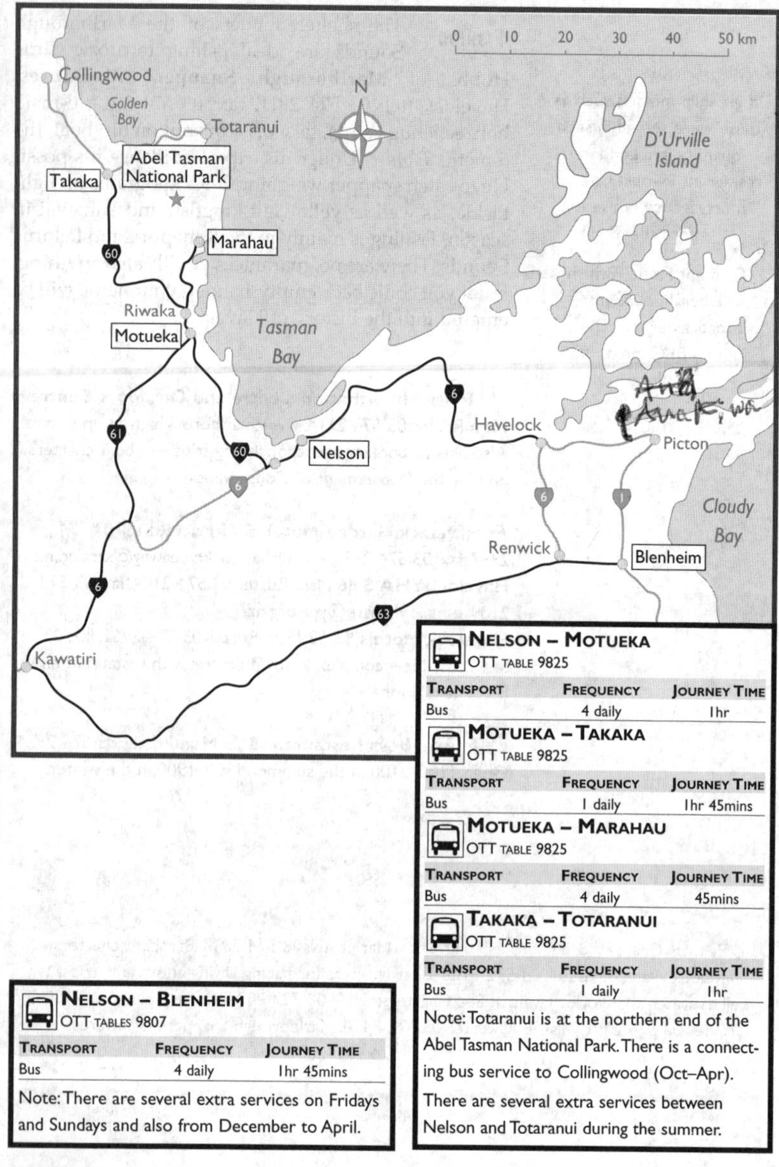

NELSON – MOTUEKA
OTT TABLE 9825

TRANSPORT	FREQUENCY	JOURNEY TIME
Bus	4 daily	1hr

MOTUEKA – TAKAKA
OTT TABLE 9825

TRANSPORT	FREQUENCY	JOURNEY TIME
Bus	1 daily	1hr 45mins

MOTUEKA – MARAHAU
OTT TABLE 9825

TRANSPORT	FREQUENCY	JOURNEY TIME
Bus	4 daily	45mins

TAKAKA – TOTARANUI
OTT TABLE 9825

TRANSPORT	FREQUENCY	JOURNEY TIME
Bus	1 daily	1hr

Note: Totaranui is at the northern end of the Abel Tasman National Park. There is a connecting bus service to Collingwood (Oct–Apr). There are several extra services between Nelson and Totaranui during the summer.

NELSON – BLENHEIM
OTT TABLES 9807

TRANSPORT	FREQUENCY	JOURNEY TIME
Bus	4 daily	1hr 45mins

Note: There are several extra services on Fridays and Sundays and also from December to April.

NELSON – BLENHEIM

The northern territories of the South Island are among the most pleasant spots in the hemisphere. Nelson, the main town, is one of the sunniest places with lots of well-designed green spaces. Blenheim is the centre of the most important wine-growing region of New Zealand. Over to the west are two national parks, Abel Tasman and Kahurangi, as well as the impressive Wakamarama Range and the Farewell Spit bird sanctuary. It's relatively easy to get around and explore and you'll find all kinds of hidden surprises.

From Havelock, State Highway 6 runs inland and west through Canvastown, Pelorus Bridge, Whangamoa, then down to the sea at Wakapuaka before reaching Nelson at the edge of Tasman Bay. From here the road passes through Stoke to reach Richmond, where you make a sharp right-hand turn onto State Highway 60, leading to Tasman and Motueka.

A worthwhile detour from here is to follow the track along the coast towards the Abel Tasman National Park. After 13 kilometres you'll come to Kaiteriteri and its crescent-shaped golden beach. The scenery here is stunning, the lush green hills the backdrop to the blue waters of Tasman Bay. Nine kilometres further along the track is Marahau, access point to the Abel Tasman National Park.

ROUTE DETAIL

From Havelock, take State Highway 6 through Canvastown, Pelorus Bridge, Whangamoa, and Wakapuaka to Nelson.

To Tasman and Motueka: At Richmond make a sharp right-hand turn onto State Highway 60, which leads to Tasman and Motueka directly. (See the introduction above for details about a detour to Abel Tasman National Park.)

To Collingwood: From Motueka take State Highway 60 through Upper Takaka, returning to the coast at Takaka.

Takaka – Collingwood	25 km

To return to Blenheim: Go back to Motueka, then take State Highway 61, through Stanley Brook, before rejoining State Highway 6 to cross the Hope Saddle. At Kawatiri turn sharp left onto State Highway 63, which leads to the ski resort of St Arnaud, at the tip of the Nelson Lakes National Park. The road drops slowly to Hillersden, from where it runs through the Wairau Valley to Renwick and Blenheim.

Nelson – Blenheim

Leave Motueka and take State Highway 60 inland through Upper Takaka, before returning to the coast at Takaka. Twenty-five kilometres further on is the town of Collingwood.

Return to Motueka, then take State Highway 61, through Stanley Brook, before rejoining State Highway 6 to cross the Hope Saddle. Turn sharp left onto State Highway 63, which leads to the ski resort of St Arnaud, at the tip of the Nelson Lakes National Park. The road drops slowly to Hillersden, from where it runs through the Wairau Valley to Renwick and Blenheim.

Nelson

Nelson is one of the most attractive cities in New Zealand, with numerous gardens and wonderful views of the Tasman Bay. The whole town has a nautical flavour: many of the streets are named after the great seadog's battles as well as the ships that brought pioneer settlers to the region. The pakeha name is more imaginative than the decidedly prosaic Maori alternative of Whakatu, which can be translated as 'the place where you dump broken canoes'.

Nelson is a fertile area with a backdrop of green hills and a coastline of stunning beaches and tidal estuaries. The population of just over 40,000 enjoys more than 2400 hours of sun a year, making it the sunniest spot in New Zealand together with neighbouring Blenheim. The town's most important building is the neo-Gothic **Christ Church Cathedral** at the top of Trafalgar St, the main thoroughfare. Construction began in 1925, but dragged on for many years while arguments raged about the safety of the tower, which was not earthquake-proofed. A modified design was eventually completed in 1967. (Open daily 0800–1900.)

'Every house [in Nelson] was neat and pretty. The site is, I think, as lovely as that of any town I ever saw. Merely to breathe there, and to dream, and to look around was a delight. Nobody seemed to be either rich or poor, – to be either great or humble ... I was very much in love with Nelson during the few hours that I passed there.'

Anthony Trollope, *Australia and New Zealand*, 1873

The **Bishops School**, in Nile St East, served the community for nearly a century from 1844 until the 1930s (open by appointment, tel: 03 548 4043). The **Suter Art Gallery** at 208 Bridge St (tel: 03 548 4699, fax: 03 548 1236; www.thesuter.org.nz) was founded in 1899 as an exhibition hall for art and crafts. Today there's an excellent collection of Maori art here, although the most well-known painting, of Maori heroine Huria Matenga, is by Gottfried Lindauer, a pakeha. (Open daily 1030–1630.) **Founders Historic Park** at 87 Atawhai Drive, 2 kilometres from town (tel: 03 548 2649), is an

BEACHES

The best of Nelson's many beaches is Tahuna, some 5 kilometres from the centre of the town. Further out (25 kilometres) is Rabbit Island with 13 kilometres of uninterrupted sand.

outdoor museum that aims to re-create a typical late-19th-century village. The reconstructed buildings include Rutherford's boyhood home, a newspaper office, a bakery and a wind-powered flour mill, while local craftsmen demonstrate traditional skills such as glass blowing. (Open daily 1030–1630.) The **Nelson Provincial Museum** lies just outside the city, at **Isel Park**, and claims to have the largest photographic collection in New Zealand. (Open Mon–Fri 1000–1600, Sat–Sun 1400–1600; tel: 03 547 9740; e-mail: museum@iconz.co.nz.) Also in the park is **Isel House**, a stone mansion built before the turn of the 20th century that has collections of china and handcarved furniture. The house is closed until further notice, though Isel Park is open daily 0800–dusk and is well worth a visit.

Brightwater, 19 kilometres south-west of Nelson, was in 1871 the birthplace of one of the world's greatest scientists, Ernest Rutherford, the father of nuclear physics. Rutherford studied at Nelson College before making a name for himself at Cambridge University in England. After splitting the atom, he won the Nobel Prize for Chemistry in 1908 and was elevated to the British peerage in 1931. He died in 1937 and is buried in Westminster Abbey, London.

FIRSTS

Nelson can claim many firsts: the first 8-hour working day in the world (1842); and in New Zealand, the first commercial brewery (1842), the first recognised racecourse (1845), the first railway line (originally a horse-drawn tramway) and the first rugby club (14 May 1870).

EN ROUTE

Broadgreen (276 Nayland Rd, Stoke; tel/fax: 03 546 0283; www.geocities.com/broadgreen_house), built in 1855, was designed to look like a Devon farmhouse. It has now been restored with its 19th-century fixtures and fittings. (Open daily 1030–1630.)

NO MONEY!

In 1839 Colonel William Gibbon Wakefield of the New Zealand Company arrived in Nelson with the intention of settling the area but found 'too few gentlemen with too little money' to buy the allotments. Five years later the Company itself went bankrupt leaving the Nelson project in a parlous state. The area eventually prospered thanks to German immigrants.

Nelson Visitor Information Centre cnr Trafalgar and Halifax St; tel: 03 548 2304, fax: 03 546 7393; e-mail: vin@latitudenelson.co.nz.

Department of Conservation Office 186 Bridge St; tel: 03 546 9335.

Admirals Motor Inn $$ 26 Waimea Rd; tel: 03 548 3059 or 0800 745 755, fax: 03 548 3057; www.nzmotels.co.nz/admirals; e-mail: admiralsnn@xtra.co.nz. Close to the city centre and adjacent to a restaurant and bar. Swimming pool and spa.

California House Inn $$$ 29 Collingwood St; tel: 03 548 4173, fax: 03 548 4184; www.californiahouse.co.nz; e-mail: info@californiahouse.co.nz. Treat yourself to a bit of luxury in this beautifully restored 1893 villa. Price includes a delicious breakfast.

Cambria House $$$ 7 Cambria St; tel: 03 548 4681 or 0800 548 4681, fax: 03 546 6649; www.cambria.co.nz; e-mail: cambria@cambria.co.nz. Wooden house in a pretty garden setting. Good breakfasts.

Leisure Lodge $$ 40 Waimea Rd; tel: 03 548 2089 or 0800 333 089, fax: 03 546 8502; www.leisurelodge.co.nz; e-mail: stay@leisurelodge.co.nz. Well-appointed units near the centre. Restaurant and bar.

Nelson Central YHA $ 59 Rutherford St; tel: 03 545 9988, fax: 03 545 9989; e-mail: yhanels@yha.org.nz. One of the best hostels in New Zealand.

Rutherford Hotel Nelson $$$ Trafalgar Sq.; tel: 03 548 2299 or 0800 437 227, fax: 03 546 3003. Smart hotel with bar and three restaurants.

Trailways Motor Inn $$$ 66 Trafalgar St; tel: 03 548 7049 or 0800 872 459; www.trailways.co.nz; e-mail: trailway@ts.co.nz. Quiet riverside motel with licensed restaurant.

Faces Café Bar $ 136 Hardy St; tel: 03 548 8755. Licensed sidewalk café offering Mediterranean-inspired dishes. Open daily from 1100.

The Grape Escape $$ McShane Rd; tel: 03 544 4341. The vineyard café of two wineries – Te Mañia Estate and Richmond Plains, one of only two organic wine producers in the Nelson region.

Boat Shed Café $$ 350 Wakefield Quay; tel: 03 546 9783. Open daily breakfast, lunch and dinner. In an area of superb fish restaurants this one stands out. You have to book as it is always busy. In summer try to get a seat outside on the balcony over the water so that you can watch the sun set over Tasman Bay. A short taxi ride from the city centre. Licensed.
The Forum $–$$ 223 Hardy St; tel: 03 546 6691. All-day snack menu, and evening dining in converted old bank building. Dancing until late.

MOTUEKA

Motueka, meaning 'wood hens in a grove of trees', 'crippled wood hen' or even 'land of the wood hens' (you pays your money and you takes your choice), lies on the Tasman Bay coast, and is part of the Nelson fruit belt. The local orchards grow apples, pears, kiwifruit, berryfruit, stonefruit and the country's finest hops.

The first Europeans arrived here in the 1840s. One reminder of those early days is the **Te Ahurewa Maori Church** on Pah Street, opposite the Post Office, a simple structure built in 1897. A female settler wrote of Motueka:

'The climate is delightful. It has neither the rains of Auckland nor the winds of Port Nicholson. The waters abound in fish of excellent quality, and the land with birds, pigeons, quails, wild duck and parrots.'

Nowadays, if you want to see birds, drive out of town by way of Staples St to the Motueka Sandspit, which boasts a large variety of seabirds, including pied oystercatchers, banded dotterels and bar-tailed godwits.

i **Visitor Information Centre** Wallace St; tel: 03 528 6543, fax: 03 528 6563; e-mail: mzpvin@xtra.co.nz; www.motueka.net.nz.

Abel Tasman Motel & Lodge $–$$ 45 High St; tel/fax: 03 528 6688 or 0800 845 678; e-mail: abel.tasman. motel@ xtra.co.nz. Five minutes' walk from the town centre.
Bakers Lodge $ 4 Poole St; tel: 03 528 0102, fax: 03 528 0103; e-mail: bakerslodge@motueka.co.nz. Award-winning youth hostel.
Equestrian Lodge Motel $ Tudor St; tel: 03 528 9369 or 0800 668 782, fax: 03 528 6369; www.equestrianlodge.co.nz; e-mail: equestrianlodge@xtra.co.nz. Spacious units in park setting close to the centre. Swimming pool and children's playground.

TONGA ISLAND

A boat leaves Marahau every day at 0845 and 1300 to take visitors to Tonga Island Marine Reserve, off the Abel Tasman National Park coast. On arrival passengers don wetsuits, snorkels, masks and fins for a guided swim with seals (dolphins too sometimes). Abel Tasman Seal Swim (tel: 0800 527 8136, fax: 03 527 8136; www.nelson.net.nz/web/sealswim) has the requisite Marine Mammal Licence.

Motueka Garden Motel $ 71 King Edward St; tel: 03 528 9299 or 0800 101 911, fax: 03 528 6284; e-mail: romelaine@hotmail.com. Facilities include children's playground, mini-golf, swimming and spa pools.

Hot Mamas Café $ 105 High St; tel: 03 528 7039. Relaxed atmosphere with a blackboard menu as well as *à la carte*. There's a sheltered patio garden with herbs, roses and lavender and live music at weekends. Licensed and BYO. Open daily 0830–late.

Jacaranda Park Garden Café $$ off College St West, 4 km from town; tel: 03 528 7777. Beautiful garden with great views of the countryside. Excellent food including home-made specialities and extensive wine list. Open daily 0930–1630.

MARAHAU

Marahau lies at the eastern entrance to the Abel Tasman National Park. There's accommodation here at all price levels as well as two cafés so an overnight stay is definitely on the cards.

South of Marahau, Highway 60 crosses Takaka Hill – known as the Marble Mountain – which offers splendid views of the sea.

Abel Tasman Marahau Lodge $$ Marahau Beach Rd; tel: 03 527 8250, fax: 03 527 8258; www.abeltasmanmarahaulodge.co.nz; e-mail: jan@abeltasmanmarahaulodge.co.nz. Motel in beautiful surroundings. Ensuite luxury units and room service.

Ocean View Chalets $ Marahau Beach Rd; tel: 03 527 8232, fax: 03 527 8211; www.abel.tasman.chalets.webnz.co.nz; e-mail: o.v.ch@xtra.co.nz. Wooden chalets overlooking the sea at the edge of the National Park.

The Park Café $ Harvey Rd; tel: 03 527 8270 or 03 527 8158. Open 0800–late. At the entrance to the National Park, this café with splendid views is also a shop, an information centre, art gallery, craft shop and much else. It will provide you with packed lunches and it caters for vegetarians.

NELSON LAKES NATIONAL PARK

Just over an hour's drive south of Nelson city is one of the South Island's most attractive national parks. Covering an area of 102,000 hectares, Nelson Lakes National Park encompasses long bush-clad valleys, two magnificent lakes and spectacular alpine scenery. Main entry point to the park is the sleepy little township of St Arnaud, on the shores of Lake Rotoiti. Here visitors can find accommodation and obtain further information about the park.

On first seeing the densely forested shores of Lake Rotoiti in 1860, an early explorer commented; 'The surface of the lake swarmed with birds, giving life to this magnificent scene.' However, not long after the first Europeans arrived in the region, the animals they introduced caused havoc among the local wildlife. Having never encountered such efficient predators, the birds had no defences against the stoats and rats that killed their chicks and stole their eggs. Even introduced wasps competed successfully against the birds, depriving them of the sugary honeydew, produced by a small insect that lives on the native beech trees. Fortunately, in recent years, an eradication programme carried out by the Department of Conservation has enabled a renaissance of the local bird life. Poison bait was laid out for the stoats and rats, and poison also worked successfully with the wasps, eliminating 99 per cent of their nests. An interesting side effect of the reduced wasp population was a significant increase in native insects as well.

One of the birds to benefit most from this programme is the beautiful kaka parrot. Once, large flocks of kaka were common in the area, but in more recent times you had to count yourself lucky if you heard, let alone saw one of these endangered birds. Now trampers have an excellent chance of actually seeing the parrots. The best time for kaka spotting is early in the morning, when they are most active. Other birds that can be seen on a walk through the park include bush robins, bellbirds and in the higher regions the kea, a mountain parrot. Only a short stroll is the Bellbird Walk, which takes 15 minutes and is accessible for wheelchairs. Other walks of less than 2 hours include the Peninsula Nature Walk and Loop Track. Both offer a good introduction to the native beech forest that predominates here. A more ambitious walk, and a great introduction to tramping in alpine regions for those with limited experience, is the Travers-Sabine Circuit. It takes five to six days and starts and finishes in St Arnaud.

Other activities in the park include skiing on the Mt Robert and Rainbow ski fields in winter, angling for brown trout in lakes Rotoiti and Rotoroa, boat trips on both lakes and guided ecotours. More information on what to do in the region is provided by the website www.starnaud.co.nz.

Information: Nelson Lakes Area Office and Visitor Centre, at the DOC camping ground on Lake Rotoiti, a short stroll from St Arnaud township; tel: 03 521 1806, fax: 03 521 1891; e-mail: starnaudao@doc.govt.nz.

Transport to St Arnaud is provided by Nelson Lakes Transport in Nelson and St Arnaud; tel: 03 547 5912, fax: 03 547 5914; e-mail: nlt@xtra.co.nz.

THE ABEL TASMAN NATIONAL PARK

Abel Tasman is one of the smaller National Parks of New Zealand, covering an area of 23,000 hectares, and can be explored by a mixture of cruising and walking. Some of the tramps can take days, but there are also several walks of less than 4 hours. However, because the park boasts absolutely stunning coastal scenery, it is very popular, and tracks and huts can be crowded in summer. **Abel Tasman National Park Enterprises**, at 265 High St, Motueka (tel: 03 528 7675 or 0800 223 582, fax: 03 528 0297; www.abeltasman.co.nz), has details of combined cruise and walk options. The shortest trip starts from the settlement of Marahau and cruises to Anchorage, beyond Pitt Head in Torrent Bay. From here there's a walk via Te Pukatea Bay to Pitt Head itself where the boat is waiting. Slightly more exerting is the trip that starts with a cruise to Tonga Bay by way of the seal colony on **Tonga Island**. The walk leads back down the coast, past the Tonga Arches to Bark Bay and the boat.

The main tramp in the park is the beautiful three- to four-day Coast Track. Classified as a 'Great Walk', it is also one of the country's easier multi-day walks. Tougher is the three- to five-day Inland Track, which is much less crowded than its coastal counterpart.

Sea kayaks, however, are the ideal way to explore the islands and bays of this ecologically sensitive area. For beginners, the best bet is a tour led by a guide with sound local knowledge who can lead you straight to the seals and dolphins. The kayaks are one- and two-seaters and come fully equipped. A half-day tour is probably about right if you've never been canoeing before. Contact **Abel Tasman Kayaks** (Marahau Beach; tel/fax: 03 527 8022 or 0800 527 8022; www.kayaktours.co.nz) or **Ocean River Sea Kayaking** (Marahau Beach; tel: 03 527 8266 or 0800 732 529, fax: 03 527 8006; www.seakayaking.co.nz).

i **Department of Conservation** cnr High St and King Edward St, Motueka; tel: 03 528 9117, fax: 03 528 6751.

TAKAKA AND GOLDEN BAY

From Motueka head north-west for a scenic drive over the 'Marble Mountain', and you'll drop down into the main town of the area, Takaka, a rural service centre with a population of around 1100 out of season.

The Dutch explorer, Abel Tasman, arrived off the coast of Golden Bay on 13 December 1642, anchoring off the Tata Islands. Six days later members of his crew became involved in an altercation with the local Maoris, and four of the sailors were killed. A chastened Tasman christened the place 'Murderers Bay' before moving on

KAHURANGI NATIONAL PARK

Established in 1996, the Kahurangi National Park covers some 452,000 hectares, and encompasses glaciated mountain ranges and dense forest. More than half of New Zealand's plant species are to be found here, 67 of which exist nowhere else in the country. Kahurangi is also home to more than 18 species of native bird, including the great spotted kiwi, blue duck and rock wren.

The 82 kilometre-long **Heaphy Track**, which passes through the Kahurangi National Park to Kohaihai Bluff, is one of New Zealand's Great Walks. It takes four to six days to complete and will introduce you to a wide diversity of landscapes. For maps, hut passes and detailed information, contact one of the local visitors centres or DOC offices.

'as no friendship could be made with these people, nor water nor refreshments be obtained.'

Don't miss a trip to **Te Waikoropupu (Pupu) Springs**, just beyond Takaka, which is claimed to be the world's clearest freshwater spring. Further on you'll discover **Collingwood**, a small beachside township with its roots firmly in the gold rush of the 1840s.

Cape Farewell Horse Treks (Puponga, tel/fax: 03 524 8031; www.horsetreksnz.com), at the base of Farewell Spit, offers trips through superb trekking countryside, lasting from 90 minutes to ten days. Horses for all abilities.

There are several craft studios in Golden Bay not far from Collingwood. **Tim Jessep Pottery**, Lookout Rd (take State Highway 60 to Parapara Beach) specialises in large patio ware (tel: 03 524 8663; open daily 1000–1700), while nearby **Estuary Arts** is noted for its distinctive, brightly coloured art work (tel: 03 524 8466; open Sept–Apr Wed–Sun 1000–1700). **Living Light Candles** on Tukurua Rd (tel: 03 525 7575; open daily, summer 0900–1800, winter 0900–1700) sells hand-made candles of every shape, size and colour. **Eckert Art Works**, also on Tukurua Rd, sells sculpture and furniture by Tim Eckert (tel: 03 525 7257; open daily 1030–1700).

FAREWELL SPIT

Farewell Spit extends for 35 kilometres to the east of **Cape Farewell**. Both were named by Cook as he left for Australia at the end of his first visit in March 1770. The best way to see the spit is by guided tour (Farewell Spit Tours, tel: 03 524 825 7 or 0800 808 257, fax: 03 524 8939 or Farewell Spit Nature Tours, tel: 0800 250 500; www.farewell-spit.co.nz). You'll be shown some of the most spectacular sand dunes in the world, upwards of 20 metres in height. Farewell Spit is also a wildlife refuge for the protection of birds, specifically the bar-tailed godwit and other migratory species that spend the summer here before moving on to Siberia and Alaska.

Department of Conservation 62 Commercial St, Takaka; tel: 03 525 8026, fax: 03 525 8444; e-mail: goldenbayao@doc.govt.nz.
Visitor Information Centre Willow St, Takaka; tel: 03 525 9136, fax: 03 525 9288; e-mail: gb.vin@nelsonnz.com.

Anatoki Lodge Motel $$ 87 Commercial Street, Takaka; tel: 03 525 8047 or 0800 262 333, fax: 03 525 8433; www.nzmotels.co.nz/anatoki; e-mail: anatoki@xtra.co.nz. Central to local attractions.
Collingwood Beachcomber Motels $ Tasman St, Collingwood; tel: 03 524 8499 or 0800 270 520, fax: 03 524 8599; e-mail: promotionmedia@paradise.net.nz. Views over the river estuary. Will organise excursions to Farewell Spit.
Collingwood Homestead $$ Elizabeth St, Collingwood; tel: 03 524 8079, fax: 03 524 8979; www.collingwoodhomestead.co.nz; e-mail: maggie@collingwoodhomestead.co.nz. Spacious rooms in large colonial-style house, with breakfasts and dinners.
Pioneer Motels $ Tasman St, Collingwood; tel: 03 524 8109 or 0800 180 109, fax: 03 524 8394. New motel close to the beach.
Sans Souci Inn $$$ Richmond Rd, Pohara; tel/fax: 03 525 8663. Unique Mediterranean-style accommodation, just 2 mins from the beach, with award-winning food and wine.
Skara Brae $$ Elizabeth Street, Collingwood; tel: 03 524 8464, fax: 03 524 8474; www.accommodationcollingwood.co.nz; e-mail: skarabrae@xtra.co.nz. Bed and breakfast in an historic home.

BLENHEIM

The largest town in the Marlborough region owes its prosperity almost entirely to the wine industry. It seems that the entire Wairau Plain (26,500 hectares all told) was bought up around 1830 by a whaling captain, John Blenkinsopp, who pulled a fast one on the local Maoris. When the settlers began surveying the land, confrontation ensued, culminating in the 'Wairau Affray' when 22 Europeans and six Maoris were killed. The terms of the 'agreement' were renegotiated in 1847 when the new owners handed over the sum of £3000.

The first building was almost certainly a pub – 'the resort of all the disorderly characters' – but the discovery of gold in 1864 gave the locals a purpose in life, at least for a while. Today the population is around 26,500. It's a pleasant town with a lot of lush green spaces. In the centre is Seymour Square with a spectacular fountain and Blenkinsopp's cannon. Cross the footbridge over the Taylor River to **Pollard Park**, irrigated by Fulton Creek and with a duck pond surrounded by colourful flower beds and native plants. Two kilometres from the centre of Blenheim at Arthur Baker Place, off New Renwick Road, is the **Brayshaw Historic Museum Park**, where you'll find displays of old farming equipment, relocated colonial buildings re-creating an early 20th-century street, and a museum of local history (tel: 03 578 1712; open daily 1000–1600).

Five kilometres south of Blenheim, on State Highway 1, is Riverlands Cob Cottage, a mud-walled, shingle-roofed pioneer house dating from the 1860s and furnished in the style of the period (open continuously).

EN ROUTE

The Richmond Range lies some 26 kilometres west of Blenheim and the Department of Conservation has produced several excellent leaflets detailing the facilities and the walks in the area. It's a fairly unexacting climb to the summit of Mount Richmond (1760 metres) – you can easily manage it in a day trip from Blenheim.

WINE TOURS

Most of the major wineries cluster between Blenheim and Renwick. Avoid the kind of organised wine tour that carries busloads of tourists at breakneck speed from one vineyard to the next, allowing hardly any time to enjoy the product. Far better to plan your own itinerary. Listed in the next section are some wineries that welcome visitors.

i **Visitor Information Centre** 2 High St; tel: 03 578 9904, fax: 03 578 6084; e-mail: blm_info@clear.net.nz.

Aorangi Lodge Motel $$ 193 High St; tel: 03 578 2022 or 0800 507 050, fax: 03 578 2021; e-mail: aorangi.lodge.motel@xtra.co.nz. Central motel with swimming pool.

Colonial Motel $$ 66 Main St; tel: 03 578 9284 or 0800 105 789, fax: 03 578 2233. Motel in garden setting with swimming pool and children's playground.

The Grapevine $ 29 Park Tce; tel: 03 578 6062; e-mail: rob.diana@xtra.co.nz. Backpackers located in an old villa with views over river and park.

Henry Maxwell's $$ 28 Henry St; tel: 03 578 8086 or 0800 436 796, fax: 03 578 8089; www.henrymaxwells.co.nz. Bed and breakfast rooms with TVs. Outdoor spa, restaurants nearby.

Marlborough Hotel $$$ 20 Nelson St; tel: 03 577 7333 or 0800 115 533, fax: 03 577 7337; www.the-marlborough.co.nz; e-mail: themarlborough@xtra.co.nz. Modern hotel with large comfortable rooms, two restaurants and a bar.

Some of the best food is served in the vineyards listed in the following section.

D'urville Wine Bar & Brasserie $$ 52 Queen St; tel: 03 577 9945. Fresh local produce, great selection of local wines. Open every day for breakfast and dinner, Mon–Fri for lunch.

Rocco's Italian Restaurant $$ 5 Dodson St, Blenheim; tel: 03 578 6940 or 0800 100 948. Open Mon–Sat from 1730. Fresh pasta made daily by the Rocco brothers, who give the New Zealand cuisine – mainly fish – an Italian facelift. Try the crayfish or mussels alla pizzaiola (made with greenshell mussels on the half-shell, topped with a mild chilli-tomato sauce, sprinkled with cheese, and browned under the grill).

Whitehaven Winery Café $$ 1 Dodson St; tel: 03 577 6634. Garden setting. Formal evening dining in the Whitehaven Winery. Open all day every day.

THE REGION'S VINEYARDS

Nature has smiled on Marlborough, providing it with the ideal climate and soil for wine growing. Grapes were grown by the early settlers but its only in recent years that the wine industry has really taken off. Montana Wines of Auckland took the critical decision in the 1970s when they chose to expand here rather than Canterbury because of the more attractive land prices. At first the grapes were transported to Montana's Gisborne winery for processing, but in 1977 they built their own plant in Marlborough and other companies quickly followed suit: Swiss, French, and Australian interests now contribute to the native wine industry.

Currently there are more than 4000 hectares of vineyards under cultivation and over 40 wineries. The varieties grown include Sauvignon Blanc, Chardonnay, Riesling, Pinot Noir, Pinot Gris, Cabernet Sauvignon and Merlot.

WINE AND FOOD FESTIVAL

The Marlborough Wine and Food festival takes place annually on the second Saturday in February and attracts crowds of up to 7000. Besides wine tastings there are food stalls, craft exhibitions, music and special events.

If you're into wine, you'll find the book, *The Wines and Wineries of Marlborough*, on sale at Blenheim Information Office a worthwhile investment.

Alan Scott Wines Jacksons Rd; tel: 03 572 9054, fax: 03 572 9053; www.allanscott.com; open daily 0900–1700. Has the award-winning Twelve Trees restaurant on the premises, tel: 03 572 7123.

Cairnbrae Jacksons Rd; tel: 03 572 8018, fax: 03 572 7018; www.cairnbrae.co.nz. Vineyard owned by the family of Murray and Daphne Brown for several generations. The 'stony ridges' of the name refer to the exposed stone of the hillside which reflects heat onto the ripening grapes.

Cellier Le Brun Terrace Rd, Renwick; tel: 03 572 8859, fax: 03 572 8814; www.lebrun.co.nz; open daily 0900–1700. Offers tastings of its 'sparkling white' in a small café. This is a most elegant drop of bubbly, possibly because the winemaker is French and comes from a family that has been in the business since 1640.

Clifford Bay Estate 626 Rapaura Rd; tel: 03 572 7132, fax: 03 572 7138; www.cliffordbay.co.nz. Open daily 0930–1630 (summer), 1000–1630 (winter). Tastings and cellar door sales. The attached restaurant is open for lunches.

Cloudy Bay Jacksons Rd; tel: 03 520 9140, fax: 03 520 9040; www.cloudybay.co.nz; open daily 1000–1630. The Sauvignon Blanc and the Chardonnay produced by this vineyard have been called two of the greatest white wines to come out of New Zealand.

Seafood platters are a local speciality: rainbow and brown trout, greenshell mussels, snapper, tarakihi and blue cod, washed down with a local wine – delicious!

Framingham Wine Co. Conders Bend Rd, Renwick; tel: 03 572 8884; www.framingham.co.nz; open daily 1000–1700. Prize-winning Riesling.

Gillan Estate Rapaura Rd; tel: 03 572 9979, fax: 03 572 9980; e-mail: gillanwines@voyager.co.nz; open daily 0930–1630 (summer), otherwise by appointment. Tastings with tapas and sales.

Grove Mill Waihopai Valley Rd, Renwick; tel: 03 572 8200, fax: 03 572 8211; www.grovemill.co.nz; open daily 1100–1700. Tastings and sales; also an art gallery!

Herzog Winery & Restaurant 81 Jeffries Rd; tel: 03 572 8770, fax: 03 572 8730; www.herzog.co.nz. The gourmet restaurant is open 4 Oct to end of April. Closed Mon during high season.

Highfield Estate Brookby Rd; tel: 03 572 8592, fax: 03 572 9257; www.highfield.co.nz; open daily 1000–1700. Offers tastings with tapas.

Hunter's Wines Rapaura Rd; tel: 03 572 8489, fax: 03 572 8457; www.hunters.co.nz; open Mon–Sat 0930–1630, Sun 1030–1600. Broad range of wines, but here you pay a nominal fee for the tastings. The restaurant, of a high international standard, is open for both lunch and dinner.

Johanneshof Cellars Koromiko; tel: 03 573 7035, fax: 03 573 7034; e-mail: johanneshofcellars@xtra.co.nz, open Tues–Sun 1000–1600 (summer), winter by arrangement. Underground cellars, free tastings and cellar door sales.

Lawson's Dry Hills Alabama Rd; tel: 03 578 7674, fax: 03 578 7603; www.lawsonsdryhills.co.nz; open daily 1000–1700. Tastings and sales with a restaurant open during the summer.

Montana Brancott Winery Marlborough, on State Highway 1, 5 km south of Blenheim; tel: 03 578 2099, fax: 03 579 1067; www.montanawines.com; open daily 0900–1700. Tours on the hour, tastings and sales. One of the oldest – originally established in 1934 near Auckland – certainly the largest local winemaker, supplying about 40 per cent of the country's wine.

Nautilus Estate 12 Rapaura Rd; tel: 03 572 9364, fax: 03 572 9374; www.nautilusestate.com. Cellar door sales. Open 1000–1700 (summer), 1030–1630 (winter).

Ponder Estate New Renwick Rd; tel: 03 572 8642, fax: 03 572 9034; www.ponder.co.nz; open daily 1000–1630 (May–Sept), 0930–1700 (Oct–Apr). Produces olive oil as well as award-winning wines.

The Wither Hills Walkway

Just 7 kilometres from Blenheim, off Taylor Pass Road, is the Wither Hills Walkway. The network of paths allows you to view the whole of the town and the Wairau Plain.

At one time the walkway was a barren area but it has since been replanted and is now a nature reserve with short, well-signposted walks. You can complete a circuit of the park (6 kilometres) in less than 3 hours.

Seresin Estate Bedford Rd; tel: 03 572 9408, fax: 03 572 9850; www.seresin.co.nz; open daily 1000–1630 (summer), Mon–Fri 1000–1630 (winter). A strong body of opinion has it that the Sauvignon Blanc and the Chardonnay produced here are the definitive wines of the area.

Shingle Peak Rapaura Rd; tel: 03 572 7150, fax: 03 572 9885; open daily 1000–1700. Tastings and sales. Indoor and outdoor dining in the brasserie.

Stoneleigh Jacksons Rd; www.stoneleigh.com; open daily 1000–1630. Very distinctive, individual wines.

Wairau River Wines Rapaura Rd; tel: 03 572 9800 or 0800 924 728, fax: 03 572 9885; www.wairauriverwines.com; open daily 1000–1700. Free tastings and good lunches in the restaurant.

A Wine Story

The first vines were planted by the British Resident, James Busby, in his back garden at Waitangi in 1836, but it has only really been in the last decade that the New Zealand wine industry has come of age.

The effort seems to have paid off. Nowadays there are over 40 wineries in the Blenheim area, ranging from the biggest producers in New Zealand to very small, specialist vineyards. Most of the major ones are between Blenheim and Renwick. The area is famous for its Sauvignon Blanc, but also for its Chardonnay. As a complement to the wine there is now a movement to produce a wide variety of gourmet food. All of this comes together at the annual Marlborough Food and Wine festival on the second Saturday in February.

Many of the grapes produced in this area find their way to North Island wineries to be blended with other varieties – a fact not widely publicised.

'I have no intention of living in France and not drinking New Zealand Sauvignon Blanc. I have arranged for regular consignments to be delivered. I cannot go back to drinking French white wine. No. Never. It is too much to ask.'

A French official on being given a home posting.

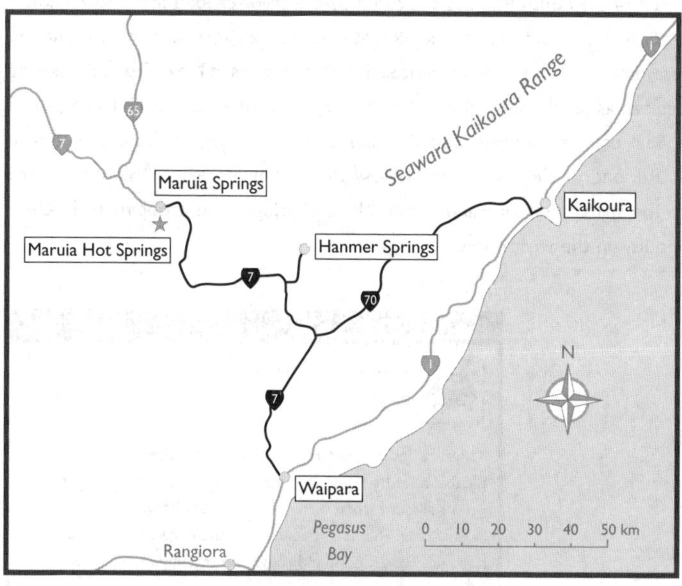

KAIKOURA – WAIPARA OTT TABLE 9800/9806		
TRANSPORT	**FREQUENCY**	**JOURNEY TIME**
Train	Daily	2hrs
Bus	3 daily	2hrs

Note: Additional bus services operate between December and February.

Notes

On Tuesdays, Thursdays and Saturdays there is a bus service between Kaikoura and Hanmer Springs; OTT table 9809. Between Waipara and Hanmer Springs there is a service twice daily with an extra bus on Fridays and Sundays; OTT table 9806.

Kaikoura – Waipara

The east coast of the South Island is sheltered by the snow-capped Seaward Kaikoura Range and boasts a sea so rich in nutrients that it attracts an amazing variety of marine life. Kaikoura, now one of the leading ecotourism destinations in New Zealand, has long been recognised as an abundant food source by the Maoris – *kai* means to eat, *koura* is crayfish. Seal colonies, whales, dolphins and albatrosses are also found here. The Lewis Pass Rd, one of the few routes across the mountains, leaves Waipara before climbing to the spa resorts of Hanmer and Mariua Springs, then dropping to Reefton and Greymouth on the west coast.

Route Detail

Kaikoura to Blenheim	126 km
Kaikoura to Christchurch	191 km

Kaikoura lies on State Highway 1, the east coast road from Blenheim in the north to Christchurch. Take Highway 1 south from Kaikoura, then turn right on State Highway 70 towards Swyncombe. This scenic road skirts the edge of the Seaward Kaikoura Range, passing through the settlements of Waiau and Rotherham.

Just after Rotherham, and before reaching Culverden, turn right onto State Highway 7, which follows the Waiau River. Turn right onto State Highway 7A, crossing the Waiau Ferry Bridge, then follow the signs for Hanmer Springs and the Forest Park.

Back on State Highway 7 you can take a detour westwards over the spectacular Lewis Pass to the less visited Maruia Springs. Return on the same road, past Marble Point where pink Hanmer marble is quarried, and through the village of Waikari to Waipara where State Highway 7 joins State Highway 1.

detour: 70 km

KAIKOURA

Kaikoura is famous for the variety of marine mammals that can be seen from its shores. The town itself (population of 2500) sits on a peninsula jutting out from the rugged coastline. In the 19th century, the local whaling stations used the cliffs as lookouts. You can see relics of those days in the **Kaikoura District Museum** (tel: 03 319 7440) at 14 Ludstone Rd (open Mon–Fri 1230–1630, Sat–Sun 1400–1600). More evocative though is **Fyffe House** (tel: 03 319 5835) at 62 Avoca St (on the peninsula), an old whaler's cottage, built on whalebone foundations with walls made from timber salvaged from shipwrecks. Open daily 1000–1800 (Nov–April), Thur–Mon 1000–1800 (May–Oct).

Two kilometres south of Kaikoura on State Highway 1 is the limestone Maori Leap Cave. You can go on a 35-minute tours among the stalagmites and stalactites, tinged red with iron oxide (tel: 03 319 5023).

Kaikoura's esplanade is reminiscent of a typical English seaside town but all similarities stop at the shoreline, where two strong ocean currents converge, dropping into a sheer canyon a few kilometres out to sea – the deep water provides a rich feast of marine organisms that attracts an astonishing variety of sealife. Pride of place belongs to the giant sperm whale, which can grow up to 20 metres in length. Sperm whales were once close to extinction, but can now be viewed nearly all the year round. You might also see humpback and southern right whales.

From October to April, dusky dolphins arrive in pods several hundred strong. New Zealand fur seals also make an appearance. There are opportunities to go wetsuit swimming with the seals and dolphins and the scuba-diving is also superb. Whale-watching trips are organised from the coast, by boat, light aircraft or helicopter.

Of the many operators, the Maori-owned **Whale Watch Kaikoura** (Whaleway Station; tel: 0800 655 121, fax: 03 319 6545; www.whalewatch.co.nz) are the most environmentally conscious. They run up to four 3½-hour trips daily in vessels specially built for the purpose. If they're booked up, try **Top Spot Seal Swim** Deal St; tel: 03 319 5540, fax: 03 319 6587; e-mail: topspot@xtra.co.nz. **Seal Swim Kaikoura** 202 Esplanade; tel: 03 319 6182, fax: 03 319 6186; www.kaikoura.co.nz/sealswim. **Dolphin Encounter** 58 West End; tel: 0800 733 365; www.dolphin.co.nz.

Flights can be arranged through **Wings Over Whales** Peketa Airfield; tel: 0800 226 629; www.whales.co.nz

SKIING

Another facility near Kaikoura is the Mt Lyford Ski Area, just 45 minutes from the town. It offers beginner and advanced slopes and there's a ski school, hire facilities and a shuttle bus from Kaikoura. Tel: 03 315 6178, fax: 03 315 6158; www.mtlyford.co.nz.

(30-minute flight) or **Kaikoura Helicopters**, Whaleway Station; tel: 03 319 6609, fax: 03 319 6814; www.worldofwhales.co.nz.

Keep your eyes open for the **Kaikoura Peninsula Walkway**, which leads from the town on a circuit of the peninsula. The sea caves and stacks are the breeding ground of red-billed and black-backed gulls as well as seals and you'll also encounter shags, herons and oystercatchers.

i **Kaikoura Visitor Centre** Westend Esplanade; tel: 03 319 5641, fax: 03 319 6819; e-mail: info@kaikoura.co.nz. Open daily 0900–1730 (summer), 0900–1700 (winter).

Kaikoura Top 10 Holiday Park $ –$$ 34 Beach Rd; tel/fax: 03 319 5362 or 0800 363 638; www.kaikouratop10.co.nz. Cabins, flats, motel and tent sites, near the centre of town.
Maui YHA $ 270 Esplanade; tel: 03 319 5931, fax: 03 319 6921; e-mail: yhakaikr@yha.org.nz.
White Morph Motor Inn $$$ 92–94 Esplanade; tel: 03 319 5014 or 0800 803 666, fax: 03 319 5015; www.whitemorph.co.nz; e-mail: info@whitemorph.co.nz. Waterfront motel close to town centre with own licensed restaurant.

There are a number of kiosks on State Highway 1 that sell crayfish. Restaurants in the area are quite expensive, but most sell superb local seafood.
Caves Restaurant $$$ State Highway 1 (2 km south of town); tel: 03 319 5023. Serves generous helpings of fish and seafood as well as local farm produce. Open Sun–Fri 0700–2000, Sat 0700–1800. Licensed and BYO.

HANMER SPRINGS

Ninety minutes north of Christchurch is the spa of Hanmer Springs, an alpine village in an active thermal area. Hanmer, with its snow-capped peaks, has always been popular with the people of Christchurch but it's now part of the international tourist circuit. The activities available in the resort range from bathing in the thermal-pools complex, with its adjacent health and fitness centre, to rafting and jet boating in the Waiau Canyon. The Hanmer Springs (on Mt St Patrick) and Mt Lyford ski fields are also within easy driving distance.

The thermal springs were discovered nearly 150 years ago and their therapeutic properties immediately recognised. **Thermal Reserve** (Amuri Ave; tel: 03 315 7511; www.hotfun.co.nz) is a modern complex with seven different open-air thermal pools and three sulphur pools (the hottest is 40°C), as well as free-form rock pools, a freshwater 25-metre swimming pool, toddler's pool, sauna and steam rooms. There are picnic areas, or you can visit the licensed Garden House Café and undo all the good work! Open daily 1000–2100.

Hanmer Springs also offers walking trails in the mountains, which are exceptionally beautiful during the autumn when the forests blaze with colour. One of the best routes is to the summit of **Conical Hill** (about 30 minutes each way), with rewarding views of the Hanmer Plains.

AN ALTERNATIVE TO THE CONICAL HILL WALK
Less demanding, and suitable for wheelchairs, is Woodland Walk, 45 minutes through beech woods and native scrub.

SPORT **Thrillseekers Canyon Adventure Centre** (tel: 03 315 7046, fax: 03 315 7057; www.thrillseeker.co.nz) offers bungy jumping, jet boating and other excitements.

Rainbow Adventures on the Jacks Pass Rd leads rafting trips on the Clarence, Jurunui and Waiau Rivers, also fun-yaking (in one- or two-seater inflatable kayaks), canyoning (scrambling up river banks and sliding down waterfalls) and tandem paragliding (including a helicopter trip) - tel: 03 315 7401 or www.rainbowadventures.co.nz for details.

Bikes can be hired from **Dust 'n' Dirt**, 20 Conical Hill Rd; tel: 03 315 7233. (Route maps are provided.)

Rainbow Horse Trekking tel: 03 315 7444 offers guided rides of varying degrees of difficulty.

Hanmer Springs Ski Area, on Mt St Patrick, is run by the Amuri Ski Club; tel/fax: 03 315 7201; www.snow.co.nz/hanmersprings.

i **Hurunui Visitors Information Centre** 42 Amuri Ave West; tel: 03 315 7128 or 0800 733 426; fax: 03 315 7658; e-mail: info@hurunui.com.

Alpine Garden Motel $$ 3 Leamington St; tel: 03 315 7332, fax: 03 315 7334; e-mail: alpinegardens@xtra.co.nz. Quiet location despite being close to spa pools. Comfortable rooms with verandas.
Forest Peak Motel $$ 4 Torquay Tce; tel/fax: 03 315 7132. Wooden cabins in attractive park setting. Some with open fires.
Hanmer Resort Motel $$$ 7 Cheltenham St; tel: 03 315 7362, fax: 03 315 7581. Clean, spacious units in central location, close to the thermal pools.
Kakapo Backpackers $ 14 Amuri Ave; tel/fax: 03 315 7472; e-mail: stay-kakapo@xtra.co.nz. Brand-new youth hostel 250 metres from the springs.

Kaikoura – Waipara

Jollie Jack's Café & Bar $$ The Mall, Conical Hill Rd; tel: 03 315 7388. Tasty dishes served inside or al fresco. Children's menu. Fully licensed. Open daily 1100–late.
The Old Post Office $$$ 2 Jacks Pass Rd; tel: 03 315 7461. Stylish restaurant in former post office. Open daily 1800–2300. Full range of local wines.

Bungy Jumping

New Zealand is without doubt the home of the bungy jump. The famous Kiwi A J Hackett launched his first commercial bungy jumping operation in Queenstown, and the activity has rocketed from there and is now available nationwide. To ensure that an operator you might use is safe and reliable, check with your local tourist office. The Waiau Ferry Bridge, constructed in 1887, is now a popular spot for bungy jumping. If you want to feel the adrenalin surge, contact: Thrillseekers Canyon Adventure Centre, tel: 03 315 7046, fax: 03 315 7057; www.thrillseeker.co.nz.

MARUIA SPRINGS

One hour's drive from Hanmer is the quieter thermal resort of Maruia. Facilities here include three natural outdoor pools, plus a cold plunge pool, traditional segregated Japanese-style bath-houses with soaking pool and jacuzzi, and private spa pools. There is a bar, café and restaurant, spectacular views and accommodation if you want to stay. Tel/fax: 03 523 8840; e-mail: enquiries@maruia.co.nz; open 0900–2100.

WHERE NEXT?

Continuing along State Highway 7 leads straight to the coastal town of Greymouth (see p. 326), the former gold and coal centre that now forms the largest commercial centre and town on the west coast.

CHRISTCHURCH

Despite its conservative face, Christchurch is a rather quirky place – surely no other city in the world can boast an official wizard paid for by the council and recognised by the Prime Minister? Its apparent 'Englishness' stems partly from the Gothic-revival architecture so popular in 19th-century Britain, partly from the Anglicised gardens, planted with oaks and daffodils, and partly from the climate which, in winter at least, is as cold and wet as the home country. Christchurch was the last and most successful colonising project inspired by Edward Gibbon Wakefield's New Zealand Company. Named Canterbury initially, it was rechristened after Christ Church College, Oxford – appropriately enough for a university town. It is now New Zealand's second-largest city with a population of 310,000.

THE CANTERBURY PILGRIMS

When the first official settlers arrived in December 1850 they called themselves the Canterbury Pilgrims to signify they were serious-minded, God-fearing followers of the Church of England. The Pilgrims looked down on earlier settlers, who they called 'Pre-Adamites', and a certain snob value still attaches to being descended from families who arrived in the First Four Ships.

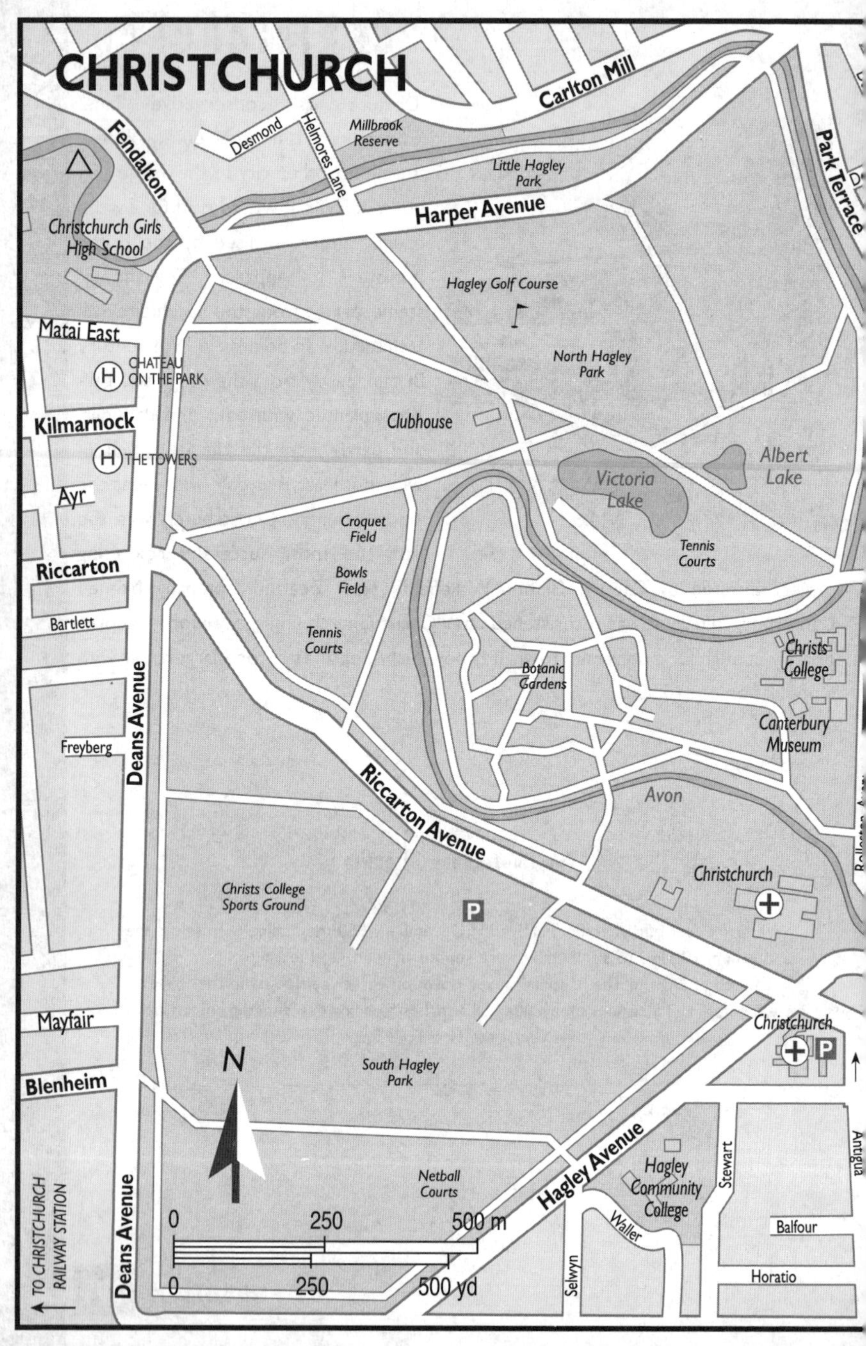
CHRISTCHURCH
Carlton Mill
Desmond
Helmores Lane
Millbrook Reserve
Little Hagley Park
Park Terrace
Fendalton
Harper Avenue
Christchurch Girls High School
Hagley Golf Course
Matai East
CHATEAU ON THE PARK
North Hagley Park
Kilmarnock
Clubhouse
THE TOWERS
Victoria Lake
Albert Lake
Ayr
Croquet Field
Tennis Courts
Riccarton
Bowls Field
Bartlett
Tennis Courts
Christs College
Botanic Gardens
Deans Avenue
Canterbury Museum
Freyberg
Riccarton Avenue
Avon
Christchurch
Christs College Sports Ground
P
Christchurch
Mayfair
N
South Hagley Park
Blenheim
Hagley Avenue
Hagley Community College
Stewart
Antigua
Netball Courts
Waller
Balfour
0
250
500 m
Selwyn
Horatio
0
250
500 yd
Deans Avenue
TO CHRISTCHURCH RAILWAY STATION

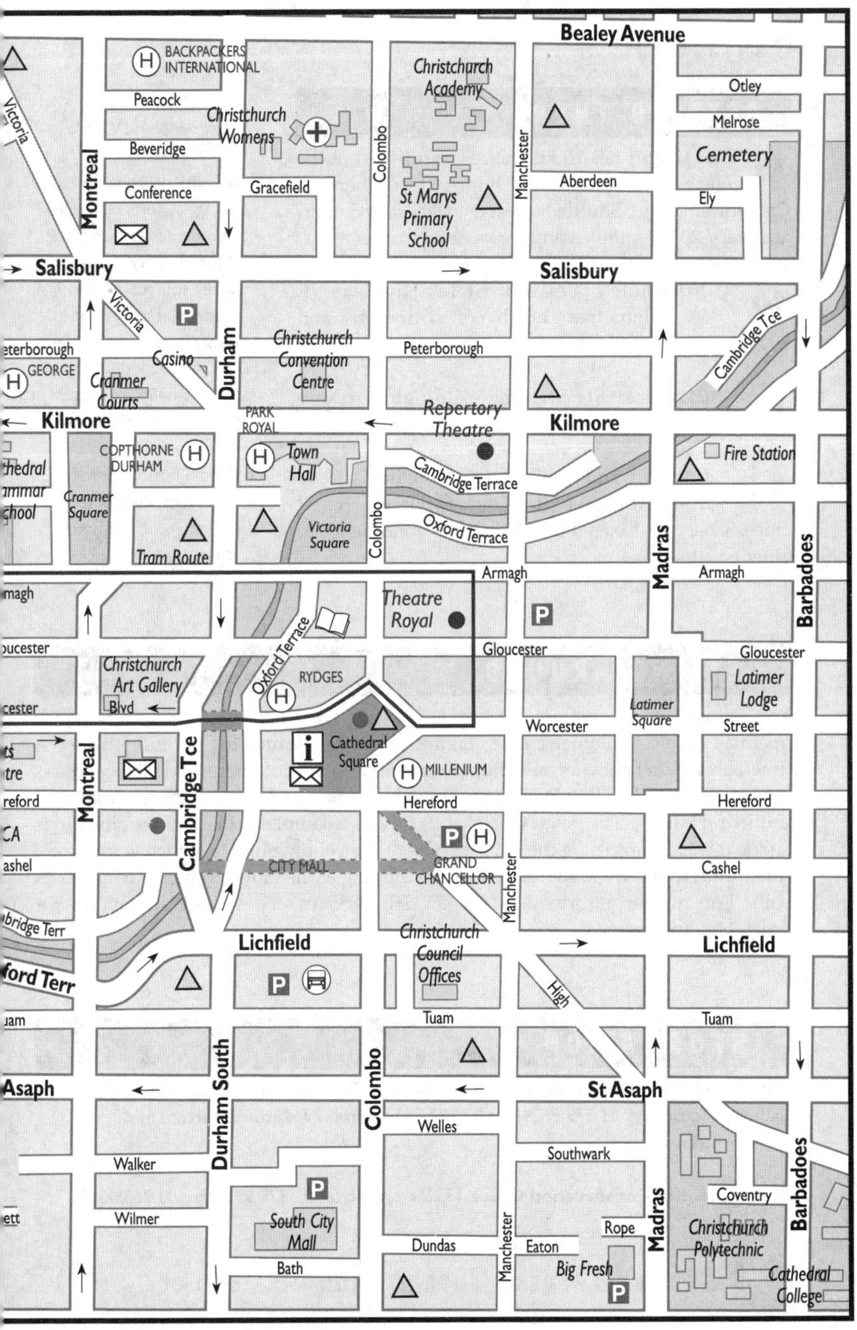

Bealey Avenue
BACKPACKERS INTERNATIONAL
Peacock
Christchurch Womens
Christchurch Academy
Otley
Melrose
Victoria
Beveridge
Colombo
Manchester
Cemetery
Montreal
Conference
Gracefield
St Marys Primary School
Aberdeen
Ely
Salisbury
Salisbury
Victoria
Christchurch Convention Centre
Peterborough
Peterborough
GEORGE
Casino
Cranmer Courts
Durham
Cambridge Tce
PARK ROYAL
Repertory Theatre
Kilmore
Kilmore
COPTHORNE DURHAM
Town Hall
Cambridge Terrace
Fire Station
Cranmer Square
Victoria Square
Oxford Terrace
Tram Route
Madras
Barbadoes
Armagh
Armagh
Theatre Royal
Oxford Terrace
Gloucester
Gloucester
Christchurch Art Gallery
Blvd
RYDGES
Latimer Lodge
Latimer Square
Worcester
Street
Cathedral Square
MILLENIUM
Montreal
Cambridge Tce
Hereford
Hereford
CITY MALL
GRAND CHANCELLOR
Manchester
Cashel
Christchurch Council Offices
Lichfield
Lichfield
High
Tuam
Tuam
Durham South
Colombo
St Asaph
Welles
Southwark
Walker
Coventry
Wilmer
South City Mall
Rope
Madras
Christchurch Polytechnic
Barbadoes
Dundas
Eaton
Manchester
Bath
Big Fresh
Cathedral College

GETTING THERE

AIR **The Airport** lies 10 kilometres north-west of the centre. City buses run hourly from here to Cathedral Square. Shuttle buses tel: 0800 748 885 operate every 20–30 minutes and make hotel stops.

CAR Christchurch lies on **State Highway 1**, 366 kilometres north of Dunedin and 350 kilometres south of Picton.

RAIL **Clarence St Station**, Addington. Daily services from Picton and Greymouth.

BUS **InterCity and Mt Cook Landline buses** leave from Worcester St to the major east coast cities. Coast to Coast buses cross the mountains to Greymouth.

Before World War II, Christchurch's prosperity depended on the rich agricultural land that surrounded it. After 1945 the availability of cheap energy sources, especially hydroelectric power, transformed it into New Zealand's second industrial city. As befits its status Canterbury has its own international airport and a splendid port in Lyttelton, a natural deepwater anchorage 11 kilometres south-east of the city.

GETTING AROUND

You can get about town on foot or you can take the refurbished 1905 tram, which operates on a 2.5-kilometre loop, taking about 30 minutes for the full journey. A time-based ticket allows you to hop on and off at points of interest. Most local buses now leave from **The Bus Exchange**, 71 Litchfield St, but some still depart from near Cathedral Square. The green **Orbiter** bus travels a complete circuit of the city and is an ideal way of accessing the suburbs. Catch the yellow **Shuttle**, which is free, for a ride through the city to Moorhouse Ave, stopping at the Hoyts 8 cinema complex as well. For further information tel: 03 366 8855 or try www.ecan.govt.nz for timetables and maps.

INFORMATION

The Christchurch & Canterbury Visitor Centre Old Chief Post Office Building, Cathedral Square; tel: 03 379 9629, fax: 03 377 2424; e-mail: info@christchurchnz.net; www.christchurchnz.net.

Department of Conservation Office 133 Victoria St; tel: 03 379 9758, fax: 03 365 1388.

Christchurch Airport Travel and Information Centre Christchurch Airport; tel: 03 353 7774 (domestic), 03 353 7783 (international), fax: 03 353 7754; e-mail: pamela.williams@cial.co.nz.

POST AND PHONES There is a post office (known as a 'post shop') at 3 Cathedral Square, tel: 03 531 666 or 0800 501 501; open Mon–Fri 0800–1800, Sat 1000–1600. Pick up poste restante mail from main counter.

ACCOMMODATION

A GOTHIC REVIVAL

Wandering around Christchurch you'll see many examples of the Gothic Revival architecture that gives the city such an English look and feel. There are about 30 distinguished buildings within the city; the Historic Places Trust describes them in its free leaflet 'Historic Christchurch', available at the Visitor Information Centre.

Adelphi $$ 49 Papanui Rd, Merivale; tel: 03 355 6037 or 0800 335 560, fax: 03 355 6036; www.adelphimotel.co.nz; e-mail: adelphi@xtra.co.nz. Spacious units, sauna and spa. Close to shops and restaurants.

Alcala Motor Lodge $$ 100 Sherborne St; tel: 03 365 8180 or 0800 224 441, fax: 03 365 8378; e-mail: alcala@ihug.co.nz. New, central motel. Suites with spas.

Alglenn Motel $ 59 Papanui Rd; tel: 03 355 7010 or 0800 254 536, fax: 03 355 6130; e-mail: alglennmotel@xtra.co.nz. Quiet accommodation close to the centre.

Cashel Court Stadium Motel $$ 457 Cashel St; tel/fax: 03 389 2768. Motel in a pleasant setting on the road to New Brighton, with outdoor pool.

Chateau on the Park $$$ 189 Deans Ave; tel: 03 348 8999 or 0800 808 999, fax: 03 348 8990; www.chateau-park.co.nz; e-mail: res@chateau-park.co.nz. Heated outdoor pool and superb setting overlooking Hagley Park. Two restaurants and bar.

Christchurch City YHA $ 273 Manchester St; tel: 03 379 9535, fax: 03 379 9537; e-mail: yhachch@yha.org.nz. Right in the centre, with great facilities. Another YHA hostel, Rolleston House, is also in town; tel: 03 366 6564, fax: 03 365 5589; e-mail: yhachrl@yha.org.nz.

Cokers Garden City Hotel $$ 52 Manchester St; tel: 03 379 8580 or 0800 123 939, fax: 03 379 8585; e-mail: cokers@xtra.co.nz. Popular hotel with 43 rooms, most with ensuite bathrooms. Bar serving meals.

Colonial Inn Motel $$ 43 Papanui Rd, Merivale; tel: 03 555 9139 or 0800 111 232, fax: 03 355 5457; www.colonialinnmotel.co.nz; e-mail: colonialinn@xtra.co.nz. Pleasant modern motel close to the centre. Cooked and continental breakfasts available.

Croydon House $$ 63 Armagh St; tel: 03 366 5111, fax: 03 377 6110; www.croydon.co.nz; e-mail: welcome@croydon.co.nz. Comfortable bed and breakfast in a former rest home for soldiers. Excellent breakfasts. On the tram line.

Diplomat $$ 127 Papanui Rd, Merivale; tel: 03 355 6009, fax: 03 355 6007; e-mail: diplomatchch@xtra.co.nz. Motel in pleasant garden setting with swimming pool, heated spa and spacious well-equipped units.

Elm Tree House $$$ 236 Papanui Rd, Merivale; tel: 03 355 9731, fax: 03 355 9753; www.elmtreehouse.co.nz; e-mail: stay@elmtreehouse.co.nz. Spacious bed and breakfast in an historic house.

Foley Towers $ 208 Kilmore St; tel: 03 366 9720, fax: 03 379 3014; e-mail: foley.towers@backpack.co.nz. Clean, comfortable backpackers' hotel with dormitories and rooms.

Millbrook 60 $$ 60 Carlton Mill Rd; tel: 03 366 9529, fax: 03 366 8606; www.manz.co.nz/millbrook60; e-mail: millbrook60@xtra.co.nz. Comfortable motel located on the banks of the Avon River (canoes for hire).

Occidental Backpackers $ 208 Hereford St; tel: 03 379 9284 or 0800 847 467; www.occidental.co.nz; e-mail: freebreakfast@occidental.co.nz. The closest hostel to Cathedral Square.

Redcliffs on Sea B&B $$ 125 Main Rd, Redcliffs; tel: 03 384 9792, fax: 03 384 9703; www.nzhomestay.co.nz/ebert.htm; e-mail: redcliffs@nzhomestay.co.nz. Rooms in beautiful seaside home with garden. Restaurants nearby.

Round the World Backpackers $ 314 Barbados St; tel: 03 365 4363.

Sherborne Motor Lodge $$ 94 Sherborne St; tel: 03 377 8050 or 0800 743 267, fax: 03 377 0696; www.canterburypages.co.nz/sherborne; e-mail: sherborne@clear.net.nz. New complex with well-equipped apartments, some with spa baths.

Stonehurst Hotel Backpackers $ 241 Gloucester St; tel: 03 379 4620 or 0508 786 633, fax: 03 379 4647; www.stonehurst.co.nz; e-mail: accom@stonehurst.co.nz. Award-winning hostel with solar-heated pool.

Vagabond Backpackers $ 232 Worcester St; tel: 03 379 9677; e-mail: vagabondbackpackers@hotmail.com. A small, friendly hostel with a pleasant garden. Only a ten-minute walk from town.

FOOD AND DRINK

Some delicious local specialities to look out for are artichokes stuffed with prawns, seared salmon or rack of Canterbury lamb. These delicacies are highly recommended washed down with a bottle of Chardonnay or Pinot Noir.

Azure $$$ 128 Oxford Terrace; tel: 03 365 6088; open daily 1000–late. In a great position on leafy Oxford Terrace overlooking the River Avon. Mediterranean/Pacific Rim food with wine available by the glass. Try the carpaccio of cervena (venison), sprinkled with shaved parmesan, capers, a light balsamic oil and cracked pepper. Licensed.

Casey Jones Café and Bar $ 392 Moorhouse Ave; tel: 03 379 4889; open daily 0700–0300. Strong rail theme and specialises in fast service for the movie-going public. Serves Sumatran coffee guaranteed to keep you awake in the wee, small hours.

Dux de Lux $$ 41 Hereford St; tel: 03 366 6919. If you are a vegetarian most of the restaurants in Christchurch will make a special effort. But this splendid restaurant specialises in vegetarian dishes and seafood. It also brews its own beers. Booking advised. Licensed.

E-Caf $ 28 Worcester St; tel: 03 372 9436; e-mail: e-caf@theartscentre. Internet café where you can check up on your e-mail, while enjoying coffee and snacks.

Hay's Café $$ 63 Victoria St; tel: 03 379 7501. Restaurant specialising in Canterbury lamb. Has won the NZ Beef and Lamb Bureau Hallmark of Excellence each year since 1997.

Le Bon Bolli $$$ cnr Montreal St and Worcester Blvd; tel: 03 374 9444 or 03 374 1997. Upmarket French cuisine in early 20th-century French-style surroundings. Awarded National Restaurant of the Year, so it must be doing something right.

Mona Vale $$ 63 Fendalton Rd; tel: 03 348 9660. Late-Victorian homestead in lovely gardens with the Avon flowing through. Ideal for a tea break and offers food daily 0930–1600.

Oxford On Avon $$ 794 Colombo St; tel: 03 379 7148. A restaurant and bars overlooking the Avon River.

Palazzo del Marinaio $$ Shades Arcade, 108 Hereford St; tel: 03 365 4640; open daily 1200–1500, 1730–late. The name means Palace for the Fishermen. The owners came to New Zealand from Malta in 1977. Serves rock lobster, oysters, scallops, mussels, scampi, squid, octopus, crab and anything else freshly caught. It also serves Canterbury lamb. Licensed.

Retour Restaurant $$$ cnr Cambridge Tce and Manchester St; tel: 03 365 2888. Once a band rotunda, this restaurant specialises in European cuisine and has an attractive riverside setting. Licensed and BYO.

Vesuvio Bar and Café $$$ 182 Oxford St; tel: 03 365 4183. Overlooking the Avon River, this is first and foremost a jazz bar which is open daily 1800–late. Attached is Vesuvio Teppanyaki, a very fair Japanese restaurant with flashy service. Unusual but pleasant.

THE WIZARD OF CHRISTCHURCH

The Wizard of Christchurch is, in fact, a British-born academic – real name, **Ian Brackenbury Channell**. He materialises in Cathedral Square during the summer, usually at lunch times, in full wizardly regalia. Perched on a small stepladder, the eccentric crusader by turns eggs on and castigates the local population for its alleged shortcomings and makes a speciality of defending lost causes. For his highly individual contribution to tourism, Channell received the official title Wizard of New Zealand in 1990.

It's not just the Wizard who goes on show in Cathedral Square. Atheists and religious fundamentalists mount their stepladders to battle it out verbally on the cathedral's steps – this is the city's free-speech corner, where anything and everything goes.

HIGHLIGHTS

Christchurch is tailor-made for tourists. The centre is compact and therefore well suited to walking. It's also flat so getting about by bike is a definite possibility. You're unlikely to get lost as the city is laid out on a grid pattern (the River Avon is the only feature that's likely to lead you off the straight and narrow). The hub of Christchurch is Cathedral Square, once a busy bus terminal, but now pedestrianised. There's a small market here on Saturdays and food stalls selling satay and other fast food during the week. In the summer months the square becomes an open-air stage for buskers and there are free concerts every Friday at midday. Look out for impromptu performances by the Wizard, one of Christchurch's more eccentric characters.

CHRISTCHURCH CATHEDRAL

The tall, copper-covered spire of the Anglican Cathedral dominates Cathedral Square. The foundation stone was laid in 1864 – just 14 years after the arrival of the first organised settlers. For a small donation you can climb the 134 steps to the top of the **Bell Tower** (open daily except Sun 0830–1600) for panoramic views of the city, the surrounding plains and the distant Southern Alps.

CIVIC BUILDINGS

The modern **Town Hall** in Kilmore St is more a cultural complex than an administrative centre with a magnificent 2584-seat auditorium. On the south side is the **Ferrier Fountain** and a small lake, which provides a backdrop for millions of tourist snapshots every year.

MOA

Far bigger than an ostrich, and slower, the now extinct giant moa (*Dinornis giganteus*) once browsed scrub lowlands and forests mainly in the South Island. Because New Zealand was isolated from other major landmasses, it was able to occupy a niche left vacant by the absence of large herbivorous mammals. At first its only enemy was the giant Haast's eagle, a gigantic raptor with talons like a tiger's claws and a wingspan of 3 metres. Then, when the first Maoris arrived, it became a sought-after source of food. Unable to defend itself properly against these moa-hunters, as the early Maori settlers were known, the great flocks of giant moa were soon decimated. It is assumed that it was already long extinct before the first Europeans arrived.

Like a number of other native birds, the moa were unable to fly. They did not even have vestigial wings like kiwi and ostriches. It seems there were 11 different species of moa, ranging from the 3 metre-high (if it stretched its neck to browse), 270-kilogram giant moa, to the 1 metre-high, 20-kilogram coastal moa. The eggs were also prodigious: one giant moa egg that was discovered at Kaikoura had a capacity of close to 4 litres! Eating an omelette made from that would be equivalent to digesting roughly 60 hens' eggs. Great for your cholesterol!

Though it was long believed that the various types of moa had died out owing to dramatic climate change, more recent research has proved otherwise. It is now considered a fact that their extinction was precipitated by human interference. The early Maori settlers didn't only hunt all species of moa, they also changed vital habitat by burning down forests to make room for their settlements. Some of the smaller bush moa may have survived into European times, but it is generally assumed all moa species became extinct between 300 and 500 years ago. Nevertheless, up to the present day there have been reported sightings of moa in remote bush locations.

As your chances of rediscovering a hidden population of moa are infinitely remote, your best bet is to visit one of the museums where replicas of the bird are on view. Possibilities include Auckland Museum and Canterbury Museum in Christchurch.

Christchurch

The Arts Centre occupies former University buildings now converted to accommodate a number of small theatres, galleries, shops and cafés on a single site. Not far away on the corner of Worcester Blvd and Montreal St is the brand-new **Christchurch Art Gallery** (www.christchurchartgallery.org.nz). It replaces the former Robert McDougall Art Gallery, and now houses its collection of New Zealand paintings and prints, as well as pottery and sculpture. At the time of writing, opening times and contact numbers had not yet been finalised.

The **Canterbury Museum**, in Rolleston Ave, covers New Zealand history, geology and ethnography. The section on pre-settler New Zealand – 'Ancient People, New Lands' (Iwi Tawhito, Whenua Hou) – includes a stuffed moa. This bird, now extinct, was an irresistible source of food for the Maoris (see p. 299). The highlight of the exhibition is the **Hall of Antarctic Discovery**, devoted to Polar exploration (many expeditions used New Zealand as a jumping-off point). Open daily 0900–1730 (summer), 0900–1100 (winter); tel: 03 366 5000.

The Canterbury Museum was founded in 1867 by the famous geologist Julius von Haast. The museum often built up its collection by exchanging the moa bones von Haast found for artefacts from overseas.

Parks and Gardens

Canterbury's two best-known green spaces are Hagley Park and the Botanic Gardens. **Hagley Park**, which lies within a loop of the Avon River, is laid out in English style with lawns and woodland, spiced up with a variety of native and exotic trees and plants. The **Botanic Gardens** boasts one of the finest collections of exotic and indigenous plants in New Zealand and are spectacular when the flowers bloom in the spring. The **Cockayne Memorial Garden** is devoted solely to native plants. Grounds open daily 0700 to 1 hour before sunset; conservatories open 1015–1600.

Ferrymead Historic Park

The Ferrymead Historic Park is a working museum of transport and technology, with restored steam engines and a wonderful collection of fire engines. The park also aims to re-create a New Zealand township as it might have looked before 1920. Period trams trundle through the main street, past the bakery, printing shop, blacksmith and carpenters. Be sure to pop into the antique restoration workshop to see the wonderful mechanical pianos. 269 Bridle Path Rd; tel: 03 384 1970, fax: 03 384 1725; www.ferrymead.org.nz; open daily 1000–1630.

Damp Outside?

Then watch the fish enjoy the water at **Southern Encounter Aquarium**, in the middle of Cathedral Square (enter via the Visitor Centre). Be awed by the giant eels, touch the smaller fry (there's a Touch Tank) and watch the fish being fed. Above all, it's great to see what the local marine life looked like before it ended up on your plate. The aquarium is open daily 0900–1700; tel: 03 359 0581.

The Te Huingi Manu Wildlife Reserve is popular with bird watchers and sailors. It lies on the estuary of the Avon and Heathcote rivers. Open daily, dawn to dusk.

Mona Vale Gardens, at 63 Fendalton Rd, retain their original Edwardian character with fabulous displays of roses, azaleas, irises and fuchsias as well as a fernery and lily pond. The land, on the banks of the Avon River, originally belonged to Deans Cottage, Kahu Rd, built from local pit-sawn timber in 1843 by two Scottish settlers, the brothers William and John Deans (being restored). Adjacent is the larger **Riccarton House**, built by the Deans family in 1856–1900.

The **Gondola** on Bridle Path Rd ascends 500 metres to the crater rim of Mount Cavendish, the sunken, now defunct volcano on which Christchurch was founded. From the top there are views of the city, Banks Peninsula and the wide expanse of the Canterbury Plains – on a clear day you can make out the white peaks of the Southern Alps. Also at the summit is a restaurant and a multi-media **Time Tunnel**, which presents the history of the area in a novel way. A free shuttle bus, departing opposite Cathedral Square tram stop, takes you to and from the Gondola. Open daily 1000–late; tel: 03 384 0700.

BEACHES The extensive sandy beach at New Brighton is popular with Christchurch residents and suitable for swimming, windsurfing and strolling.

There's another large stretch of beach at Redcliffs, in front of Cave Rock – cliffs pitted with small caves. Alternatives are Port Hills to the south and Waimari Beach to the north.

INTERNATIONAL ANTARCTIC CENTRE

The International Antarctic Centre, right next to the airport, is the base for the Antarctic discovery and development programmes sponsored by New Zealand, the United States, Italy and other countries. The museum is extraordinarily evocative – even members of the museum staff have wintered in this inhospitable region. Look out for the hologram of Scott of the Antarctic, writing his diary in his hut while awaiting his doom. Orchard Rd, served by the Super Shuttle running to and from airport. Tel: 03 358 9896 or 0508 736 4846, fax: 03 353 7799; www.iceberg.co.nz; open daily 0900–2000 (summer), 0900–1730 (winter).

SPORT

SKIING Some of New Zealand's best ski slopes can be found on **Mount Hutt,** only an hour from Christchurch airport (tel: 03 308 5074, fax: 03 302 8811; www.nzski.com/mthutt). The season runs from May to October and there are snow-making machines to ensure the slopes are always well covered. If you're an intermediate or advanced skier (and can afford it), heli-skiing is also available here.

An alternative ski resort, smaller and less frenetic than Mount Hutt, is **Hanmer Springs Ski Area** on Mt St Patrick, where the slopes are better suited to skiers with intermediate skills (see p. 289). North of Hanmer Springs is the historic **Molesworth Station**; covering an expanse of 182,000 hectares, it is the country's largest high-country sheep and cattle station. From January to February it is possible to cycle or drive through breathtaking scenery, along a four-wheel drive road that passes through the station and links Hanmer Springs to Blenheim. Those without transport have a choice of four-wheel drive, bike or horseback tours starting from either Blenheim or Hanmer Springs. Enquire at the respective visitor centres for details or contact Molesworth Station Tours, tel/fax: 03 315 7401; e-mail: rick.j.stirling@xtra.co.nz, or Hurunui Horse Treks, tel/fax: 03 314 4204; www.hurunui.co.nz.

'It was Junior England all the way to Christchurch – in fact, just a garden. And Christchurch is an English town, with an English park annex, and a winding English brook just like the Avon – and named the Avon; but from a man, not from Shakespeare's river... If it had an Established Church and social inequality it would be England all over again with hardly a lack.'

Mark Twain, *More Tramps Abroad*, 1897

BOATING Punting on the Avon River is one of the pleasures of a stay in Christchurch and should not be missed. Punts are rented out from the jetty behind the Municipal Buildings, cnr Worcester Blvd and Oxford Terrace. (0900–dusk (summer), 1000–1600 (winter); for bookings tel: 03 379 9629). The Antigua Boatsheds on Rolleston Ave, near the hospital (tel: 03 366 5885) hires out canoes and paddle boats.

The Rangitata river is ideally suited to rafting. One of the specialist firms in the area is Rangitata Rafts, Peel Forest; tel/fax: 03 696 3534 or 0800 251 251; www.rafts.co.nz. Rivers are graded from 1 to 6 in ascending order of difficulty: Rangitata is graded 5, which means that wearing wetsuits, life jackets and protective helmets is compulsory. Rafting Canterbury offers grade 3 to 5 rafting, tel: 03 318 1813; e-mail: raftriver@cyberxpress.co.nz.

PARAGLIDING

Nimbus Paragliding, tel: 0800 111 611; www.nimbusparagliding.cjb.net, and Phoenix Paragliding, tel/fax: 03 326 7634; www.paragliding.co.nz, both transport you to the mountains for a tandem flight. Perfect for the inexperienced.

FISHING The Rakaia River, only 50 kilometres south of Christchurch, is New Zealand's salmon capital. The river is crossed by a 1.8-kilometre bridge, one of the longest in the southern hemisphere. During the season (Oct–Apr) anglers can be seen lining the river banks to the east of the town. As always, professional guides can lead you to the best spots. Try Rakaia Salmon Safaris, tel/fax: 03 302 7389; e-mail: r.j.watts@xtra.co.nz. More information is available from either the **Ashburton Information Centre**, tel: 03 308 1050; e-mail: ashinfo@actrix.co.nz, or the **Methven Information Centre**, tel: 03 302 8955 or 0800 764 444; e-mail: methven@clear.net.nz.

WILDLIFE PARKS

The excellent **Willowbank Wildlife Reserve** is only 15 minutes from downtown Christchurch. Here you can see a good selection of native wildlife, including the normally nocturnal kiwi in a daytime setting – a rare opportunity. Willowbank is located on Hussey Rd, Harewood; tel: 03 359 6226; www.willowbank.co.nz; open daily 1000–2200.

Can't get enough? Then have a look at **Orana Wildlife Park** (tel: 03 359 7109; www.oranawildlifepark.co.nz). This is the country's only open-range zoo specialising in endangered African and native fauna. It's situated about 10 minutes from the airport, along McLeans Island Rd. Open daily 1000–1700.

HORSERIDING For romantic trekking through the Port Hills, including evening rides, contact **Heathcote Valley Riding School**, 131 Bridle Path Rd, by the Gondola terminal; tel: 03 384 1971.

RUGBY & CRICKET The former Lancaster Park is now known as **Jade Stadium** (tel: 03 379 1765; www.jadestadium.co.nz) and has been redeveloped into a world class sports stadium. As the city's main cricket and rugby venue, it's the place to go for national and international standard matches in both sports. Especially exciting are the international matches that are played here, but the atmosphere is also great when the local rugby team, 'The Crusaders', takes on all-comers in the winter rugby season.

SHOPPING

Shopping in Christchurch couldn't be easier as many of the stores are concentrated in central malls. Contemporary New Zealand art is undergoing something of a renaissance - a good place to suss the scene and possibly buy a small sketch is in the **CoCA Art Gallery,** 66 Gloucester St; tel: 03 366 7261; www.coca.org.nz. Admission is free although there are sometimes charges for special exhibitions.

CHARLES UPHAM

Charles Upham is the only fighting soldier ever to be awarded the Victoria Cross twice. He was born in Christchurch in 1908 and earned his first VC in Crete in May 1941. The second was awarded at Ruweisat Ridge, Egypt, in July 1942, where he was severely wounded. Captured by the Germans, he ended the war in Colditz Castle. When he returned to New Zealand he went back to being a sheep farmer at Hundalee, North Canterbury, refusing all honours and shunning the limelight. He died in 1994.

CULTURE AND NIGHTLIFE

Christchurch has a lively theatre scene, fed by **Canterbury University**. The magnificent **Arts Centre;** tel: 03 366 0989; www.artscentre.org.nz, is the focal point for the performing arts, with cinemas and galleries as well as theatres.

The **Town Hall** on Victoria Square; tel: 03 366 8899, is the main venue for classical music concerts, and includes the **James Hay Theatre**.

CLUBS AND BARS

Christchurch is well served by pubs and bars. If you don't want to walk too far between drinks, the area to the south of the Cathedral at the crossroads of Colombo and Cashel Streets is the best place to head.

Azure Restaurant and Bar 128 Oxford Tce; tel: 03 365 6088. Excellent Mediterranean fare, good DJs and music, dancing until late.

Dux de Lux cnr Hereford St & Montreal St; tel: 03 366 6919. Popular brewery pub, with outdoor seating, good food, real ale and live music.

Holy Grail 88 Worcester Blvd; tel: 03 365 9816; www.holygrail.co.nz; open daily 1100–late. Enormous sports bar, with dancing, games room, two restaurants and a 70-seat grandstand.

The Loaded Hog cnr Manchester and Cashel St; tel: 03 366 6674. Dancing, DJs, live music and a mature crowd. Beers brewed on site.

MARAE OF THE FOUR WINDS

For the Maori experience, visit the Nga Hau E Wha Marae or 'Marae of the Four Winds' – the name expresses a desire for cultural harmony throughout the world. There are two tour options, both starting daily at 1845, which explain Maori culture and traditions and offer performances of song and dance; one of the tours also provides a hangi dinner. One of the attractions of the village is the spectacularly carved Aoraki meeting house, one of the largest in New Zealand. The elaborate gateway (1982) is decorated with representations of the ancestors, while the carved arch symbolises Kahukura, god of the rainbow. At 250 Pages Rd; tel: 03 388 7685 or 0800 456 898.

OFF TO AKAROA?

No problem with the **Akaroa Shuttle** (tel: 0800 500 929). Departs daily from the Christchurch Visitor Information Centre 0900, 1030 and 1400 (Nov–Apr), 1000 (May–Oct).

INSPECTOR RODERICK ALLEYN

Dame Edith Ngaio Marsh was born in Christchurch in 1895 and died in her 87th year. She had two separate careers, each of which brought her fame and respect. Outside New Zealand she is known for the meticulously constructed detective stories featuring Inspector Roderick Alleyn of Scotland Yard. What isn't so well known is that she was also a highly successful Shakespearean actress and producer on the New Zealand stage. Dame Marsh's house, at 37 Valley Rd and kept just as she left it, can be viewed by appointment – tel: 03 337 9248.

CINEMAS

There are several large cinemas in Christchurch, including the **Regent on Worcester** at 94 Worcester St and the **Rialto** at 250 Moorhouse Ave. Arthouse films are shown at the Arts Centre.

LISTINGS

Christchurch's daily newspaper *The Press* has comprehensive listings; see also the free listings brochure, 'Today & Tonight – Christchurch & Canterbury', which is available at the Visitor Centre and is updated throughout the year.

WHERE NEXT?

Visit the nearby Canterbury Plains, or head south to Timaru (see p. 313) via Highway 1 – OTT table 9816 for bus – or north to Kaikoura (p. 287). See OTT tables 9800/6. The TranzAlpine express takes you to Greymouth in 4½ hrs (OTT table 9800), or enjoy the scenery from the trans-alpine Coast to Coast Daily Bus Service (no tunnels; OTT table 9805).

Banks Peninsula extends from the northern end of the Canterbury Bight. One thousand years ago it attracted moa hunters; later settlers chased seals and whales. Today it's inhabited mainly by sheep farming communities. The name commemorates Joseph Banks, the botanist on Cook's expedition.

The peninsula was formed by volcanic action and from the road along its spine there are wonderful views over Akaroa and back towards Christchurch. The Peninsula is excellent tramping territory and the 35-kilometre **Banks Peninsula Track**, a four-day hike, is outstanding, although it is definitely for serious trampers. Along the way you might catch a glimpse of the Hector's dolphin, the world's smallest.

The first Frenchman to arrive on the Banks Peninsula was Captain Jean Langlois, the master of a whaling vessel, who bought a piece of land from the Maoris in 1838. He returned to France to form the Nanto-Bordelaise Company and arrived back in New Zealand two years later with 80 would-be colonists to establish a beachhead, as it were, for the planting of the tricolour.

Unfortunately for the French, however, the British had already found out what was afoot and seven days before Langlois' arrival they despatched a warship to Akaroa and hoisted the Union Flag. Dreams of French dominion over the whole of New Zealand evaporated overnight.

Spotting Dolphins

Watch out for regular splashes in the water surface: as they travel dolphins break surface about every 2 minutes to make a short and explosive exhalation, followed by a longer inhalation before submerging again.

Dolphins are superbly streamlined and can sustain speeds of up to 30 kph, with bursts of more than 40 kph.

AKAROA

The pretty seaside town of Akaroa is the only settlement in New Zealand to have been colonised by the French and the Visitors Centre still makes great play of the fact - especially that it was a failed attempt. Apart from a few restaurants, the French connection is confined mainly to street and house names, although Akaroa does have its own little artists' colony.

While Akaroa itself is attractive, the jewel in the crown is the **Langlois-Eteveneaux House and Museum**. The oldest house in Canterbury, it dates from around 1840 and was designed along French colonial lines – it may even have been prefabricated and shipped to New Zealand on behalf of its original owner, Captain Langlois' brother, Aimable. Open daily 1030–1600.

Akaroa harbour is the departure point for cruises to see the world's smallest dolphins, only found on this part of the coast. The season for Hector's dolphin spotting is November to April. **Akaroa Harbour Cruises**, Akaroa Wharf; tel: 03 304 7641; www.canterburycat.co.nz, runs 2-hour catamaran trips; alternatively try **Dolphin Experience**, 61 Beach Rd; tel/fax: 03 304 7726 or 0508 365 744; www.dolphinsakaroa.co.nz. This trip lasts three hours and is relatively expensive but the price includes hot showers and refreshments after your swim.

i Akaroa Information Centre 80 Rue Lavaud; tel: 03 304 8600.

Chez La Mer $ 50 Rue Lavaud; tel/fax: 03 304 7024; e-mail: chez_la_mer@clear.net.nz. Historic lodge with a secluded garden and close to beach.

Driftwood Motel $$ 56 Rue Jolie (North End); tel: 03 304 7484 or 0508 928 373, fax: 03304 5858; www.driftwood.co.nz; e-mail: driftwood@caverock.net.nz. Seafront units with balconies and superb views. Spa and kayak hire.

L'Hotel Motel $$ 75 Beach Rd; tel: 03 304 7559 or 0800 454 6835, fax: 03 304 7455; e-mail: hotel-akaroa@xtra.co.nz. Delightful French-style bed and breakfast on the waterfront. Licensed restaurant.

La Belle Villa $$ 113 Rue Jolie; tel/fax: 03 304 7084. Spacious airy rooms in an historic wooden house with swimming pool and large garden.

Le Bons Bay Backpackers $ tel: 03 304 8582. Located in an old farmhouse set in rambling country gardens. Free pickup from Akaroa, free breakfast and scrumptious evening meals (not free!). Excellent value.

Onuku Farm Hostel $ tel: 03 304 7612; www.onukufarm.co.nz. This backpackers is situated on a coastal sheep farm, 6 km from Akaroa – free pickup from Akaroa. They organise kayak trips and also provide huts and tent sites. At the start of the Banks Track.

C'est La Vie $$$ 33 Rue Lavaud; tel: 03 304 7314. Superb French cuisine served up with style. Live music. Open evenings only. BYO.
Harbour Seventy One $$ 71 Beach Rd; tel: 03 304 7656. Fresh fish daily, formal dining. Licensed.

BARRY'S BAY

Banks Peninsula was one of the first areas in New Zealand to produce cheese (commercial shipments were sent to Australia as early as the 1850s). You can get to Barry's Bay from Akaroa across the water, by taking the shuttleboat from Akaroa harbour – departures are twice daily.

Barry's Bay Traditional Cheese Ltd
Akaroa (tel: 03 304 5809). Open Mon–Fri 0800–1700 (May–Sept), viewing only on alternate days Oct–Apr.

OKAINS BAY

This beautiful beach and lagoon on the Banks Peninsula offers safe swimming and boating. Nearby is the **Okains Bay Maori and Colonial Museum**, tel: 03 304 8611 housed in a former cheese factory, which contains some interesting Maori artefacts including a 15th-century god stick, a restored war canoe from 1867, a carved *patu* (club) and other weapons. There's also a meeting house with figures carved by John Rua. Open to visitors daily 1000–1700.

METHVEN AND THE CANTERBURY PLAINS

Until recently the lively resort of Methven, 95 kilometres from Christchurch, was a quiet village on the chequerboard fields of the Canterbury Plains. Today it's a mecca for sports lovers. Apart from the excellent skiing on Mt Hutt, there's summer fishing, golfing, jetboating, tramping, mountain biking and the supreme experience – a balloon flight over the Canterbury Plains! The inland location and the prevailing breeze flowing from the Southern Alps make for perfect flying conditions.

The Plains are also well away from commercial flight paths, giving the balloon pilots more freedom to manoeuvre. From this superb vantage point, the Canterbury Plains open up beneath you. This is a major food-producing area with many of the crops destined for markets in the northern hemisphere. The Rakaia, a rare example of a braided river, flows across mid-Canterbury, making its own distinct mark on the landscape. You'll also see sheep, deer, beef cattle, even llama dotting the fields, all

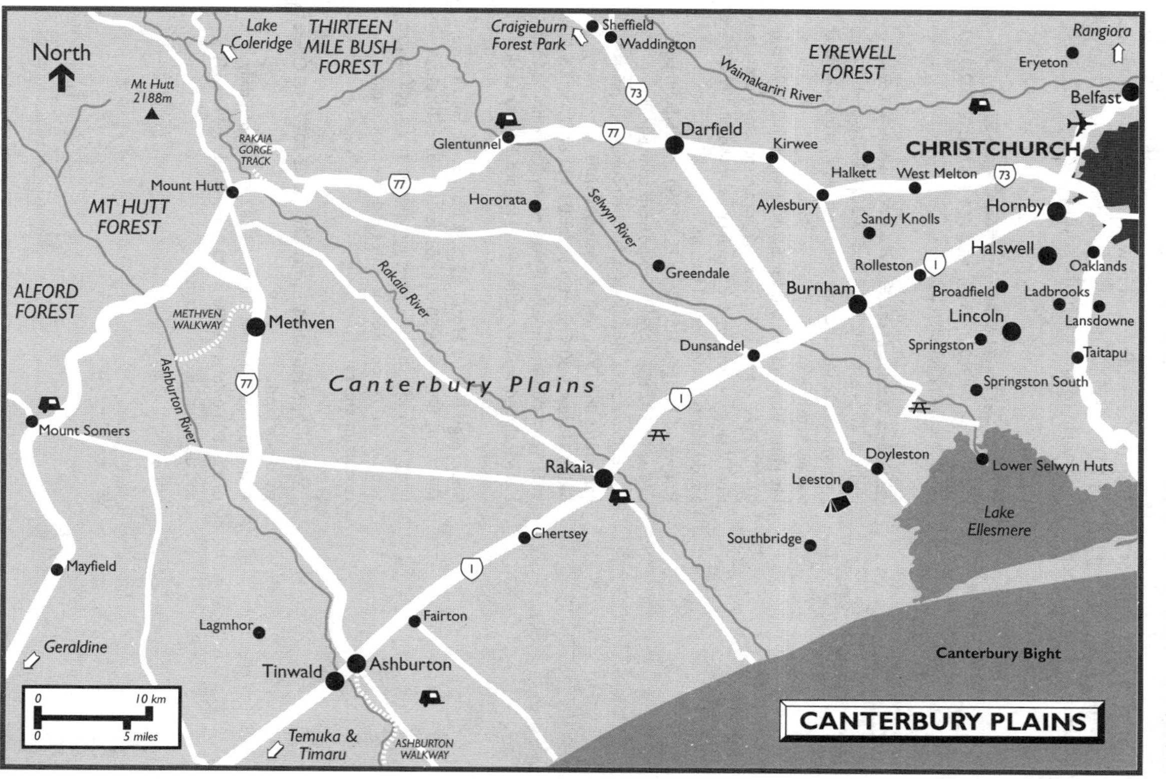
North
Lake Coleridge
THIRTEEN MILE BUSH FOREST
Craigieburn Forest Park
Sheffield
Waddington
EYREWELL FOREST
Rangiora
Eryeton
Waimakariri River
Belfast
Mt Hutt 2188m
73
77
Darfield
Glentunnel
Kirwee
CHRISTCHURCH
RAKAIA GORGE TRACK
Halkett
West Melton
Mount Hutt
Hororata
Aylesbury
Hornby
MT HUTT FOREST
Selwyn River
Sandy Knolls
Halswell
Oaklands
Rolleston
1
Greendale
Burnham
Broadfield
Ladbrooks
ALFORD FOREST
Rakaia River
Lincoln
Lansdowne
METHVEN WALKWAY
Methven
Dunsandel
Springston
Taitapu
Ashburton River
Canterbury Plains
Springston South
Mount Somers
Doyleston
Lower Selwyn Huts
Rakaia
Leeston
Lake Ellesmere
Chertsey
Southbridge
Mayfield
Fairton
Lagmhor
Canterbury Bight
Geraldine
Tinwald
Ashburton
0
10 km
0
5 miles
Temuka & Timaru
ASHBURTON WALKWAY
CANTERBURY PLAINS

against the magnificent backdrop of the Southern Alps with views of Mt Cook and the other peaks of the National Park. Overall the panorama extends more than 300 kilometres from Amberley in the north to Timaru in the south.

i **Methven Travel & Information Centre** 93 Main Rd, Methven; tel: 03 302 8955 or 0800 764 444, fax: 03 302 9367; e-mail: methven@clear.net.nz.

Green Gables Deer Farm $$ Waimarama Rd, State Highway 77; tel: 03 302 8308, fax: 03 302 8309; e-mail: greengables@xtra.co.nz. Bed and breakfast in attractive rural setting. Activities arranged.

Mt Hutt Bunkhouse $ 8 Lampard St; tel: 03 302 8894, fax: 03 302 9122; e-mail: mthuttbunks@xtra.co.nz. Linen provided, Sky TV, laundry facilities and two fully equipped kitchens. There are discounted rates for off season.

Redwood Lodges $ 5 Wayne Pl. (office) and 25 Southbelt; tel/fax: 03 302 8964; www.snowboardnz.com; e-mail: skired@xtra.co.nz. Both lodges feature rooms with private bathrooms and TV, as well as cheaper dorms.

Skiwi House $ 30 Chapman St; tel: 03 302 8772, fax: 03 302 9972; www.skiwihouse.com; e-mail: comfy@skiwihouse.co.nz. Linen included, laundry facilities and log fire. Popular in ski season.

Sovereign Resort Hotel $$–$$$ Main St, Mt Hutt Village; tel: 03 302 8724 or 0800 506 551, fax: 03 302 8870; e-mail: info@sovresort.co.nz. Facilities include spa, sauna, golf course and swimming pool. Rooms with good views, excellent restaurant and bar.

Blue Pub Hotel $$ Barkers Rd; tel: 03 302 8046. Offers good pub food.

Café 131 $$ 131 Main Rd; tel: 03 302 9131. Open daily 0700–1800 (winter), 0900–1600 (summer). Large breakfasts and delicious lunches. Licensed.

BALLOONING

Aoraki Balloon Safaris has been operational for six years and prides itself on a 100 per cent safety record. There are regular Civil Aviation checks on both equipment and pilots, and the Aerostar Balloons from the USA to strict FAA and CAA standards. Incidentally the company appears in the *Guinness Book of Records* for flying the oldest passenger in a Hot Air Balloon – Florence Laine at the age of 102 years and 3 months!

Most flights lift off at daybreak when the air is at its stillest although sunset flights are also available in the winter months. Flight time is around 1 hour but you'll need to set aside 4 hours for the trip. After the experience, there's a celebration 'champagne style' buffet breakfast in whichever field you drift in to land. Every flight is commemorated with a certificate, while information sheets and in-flight photos are also available.

If you become hooked on ballooning, there's an awe-inspiring flight over the Rakaia Gorge – the balloon actually descends into the river chasm, rising again to land in one of the nearby sheep stations. There are also flights over the 'Garden City' of Christchurch.

Full details from **Aoraki Balloon Safaris,** PO Box 75, Methven; tel: 03 302 8172 or 0800 256 837, fax: 03 302 8162; e-mail: Calm@voyager.co.nz.

Or, you can check the website out at:

www.canterburypages.co.nz/aoraki/index.html.

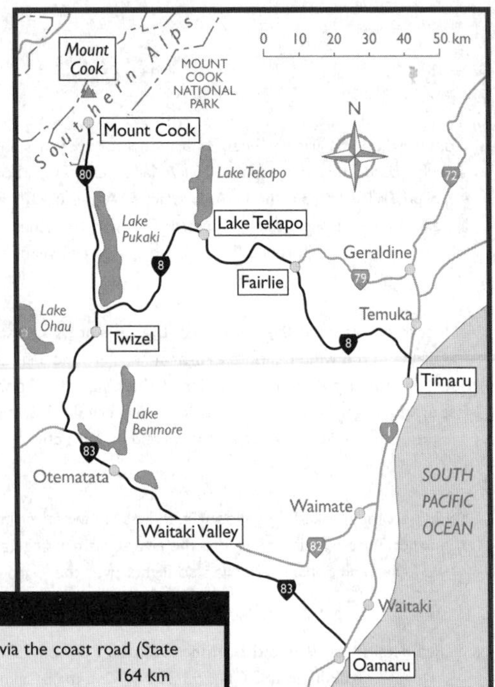

Route Detail

Timaru – Christchurch, via the coast road (State Highway 1) 164 km

Leave Timaru heading north. At Washdyke turn left onto State Highway 8 through Pleasant Point and Sutherlands. Follow the Tengawai River to Fairlie, then continue on the same road, through Kimbell to Lake Tekapo, crossing the dam to the village of the same name. Drive through Mackenzie Country and Simons Pass to the end of Lake Pukaki. Here you can detour onto State Highway 80 which follows the edge of the lake, before climbing in the direction of New Zealand's highest peak, Mount Cook, and the Information Office in the village at the edge of the National Park.

Return to State Highway 8 and continue through Twizel to Omarama. Take a left onto State Highway 83 and head for the Waitaki Valley. Continue past the dams and hydro-electric power stations at Benmore, Aviemore, and Waitaki, towards the settlements of Warekuri, Duntroon, and Georgetown, returning to the coast just north of Oamaru.

Note

There is a bus from Christchurch to Queenstown that runs via Fairlie, Mount Cook and Twizel, OTT table 9810.

This is sheep country and, perhaps more importantly, Mackenzie Country (see box, p. 317). It's a tough area even today, especially for farmers. The winters can be severe and the summers very warm. However, don't let this put you off – the area includes magical Lake Tekapo and the permanently snow-capped Mount Cook, the highest peak in New Zealand. Twizel is a growing adventure resort and a good base for exploring Mackenzie Country, while the Waitaki Valley provides a link to the seaside resorts of the east coast.

TIMARU

Carnival Time

Timaru is famous for its carnival, which takes place annually on sandy Caroline Bay for three weeks at Christmas.

Timaru, as the name implies, was a 'place of shelter' for the Maoris who travelled by canoe along this exposed stretch of coastline. The first European resident was a whaler called Samuel Williams, and on the beach at Caroline Bay there's still a massive pot (once used for rendering down whale fat) to remember him by. Timaru didn't really take off for another 20 years until the arrival in 1859 of the English ship *Strathallan*, with 120 migrants on board.

Today Timaru is the main port of South Canterbury. Probably its greatest attraction is **Caroline Bay**, with a fine sandy beach, considered one of the safest in New Zealand, and with plenty of tree cover for shade.

In the town itself is the **South Canterbury Museum** (Perth St). Hanging from the ceiling of the elegant octagonal building is the star exhibit, a replica of the first aircraft built by Richard Pearse, with an engine using horizontally opposed cylinders, as seen on modern BMW motorcycles. There are a few relics of the town's early days as a whaling station, most interestingly some examples of scrimshaw (etchings on whalebone) and the private collection of local naturalist E P Seally (mainly moths and butterflies). Less worthy, but possibly more interesting, are the antiquated slot machines, still in working order. Open Tues–Fri 1000–1630 and Sat–Sun 1330–1630.

TIMARU AMAZING RESIDENTS ... NO. 1. PHAR LAP

'Born in New Zealand, raced in Australia, died, still a winner, in America' could have been inscribed on the headstone of the famous racehorse, Phar Lap, reared in Seadown in the 1920s. Phar Lap was sold to an Australian, Hugh Telford, in 1928 for 160 guineas and went on to win 37 out of 51 starts during a career spanning just three years. He died in 1931 shortly after winning his first race in the United States. Phar Lap's achievements are commemorated in the name of Timaru's racetrack and by a statue in the paddock where he was born.

The **Aigantighe Art Gallery** on 49 Wai-Iti Rd, (pronounced 'egg and tie', Gaelic for 'At Home' or 'Welcome') has some remarkable garden sculptures by Kiwi and Zimbabwean artists as well as temporary exhibitions. Open Tues–Fri 1000–1600, Sat–Sun 1200–1600.

The **Botanic Gardens** in Queen St has an impressive collection of native plants including threatened species and a herb and rose garden. Open daily 0800–dusk.

The **airport** in Timaru is named after local pioneer aviator, Richard Pearse. There's considerable evidence to suggest that Pearse was the first to accomplish powered flight. Records show that he took to the air on 31 March 1903, some nine months before the Wright brothers, coming to earth with a bump after about 100 metres. Although Pearse went on to make several more flights he lost his place in the record books because he never successfully achieved a round trip, the accepted criterion of 'sustained flight'. Sadly, Pearse ended his days in a psychiatric hospital in Christchurch.

i **Timaru Visitor Information Centre** 2 George St; tel: 03 688 6163, fax: 03 684 0202; open Mon–Fri 0830–1700, Sat–Sun 1000–1500; e-mail:info@timaru.co.nz.

Anchor Motel $–$$ 42 Evans St; tel: 03 684 5067, fax: 03 684 5706. Central motel with off-street parking and backpackers accommodation.
Mountain View $$ Talbots Rd, off State Highway 1; tel: 03 688 1070, fax: 03 688 1069; e-mail: mvhomestay@xtra.co.nz. Farm offering comfortable rooms, breakfasts and dinners by arrangement.

Parklands Motor Lodge $$ 65 Evans St; tel: 03 688 4108 or 0800 306 030, fax: 03 688 4107; e-mail: parklands@timaru.com. Good-value accommodation close to shops and restaurants, with spa baths in all units

Timaru Motor Lodge $$ 7 Prince's St; tel: 03 688 4455 or 0800 807 750, fax: 03 688 6698. Well-equipped units with laundry and off-street parking.

Timaru Selwyn Holiday Park $ Selwyn St; tel: 03 684 7690 or 0800 242 121, fax: 03 688 1004; e-mail: topten@ timaruholidaypark.co.nz. Motel, cabins and tent sites.

Boudiccas $ 64 The Bay Hill; tel: 03 688 8550. Kebabs, felafel and other Middle Eastern standards.

Casa Italia Ristorante $$ 2 Strathallan St; tel: 03 684 5528. Restaurant in former customs house. The Italian chef makes excellent fresh pasta.

The Old Bank Café & Bars $ 232 Stafford St; tel: 03 684 4392. Open daily 1100–2100.

TIMARU AMAZING RESIDENTS ...
NO. 2. ROBERT (BOB) FITZSIMMONS

Timaru's most famous son was the boxer and prizefighter, Robert (Bob) Fitzsimmons.

Born in Cornwall, England, in 1862, Fitzsimmons came to New Zealand at the age of nine and was apprentice to his father as a blacksmith. He boxed in his spare time and after becoming champion in New Zealand and Australia, moved to San Francisco where, at the age of 28, he won the world middleweight championship by defeating Jack Dempsey.

In 1897 Fitzsimmons went one better by moving up to the heavyweight division and knocking out 'Gentleman' Jim Corbett in the 14th round of a world title fight at Carson City, Nevada. He rounded off his astonishing career in 1903, when, aged 41, he won the world light-heavyweight title on points against George Gardner. Fitzsimmons revisited Timaru in 1908 and received a hero's welcome. His statue stands in the courtyard next to the ANZ bank in the centre of the town.

FAIRLIE

Fairlie, at the crossroads of State Highways 79 and 8, is an oasis in the harsh wilderness of Mackenzie Country. It services the local sheep stations, the largest of which is Clayton, covering an area of more than 15,000 hectares. In the winter Fairlie doubles as a ski resort for Mount Dobson, 26 kilometres away and its population swells accordingly. The town is proud of its Scottish pedigree and hosts the Mackenzie Highland Show on Easter Monday. The **Museum** on Mount Cook Rd, gives a good impression of what life would have been like for the early settlers in Mackenzie Country. The old railway station has been rebuilt here along with the Mabel Binney Cottage, originally inhabited by the local blacksmith and furnished in the style of the period (c.1900). Open daily 0900–1700.

It is probably the name of a town originally called Fairlie Creek, which in turn comes from James Fairlie, who lived in a hut just outside the town centre. The town has a scottish tradition and hosts the Mackenzie Highland show on Easter Monday.

A walkway runs for 3 kilometres, starting below the Allendale Road Bridge and running along the shaded banks of the Opihi River.

Visitor Information Centre The Sunflower Centre, 31 Main St; tel: 03 685 8258.

Aorangi Motel $$ 26 Denmark St; tel/fax: 03 685 8340 or 0800 668 351; www.aorangimotel.co.nz; e-mail: j.cassie@xtra.co.nz. Central motel with well-equipped rooms, spa and golf club hire.

Fairlie Gateway Top 10 Holiday Park $ 10 Allandale Rd; tel/fax: 03 685 8375 or 0800 324 754; www.fairlietop10.co.nz; e-mail: call@fairlietop10.co.nz. Close to town in quiet surroundings. Cabins and tent sites.

Fontmell Farmstay $$ Nixons Rd; tel/fax: 03 685 8379. Small homestead in attractive rural setting, offering bed and breakfast.

Mount Dobson Motel $$ State Highway 8, 6 km west of town; tel: 03 685 8819, fax: 03 685 8898. Quiet motel, handy for the ski fields. There's a restaurant nearby.

Old Library Cafe $ 6 Allendale Rd; tel: 03 685 8999. Open 0800–late. Meals are inexpensive and filling, and include Thai curries, vegetarian choices and steaks.

Rimuwhare Country Retreat $$ 53 Mount Cook Rd; tel: 03 685 8058. Open daily lunch and dinner. Excellent Mediterranean-style food in a rural setting. Popular, so booking advised. Licensed.

A Sheep Mystery

James Mackenzie was born in Scotland, probably in Inverness sometime in the 1820s (the precise date of birth is unknown). He came to New Zealand with ambitions to become a sheep farmer but encountered some difficulties as his native language was Gaelic and his grasp of English uncertain.

In 1855 around 1000 sheep went missing from Levels Station, at Timaru. They were tracked by the overseer to the area now known as Mackenzie Country where the man himself was overpowered and arrested in the afternoon of 4 March. During the night he escaped and made his way over the rough terrain in bare feet as far as Lyttelton, where he went into hiding. He was discovered in an attic and tried and convicted of theft and of 'standing mute with malice'. Sentenced to five years in jail, he escaped not once, but twice, and was pardoned after 18 months by the Provincial Superintendent, who accepted that Mackenzie's silence under cross-examination came from his poor understanding of English. The extent of Mackenzie's actual guilt has never been established and the story has entered local folklore. After he was pardoned James Mackenzie disappeared without trace from the records – it's thought that he left New Zealand for Australia. Incidentally, the policeman who discovered Mackenzie in the loft at Lyttelton, Sergeant Seager, turns out to have been the grandfather of the crime writer, Ngaio Marsh.

LAKE TEKAPO

Covering an area of 83 square kilometres, serene Lake Tekapo is one of the most stunning sights in the country and the air round about is equally famous for its purity. For photographers and nature lovers, it's a paradise, but don't even think of taking a swim here – the water, a beautiful turquoise, is unimaginably cold for most of the year. Tekapo is now part of a major hydroelectric scheme, fed by the Godley and Cass rivers.

Lake Tekapo Village consists of little more than two rows of buildings, inhabited by a population of around 400. Most of the time people just hang around, mesmerised by the views.

The Church of the Good Shepherd on the lake shore has one of the prettiest settings in New Zealand, with a window framing the lake and the hills and mountains beyond, so that the scenery, in effect, becomes the altar. It was built in 1935 as a memorial to the pioneers of the Mackenzie Country. About 50 metres further along the waterfront is the sheepdog monument erected by local farmers in 1966.

Lake Tekapo Village makes a good base for walks in the area. For starters try the excellent 10-kilometre track to **Mount John Lookout** from the end of Lakeside Drive. As you enter the Domain you'll see a walkway map. The path climbs through to the summit from where there are wonderful views of the Mackenzie basin, the lake and the Southern Alps. Allow 3 hours.

The University of Pennsylvania chose to build its international observatory on Mount John because it enjoys so many clear, cloudless days.

i **Lake Tekapo Information Centre** State Highway 8; tel: 03 680 6686. Also a souvenir shop.

The Godley Resort Hotel $$ Tekapo River Bridge; tel: 03 680 6848 or 0800 835 276, fax: 03 680 6873; www.tekapo.co.nz; e-mail: info@tekapo.co.nz. Contains shops and restaurants and a range of rooms at different prices.
Tekapo YHA $ Simpson Lane; tel: 03 680 6857, fax: 03 680 6664; e-mail: yhatekpo@yha.org.nz. Fantastic views over the lake from the cosy lounge. Internet access.

Robin's Café $ State Highway 8; tel: 03 680 6998. Licensed.
Jade Palace $$ State Highway 8; tel: 03 680 6828. Chinese restaurant. Licensed.
Reflections $$ State Highway 8; tel: 03 680 6808. Cosy restaurant with open fire, serving award-winning dishes.

MOUNT COOK

Mount Cook Village lies within Mount Cook National Park. Despite its proximity, the snow-capped mountain (3755 metres) is not as accessible as it looks. Experienced climbers only need apply and guides are essential.

The National Park was designated a world heritage site by UNESCO in 1986. It contains 22 peaks while the foothills and lower slopes are carpeted with flowers in

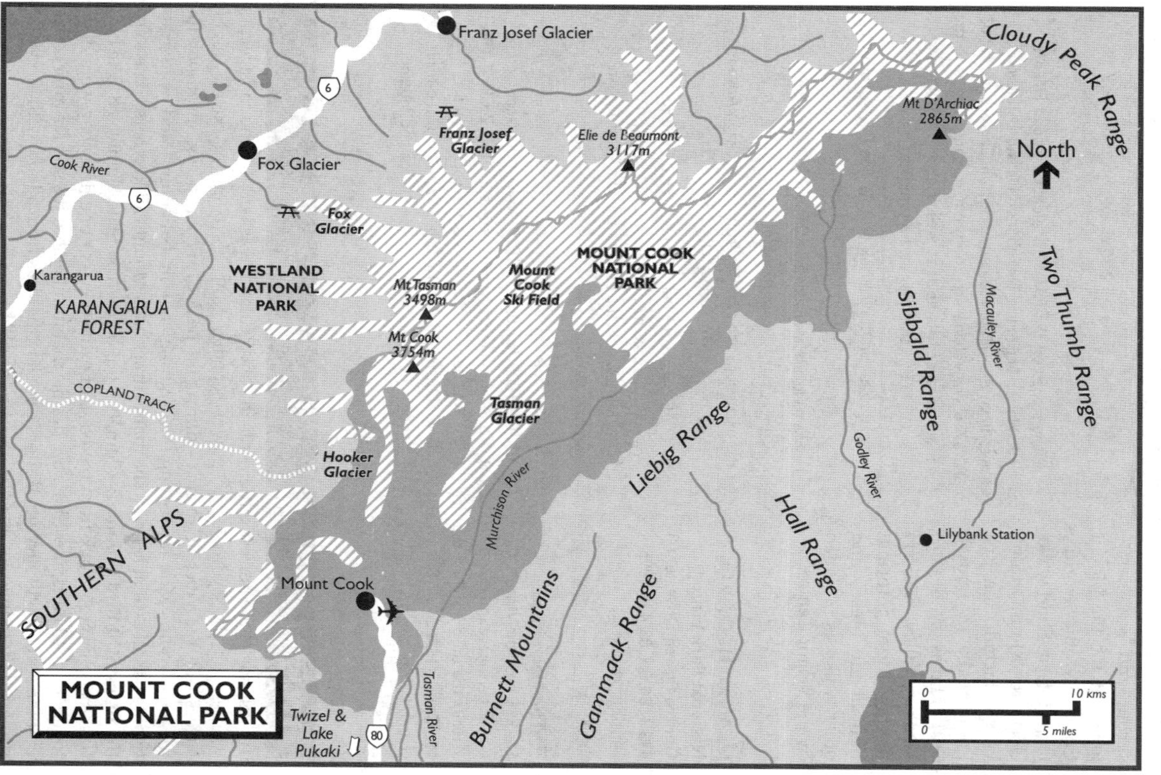
Franz Josef Glacier
Cloudy Peak Range
6
Mt D'Archiac
2865m
Franz Josef
Glacier
Elie de Beaumont
3117m
North
Cook River
Fox Glacier
6
Fox
Glacier
MOUNT COOK
NATIONAL
PARK
Mount
Cook
Ski Field
WESTLAND
NATIONAL
PARK
Karangarua
KARANGARUA
FOREST
Mt Tasman
3498m
Mt Cook
3754m
Sibbald Range
Macauley River
Two Thumb Range
COPLAND TRACK
Tasman
Glacier
Liebig Range
Hooker
Glacier
Murchison River
Godley River
Hall Range
SOUTHERN ALPS
Lilybank Station
Mount Cook
Burnett Mountains
Gammack Range
Tasman River
MOUNT COOK
NATIONAL PARK
Twizel &
Lake
Pukaki
80
0
10 kms
0
5 miles

spring and summer – look out for the Mount Cook lily, the world's largest daisy. Short walks close to Mount Cook village include the Kea Point walk (3 hours); Sealy Tarns walk and Hooker Valley walk (4 hours). More information about these, and other walks, is provided by the Visitor Centre.

SPORT

The slopes on the Tekapo ski-field on Round Hill are suitable for beginners. There's a ski lift and a shuttle bus leaves from the village. Alpine Recreation Canterbury, tel: 03 680 6736; www.alpinerecreation.co.nz, organises trips to the more advanced ski fields as well as alpine climbing and tramping in the summer.

You can skate on the ice rink on Lakeside Drive from May to August.

Horse treks are available from Mount John Station; tel: 03 680 6882.

Lake excursions are available from Lake Tekapo Adventures and Cruises; tel: 03 680 6721.

Air Safaris tel: 0800 806 880 or 03 680 6880; www.airsafaris.co.nz offer a choice of scenic flights over Mount Cook, the glaciers and the West Coast.

i Aoraki/Mt Cook National Park Visitor Centre Bowen Drive; tel: 03 435 1186, fax: 03 435 1895; e-mail: mtcookvc@doc.govt.nz.

The Hermitage
$$–$$$ near the Visitors Centre (tel: 03 435 1809, fax: 03 435 1879; www.mount-cook.com; e-mail: hermitage.mtcook@xtra.co.nz) is one of the most famous hotels in New Zealand. This is actually the third hotel on the site; the first was destroyed by floods, the second by fire.
Mt Cook YHA $ cnr Bowen and Kitchener Dr.; tel: 03 435 1820, fax: 03 435 1821; e-mail: yhamtck@yha.org.nz. Facilities include a shop, free sauna, log fires, free videos and Internet access.

TWIZEL

Twizel, one of the newest settlements in New Zealand, was built for the construction workers on the hydroelectric power scheme. Now it's being marketed (highly successfully) as a recreation area – during the peak Christmas period it's impossible to get a room. Mountaineering, ski touring, hot-air ballooning and wilderness fishing are all available here. The main attraction is Mount Cook; others come to see the **Black Stilt Bird Colony**, 3 kilometres out of town on State Highway 8. The birds have been brought back from the edge of extinction – at one time they were down to less than 40 pairs; now there are double that number, but it's still far from certain that the species will survive. Visitors can view the stilts from a hide, with binoculars provided. Bookings are essential; tel: 03 435 3124.

> 'If a person says he thinks he has seen Mount Cook, you may be quite sure that he has not seen it. The moment it comes into sight the exclamation is: 'That is Mount Cook!' – not 'That must be Mount Cook!' There is no possibility of mistake.'
>
> Samuel Butler, *A First Year in Canterbury Settlement*, 1863

i **Twizel Information Centre** Market Place; tel: 03 435 3124, fax: 03 435 0537; e-mail: info@twizel.com. Open Mon–Sat 0900–1700 (May–Sept), daily 0900–1900 (Oct–Apr).
Department of Conservation Wairepo Rd; tel: 03 435 0802, fax: 03 435 0852.

Colonial Motels $$ 36 Mackenzie Dr; tel: 03 435 0100, fax: 03 435 0499; www.twizel.com/colonial motel; e-mail: colonial@twizel.com. Eight units near the centre of town.
Mountain Chalet Motels $–$$ Wairepo Rd; tel: 03 435 0785 or 0800 629 999, fax: 03 435 0551; www.mountainchalets.co.nz; e-mail: mt.chalets@xtra.co.nz. Twenty-five recently built chalets with mountain views. Also offers backpacker accommodation in the lodge.

Hunter's Café & Bar $–$$ 2 Market Place; tel: 03 435 0303. Generous helpings of food, friendly service and lively atmosphere. Open 1100 till late. Licensed.

WAITAKI VALLEY

The appearance of the Waitaki Valley has been completely changed over the last 100 years thanks to the two massive hydroelectric power schemes, which have harnessed the power of the rivers draining into the valley from Lakes Tekapo, Pukaki and Ohau. Waitaki is divided into a series of reservoirs, separated by the dams of the three main power stations: Benmore, Aviemore and Waitaki.

OAMARU

The principal town and port of North Otago lies 115 kilometres north-east of Dunedin and 85 kilometres south-west of Timaru. The name means 'place of sheltered fire'. Oamaru limestone, quarried in the area, is used not only in local buildings but in construction throughout the country. It makes the town look coordinated and very attractive.

Oamaru serves the local farming community, which is gradually diversifying from the traditional sheep rearing. Ten kilometres out of town is Totara Estate, which produced the first shipment of refrigerated New Zealand lamb to Britain on board the *Dunedin* in 1882. You can still visit the estate.

The first settler to Oamaru was a runholder – someone who farmed sheep on a sheep run. That was Hugh Robinson, who arrived in 1853. Only five years later, they were laying out the town and eight years after it became a borough.

To see the town at its best go to **Lookout Point** at the end of Tamar St just as the sun is rising, when the beaches and the harbour positively glisten.

Don't leave without visiting the **Little Blue Penguin Observatory** at Breakwater Rd (tel: 03 434 1718), where you can see the world's smallest penguins returning home around dusk.

You'll get another sight of the penguins if you take the **Graves Walkway**, a coastal track running for 2 kilometres from Waterfront Rd. There's a hide here where you can watch the birds – the best time is late afternoon.

i **Oamaru Visitor Centre** | Thames St; tel: 03 434 1656, fax: 03 434 1657; e-mail: info@tourismwaitaki.co.nz.

EN ROUTE

The Southern Sockeye Salmon Farm lies 9.5 km out of town on the Glen Lyon Rd. The salmon bred here were introduced into the river nearly 100 years ago from Canada. The colony was threatened by the hydroelectric development and the farm is part of a plan to protect the fish and grow them commercially.

Anne Mieke Guest House $$ 47 Tees St; tel: 03 434 8051, fax: 03 434 8050; e-mail: anne.mieke@xtra.co.nz. Superb harbour views and a friendly, welcoming bed and breakfast.
Colonial Lodge Motel $$ 509 Thames Highway; tel: 03 437 0999 or 0800 102 999, fax: 03 437 0992. Cooked and continental breakfasts; there are also restaurants nearby. Close to the blue penguin colony.
Empire Hotel $ 13 Thames St; tel: 03 434 3446; www.oamaru.net.nz/empire.htm; e-mail: empirehotel_@hotmail.com. An 1867 Victorian hotel in Oamaru's historic district. Central location.
Pen-Y-Bryn Lodge $$$ 41 Towey St; tel: 03 434 7939, fax: 03 434 9063; www.penybryn.co.nz; e-mail: admin@penybryn.co.nz. Elegant Victorian mansion with comfortable rooms and excellent food and wines.
Red Kettle YHA $ cnr Reed and Cross St; tel/fax: 03 434 5008; e-mail: yhaomaru@yha.org.nz. Located in a cosy old bungalow. Open Sept–May/June.
Swaggers Backpackers $ 25 Wansbeck St; tel: 03 434 9999; e-mail: swaggers@es.co.nz. Central location with sea views from most rooms. Complimentary tea, coffee and milk.

Star and Garter $$ 9 Itchen St; tel: 03 434 5246. A music-hall revival restaurant that provides excellent fun and substantial food. Open daily 1030–late.
The Last Post $$$ 12 Thames St; tel: 03 434 8080. Restaurant and bar with garden in the former post office building. Closes Sun–Thur at 2200, Fri–Sat at midnight.

WHERE NEXT?

The natural progression of journey from Oamaru is to continue south along State Highway 1 to the lovely city of Dunedin (see p. 371) with its rich Scottish heritage. Continuing further along this Highway will lead you to Balclutha (see p. 384).

MOERAKI BOULDERS

As you drive south along the coast road from Oamaru you'll notice the Moeraki Boulders scattered along the beach. There are about 50 of them and they're huge – the largest is up to 4 metres in circumference and weighs in at an estimated 7 tonnes. According to Maori tradition they originated as gourds and food baskets, spilled from the ancestral canoe, Araiteuru, when it was wrecked nearby.

Technically, if more prosaically, the rocks are classified as septarian concretions. They were probably formed some 60 million years ago when lime salts adhered to fossil shell, bone fragment, a piece of wood or other object, forming a boulder that grew slowly in size as the minerals accumulated.

There's a Visitors Centre in the carpark overlooking the boulders, with a licensed restaurant and souvenir shop (tel: 03 439 4827).

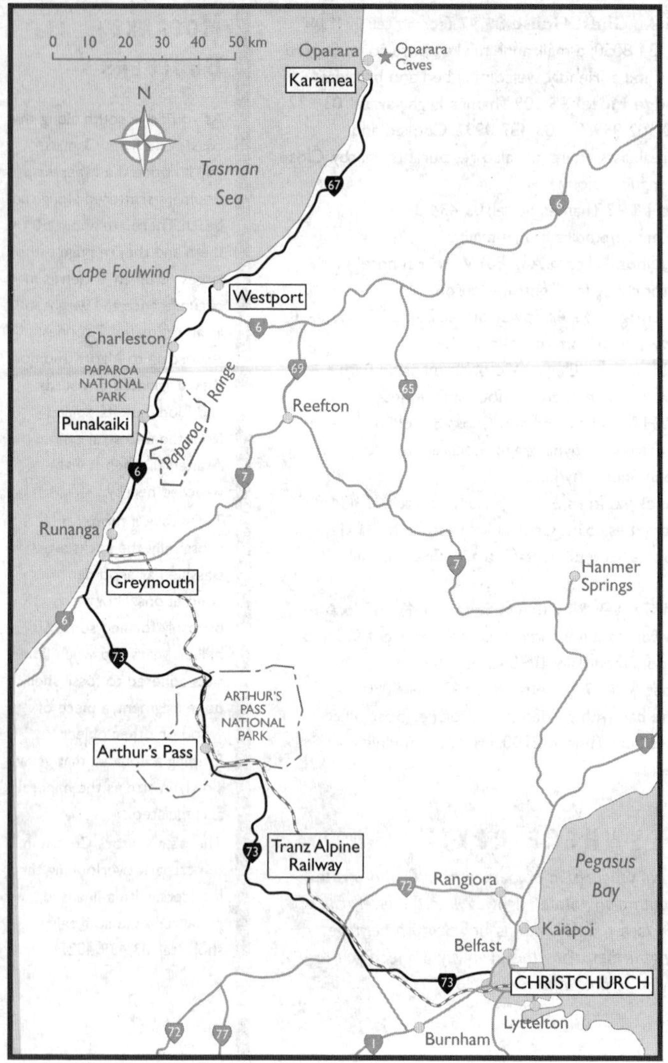
0 10 20 30 40 50 km
N
Oparara
Oparara Caves
Karamea
Tasman Sea
67
6
Cape Foulwind
Westport
6
Charleston
69
65
PAPAROA NATIONAL PARK
Paparoa Range
Reefton
Punakaiki
7
6
Runanga
7
Greymouth
Hanmer Springs
6
73
ARTHUR'S PASS NATIONAL PARK
Arthur's Pass
1
Tranz Alpine Railway
73
Pegasus Bay
72
Rangiora
Kaiapoi
Belfast
73
CHRISTCHURCH
Lyttelton
72
77
1
Burnham

GREYMOUTH – KARAMEA

Notes

The bus service from Greymouth runs only as far north as Westport before heading east to Nelson; change at Westport for Karamea. Along with the TranzAlpine Railway, three buses run daily from Christchurch to Greymouth. OTT 9805.

'… an inhospitable shore, unworthy of observation, except for its ridge of naked and barren rocks covered with snow. As far as the eye could reach the prospect was wild, craggy and desolate'.

Captain James Cook
Journal, 1770

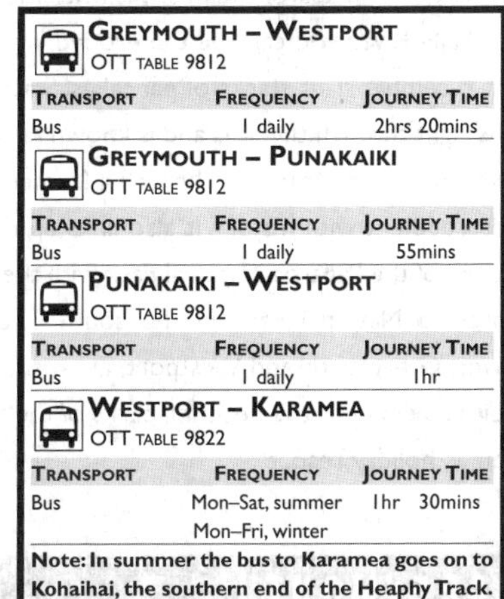

GREYMOUTH – WESTPORT
OTT TABLE 9812

TRANSPORT	FREQUENCY	JOURNEY TIME
Bus	1 daily	2hrs 20mins

GREYMOUTH – PUNAKAIKI
OTT TABLE 9812

TRANSPORT	FREQUENCY	JOURNEY TIME
Bus	1 daily	55mins

PUNAKAIKI – WESTPORT
OTT TABLE 9812

TRANSPORT	FREQUENCY	JOURNEY TIME
Bus	1 daily	1hr

WESTPORT – KARAMEA
OTT TABLE 9822

TRANSPORT	FREQUENCY	JOURNEY TIME
Bus	Mon–Sat, summer Mon–Fri, winter	1hr 30mins

Note: In summer the bus to Karamea goes on to Kohaihai, the southern end of the Heaphy Track.

ROUTE DETAIL

Greymouth – Westport 150 km
Greymouth – Hokitika 45 km

Head north from Greymouth on State Highway 6 through the coal mining town of Runanga to Rapahoe which has an 11 kilometre-long beach, perfect for bathing and gem collecting.

Continue through the former mining settlements (gold and coal) of Greigs and Barrytown to Punakaiki, which lies at the entrance to the Paparoa National Park. State Highway 6 hugs the coast as far as Charleston then heads inland to Westport.

Leave the Highway, which crosses the island at this point, and take the west coast extension, State Highway 67 through a string of settlements on the plain between the Karamea Bight and the Matiri Range. After crossing the Mokihinui River, the road returns to the coast at Te Namu and ends at Karamea. The only way to get further north from here is on foot – via the famous Heaphy Trail.

From Greymouth it is also possible to cross the South Island to Christchurch. Take State Highway 6 through South Beach and Gladstone, then turn left onto State Highway 73 which crosses Arthur's Pass.

Greymouth – Karamea

This rugged stretch of coast is sparsely populated all the way from Karamea at the edge of the Kahurangi National Park to the Mokitiki Gorge. In fact, you're more likely to come across a grey seal than a human on some beaches. The Paparoa National Park was established in 1987 and covers 27,818 hectares between the Tasman Sea and the Paparoa Range. At the mouth of the Punakaiki River you can see the eroded limestone slabs that resemble giant stacks of pancakes. State Highway 6 runs right through the area and is known as the Heritage Highway because it passes through a former gold mining area, redolent with history. It also links up the northern section of the Paparoa National Park with the magnificent Fiordland National Park in the south. The two main towns, Greymouth and Westport, are visited more for their proximity to the beautiful parks of the South Island than as holiday resorts.

The Grey River flood barrier was last tested in 1994. When the rains came, for the first time in the town's history Greymouth was not inundated. The Grey River is especially treacherous at the notorious bar where it meets the Tasman Sea.

GREYMOUTH

Greymouth, famous for its whitebait, was founded in 1863 as a government depot at the mouth of the Grey River. Like so many other settlements in New Zealand, it owed its development to the discovery of gold and, later, coal. Both commodities are now in short supply although some of the slack has been taken up by timber and cattle raising. For more than a century the people of the town have been concerned about flooding from the river – Greymouth was devastated by floods in 1988. The 'Great Wall' flood barrier was the outcome. This has now become an attractive walk from the centre of town, past Fisherman's Wharf to the breakwater – about 90 minutes all told. There are spectacular views from the wall and on a clear day you can see as far as Mount Cook. No longer a threat, the **Grey River**, has become a major attraction offering fishing and rafting.

Tourism is being encouraged at **Shantytown** (Paroa, 8 kilometres south of town). This is a replica West Coast gold-mining town of the 1860s in a native bush setting. You can even pan for gold here – everyone who does so is guaranteed to find a few flakes. Wander at leisure around the jail, livery stables (complete with gigs and horses), carpenter's shop, general store, 137-year-old church and Golden Nugget Hotel. Shantytown: tel: 03 762 6634; www.shantytown.co.nz. Open daily 0830–1700.

Greymouth is also associated with pounamu - greenstone, or to give it its technical name, nephrite jade. The **Jade Boulder Gallery**, tel: 03 768 0700, in Guinness St, has a wondrous display of the semi-precious stones in their natural state, before they are carved and polished and set. If you're looking for a souvenir, jade items, including golf putters, are on sale in the store. Open daily.

The town's coastal location makes it a good base for viewing the local marine fauna. **Scenicland-Dolphin Adventure Tours** (tel: 0800 929 991; www.dolphintours.co.nz) runs cruises all the year round and you'll get to see not only Hector's dolphins (an endangered species) but also fur seals and seabirds. Open daily.

A more energetic alternative is to go blackwater rafting through the Taniwha cavern complex with **The Wild West Adventure Company**, tel: 03 768 6649. Wetsuits, crash helmets and other equipment provided.

Nearby **Lake Brunner** is named after Thomas Brunner (1821–74), an intrepid local explorer who joined the New Zealand Company as a surveyor's assistant in 1841. During a distinguished career he discovered the source of the Grey and Buller rivers, and followed both their courses with the help of Maori guides. Brunner settled down to become a government surveyor and eventually, the Commissioner of Public Works in Nelson.

THE GREY VALLEY

The Grey Valley, inland from Greymouth, is in fact very green. It is an area of high rainfall and comprises mainly of forest. Gold prospectors once haunted the woods here and you still come across abandoned equipment, houses, and even whole settlements.

Start your exploration by driving up the valley on State Highway 7 through Dobson, Stillwater, Ngahere, Ikamatau and Reefton. Continue to Inangahua Junction, where you can still see the scars on the hillside from the great earthquake of 1968. The road then traverses the Lower Buller Gorge to Westport.

WHAT'S BREWING

Sample award-winning beers on one of Monteith's Brewery Tours.

Monteith's Brewery Company, cnr Turumaha and Herbert Sts, Greymouth; tel: 03 768 4149.

Visitor Information Greymouth, Cnr Herbert and Mackay Sts; tel: 03 768 5101, fax: 03 768 0317; e-mail: vingm@minidata.co.nz.

Ashley Hotel $$ 74 Tasman St; tel: 03 768 5135 or 0800 807 787, fax: 03 768 0319; www.hotelashley.co.nz; e-mail: ashley.grey@xtra.co.nz. Facilities include bar, restaurant and brasserie, heated pool, spa and sauna.

Charles Court Motel $$ 350 Main South Rd; tel: 0800 800 619, fax: 03 762 6594. Spacious grounds with children's playground and close to the beach.

Greymouth Seaside Top 10 Holiday Park $–$$ Chesterfield St; tel: 03 768 6618 or 0800 867 104, fax: 03 768 5873; www.top10greymouth.co.nz; e-mail: info@top10greymouth.co.nz. Standard flats, cabins and motel units close to the beach. Also bunkhouse with dormitory.

Noah's Ark Backpackers $ 16 Chapel St; tel: 03 768 4868 or 0800 662 472. Old monastery building with loads of character. Dormitory, single, twin and double rooms available.

MOANA (ON THE SHORES OF LAKE BRUNNER)

Moana is a small township on the shores of Lake Brunner, 42 kilometres from Greymouth. It boasts some of the best trout fishing on the South Island and anglers are practically guaranteed a catch all year round.

The best time for fly-fishing and spinning is from October to April. The town is also the centre for some splendid sightseeing. Cross the Arnold River footbridge for access to the shores of Lake Brunner where there's swimming.

Native wildlife can be seen in natural bush surroundings at the Conservation Park, 1 kilometre out of town on the road back to Greymouth. To get there drive inland on State Highway 17 to Stillwater, then take the turning to Moana. You can either return the same way or continue to Te Kinga, Rotamanu and Inchbonnie as far as the Arthur's Pass Road. From here drive down to Kumara Junction on State Highway 73, then back along State Highway 6 to Greymouth.

The Hog's Head Bar & Grill $$ 9 Tainui St; tel: 03 768 4093. House speciality is whitebait (in season).

Jones's Licensed Café & Bar $$ 37 Tainui St; tel: 03 768 6468. Superb menu providing quick, light meals. Has a welcoming atmosphere with music in the evenings. Open daily for lunch and dinner.

The Smelting House Café $ 102 MacKay St; tel: 03 768 0012. Breakfasts and lunches and afternoon snacks. Specialises in home-made food. Open 0730–1630.

PUNAKAIKI

Punakaiki, at the mouth of the river of the same name, is the gateway to **Paparoa National Park**, New Zealand's smallest. At its heart, a subtropical microclimate around the limestone bluffs produces lush vegetation. Paparoa is also the world's only breeding-ground of black petrels. **Paparoa Nature Tours**, tel: 03 731 1826, organises 2-hour trips between April and December to view the petrels as they come to land by their burrows.

Equally diverting are the blowholes by **Pancake Rocks**, formed as the sea surges into caverns beneath the cliffs before forcing the water up through holes in the limestone. The reason for the name is that this stratified limestone has been weathered into a dramatic formation that looks just like a stack of giant pancakes. There are several tracks through the park. Dolomite Point and the blowholes are a 15-minute walk, suitable for wheelchairs.

Punakaiki Cavern, also close to the Visitor's Centre, is a limestone cave, about 70 metres deep. Wooden steps and a walkway help you find your way to the glow-worms (take a torch). **Truman Track** (30 minutes return) leads to a small beach backed by

CHARLESTON

Charleston, north of Punakaiki and en route to Westport, was an area of intensive mining activity in the 1860s. Its population at one time reached 18,000 (it's now down to 30!). Mitchells Gully Gold Mine has been mined by one family since 1866. It has recently reopened as a working museum to reveal how gold was extracted. Open daily 1000–1500; tel: 03 789 6553.

PANCAKE ROCKS

Don't miss the pancake rocks when you are in Punakaiki – they make the town famous, and are just a 15-minute walk from the main road.

rock platforms. If you're looking for an alternative way of exploring the park, **Punakaiki Canoe and Cycle Hire** tel: 03 731 1870 provide kayaks, canoes and mountain bikes.

i **Punakaiki Visitor Information and DOC** Office, by Pancake Rocks tel: 03 731 1895.

WESTPORT

Westport lies 105 kilometres north-east of Greymouth, near the mouth of the Buller river. Westport benefitted from the gold rush of the 1850s, but coal proved a more lasting source of mineral wealth – the mines around the town are still an important source of bituminous coal. You can discover more about the history of mining in the area at Coaltown, Queen St; open daily 0900–1630.

For a more out-of-doors experience head for the **Westland National Park**, which embraces more than 117,000 hectares of rugged mountain and dense forest terrain.

i **Westport Visitor Information Centre** 1 Brougham St; tel: 03 789 6658, fax: 03 789 6668; e-mail: westport.info@xtra.co.nz.

Department of Conservation Office 72 Russell St; tel: 03 788 8008.

Ascot Motor Lodge $$ 74 Romilly St; tel: 03 789 7832, fax: 03 789 6311. Away from traffic and train noise.

Marg's Travellers Rest $$ 56 Russell St; tel: 03 789 8627, fax: 03 789 8396. Clean, comfortable accommodation close to the centre. Breakfasts on the terrace.

Seal Colony Tourist Park $$ Marine Parade, Carters Beach; tel: 03 789 8002, fax: 03 789 6732. Closest accommodation to the seal colony. Also located by safe swimming beach and an 18-hole golf course.

Bay House Cafe $$ Tauranga Bay; tel: 03 789 7133. Restaurant and café at the end of Cape Foulwind Walkway. Excellent sea views and good food. Open daily.

Baillie's Bar and Restaurant $$ 187 Palmerston St; tel: 03 789 7289. Great seafood platters, home-made pizza and a full New Zealand wine list. Open daily.

A SEAL COLONY

Westport is also close to the major seal colony on Cape Foulwind, 12 kilometres west of town. The coastal views, accessible from a 4-kilometre long walkway, are superb. At the Tauranga Bay Seal Colony platforms overlook the seals. (The best time to see them is October to January.)

KARAMEA

Karamea is the last stop on the Heritage Highway and the gateway to the Kahurangi National Park. The town lies on the estuary of the Karamea river, over 100 kilometres north-east of Westport. The Nelson Provincial Government founded Karamea as a special farm settlement in 1874, but the land was infertile and hundreds of the assisted migrants left the area, unable to make a living. Nowadays the town owes its livelihood to tourists visiting the **Kahurangi National Park** to the north and the beaches overlooking the Tasman Sea.

Another attraction is the **Heaphy Track**, which follows the coast north from Karamea before crossing the Wakamara Mountains and winding up at Collingwood. Even if you don't feel up to walking the whole track, the first few kilometres are truly scenic. The Nikau Loop Walk, 15 kilometres north of Karamea on the Kohaihai river, takes about 40 minutes and has well-graded paths. If you do walk the whole track, you can get a bus back from Collingwood between April and October to Takaka, with a connection to Nelson.

Scotts Beach is another local walk with magnificent views; allow an hour and a half for the return trip.

It is unusual for a resort to make a destination worthwhile in itself, but this is true of the Last Resort at Karamea. This is a very unusual and well-thought-out resort (with grass on the roof to cut out the noise when it rains!). It is mainly hand-built, eco-friendly and offers a wide range of trips to explore the surrounding countryside.

i **Karamea Information and Resource Centre** Bridge St; tel/fax: 03 782 6652.

Bridge Farm Motels $$ Bridge St; tel: 03 782 6955, fax: 03 782 6748. Spacious and comfortable motel in attractive setting overlooking the Kahurangi National Park.

Karamea Village Hotel $ Waverly St; tel/fax: 03 782 6800. Bar meals are available.

The Last Resort $–$$ 17 Waverly St; tel: 03 782 6617, fax: 03 782 6820. This unusual eco-friendly holiday complex, mainly hand-built, has grass sown on the roofs to cut down the noise when it rains! Apart from an excellent licensed restaurant, the staff help arrange trips into the surrounding countryside.

ARTHUR'S PASS

One of the world's most scenic journeys and a miracle of road and rail engineering, Arthur's Pass is the main route across the Southern Alps.

Arthur Dobson, who gave the pass its name, was told about the route by the local Maoris, who had been using it for centuries. He immediately surveyed the pass and achieved a degree of immortality in the process. Originally it was traversed by teams of horses; the railway was constructed in 1923. Bring your camera – the views are stunning.

Springfield to Arthur's Pass

Staircase viaduct, the highest and most impressive on the train line, is 73 metres high. It could easily accommodate Christchurch Cathedral with room to spare.

DRIVING Leave Greymouth on State Highway 6 passing through South Beach on the way to Kumara Junction. Here turn left onto State Highway 73. The road follows the course of the Taramakau river through broadleaved evergreen forest, then climbs to Arthur's Pass by way of Jacksons, where the old coaching inn has been refurbished in 19th-century style. Otira is at its best in the spring when the scarlet rata trees (unique to the slopes of the Southern Alps) come into bloom.

Beyond Arthur's Pass, State Highway 73 descends via Lake Pearson and the ski fields of the Craigieburn Forest, to dramatic Porters Pass on the way to Springfield. Here the road joins the railway to cross the plains along the banks of the River Waimakariri to Christchurch.

The **Tranz Alpine Express**: The TAE leaves Christchurch every day at 0900 on its 4½-hour journey to Greymouth. As you cross the Canterbury Plains, you'll notice lines of tall trees running at right angles to the path of the train – these windbreaks are vital in protecting the plains from damage and erosion. The track now begins its long climb over the Waimakariri Gorge towards Arthur's Pass. Here there's normally a change of engine, allowing enough time to photograph the dazzling views.

The 8.5 kilometre-long tunnel at Otira is one of 19 on the 231-kilometre journey. Eventually the track begins the descent to Lake Brunner passing through the dense, podocarp forest of the west coast to Greymouth. The TAE has viewing windows and an observation car. Snacks and morning tea are also served. If you don't want to go all the way to the west coast, it's possible to get off at Arthur's Pass and spend five hours there before catching the train on its return journey, to arrive in Christchurch in the early evening.

QUICK FACTS ABOUT ARTHUR'S PASS

It was established as New Zealand official parkland in 1929.

The park covers about 980 square kilometres (about 380 square miles) of mountainous landscape.

The peaks inside the park's boundaries include Mount Murchison (2400 metres/7874 feet), Mount Rolleston (2271 metres/7451 feet), and 28 others taller than 1800 metres (6000 feet).

The park features glaciers, forest, chamois (a type of goat) and deer.

Arthur's Pass National Park takes its name from a pass between the Canterbury and Westland regions, 926 metres (3083 feet) above sea level, discovered by Sir Arthur Dudley Dobson in 1864.

ARTHUR'S PASS NATIONAL PARK

Arthur's Pass is also the name given to the fourth-largest national park in New Zealand, with an area of more than 100,000 hectares. The two main peaks in this upland region are Mount Rolleston (2271 metres) and Mount Pfeifer (1705 metres). Often shrouded in mist and cloud, the rich vegetation includes the crimson rata and other alpine flowers. Arthur's Pass Village started out in the early 1900s as a settlement for navvies and railway engineers. Now it caters for walkers, climbers and skiers.

ARTHUR'S PASS STOPOVER

Arthur's Pass was once the changeover point from steam to electric locomotives, as the next section is the steepest on the route.

There are several walks from the village: **Devil's Punchbowl** is a 2-kilometre track leading to a waterfall, while Bridal Veil Nature Walk (about the same distance) climbs through mountain beeches to a lookout point before returning via the main road. Allow 4 hours to complete the Temple Basin Walk, which starts at the car park, more time if you intend to photograph the stunning mountain views.

i **Arthur's Pass Visitor Centre** State Highway 73, tel: 03 318 9211, fax: 03 928 9271; open daily 0800–1700. Sells two immensely useful and inexpensive brochures: *Walks in Arthur's Pass National Park* and *Arthur's Pass Village Historic Walk*, which takes you past a series of viewpoints with plaques telling the history of the area.

Coast to Coast tel: 0800 800847 have details of minibuses running over the Pass.

SPORT

There are several skifields in the area all offering spectacular views.

Mt Olympus is small, but there are runs here for all levels. The slopes at Craigieburn Valley and Mount Cheeseman are more challenging and better suited to intermediate and advanced skiers. Broken River and Temple Basin are suitable for snowboarding, while Porter Heights can claim to have the longest run in the southern hemisphere.

Bealey Hotel $$ State Highway 73 (12 km east of Arthur's Pass); tel: 03 318 9277, fax 03 318 9014. Beautiful views over the Waimakariri River from this complex, which offers a range of accommodation from budget to ensuite rooms. Licensed restaurant and bar.

The Chalet $$$ State Highway 73; tel: 03 318 9236, fax: 03 318 9200. Comfortable bed and breakfast in attractive chalet-style hotel with restaurant and bistro.

Flock Hill Lodge $–$$ Hwy 73 (40 km east of Arthur's Pass); tel: 03 318 8196, fax: 03 318 8856; www.flockhill.co.nz. Stay on a high-country station amidst magnificent alpine scenery! There is a range of accommodation, from backpackers to comfortable cottages and motel units. Various activities can be arranged and mountain-bikes can be hired. Those travelling on the Tranz Alpine Express can get off at Mt White Bridge; a courtesy car will then bring you to the lodge (arrange beforehand).

Mountain House Backpackers $ Main Rd; tel: 03 318 9258, fax: 03 318 9058; www.trampers.co.nz; e-mail: mountain.house@xtra.co.nz. Centrally located in Arthur's Pass Village. Also tent sites.

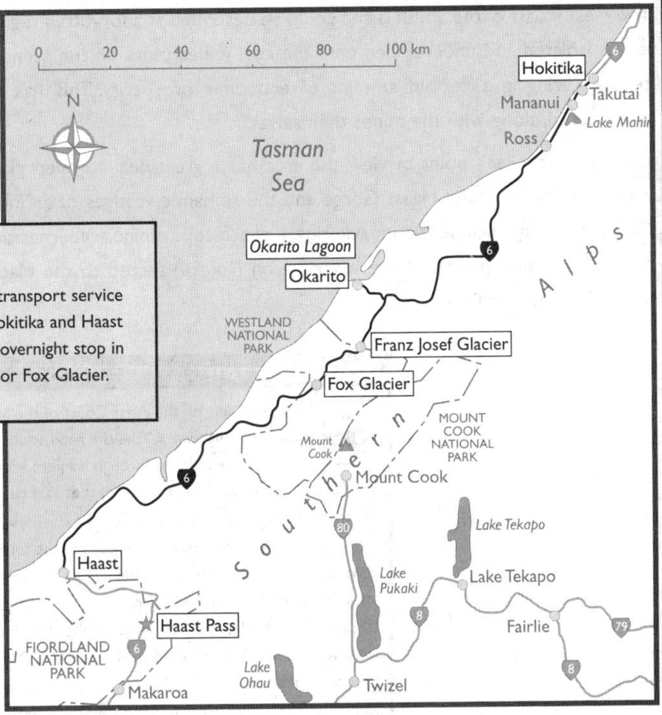

Note
The public transport service between Hokitika and Haast involves an overnight stop in Franz Josef or Fox Glacier.

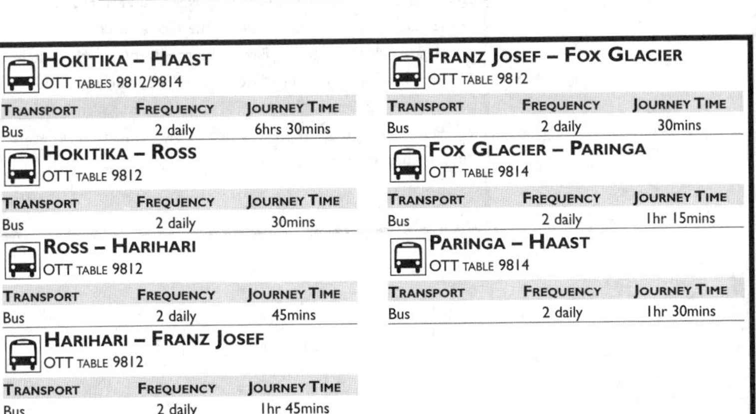

Hokitika – Haast
OTT tables 9812/9814

Transport	Frequency	Journey Time
Bus	2 daily	6hrs 30mins

Hokitika – Ross
OTT table 9812

Transport	Frequency	Journey Time
Bus	2 daily	30mins

Ross – Harihari
OTT table 9812

Transport	Frequency	Journey Time
Bus	2 daily	45mins

Harihari – Franz Josef
OTT table 9812

Transport	Frequency	Journey Time
Bus	2 daily	1hr 45mins

Franz Josef – Fox Glacier
OTT table 9812

Transport	Frequency	Journey Time
Bus	2 daily	30mins

Fox Glacier – Paringa
OTT table 9814

Transport	Frequency	Journey Time
Bus	2 daily	1hr 15mins

Paringa – Haast
OTT table 9814

Transport	Frequency	Journey Time
Bus	2 daily	1hr 30mins

Hokitika – Haast

The West Coast of the South Island could be described as a forgotten region. Certainly it was isolated and undeveloped until the coal mines came on the scene in the 19th century, bringing a certain amount of economic prosperity. This has now all but disappeared, along with the mines themselves.

From the traveller's point of view the area has a great deal to offer: glaciers, scenic waterfalls, the dramatic Haast Gorge and the romantic vestiges of an industrial past. Other highlights include Mount Aspiring, a spectacular alpine wilderness; the Okarito Lagoon, breeding ground of the white heron (*kotuku*) sacred to the Maoris; and the Westland National Park.

Route Detail

Hokitika lies on the West Coast of the South Island on State Highway 6. Take the road south as it rounds the Hokitika Gorge through Kaniere – once a major goldfield – before returning to the coast at Takutai.

Continue through Mananui, past Lake Mahinapua, where the scenery becomes more impressive. Beyond the former gold town of Ross and the forested Lake Ianthe is Harihari, a farming and timber milling community.

Continue past Mt Hercules and Lake Wahapo to the Forks, from where there's a side road to the peaceful Okarito Lagoon. Return to State Highway 6.

Past Lake Mapourika is the Westland National Park and the Franz Josef and Fox Glaciers. Cross the Cook and the Karangarua rivers to Bruce Bay at the mouth of the Mahakitahi. Continue past Lakes Paringa and Moeraki, popular with trout and salmon fishermen. On the final stretch from Knight's Point to Haast, the road follows the shore of the Tasman Sea, offering superb coastal views.

240 km

HOKITIKA

CRAFTS IN HOKITIKA

There are numerous little outlets in Hokitika selling arts and crafts, including pottery, textiles, wood carvings and handcrafted jewellery made from gold nuggets found in the area.

Hokitika, 40 kilometres from Greymouth, at the mouth of the Hokitika river, was once the provincial capital; today the town has a population of less than 4000. The first European settlers arrived in the 1860s to scramble for gold. There were soon more than 6000 miners and prospectors in the makeshift town, panning the river for the precious metal.

Today's miners also extract greenstone (jade), the rock highly valued by the Maoris, who used it to make weapons and ornaments. It's now sold in the local shops. You can watch cutting demonstrations at **Mountain Jade**, 41 Weld St. The **West Coast Historical Museum** in Hamilton St has an interesting greenstone collection, as well as historic goldmining memorabilia. The old Gold Rush days are recaptured in the 'Greenstone and Gold' audio visual show and added fun is provided by the chance to try gold panning or to go on a treasure hunt. Open daily.

WILD FOODS FESTIVAL

If you're around Hokitika in March, don't miss out on this festival! There's gourmet food to enjoy, and some more unusual delicacies – how about *kuia* (sea urchin) or huhu grubs? There's also plenty of good South Island beer, live music and a generous chunk of West Coast culture. All in all, it's loads of fun. Website: www.hokitika.com/wildfoods.

i **Westland Visitor Information Centre** Carnegie Building, cnr Hamilton and Tancred St; tel: 03 755 6166, fax: 03 755 5011; e-mail: hkkvin@xtra.co.nz.

Beach House Backpackers $ 137 Revell St; tel: 03 755 6859. Friendly place with a restaurant and unique garden. Enjoy the hot tubs!

Black Sands Motor Lodge $$ 252 Revell St; tel: 03 755 8773, fax: 03 755 8772. Smart, clean motel in quiet location with spa and swimming pool.

Café de Paris $$ 19 Tancred St; tel: 03 755 8933. Good food, from breakfasts to Mediterranean cuisine, in relaxed atmosphere. Licensed and BYO.

Trappers $$ 79 Revell St; tel: 03 755 5133. Good food, although the theme suggested by the name may not be totally to your taste. Licensed.

OKARITO LAGOON

This beautiful lagoon lies 35 kilometres south of Harihari (turn off State Highway 6 at the signs 3 kilometres beyond Lake Wahapo). At Waitangiroto, at the northern end of the lagoon, there's a protected breeding ground for the kotuku (white heron), sacred to the Maori for its rarity, grace and beauty.

Access to the sanctuary is permitted only in the company of a Department of Conservation guide and booking is essential. Contact **White Heron Sanctuary Tours**, tel: 03 753 4120 (Nov–Feb, 1500–1800; duration 2½ hours).

EN ROUTE

Lake Matheson, 6 kilometres from the Fox Glacier, has become a major tourist attraction in its own right. When the weather is clear, the reflections of Mounts Tasman and Cook are a magnificent sight in the still waters of the lake. The view often appears on postcards.

FOX GLACIER

The dimensions of the Fox Glacier are truly impressive: the 13 kilometre-long river of ice flows from a snowfield below the Douglas and Glacier Peaks. Starting at 2750 metres above sea level, it drops about 200 metres per kilometre until it melts away at about 245 metres above sea level.

Among the remarkable features of the glacier are the deep-blue kettle lakes, formed by the slow melting of dead ice left behind as the glacier retreats. Alpine parrots (kea) have also made their home here and take great delight in attacking the windscreen wipers and windscreen sealing of parked cars. To reach the glacier on foot (30 minutes), take the track from the car park, about 8 kilometres from town. Perhaps even better is the river walk, which is along the glacier road before you get to the car park and runs for 2 kilometres, taking about 30 minutes.

From either village you can drive or walk out to the 'snout' of each glacier. Looming above, the towering blocks of ice, known as 'seracs', lie jumbled together in a mass that creaks and heaves as the blocks tumble into the moraine below.

The Fox Glacier is unusual as blocks of ice remain buried beneath rock debris downstream of the terminal face, and melt to create the milky lakes nestled around the Fox River.

The town of Fox lies at the western foot of the Victoria Range and exists solely for tourists. By the way, the constant 'thud-thud' you can hear in the area is from the choppers constantly taking off in the towns of Fox and Franz Josef.

i **Department of Conservation Visitor Centre**
State Highway 6; tel: 03 751 0807, fax: 03 751 0858.

Fox Glacier Hotel $$ cnr State Highway 6 and Cook Flat Rd, Fox Glacier; tel: 03 751 0839, fax: 03 751 0868. Rooms at a variety of prices. Good restaurant and bar.
Fox Glacier Holiday Park $–$$ Fox Glacier; tel: 03 751 0821, fax: 03 751 0813. Dormitory accommodation, cabins, flats and tent sites.

Café Neve $ State Highway 6. Wholefood snacks and pizzas outside on the terrace and indoors.
Cook Saddle Café and Saloon $$ State Highway 6. Mountain lodge-style café and bar.

WHAT'S A GLACIER?

A glacier is a river formed from giant blocks of snow crystals that have accumulated over thousands of years through mounting pressure. The river of ice slides slowly down the mountainside until it melts in the warmer valleys, but is continually renewed at its source.

When Julius von Haast first saw the Fox Glacier in 1865, it was 3 kilometres nearer the main highway than it is today and its surface was up to 300 metres higher. Although there have been some 'surges' in the years since, when the glacier advanced, the general trend has been an overall retreat. It is not known what further effect global warming will have on this.

THE AMAZING THOMAS BRUNNER

Thomas Brunner lived from 1821 to 1874, was an explorer and was, it seems, as tough as old boots. He went through a series of amazing adventures and appears to have regarded them as all in a day's work.

He came to New Zealand as a survey assistant with the New Zealand company in 1841. First he made two journeys of exploration – one with William Fox and Charles Heaphy, and the second with Heaphy. In December 1846 he set out with two Maori guides and their wives to find out what was the source of the Buller River. The party ran out of food and so Thomas cooked his dog for rations until the party reached a Maori settlement at Arahura. Thomas Brunner wintered there, living on fern root and walking barefoot.

He arrived back at Nelson on 15 June 1848, 560 days after his departure and long after he had been presumed dead. He had traced the Grey and Buller rivers from source to mouth, and the Inangahua from its source to its junction with the Buller. During the last few weeks of his journey, he had lost the use almost entirely of one leg.

After a period of unemployment, Brunner settled down to become a government surveyor, then Chief Surveyor for Nelson Province, and later Nelson's Commissioner of Public Works.

FRANZ JOSEF GLACIER

The Franz Josef is one of the most accessible glaciers in New Zealand. To view it on foot, follow one of several walks, which leave from the car park 5 kilometres south of the village. The terrain is fairly flat, so it'll take about 30 minutes. You'll get a better understanding of the glacier if you have a trained guide with you (contact the Department of Conservation). If money's no object, you can fly to the top by helicopter or light aircraft and land on the glacier itself.

Europeans have known about the glacier since Tasman's voyage of 1642. The pioneering geologist, Julius von Haast, named it after the reigning Austro-Hungarian emperor..

FLIGHTS OVER THE GLACIER

Air Safaris tel: 03 752 0716 offer flights over the Glaciers (25 minutes) and Mt Cook (40 minutes).

Alpine Guides Fox Glacier, tel: 03 751 0825, link a helicopter tour with a walk on the Fox Glacier. Other helicopter flights with touchdowns in the snow are offered by

WHY ARE THE GLACIERS UNUSUAL?
The Fox Glacier and the Franz Josef Glacier are unusual because they extend right down through the coastal temperate zone, a phenomenon found nowhere else in the world.

Fox & Franz Josef Heliservices, tel: 03 752 0793, **Glacier Southern Lakes Helicopters**, tel: 03 752 0755 and **Helicopter Line**, tel: 0800 807 767.

Department of Conservation Visitors Information Centre Westland National Park, State Highway 6; tel: 03 752 0796, fax: 03 752 0797.

Chateau Franz $ 8 Cron St, Franz Josef; tel: 03 752 0738. Popular backpacker hotel with dormitories, rooms and a pool table.

Franz Josef Mountain View Top 10 Holiday Park $–$$ State Highway 6; tel: 03 752 0735, fax: 03 752 0035; e-mail: bookings@mountain-view.co.nz. Just over 1 km north of the village. Great views and the usual excellent facilities.

Terrace Motel $$ Graham Pl.; tel: 03 752 0130, fax: 03 752 0190. New, well-equipped motel, close to the centre.

Blue Ice Café $$ State Highway 6. Serves excellent main meals and light snacks. Bar open until 0200.

THE HAAST PASS

This famous pass crosses the Southern Alps to connect Central Otago with Westland and at 565 metres is the lowest of the routes to bridge the main divide. The road was not completed until 1965, but the Maoris had known about the pass for centuries – they called it Tiori-patea, meaning 'the way ahead is clear'.

The most dramatic stretch of the road is through the towering **Gates of Haast Gorge**, involving a climb of 450 metres in less than 3 kilometres. It's an easy drive, and there are plenty of places to pull over and watch the river as it crashes over the boulders below. If it has been raining there's an amazing 28 metre-high waterfall just off the main road at Thunder Creek Falls.

At 732 metres, the Haast Bridge is the longest on the West Coast. Before it opened in 1964, travellers making the crossing risked life and limb. According to the explorer Charles Douglas: 'The Haast was navigated in bakers' dough troughs, sluice boxes, tin pumps and other impossible looking contrivances.'

Haast itself is little more than an information centre and a couple of petrol stations. If you're looking for somewhere to stay, you'll have to settle for the Haast Hotel. The nearest general store and post office is 4 kilometres south of the bridge at Haast Beach, a wild sweep of sand covered with driftwood and frequently assailed by stormy waters.

i **World Heritage Centre** Haast Junction, cnr State Highway 6 and road to the beach; tel: 03 750 0809. Maps, displays and information.

THE HAAST WORLD HERITAGE VISITOR CENTRE

Recently, the Haast area has achieved much greater recognition for the magnificent rainforests, coastal lagoons and wetlands (the most extensive in the country) that surround it. The area was designated the South West New Zealand Heritage area by UNESCO in 1991, and the excellent World Heritage Centre opened on the banks of the Haast river in 1993.

The centre has a series of excellent displays on early Maori settlers, the abundant local wildlife, swamp forests and the unusual sanddune forests nearby. Staff can also furnish you with information on local walks, jetboating on the Haast river, fishing, hiking and helicopter rides.

EN ROUTE

The west coast road peters out at Jackson Bay, 50 kilometres from Haast. In 1875 there were ambitious plans to transform what was an unremarkable whaling station into a port to rival Greymouth. Unfortunately no account was taken of the swampy terrain and the absence of a wharf, and the scheme foundered. Today, the main attraction of the harbour is Jackson's Head, which boasts one of the world's largest colonies of Fiordland crested penguins. Signs along the route warn drivers to: 'Please watch out for penguins crossing the road.'

WHERE NEXT?

From Haast, you can take State Highway 6 South to Wanaka, travelling through the Southern Alps, or continue on that route a little further to reach Arrowtown and the lively centre of Queenstown (see p. 343).

QUEENSTOWN

This compact alpine resort has a stunning setting at the edge of luminous Lake Wakatipu, the serrated peaks of the Southern Alps rising in the distance. There are excellent skiing facilities here and Queenstown is also a good touring base for exploring Fiordland and Central Otago. What's more, it's on the go more or less 24 hours a day. If you're not shattered after a day on the slopes, sailing the lakes, rock climbing, bungy jumping, jet-boating or river rafting, you can dance the night away in one of the town's many nightclubs. It's no surprise that in a recent Condé Nast *Leisure and Travel* magazine survey, Queenstown was a world-beater for fun, friendliness and environment.

GETTING THERE

AIR The **Airport** is at Frankton, 7 kilometres northeast of town. A Super Shuttle bus meets most flights; tel: 03 442 3639. For taxis phone either **Queenstown Taxis** (tel: 03 442 7788) or **Alpine Taxis** (tel: 03 442 6666).

BUS The Clocktower Building in Camp St acts as the main departure and pickup point for **InterCity** and **Newmans** buses. Bookings can be made here as well; tel: 03 442 4100.

GETTING AROUND

BUS The **Shopper Bus** leaves from the top of the Mall with regular services to Fernhill, Frankton, Arrowtown, the Shotover Jet and a limited service to the airport; tel: 03 442 6647. **Kiwi Discovery** operates a service to the main ski resorts in winter; tel: 03 442 7340; www.kiwidiscovery.com.

INFORMATION

There are three tourist offices at the major Queenstown crossroads. Two are there mainly to sell excursions – you'll get a more comprehensive service from the Queenstown Travel and Visitors Centre (look for the green triangle), Clocktower Centre, cnr of Shotover and Camp Sts; tel: 03 442 4100 or 0800 66 8888, fax: 03 442 8907; e-mail: qvc@xtra.co.nz.

Department of Conservation Office 37 Shotover St; tel: 03 442 7933, fax; 03 442 7932.

POST AND PHONES

The main **Post Office** (and address for poste restante mail) is on the corner of Camp St and Ballarat St. Open Mon–Fri 0830–2000, Sat 0900–2000, Sun 1000–1800.

ONE OF NEW ZEALAND'S MOST POPULAR RESORTS

Queenstown's annual influx of visitors is over half a million.

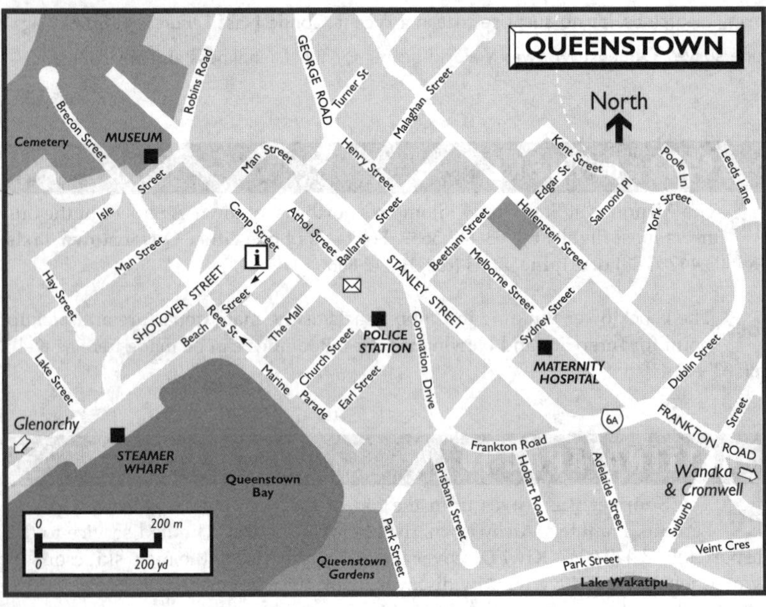

ACCOMMODATION

Queenstown has beds for about 20,000 visitors and prices range from backpacker inexpensive to serious luxury.

Alpha Lodge $$ 62 Frankton Rd; tel: 03 442 6095, fax: 03 442 8010. Good-value motel with welcoming hosts.

The Black Sheep $ 13 Frankton Rd; tel: 03 442 7289, fax: 03 442 7361; www.blacksheepbackpackers.co.nz; e-mail: theblacksheep@queenstown.co.nz. Close to downtown, internet, licensed bar, open 24 hours, free pool and more besides.

Bungi Backpackers $ cnr Sydney and Stanley Sts; tel: 03 442 8725.

Deco Backpackers $ 52 Man St; tel: 03 442 7384, fax: 03 442 6258; www.decobackpackers.co.nz. A small hostel near a reserve with beautiful lake views.

Garden Court $$$ 41 Frankton Rd; tel: 03 442 9713, fax: 03 442 6468. Delightful motel in attractive garden setting. Rooms with mountain or lake views, licensed bar, spa, video.

Hippo Lodge $ 4 Anderson Heights; tel: 03 442 5785; www.ebits.co.nz/hippolodge/main.html#top (for online bookings). Lake and mountain views.

Hotel Esplanade $–$$ 78 Park St; tel: 03 442 8611, fax: 03 442 9635. En suite rooms with spectacular lakeside views.

Lakeside Motel & Backpackers $–$$ 18 Lake Esplanade; tel: 03 442 8976, fax: 03 442 8930. Only a 3-minute walk to the centre. Well-equipped units and superb views.

Queenstown House $$$ 69 Hallenstein St; tel: 03 442 9043, fax: 03 442 8755. Bed and breakfast with clean well-equipped rooms.

Queenstown Top 10 Holiday Park Creeksyde $ 54 Robins Rd; tel: 03 442 9447, fax: 03 442 6621; www.camp.co.nz; e-mail: creeksyde@camp.co.nz. Excellent facilities and booking office for activities. Close to town.

Scallywags Guesthouse $ 27 Lomond Crescent; tel: 03 442 7083, fax: 03 442 5885. Superb views of the lake and mountains. Dormitories and rooms with use of kitchen.

Southern Laughter $ 4 Isle St; tel: 03 441 8828, fax: 03 441 8834; www.southernlaughter.co.nz. A good hostel with internet, its own spa and a games room.

Thomas' Hostel $ 50 Beach St; tel: 03 442 7180, fax: 03 441 8417; www.thomashotel.co.nz; e-mail: thecat@xtra.co.nz. A large hostel with a variety of rooms to suit various budgets.

Turner Lodge $$ 2 Turner St; tel: 03 442 9432, fax: 03 442 9409. Modern bed and breakfast with some self-catering rooms. Sun deck.

FOOD AND DRINK

There are over 100 restaurants in Queenstown and new ones open and close every day. The standard is high and this can be reflected in the prices.

Boardwalk Seafood Restaurant $$$ Steamer Wharf; tel: 03 442 5630. Probably the best restaurant in Queenstown, on the shores of Lake Wakatipu. Serves the freshest food in the Asian/Pacific style. Worth paying for a special night out.

The Cow $$ Cow Lane; tel: 03 442 8588; open daily 1200–2300. Popular pizzeria, reputed to be the best in New Zealand. The special, 'Her Majesty's Pleasure', will destroy your diet for a year. In season it's packed with noisy skiers. BYO and licensed.

Gantleys $$$ Arthurs Point Rd, Arthurs Point; tel: 03 442 8999. About 7 km from town in an elegant 19th-century inn, this restaurant has an award-winning wine list. Taxi service to and from Queenstown.

Pasta Pasta Cucina $$ 6 Brecon St; tel: 03 442 6762. One of the better Italian restaurants, offering interesting and varied pasta sauces. Takeaway and licensed.

Red Rock $$ 48 Camp St; tel: 03 442 6850. Open 0700 until late (especially in the skiing season). BBQ food.

Roaring Megs $$$ 57 Shotover St; tel: 03 442 9676; open 1830 for dinner only. Former gold miner's cottage that was transported to this site from Skippers in 1922. Candlelit dining and arguably the best New Zealand lamb on the South Island. Licensed.

Skyline Restaurant and Café $$–$$$ tel: 03 441 0101. Indoor tables, or cheaper terrace seats on Bob's Peak, with fabulous views of mountains and active people!

Check which restaurants are hip and trendy by looking in *Queenstown Today and Tonight*, a free publication available at the information centres.

Sombrero's Mexican Restaurant and Bar $–$$ Upstairs, Beech Tree Arcade, Beach St; tel: 03 442 8240. Queenstown's only authentic Mexican eatery, although the tastes have been modified to suit local palates. Has a good line of vegetarian specials.

Tatlers $$ The Mall; tel: 03 442 8372. Popular restaurant and bar with blackboard menu. Open late.

Winnie Bagoes $$ 7 The Mall; tel: 03 442 8635. Open for lunch and dinner. Very busy during the skiing season. Serves truly great pizza and there's an outside balcony. Late-night bar.

PARADISE

A major newspaper in Australia sent a photographer to cover a story in Queenstown in 1993. He never returned. When he eventually phoned in his resignation, he explained, 'It's taken me long enough to find paradise and I'm not moving.'

HIGHLIGHTS

Queenstown was first settled by a Welshman, William Rees, who farmed the edge of Lake Wakatipu undisturbed until gold was discovered in the Arrow River. Rees began honing his entrepreneurial skills, opening a general store and running a ferry across the lake. His farm buildings served as the 'town' while his woolshed became the Queen's Arms Hotel (now **Eichardt's**). It's said that during the great floods of 1879, when the water rose to within 8 centimetres of the top of the bar, customers still came in to be served and were not disappointed.

Queenstown's oldest house, on the corner of **Marine Parade and Earl St**, dates from 1864 and is now a museum to the early settlers and explorers of the area (tel: 03 442 5687).

Modern Queenstown is best enjoyed by taking a stroll through Queenstown Gardens overlooking Lake Wakatipu. A walkway, starting at **Marine Parade**, follows the tree-lined promontory past a bowling green, tennis courts and rollerskating rink.

KIWI AND BIRDLIFE PARK

Located on Brecon St, this is the place to go if you're interested in the country's endangered birds. Not only do you get to see rare birds such as kiwis, black stilts and parakeets, but your entry fee goes towards the National Breeding Programme – a vital project if these birds are to survive. For more details tel: 03 442 8059.

LOCAL PEAKS

A ski lift runs to the top of Coronet Peak and is open all year round. If you like you could even take a mountain bike up with you and cycle down. If that's not enough of a challenge, try the 600 metre-long Cresta Run – the sledge is equipped with a brake and you'll need it as you hurtle down the oversized guttering at speeds of up to 65 kph!

For something a bit less taxing, ride the gondola to Bob's Peak (446 metres) and enjoy the view. The gondola operates daily between 0900 and midnight from Brecon St.

SPORT

Some firms offer combination Adventure Trips where you try three or four activities in one day. The 'Shotover Triple Challenge', for example, involves a plane trip, a helicopter trip and a spot of white-water rafting, while 'Awesome Foursome' offers jetboating, rafting, a helicopter ride and a bungy jump. For more details contact **Totally Tourism**, tel: 03 442 7318 or 0800 500 575.

WATER SPORTS Try to imagine hurtling through a canyon on a well-greased tea tray and you'll get the general idea of Jet Boat rides on the Shotover River (see box on p. 349)! It's popular so reservations are essential. One of the best known operators is **Shotover Jet Boat Rides**, tel: 03 442 8570.

The Kawarau and Shotover Rivers are also tailor-made for whitewater rafting and (mid-Sept to mid-May) for river surfing and white water sledging (you wear a padded wetsuit for protection!) **Challenge Rafting**, Cnr Shotover and Camp Sts; tel: 0800 423 836/ 03 442 7318 offer rafting and sledging; while **Serious Fun**, tel: 03 442 5262 is for surfers.

BUNGY JUMPING Queenstown was the site of the first ever bungy jump and there are five spectacular leaps within striking distance. Prices include a certificate, T-shirt and photo (or video) to commemorate the jump.

To find out more call at the **Queenstown Bungy Centre**, Shotover St (in the centre of town); tel: 03 442 7100 or

SHOPPING IN QUEENSTOWN

The resort also has an excellent range of shops, most staying open until 2100, seven days a week.

THE SHOTOVER JET

Jet boating is a New Zealand invention. The Shotover Jet has been custom-built for use in the canyon and reaches speeds of up to 70 kph as it skims the surface of the water. The boat is powered by a gas turbine that pumps out water at high velocity through a steerable nozzle. The helmsman is able to skid the boat from one side of the canyon to the other and spin it in a 360-degree turn – an exhilarating experience for passengers.

0800 286 495. There you will be told of the delights of the 71-metre Skippers Canyon Bridge, the 43-metre Kawarau Bridge and the relatively new jump from The Ledge (35 metres) by the Skyline Gondola on Bob's Peak. For the completely fearless there's also the 102-metre plunge over the Shotover River, contact **Pipeline Bungee**, 27 Shotover St; tel: 03 442 5455.

HORSE RIDING Shotover Stables on Malaghans Rd, 7 kilometres north of town, offers treks through the historic Otago gold mining area etc. Tel: 03 442 7486.

FLYING Paragliding, hang-gliding, parasailing, parapenting (two-person manoeuvrable parachute) and skydiving are all available over Lake Wakatipu and the Remarkables.

Among the companies specialising in these feats of daring are **Skytrek Hangliding**, tel: 03 442 6311, **Queenstown Tandem Parapent**, tel: 025 324 663, or **Flight Park**, tel: 0800 467 325. **Paraflight**, tel: 03 442 8507 will winch you 80 metres into the sky to parasail over the lake. Trips leave from the main town pier between August and May. For 'The Ultimate Jump', you will be in good hands with the professional skydiving team, **Skydive Tandem,** tel: 021 325 961 or 03 442 5867.

You can fly to the Fox and Franz Josef Glaciers (see pp. 338–341) by light aircraft or by helicopter. Each has its advantages: the helicopter hovers over interesting

BUNGY SUPPORT

A J Hackett first offered bungy jumping from the Kawarau Bridge in 1988 and people have been flinging themselves off ever since. If you'd feel happier with the support of a friend, tandem jumps are available. The routine is always the same. First your ankles are lashed to a length of multi-stranded rubber rope, called a bungy. Then, after shuffling to the edge of the platform, and encouraged by shouts from friends and spectators, you make the leap into the unknown, avoiding a spectacular death at the last moment as the rope hauls you up by your ankles.

parts of the glaciers for a closer look; while the aircraft shuts down its engines on landing so that you can enjoy the silence. Be aware that adverse weather conditions can lead to cancellation of flights to the glaciers for days at a time in the winter, so check you're flying before you set off. Contact: **Air Fiordland**, tel: 03 442 3404 or 0800 103 404, **Southern Lake Helicopters**, tel: 03 442 3016 or **The Helicopter line**, tel: 03 442 3034.

SKIING Queenstown offers every type of skiing, from beginner's slopes to heli-skiing with guides in remote areas, such as **Harris Mountain**. There are three internationally rated ski fields – Treble Cone, Cardrona and Waiorau Nordic – all within an hour's drive of Queenstown.

While The Remarkables are ideal for children and beginners, there are enough challenges to keep even an experienced skier happy. This is also one of the few commercial ski areas in New Zealand to offer cross country and Nordic skiing. To reach the ski centre you can either drive or take one of the frequent buses.

The best time to ski on Coronet Peak is July to September. This well-established field lies 15 kilometres from Queenstown up a sealed access road. There are groomed slopes and trails to suit everyone from beginner to expert, and deep powder in the back bowls. Night skiing is also available in season.

WALKING There are a number of enjoyable 1- or 2-hour walks, within easy access of Queenstown. (Leaflets and information from the Visitor Centre.) Try the flat, tree-lined **Frankton Arm Track**, which leaves from the Peninsula and follows the shores of Lake Wakatipu, returning to town along the banks of the Kawarau River; or the Sunshine Bay Track, which ends up at the popular lakeside picnic area.

For a more energetic walk, involving a climb into the mountains, take the well-signposted **Queenstown Hill**

LAKE WAKATIPU

To get to the bottom of Lake Wakatipu, visit Queenstown Underwater World, an aquarium with an underwater window where you can see brown and rainbow trout close up and feed them by dropping a coin into a slot.

HIGHEST BUNGY

Queenstown's highest jump at 134 metres is the Nevis Highwire Bungy. It's situated in the splendid scenery of Nevis Canyon, about 32 kilometres from Queenstown. Tel: 03 442 7100.

THE SHOTOVER RIVER

For two years after the discovery of gold, the Shotover was 'The Richest River in the World'. It rises in the Richardson Mountains and gathers momentum as it passes through Skippers Canyon before flowing into the Kawarau River.

DAY TRIP TO MILFORD

From Queenstown you can catch a bus or fly to Milford Sound. It's also possible to do a combination of both – cruise on the Sound included. Contact **Real Journeys**, tel: 03 442 7500 or 0800 656 501, fax: 03 442 7504; www.realjourneys.co.nz; e-mail: reservations@realjourneys.co.nz.

Track, which rises steeply through bush to the summit of the 907-metre hill to reveal a view across the entire Wakatipu basin. (Allow about 3 hours return with rests and viewing time.)

With one or two exceptions, all the ski fields in New Zealand are some distance from the resorts. Before you can even think of a chair lift, you have to get to the ski field by car or bus. The advantage is the range of facilities available – shops, restaurants, nightlife etc. The downside is that you have to get up early because the drive to the ski field will often take more than 30 minutes.

The best-known walk in the area is **12 Mile Track**, which starts at the Mount Crichton Scenic Reserve, 11 kilometres west of Queenstown (look out for the signpost and parking area on your right). This loop track takes 3–4 hours at a reasonable pace and passes Sam Summer's stone hut, which still looks much as it did when the gold miner lived here.

SHOPPING

You can buy everything you need for the slopes in Queenstown. For designer leisure wear New Zealand style, try **Wild South**, Beach St; tel: 03 441 8950, an alternative is Timberland, just around the corner in O'Connells Shopping Centre, tel: 03 442 4021. For climbers and hill walkers **The Mountaineer Shop**, on the corner of Beach and Rees Sts, sells genuine Swannies Swandris (outer gear unique to New Zealand, but a bit like the Australian Drizabone).

CLUBS AND BARS

The lively après-ski atmosphere in the bars and nightclubs throughout Queenstown (most of which have live music every night) earns it the reputation of 'party town'. For the latest information, check out the free publication, *Queenstown Today and Tonight.*

Chico's 15 The Mall; tel: 03 442 8439. 'The' late night bar at the time of writing. Live music most nights.

Lone Star Café and Bar 14 Brecon St; tel: 03 442 9995. Live New Zealand bands.

McNeills's Cottage Brewery 14 Church St; tel: 03 442 9688; open 1130–late. Excellent beer, tonnes of ambience and generally a pleasant place to idle away an evening.

Red Rock 48 Camp St; tel: 03 442 6850. Popular beer bar, serving BBQ food. Happy hours 1700–1900 and 2100–2300.

EVENTS

The annual **Queenstown Winter Carnival** is a week-long festival held in mid-July with ski races, other sporting events and lots of entertainment.

In September look out for the **Remarkables Spring Ski Carnival.**

DAY TRIPS

LAKE WAKATIPU (Or Whakatipua, 'the hollow of the giant'.) According to Maori legend the lake was formed by the burning body of a slain giant. Only his heart was not reduced to ashes, and to this day its rhythmic beating causes a slight rise and fall in the lake's level every 5 to 50 minutes. The prosaic scientific explanation is that this unusual phenomenon (known as a seiche) is caused either by the wind or by variations in atmospheric pressure.

You can explore the lake (total area 293 square kilometres) by signing up for a cruise on the TSS *Earnslaw* (tel: 03 442 7500), a 75-year-old twin-decker with coal-fired boilers that carries mail, provisions etc to the less accessible sheep stations. You can watch the stokers fuelling the fireboxes and you're encouraged to explore the ship's bridge, engine room etc.

Colour Section

(i) Dunedin (pp. 371–381): the railway station; Puzzling World, Wanaka (p. 358)

(ii) Lunch break at Mahara Island, Lake Manapouri (p. 365); a walker in the rainforest, Milford Track (p. 368)

(iii) Queenstown (pp. 343–353): jetboating; dining downtown

(iv) Close to Franz Josef Glacier (p. 340)

Valentines
PUZZLING WORLD!
15

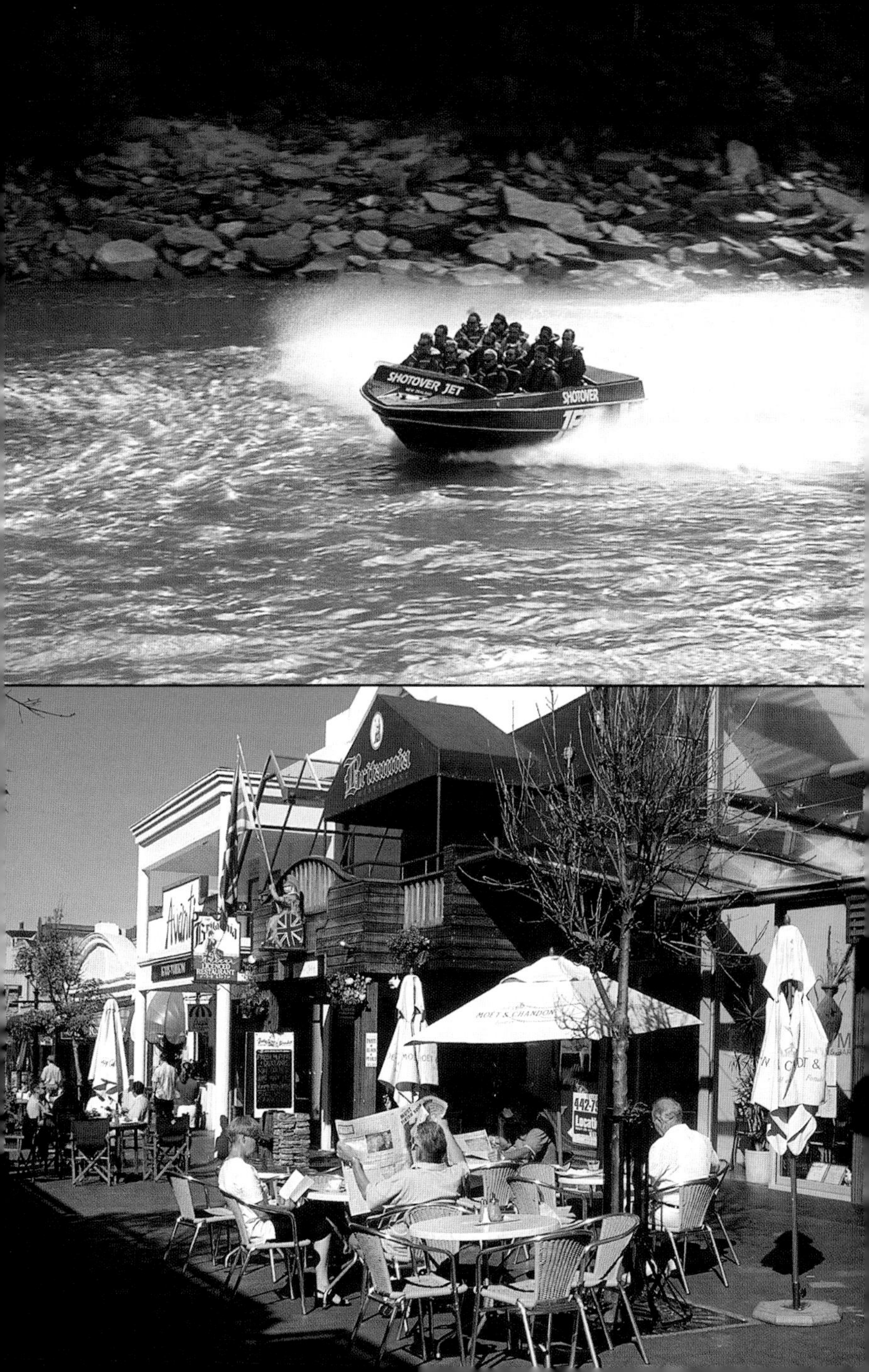
SHOTOVER JET
SHOTOVER
LICENCED RESTAURANT
MOET & CHANDON

If you want you can disembark at **Steamer Wharf Village** (a charming tourist development) or Walter Peak High Country Farm for a guided tour and a meal at the homestead restaurant with meat served from a carvery, poached salmon, freshly baked bread and other home-made specialities.

During summer cruises leave at 1000, 1200, 1400, 1600, 1800 and 2000 (the magical moonlit sailing). Note that for a couple of weeks at the end of May and beginning of June the *Earnslaw* undergoes its annual overhaul and is replaced by a fiordlander launch.

THE KINGSTON FLYER A must for steam buffs and romantics, the ride on board the Kingston Flyer is a short, but enjoyable journey into the past. The line runs for 14 kilometres from Fairlight to Lake Wakatipu on what remains of the Lumsden to Kingston line. The track was originally laid down in 1863 so that train passengers could connect with the lake steamers. The Kingston Flyer operated locally and was capable of speeds of up to 80 kph – a big deal at that point in the 19th century.

DON'T MISS THE KINGSTON FLYER!

The Kingston Flyer is a lovingly restored early 20th-century steam train that runs during the summer season.

Nowadays, Pacific Class AB locomotives haul refurbished carriages dating from 1898 and painted in the old green livery. The pièce de resistance is the restaurant and gallery car where tea and coffee are sold in chunky railway cups along with souvenirs.

The Kingston Flyer, tel: 03 248 8848, leaves Kingston daily 1015 and 1545. The return trip takes 45 minutes and the service usually runs from October through to April, other months by demand.

GLENORCHY The Dart and Rees Rivers both drain into Lake Wakatipu at Glenorchy, 40 minutes from Queenstown, making this an ideal base for anglers. Fishing gear is available for hire to guided or approved fishermen, and the season is open ended. Local experts are also available for hunting trips (deer, goats and duck shooting in season). If this doesn't turn you on you could try horse trekking, canoeing or windsurfing – conditions are so good on the lake that world records have been set here. Last but not least, it's also a great base for walking, as such major tramps as the Routeburn, Rees-Dart and Caples can be started here.

CENTRAL OTAGO

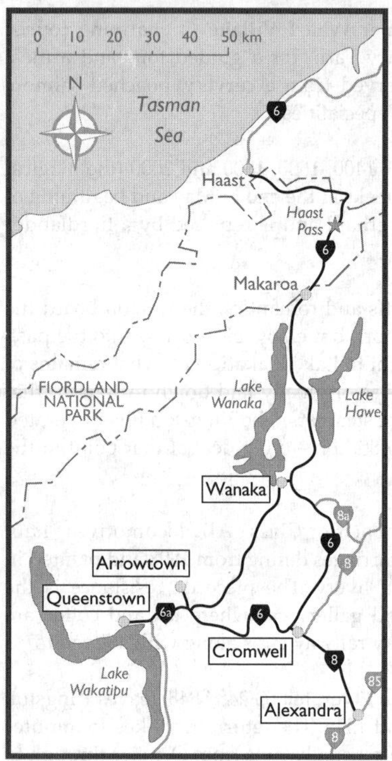

Note

Intercity Coach Lines will call at Arrowtown if booked in advance.

Queenstown – Alexandra
OTT table 9813

Transport	Frequency	Journey Time
Bus	3 daily	1hr 30mins

Queenstown – Cromwell
OTT tables 9813/9814

Transport	Frequency	Journey Time
Bus	5 daily	1hr

Cromwell – Alexandra
OTT table 9813

Transport	Frequency	Journey Time
Bus	3 daily	35mins

Queenstown – Haast
OTT table 9814

Transport	Frequency	Journey Time
Bus	2 daily	5hrs

Cromwell – Wanaka
OTT table 9814

Transport	Frequency	Journey Time
Bus	2 daily	45mins

Wanaka – Haast
OTT table 9814

Transport	Frequency	Journey Time
Bus	2 daily	3hrs 15mins

Central Otago is two contrasting experiences – Queenstown and the rest. While Queenstown appeals mainly to tourists craving a bit of nightlife, other towns such as Arrowtown, Wanaka and Cromwell are much quieter but offer a similar range of adventure activities. Scenically there's everything from mountain peaks and rolling hills to lakes and rivers. Traditionally, this is gold country and the area is riddled with old workings and mine settlements – there's even a ghost town.

You may find that New Zealanders have ambivalent feelings about Queenstown and the surrounding area. This is merely because the area has been criticised by folklore. The area certainly has its charms: you can go skiing, sail on several different lakes, ride on a steam train, eat at some of New Zealand's top restaurants, go fishing or dance the night away. In fact, it's got pretty much everything you could need on a holiday except for a beach.

Route Detail

Leave Queenstown on State Highway 6A to Frankton, turning left onto State Highway 6, which runs through the Kawerau Valley with the Remarkables rising to the south. Beyond Gibbston the Kawerau River continues to Cromwell where you pick up State Highway 8, which follows the banks of Lake Dunstan through the bleak Cromwell Gorge to the Clyde Dam, and from here to Alexandra. 135 km

Return to State Highway 6 and continue through the valley created by the Pisa Range and the Dunstan Mountain. Here the road turns west to join State Highway 8A on the way to Wanaka, a pretty resort at the end of the lake of the same name.

From here it's possible to continue on State Highway 6 to the west coast via the Haast Pass, and Lakes Hawea and Wanaka. Alternatively, to make a round trip, follow the signs to Cardrona (Crown Range Road), past the ski slopes to Lake Hayes. Here take the short detour to Arrowtown before heading to State Highway 6 and Queenstown.

CROMWELL

Cromwell is 63 kilometres east of Queenstown and 57 kilometres south of Wanaka. When the Clyde Dam was built in 1989, part of Cromwell disappeared beneath Lake Dunstan. There is no doubt that the dam completely changed the character of the River Clutha and there was some local opposition at the time: originally, for example, there were going to be five power stations, but now it seems unlikely that there will be any further development. The upside for the town, though, was a growth in tourism. However, the lake now offers a splendid range of water sports from fishing to water-skiing and jet boating. If you want to spend time on the lake you can get more information from the visitor centre or contact: **Boating Unlimited**, tel: 03 445 0327, or **Trout Fishing Services**, tel: 03 445 1745.

The history of Cromwell from the time of the gold rush to the construction of the dam can be seen at the **Information Centre and Museum** on pedestrianised Melrose Terrace, in the centre of town. Several historic buildings were salvaged before the waters rose and rebuilt to form Old Cromwell Town on the lake shore next to the **Victoria Arms Hotel** (tel: 03 445 0607).

CROMWELL'S FIRST MAYOR

Cromwell's first mayor was the supremely egotistical Captain Jackson Barry. He arrived in Cromwell in 1863, after having been variously a drover in New South Wales, a trader in Malaysia, a whaler in the Pacific, a miner in California and a coach driver in Victoria, Australia. Barry opened the Victoria and Sydney Butchery and earned himself considerable popularity by offering cut-price meat. The grateful citizens duly elected him mayor, but some lived to regret it, including the councillor who once had the temerity to oppose him. After striking him, Barry said in his own defence, 'I still think I took the proper course, if a forceful one, of putting my councillors straight.'

EN ROUTE

The wine industry only put down roots in Central Otago in the 1980s but it's already winning awards. Try the Chardonnay, Pinot Noir or Pinot Gris produced in the Kawarau Valley. Chard Farm Winery (tel: 03 442 6110; www.chardfarm.co.nz), near the bungy bridge off State Highway 6, is open 1100–1700 daily. Gibbston Valley Winery (tel: 03 442 6910; www.gvwines.co.nz), 14 kilometres east of Arrowtown, on State Highway 6, has the largest underground wine cellar in New Zealand (open for 30-minute tours between 1000 and 1600). It's also known for its superb restaurant. Open for lunch only, booking essential, tel: 03 442 6910.

EN ROUTE

The Kawerau Gorge Mining Centre, 8 kilometres west of the town on State Highway 6, lies in a 25-hectare reserve once known as Gees Flat, which has been mined on and off for nearly a century. You learn about how gold was recovered using a stamper battery and water races and see the rusting remains of the gold mining operations of the 1860s. You can even pan for gold yourself – most visitors find traces of the metal. Open daily 0900–1730, with mining demonstrations at 1200 and 1500.

i **Cromwell and District Information Centre and Museum** 47 The Mall; tel: 03 445 0212, fax: 03 445 1319; e-mail: cromwellvin@xtra.co.nz.

Anderson Park $$ Gair Ave; tel: 03 445 0321 or 0800 220 550, fax: 03 445 1523. Good-value modern motel in pleasant grounds and with children's playground.
Cromwell Top 10 Holiday Park $ 1 Alpha St; tel: 03 445 0164 or 0800 107 275, fax: 03 445 0431; www.cromwellholidaypark.co.nz; e-mail: info@cromwellholidaypark.co.nz. Motels, cabins, tent sites and campervan sites. Internet access.
Gateway Lakeside Motel $$ Alpha St; tel: 03 445 0385, fax: 03 445 1855. Spacious units on the shores of Lake Dunstan.
Golden Gate Lodge $$$ Barry Ave; tel: 03 445 1777 or 0800 104 451, fax: 03 445 1776; e-mail: stay@goldengate.co.nz. Comfortable motel in the heart of the former gold mining area.

Victoria Arms $$ Melmore Terrace; tel: 03 445 0607. Lashings of atmosphere in this restaurant located in a reconstructed building of Old Cromwell.

ALEXANDRA

An attractive town at the junction of the Manuherikia and Clutha Rivers, Alexandra is at its best in the spring and autumn when the trees are ablaze with colour. For views of the town, cross the Shaky Bridge, erected in 1879, to the Tucker Hill lookout point.

Every Good Friday, Alexandra plays host to the traditional Easter Bunny Shoot. The sad history of these over-fecund creatures and the annual hunt instigated to control them is told at the **Alexandra Museum and Art Gallery** on the corner of Walton and Thomson Street, open Mon–Sat 1100–1700, Sun 1300–1600.

Horse trekking or four-wheel drive safaris through goldmining country, or canoeing through the Roxborough Gorge are some of the activities offered by **Central Outdoor Adventures**, tel: 03 448 6360; while there are several outlets hiring mountain bikes, for example **Henderson Cycles** Limerick St; tel: 03 448 8917.

> 'There is nothing soft about New Zealand, the country. It is very hard and sinewy, and will outlast many of those who try to alter it.'
>
> John Mulgan, *Report on Experience*, 1947

Central Otago Visitor Information Centre
22 Centennial Ave; tel: 03 448 9515, fax: 03 440 2061; e-mail: info@tco.org.nz.

Alexandra Garden Court Motel $–$$ Manuherikia Rd; tel: 03 448 8295, fax: 03 448 8200; e-mail: alex.gardencourt@xtra.co.nz. Quiet motel with extensive gardens, playground, swimming pool, BBQ and aviary.
Alexandra Holiday Park $ Manuherikia Rd; tel: 03 448 8297, fax: 03 448 8294. Cabins and tent sites near the river.
Centennial Court Motor Inn $$ 96 Centennial Ave; tel: 03 448 6482 or 0800 802 909, fax: 03 448 9012; e-mail: centennialcourt@nzsouth.co.nz. Small, but well-equipped units. Also large restaurant and bar.
Kiwi Motel $$ 115 Centennial Ave; tel: 03 448 8258, fax: 03 448 6201. Friendly motel close to the centre, offering continental and cooked breakfasts.

Briar and Thyme $$ 26 Centennial Ave; tel: 03 448 9189. Restaurant and wine bar. Superb food served up with style in an atmospheric old house. Booking advised.

WANAKA

Wanaka, 120 kilometres north of Queenstown, lies on the lake of the same name and is close to **Mount Aspiring National Park** with its superb alpine scenery. There's excellent fishing in the lake, the fourth largest in New Zealand. The town takes off in the winter when the ski slopes open on Cardrona and Treble Cone, creating a demand for nightlife that is more than satisfied. No one knows where the name Wanaka came from. It may derive from Wananga, meaning 'sacred knowledge', or from the name of a Maori chief who used to fish here. The pakeha name, Pembroke, is no longer in use.

The **New Zealand Fighter Pilots Museum** at the airport has some interesting exhibits, including historic aircraft. If money is no object, you can hitch a ride in a Tiger Moth, a Pitts Aerobatic or a Mustang dating from the 1940s. Open daily 0930–1600 (Mar–Christmas), 0930–1800 (Christmas–Feb).

EN ROUTE

Stuart Landsborough's **Puzzling World**, 2 kilometres from Wanaka (tel: 03 443 7489) is home to an eccentric three-dimensional maze, equally challenging for children and adults. The object is to visit the four corners of the maze in order (allow at least an hour). If you get completely lost, don't panic, there are emergency exits. Other diversions here include the Tilted House, Hall of Holograms and Puzzle Centre.

THE SIBERIA EXPERIENCE

This top-notch 4-hour adventure tour starts from Makarora, only a 45-minute drive north of Wanaka township. It involves a 25-minute flight to the remote Siberia Valley in Mount Aspiring National Park, a 3-hour bush walk (without a guide), and then a 30-minute jetboat trip back to Makarora. It's an unforgettable experience. Contact Southern Alps Air Ltd; tel: 03 443 8666 or 0800 345 666; www.siberiaexperience.co.nz, or check www.makarora.co.nz for other activities in the region.

Next door to the New Zealand Fighter Pilots Museum is the **Wanaka Transport Museum** with its collection of vintage cars and bikes – the dry mountain air helps prevent rust. Open daily, 0830–1700; tel: 03 443 8765.

Wanaka is famous for its **War Birds over Wanaka** air show, which comes to town every even-numbered year at Easter.

i **Wanaka Visitor Information Centre** The Lake Front, 100 Ardmore St; tel: 03 443 1233, fax: 03 433 1290; e-mail: info@lakewanaka.co.nz.

Department of Conservation Ardmore St; tel: 03 443 7660, fax: 03 443 8777.

Wanaka has a good range of accommodation, generally better value than Queenstown.

Brook Vale Manor $$ 35 Brownston St; tel: 03 443 8333 or 0800 438 333, fax: 03 443 9040; e-mail: info@brookvale.co.nz. Rooms with balconies and views, close to the centre.

Bullock Creek Lodge $ Brownston St; tel/fax: 03 443 1265; e-mail: bullockcreeklodge@clear.net.nz. Log fires, barbeques, well-equipped kitchen and mountain views.

Panorama Court $$ 29–33 Lakeside Rd; tel: 03 443 9299 or 0800 433 554, fax: 03 443 8702. Well-equipped apartments with lake and mountain views. Two minutes to shops etc.

The Purple Cow $ 94 Brownston St; tel: 0800 772 277; www.purplecow.co.nz; e-mail: stay@purplecow.co.nz. All rooms have en suite bathrooms. Internet access.

Wanaka Bakpaka $ 117 Lakeside Rd; tel: 03 443 7837; e-mail: wanakabakpaka@xtra.co.nz. Close to lake with spacious lawns and Internet access. A place to get away from it all.

Wanaka YHA $ 181 Upton St; tel/fax: 03 443 7405; e-mail: yhawnka@yha.org.nz. A small hostel set in spacious grounds. Tent sites, Internet access and bike hire available.

Muzza's Bar & Café $ Helwick St; tel: 03 443 7296. Roast lamb with local veggies is a speciality.

Relishes $$ 99 Ardmore St; tel: 03 443 9018. Popular restaurant with outside tables. Good local wine list.

Sweet Retreat $ 105 Ardmore St; tel: 03 443 7669. All-day breakfasts, giant sandwiches and home-made muffins to go with your freshly ground coffee.

Tuatara Pizzeria $ 76 Ardmore St; tel: 03 443 8186. For takeaways or restaurant service – a friendly establishment with a pool table and log fire in the winter.

ARROWTOWN

HISTORIC ARROWTOWN

From the Lakes District Centennial Museum you can pick up the leaflet *Historic Arrowtown* which will guide you around over 40 historic buildings in the township. Note, however, that many of the buildings are private houses and can only be viewed from the street.

This historic gold rush town is still pretty much as it was at the turn of the century – more than 50 of the town's buildings are listed. Particularly attractive is the **Avenue of Trees**, a row of cottages overshadowed by sycamores and oaks. The **Lakes District Centennial Museum**, in Buckingham St, is mainly devoted to gold mining. Look out for the portrait of the notorious pub landlord, Bully Hayes (see box below). Open daily 0900–1700; tel: 03 442 1824.

Originally the small town consisted of more taverns than anything else. Of these early taverns, the **Royal Oak** still exists. In 1864, the proprietor ran a raffle with a golden nugget as a prize. The winner, who in the end had to prove his claim in court, was Albert Eichardt, a German who was making a living selling ginger beer. He sold the nugget and used the proceeds to buy Eichardt's pub, in Queenstown, which exists to this day.

At the western end of town is the **Chinese settlement**. Chinese miners began arriving from the Victoria goldfields in the 1860s at the invitation of the Otago

BULLY HAYES

One early settler in Arrowtown was the American adventurer, Bully Hayes, who, in his time, was accused of murder, rape, piracy and bigamy. Burly and very strong, he kept his long hair crimped to hide the fact that one ear had been cut off for cheating at cards.

In 1860, he arrived in Arrowtown from Sydney, Australia, where he was accused of sexually assaulting a 15-year-old girl. He found work as a gold miner and started his own bar, 'The United States Hotel'. It was not long before he had seduced and bigamously married the daughter of a rival landlord, Rose Buckingham. Together they fled to Nelson, but she and her child drowned in 1864 in a boating accident. (Hayes managed to swim to safety, but the newspapers openly accused him of murdering his family.) Hayes continued to roam the Pacific, eventually dying in a brawl.

A GOLD RUSH START

Arrowtown grew up with the gold rush of the 1860s. The first find in the Arrow River was made by the Maori, Jack-Tewa, in 1862, although an American prospector, William Fox, claimed that he was the first. Though William Fox managed to keep the finds secret for some months, the news eventually leaked out and gold miners flooded to the region, creating mayhem. Problems with claim jumpers led to some gun play, and the area was not brought under control for some years.

Provincial Council. They were ostracised by the locals, possibly because, according to the newspapers, they were 'orderly and sober, upright and straightforward'. The stone and mud-brick dwellings have now been excavated and restored, along with Ah Lumb's store. The leader of the Chinese community until his death in the 1920s, Ah Lumb did a brisk trade in opium, which was legal in New Zealand until 1901.

Outside the store is Ah Wak's lavatory, also listed as an Historic Place – the only outdoor lavatory in New Zealand to be accorded this honour.

Arrowtown Holiday Park $ 11 Suffolk St; tel/fax: 03 442 1876. Central location. Cabins, tent sites and a tennis court.
Golden View Motel $$ 48 Adamson Dr.; tel/fax: 03 442 1833 or 0800 246 538; e-mail: goldview@southnet.co.nz. Motel in quiet location close to the centre. Mountain bikes for hire.
Viking Lodge Motel $$ 21 Inverness Cres.; tel/fax: 03 442 1765 or 0800 181 900. Well-equipped chalets in spacious grounds with swimming pool.

Arrowtown Organic Bakery $ Ballarat Arcade, Buckingham St; tel: 03 442 1507. Superb variety of bread, rolls and snacks.
The Stables $$ 28 Buckingham St; tel: 03 442 1818. Beautiful food served up in a stylish old stone building. Closed Mon.

MACETOWN

On a grassy plateau, 15 kilometres up the River Arrow, is Macetown, Otago's ghost town. At its height during the boom days of the gold rush, Macetown was large enough to support a couple of hotels and even a school. Now amongst the stone walls and broken, rusting batteries there's few buildings left standing, although one cottage and the bakery have had their exteriors restored.

Macetown can only be reached via the **Arrow Gorge** – on foot (6 hours return), on horseback or by four-wheel drive. The route involves many river crossings and should not be taken lightly. **Nomad Safaris** (tel: 03 442 6699) and **Outback NZ** (tel: 03 442 7386; www.outback.net.nz) both run day trips to the area.

SPORT IN CENTRAL OTAGO

There are plenty of opportunities for sport in Central Otago. Here are a few ideas.

Good Sports, Dunmore St, Wanaka; tel: 03 443 7966.

This one-stop adventure shop offers just about every activity you can think of:

Canyoning (scrambling up canyons, then abseiling down waterfalls) – available at Emerald Creek (ideal for beginners) or Twin Falls (for the experienced).

Rock climbing and abseiling courses – half- and full-day courses in the Matukituki Valley.

Sky diving, paragliding and scenic or stunt flights (acrobatic joy rides) in Tiger Moths.

Tours – mountain biking, horse-riding, lake cruises, trout fishing (licences arranged) and photographic tours.

Water sports – everything from water skiing and banana boat riding, to canoeing, windsurfing, sailing, jet boating, rafting, white water sledging and kayaking.

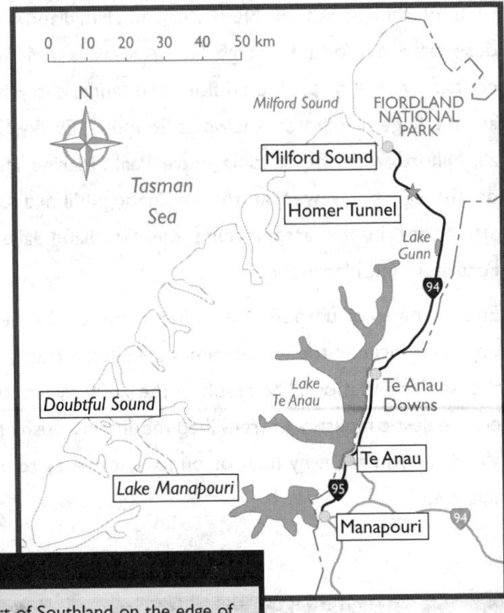

ROUTE DETAIL

Manapouri lies in the heart of Southland on the edge of the Fiordland National Park. Follow State Highway 95 northwards along the edge of Lake Manapouri to the resort of Te Anau, from where the road follows the bank of Lake Te Anau to Pleasant Bay. Beyond the sheltered harbour of Te Anau Downs (the starting point for walkers intending to tackle Milford Track), is Mirror Lakes (on your left), and further on is Lake Gunn. 75 km

You will then come to The Divide, the lowest east–west pass in the Southern Alps at 534 metres. This is where the Routeburn Track branches off through the Upper Hollyford Valley while State Highway 95 descends towards the Homer Tunnel. 85 km

The road continues to The Chasm, a spectacular falls at the Cleddau River (walkways from the road lead to the gorge). The car park at Milford is just a few minutes walk from the visitor centre.

TE ANAU – MILFORD SOUND

OTT TABLE 9811

TRANSPORT	FREQUENCY	JOURNEY TIME
Bus	2 daily	2hrs 45mins

Note: These buses start from Queenstown. There are additional services from November to April starting from Te Anau.

MANAPOURI – MILFORD SOUND

One of the glories of New Zealand, Fiordland's 1.25 million hectares has been designated a World Heritage Site. Access is strictly controlled and in some areas containing rare or protected flora and fauna, entry is by permit only. Along the coast are the finger-like fiords, known as Sounds – Dusky, Doubtful and, most magnificent of all, Milford, with the dazzling Mitre Peak. Marine life usually found at much greater depths can be viewed at the fascinating Milford Underwater Observatory. Other attractions in the area include the Fiordland lakes: Te Anau, Monowai, Hauroko, Poteriteri and Manapouri.

Endless miles of unspoilt bush offer some of the best tramping in the world. Walks on offer include the world-famous Milford Track, the Rees-Dart, the Routeburn, the Kepler and more. The result of the 7600 millimetres of rainfall per year has created a majestic tapestry of tree-lined mountains, bushy trails and piles and piles of water. Whether you see it by boat or on foot, it is easy to appreciate the stunning beauty of this area.

MANAPOURI

While the facilities at this pretty lakeside settlement amount to little more than a general store-cum-post office and café, it's a delightful spot for anyone wishing to explore the Sounds and Fiordland.

You can pick up the useful Department of Conservation leaflet *Manapouri Tracks,* describing walking trails around the lake, from **Real Journeys**, Pearl Harbour; tel: 03 249 7416 or 0800 656 501; www.realjourneys.co.nz.

Here are a couple of ideas for local water sports:

Fiordland Ecology Holidays, 5 Waiau St; tel: 03 249 6600, organises natural history cruises for three to ten days, aboard *Breaksea Girl*, a 20-metre yacht. Maximum of 12 passengers.

Adventure Charters, tel: 03 249 6626, leads sea and lake kayaking expeditions on Manapouri and Doubtful Sound - day trips and overnight adventures.

DOUBTFUL SOUND AND LAKE MANAPOURI

Doubtful Sound and Lake Manapouri go hand in hand. The 'Lake of the Sorrowing Heart' is one of the largest in New Zealand and, at 444 metres, the second deepest. It's a natural asset in two senses – aesthetically Manapouri is an area of outstanding natural beauty, while commercial considerations have led to the building of a hydro-electric power plant on the western shore. To reach the Sound you'll need to cross the lake, then transfer to a bus, which will take you over the Wilmot Pass. Boats leave Deep Cove wharf and sail past the Lady Alice Falls along the **Malaspina Reach** into the heart of the Sound itself – a hanging valley created by the action of glaciers.

Access to the Fiordland National Park is strictly controlled. Cars are confined to one or two roads on the perimeter so you're expected to get about on foot. Areas classified as 'natural environment', while unspoilt, have been provided with tramping huts, bridges and tracks to facilitate access. Other amenities are restricted to 'facilities areas' where controlled development is allowed.

Glade Motel and Motor Park $$ Murrell Ave; tel: 03 249 6623. A range of non-smoking accommodation is available in this quiet motel on the bank of the Waiau River.

Lakeview Motor Inn $$ 68 Cathedral Drive; tel: 03 249 6652, fax: 03 249 6650. Everything from backpacker rooms to fully equipped units, this motel also offers a café, restaurant and bar and stunning views of the lake.

Murrell's Grand View House $$$ 7 Murrell Ave; tel/fax: 03 249 6642. Non-smoking bed and breakfast accommodation in a 19th-century wooden inn. Excellent dinners by arrangement.

WHERE SOME OF THE NAMES COME FROM ...

The Spanish place names around Doubtful Sound recall the explorers, Malaspina, Nec, and Bauza, who were members of a mapping expedition in 1793–94. A fourth member of the party, Marcaciones, conducted experiments to test the force of gravity in the southern hemisphere and gave his name to the Point where he took his measurements.

'Doubtful Sound' was Cook's choice. When he arrived in 1770, he thought it 'a very snug harbour', but was doubtful about sailing into the Sound because of the prevailing winds.

TE ANAU

Te Anau is 167 kilometres south-west of Queenstown and on the second-largest lake – 342 square kilometres in area – in New Zealand. It claims to be the 'walking capital' of the world largely because, lying on the shores of **Lake Te Anau**, it's on the doorstep of Fiordland and is handy for the main southern walking tracks. There's a choice of accommodation as well as restaurants, shops and other amenities.

Te Anau is a mecca for ornithologists as this section of the lake is home to a colony of takahe, long thought to be extinct until they were rediscovered in 1948 by a local doctor. There are currently 160 birds and it's hoped that a full breeding colony will eventually be established – predatory stoats are the main threat to this burgeoning community nowadays.

LAKE TE ANAU EXCURSIONS

The most interesting of the lake excursions is the 2-hour trip to the Te Ana-au Caves where the glow-worm grotto can only be entered by boat.

To see a takahe head for the **Te Anau Wildlife Park** on the road to Manapouri, where the birds are bred using eggs taken from the conservation area. Each female takahe raises only a single chick, despite laying a whole clutch of eggs, so the surplus is brought to the Park for hatching. The chicks are then raised in conditions approximating as closely as possible to those in the wild. (Open daylight hours.)

If you want to explore the area on foot, the closest tracks are **Hollyford**, **Routeburn**, **Milford**, **Kepler** and **Dusky**. Note, however, that these are all serious tramps, definitely not for the faint-hearted. Each walk takes from three to seven days, with accommodation in DOC huts. You'll need to book in advance during the summer (contact the Fiordland National Park Visitor Centre, see p. 367). Most tracks are open from late October until late March.

FIORDLAND ECOTOURS OPERATORS **Tawaki Dive**, tel: 03 249 9006. Arranges scuba diving in the area. **Fiordland Wilderness Experiences and Kayaking**, 66 Quinton Drive; tel: 03 249 7700. Sea kayak exploration of Doubtful, Milford and Dusky Sounds. **Real Journeys** (tel: 03 249 7416 or 0800 656 501; www.realjourneys.co.nz) run cruises which sail into the glow-worm caves.

FLYING If you can afford it, scenic flights offer a spectacular overview of the Fiordland. An operator specialising in flights over Milford Sound is **Air Fiordland**, tel: 03 249 7505. **Waterwings Airways**, tel: 03 249 7405, use floatplanes, which add a new dimension to the experience.

Te Anau Visitor Centre cnr Town Centre and Lake Front Drive; tel: 03 249 8900. Opposite the visitor centre is an underground trout observatory where you can feed the fish.
Fiordland National Park Visitor Centre (DOC) Lakefront; tel: 03 249 7921.

Campbell Autolodge $$$ 42–44 Lakefront Drive; tel: 03 249 7546, fax: 03 249 7814. Units with full facilities and lake views. Staff will arrange tours.
Explorer Motor Lodge $$$ 6 Cleddau St; tel: 03 249 7156, fax: 03 249 7149. Motel in landscaped garden setting, two minutes from town.
Lake Front Lodge $$ 58 Lake Front Drive; tel: 03 249 7728, fax: 03 249 7124. New motel with well-equipped non-smoking units.
Te Anau Backpackers $ 48 Lakefront Dr; tel: 03 249 7713. Dorm, twin and double rooms available.
Te Anau Downs $$ tel: 0800 500 706 or 03 249 7510, fax: 03 249 7753.Bed and breakfast with en suite rooms, a restaurant and bar. Close to the Milford Track.
Te Anau Lakeview Holiday Park $ Te Anau–Manapouri Hwy; tel: 03 249 7457, fax: 03 249 7536; www.teanauholidaypark.co.nz; e-mail: reservations@destinationnz.com. Tent sites, cabins and a motel. A good base for walking the local tracks. Ten-minute walk to town.

Keplers $$ Town Centre; tel: 03 249 7909. Serves venison, lamb and seafood.
La Toscana $$ Milford Rd; tel: 03 249 7756. Friendly service and large portions in this Italian restaurant. Licensed and BYO.

PROTECTING THE NATIONAL PARK

Some areas are retained as wilderness by the simple expedient of only allowing access on foot. If you are not dedicated enough or able to walk, you will not see them. Then there are areas that are classified as 'natural environment'; the intent here is that they will remain pretty much as nature fashioned them, but with some additions by the park authorities, such as huts, bridges or tracks to make access slightly less arduous. Finally, some places are classified as 'facilities areas' where controlled development is allowed.

MILFORD TRACK

This 53-kilometre tramp from Lake Te Anau to Milford Sound over the Mackinnon Pass is justly celebrated. Apart from a steep climb (1073 metres) to the Pass itself, the ground is fairly flat; even so most walkers take three or four days, travelling light and staying overnight in huts. The first pakeha to take this route was Quintin Mackinnon, who made the crossing in 1888. Tourists began following in his wake almost immediately - the first huts appeared within 12 months. In 1908 the London magazine, *The Spectator* described Milford Track as the 'Greatest Walk in the World' a view since endorsed by thousands of contented trampers.

PREBOOK HUT ACCOMMODATION

Milford is New Zealand's best-known track, and for that reason is the only one that requires pre-booked hut accommodation. It is quite highly regulated (you can only walk in one direction, and you must complete it in the alloted time – so no breaks for bad weather). Despite these regulations it is still worth doing as it affords some spectacular views.

UPPER HOLLYFORD VALLEY

The granite hills on either side of the Hollyford Gorge are almost without vegetation. Consequently, when it rains there is nothing to soak up the water and the result is hundreds of spectacular waterfalls and cascades. In some places, the rock wall is covered by a solid sheet of water; in others, waterfalls spill out in foaming torrents. The river, by the side of the road, rushes furiously over the rocks towards Lake McKerrow.

The **Hollyford Track** is a four- or five-day tramp through the valley and along the shore of the lake. Hollyford Valley Walk, tel: 03 442 3760, organises tramps in the valley as well as jet boating and flights to points en route.

MILFORD DAY WALK

It's now possible to walk the first section of the Milford Track on a guided 9-hour walk. The walk includes transport from Te Anau and a cruise on Lake Te Anau. As the walk is restricted to 24 trampers per day, make sure you book early. Real Journeys, tel: 03 249 7416 or 0800 656 501; www. realjourneys.co.nz.

HOMER TUNNEL

Driving through the Homer Tunnel can be an unnerving experience. More than 1200 metres long and with a very steep gradient (averaging 1 in 11), it's completely unlit, making the unlined rock walls seem

The tunnel was named after Henry Homer, the geologist-engineer who originally proposed the tunnel route.

dangerously close. Once you are in, however, there's no turning back – your car headlights pick out a single track with what are optimistically called passing places along the way. Watch out for tour buses travelling in the opposite direction!

Constructed to take the road from Hollyford Valley to Cleddau Valley and on to Milford Sound, the tunnel suffered considerable delays in its construction. The route was proposed in 1889, but work did not get underway for another 50 years and it took five years to cut through the rock. After World War II intervened, the tunnel was eventually completed in 1953.

MILFORD SOUND

Known to the Maoris as Piopiotahi or 'the place of the single thrush', an indigenous bird now extinct, Milford Sound is the most visited part of the park. 'Sound' is technically a misnomer as Milford is not a sunken valley but a fiord, created by the scraping action of a glacier. The shores are steep and rocky, little vegetation. Apart from the temporary waterfalls, created by storms, there's the dramatic **Bowen Falls** which drop 160 metres from a hanging valley in the **Darren Ranges** – most cruise boats nose right into the spray – and the **Sterling Falls** (146 metres) near a rocky cliff called **The Elephant**. At the far end of the fiord is **Mitre Peak**, which rises 1694 metres above sea level and is said to resemble a bishop's mitre if you approach it from the right angle.

John Grono

Milford Sound was given its name by the sealer, John Grono, who wanted to commemorate the Welsh harbour of Milford Haven. However, most of the early settlers were Scottish, including the eccentric Donald Sutherland, who claimed not to have set eyes on a single other human being for two years. Eventually he built the John O'Groats hotel and gave his name to the falls, which, at 580 metres, were for a long time thought to be the highest in the world.

An Additional Inhabitant

Cascade Creek is home to the long-tail bat, New Zealand's only native land mammal apart from one other bat.

The Sound looks most impressive immediately following a storm, when the sky fills with rainbows. (The odds on seeing it through a downpour are in your favour, as it rains on average 200 days of the year.) Because of the heavy rainfall, there's a permanent layer of freshwater above the seawater, encouraging marine life to congregate in the upper levels of water. By visiting the **Milford Sound Underwater Observatory** (reached by cruise or water taxi from the wharf, see below) it's possible to see creatures normally beyond the reach of divers. A circular gallery 9 metres below the surface looks out onto specially created gardens where starfish, sea fans, perch, pigfish and myriads of luminous species swim among rare red and black coral.

All boats depart from the ferry wharf. The smaller boats tend to be more stable and are better in rough water – Milford Sound is uncomfortably close to the Roaring Forties. Try **Mitre Peak Cruises,** tel: 03 249 8110; www.mitrepeak.com. Cruises are also offered by **Real Journeys** (tel: 03 249 7416 or 0800 656 501; www.realjourneys.co.nz) and **Red Boat Cruises** (tel: 0800 657 444; www.redboats.co.nz). It is wise to book all cruises a few days in advance.

WILDLIFE IN THE SOUND

Up to a depth of 10 metres below the surface of Milford Sound the water is fresh. Stained with tannin and therefore light-absorbent, it encourages light-avoiding species to become established in the saltwater underneath. Already more than 50 have been discovered and marine biologists are still exploring.

Milford Sound also boasts the world's largest accessible collection of black coral – more than 7 million colonies existing at depths of as little as 5 metres (40 metres is usually the minimum). Red hydro corals are found from 15 metres down.

PADDLE MILFORD

Rosco's Milford Sound Sea Kayaks (tel: 03 249 8500; www.adventurefiordland.co.nz; e-mail: info@adventurefiordland.co.nz) are a great way to get closer to the marine life. On a paddle through the Sound there's a good chance of glimpsing dolphins, fur seals and penguins. Fiordland Wilderness Experiences (see p. 366) also offer similar kayak trips.

Dunedin is the old Gaelic name for Edinburgh, underlining the Scottish origins of the settlement – some people here still speak with a burred 'r'. Founded, like so many other towns, by the New Zealand Company (in 1848), Dunedin really took off during the gold rush – while the fields were more than 100 kilometres inland, this was the nearest port. In the space of just four years the population grew five-fold and Dunedin became one of New Zealand's wealthiest cities. The architecture in Dunedin is striking: the railway station on Anzac Avenue, which boasts an intricate collection of stained glass; the fine Art Gallery; the Otago Museum and the Hocken Library, to name a few.

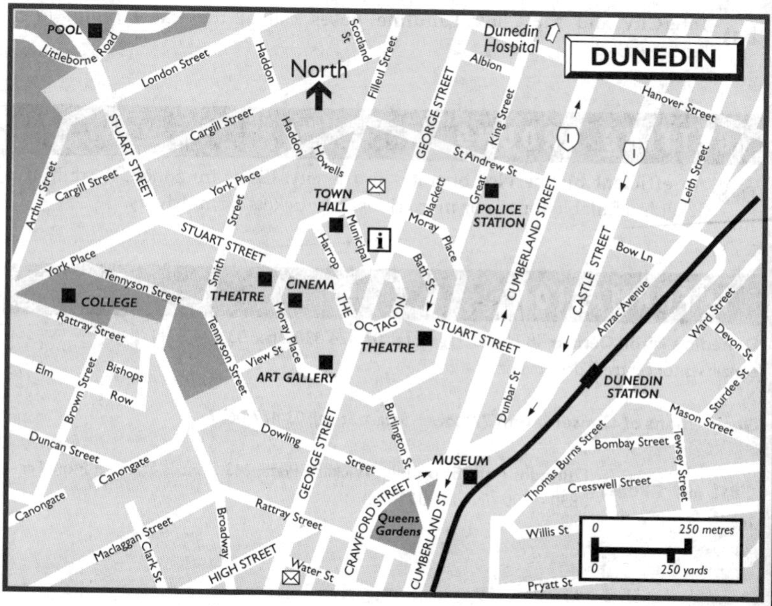

DUNEDIN

The country's first university was also founded here. (The 17,000-strong student community still makes an important contribution to the city's energy levels.) Dunedin is an arty sort of place and the floating population of poets, writers, crafts people and painters add to the colour.

Scenically, the city's characteristics are the long natural harbour, which attracted the attention of the Maoris back in the 16th century, and the bush-covered hills, which provide numerous vantage points and walks.

GETTING THERE

AIR The **Airport** lies 30 kilometres from the city (off State Highway 1). International flights arrive from Sydney and Brisbane, as well as domestic flights from all over New Zealand. Regular shuttle buses leave from the airport to the city centre.

RAIL The historic **railway station** is on Anzac Ave off Stuart St. *The Taieri Gorge Limited* is the only train running from this station now (see p. 378; OTT table 9802).

BUS **InterCity and Mt Cook Landline buses** call at the travel centre in St Andrew St.

GETTING AROUND

BUS An **efficient bus service** operates in the city. Fares are zoned. A multi-trip ticket is available for ten or more rides. Buy tickets from drivers.

INFORMATION

Dunedin Visitor Centre 48 The Octagon; tel: 03 474 3300, fax: 03 474 3311; e-mail: visitor.centre@dcc.govt.nz.

Department of Conservation 77 Lower Stuart St; tel: 03 477 0677.

POST AND PHONES **Dunedin Post Shop** John Wickliffe Plaza, 243 Princes St; open Mon–Fri 0830–1700 (from 0900 Wed).

ACCOMMODATION

Abbey Lodge $$$ 900 Cumberland St; tel: 03 477 5380, fax: 03 447 8715. Motel units and hotel rooms, close to the centre. Facilities include swimming pool, spa and sauna and award-winning restaurant and bar.

Albatross Inn $$ 770 George St; tel: 03 477 2727, fax: 03 477 2108. Central Edwardian town house with comfortable rooms, some with self-catering facilities.

Allan Court Motel $$ 590 George St; tel: 03 477 7526, fax: 03 477 4937. One- and two-bedroomed units on main street. Cooked and continental breakfasts.

Aunty's Backpackers $ 3 Union St; tel: 03 474 0708 or 0800 428 689; www.auntysbackpackers.co.nz. Located in a lovely old villa.

Beach Lodge Motel $$ 38 Victoria Rd, St Kilda; tel: 03 455 5043. Convenient for the beach but only a few minutes from the city centre. Spa pool and children's playground.

Bentleys $$ 137 St Andrew St; tel: 03 477 0572. Comfortable, centrally situated hotel with à la carte restaurant, garden café and bar.

Castlewood B&B $$ 240 York Place; tel/fax: 03 477 0526. Central hotel with spacious, comfortable rooms.

Chalet Backpackers $ 296 High St; tel: 03 479 2075.

Elm Lodge $ 74 Elm Row; tel: 03 474 1872 or 0800 356 563.

Farry's Motel $$ 575 George St; tel: 03 477 9333, fax: 03 477 9038. Well-equipped units set in pleasant landscaped gardens, close to centre.

Leviathan Hotel $$ 27 Queens Gardens; tel: 03 477 3160, fax: 03 477 2385. Close to the Octagon. Rooms with good facilities and motel units. Large licensed restaurant.

Manor House $ 28 Manor Place; tel: 03 477 0484, fax: 03 477 8145; www.manorhousebackpackers.co.nz; e-mail: mail@manorhousebackpackers.co.nz. Located in two of Dunedin's lovely historic homes. E-mail service. Nice gardens.

Next Stop Dunedin Backpackers $ 2 View St; tel: 03 477 0447.

Sahara Guesthouse and Motels $–$$ 619 George St; tel: 03 477 6662, fax: 03 479 2551. Rooms and motel units. Friendly, helpful hosts.

Shoreline Hotel $$ 47 Timaru St; tel: 03 455 5196, fax: 03 455 5193. Comfortable rooms. Large grounds, two bars and licensed restaurant.

FOOD AND DRINK

'119' Coffee Shop $ 119 Stuart St; tel: 03 477 3284. Breakfasts, snacks (including home made soups) and hot meals.

A Cow Called Berta $$$ The Terraces, 199 Stuart St; tel: 03 477 2993. Popular restaurant in beautiful Victorian terraced house, serving country-style food. Open Mon–Sat from 1800. Licensed.

Arc Internet Café and Bar $ 135 High Street; tel: 03 474 1135. Free internet access while you enjoy coffee and snacks.

Cargills 'Atrium' Restaurant $$ Cargills Hotel, 678 George St; tel: 03 477 7983. Excellent international cuisine, served up al fresco in the courtyard, often to live music. Open daily 0700–2200. Booking advised.

Etrusco $$ 8 Moray Pl; tel: 03 477 3737. Located upstairs in the Savoy Building. Excellent Italian cuisine in elegant surroundings.

High Tide Restaurant $$ 29 Kitchener St; tel: 03 477 9784. Good-value bistro-style restaurant in garden setting with harbour views. BYO and licensed.

The London Lounge $ 387 George St; tel: 03 477 8035. Restaurant above the Albert Arms Tavern. Large pub meals at very reasonable prices.

Ombrellos Courtyard Caffè and The Bar $$ 10 Clarendon St, tel: 03 477 8773. Mediterranean-style restaurant set in two cottages and the courtyard in between. Open fires in the winter. Open Tue–Sat brunch and dinner, Sun lunch only. Licensed.

Portraits $$$ Abbey Lodge, 900 Cumberland St; tel: 03 477 5380. Award-winning restaurant and bar, serving New Zealand cuisine. Reservations advised. Licensed and BYO.

Ports O'Call $$$ 118 High St; tel: 03 474 6003. Steak and seafood grills with sauces etc. from around the world. Licensed.

Potpourri Natural Foods $ 97 Stuart St; tel: 03 477 9983. Vegetarian café with extensive salad bar and freshly baked wholemeal cakes and desserts.

Sirenz Espresso & Panini Bar $ 263 George St; tel: 03 474 9200. Excellent coffee and panini with a good range of herbal teas.

HIGHLIGHTS

FLETCHER HOUSE

Fletcher House, 727 Portobello Rd, on the Otago Peninsula is a restored Edwardian Villa, built 1909, furnished in period style. Open Christmas–Easter and weekends and holidays 1100–1600.

The heart of Dunedin is the **Octagon**. Refurbished in 1989, this is the place to watch the world go by over a coffee or while browsing in the Friday craft market. The Robbie Burns statue has its 'back to the kirk and face to the pub' – the kirk in this case being St Paul's Cathedral, a splendid example of the Gothic Revival designed by English architect, Edmund Spedding, in 1919. The interior of the twin-spired building is light and spacious, an effect created by the use of creamy Oamaru stone and the 65 metre-high, vaulted ceiling. On the north side of the Octagon is the Classical municipal chambers, dating from 1880. The **Dunedin Public Art Gallery**, 30 The Octagon; tel: 03 474 3450, has one of the best picture collections in the country, especially good on works by contemporary New Zealand artists. Open Sat, Mon–Thur 1000–1800, Fri 1000–2000, Sun 1000–1700.

The **railway station** was designed in a flamboyant style reminiscent of the Flemish Renaissance by George Troup, whose architectural excesses earned him the nickname 'Gingerbread George'.

The **Otago Settlers Museum**, at 230 Cumberland St; tel: 03 477 5052, relates the social history of the Otago from the early Maori settlements, through the gold mining era to the present. The museum has expanded into the former bus station next door and the gorgeous art deco booking hall now houses a permanent transport exhibition. Open Mon–Fri 1000–1700, weekends 1300–1700.

The Otago Museum 419 Great King St; tel: 03 474 7474, has an outstanding collection of Maori and Pacific Island cultural artefacts, including beautifully carved figures; it is also home to 'Discovery World', an exciting hands-on science centre for children. Open Mon–Fri 1000–1700, Sat–Sun 1200–1700.

BEACHES

Four kilometres south of Dunedin is St Clair beach, a windswept, sandy expanse, especially well-suited to surfing and with lifeguard patrols. There's a heated outdoor saltwater pool, otherwise you have to go to the St Kilda end of the beach for more sheltered swimming – flags mark the safe zones. Brighton Beach, 20 minutes south of Dunedin, beyond the Kaikorai Estuary and Warrington Beach, to the north of the city, are popular weekend escapes for the locals.

The Jacobean-style house known as **Olveston** (at 42 Royal Terrace) was built in 1906. Its 30 rooms have been preserved as they were when the Theomins family left in 1933 and there's an unmistakable air of elegance and prosperity in the décor, which includes stained-glass windows, ornate brass fittings and ornaments and antiques collected from round the world. Don't miss the English oak staircase and gallery, assembled without the use of nails. Open daily with guided tours at 0930, 1045, 1200, 1330, 1445 and 1600. To book, tel: 03 477 3320; e-mail: olveston@xtra.co.nz.

Baldwin Street has a place in the *Guinness Book of Records* as the world's steepest street. It climbs at a gradient of 1 in 2.7 and there are 270 steps to the top. As you struggle to the top, consider that the current record for running up and down again is just two minutes.

Dunedin's Botanic Garden, on the corner of Cumberland St and Lovelock Ave, was established in 1863 and is the oldest in New Zealand. As well as a superb rhododendron collection, there's a rock garden, alpine house, aviary, and the Café Croque-o-dile, a pleasant spot to linger over coffee. Open daily sunrise to sunset; tel: 03 477 4000.

SPORT

The sheltered waters of the **Otago harbour** are tailor-made for water sports, including windsurfing, yachting, canoeing and rowing. The quinnat salmon season is between December and April. Fishing is by rod and line from the banks of the harbour or from a chartered boat. No licence is required.

Dunedin is really a city for exercise through walking – there are several excellent waymarked walks, including the Tunnel Beach Walkway.

SURFING

The Dunedin area has some excellent surf breaks. Good beaches include St Clair, Tomahawk, Aramoana, Karitane and many others in between.

SPEIGHTS BREWERY

Speights Brewery, one of New Zealand's oldest, has a working museum illustrating 100 years of brewing history. The tour culminates in the boardroom with tastings of the various ales. 200 Rattray St; tel: 03 477 9480. Tours start Mon–Sun 1000, 1145, 1400. Evening tours Mon–Thur 1900. Booking essential.

WALKS

The maps and leaflets available from the Visitors Centre will give you a good idea of what's possible. One of the easiest and most scenic routes is the Tunnel Beach Walkway, which you can easily manage in an hour. The starting point is **Blackhead Rd** (7 kilometres south of the city) from where the path leads down a stairway tunnel with direct access to the beach. (This is private property and is closed during the lambing season, in September and October.)

For panoramic views, head for **Mount Cargill** with its network of easy tracks. (There's a car park at the summit, reached via Pine Hill Road.) One recommended walk is to the rock formation known as Organ Pipes (3 kilometres, 90 minutes, return). The track passes the Cargill and Holmes peaks and crosses the Buttar saddle to the 10 million-year-old columns, formed from molten lava.

SHOPPING

The best place to look for souvenirs is the **Octagon craft market** on Fridays. Other days try the following: **Blackbird Pottery**, cnr Highcliff Rd and Sandymount Rd; tel: 03 476 1690, sells hand-painted ceramic birds, including albatrosses. **Happy Hens**, The Octagon; tel: 03 474 5151, specialises in brightly painted pottery hens. **Clifton Wool 'n' Things**, Highcliff Rd; tel: 03 454 4224, also produces woollen goods – all in natural colours. T-shirts, baseball caps etc. can be found in **NZ Shop**, The Octagon; tel: 03 477 3379.

ENTERTAINMENT

Dunedin's vibrant music and theatre scene draws heavily on the support of the student population. (Look out for lunchtime concerts and other performances at the University.) Listings appear in the *Otago Daily Times* and the free weekly magazine, *Fink*. Tourist Information also publish a free monthly, *Otago happenings*.

VENUES

The Empire 396 Princes St; tel: 07 474 9326. Venue for live bands.

Fortune 231 Stuart St; tel: 03 477 1292. Dunedin's professional theatre company performs in a converted Victorian church.

Hoyts 33 The Octagon; tel: 03 477 7019. Central six-screen multiplex which shows the latest English- language films.

The Regent The Octagon; tel: 03 477 8597. The New Zealand Royal Ballet appears here; also comedy, musicals and other popular entertainment.

Town Hall Moray Pl; tel: 03 474 3614. Concerts by the New Zealand Symphony Orchestra and Dunedin Sinfonia.

Westpac Trust Mayfair Theatre 100 King Edward St; tel: 03 455 4962. Performances by the Dunedin Opera Company.

EVENTS

Scottish Week. Every March Dunedin celebrates its Gaelic origins with bagpipes, haggis, Scottish dancing and recitals of Robbie Burns' poetry. In this sense, Dunedin retains its distinctive Scottish history: after all, it does have the country's only whisky distillery! Scottish week means anything goes as long as it's celtic – you can even arrange a haggis ceremony or buy a kilt here.

Rhododendron Festival, third week in October. Dunedin is famous for this flower, which grows particularly well in gardens here.

THE TAIERI GORGE RAILWAY

Train buffs should not miss the chance of a ride on the Taieri Gorge Railway. The track was laid in 1879 and runs for 77 kilometres over viaducts spanning ravines and through old mountain tunnels into the high country: all in all, an exhilarating journey through remote countryside inaccessible by road. There's a licensed snack bar on board and plenty of storage space for packs and bicycles. All the carriages are air conditioned. Trips depart from the Dunedin railway station, bookings are essential; tel: 03 477 4449; e-mail: reserve@taieri.co.nz. Timetable information can be found on their website at www.taieri.co.nz.

BARS AND NIGHTCLUBS

The centre of Dunedin, especially around George, Princes and Stuart Sts, is a haven of cafés, restaurants and late-night bars.

Albert Arms 387 George St. Popular student bar with restaurant upstairs. Live music and DJs. Theme nights.

Captain Cook cnr of Albany St and Gt King St. A student pub with pool tables and garden. Bar snacks available. Open till 0230 Thur–Sat.

Robbie Burns Hotel 374 George St. Live jazz on Friday night.

Statesman 91 St Andrew St. Large pub with rock bands at weekends. Open until 0300 Fri and Sat.

HARBOUR TRIPS

Taking a boat trip round the harbour is by far the best way to view the royal albatross nesting area, plus seals, penguins and the other wonders of the Otago Peninsula.

The **Westpac Trust Aquarium**, Hatchery Rd, Portobello; tel: 03 479 5819, presents the marine life of New Zealand's southern waters, with 'touch tanks', where you can feel as well as see the creatures. Open Dec–Feb, daily noon–1630; Mar–Nov Sat–Sun noon–1630.

Monarch Wildlife Cruises cnr Wharf and Fryatt Streets; tel: 03 477 4276, or 0800 666 272. Offers daily trips to Wellers Rock and beyond.

Wild Earth Adventures (tel: 025 721 931) organise sea kayak trips around the Otago Peninsula. Visit them on the Internet at www.nzwildearth.com.

A Story of Obsession

Obsession can take many forms. In the case of banker William Mudie Larnach, it was the building of the perfect house. Construction began in 1871 and it took 200 workmen 15 years to complete. The cost was estimated at £125,000, a huge sum in those days. Unfortunately, Larnach was not to live happily in his dream home. In 1898, facing financial ruin and in the knowledge that his third wife had run off with his eldest son, he dressed himself in silk topper and tail coat and blew his brains out in a committee room in Wellington's Parliament House.

Visitors to Larnach Castle can admire the lavish furnishings, including magnificent carved ceilings and panelling, and the superb views of the sea, 300 metres below the castellated tower. There's a gift shop and tearooms in the 14-hectare grounds, but if you want to eat in the formal surroundings of the castle dining room, you'll have to book well in advance, tel: 03 476 1616.

DAY TRIPS

MOERAKI North of Dunedin, on the road to Christchurch, you'll find the beach of Moeraki. The attractions are the giant spherical boulders tossed along the sand like giant marbles, said by legend to have been washed ashore from a Maori canoe. The basic geological explanation is that the boulders emerged from the mudstone cliffs behind (see p. 323).

THE OTAGO PENINSULA ROAD For a splendid drive from Dunedin, head out on the Otago Peninsula road, along the southern edge of the harbour. There are panoramic views out to the Pacific Ocean, but this is also an opportunity to see some of the world's rarest birds in their natural habitat. All along the shores of the Peninsula you'll see the common cormorant, or shag, as well as herds of southern sea seals – keep your distance, the seals become angry with tourists who take liberties.

This is just an appetiser, though, for the main dish at Taiaroa Head (at the very tip of the Peninsula – about 30 minutes' drive from the centre of town), with the world's only mainland colony of royal albatross. The visitor's centre here (open daily) has videos of these rare birds and organises guided tours to the nests, which is the only way you're guaranteed to see them (closed during the breeding season from mid-Sept to late Nov); tel: 03 478 0499. However, the **Taiaroa Head sanctuary** is also home to yellow-eyed penguins, which have their own Conservation Reserve. There's a hide for viewing and photographing these rare birds. Open Oct–Mar all day, Apr–Sept for 3–4 hours before sunset; tel: 03 478 0286.

Larnach Stables $ & Lodge $$$ Camp Rd; Otago Peninsula; tel: 03 476 1616, fax: 03 476 1574. Stay in the converted stables, or in stylish themed rooms in a re-created colonial lodge, all in the grounds of Lanarch Castle. If you decide to eat out in the stylish (but expensive) restaurant, book ahead.

Nisbet Cottage $$ 6a Elliffe Place; tel: 03 454 5169. Bed and Breakfast in quiet house. Ensuite rooms with TV and phone. Offer a guided 'Sunrise Penguin Walk' on the Peninsula.

Fish and Chips $ There are two excellent fish and chip shops in both Portobello and MacAndrew Bay. Get your order in, then go out and sit on one of the jetties and watch the sun set over Dunedin.

WHERE NEXT?

Hwy 1 links Dunedin to Balclutha (p. 384) and Oamaru (p. 321). They are also linked by bus services – see OTT table numbers 9816 and 9819.

BALCLUTHA – INVERCARGILL

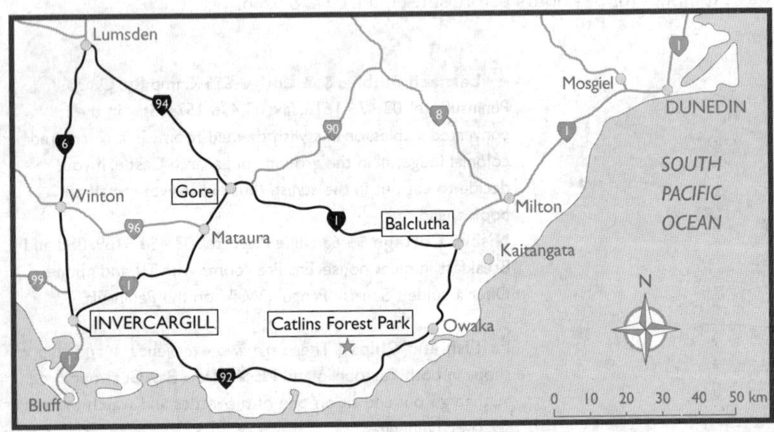

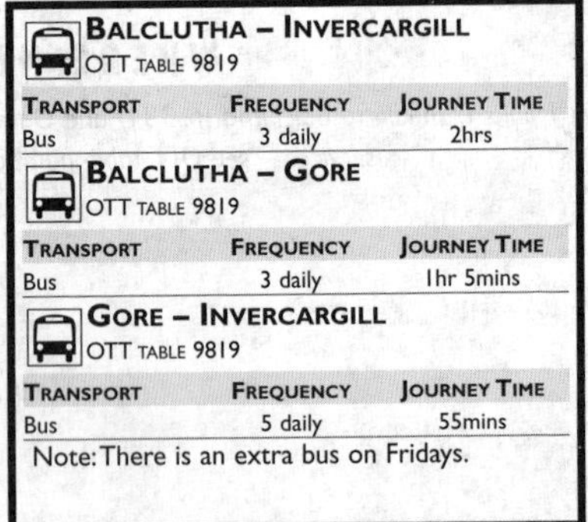

BALCLUTHA – INVERCARGILL
OTT TABLE 9819

Transport	Frequency	Journey Time
Bus	3 daily	2hrs

BALCLUTHA – GORE
OTT TABLE 9819

Transport	Frequency	Journey Time
Bus	3 daily	1hr 5mins

GORE – INVERCARGILL
OTT TABLE 9819

Transport	Frequency	Journey Time
Bus	5 daily	55mins

Note: There is an extra bus on Fridays.

BALCLUTHA – INVERCARGILL

The east coast town of Balclutha lies 85 kilometres south of Dunedin. There's a choice of two routes from here to Invercargill, the first heading westwards through farmland, the other, known helpfully as the Southern Scenic Route, following the coast.

For tourists, the main attraction of this area, known somewhat unimaginatively as Southland, is Catlins Forest Park.

The abundant wildlife supported by dense forest vegetation is an area of highly productive agricultural land, with sheep farming predominant, and a population of around 100,000 – just three people to every square kilometre. Neither is it overcrowded with tourists. Very few venture beyond Milford Sound and Queenstown, leaving the rolling green hills, dense rainforests, spectacular waterfalls and rugged coastline of the south to be enjoyed by the abundant wildlife, including many rare species. At the heart of the area is the Catlins Forest Park, with caves, a petrified forest and many good tramps.

The First Settler

There is some argument as to the identity of the first European to settle in the area. One claimant is Thomas Redpath, who is said to have settled there in 1849. In 1852 James McNeil built a hut that became the first house. He started a ferry service, which grew into a town when gold was discovered.

Route Detail

To travel inland, start on State Highway 1, following the Waiwera River from Balclutha to Clinton. Pass through Waipahi, Arthurton and Pukerau to Gore.

Balclutha – Gore 70 km

From Gore, continue on State Highway 1 to Invercargill via Mataura, or turn right onto State Highway 94 along the banks of the River Mataura through the sleepy agricultural communities of Mandeville, Riversdale and Balfour to Lumsden. Turn left here onto State Highway 6 and drive through the fertile farmland of the Oreti Valley to Invercargill.

Balclutha – Invercargill via Matura 110 km

Or, to follow the coast route, take State Highway 92 south from Balclutha to Romahapa – where there's a possible detour, turning off to the superb beach at Kaka Point – then continue through Glenomaru to Owaka on the Catlins estuary. From here the road skirts round the edge of the Catlins Forest Park on its way through Papatowai, Tokanui and Fortrose to Invercargill.

BALCLUTHA

Balclutha (population 4000) is a small town serving the local sheep-farming communities. It's a Gaelic word, meaning 'town on the Clyde' – in Maori mythology the River Clutha is personified as two people journeying to the sea from Lake Wanaka. The story goes that at Balclutha they fought and went their separate ways, only to be reconciled as they entered the sea.

The Clutha was a rich source of gold, and by the end of the 19th century more than 100 dredgers were working the river. A devastating flood in 1878 destroyed the first road bridge, taking away much of the settlement with it. The townsfolk learnt their lesson and since the building of the ferroconcrete bridge in 1935, now a local landmark, flood banks have been added to the defences.

LOVELL'S COTTAGE

There's not much to see in town, but if you head north on State Highway 1, then after 12 kilometres you will come to Lovell's Flat Sod Cottage, a typical single-room colonial house with period furnishings. Ask about opening times at the Visitor Information Centre before you set out.

Of a number of possible walks, the most suitable for day trippers is the **Blair Athol Walkway** (about 2 hours return) starting at Naish Park in Charlotte St and following the banks of the Clutha to Blair Athol farm. An alternative (also 2 hours) is the Awakiki Bush Walkway, beginning on Awakiki Rd, off State Highway 92, by Telford. This is a fine example of podocarp forest, with some 300-year-old totara trees to admire en route.

i **Clutha Information Centre** 4 Clyde St; tel: 03 418 0388, fax: 03 418 1877; e-mail clutha.vin@cluthadc.govt.nz.

Helensborough Motor Inn $$ Main North Rd (SH1); tel/fax: 03 418 1948 or freephone 0800 444 778. Friendly motel in beautiful garden setting within walking distance of the town.

Naish Park Motor Camp $ 56 Charlotte St; tel: 03 418 0088, fax: 03 418 0767. Close to town with cabins and tent sites.

Nugget View Motel $$ Rata St, Kaka Point (15 km from Balclutha); tel: 03 412 8602, fax: 03 412 8623; www.catlins.co.nz; e-mail: nugview@catlins.co.nz. Well-appointed units with superb views of the coast. Close to the wildlife sanctuary and swimming in the Clutha estuary. Boat cruises and fishing trips arranged.

Rosebank Lodge $$ 265 Clyde St; tel: 03 418 1490, fax: 03 418 1489; e-mail: reception@rosebanklodge.co.nz. New motel with luxury units, spa, sauna, bar and restaurant.

265 Restaurant $$ Rosebank Lodge, 265 Clyde St; tel: 03 418 1490. Moderately priced motel restaurant.

Hotel South Otago $ 13 Clyde St; tel: 03 418 2100. Bar serving snacks and meals.

CATLINS

Catlins Forest Park stretches from Waipapa Point to Nugget Point. The Maoris hunted the moa here until the giant bird became extinct around 500 years ago, forcing them to move on to other hunting grounds.

The name is actually a misspelling. The area was named after Edward Catlin, who, in 1840, surveyed the Clutha River. It is not known how the spelling mistake crept in.

Logging depleted the forest here, but since it was outlawed, following intense pressure from the green lobby, the forest has been regenerated with rimu, rata, matai and beech trees. The eastern edge of the park is defined by rugged coastline, a refuge for rare and endangered marine life including Hooker sea lions in **Surat Bay**, yellow-eyed penguins and elephant seals at **Nugget Point** and Hector's dolphins almost anywhere. **Cathedral Caves**, named from their 30–50 metre-high pointed roofs, are only accessible for an hour either side of low tide, but they're worth visiting to see the imprints of fossilised trees and shells (take a torch). To get there, turn off State Highway 92 some 10 kilometres beyond Papatowai and follow the track to the beach. If you're interested in fossilised remains, you could also drive to Curio Bay, where the stumps and logs of a prehistoric forest are revealed at low tide. In Porpoise Bay it is possible to swim with porpoises.

FUEL IN THE CATLINS

Note that in the Catlins the petrol stations tend to be few and far between – always fill up when you have a chance.

The **Department of Conservation Centre** at Owaka has detailed route maps of walks in the Catlins, Forest Park. Highlights include the sweeping sands at

JACKS BAY
Don't miss Jacks Bay Blowhole, which surprises passers-by as it spurts water over farmland more than 200 metres from the sea.

Tahakopa and Tautuku Bays; Tunnel Hill Historic Reserve, a section of abandoned railway track including a 200 metre-long tunnel; and the beautiful Purakaunui Falls, where the Maoris used to catch eels. The eastern edge of the park is defined by a rugged coastline and this has always been a haven for marine life, much of it rare, some of it for years endangered.

Several companies operate tours in the Catlins. **Catlins Wildlife Trackers**, Balclutha; tel: 03 415 8613 or 0800 228 5467; www.catlins-ecotours.co.nz offers award-winning ecotours, with overnights in homestays. **Dolphin Magic**, Waikawa; tel: 03 246 8444, arranges dolphin (and other marine life) watching trips.

i **Catlins Information Centre** 20 Ryley St, Owaka, South Otago; tel/fax: 03 415 8371.
Department of Conservation Field Centre 20 Ryley St; tel: 03 419 1000, fax: 03 419 1003.

GORE

Southland's second town (population 13,000), Gore claims to be the 'Brown Trout Capital of the World'. There are more than 40 streams in the area and the local fishermen will defy anyone to miss out on a catch. Gore's other claim to fame is its status as New Zealand's Country Music Capital – a sort of antipodean Nashville writ small – don't miss the Golden Guitar festival, held every June.

The town was named after Sir Thomas Gore Browne, one of the first governors of New Zealand. In 1885 settlers arrived in the Gore area to start sheep farming. At the time, the area was known as Longford, after a long ford across the Mataura River. Later the town was surveyed and subdivided and in 1885 became a borough. For all those years there was a settlement on the other side of the Mataura River called Gordon. In 1890 it joined Gore to become East Gore.

Croydon Aircraft Services, Mandeville (17 kilometres north of Gore on Highway 94) has a collection of vintage aircraft. You can take a flight in a 1930s Tiger or Gypsy Moth. Tel: 03 208 9755; www.themoth.co.nz.

Hokonui Pioneer Park on the corner of Waimea St and Highway 94 is home to a collection of restored buildings, antiquated farm machinery and vintage cars. Hokonui Moonshine Museum has opened recently on the site to tell the story of the Scottish settlers who distilled illicit whisky in the Hokonui Hills between 1880 and 1920. Open daily 1400–1600; tel: 03 208 9908.

i **Gore Visitor Information Centre** cnr Hokonui Dr. and Norfolk St; tel/fax: 03 208 9908; e-mail: goreinfo@esi.co.nz.

Croydon Lodge Motor Hotel $$ Queenstown Highway; tel: 03 208 9029 or 0800 280 280, fax: 03 208 9252; e-mail: thelodge@esi.co.nz. Recently renovated motel with golf course, children's playground, two bars and a licensed restaurant.

Old Fire-Station Backpackers $ 19 Hokonui Dr.; tel/fax: 03 208 1925; e-mail: oldfirestation@ispnz.co.nz. Central location.

Riverlea Motel $$ 46–48 Hokonui Dr; tel/fax: 03 208 3130 or 0508 202 780; e-mail: riverleamotel@xtra.co.nz. Short walk from town, ten ground-floor units. Cooked and continental breakfasts.

The Green Room Café $ 59 Irk St; tel: 03 208 1005. An Internet café and art gallery combined. Good coffee and food.

The Moth Restaurant & Bar $$ Old Mandeville Airfield, SH 94, Mandeville; tel: 03 208 9662. Offers morning or afternoon coffees, and an *à la carte* menu for lunch and dinner. Before a meal you can even go for a ride in a Tiger Moth! Open Tues–Sun 1100–late.

WHERE NEXT?

From Invercargill you can link up via State Highway 6 through Southland to Queenstown (see p. 343). Or take the left turn-off at Lumsden, and head to link up with the Manapouri – Milford Sound route (see p. 363). If you have taken this route in reverse, Dunedin is 85 km from to Balclutha via Highway 1.

INVERCARGILL

Like Dunedin, Invercargill, the southernmost city in New Zealand, was originally a Scottish settlement, although the area was known to the Maoris as Murikiku, 'the tail end of the land'.

The gateway to Fiordland in the west and to Catlins Forest Park in the east, Invercargill also lies at the heart of a rich agricultural area where sheep and dairy farming flourish. Fishing also makes an important contribution to the local economy – the famous Bluff oysters are harvested in the Foveaux Strait, which separates the mainland from Stewart Island.

While Invercargill is somewhat provincial, it's a pleasant town nonetheless with good shopping, a choice of restaurants and friendly, hospitable people with time for visitors.

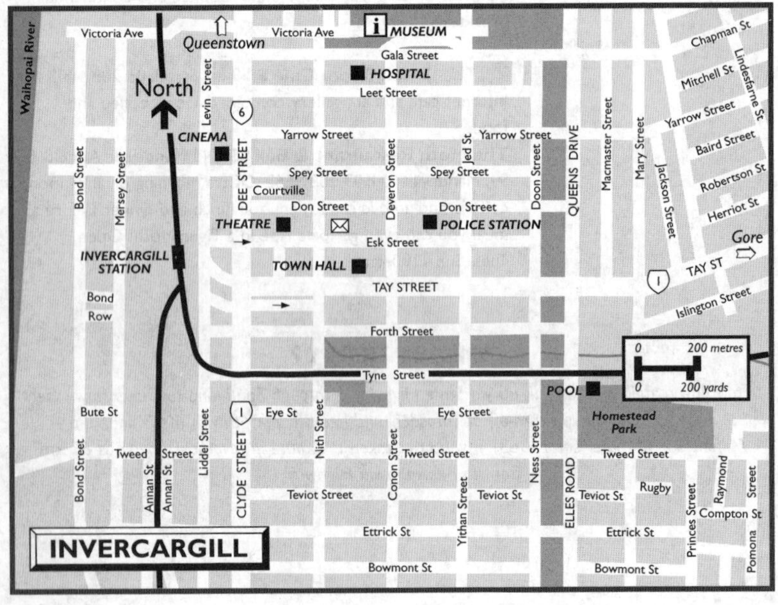

GETTING THERE

AIR Invercargill's **Airport** lies 3 kilometres from the city centre. Air New Zealand flies to Dunedin, Christchurch, Wellington and Auckland; Stewart Island Flights fly daily to Stewart Island. Spitfire shuttle buses and taxis take passengers to and from the city; tel: 03 214 1851.

BUS **InterCity Coachlines** leave the Travel Centre at the former railway station daily for Te Anau, Queenstown and Christchurch (via Dunedin).

GETTING AROUND

Local buses are operated by Invercargill Passenger Transport and run regulary Mon–Sat. Campbelltown Passenger Service runs a regular bus service between Invercargill and Bluff that connects with the catamaran service to Stewart Island.

INFORMATION

Invercargill Visitor Information Centre Southland Museum and Art Gallery, 108 Gala St; tel: 03 214 9133, fax: 03 218 4415; e-mail: tourismandtravel.invercargill@thenet.net.nz.

Department of Conservation Office PO Box 743, Don St; tel: 03 214 4589, fax: 03 214 4486.

POST AND PHONES The central Post Office is in Don St. Open Mon–Fri 0830–1700.

THE HISTORY OF THE NAME

Invercargill is, in fact, a misnomer. The Gaelic prefix Inver meaning 'mouth of' is normally applied to a river (e.g. Inverness). In this case it was added to Cargill in a mistaken attempt to honour the superintendent of Otago province – William Cargill.

ACCOMMODATION

Aachen Motel $$ 147 Yarrow St; tel/fax: 03 218 8185 or 0800 588 185; e-mail: aachen@southnet.co.nz. Spacious units in quiet surrounding, close to Queens Park. Breakfast available.

Admiral Court Motor Lodge $$ 327 Tay St; tel: 03 217 1117 or 0800 111 222, fax: 03 217 4447; e-mail: nicebeds@ xtra.co.nz. New motel on State Highway 1. Studio and family units with easy access to town centre. Breakfast included.

Birchwood Manor Motel $$ 189 Tay St; tel: 03 218 8881 or 0800 888 234, fax: 03 218 8880; www.birchwoodmanor.co.nz; e-mail: birch@birchwood.co.nz. Comfortable motel with spa bath units.

Chelmsford Court Motel $$ 88 Salford St; tel: 03 217 5807, fax: 03 217 8732; e-mail: anna.andrews@clear.net.nz. Non-smoking motel in quiet suburb.

Coachmans Inn $–$$ 705 Tay St; tel: 03 217 6046 or 0508 426 224, fax: 03 217 6045. Large motel with en suite units, cabins and camping and caravan places. Restaurant and bar.

Gerrard's Hotel $$$ 3 Leven St; tel: 03 218 3406, fax: 03 218 3003; www.gerrards.co.nz; e-mail: info@gerrards.co.nz. Small family-run hotel in an historic building. Bar and licensed restaurant.

Monarch Motel $$ 633 Tay St; tel/fax: 03 217 6114 or 0800 287 666; www.monarchmotel.co.nz; e-mail: monarchmotel@ xtra.co.nz. Comfortable units in central motel with spa and sauna.

Queens Park Motels $$ 85 Alice St; tel: 03 214 4504 or 0800 800 504, fax: 03 214 4503; www.queensparkmotels.co.nz; e-mail: queens.park.motels@xtra.co.nz. The only motel in the park.

Surrey Court Motels $$ 400 Tay St; tel/fax: 03 217 6102 or 0800 188 333; e-mail: surreycourt@xtra.co.nz. Close to the town centre and Queens Park.

Southern Comfort Backpackers $ 30 Thomson St; tel: 03 218 3838; e-mail: coupers@xtra.co.nz. Non-smoking hostel. Free bikes.

Tuatara Backpackers Lodge YHA $ 30–32 Dee St; tel: 03 214 0954, fax: 03 214 0956; www.stayyha.com; e-mail: tuataralodge@xtra.co.nz. Facilities include Internet access, two TV lounges and a kitchen.

FOOD AND DRINK

148 on Elles $$$ 148 Elles Rd; tel: 03 216 1000. Housed in a 1912 building, this smart restaurant offers such specialities as venison and freshly caught seafood. Dinner only (except Sun brunch). Licensed.

HMS King's Restaurant **$$** 80 Tay St; tel: 03 218 3443. Superb seafood. Not open for lunch on Sat or Sun. Licensed.

Louie's **$$$** 142 Dee St; tel: 03 214 2913. Very popular with locals and has excellent Pacific Rim-style food.

Rock's Café and Restaurant **$$** 101 Courtville Place; tel: 03 218 7597. Trendy, noisy and popular. Licensed.

Tillermans Café and Bar **$$** 16 Don St; tel: 03 218 9240. Open for lunch only Sun and Mon. Relaxed, quiet atmosphere and friendly service. Licensed.

Zookeepers Cafe **$$** 50 Tay St; tel: 03 218 3373. Popular café-bar offering good-value food and a lively atmosphere.

HIGHLIGHTS

Southland Museum and Art Gallery (on Gala St), with its distinctive white pyramidal roof, is home to several fascinating exhibitions including the audio-visual experience, 'Beyond the Roaring Forties', featuring the sub-antarctic islands south of New Zealand, and the 'Tuatara House'. The tuatara, a nocturnal reptile and a lineal descendant of the dinosaur, is so much smaller than its ancestors that you have to be sharp-eyed to spot it at all. The museum is the proud owner of 50 of these creatures, the oldest of which is a centenarian. There's also a section devoted to Maori culture and a picture gallery. The museum's original benefactor and 'curator' was local barber, Alexander McKenzie, who exhibited the artefacts in his shop window. His collection was acquired by Southland Museum Board in 1915. Tel: 03 218 9753; open Mon–Fri 0900–1700, Sat–Sun and holidays 1000–1700.

Queens Park

Queens Park, the huge gardens to the north of the Southland Museum, supports a small animal sanctuary, an 18-hole golf course, a children's playground and an aquatic centre with a 50-metre swimming pool as well as a stunning rhododendron display.

Just off Tramway Road is the Murihiki Urban Marae which is both the meeting point for the local Maoris and also a wonderful place to see their carvings.

Anderson Park is a Georgian-style mansion set in 24 hectares of parkland, 7 kilometres north of the city. It's now an art gallery devoted to contemporary New Zealand painting. Entrance is free, but there's a charge for special exhibitions; open Tues–Sun 1330–1700. In the grounds is a Maori house with carvings by master craftsman, Tene Waitere; tel: 03 215 7432.

A Good View of the Town

There are good views of Invercargill (Sunday afternoons only) from the 40 metre-high Water Tower on the Doon St Reserve. (Open 1330–1630.)

SURVIVORS FROM A BYGONE AGE

TUATARA

Some 220 million years ago, when dinosaurs stalked the earth, the ancestors of the tuatara also roamed the Jurassic forests. Virtually unchanged today, it looks like a lizard but belongs to another reptilian order. It is, in fact, the last of its kind. Now found only on a few offshore islands, the slow-moving tuatara once lived on the mainland, but it proved to be no match for introduced predators such as cats and rats. It tends to hunt at night, feeding mainly on such slow-moving creatures as wetas and slugs, or the eggs and chicks of the birds it sometimes shares its burrows with.

Like other reptiles, the tuatara has a very leisurely approach to life. Eggs are laid some eight months after mating and may require over a year to hatch. After hatching the tuatara grows slowly, not reaching sexual maturity much before it is 20, and attaining its full size of roughly 60 centimetres and 600 grams at around 35 years. A tuatara can live to be at least 60, although some might even reach the ripe old age of 100 or more.

Another interesting fact about the reptile is the existence of a vestigial third eye on its head. Some scientists think it might be a kind of biological clock, sensitive to light and controlling cycles of sleeping, hibernation and mating. On the topic of sex … the tuatara is the only reptile without a penis! After mounting the female, the male simply transfers sperm from his cloaca to that of his partner. Sounds about as exciting as passing the coffee, doesn't it?

WETA

With its long antennae, spiked hind legs and large jaws, it appears like a monster from a horror film. But though it can inflict a painful bite if disturbed (okay, *it* decides when it's disturbed), the weta is an otherwise harmless insect. Related to grasshoppers and locusts, it is also vegetarian. The weta is unable to fly, though a few species can jump at least as well as any grasshopper.

Various species of weta are found throughout the country in a variety of habitats, ranging from bush to caves. Perhaps the most fascinating of all weta are those belonging to a group known as the giant weta. Giant weta are almost unchanged from their ancestors, which lived over 190 million years ago. The largest species within this group is the wetapunga, up to 82 millimetres long. Now only found on Little Barrier Island, it can weigh as much as 71 grams, which is about as heavy as a thrush. The only insect that is heavier is the African goliath beetle.

The most common type of weta is the tree weta. Only slightly smaller than the giant weta, it usually lives in the forest, but it is not uncommon to find in gardens, or just about any dark, damp place – including your tramping boots!

ENTERTAINMENT

The *Southland Times* has a small listings section.

The night scene in Invercargill is fairly limited. There's a Hoyts cinema in Dee St and two small theatres. A couple of bar-clubs stay open later at weekends:

Embassy 112 Dee St; tel: 03 214 0050. Live music.

Frog 'n' Firkin $ 31 Dee St; tel: 03 214 4001. Café and bar with a casual atmosphere. Live entertainment most nights; open until late.

DAY TRIPS

BLUFF

Bluff, Invercargill's port, lies 27 kilometres south of the city. This is where you pick up the ferry to Stewart Island and, if you're here between March and August, where you can sample the succulent Bluff oysters which breed in the deep waters of the Foveaux Strait.

Bluff is the oldest European town in New Zealand (the land has been permanently settled since 1824). Although the dock has been modernised, the traditional fishing fleet remains and there's always plenty of activity on the quayside in the mornings as the boats unload their catches, to be sold from the sheds on Foreshore Rd.

BLUFF OYSTER & SOUTHLAND SEAFOOD FESTIVAL

Fine wines and mouth-watering seafoods await visitors lucky enough to be in Bluff during this festival (Apr/May). Delicacies especially worth trying are the local oysters, Fiordland lobsters and muttonbird. Highlights of the festival include the Oyster Eating Competition and the Southern Seas Ball. For more information visit www.bluff.co.nz.

Just outside the port, **Bluff Hill** (265 metres high) offers fabulous views of the harbour, and Foveaux Strait with Stewart Island in the distance (leave the town at Lee St for a 30-minute walk to the top). **Sterling Point** is the southernmost point on the South Island. A 7-kilometre walk leads from Ocean Beach to the cliff top, where tourists like to be photographed under a signpost that indicates the distances to various major cities of the world.

West of Invercargill the road passes Oreti Beach. On calm days the long sweep of white sand attracts swimmers, yachtsmen, water skiers and sunbathers, but when the wind whips up a sand storm and the waves roll in, it's the turn of the windsurfers.

RIVERTON The village of Riverton is a pleasant holiday spot that even has its own pier. Fishing is the main industry here and for souvenir shopping there's the Te Maori Arts & Craft Studio, with a good collection of traditional hand-made items including wood and bone carvings. Open daily; tel: 03 234 9965.

COLAC BAY

Just beyond Riverton, outside Invercargill, is Colac Bay – it was near here that the famous Maori canoe, Takitimu (one of the original fleet to sail from Hawaiki), ran aground at the mouth of the Waiau River.

TUATAPERE The former logging town of Tuatapere, the gateway to south Fiordland, is tramping territory. From here the road continues through Clifden, with its 100-year-old suspension bridge (now a tourist sight) to Manapouri.

i **Tuatapere Visitors Centre** 31 Orawia Rd; tel: 03 226 6399; also a craft shop and logging museum.
Riverton Information Centre Palmerston St, Riverton; tel: 03 234 9991.

Globe Backpackers & Bar $ 144 Palmerston St, Riverton; tel/fax: 03 234 8527 or 0800 248 886; e-mail: globebackpackers@xtra.co.nz. Features a huge kitchen with a twin coal range. In the middle of town.
Riverton Beach Motel $ 4 Marne St, Riverton; tel/fax: 03 234 8181. Units with sea views, 2-minute walk to the beach.
Riverton Rock Guest House $$ 136 Palmerston St, Riverton; tel: 03 234 8886, fax: 03 234 8816; e-mail: guesthouseriverton@xtra.co.nz. Old-fashioned hotel, recently restored with en-suite rooms, dormitory, kitchen and lounge. Wheelchair access.
Waiau Hotel $$ 49 Main St, Tuatapere; tel: 03 226 6409, fax: 03 226 6354; www.waiauhotel.co.nz; e-mail: info@waiauhotel.co.nz. Bed and hearty, cooked breakfast. Trips arranged to Southland sights.

TUATAPERE HUMP RIDGE TRACK

This beautiful new track starts near Tuatapere and includes coastal scenery along with expanses of native forest. It's a 53-kilometre circuit requiring three days to complete. Accommodation is in two huts along the route, which starts at the western end of Blue Cliffs Beach on Te Waewae Bay. Bookings are essential; tel: 03 226 6739, fax: 03 226 6074; www.humpridgetrack.co.nz; e-mail: info@humpridgetrack.co.nz.

A Bankrupt Province

Southland became a province in 1861 by achieving its independence from Otago Province, which had been established in 1853. The new province had based its spending levels on the flow of money from the northern goldfields. When this source of revenue dried up, Southland went bankrupt. As a result it was forced to rejoin Otago province in 1870.

Now Southland is technically a local government region, although it is known as a province by the inhabitants, and it is considered slightly vulgar to bring up the unfortunate fact of the bankruptcy.

WHERE NEXT?

Invercargill is the main gateway to Stewart Island (p. 396) and is the starting (or finishing) point of the 'Southern Scenic Route' (Balclutha–Invercargill, see p. 382). This route can also be continued beyond Invercargill to Te Anau at the edge of the Fiordland National Park (see p. 366).

STEWART ISLAND

Stewart Island is separated from the South Island by Foveaux Strait. It was first colonised by the Maoris in the 13th century, when they made a good living from fishing for blue cod, crayfish and paua and from hunting the titi (muttonbird). Wrongly identified as a peninsula by Captain Cook, the island was explored more thoroughly by William Stewart, who produced charts of the waters around Port Pegasus in 1809. Stewart Island is famous for the night-time displays of the aurora australis (southern lights) and for its sunsets – the Maoris called it the 'Land of the Glowing Skies'.

Only short stretches of the 700 kilometre-long coastline are easily accessible, although the rugged, densely forested interior offers some challenging tramps, and since March 2002 is now protected as **Rakiura National Park**. Stewart Island is also a haven for bird life and home to a local variety of the brown kiwi.

GETTING THERE

Stewart Island Ferry Service operates the *Foveaux Express* catamaran service twice daily between Bluff and Halfmoon Bay (journey time approximately 1 hour). Wheelchair facility. Tel: 03 212 7660; www.foveauxexpress.co.nz; e-mail: foveauxexpress@southnet.co.nz. Times are given in the *Thomas Cook Overseas Timetable*, table number 9782.

For about twice the price and a fraction of the time you can get there by air. **Stewart Island Flights** flies from Invercargill airport three times a day and the shuttle bus from the airfield on Stewart Island to Oban is included in the price. The planes are small, so arrive early to be sure of a place. Tel: 03 218 9129, fax: 03 214 4681; www.stewartislandflights.com; e-mail: info@stewartislandflights.com.

GETTING AROUND

On Foot You can get round most of the inhabited part of the island on foot.

Moped Mopeds can be rented from **Oban Tours and Taxis** (tel: 03 219 1456) or **Stewart Island Travel** (tel: 03 219 1269), or mountain bikes from **Innes' Backpackers** on Argyle St (tel: 03 219 1080).

Water Taxi Water Taxis are useful if you want to fish or go diving in the more inaccessible spots. Regular departures from Halfmoon Bay, Golden Bay and Thule with **Seaview Water Taxi** (tel: 03 219 1014 or 03 219 1078).

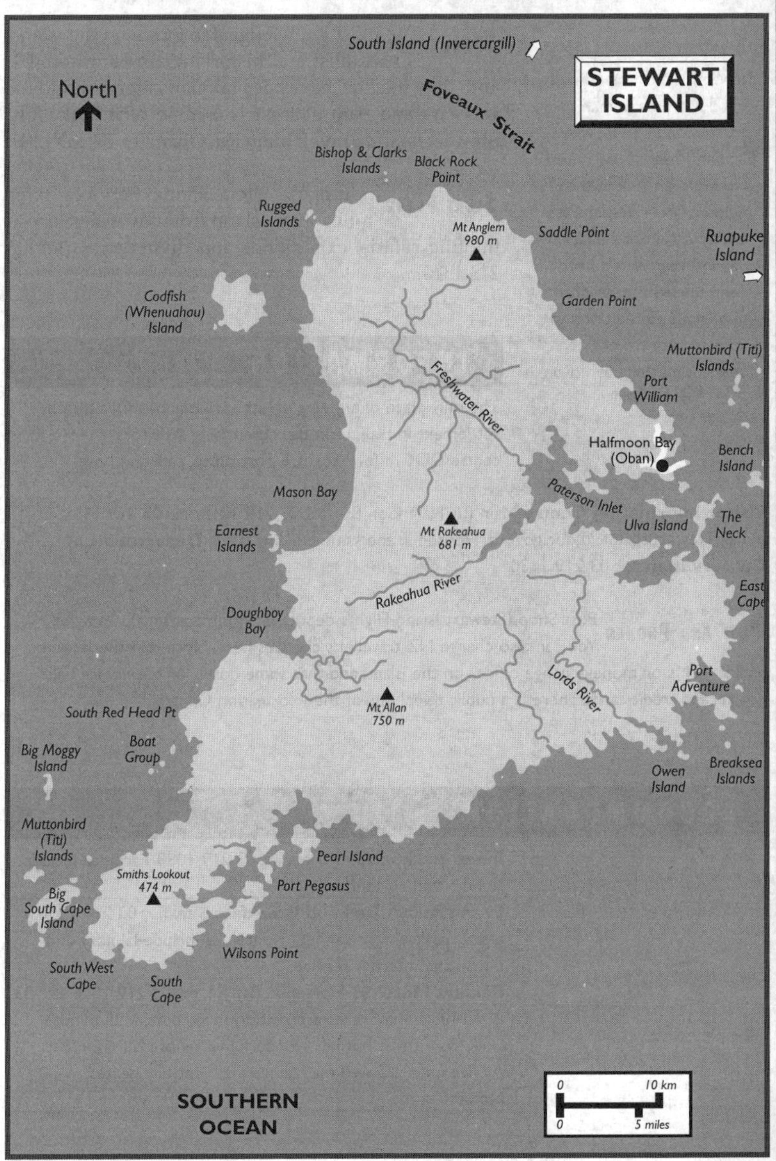
South Island (Invercargill)
STEWART ISLAND
North
Foveaux Strait
Bishop & Clarks Islands
Black Rock Point
Rugged Islands
Mt Anglem 980 m
Saddle Point
Ruapuke Island
Codfish (Whenuahau) Island
Garden Point
Muttonbird (Titi) Islands
Port William
Freshwater River
Halfmoon Bay (Oban)
Bench Island
Paterson Inlet
Mason Bay
Ulva Island
The Neck
Earnest Islands
Mt Rakeahua 681 m
Rakeahua River
East Cape
Doughboy Bay
Port Adventure
Lords River
South Red Head Pt
Mt Allan 750 m
Big Moggy Island
Boat Group
Owen Island
Breaksea Islands
Muttonbird (Titi) Islands
Pearl Island
Smiths Lookout 474 m
Port Pegasus
Big South Cape Island
Wilsons Point
South West Cape
South Cape
SOUTHERN OCEAN
0 10 km
0 5 miles

Stewart Island

Stewart Island was officially declared a British possession in 1840, when Captain Joseph Nias raised the Union Jack in the region of Port Pegasus. It's said that the proclamation was inserted into a bottle and buried but despite numerous expeditions to the site, it's never been found. Something to do on your travels?

Tours The most knowledgeable guide on the island is naturalist and historian Sam Sampson. He and 'Billy the Bus' have been taking visitors around for 16 years and Sam at least is a mine of information. **Stewart Island Travel**; Main Rd, Oban; tel: 03 219 1269.

Float Plane Southland Float Plane Services offer tours of the island from Invercargill; also hunting safaris, expeditions and diving trips (tel: 03 213 1310).

Information

The only place of any size on Stewart Island is Oban, a tiny settlement in Halfmoon Bay comprising a visitors centre/DOC, a few stores, a post office, café and hotel.

Visitor Information Centre Main Rd, Halfmoon Bay; tel: 03 219 1218, fax: 03 219 1555; e-mail: stewartislandfc@doc.govt.nz. Housed in the same building is the **Department of Conservation**, tel: 03 219 1130.

Post and Phones Post Shop (Stewart Island Flights depot), Elgin Terrace; tel: 03 219 1090. You can also change NZ traveller's cheques here. Note that there are no banks, ATMs or money-change offices on the island and that some hotels or businesses will not accept credit cards. There is a public telephone at the Information Centre.

Accommodation

Innes' Backpackers $ tel/fax: 03 219 1080. Facilities include laundry and TV lounge.

Jo and Andy's Bed and Breakfast $ tel/fax: 03 219 1230; e-mail: jariksem@clear.net.nz. Facilities include laundry and e-mail and Internet service.

Rakiura Motel $$ Horsehoe Bay Rd, tel: 03 219 1096, fax: 03 219 1408; e-mail: rakiuraretreat@yahoo.co.nz. A 25-minute walk from town, but has wonderful views of Halfmoon Bay. All five units are well maintained and centrally heated. No restaurant.

Kayaking

Experienced kayakers (the weather here is unpredictable) can explore the rivers feeding into Patterson Inlet. It's a great way to see native shore birds and you may even spot bottle-nosed dolphins further out to sea. Innes' Backpackers, tel: 03 219 1080, suggests tours and rents out kayaks and camping equipment. (There are several DOC huts in the inlet but you'll need to book in advance.)

South Sea Hotel $$ Main Rd, Elgin Terrace; tel: 03 219 1059, fax: 03 219 1120; www.stewart-island.co.nz; e-mail: southsea@stewart-island.co.nz. On the waterfront in Halfmoon Bay, this is the liveliest place on the island, priding itself on its pub atmosphere and restaurant, and specialising in sea food. Come here to meet the locals.

Stewart Island Backpackers/Shearwater Inn $–$$ Ayr St; tel: 03 219 1114, fax: 03 219 1516; e-mail: shearwaterinn@stewart-island.co.nz. Reasonably priced and centrally located, with dormitories, single and double rooms. Facilities include TV lounge, laundry, full cooking facilities and pool table.

Stewart Island Lodge $$$ 14 Nichol Rd; tel: 03 219 1085. Luxury accommodation with en suite bath and shower, tea and coffee facilities and views of Halfmoon Bay. B and B or full board terms with gourmet cooking (seafood specialities).

FOOD AND DRINK

South Sea Hotel (see above) is one of only a few public places on the island where you can get a meal, including mussels and the local speciality, muttonbird.

The muttonbird, or titi, is a member of the petrel family. Adult muttonbirds fly to Siberia for the summer, leaving their young in deep burrows until they return. The two main breeding grounds (helpfully called Muttonbird Islands) lie off the coast of Halfmoon Bay and not far from the South West Cape. Long appreciated by the Maoris as a delicacy, they're traditionally boiled and then roasted or grilled.

SHOPPING

If you're self-catering you'll find all the basics at **Ship to Shore** on Elgin Terrace; tel: 03 219 1069; open seven days. Ask here about fresh fish.

The Fernery, Golden Bay Rd (nr Observation Rock) sells local craft items, ferns-in-eggs, T-shirts, paintings and etchings, prints, cards etc. Tel: 03 219 1453.

WALKING

If you're not planning on staying long, there are plenty of undemanding strolls and walks that won't consume too much of your time. One of the loveliest is the Fuchsia Walk, leaving from Dundee St and taking just 10 minutes. During that time you'll be treated to a concert of birdsong by tui, bellbirds and the like. For panoramic views of Stewart Island, including Paterson Inslet, Horseshoe Bay, Mount Anglem and Ulva Island, head for Observation Rock (great for sunsets!). The Raroa Walk (20 minutes) is a chance to enjoy the splendours of natural rainforest without over-taxing yourself. There are wonderful views of the Foveaux Strait from Ackers Point, while a good half-day excursion is to Ringaringa Beach (Golden Bay).

For experienced walkers, there are two major tramps within the brand-new **Rakiura National Park**:

The Rakiura Track is a round trip of 36 kilometres and usually takes three days. It's a real adventure involving steep climbs to lookout points with superb views, encounters with abandoned Maori settlements, untamed stretches of bush and forest and plunges to desolated beaches. You'll need passes for the two huts and three official campsites along the way.

For a real test of endurance, trampers take on the **North-West Circuit**. Allow 10–12 days to complete the walk of 125 kilometres. It's the terrain that's the problem, with deep mud often obscuring the track. There are side trips to Mount Anglem (980 metres) and Masons Bay, home of the kiwis. Don't forget to bring insect repellent, waterproofs and warm clothes.

BIRDWATCHING

Twitchers come to Stewart Island to see the brown kiwi, unusual because it shows itself in daylight. However, it's a nocturnal adventure that's served up by Bravo Adventure Cruises, tel/fax: 03 219 1144; e-mail: philldismith@xtra.co.nz. Every other evening at dusk visitors are taken on a 4-hour trip from Oban. After a short boat ride there's a walk to a windswept beach to watch the kiwi feeding on crustaceans. Although kiwi are wary of humans, they're too busy eating to be overly self-conscious! You'll need warm clothing, a decent pair of walking boots and a flashlight.

Ulva Island Reserve is visible from Oban. Southern Isle Charters, tel/fax: 03 219 1133, runs regular cruises to Ulva Island and also offers a visit to a salmon farm. Otherwise, take a water taxi from Oban and pack some lunch. You get to see weka, bellbirds, oystercatchers, kaka, parakeets, tui and fantails among others and the vegetation is also remarkable.

THE KIWI

The kiwi is a ubiquitous bird. In New Zealand you are confronted by its image on countless PR posters and tourist brochures. It has lent its name to the furry kiwi fruit, the population as a whole, and the national rugby league team – to mention but a few. In short, it has become a major national symbol.

This is in no small part due to the fact that it is also a bit of a strange bird. Roughly the size of a plump chicken, it has a rounded form, big feet and a long, curved bill with nostrils at the end of it. As if this were not enough, its brownish feathers resemble hair, it has whiskers like a cat and, of course, it cannot fly. It almost goes without saying that this avian curiosity is found nowhere else but here. The name, by the way, derives from the peculiar, shrill call of the male bird.

Kiwis have been around in New Zealand for some 70 million years, thus making them the country's most primitive bird. Three species have been identified: the **brown** or **common kiwi** (*Apteryx australis*), found on both main islands and Stewart Island; the **little spotted kiwi** (*A. oweni*), restricted to the South Island's west coast; and finally the **great spotted kiwi** (*A. haasti*), which is found in the northern region of the South Island's west coast.

Because kiwis are mainly nocturnal and very shy, it is very difficult to spot them in the wild. Furthermore, they tend to dwell in dense forest, though they have managed to adapt to areas of rugged farmland. Their diet consists of grubs and other ground insects, as well as fruit they find lying on the ground. The female bird usually lays only one egg, which because of its size is also quite amazing. Not only is it big in relation to the bird, but it may weigh up to a quarter of the weight of the parent. It's usually the male that then takes care of incubation.

If you are keen on spotting a kiwi in its natural habitat, it is probably best to head for Stewart Island. Here the birds may be seen foraging on the beach, even in broad daylight! Otherwise, there are a number of nocturnal houses scattered around the country.

CONDUCT

New Zealanders are an open, friendly people with a distinct preference for informality in their relations with others. This is especially the case outside the main centres where, for instance, a local shopkeeper might take the time for a short chat, at the end of which you are likely to come away with plenty of information about the locality you are visiting. Or, if you have a breakdown and are miles from the nearest phone, the chances are that some Kiwi motorist will stop and lend you a hand. In fact, many overseas visitors come away with the impression that every second New Zealander is a trained mechanic!

Of course, relaxed attitudes and friendliness are based on reciprocity, and you will find that your dealings with Kiwis will go very well if you approach them in the same spirit. Perhaps the only really sore points that they have as a people are to do with national pride. Well aware of their nation's small size and insignificance on the world stage, they are nevertheless immensely proud of their country, of its physical beauty and of any achievements, in particular sporting achievements, that have brought the land international acclaim. Therefore, it should come as no surprise that they react quite sensitively to any overt criticism of their land. Visitors should bear this in mind and be tactful in this respect. And finally, when visiting a Maori marae (the open space in front of a meeting house), remember that this is a place of great spiritual importance and should be treated with due respect. Outside tourist attractions that especially welcome visitors, never enter a marae without first seeking permission.

CULTURE

Some New Zealanders are convinced that their country is tantamount to a cultural desert. Nothing could be further from the truth. There's a thriving theatrical scene, with companies playing to packed auditoriums. It's also worth noting that there are more bookshops per head of population in New Zealand than anywhere else in the world. New Zealand has a vibrant rock and pop scene with no fewer than 100 groups around at any one time. The standard varies of course, but at the quality end New Zealand groups can compete with any in the world.

New Zealand is less noted (Dame Kiri Te Kanawa excepted) for its classical music, although there are concert halls in the major cities offering varied programmes, including opera.

The country prides itself on its museums and art galleries. European, New Zealand and Maori art are all represented as are the various strands of their history and cultures.

ECO-TOUR OPERATORS

With 14 national parks, numerous forest parks and some of the world's most unique flora and fauna, New Zealand is a veritable paradise for those who appreciate nature in its most pristine form. However, if you really want to understand the country's natural environment, and see things most visitors miss, then it is best to enlist the help of experts. Ecology or nature tours in New Zealand cover everything from bird-watching to whale-watching. For an overview on the Internet visit www.ecotours.co.nz. Many local operators are also listed at the relevant places in this guide. Listed below is a selection of those who operate nationally.

Canterbury Trails
PO Box 12206, Christchurch; tel: 03 337 1185, fax: 03 337 5085; www.canterburytrails.co.nz; e-mail: trails@xtra.co.nz.
Guided nature tours through the North and South Islands. Maximum group size is six. Part of the tour costs go towards conservation efforts in New Zealand.

Heritage Expeditions (NZ) Ltd
PO Box 6282, Christchurch; tel: 03 338 9944, fax: 03 338 3311; phone toll-free: 0800 262 8873 (within NZ) or 1800 143 585 (within Australia); www.heritage-expeditions.com; e-mail: info@heritage-expeditions.com.
Offers natural history tours through NZ and cruises to the sub-antarctic islands and Antarctica. Winner of various tourism awards and a licensed DOC operator.

Nature Quest New Zealand Ltd
PO Box 6314, Dunedin; tel/fax: 03 489 8444; www.naturequest.co.nz; e-mail: nature@naturequest.co.nz.
Specialises in guided birding trips for individuals and couples. Will also help organise self-drive itineraries.

New Zealand Nature Safaris
PO Box 93, Lyttleton 8033; tel: 025 360 268, fax: 03 328 8173; phone toll-free: 0800 697 232 (in NZ) or 1800 141 242 (in Australia); www.nzsafaris.co.nz; e-mail: info@hikingnewzealand.com.
Offers small group ten-day hiking safaris and four-day hikes. Maximum group size is 12.

New Zealand Electricity

50Hz
AC
230–240V

ELECTRICITY

The supply nationally is AC, 230–240V. The usual 110–120V AC shaver sockets are fitted in hotel and motel bathrooms. Other sockets are of the three-pronged, angled variety also used in Australia. Adapter plugs are required for American and UK appliances.

Adapters can be bought from the electronic chain Dick Smith's (cheaper than buying them at the airport). Note that these days almost every notebook computer handles dual voltage, so you won't need a transformer.

ENTRY AND CUSTOMS

Check with your travel agent or with the embassy or consulate in your home country as to precise requirements. All travellers will need a valid passport extending for at least three months beyond the duration of stay. UK visitors do not require a visa, but are issued with a permit for six months on arrival. Nationals from the USA, Canada and most European countries do not require a visa for a stay of three months or less.

There are restrictions on the quantities of tobacco and alcohol each individual is allowed to bring in. Check before you travel (www.customs.govt.nz), but currently these are as shown in the box below.

RESTRICTIONS ON TOBACCO AND ALCOHOL COMING INTO NEW ZEALAND

(minimum age is 17 to qualify)

200 cigarettes or 50 cigars or 250 g tobacco;

one bottle of spirits not exceeding 1.125 litres;

4.5 litres wine or beer, for example six 750 ml bottles.

The importing of all narcotics as well as fruit, vegetables, plants, seeds, meat and pornographic material is strictly forbidden. Any violation will result in a heavy fine.

HEALTH

Hospital dispensaries operate outside the normal opening hours of chemists/ pharmacies. If you intend to bring in large quantities of medication, you should carry the prescription as proof that it's for your own use.

Never drink water from lakes and streams without boiling it well first or treating it wih iodine drops or tablets. The waterborne parasite, giardia, is a major problem and giardia-rated filters are available.

As the protective ozone layer is thinner here than in other parts of the world, you need to take even greater precautions against sunburn – not only on the beach, but on the ski slopes and mountain tops (cloud cover is no protection in itself). Always wear a hat and use liberal quantities of sunscreen, especially on areas not usually exposed, including your feet and on delicate parts e.g. nose and ears. Maximum burn times during summer are published in the weather section of the newspaper – take note that they can be as little as ten minutes!

Sandflies can drive you to distraction if you are unprepared! Unlike the mosquitoes that appear at dusk, these tiny black insects operate in daylight and deliver an even more irritating bite. They thrive in coastal areas and inland on bushes, grass and trees. Bites (which can become infected) are usually on the ankles and feet, so shoes and thick socks are a sensible precaution.

Insect repellents with a 28 per cent minimum concentration of DEET are the most effective – however, DEET 'melts' plastics e.g. glass frames, rubber and synthetic materials, so thorough washing is needed after use. Other repellents are Off! and Repel – both come in spray and stick form, but are not as destructive as DEET.

HIGH COMMISSIONS

• Always keep a photocopy of your passport and your return tickets in a place separate from the originals. When you are in a panic because you've lost them this will help you out!

• If your passport has been stolen please go to the local police and report the loss/theft. Consular staff will be able to help you quicker if this is done before you contact them. For US citizens a personal appearance is required in Auckland prior to the replacement of a passport.

• Consular services are generally unable to offer you financial help on the spot. However, they are able to contact family and friends abroad on your behalf so that you can obtain the help you need.

• After-hours consular services are available at the following: UK, Australian and Canadian High Commissions; and the US Embassy – just phone and listen to details of how to contact the duty officer.

AUSTRALIA	Australian High Commission – Consular Services at either: 72–78 Hobson St, Wellington; tel: 04 473 6411, fax: 04 498 7135; or 186–194 Quay St, Auckland; tel: 09 921 8800, fax: 09 921 8820; www.australia.org.nz.
CANADA	Canadian High Commission, 61 Molesworth St, PO Box 12049, Wellington; tel: 04 473 9577, fax: 04 471 2082; or toll-free from Auckland; tel: 09 309 8516; www.dfait-maeci.gc.ca/newzealand; e-mail: wlgtn@dfait-maeci.gc.ca.
REPUBLIC OF IRELAND	Consulate Section, Level 6, 18 Shortland St, Auckland; tel: 09 977 2252, fax: 09 977 2256; www.irlgov.ie/iveagh; e-mail: consul@ireland.co.nz.

SOUTH AFRICA	Within New Zealand, contact: Honorary Consul, 22 The Anchorage, Whitby, Wellington; tel: 04 234 8006, fax: 04 234 8075; e-mail: gregoryf@hrc.co.nz.
	South African High Commission, State Circle, Yarralumla, Canberra, Australia; tel: 61 2 6273 2424, fax: 61 2 6273 4994; www.rsa.emb.gov.au; e-mail: consular@rsa.emb.gov.au.
UNITED KINGDOM	British High Commission, 44 Hill St, PO Box 1812, Wellington; tel: 04 924 2888, fax: 04 473 4982; www.britain.org.nz. After-hours duty officer (emergencies only) tel: 029 924 2888.
USA	Consular Services, 3rd Floor, Citibank Centre, 23 Custom St East, Auckland; tel: 09 303 2724, fax: 09 366 0870; www.usembassy.org.nz. After-hours duty officer (emergencies only) tel: 04 472 6000.

HOTEL CHAINS, HOSTELS, HOLIDAY PARKS

Most hotel groups produce their own brochures and can be booked from the UK through a travel agent. Almost all have e-mail or websites (see below). Many of the smaller groups are marketed within New Zealand by Reservation Service providers like Accommodata, e-mail: reservations@accommodata.co.nz or website: www.accommodata.co.nz

MANZ (Motel Association of New Zealand) has nearly 1000 members (mainly independently owner-operated motels) all of whom have signed a 12-point code of ethics. For further information, tel: 04 499 6415, fax: 04 499 6416; www.manz.co.nz or www.nzmotels.co.nz; e-mail: motel@manz.co.nz. Many of their members also belong to other marketing groups such as Best Western, or Flag Choice.

Rural Holidays NZ Ltd gives visitors to New Zealand an insight into NZ's unique rural life – guests stay with New Zealanders in the comfort of their own home. For contact details see p. 408.

Hotel Passes or **'Go as you please'** voucher schemes are offered by **Best Western, Flag Choice** and **Pacifica Lodges** groups and give visitors the option of purchasing vouchers in their local currency prior to leaving for New Zealand. These vouchers are not available in New Zealand and must be prepurchased. They give visitors the flexibility to travel around on a go-as-you-please basis or can be pre-booked to secure a reservation. Any unused vouchers are refundable (less a handling charge). Each property requires a certain number of vouchers depending on the season and classification of the property – details are shown in an accompanying booklet. There are often conditions attached to these schemes as only a certain number of rooms are allocated to them. In peak seasons (Oct–Mar), however, it advisable to book in advance to avoid disappointment. Full details via either organisation in the UK.

Best Western Hotels
190 Great South Rd, Remuera, Auckland; tel: 0800 BEST WEST (0800 237 893) or 09 520 5418, fax: 09 248 7653; www.bestwestern.com.
Over 70 independently owned quality motels from the world's largest group of independently owned hotels and motels. Online booking possible.

Budget Backpacker Hostels NZ
www.backpack.co.nz.
Over 300 independent hostels representing almost all the owner operated hostels in NZ. Each hostel has a Backpackers Perception Rating based on guest surveys following stays at the hostels. Also has a BBH Club Card which offers travel discounts – it costs $40 but gives you a $20 phone card.

Budget Motel Chain
Budget House, 435 Raymond St, Sale, Victoria 3850, Australia; tel: 0800 8112 2333 (New Zealand only); www.budgetmotelchain.com.au; e-mail: reservations@budgetmotelchain.com.au.
Motels offering good, comfortable, clean accommodation at an affordable tariff.

CDL Hotels
Tel: 0800 808 228, fax: 09 309 0553; www.cdlhotels.co.nz; e-mail: central.res@cdlhms.co.nz
Thirty hotels across NZ. Freephone in NZ is 24 hours, voice activated direct to your chosen location. Chain consists of five-star Millennium hotels, mid-range Copthorne hotels and NZ's largest three-star group Quality hotels. Online booking.

Flag Choice Hotel
PO Box 3654, Auckland 1; tel: 0800 803 524; www.flagchoice.com.au; e-mail: reservations@flagchoice.com.au.
A choice of over 60 hotels, motels and appartments in NZ. Online booking possible.

Golden Chain Motels
PO Box 5341, Christchurch; tel: 0800 8046 5336 or 03 358 0821, fax: 03 358 5012; www.goldenchain.co.nz; e-mail: res@mchg.co.nz.
Motels and apartments throughout NZ in all main cities and tourist resorts. Online booking.

Holiday Accommodation Parks New Zealand
Tel: 04 298 3283, fax: 04 298 9284; www.holidayparks.co.nz; e-mail: hapnz@holidayparks.co.nz.
Holiday parks belonging to this association can be found throughout the country.

Hostelling International
YHA NZ, Reservations, PO Box 436, Christchurch; tel: 03 379 9808, fax: 03 379 4415; www.yha.org.nz; e-mail: book@yha.org.nz.
Sixty-four hostels across the country. During peak times advance booking is recommended for Auckland, Christchurch, Queenstown and Nelson.

Mainstay International Hotels
Operated by Mitchell Corporation NZ, PO Box 5341, Christchurch; tel: 0800 MAIN HOTELS (0800 624 646) or

03 358 7900, fax: 03 358 5012; www.mainstay.co.nz; e-mail: res@mchg.co.nz. Forty-four independently owned and operated hotels and apartments NZ wide, all with Qualmark ratings. Individual 0800 Nos. Online booking possible.

Manor Inns
PO Box 3051, Auckland;
tel: 0800 MANOR INNS (806 688) 24 hours or 09 302 4808, fax: 09 307 0870;
www.manorinns.co.nz;
e-mail: manorinns@xtra.co.nz.
A group of nine North Island hotels in Auckland (city and airport), Whakatane, Hamilton, Rotorua, New Plymouth, Wanganui, Wellington and Dunedin. Also has 31 affiliated properties.

Novotel Hotels & Resorts
Accor Asia Pacific, Level 46, 19–29 Martin Place, Sydney, NSW 2000, Australia; tel: 0800 444 422 (New Zealand) or 1300 656 565 (Australia) or 61 2 8584 8666 (outside Australia and NZ);
www.accorhotels.com.au/Novotel.
Six hotels, including Auckland, Wellington, Hamilton, Rotorua and Queenstown. Online booking.

Pacifica Lodges & Inns
PO Box 90916, AMSC, Auckland;
tel: 0800 800 112 (New Zealand) or 09 303 3566, fax: 09 303 3564;
www.pacificalodges.co.nz;
e-mail: pacifica@pacificalodges.co.nz.
Eighty hotels/motels across NZ. Reservations operate 0830 to 1700 Mon to Fri.

Rural Holidays NZ Ltd
PO Box 2155, Christchurch;
tel: 0800 883 355 or 03 355 6218, fax: 03 355 6271; www.ruralhols.co.nz; e-mail: enquiries@ ruralhols.co.nz. Online booking possible.
Operates the 'Homestay Collection' – a wide choice of holidays on the farm, country homes and city stays. In USA bookable through Discover Downunder tel: 1 888/836-9836 or 1 888/8DOWNUNDER;
e-mail: mail@discoverdownunder.com.

Rydges Hotels & Resorts
Level 2, 49 Market St, Sydney, NSW 2000, Australia; tel: 61 2 9261 4929 (outside Autralia and NZ) or 0800 446 187 (New Zealand) or 1 800 226 466 (Australia);
www.rydges.com.au; e-mail: info@rydges.com.
Upmarket group of hotels with properties in Auckland, Rotorua, Christchurch and Queenstown. Online bookings.

Scenic Circle Hotels
Tel: 0800 696 963 or 03 357 1919, fax: 03 357 1901; www.scenic-circle.co.nz;
e-mail: reservations@scenic-circle.co.nz.
NZ owned and operated. Fourteen quality hotels in Christchurch, Queenstown, Wanaka, Dunedin, The Glaciers, Punakaiki, Wellington, Hamilton, Napier and Auckland. Online booking.

Six Continents Hotels
Tel: 0800 801 111 (NZ only); 1300 363 300 (Australia); 0800 897 121 (UK); 800/835-7742 (USA & Canada); www.sphc.com.au.
Part of the Bass Hotels group (Holiday Inn), with six hotels in Auckland, Rotorua, Christchurch and Queenstown.
Online booking possible.

Small Luxury Hotels of the World
Tel: 0800 441 098 (New Zealand); 1800 251 958 (Australia); 0800 525 48000 (UK); 800 525 4800 (USA & Canada); www.slh.com.
Thirteen luxury lodges and luxurious retreats, including the George Hotel in Christchurch. Online booking possible.

Superior Inns of New Zealand
PO Box 32 130, Devonport, Auckland; tel/fax: 09 445 4131; www.superiorinns.co.nz; e-mail: admin@superiorinns.co.nz.
A selection of 42 of the finest bed and breakfast hosted accommodation in New Zealand. Online booking possible.

Top 10 Holiday Parks
PO Box 959, Christchurch; tel: 0800 TOP TEN (0800 867 836), fax: 03 377 9950; www.topparks.co.nz; e-mail: info@top10.co.nz.
Forty-six locations offering campsites with self-contained units – all with at least a three-star Qualmark rating, providing a good range of facilities and services.

VIP Backpackers Resorts Int. NZ
PO Box 80021 Greenbay, Auckland; tel: 09 827 6016, fax: 09 827 6013; www.vip.co.nz; e-mail: backpack@vip.co.nz.
Network of hostels with a discount card giving travel-related discounts.

LANGUAGE

The official languages are English and Maori, though in daily life Maori is rarely spoken outside the home or marae (open space in front of a meeting house). While it is unlikely that you will be required to speak Maori, it can be useful to know a few words, as many place names and geographical features have Maori names. These place names either refer to a local event, legendary or otherwise, or are of a descriptive character. For instance, Rotorua means 'second lake', Ohakune means 'a place to take care in' (nobody knows why anymore) and Otaihape (the original name of Taihape) can be translated as 'the abode of Tai the Hunchback'. See also 'Speaking New Zealand Style' (p. 53).

Common greetings and phrases:

Haere mai	welcome
Haere ra	goodbye (spoken by person staying, to person going)
E noho ra	goodbye (spoken by person going, to person staying)
Morena	good morning
Ka pai	thank you
Kia ora	hello or good luck
Tena koe	hello (to one person)
Tena korua	hello (to two people)
Tena koutou	hello (to three or more people)

Some words encountered in Maori place names:

ao	cloud
awa	river
ika	fish
kai	food

koura	crayfish
manga	stream
maunga	mountain
moana	sea or lake
motu	island
nui	big
pa	fortified settlement
papa	flat rock
puke	hill
rangi	sky
roa	long
roto	lake
wai	water
waka	canoe
whanga	bay
whenua	land or country

MAPS

Tourist Information offices, such as the Visitor Information Network – look for the green triangle logo – and the Department of Conservation (DOC), stock maps and guides.

Members of the British Automobile Association can, on presentation of their membership card, obtain road maps from the New Zealand offices.

Serious walkers will probably want the detailed maps produced by the Department of Land and Survey Information, available from their offices as well as some DOC offices and better bookshops. In fact, New Zealand is one of the best mapped countries in the world because of the tendency of the population to go tramping through the countryside. Sketch maps are available at a minimal cost, but proper topographical maps are recommended.

NATIONAL PARK VISITOR CENTRES

An excellent source of information, Park Visitor Centres are located at, or near, the main entrances of most national parks. Apart from offering all the necessary practical information about various walks and huts, they often function as small natural history museums as well, with an emphasis on the local fauna and flora. Walking maps, brochures and books concerning the park in question can be purchased here. These park books are superbly illustrated and would make a great souvenir of your visit.

More information on both national and forest parks can be had from Department of Conservation (DOC) offices. They are located in many towns and cities throughout the country and will be able to supply all the necessary details on parks and walks in their vicinity. Addresses of DOC offices and Visitor Centres are listed at the appropriate places throughout this guide. For tips about hiking, see p. 38.

OPENING TIMES

Normal business hours: 0830–1700 Monday–Friday, although some tourist agencies and airlines are open longer.

Shops: 0900–1730 on weekdays, with the exception of Thursdays or Fridays in larger towns and cities, when some stores stay open until 2030 or 2100. Some shopping centres close at lunchtime on Saturdays, but tourist shops usually stay open longer. Increasingly, stores in major centres are open on Saturday afternoons and Sundays. Petrol stations are usually open daily, except in rural areas, but may close in the early evening.

Banking hours: 0930–1630 Monday–Friday. Closed public holidays.

Museums: opening times vary according to size and locality. Many of the small, local museums are staffed by volunteers who operate a flexible roster. It is as well to check before setting out.

Towns, such as Queenstown, whose livelihood depends on tourism, have a much more flexible approach to opening times. There is some Sunday opening. There are also food outlets within 24-hour petrol stations and some convenience stores that open 0700–2200.

POSTAL SERVICES

Stamps are widely available in supermarkets, grocery stores and bookshops as well as post offices, which are now usually known as 'post shops'. Local mail is designated standard or Fast Post according to the value of the stamp. For international mail, post in the Fast Post letter slot. Post shops open 0900–1730 Mon–Fri.

PUBLIC HOLIDAYS

Businesses and banks are closed on all public holidays listed here. With the exceptions of Christmas Day and Good Friday, shops, museums and other attractions may be open.

PUBLIC HOLIDAYS

1–2 Jan New Year

6 Feb Waitangi Day

Mar/Apr Good Friday

Mar/Apr Easter Monday

25 Apr Anzac Day

1st Mon in June
Queen's Birthday

4th Mon in Oct
Labour Day

25 Dec Christmas Day

26 Dec Boxing Day

There are also regional anniversary days, which are marked by local festivities, as well as events associated with local culture, produce and recreation. These dates tend to crop up between November and March and vary from year to year.

The main school holiday begins just before Christmas and ends in the last week of January. There is a two-week break over the Easter period, a further two-week winter break in mid-July, and another two-week break at the end of September/beginning of October.

SHOPPING

If you're looking for presents and souvenirs to take home, here are some suggestions.

Maori art, normally carving on either wood or greenstone, can be highly decorative. Before buying have a look at some of the art work exhibited in museums and you'll soon be able to tell good carving from dross. Museum shops are also reliable places to buy.

Jewellery is big in New Zealand – bone-carving pendants, paua-shell necklaces etc. are typical popular purchases.

If you're buying clothing, you might as well take back something practical: as parts of New Zealand can claim the highest rainfall in the world, wet-weather gear tends to be of high quality. The most famous line is Swandri – swannies.

New Zealand became famous as a wool-exporting country in the 19th century, and sheepskin coats and rugs are still sold widely. Woollen sweaters and other knitted items are also a good bet.

Instead of the predictable T-shirt, why not treat yourself to an authentic All Black jersey? It will make you very popular with rugby fans – Australians excepted.

While wine is undoubtedly a good buy, it's awkward and expensive to transport, especially as you will probably have to pay duty to take it home. It may be worth making an exception for Cloudy Bay, a delightful white wine from the Marlborough region, rarely encountered outside New Zealand. It travels well and can be shipped ahead.

TAXES

New Zealand has its own form of purchase tax, similar to the iniquitous VAT in Europe and sales tax in part of the US. The local form of impost is called GST (Goods and Service Tax) and it is added (12.5 per cent) to pretty much everything. However, it is the practice to quote all prices inclusive of GST. Visitors can recover GST at the exit airport if the amount is sufficiently large – ask for details of the scheme at the time that you make your purchase.

TELEPHONES

Most public payphones operate by way of prepaid card, which you can buy at supermarkets, petrol stations, newsagents and other retail outlets. Coin-operated phones are rare, but there are boxes that take credit cards. You can find out the per-minute cost of your call by lifting the receiver and dialling the number without inserting money or card. The cost will show on the LCD screen.

GSM mobile phones work throughout New Zealand – the coverage is excellent in cities, and along state highways, but patchy in remote and hilly areas. Consult your service provider before you leave to see whether your phone is enabled for use in New Zealand.

USEFUL TELEPHONE NUMBERS

111 for emergencies

010 for local operator

0170 for international operator

018 national directory enquiries (50 cent fee)

0172 international directory enquiries ($1.50 fee)

0+full area code and local number for national direct-dialled calls

00+country code, area code (without the initial 0) and local number for international calls

0800 and 0508 numbers are toll-free within New Zealand

0160 instead of 00 for international calls will have the operator call you back with the cost of the call after you have finished, though there will be a small charge for this service.

TIME

New Zealand is 12 hours ahead of GMT. Daylight Saving Time is observed from the last Sunday in October through to the first Sunday of March, advancing the clocks by 1 hour.

TOILETS

Every small town has public toilets and these are kept very clean. In some places you will come across automatic Supaloos. Check out Hundertwasser's loo in Kawakawa!

TOURIST INFORMATION WEBSITES

Listed here are not just 'official' websites, but also any commercial sites that offer tourists useful information for planning their trip.

New Zealand Tourism Website
www.purenz.com

General Information
www.travelplanner.co.nz
www.zealand.org.nz
www.newzealandnz.co.nz
www.nz.com
www.kiwitourism.com
www.jasons.co.nz
www.nzcentre.co.nz

NORTH ISLAND SITES

Tourist Highways
www.centralnorthnz.co.nz
www.pacificcoast.co.nz
www.thermalnz.co.nz

Regions

Bay of Islands
www.nzinfo.com
www.bay-of-islands.co.nz

Bay of Plenty
www.nztauranga.com

Centre Stage
(Wellington, Wairarapa, Nelson, Marlborough)
www.centrestage.co.nz

Coromandel and Thames Coast
www.thepeninsula.co.nz
www.thecoromandel.com

Gisborne and Eastland
www.eastland.tourism.co.nz
www.gisbornenz.com

Great Barrier Island
www.gbi.aotea.org

Hawkes Bay
www.napieronline.co.nz
www.hawkesbaynz.com
www.hb.co.nz
www.hawkesbay.com

Horowhenua Region (Levin, Otaki)
www.horowhenua.org.nz

Kapiti Coast
www.kcdc.govt.nz
www.kapititourist.co.nz

Kauri Coast (Northland)
www.kauricoast.co.nz

Manawatu Region
www.manawatu.com

Northland
www.northland.org.nz
www.twincoast.co.nz

Rangitikei Region
www.rangitikei.co.nz

River Region
(Wanganui and Rangatikei Districts)
www.river-region.org.nz

Taranaki (New Plymouth)
www.taranakinz.com
www.stratford.org.nz
www.stdc.co.nz
www.tourismtaranaki.org.nz

Tararua Region
(Dannevirke/Woodville)
www.tararua.net

Tongariro Region
www.mtruapehu.com
www.ruapehu.tourism.co.nz
www.url.co.nz/ruapehu.html

Waiheke Island
www.waiheke.co.nz

Waikato Region
www.chemistry.co.nz/waikato.htm
www.waikatonz.co.nz

Wairarapa Region
www.destination.co.nz/wairarapa
www.wairarapa.co.nz

Towns and Cities

Auckland
www.aucklandnz.com
www.aucklandcity.govt.nz
www.gotoauckland.com

Devonport
www.tourismnorthshore.org.nz
www.devonport.co.nz

Feilding
www.webweavers.co.nz/Feilding
www.feilding.co.nz

Hahei
www.hahei.co.nz

Hamilton
www.hamiltoncity.co.nz

Hawera
www.hawera.net.nz

Kerikeri
www.kerikeri.co.nz

Napier
www.napier.govt.nz

New Plymouth
www.newplymouthnz.com

Ohakune
www.ohakune.info
www.travelink.co.nz/nz/Ohakune.html

Opotiki
www.opotiki.net

Palmerston North
www.pncc.govt.nz
www.manawatunz.co.nz

Paraparaumu and Paraparaumu Beach
www.communities.co.nz/Paraparaumu
www.kapititourist.co.nz/docs/paraparaumu.asp
www.tranzmetro.co.nz/wellington/paraparaumu/default.asp
www.jasons.co.nz/destinations/paraparaumu_beach

Rotorua
www.rotoruanz.com

Russell
www.russell.gen.nz

Taumarunui
www.middle-of-everywhere.co.nz

Taupo
www.laketauponz.com

Tauranga
www.tauranga-dc.govt.nz
www.nztauranga.com

Te Aroha
www.tearoha-info.co.nz
www.visittearoha.com

Thames
www.thames-info.co.nz

Turangi
www.laketaupo.co.nz

Waihi
www.waihi.co.nz

Waitomo (Te Kuiti)
www.waitomo-museum.co.nz
www.waitomo.govt.nz
www.tourism.waitomo.govt.nz

Wanganui
www.wanganui.co.nz
www.wanganui.com

Warkworth
www.warkworth-information.co.nz
www.warkworthnz.co.nz

Wellington
www.wellingtonnz.com
www.wellington.net.nz
www.wcc.govt.nz

Whangamata
www.whangamata.co.nz

Whangarei
www.whangareinz.org.nz
www.wdc.govt.nz
www.whangarei.co.nz
www.cityofwhangarei.co.nz

Whitianga and Mercury Bay
www.whitianga.co.nz

SOUTH ISLAND SITES

General
www.nzsouth.co.nz
www.atoz-nz.com
www.southernscenicroute.co.nz
www.southisland.org.nz

Regions

Canterbury Region
www.canterburypages.co.nz
www.canterbury.net.nz

Catlins
www.catlins.org.nz
www.catlins-nz.com

Chatham Islands
www.chathams.com

Fiordland Region (Te Anau)
www.fiordland.org.nz
www.fiordlandtravel.co.nz

Golden Bay Region
www.goldenbayindex.co.nz

Hurunui Region (Hanmer Springs, Kaikoura)
www.hurunui.com

Marlborough Region
www.marlborough.co.nz
www.destination.co.nz/marlborough
www.destinationmarlborough.com

Otago Region
www.centralotagonz.com
www.nzsouth.co.nz/goldfields
www.tco.org.nz
www.otagowine.com/winetrail

Southland Region
www.southland.org.nz

Stewart Island
www.stewartisland.co.nz
www.commercial.co.nz/~rakiura

Waimakariri District
(Rangiora, Kaiapoi, Oxford)
www.waimakariri.co.nz

Waimate Region
www.waimate.org.nz

West Coast & Glaciers
www.west-coast.co.nz
www.nz-holiday.co.nz/glacier.country

Towns and Cities

Akaroa
www.akaroa.com
www.nz-holiday.co.nz/akaroa

Alexandra
www.alexandra.co.nz

Arrowtown
www.arrowtown.org.nz
www.destination.co.nz/arrowtown

Ashburton
www.ashburton.co.nz

Bluff
www.bluff.co.nz

Christchurch
www.ccc.govt.nz
www.christchurchnz.net
www.canterburypages.co.nz/explore/chch
www.cae.canterbury.ac.nz/chchtour.htm

Cromwell
www.cromwell.org.nz

Dunedin
www.cityofdunedin.com
www.visit-dunedin.co.nz

Geraldine
www.canterburypages.co.nz/explore/geraldine
www.nz-holiday.co.nz/geraldine/index.html

Glenorchy
www.glenorchyinfocentre.co.nz
www.destination.co.nz/glenorchy

Travel Directory

Gore and Districts
www.mataura.com

Greymouth and District
www.greymouthnz.co.nz

Hanmer Springs
www.hanmer.com
www.nz-holiday.co.nz/hanmer.springs

Hokitika
www.hokitika.com

Invercargill
www.invercargill.org.nz
www.cityevents.co.nz

Kaikoura
www.kaikoura.co.nz

Methven
www.nz-holiday.co.nz/Methven

Mount Cook
www.mount-cook.com

Nelson
www.nelsonnz.com
www.nelson.co.nz
www.nelsonnz.co.nz

Oamaru
www.oamaru.org

Picton
www.picton.co.nz

Punakaiki
www.punakaiki.co.nz

Queenstown
www.queenstown-nz.co.nz
www.queenstown-vacation.com
www.queenstownadventure.com

Timaru
www.southisland.org.nz/timaru.asp
www.home.timaru.com

Wanaka
www.wanaka.co.nz

Westport
www.westport.org.nz

VISITORS CENTRES

Every town has a Visitors Centre, identified by a sign with the letter 'i' and a green triangle ('i' without the triangle denotes a commercial organisation, usually with some free information as well as tours on offer). All information centres will make bookings.

WEB ACCESS

In New Zealand many libraries offer internet facilities, as do many backpacker hostels and HI/YHA hostels. There are also numerous cybercafés scattered around the country in the larger towns and cities. Over 30 New Zealand cybercafés are listed on the website www.cybercafes.com.

CONVERSION TABLES

DISTANCES (approx. conversions)

1 kilometre (km) = 1000 metres (m) 1 metre = 100 centimetres (cm)

Metric	Imperial/US	Metric	Imperial/US	Metric	Imperial/US
1 cm	⅜ in.	10 m	33 ft (11 yd)	3 km	2 miles
50 cm	20 in.	20 m	66 ft (22 yd)	4 km	2½ miles
1 m	3 ft 3 in.	50 m	164 ft (54 yd)	5 km	3 miles
2 m	6 ft 6 in.	100 m	330 ft (110 yd)	10 km	6 miles
3 m	10 ft	200 m	660 ft (220 yd)	20 km	12½ miles
4 m	13 ft	250 m	820 ft (275 yd)	25 km	15½ miles
5 m	16 ft 6 in.	300 m	984 ft (330 yd)	30 km	18½ miles
6 m	19 ft 6 in.	500 m	1640 ft (550 yd)	40 km	25 miles
7 m	23 ft	750 m	½ mile	50 km	31 miles
8 m	26 ft	1 km	⅝ mile	75 km	46 miles
9 m	29 ft (10 yd)	2 km	1½ miles	100 km	62 miles

24-HOUR CLOCK

(examples)

0000 = Midnight	1200 = Noon	1800 = 6 pm
0600 = 6 am	1300 = 1 pm	2000 = 8 pm
0715 = 7.15 am	1415 = 2.15 pm	2110 = 9.10 pm
0930 = 9.30 am	1645 = 4.45 pm	2345 = 11.45 pm

TEMPERATURE

Conversion Formula: °C x 9 ÷ 5 + 32 = °F

°C	°F	°C	°F	°C	°F	°C	°F
-20	-4	-5	23	10	50	25	77
-15	5	0	32	15	59	30	86
-10	14	5	41	20	68	35	95

WEIGHT

1kg = 1000g 100 g = 3½ oz

Kg	Lbs	Kg	Lbs	Kg	Lbs
1	2¼	5	11	25	55
2	4½	10	22	50	110
3	6½	15	33	75	165
4	9	20	45	100	220

FLUID MEASURES

1 ltr.(l) = 0.88 Imp. quarts = 1.06 US quarts

Ltrs.	Imp. gal.	US gal.	Ltrs.	Imp. gal.	US gal.
5	1.1	1.3	30	6.6	7.8
10	2.2	2.6	35	7.7	9.1
15	3.3	3.9	40	8.8	10.4
20	4.4	5.2	45	9.9	11.7
25	5.5	6.5	50	11.0	13.0

MEN'S SHIRTS

NZ/UK	Eur	US
14	36	14
15	38	15
15½	39	15½
16	41	16
16½	42	16½
17	43	17

MEN'S SHOES

NZ/UK	Eur	US
6	39⅓	6½
7	40½	7½
8	42	8½
9	43	9½
10	44½	10½
11	46	11½

LADIES' CLOTHES

NZ UK	France	Italy	Rest of Europe	US
10	36	38	34	8
12	38	40	36	10
14	40	42	38	12
16	42	44	40	14
18	44	46	42	16
20	46	48	44	18

MEN'S CLOTHES

NZ/UK	Eur	US
36	46	36
38	48	38
40	50	40
42	52	42
44	54	44
46	56	46

LADIES' SHOES

NZ/UK	Eur	US
3	35½	5½
4	37	6½
5	38	7½
6	39½	8½
7	40½	9½
8	42	10½

AREAS

1 hectare = 2.471 acres

1 hectare = 10,000 sq metres

1 acre = 0.4 hectares

INDEX

This index lists places and topics in alphabetical sequence. All references are to page numbers. To find routes between cities, see pp. 16–17.

AFFIX
STAMP
HERE

Thomas Cook Publishing
PO Box 227
Unit 15/16
Coningsby Road
Peterborough PE3 8SB
United Kingdom

Please help us improve future editions by taking part in our reader survey. Complete and return this card to the address on the reverse or e-mail your feedback to books@thomascook.com or visit www.thomascookpublishing.com. Any suggestions which are used for updating will be acknowledged in future editions.

1. Which Independent Travellers title did you purchase?

....

2. Is this the first Independent Travellers guidebook you have bought?

☐ YES ☐ NO

3. Why is this your preferred choice of budget travel guide?

....

....

4. In your opinion, how could future editions of this book be improved?

....

....

....

5. What other titles would you like to see in this series?

....

Full Name ....

Age ☐ under 21 ☐ 21-30 ☐ 31-40 ☐ 41-50 ☐ over 50

Address ....

.... Postcode ....

Daytime telephone number ....

E-mail address ....

☐ Please tick here if you do not wish to receive details of products and services from Thomas Cook Publishing.